Mountain Dharma

The Library of Tibetan Classics is a special series being developed by the Institute of Tibetan Classics aimed at making key classical Tibetan texts part of the global literary and intellectual heritage. Eventually comprising thirty-two large volumes, the collection will contain over two hundred distinct texts by more than a hundred of the best-known authors. These texts have been selected in consultation with the preeminent lineage holders of all the schools and other senior Tibetan scholars to represent the Tibetan literary tradition as a whole. The works included in the series span more than a millennium and cover the vast expanse of classical Tibetan knowledge—from the core teachings of the specific schools to such diverse fields as ethics, philosophy, linguistics, medicine, astronomy and astrology, folklore, and historiography.

Mountain Dharma: An Ocean of Definitive Meaning

Mountain Dharma: An Ocean of Definitive Meaning (*Ri chos nges don rgya mtsho*) is the magnum opus of Dölpopa Sherab Gyaltsen (1292–1361). This unique treatise presents a controversial interpretation of two of the key principles of Mahāyāna Buddhism—namely, emptiness and the theory of buddha nature. Dölpopa identified the *Kālacakra Tantra* and the Shambhala king Kalkī Puṇḍarīka's *Stainless Light* as his primary sources of inspiration. Also crucial were certain Mahāyāna sūtras, the teachings of Maitreya, and those of the fourth-century masters Asaṅga and his brother Vasubandhu. These and other Vajrayāna and Mahāyāna works represented for Dölpopa the culmination of Buddhist philosophical thinking, which he refers to as Great Madhyamaka, the middle way transcending all extremes of existence, nonexistence, both, and neither. Dölpopa first formulated the view known as *shentong* ("emptiness of other"), which says ultimate reality is not empty of self-nature but only empty of relative phenomena other than itself. Later sustained by Tāranātha (1575–1635) and others in Dölpopa's Jonang tradition, the influence of the *shentong* view also extends beyond his tradition and is discernible in the writings of such eminent Tibetan masters as Shākya Chokden (1428–1507) of the Sakya tradition, Karmapa Mikyö Dorjé (1507–54) of the Kagyü tradition, the nonsectarian master Jamgön Kongtrul (1813–1900), and the Nyingma master Ju Mipham (1846–1912).

HE LIBRARY OF TIBETAN CLASSICS • VOLUME 7

Thupten Jinpa, General Editor

MOUNTAIN DHARMA

An Ocean of Definitive Meaning

Dölpopa Sherab Gyaltsen

Translated by Cyrus Stearns

Wisdom

in association with the Institute of Tibetan Classics

Wisdom Publications
132 Perry Street
New York, NY 10014 USA
wisdom.org

Library of Congress Cataloging-in-Publication Data
Names: Shes-rab-rgyal-mtshan, Dol-po-pa, 1292–1361 author. | Stearns, Cyrus, 1949– translator.
Title: Mountain Dharma: an ocean of definitive meaning / Dölpopa Sherab Gyaltsen ; translated by Cyrus Stearns.
Other titles: Ri chos nges don rgya mtsho. English
Description: First edition. | New York: Wisdom Publications, 2025. | Series: The Library of Tibetan Classics; 7 | Includes bibliographical references and index.
Identifiers: LCCN 2024005196 (print) | LCCN 2024005197 (ebook) | ISBN 9780861714469 (hardcover) | ISBN 9781614298076 (ebook)
Subjects: LCSH: Jo-nang-pa (Sect)—Doctrines. | Shes-rab-rgyal-mtshan, Dol-po-pa, | d 1292–1361. Ri chos nges don rgya mtsho. | Mādhyamika (Buddhism) | Sunyata.
Classification: LCC BQ7674.4 .S4713 2025 (print) | LCC BQ7674.4 (ebook) | DDC 294.3/92—dc23/eng/20241107
LC record available at https://lccn.loc.gov/2024005196
LC ebook record available at https://lccn.loc.gov/2024005197

ISBN 978-0-86171-446-9   ebook ISBN 978-1-61429-807-6

29 28 27 26 25   5 4 3 2 1

Cover and interior design by Gopa & Ted2, Inc. Cover typeset by Tony Lulek.

Printed on acid-free paper that meets the guidelines for permanence and durability of the Production Guidelines for Book Longevity of the Council on Library Resources.

Printed in Canada.

Message from the Dalai Lama

THE LAST TWO MILLENNIA witnessed a tremendous proliferation of cultural and literary development in Tibet, the "Land of Snows." Moreover, due to the inestimable contributions made by Tibet's early spiritual kings, numerous Tibetan translators, and many great Indian paṇḍitas over a period of so many centuries, the teachings of the Buddha and the scholastic tradition of ancient India's Nālandā monastic university became firmly rooted in Tibet. As evidenced from the historical writings, this flowering of Buddhist tradition in the country brought about the fulfillment of the deep spiritual aspirations of countless sentient beings. In particular, it contributed to the inner peace and tranquility of the peoples of Tibet, Outer Mongolia—a country historically suffused with Tibetan Buddhism and its culture—the Tuva and Kalmuk regions in present-day Russia, the outer regions of mainland China, and the entire trans-Himalayan areas on the southern side, including Bhutan, Sikkim, Ladakh, Kinnaur, and Spiti. Today this tradition of Buddhism has the potential to make significant contributions to the welfare of the entire human family. I have no doubt that, when combined with the methods and insights of modern science, the Tibetan Buddhist cultural heritage and knowledge will help foster a more enlightened and compassionate human society, a humanity that is at peace with itself, with fellow sentient beings, and with the natural world at large.

It is for this reason I am delighted that the Institute of Tibetan Classics in Montreal, Canada, is compiling a thirty-two-volume series containing the works of many great Tibetan teachers, philosophers, scholars, and practitioners representing all major Tibetan schools and traditions. These important writings are being critically edited and annotated and then published in modern book format in a reference collection called *The Library of Tibetan Classics*, with their translations into other major languages to follow later. While expressing my heartfelt commendation for this noble project, I pray and hope that *The Library of Tibetan Classics* will not only make these important Tibetan treatises accessible to scholars of Tibetan studies, but will create a new opportunity for younger Tibetans to study and take interest in their own rich and profound culture. Through translations into other languages, it is my sincere hope that millions of fellow citizens of the wider human family will also be able to share in the joy of engaging with Tibet's classical literary heritage, textual riches that have been such a great source of joy and inspiration to me personally for so long.

The Dalai Lama
The Buddhist monk Tenzin Gyatso

Special Acknowledgments

The Institute of Tibetan Classics expresses its deep gratitude to the Tsadra Foundation for the core funding for the translation of this important volume. We also thank the Ing Foundation for its long-standing patronage of the Institute, making it possible for the Institute and its general editor to oversee the ongoing translation projects of the thirty-two-volume *Library of Tibetan Classics* series.

Publisher's Acknowledgment

THE PUBLISHER WISHES TO EXTEND a heartfelt thanks to the following people who have contributed substantially to the publication of *The Library of Tibetan Classics*:

Tsadra Foundation
Pat Gruber and the Patricia and Peter Gruber Foundation
The Hershey Family Foundation
The Ing Foundation

We also extend deep appreciation to our other subscribing benefactors:

Anonymous, dedicated to Buddhas within
Anonymous, in honor of Dzongsar Khyentse Rinpoche
Anonymous, in honor of Geshe Tenzin Dorje
Anonymous, in memory of K. J. Manel De Silva—may she realize the truth
Anonymous, in memory of Gene Smith
Dr. Patrick Bangert
Nilda Venegas Bernal
Serje Samlo Khentul Lhundub Choden and his Dharma friends
Nicholas Cope
Kushok Lobsang Dhamchöe
Diep Thi Thoai
Tenzin Dorjee
Richard Farris
Gaden Samten Ling, Canada
Evgeniy Gavrilov & Tatiana Fotina
Petar Gesovic
Great Vow Zen Monastery
Ginger Gregory
the Grohmann family, Taiwan
Gyaltsen Lobsang Jamyang (WeiJie) and Pema Looi
Rick Meeker Hayman
Steven D. Hearst
Jana & Mahi Hummel
Curt and Alice Jones
Julie LaValle Jones
Heidi Kaiter
Paul, Trisha, Rachel, and Daniel Kane

Land of Medicine Buddha
Dennis Leksander
Diane & Joseph Lucas
Elizabeth Mettling
Russ Miyashiro
Kestrel Montague
the Nalanda Institute, Olympia, WA
Craig T. Neyman
Kristin A. Ohlson
Arnold Possick
Magdalene Camilla Frank Prest
Quek Heng Bee, Ong Siok Ngow, and family
Randall-Gonzales Family Foundation
Erick Rinner
Andrew Rittenour
Dombon Roig Family
Jonathan and Diana Rose
the Sharchitsang family
Nirbhay N. Singh
Wee Kee Tan
Tibetisches Zentrum e.V. Hamburg
Richard Toft
Alissa KieuNgoc Tran
Timothy Trompeter
the Vahagn Setian Charitable Foundation
Ellyse Adele Vitiello
Jampa (Alicia H.) Vogel
Nicholas C. Weeks II
Richard and Carol Weingarten
Claudia Wellnitz
Bob White
Kevin Michael White, MD
Eve and Jeff Wild

and the other donors who wish to remain anonymous.

Contents

Mountain Dharma: An Ocean of Definitive Meaning
Consummate, Uncommon Esoteric Instructions

TWO: RELYING ON THE SUBLIME, PROFOUND PATH BY WHICH THAT CAN BE OBTAINED

THREE: EXPLANATION OF THE RESULTS OF SEPARATION
AND PRODUCTION BY MEANS OF THAT PATH

Illustrations

General Editor's Preface

If I were asked to name five Tibetan texts with lasting impact on Buddhism in Tibet, without a doubt, the work translated in this volume, Dölpopa's *Mountain Dharma: An Ocean of Definitive Meaning*, would be on that list. Appearing in the fourteenth century, the book proposes an understanding of emptiness, the defining philosophical concept of Mahāyāna Buddhism, that is radically at odds with Nāgārjuna's influential treatise *Root Verses on Madhyamaka*. Contrary to Indian Madhyamaka's rejection of any notion of an irreducible primitive—a metaphysical truth that is independent and possesses true existence—Dölpopa's text advocates the existence within all beings of an eternal enlightened essence that is endowed with the full attributes of a buddha. This ultimate reality, though empty of relative phenomena other than itself, is in itself said to be an indivisible union of gnosis (primordial awareness) and ultimate reality that is eternal, absolute, and independent of everything else. This understanding of emptiness came to be known as *shentong*, the "emptiness of other" view. At the heart of Dölpopa's project is an important hermeneutic move, one that involves (1) prioritizing the writings of Asaṅga and Vasubandhu, taking them to represent the apex of Mahāyāna Buddhist philosophy, (2) absolutizating nondual gnosis (primordial awareness) as ultimate truth and equating it with buddha nature, and (3) seamlessly incorporating the language of unsurpassable yogatantra into the exegesis of the two foundational concepts of the Mahāyāna—emptiness and buddha nature.

Even though he does not explicitly state it, to an extent, Dölpopa's innovative (or—depending on one's perspective—heretical) views can be seen as a strong response to Sakya Paṇḍita's (1182–1251) critique of the concept of buddha nature. The latter forcefully argued that this teaching must be considered "provisional" in meaning, and that it was taught by the Buddha to assuage the fears of those deeply predisposed to grasp at self-existence. To take the teaching literally, according to Sakya Paṇḍita, would be tantamount to espousing an eternal self. While Dölpopa's emptiness of other view came under extensive critique by numerous Tibetan thinkers, it also shaped the philosophical perspectives of celebrated masters like Shākya Chokden and key figures in the nineteenth-century Rimé ("nonectarian") movement.

In our volume, Cyrus Stearns has produced a masterful new translation of Dölpopa's text. When I conceived the thirty-two-volume *Library of Tibetan Classics* and was assigning translators to the individual volumes, I was set on having Cyrus take on this volume. I have long admired his book *The Buddha from Dolpo*, which introduced the Tibetan master and his work to the English-speaking world in a clear and thoughtful way. So it is a real joy to see today Dölpopa's famed text made available to contemporary readers in an accessible and accurate translation.

Two primary objectives have driven the creation and development of *The Library of Tibetan Classics*. The first aim is to help revitalize the appreciation and the study of the Tibetan classical heritage within Tibetan-speaking communities worldwide. The younger generation in particular struggle with the tension between traditional Tibetan culture and the realities of modern consumerism. To this end, efforts have been made to develop a comprehensive yet manageable body of texts, one that features the works of Tibet's best-known authors and covers the gamut of classical Tibetan knowledge. The second objective of *The Library of Tibetan Classics* is to help make these texts part of global literary and intellectual heritage. In this regard, we have tried to make the English translation reader-friendly and, as much as possible, keep the body of the text free of unnecessary scholarly apparatus, which can intimidate general readers. For specialists who wish to compare the translation with the Tibetan original, page references of the critical edition of the Tibetan text are provided in brackets.

The texts in this thirty-two-volume series span more than a millennium—from the development of the Tibetan script in the seventh century to the first part of the twentieth century, when Tibetan society and culture first encountered industrial modernity. The volumes are thematically organized and cover many of the categories of classical Tibetan knowledge—from the teachings specific to each Tibetan school to the classical works on philosophy, psychology, and phenomenology. The first category includes teachings of the Kadam, Nyingma, Sakya, Kagyü, Geluk, and Jonang schools, of miscellaneous Buddhist lineages, and of the Bön school. Texts in these volumes have been largely selected by senior lineage holders of the individual schools. Texts in the other categories have been selected primarily in recognition of the historical reality of the individual disciplines. For example, in the field of epistemology, works from the Sakya and Geluk schools have been selected, while the volume on buddha nature features the writings of Butön Rinchen Drup and various Kagyü masters. Where fields are of more common interest, such as the three codes or the bodhisattva ideal, efforts have been made to represent the perspectives of all four major Tibetan Buddhist schools. *The Library of Tibetan Classics* can function as a comprehensive library of the Tibetan literary heritage for libraries, educational and cultural institutions, and interested individuals.

It has been a privilege to be part of this important translation project. I had the pleasure of editing the Tibetan source text, offering me a chance to closely engage with Dölpopa's masterpiece. I wish first of all to express my deep personal gratitude to H. H. the Dalai Lama for always being such a profound source of inspiration. I would like to say thank you to Cyrus Stearns for rendering this important Tibetan text with such care, diligence, and clarity. I owe thanks our long-time editor at Wisdom, David Kittelstrom, and, for taking on the numerous administrative chores that are part of a collaborative project such as this, my wife, Sophie Boyer-Langri.

Finally, I would like to express my heartfelt thanks to the Tsadra Foundation for sponsoring the direct costs of the translation of this volume; and to Nita Ing and the Ing Foundation for their long-standing patronage of the Institute of Tibetan Classics, making it possible for me to continue to oversee this translation series. It is my hope that this volume will be a source of joy, intellectual enrichment, and philosophical and spiritual insights for many people.

Thupten Jinpa
Montreal, 2024

1. Dölpopa Sherab Gyaltsen (1292–1361).

Translator's Introduction

If buddhahood will be reached even by hearing just the term "sugata essence," what need to mention what will happen with faith and devotion, and by actualizing it through meditation? So compassionate experts should teach it even if they may lose their lives, and so on, and those striving for liberation should seek it out, listen, and so forth, even if they must cross a great pit of fire.

—Dölpopa Sherab Gyaltsen, *Mountain Dharma*[1]

SOME PEOPLE THOUGHT he was a demonic genius. Others believed he was the incarnation of the Shambhala king Kalkī Puṇḍarīka. Still, everyone recognized his realization and brilliance and called him The Omniscient One.[2] No other thinker shook the Buddhist world of fourteenth-century Tibet as deeply as Dölpopa Sherab Gyaltsen (1292–1361), who taught that an eternal enlightened essence, or buddha nature, exists in all living beings, and that ultimate reality is empty only of relative phenomena other than itself, unlike relative phenomena that are empty of self-nature.

The most famous (or infamous) book Dölpopa wrote to present his unprecedented interpretations of Buddhist doctrine is called *Mountain Dharma: An Ocean of Definitive Meaning* (*Ri chos nges don rgya mtsho*). Few controversial books remain controversial a hundred years after they were written. This one has. After nearly seven hundred years, the ideas discussed in *Mountain Dharma* are still as provocative as when Dölpopa first openly taught them in 1330. Written for learned practitioners of Vajrayāna Buddhism who were meditating in mountain retreats, Dölpopa's masterpiece is filled with an ocean of quotations selected from the Indian Buddhist scriptures and treatises translated into Tibetan and preserved in the canonical collections of the Kangyur and Tengyur. When deciphering the true intent of these passages of definitive meaning, he never mentions another Tibetan author or book. His only goal is to establish the validity of his theories based on Indian works of indisputable authority.

Dölpopa's ideas spread widely and have had an enduring impact on Tibetan Buddhism to the present day. He taught that the ultimate and the relative are both empty, but they must be empty in different ways. Phenomena at the relative level are empty of self-nature and no more real than the fictitious horn of a rabbit or the child of a barren woman. In contrast, the reality of ultimate truth is empty only of those other relative phenomena. Dölpopa was not simply setting up these viewpoints of emptiness of self-nature, or *rangtong* (*rang stong*), and emptiness of other, or *shentong* (*gzhan stong*), as opposed theories located on the same level. He saw them as complementary, making the distinction that the view of the emptiness of other applied only to the ultimate and the emptiness of self-nature only to the relative. Both approaches are essential for a correct understanding of the nature of saṃsāra and nirvāṇa. He disagreed with those who said both the ultimate and the relative are empty of self-nature and did not accept that anything was not empty of self-nature. Many masters in India and Tibet had held opinions similar to Dölpopa's in the past, but he was the first to write about such ideas in detail, using terminology that was new and shocking for many of his contemporaries.

Dölpopa, who was also known as The Buddha from Dölpo and The Omniscient Dölpopa Who Embodies the Buddhas of the Three Times, identified the ultimate with the buddha nature, or sugata essence, which he held to be eternal and not empty of self-nature, but only empty of other. The buddha nature is perfect, with all its characteristics inherently present in all living beings. It is only the impermanent and temporary afflictions veiling the buddha nature that are empty of self-nature and must be removed through the practice of the path to allow it to manifest. He often remarked that most buddhas and bodhisattvas agreed with him, but most scholars in Tibet opposed him. They viewed similar statements in the scriptures to be of provisional, not definitive, meaning and in need of interpretation for the true intent to be correctly understood. This was the opinion of the Sakya tradition to which Dölpopa belonged before he moved to Jonang. He thus kept his new viewpoint secret for some time, knowing it would be misunderstood by those who had closed minds and were accustomed to different interpretations.

Dölpopa also asked if a relative truth were possible without an ultimate truth, the incidental possible without the primordial, and phenomena possible without a true nature. If their existence were possible without an ultimate, primordial, true nature, would these relative, incidental phenomena then not constitute an omnipresent reality or true nature? But if it were impossible for there to be no ultimate, would that not contradict the notion of an ultimate that is totally unestablished? Everything cannot be just empty of self-nature, because there would be no fundamental difference between the ultimate and the relative. For Dölpopa, the ultimate is a true, eternal, and established reality, empty merely of other relative phenomena.

Such descriptions of reality and the buddha nature are found in many Mahāyāna scriptures that the Tibetan tradition places in the third turning of the Dharma wheel, and in the Buddhist tantras. But no one in Tibet before Dölpopa had specifically emphasized that ultimate reality was not empty of self-nature. And he admitted that his teachings and the Dharma language he was using were new, but only in the sense that they were not well known in Tibet. They had come from the realm of Shambhala to the north, where they had been widespread from an early time.[3] He explicitly linked his ideas to the *Kālacakra Tantra* and its great commentary, the *Stainless Light*, composed by the Shambhala king Kalkī Puṇḍarīka.

Dölpopa Sherab Gyaltsen

Dölpopa (as his nickname indicates) was born in the Dölpo region of present-day Nepal in 1292.[4] He received ordination as a novice monk in 1304, and five years later traveled to upper Mustang, where he met his main teacher, Kyitön Jamyang Drakpa, from whom he received many teachings on the Vehicle of the Perfections, epistemology, and cosmology and psychology. Kyitön soon moved to the great monastery of Sakya, in the Tibetan province of Tsang, where Dölpopa eventually joined him in 1312, when he was twenty years old. By this point he had clearly been recognized as a very precocious student.

Dölpopa received countless teachings at Sakya, especially the *Kālacakra Tantra*, the Bodhisattva Trilogy,[5] the Ten Sūtras on the Essence,[6] the Five Sūtras of Definitive Meaning,[7] and the Five Treatises of Maitreya.[8] These are the main scriptures and treatises he would teach for the rest of his life and cite as scriptural sources for his theories. His teacher Kyitön praised the Kālacakra and the practice of meditation, specifically the Six-Branch Yoga.[9] Having received from Kyitön all the Kālacakra initiations, textual explanations, and esoteric instructions, Dölpopa became an expert in this tradition.

In 1313 Dölpopa traveled to the monastery of Tanak and studied the Five Treatises of Maitreya with the master Rinchen Yeshé, who was perhaps influential in the development of his views.[10] On his return to Sakya he was invited to teach a large audience on the four major topics of the Vehicle of the Perfections, epistemology, cosmology and psychology, and monastic discipline.[11]

The next year Dölpopa visited teaching institutes in Tsang and Central Tibet to further his education, undergo scholastic examinations, and meet the best teachers of other regions. During this period he became famous and received the epithet The Omniscient One because of his mastery of scriptures such as the *Sūtra on the Perfection of Wisdom in One Hundred Thousand Lines*.[12] He also received full monastic ordination from the abbot Sönam Drakpa (1273–1352) of Chölung Monastery and made the vow to never eat slaughtered meat for the rest of his life. And he received many teachings of the Kagyü, Nyingma, and other traditions during his travels. At some point he visited the monastery of Trophu and made offerings and prayers at the great Maitreya image and the large stūpa there, both constructed by the Sanskrit scholar and translator Trophu Lotsāwa Jampa Pal (1172–1236). In front of the stūpa Dölpopa prayed that he would someday be able to build one like it, or even larger.[13] After returning to Sakya, at the age of only twenty-eight he ascended to the monastic seat of Sakya Monastery, becoming the head of the monastic community and thus recognized as one of the foremost teachers of Sakya.[14]

In 1321 Dölpopa visited the great hermitage of Jonang for the first time. The practice of the Six-Branch Yoga and the teachings of the *Kālacakra Tantra* and other scriptures and treatises that emphasized the definitive meaning were the specialty of the Jonang tradition. Dölpopa was deeply impressed by the meditation practice and realization of the men and women there. According to the later Jonang master Tāranātha (1575–1635), he then traveled to Central Tibet, where he met the third Karmapa, Rangjung Dorjé, who prophesied that Dölpopa would soon have a better view, practice, and Dharma language than what he had then.[15]

The next year he left Sakya and returned to Jonang to meet the master Yönten Gyatso (1260–1327), from whom he requested the full transmission of the *Kālacakra Tantra* and many lineages of the Six-Branch Yoga.[16] The night before he arrived there, Yönten Gyatso dreamed of the Shambhala king Kalkī Puṇḍarīka raising the victory banner of the Buddhist teachings at Jonang. This auspicious dream caused him to give Dölpopa the complete

Kālacakra initiation, the transmission of the Bodhisattva Trilogy, and the profound instructions of the Six-Branch Yoga.[17] He then offered the use of the hermitage of Khachö Deden to Dölpopa, who immediately began a meditation retreat.

Yönten Gyatso soon convinced Dölpopa to teach in the assembly, and also taught him many other systems of esoteric knowledge, such as the Path with the Result, and the Five Stages of the *Guhyasamāja Tantra* and the *Cakrasaṃvara Tantra*. After some time, Dölpopa began another strict retreat at Khachö Deden, meditating on the Six-Branch Yoga of Kālacakra for one year and achieving the results of the first four of the six branches.[18] Realization of the *shentong* view of the emptiness of other first arose in his mind during this retreat, but he would not teach it to anyone until at least five more years had passed.[19]

In 1325 Yönten Gyatso urged Dölpopa to become his Dharma heir and accept the monastic seat of Jonang. This was completely against Dölpopa's wish to meditate in isolated places, without the responsibilities and restrictions of such a position.[20] But when he traveled to Lhasa to make prayers and request guidance from the holy image of Avalokiteśvara in the Jokhang temple, he was urged to become the leader of Jonang in order to benefit the Buddhist doctrine.

When Yönten Gyatso passed away in 1327, Dölpopa decided to build a monumental stūpa to fulfill the prayer he had previously made at the stūpa of Trophu and to repay his master's kindness.[21] Work began in the spring of 1330, one hundred years after Trophu Lotsāwa had begun his stūpa. Many skilled artisans and laborers gathered from different parts of Tibet, and building materials and food were brought from all directions. Kitchens and rest areas were set up for the hundreds of workers who labored while chanting maṇis and praying to the masters of the lineage. Dölpopa himself sometimes carried earth and stones and sometimes worked on the building of the walls. He had a ramp built from the west side of the stūpa so donkeys could carry earth and stone up onto the main body of the structure, and long ramps made on the south and north sides so that those carrying loads could come up one side and then go down without their loads on the other. The artisans continually circled the structure, and if the work was even a little out of alignment it was torn down and rebuilt. As word of the project spread, great offerings of gold, silver, copper, iron, silk, tea, cloth, medicines, and so on began to flow in from all regions of Tibet.[22]

2. The great stūpa of Jonang.

By this time Dölpopa had gathered an exceptional group of yogins, scholars, and translators, such as Kunpang Chödrak Palsang, Mati Paṇchen Lodrö Gyaltsen (1294–1376), Lotsāwa Lodrö Pal (1299–1354), and Choklé Namgyal (1306–86), all of whom participated in the construction of the stūpa.[23] The intense labor of the construction of the stūpa was accompanied by many extraordinary discourses by Dölpopa on the ultimate significance of the Buddha's teachings. According to Kunpang, who witnessed the events, prior to the winter of 1330 the long central poles were placed in the stūpa and Dölpopa taught the Bodhisattva Trilogy to a huge assembly. On this occasion he took great pleasure in drawing for the first time the clear distinction between the relative as empty of self-nature and the ultimate as empty only of other relative phenomena. Tāranātha, however, says that after laying the foundation for the stūpa, Dölpopa first taught the *shentong* view when giving a detailed explication of the Ten Sūtras on the Essence to an audience of about ten persons.[24] In either case, it was during the building of the stūpa, which Dölpopa himself later linked to his realization, that he first openly taught the *shentong* and related topics.

The stūpa at Jonang was carefully based on descriptions in Puṇḍarīka's *Stainless Light*, so that it could be considered the same as the Glorious Stūpa of the Planets, where the Buddha had first taught the *Kālacakra Tantra*.[25] Dölpopa said his realization of "the ultimate as empty of other, which was previously unknown in Tibet,"[26] arose by the kindness of his teachers and the Three Jewels, whose blessings he had received because of his devotion to them and their representations, and because he had worked for the benefit of the Buddhist teachings. His biographer Lhai Gyaltsen is more specific, saying Dölpopa's precise realization of the nature of ultimate reality was due to "the blessings of his construction of inconceivably marvelous threefold representations, such as those of the masters, buddhas, bodhisattvas, and the great stūpa temple."[27]

After first teaching the *shentong* view, Dölpopa wrote some minor works to explain it. According to Tāranātha, when these texts were initially circulated they were incomprehensible to most scholars because of the unusual Dharma language (*chos skad*) he was introducing. In another text, however, he says all fortunate and open-minded people were delighted by the *shentong* teachings, and it was not until much later that adherents of the Sakya, Geluk, Kadam, Shalu, Bodong, and some followers of the Nyingma tradition became so disturbed about it.[28]

Some later authors attributed the negative reaction to outrage by Sakya scholars who felt betrayed when Dölpopa began to teach an unprecedented view that contradicted the teachings of the early masters of Sakya. He had been educated as a Sakya monk, had ascended to the monastic seat of Sakya Monastery, and had upheld the ancient teachings of that tradition. Thus many in the Sakya tradition now saw him as a great apostate. Nevertheless, Sakya masters of the Khön family such as Tishri Kunga Gyaltsen (1310–58) and his two sons Ta En Chökyi Gyaltsen (1332–59) and Ta En Lodrö Gyaltsen (1332–64), as well as Dönyö Gyaltsen (1310–44) and his brother Lama Dampa Sönam Gyaltsen (1312–75), all requested teachings from Dölpopa at different times.[29]

Tāranātha also says the people who came to Jonang to discuss or argue the issues with Dölpopa gained confidence in his theories and faith in him. Others who sent written objections were said to have reached understanding after receiving his well-reasoned replies.[30] A clear example is the Kagyü master Barawa Gyaltsen Palsangpo (1310–91), who had doubts about the distinction Dölpopa made between the universal-ground primordial awareness (*kun gzhi'i ye shes*) and the universal-ground consciousness (*kun gzhi'i rnam shes*). He sent written questions to Dölpopa and some of his main disciples, and received replies from the disciples, but his doubts were not resolved. Later he received a reply from Dölpopa that was more satisfying, but different from what the disciples had written. Then he went to meet Dölpopa, whose explanations were consistent with his previous letter, and Barawa understood the true meaning of his teachings.[31] Such examples suggest that Dölpopa composed *Mountain Dharma* and other works after establishing his viewpoint through discussion with different masters and practitioners, and that his unprecedented theories that have so strongly influenced Buddhism in Tibet to the present day arose around groups of individuals and from extended conversations and disputes of which we now have only traces and fragments.[32]

The great stūpa of Jonang was finally consecrated in late October 1333.[33] In 1334 Dölpopa and Kunpang Chödrak Palsang urged Lotsāwa Lodrö Pal and Mati Paṇchen Lodrö Gyaltsen to prepare a revised Tibetan translation of the *Kālacakra Tantra* and the *Stainless Light*. Then he composed a topical outline and annotations to the *Stainless Light*.

In the following years Dölpopa traveled to many different areas, where he mostly stayed in meditation retreat. During this period he constructed many shrines, closely examined the scriptures in the Tibetan canon, and wrote significant treatises. He also had several visions, both of pure lands and tantric deities. In particular, he directly beheld the pure land of Shambhala, the source of the Kālacakra teachings, and once claimed to have actually gone there by visionary means.[34]

In the fall of 1336 Dölpopa was invited to return to Sakya Monastery, where he gave extensive teachings to several thousand people and engaged in much debate about philosophical viewpoints. Using the sūtras and tantras as witnesses, especially the set of sūtras on the perfection of wisdom, he distinguished between relative and ultimate truth by means of the categories of an emptiness of self-nature and an emptiness of other.[35] In 1338 he retired from the monastic seat of Jonang and appointed Lotsāwa Lodrö Pal as his successor. Lodrö Pal would hold this position for the next seventeen years.[36]

In 1344 two Mongolian imperial envoys arrived in Tsang with decrees from the Yüan emperor Toghon Temür, inviting both Dölpopa and Butön Rinchen Drup to China.[37] Both Dölpopa and Butön evaded the imperial invitations and retreated to isolated hermitages for meditation. To avoid the possibility of a second invitation, Dölpopa stayed in remote areas for the next four years, until a message came from the emperor allowing him to remain in Tibet and work for the Buddhist doctrine there.[38]

Dölpopa had previously taught Dharma to many of the great figures of the Tibetan intellectual and political world, but now mostly stayed in the Jonang area.[39] During the power struggle between the Sakya rulers in Tsang and the newly arisen Phakmodru in Central Tibet, serious damage had occurred to Buddhist communities, temples, and shrines. Disturbed by this, he decided to travel to Lhasa and make prayers to the Jowo image, which he felt to be the same as the Buddha. He was now sixty-six years old and had become extremely heavy in his later years, so it was very difficult for him to travel. His body was about twice the size of an average person (*phal pa nyis 'gyur tsam gyis sku che*) and his physical presence dominated any gathering, even when there were hundreds of people. Important and charismatic figures became like children when they arrived before him. Departing from Jonang in the summer of 1358, he traveled by boat down the Tsangpo River, staying for extended periods at different places along the way to give extensive teachings. After nearly a year, he began to travel by palanquin, proceeding slowly through Tsang and into Central Tibet, welcomed by all the people and the clergy, who lined the roads to greet him and escort him into the different monasteries. The crowds were often so large that people at the edges could not hear him teach, so his words had to be relayed through "interpreters" (*lo tsā ba cug gin gsungs*).

Dölpopa finally arrived in Lhasa about two months later. There he gave the instructions of the Six-Branch Yoga many times to countless teachers who came from all different monasteries. Because too many people requested teachings and were having strange physical experiences, Dölpopa had to come out from the Ramoché Khangsar temple and stay at Shöl. The audiences were so large that doors were broken and stairways collapsed. Even the extreme measure of tying dogs at the head of the stairways to prevent too many people from entering did not control the crowds.[40]

In the spring of 1360 a party arrived to invite Dölpopa back to Jonang. The people of Lhasa were distraught at his departure, and when his palanquin could not get through the crowd of people and horses, many members of the Saṅgha joined hands in a circle around it. Those wanting his blessing were made to join hands and go single file under his palanquin. The Saṅgha members chanted supplications such as Dölpopa's *General Commentary on the Doctrine*,[41] while the entire mass of people wailed hysterically. Most of the crowd had lost their senses and many could not even walk. The sun was warm and the sky was clear, but the atmosphere was filled with rainbows. When Dölpopa got into a boat to cross the river, many people jumped into the water after him and had to be saved by others.

According to Tāranātha's history of the Nyang region, the ruler Phakpa Palsang and his younger brother, Phakpa Rinchen (1320–76), had for some time wished to request Dharma teachings from Dölpopa, and now invited him to Jangra. Because of his weight, it was too difficult for him to climb the long stairs up to Jangra, so he stayed for a long time below on the battlefield of Dzingkha. There he had a huge silk maṇḍala of Kālacakra spread out and bestowed an extensive Kālacakra initiation. He also had a vision of the nearby mountain slope of Tsechen as the palace of Shambhala, and prophesied a future monastery there in which only the Six-Branch Yoga would be practiced. When he left Jangra, he was escorted to Nesar by Phakpa Palsang, and instructed the ruler, "Honor the Buddha as permanent, the Dharma as true, and the Saṅgha as infallible! This will always be beneficial, now and in the future, and your realm will also be stable."[42]

As Dölpopa continued to stop along the way and give teachings, large crowds escorted him through the valleys, chanting the six-syllable mantra of Avalokiteśvara, offering prayers, and weeping from faith.[43] In the summer of 1360 he arrived back at Jonang in excellent health and stayed in meditation at his residence of Dewachen.

On the fourth day of the eleventh lunar month in 1361 Dölpopa began to teach *Mountain Dharma: An Ocean of Definitive Meaning*. On the sixth day he had finished about half the book, said that was all he would teach, and instructed his students to take good care of the text. He seemed more radiant and healthy than ever, and wanted to walk to the stūpa, but his attendants said snow had fallen and the path was unsafe, and helped him to his residence.[44] Tea was served, his senior disciples gathered, and he gave a detailed explanation of the "powerful tenfold anagram."[45] That evening he was pleased with everyone, and there was much joking and laughter. Then he went to sleep. At dawn his attendant served him, and after a short while asked, "Will you stand up now?"

Dölpopa did not reply. The attendant thought he was in meditation and did not ask again. But when the sun came up, he pulled at Dölpopa's hand and asked, "Will you stand up now?" Dölpopa sat staring straight ahead, appearing to be in deep meditation, and did not speak. The attendant called for some elder disciples, who thought Dölpopa was perhaps affected by the intense cold and took him out into the sun and massaged him. After about midday his eyes closed and, without any sign of illness, he passed into deep meditation. He was then carried back into his room. After a few minutes he adjusted his position into that of Vajrasattva and passed away into bliss.

Dölpopa's body was kept on his bed for several days, and offerings, prostrations, and circumambulations were made day and night. Then he was put into a wooden casket anointed with perfume and adorned with silk and precious ornaments, and placed inside the crematorium. His body was extremely flexible, like a piece of cotton wool.[46] From the twenty-first day until the full moon, services were conducted by more than one hundred masters, led by Mati Panchen, Choklé Namgyal, and other major disciples.

In early 1362 the cremation ceremony was performed. As Dölpopa's body was consumed by the fire, smoke rose up only about the length of a spear, then went to the stūpa like a streaking arrow, circled it many times, and finally disappeared to the west. Huge offerings of incense, butter lamps, music, and so on were made. The men and women practitioners offered butter lamps on the roofs of their individual meditation huts, so that the entire valley sparkled. Until the smoke had faded away, each of them made prayers with tears flowing down their faces.

When the crematorium was later opened, some remains were distributed to disciples who had received the transmission of the *Stainless Light* from Dölpopa. Among the ashes were many relics that were clear like crystal. Molded images covered with gold leaf were made from the remains. Some of the images and relics were taken to Sakya, where most of the teachers and members of the Saṅgha were disciples of Dölpopa, and were welcomed with music and a great procession of the Saṅgha led by the master of the Sharpa family of Sakya. A memorial ceremony was held in the main Sakya assembly, and also in many monasteries throughout Central Tibet and Tsang.[47] Ashes from the cremation were gathered at Jonang and put with other relics into an image of Dölpopa that was placed in the great stūpa he had built.[48]

By the end of his life Dölpopa's influence was enormous. His teachings were controversial, but he taught with great love and compassion. Eyewitness accounts say that even when he was criticizing philosophical opinions that he felt were incorrect, he never did so in an angry manner, and in Dharma discussions that entailed the identification of opponents, wrong positions, and so on, he never used harsh words or made physically aggressive gestures.[49] Although he lived during a time of great political turmoil in Tibet, he had never taken sides, but did take a strong stand against all prejudice and bias. He once commented, "Here at Jonang we do not take any sides. Buddhahood is not reached through prejudicial Dharma. So we do not take part in worthless evil. Like the clouds in the sky, we do not take any sides."[50] Because of this attitude, Dölpopa is said to have been deeply respected by everyone and recognized as a great master whose goal was to revive the definitive meaning of the Buddha's message, which he felt was in danger of being lost.

Mountain Dharma: An Ocean of Definitive Meaning

Soon after the great stūpa had been consecrated at Jonang in late October 1333, Dölpopa stayed in his residence of Dewachen. There, in 1334 he and Kunpang Chödrak Palsang urged Lotsāwa Lodrö Pal and Mati Paṇchen Lodrö Gyaltsen (two of the greatest Sanskrit grammarians in Tibetan history) to prepare a revised translation of the *Kālacakra Tantra* and the *Stainless Light*. Their work was witnessed by Dölpopa and Kunpang (also a translator of Sanskrit texts), at whose request he then composed a topical outline, or summary, and annotations to the *Stainless Light*.[51] The *Kālacakra Tantra* and the *Stainless Light* were the ultimate scriptural sources for Dölpopa. Perhaps in discussions with his bilingual disciples he had concluded that the earlier Tibetan translation of Dro Lotsāwa Sherab Drak and its revision by Shongtön Dorjé Gyaltsen did not allow the profound definitive meaning to fully emerge.

At the end of his annotations to Kalkī Puṇḍarīka's *Stainless Light*, Dölpopa connects his discovery of the *shentong* view and related theories, the teachings of the *Kālacakra Tantra*, and the great stūpa of Jonang:

> Alas, my share of good fortune may be
> totally inferior, but I think a discovery
> like this is good fortune. Was this discovery
> by a lazy fool not a blessing by the Kalkī king?
>
> Though my body did not arrive at Kalāpa,[52]
> did the Kalkī enter my faithful mind, or what?
> Though my intellect was not refined in the three wisdoms,
> I think raising Mount Meru caused the Ocean to gush forth.[53]
>
> I bow down in homage to all the masters, buddhas,
> and kalkīs, by whose kindness the key points difficult
> for even the exalted ones to realize are precisely realized,
> and to their great stūpa.[54]

The raising of Mount Meru refers to Dölpopa's construction of the stūpa at Jonang, and the Ocean that flowed out from the blessings and energy awakened during that project was his most famous work, *Mountain Dharma: An Ocean of Definitive Meaning*. The external construction of the great monument was for him a reflection of the simultaneous internal process that produced some of his most significant literary works. Dölpopa was deeply inspired by the Kalkī kings of Shambhala and believed he was an incarnation of Kalkī Puṇḍarīka, as did many other people.[55]

The passages of the *Kālacakra Tantra* and the *Stainless Light* quoted in *Mountain Dharma* are from the new Jonang translations of 1334, and Dölpopa refers to *Mountain Dharma* in the verses at the end of his annotations to the *Stainless Light*. Therefore, he wrote *Mountain Dharma* after the translations of 1334, but before composing the annotations to the commentary. He probably completed the book in 1334 or 1335, perhaps even working on it while the new translations were in progress. We also know how pleased he was after his disciple Choklé Namgyal assisted by gathering quotations from profound sūtras and tantras while he was composing many treatises such as the *Ocean of Definitive Meaning*.[56] In the colophon of *Mountain Dharma*, he specifically says Choklé Namgyal urged him to compose the work.

In early 1337 Dölpopa taught *Mountain Dharma* at Jonang at the request of Kunpang Chödrak Palsang, other major disciples, and great scholars from different regions.[57] In Lhai Gyaltsen's biography of Dölpopa, just after the completion of the great stūpa, it is said that at a later point (but before 1338) Tishri Kunga Gyaltsen of the Khön family of Sakya sent offerings of the materials needed to create many works of art and volumes of scripture, among which were manuscripts of the *Stainless Light* and *Mountain Dharma* written in gold.[58] Perhaps these were commissioned to commemorate the recently completed Jonang translations and Dölpopa's new masterpiece. Soon after these events, Dölpopa spoke of his motive for composing both the annotations and the outline or summary of the *Stainless Light*: "Because all the key points of the profound definitive meaning were discovered in the great commentary on the *Kālacakra Tantra*, it has been remarkably kind. To prevent confusion about the source text I also composed a summary and exceptional annotations, as well as many other works."[59]

Another early mention of *Mountain Dharma* is found in a brief account of the life of Phuntsok Palsangpo, an important disciple of Dölpopa. When he received many transmissions from Karmapa Rangjung Dorjé (1284–1339) and Tokden Drakseng at the Kagyü monastery of Tsurphu, Phuntsok

Palsangpo saw a copy of the *Ocean of Definitive Meaning*. Reading it, he felt such faith that the hairs of his body stood on end and he was moved to tears. He prayed to be able to receive such a teaching, realize it, and teach it to others. This experience prompted him to quickly meet Dölpopa for the first time.[60] So the text was clearly being studied and discussed in Central Tibet before the death of Karmapa Rangjung Dorjé in 1339.

As noted in the historical accounts, Dölpopa wrote a separate topical outline of *Mountain Dharma*.[61] In the book itself, however, he specifically mentions only the three main sections of the ground, the path, and the results. Although many texts are quoted throughout, the *Kālacakra Tantra*, the *Stainless Light*, the Ten Sūtras on the Essence, the Ten Sūtras of Definitive Meaning, and the Five Treatises of Maitreya are the most important sources he uses to explain these three crucial topics.[62]

Ground

The ground and basis of all phenomena is the awakened state of the ultimate Buddha known by many names, such as dharmakāya, tathāgata essence, ultimate luminosity, dharmadhātu, self-arisen primordial awareness, and great bliss. It is also the ground empty of and isolated from all relative phenomena, the ground in which all stains are primordially absent. The qualities of the dharmakāya, exceeding the grains of sand found in the Ganges River, are indivisible from its nature. Through presentation and interpretation of many scriptural passages, Dölpopa first establishes this true nature to be the universal-ground primordial awareness (*kun gzhi'i ye shes*). Then he explains in great detail how that is the basic element and awareness indivisible that pervades everything, how it is the ultimate Three Jewels of the true nature, how it is the sugata essence, how it is the naturally abiding family, the continuum of the indivisible essence of ground and result, and so on.

Next he offers advice about how to reject mistaken points of view, again quoting various scriptures and focusing in turn on many topics, such as the mistaken view that the teachings about the sugata essence are of provisional meaning. This is done by demonstrating the absurd consequences that would ensue if the sugata essence and the pure self were nonexistent, showing how the ultimate qualities are completely present in living beings, explaining why the sugata essence is always present as the basic ground but does not appear to ordinary consciousness, and so on. Then he gives advice to avoid the disadvantages of not believing in the sugata essence, and explains the immense advantages of having faith in it. Finally he refutes various misconceptions about the sugata essence, such as the absurd consequences that the abandonments and realizations of a buddha would therefore be complete in all sentient beings, or that they would have accumulated the two assemblies of merit and primordial awareness.

Path

In that way, the ultimate Buddha, the dharmakāya, the quintessence of limitless, inseparable qualities, is inherently present in all sentient beings. But this does not mean the path of the two assemblies of merit and primordial awareness is unnecessary, because one must remove the incidental stains, produce the relative rūpakāya, and act for the benefit of all sentient beings. Therefore, pure and excellent view, meditation, and conduct are necessary. Dölpopa begins this second section with a general presentation of the Mahāyāna path, treating various topics such as the reasons for a pure path, the pure view for realizing the emptiness of self-nature, the nature of nonconceptual meditation, recognizing what really exists and what does not, and emphasizing the need to carefully understand the intended meaning of the three Dharma wheels and their differences. As throughout the book, all discussions are based on extensive quotations from sūtras, tantras, and the treatises of great Indian masters.

Finally, Dölpopa specifically explains the uncommon view, beginning with how scriptural statements about empty and nonempty, existent and nonexistent, and so on, point to a profound emptiness that is other than an ordinary emptiness of self-nature, or *rangtong*. At this point, he introduces the term *shentong*, or "empty of other," for the first time in the book, showing how the ultimate true nature that is other than an emptiness of self-nature is established in the scriptures by way of the many synonyms for the ground of emptiness, and refuting various misconceptions about these.

Results

The third section of *Mountain Dharma* begins with a general presentation of the Mahāyāna results. By means of correct view, meditation, and conduct, the path of the two assemblies of merit and primordial awareness is utterly completed and, through extinguishing the two obscurations that are to be abandoned, the result of buddhahood will be attained. As Dölpopa describes it, that buddhahood—the quintessence of the unimaginable, infinite excellence of the wonderful kāyas, primordial awarenesses, qualities, and activities—is vast like space and is the excellent source of everything sentient beings desire. These kāyas, types of primordial awareness, qualities, and activities of a perfect buddha are then carefully described. A long series of other topics is also discussed, such as how the kāyas are obtained, how the stains are purified and the paths and levels traversed, how the flow of ordinary breath must cease through the practice of yoga in order to reach those levels, how the consummate transformation is thus achieved, how the stains to be purified are extinguished but the sugata essence is not extinguished, how ordinary confused appearances do not arise to primordial awareness in which confusion has been extinguished, and how what appears to primordial awareness does not appear to ordinary consciousness and what appears to consciousness does not appear to primordial awareness.

About This Translation

Dölpopa's *Mountain Dharma* presents any translator with countless philological and conceptual challenges. The sheer number and extent of the quotations from classical Indian sources can be overwhelming. The cryptic nature and complexity of many of these also becomes quickly apparent. *Mountain Dharma* has sometimes been inaccurately described as an anthology. It is far more than that. Dölpopa's mastery of the issues is clearly displayed as he weaves together a rich tapestry of passages from Indian literature and his own striking interpretations of them. All the works he cites were originally written in Sanskrit and later translated into Tibetan. Sanskrit versions of most of the source texts no longer exist.

Dölpopa also quotes Tibetan translations of important tantras (such as *Chanting the Ultimate Names of Mañjuśrī*, the *Hevajra Tantra*, *Sampuṭa Tantra*, *Vajra Garland Tantra*, and *Tantra of the Drop of Mahāmudrā*) that are different than the standard translations now preserved in the canonical collections of the Kangyur. He sometimes compares the translations and uses the readings that he prefers. For example, when presenting a series of verses from the *Tantra of the Drop of Mahāmudrā* and the *Vajra Garland Tantra*, he mentions in his annotations many variant readings that match the Tibetan translations preserved in the Dergé edition of the Kangyur, and sometimes notes the need to consult an original Indian manuscript to resolve discrepancies.[63] At least for these tantras, the verses he chooses to include in *Mountain Dharma* are often from the Tibetan translations that have not survived, instead of those in the Kangyur. For example, when quoting lines from *Chanting the Ultimate Names of Mañjuśrī* (one of his most important sources) he is clearly comparing the early Tibetan translation of Lochen Rinchen Sangpo and the later revised translation by Shongtön Lodrö Tenpa (included in the Dergé Kangyur), which are both extant.[64] Throughout *Mountain Dharma*, he also frequently cites both Tibetan translations of the *Mahāparinirvāṇa Sūtra*, one translated into Tibetan from Sanskrit and the other from Chinese.

Much of this English translation of *Mountain Dharma* is thus a translation of earlier Tibetan translations of even earlier Sanskrit works. Many of the texts were repeatedly translated into Tibetan before Dölpopa's time. And he was also using the new Tibetan translations that three of his main students made from Sanskrit manuscripts of the *Kālacakra Tantra*, Puṇḍarīka's *Stainless Light*, and *Brief Presentation of the Assertions of My Own View* (by Puṇḍarīka's father, Mañjuśrīyaśas). The passages from these translations of the Jonang masters that were included in *Mountain Dharma* would not have been seen before by other Tibetans.

My translation of *Mountain Dharma* is primarily guided by Dölpopa's detailed annotations found in the earliest manuscripts of his work. Some of these annotations are included in the translation. The translation of the quotations in the book is based only on the Tibetan translations; none have been translated directly from Sanskrit sources. This translation attempts to convey what Dölpopa understood to be the intended meaning of these quotes, which is often quite different than the opinions of other scholars, then and now.

Whenever possible, quoted passages in *Mountain Dharma* that Dölpopa did not gloss in his annotations have been translated according to explanations in his other works, such as his commentary and annotations to the *Uttaratantra* and his annotations to the *Stainless Light*. Writings by his major Jonang disciples, such as Choklé Namgyal's annotations to the *Kālacakra* and the *Stainless Light*, Mati Panchen and Gharungwa Lhai Gyaltsen's commentaries on the *Uttaratantra*, Manchukhawa Lodrö Gyaltsen's commentary on *Chanting the Ultimate Names of Mañjuśrī*, and the writings of Nya Ön Kunga Pal have also been indispensable.

Dölpopa wrote for advanced practitioners who were deeply familiar with the scriptural sources he cites to support his views. His readers would have memorized many of the most important texts he quotes, such as *Chanting the Ultimate Names of Mañjuśrī* and the Five Treatises of Maitreya. Most readers of this English translation will not be acquainted with the wealth of ideas and quotations in *Mountain Dharma*. Dölpopa consistently emphasizes topics such as the definitive meaning of the Buddha's intent, the eternal reality of the sugata essence, or buddha nature, the division of the two ultimate and relative truths, the meaning of the three natures, and the distinctions of emptiness of self-nature and emptiness of other. To understand this consistency, which fastens his words and images together, is to turn a key. Once that key is turned, the profound depth of his work can be explored. While many other scriptures are also essential, the *Kālacakra Tantra* and the *Stainless Light* are his primary sources of inspiration. He refers to the *Kālacakra Tantra* as "the consummate source of Great Madhyamaka" and, as mentioned above, once said, "Because all the key points of the profound definitive meaning were discovered in the great commentary on the *Kālacakra Tantra*, it has been remarkably kind."[65]

Acknowledgments

I first heard of Dölpopa Sherab Gyaltsen in 1974 while receiving Dharma from Dezhung Tulku Rinpoché and reading the biography of the great adept Thangtong Gyalpo (1361?–1485), who said, "In my last life I was called the Omniscient Dölpopa." Dezhung Rinpoché often emphasized the importance of the buddha nature, greatly respected the Jonang masters Kunga Drölchok and Tāranātha, and told stories from their autobiographies, which inspired me to read them myself. As I continued to read the literature of the Jonang and Sakya traditions I learned more about Dölpopa and became increasingly fascinated. My first direct contact with the Kālacakra teachings and special practices transmitted through Dölpopa's tradition occurred in Kathmandu in 1988. At that time, and on two later occasions, I had the honor to interpret for Chogyé Trichen Rinpoché when he gave the great initiation of Kālacakra and taught the Six-Branch Yoga of Kālacakra according to Tāranātha's manual of guiding instructions, written precisely according to the practice of Dölpopa and his major disciples. In Kathmandu, Chogyé Rinpoché also gave the reading transmission for the *Kālacakra Tantra* and the other Kālacakra scriptures in the Kangyur. And I was fortunate to receive the *Stainless Light* from Tenga Rinpoché when he gave the reading transmission of the Tengyur collection. During this period I was also able to ask Dilgo Khyentsé Rinpoché about Dölpopa and the *shentong* view, and Khyentsé Rinpoché encouraged me, saying, "Dölpopa is good. Read Dölpopa!" I am blessed to have known such wonderful teachers.

Geshé Thupten Jinpa first contacted me in 2006 about translating *Mountain Dharma* for the Library of Tibetan Classics. I was excited by the prospect of being absorbed in it for an extended period, but terrified by how difficult the project would be. Even so, I rashly accepted Jinpa's kind invitation. I appreciate his confidence that I could eventually accomplish this work. Because of previous commitments I could not start translating the book until early 2012. At that time Tsadra Foundation generously offered a grant to support my research and work on *Mountain Dharma*, which continued through 2014. I appreciate the foundation's support during that period. In 2021 I was finally able to return to this work, two years after I had mentioned it to Daniel Aitken (CEO/Publisher, Wisdom Publications). I am truly grateful to Daniel for reviving the nearly dead project and arranging the necessary funding to bring it to completion. Without his deep commitment to publish *Mountain Dharma*, years of hard work would have come to nothing. I also thank Mary Petrusewicz for her fine copyediting, especially her perceptive queries that often prompted me to make improvements in the book.

I am pleased to thank the consummate Sanskrit scholar David Reigle for his expert advice on difficult passages and terms in texts that still exist in Sanskrit, and for his exhaustive searches to find the correct Sanskrit for obscure personal and place names translated into Tibetan. I have also benefited from the earlier English translation of *Mountain Dharma* by Jeffrey Hopkins (2006).

Mountain Dharma is indeed an ocean of the profound definitive meaning of the Buddha's teachings. I have done my best to translate Dölpopa's incredible compendium of profound knowledge. Unlike its author, however, I am not omniscient, but make mistakes for which I take full responsibility.

Technical Note

THE TIBETAN title of the volume translated here is *Ri chos nges don rgya mtsho*, which means *Mountain Dharma: An Ocean of Definitive Meaning.* Three Tibetan texts were the main sources used for this translation. (1) The edition published in volume 1 of the Jo nang dpe tshogs series by the Mi rigs dpe skrun khang, Beijing, in 2007. I found this to be the most reliable edition and primarily based my translation on it. The numbers embedded in curly brackets in the translation are approximate locators for page numbers in this edition, which contains Dölpopa's own annotations to his work. This is the only Tibetan publication to include these annotations, which were previously available only in the oldest manuscripts and are not in the two other editions listed here. Some of these annotations are translated in the present book. (2) The edition prepared specifically for *The Library of Tibetan Classics* and its Tibetan equivalent, the *Bod kyi gtsug lag gces btus*. Numbers embedded in square brackets in the translation are approximate locators for page numbers in this critical Tibetan edition published in New Delhi by the Institute of Tibetan Classics (2013, ISBN 978-81-89165-07-0) as volume 7 of the *Bod kyi gtsug lag gces btus* series. I was unable to get a copy of this edition until after the first draft of my translation was complete. The *Bod kyi gtsug lag gces btus* edition of the Tibetan text is particularly useful because its annotations identify most of the nearly twelve hundred quotations in the book. I found, however, that a large number of the identifications are incorrect. After locating and correcting about half these citations myself, Thupten Jinpa kindly found almost all the rest. The present English translation is now the most reliable source for identifying the quotations in *Mountain Dharma*. (3) The edition published in volume 3 of *Kun mkhyen dol po pa shes rab rgyal mtshan gyi gsung 'bum* (The Collected Works of the Omniscient Dölpopa Sherab Gyaltsen) by the 'Dzam thang Bsam 'grub nor bu'i gling gi par khang, 'Dzam thang, in 1998. This is an excellent edition with few mistakes.

Tibetan scholarly compositions are usually structured around an outline embedded in the text by the author; a separate outline is more unusual. In the early manuscripts and prints of *Mountain Dharma* and its *Outline* the two texts are always kept separate, without any detailed outline in the treatise itself. Silent marks, however, are found in the main text to indicate where headings and subheadings in the outline apply. And annotations in the outline provide the first few words of the sections in the main work where the headings and subheadings apply. Based on these marks and annotations in the old texts, the three most recent Tibetan editions have inserted the headings and subheadings into the main text itself. So the outline is also included in the present English translation. The placement of the headings and subheadings from Dölpopa's outline throughout the translation follows the Jo nang dpe tshogs edition, which is somewhat different than the other two listed above. Curiously, the subheadings are sometimes located between clauses in the middle of long sentences. Perhaps this is just one of Dölpopa's stylistic quirks.

The full outline of *Mountain Dharma* with references to the page numbers in the translation is also included separately as appendix 1. The table of contents selectively draws from this outline to present the main topics of discussion. Unless otherwise noted, words in square brackets in the text are almost always translations of Dölpopa's annotations found in the Jo nang dpe tshogs edition. Only a few bracketed words have been added by the translator for the sake of clarification.

In the bibliography and endnotes the various references from classical Indian works in the Kangyur and Tengyur are identified according to the numbers in the Tohoku catalogue of the Dergé edition of these collections: *A Complete Catalogue of the Tibetan Buddhist Canons* (*Bkaḥ-ḥgyur and Bstan-ḥgyur*), edited by Hakuju Ui, Munetada Suzuki, Yenshō Kanakura, and Tōkan Tada (Sendai: Tōhoku Imperial University, 1934). References to the three Tibetan translations not found in the Dergé editions are identified from other sources.

The conventions for phonetic transcription of Tibetan words are those developed by the Institute of Tibetan Classics and Wisdom Publications. These reflect approximately the pronunciation of words by a modern Central Tibetan. Transliterations of the phoneticized Tibetan terms and names used in the text can be found in the table in appendix 2. Sanskrit diacritics are used throughout.

Pronunciation of Tibetan phonetics:
ph and *th* are aspirated *p* and *t,* as in *pet* and *tip.*
ö is similar to the *eu* in French *seul.*
ü is similar to the *ü* in the German *füllen.*
ai is similar to the *e* in *bet.*
é is similar to the *e* in *prey.*

Pronunciation of Sanskrit:
Palatal *ś* and retroflex *ṣ* are similar to the English unvoiced *sh.*
c is an unaspirated *ch* similar to the *ch* in *chill.*
The vowel *ṛ* is similar to the American *r* in *pretty.*
ñ is somewhat similar to a nasalized *ny* in *canyon.*
ṅ is similar to the *ng* in *sing* or *anger.*

Mountain Dharma

An Ocean of Definitive Meaning

Consummate, Uncommon Esoteric Instructions

Dölpopa Sherab Gyaltsen

Preface

Oṃ gurubuddhabodhisattvabhyonamonamaḥ[66]

Mountain Dharma: An Ocean of Definitive Meaning
Consummate, uncommon esoteric instructions

Homage to glorious Vajrasattva.

Homage to the sugata essence, the ground with stains to be purified.
Homage to the Vajrayoga, the path that purifies stains.
Homage to the dharmakāya, the result of separation, the ground with stains removed.

> First I bow to the venerable lords, the sublime masters,
> the slightest trace of the light of whose speech
> clears away infinite darkness from the heart, increasing
> the illumination of perfect realization.
>
> I bow to that which, isolated from all [relative] phenomena,
> is yet the kāya of countless, taintless [ultimate] attributes;[67]
> to that which, separate from the selves of phenomena and persons,
> is yet the self of thusness, the pure self; to that which, beyond all
> extremes of existence, nonexistence, permanence, and annihilation,
> is yet present as permanence, stability, and eternity itself; and
> to that which, without the nature of all entities, is yet by nature
> luminosity.
>
> As those having the divine eye have revealed, in accord
> with pure scripture I will reveal what is to be known,
> which is like a great treasure beneath the earth of one's home;

what is to be brought into experience, which is like diligence
as the means to obtain that; and what is to be obtained,
which is like the fulfillment of all goals when it has been obtained.

After bowing down to the rūpakāya that has the qualities
of the ripened result (arisen from the fine seed of a conqueror,
born from the assembly of merit), in accord with scripture I will
also write of the conventional kāyas of the seers, and by what and
just how these are produced, like the growth of a great tree bursting
with sublime fruit. {4}

Part One
A Brief Presentation of the Ground, Path, and Result

This has three topics.

One: A Concise Presentation of the Ground, Path, and Result of Definitive Meaning

Here is what should be known at the very first by those who wish to obtain sublime liberation, the naturally luminous dharmakāya, self-arisen primordial awareness that is consummate purity, self, bliss, and permanence, and then act for the benefit of all sentient beings by means of the rūpakāya: [4] Even though a great treasure of jewels exists beneath the earth of a poor person's home, it is obscured by seven fathoms of earth and stone, so he lives in suffering, not seeing, not realizing, and not obtaining it. In just that way, even though a great treasure of the qualities of the naturally luminous dharmakāya exists in oneself and all others at all times, it is obscured by incidental stains, so we always live in suffering, not seeing, not realizing, and not obtaining it. From stainless scripture and reasoning endowed with the exceptional esoteric instructions of excellent masters, these should be well understood to be what are to be obtained and what are to be discarded.

Then that treasure is carefully revealed by those having the divine eye. This is similar to knowing that what is to be obtained is the great treasure itself and what is to be discarded is the earth and stone covering it; it is also the same as knowing that it will not be obtained if those are not cleared away, and will be obtained merely by clearing them away.

After understanding in that way, what is to be brought into experience is diligence in accomplishing the assembly of pure primordial awareness, with its associated factors, in order to clear away all incidental stains. This is similar to clearing away those seven fathoms of earth and stone.

Having brought it into experience in that way, what is obtained is the result of separation, the dharmakāya, a great treasure of taintless and inseparable qualities. This is similar to carefully obtaining that treasure of jewels. {5}

Two: A Concise Presentation of How Those Are Established by Scripture

Here it might be asked, "How do we know those to be like that?"

We know from the elegant statements of the buddhas and bodhisattvas. Just as the *Sūtra of the Tathāgata Essence* says:

> Sons of good family, again it is like this: Suppose that in the earth beneath a storeroom in the home of a poor person there were a great treasure filled with gems and gold that was about the size of the storeroom, covered beneath seven fathoms of earth. But that great treasure would not say to that poor man, "Sir, I am a great treasure, but covered with earth," because the great treasure is not a sentient being with a very essence of mind.
>
> That poor homeowner would think with the mind of a poor person and, even though wandering around just above it, would not hear, know, or see the existence of that great treasure beneath the earth. [5]
>
> Sons of good family, in a similar way, the great treasure of the storeroom of the tathāgata essence with the powers, the types of fearlessness, the unshared [attributes], and all the attributes of a buddha exists beneath the fixated mental activity of all sentient beings, which are like the home, but since those sentient beings are attached to form, sound, odor, taste, and contact, they circle in saṃsāra, suffering. Since they have not heard of that great treasure of attributes, they have not obtained it, and do not apply diligence to fully purify it.
>
> Sons of good family, then the Tathāgata appears in the world and perfectly and fully reveals the great treasure of attributes such as this among the bodhisattvas. They also aspire to that great treasure of attributes, dig it out, and are therefore known in the world as "tathāgatas, arhats, and perfectly complete buddhas."
>
> Having [obtained] what is like a great treasure of attributes, they teach sentient beings the forms of unprecedented reasoning, examples, reasons for acting, and activities. As donors of the

storeroom of the great treasure, they have unattached confidence, having become storerooms of the powers, the types of fearlessness, and the many attributes of a buddha. {6}

Sons of good family, in this way the Tathāgata, the Arhat, the perfectly complete Buddha, also sees with the completely pure vision of a tathāgata that all sentient beings are like that, and teaches the Dharma to the bodhisattvas in order to completely purify the storeroom of a tathāgata's primordial awareness, powers, types of fearlessness, and the unshared attributes of a buddha.[68]

And the root text and commentary of the *Uttaratantra* also says:

The afflictions are similar to the depths of the earth, while the basic element of a tathāgata is like a treasure of jewels.

Suppose an inexhaustible treasure were beneath
the earth within a poor man's home, but that man
did not know it and that treasure also did not tell him
"I am here."

Likewise, a stainless treasure of jewels is contained
within the mind, with nothing to be added or removed
from its true nature, but that is not realized, so these
beings continually experience the suffering of poverty
in many forms.

Just as a treasure of jewels contained within the home
of a poor man would not say to the man, "I, the treasure
of jewels, am here," and the man would not know,
so too a treasure of attributes abides in the home of mind,
and sentient beings are like the poor man. The Seer
is perfectly born in the world in order that they obtain
that [treasure].[69]

Agreeing with that, the *Mahāparinirvāṇa* translated by Lhai Dawa also says:

"Bhagavān, are those of the twenty-five modes of cyclic existence said to have or not have a self?"[70] [6]

[The Bhagavān] replied: "'Self' means tathāgata essence. The basic element of a buddha exists in all sentient beings, but it is also obscured by aspects of the afflictions, and even while it exists in them, sentient beings are not able to see it. It is like this: Suppose there were an inexhaustible treasure of gold in the home of a poor person in a great city, but the poor woman who was there did not know a treasure was beneath the earth of her home. A skillful man there tells that woman, 'There is a treasure in your home, but if even you yourself do not know it, how can others know to look?' {7}

"Then she begs him, 'I must get it!' So he digs that treasure from within the home and gives it to her. Then she sees it and is amazed and takes refuge in him.

"Likewise, son of good family, the tathāgata essence is in all sentient beings, but they are simply not able to see it, like that poor woman who had the treasure.

"Son of good family, now I will perfectly reveal, 'The tathāgata essence exists in all sentient beings.'

"Just as it was revealed that the poor woman had a treasure but did not know, likewise the tathāgata essence exists in all sentient beings but is obscured by the aspects of the afflictions, so sentient beings do not know and do not see it. Then the Tathāgata reveals it to them, they are pleased, and go to the Tathāgata for refuge."[71]

And so on. Likewise, the *Mahāparinirvāṇa* transmitted from China also says:

Son of good family, I also say this: the buddha nature of sentient beings is, for example, similar to a treasure of jewels in the home of a poor woman, a precious diamond gem in the forehead of a strongman, and the delicious spring of a universal emperor.[72]

It contains very extensive passages such as that. The *Dhāraṇī of Penetrating the Nonconceptual* also says:

Sons of good family, it is like this: Suppose that beneath uniquely hard and solid rock there were various great, luminous, precious wish-fulfilling gems. That is, a great treasure completely filled with different types of precious silver, precious gold, and precious emerald. Then a man who wishes for a great treasure comes. [7]

A man with clairvoyant knowledge of the great treasure says to him: "Sir, beneath that uniquely hard and solid rock there is a great precious treasure completely filled with luminous precious substances. And beneath that is the treasure of a precious wish-fulfilling gem. At the very first, however, you must dig through all that has the nature of stone! Dig through that, and stone that appears to be silver will appear to you, but you should not consider that to be the great treasure. Fully understand that and dig! {8} Dig through that, and stone that appears to be gold will appear, but you should not consider that to be the great treasure. Fully understand that and dig! Dig through that, and stone that appears to be various jewels will appear, but you should not consider that to be the great treasure. Fully understand that and dig! Sir, if you work diligently in that way, without the labor of further digging and without need of effort you will see the great treasure of the precious wish-fulfilling gem.

"If you discover that great treasure of the precious wish-fulfilling gem, you will become rich, with great wealth and possessions, and have the power to benefit yourself and others."

In that way, sons of good family, this is used as an example in order for the meaning [of the incidental stains and the sugata essence] to be understood as well as possible. "Uniquely hard and solid rock" is an expression for [the obscuration of] the conditioned defilements and [the obscuration of knowledge] that closely support the duality [of apprehended and apprehender]. "Beneath is the great treasure of the precious wish-fulfilling gem" is an expression for the [ultimate] nonconceptual basic element. "A man who wishes for that great treasure of the wish-fulfilling gem" is an expression for a bodhisattva, a mahāsattva. "A man with clairvoyant knowledge of the great treasure" is an expression for the Tathāgata, the Arhat, the perfectly complete Buddha. "Rock" is an expression for conceptual marks concerning the nature. "Dig!" is an expression for [cultivating the samādhi] that does not engage in mental activity. "Stone that appears to be silver" is an expression for conceptual marks concerning the antidotes. "Stone that appears to be gold" is an expression for conceptual marks concerning emptiness and so on. "Stone that appears to be various jewels" is an expression for conceptual marks concerning [the

> result] that will be obtained. "Discover the great treasure of the precious wish-fulfilling gem" is an expression for contacting [and obtaining] the [ultimate] nonconceptual basic element.
>
> Sons of good family, in that way, through this explicit statement of examples, you should understand penetrating into the nonconceptual basic element.[73]

And so on, it states extensively. For details, one certainly must consult those precious sūtras and that profound commentary on their intent.[74] {9} [8]

Three: A Concise Presentation of the Ground, Path, and Result of Both Kāyas

In this way, that which is the true nature, the nonconceptual and luminous basic element, is the natural family.

The evolving family supported on that is the exceptional virtues perfectly acquired through planting and growing the seeds of liberation, which develop the rūpakāya of a tathāgata. This is similar to the developing of a fine fruit tree.

In that way, it is stated that the two aspects of family (consisting of the two truths, and existent and nonexistent in the abiding state of reality) form the ground from which, by having brought the path (the assembly of primordial awareness and the assembly of merit) into experience, the dharmakāya and the two rūpakāyas will be obtained as the result. Just as the *Mahāyāna Uttaratantra* says:

> Being like a treasure and a fruit tree,
> those families should be known as twofold:
> the naturally abiding one without beginning,
> and the sublime, perfectly acquired one.
>
> From these two families, it is held,
> the three kāyas of a buddha are obtained.
> By the first, the first kāya, and by the second,
> the latter two.[75]

The Great Madhyamaka source text known as *Ornament of the Mahāyāna Sūtras* also says:

The natural and the evolving
are the support and the supported,
the existent and the nonexistent.[76]

This is, for the moment, a brief presentation. Now I will also give an extensive explanation of those [i.e., ground, path, and result]. {10}

Part Two
Extensive Explanations of Each of Those

This has three sections.

One:
How the Ultimate Buddha Is Primordially Present as the Basic Ground

This has seven topics.

I. *Showing the profound true nature to be the universal-ground primordial awareness*

That consummate Buddha, dharmakāya, tathāgata essence, ultimate luminosity, dharmadhātu, self-arisen primordial awareness, and great bliss, which is the partless omnipresent pervader, is said to be the ground and basis of all phenomena. And, in reality, it is also said to be the ground empty of, and the ground isolated from, all phenomena, and the ground with all stains removed. But it is also said to have, indivisible from its nature, the qualities of the dharmakāya exceeding the grains of sand found in the Ganges River. [9]

II. *Carefully establishing that by means of pure scripture*

This has fourteen topics.

A. *How all the deities of the basic element and awareness indivisible reside pervading all that is static and mobile*

This has two topics.

1. *How the characteristic of the cause is stated in the Vehicle of the Perfections*

Furthermore, in the *Commentary on the "Mahāyāna Uttaratantra"* a sūtra is quoted and explained:

> It says:
>
> > The basic element of beginningless
> > time is the basis of all phenomena.
> > Since it exists, all forms of life and
> > also nirvāṇa are obtained.[77]
>
> Here, how is it of beginningless time?
>
> In the context of the tathāgata essence itself, what is taught and fully established is that "A prior limit is not observed."
>
> As for "basic element," it is said:
>
> > Bhagavān, this tathāgata essence is the essence of transcendent phenomena, the essence of phenomena that are naturally, utterly pure.[78] {11}

As for "is the basis of all phenomena," it says:

> Bhagavān, therefore the tathāgata essence is the basis, ground, and support of the unconditioned attributes that are connected, indivisible, and cannot be realized as being separable [from it]. Bhagavān, the tathāgata essence is also the ground, basis, and support of the conditioned attributes that are unconnected, divisible, and can be realized as being separable [from it].[79]

As for "Since it exists, all forms of life and," it says:

> Bhagavān, if the tathāgata essence exists, it is labeled with the word "saṃsāra."[80]

As for "also nirvāṇa are attained," it says:

> Bhagavān, if the tathāgata essence did not exist, there would be no weariness about suffering, and also no wish, striving, and aspiration for nirvāṇa.[81]

Thus it says in detail.[82]

And the *Uttaratantra* also says:

> Just as worlds in all [phases] arise
> and perish dependent on space,
> so too the sense faculties arise and perish
> dependent on the unconditioned basic element.
>
> Just as space has never been
> burned before by the fires, so too
> this [sugata essence] is not burned
> by the fires of death, illness, and aging.
>
> Earth is fully based on water,
> water on wind, and wind on space.
> But space is not based on the elements
> of wind, water, or earth.
>
> Likewise, the aggregates, elements,
> and sense faculties are based on karma

and the afflictions. Karma and the afflictions
are always based on improper mental engagement.

Mental engagement that is improper
is fully based on the purity of the mind.
But the nature of mind is not based on
any [relative] phenomena.[83] [10]

And so on, it says in detail. In the commentary on that a sūtra is also quoted, which takes as an example the dependence of earth, water, and so forth on space, and then says:

> Likewise, the aggregates, elements, and sensory bases are fully based on karma and the afflictions; karma and the afflictions are fully based on improper mental engagement; improper mental engagement is fully based on natural utter purity. Therefore, it is said, "The nature of mind is luminosity, unafflicted by incidental secondary afflictions."[84] {12}

And so on. The *Sūtra of the Dense Array* also says:

The various levels are the universal ground;
the sugata essence and virtue are also that.
The tathāgatas teach that essence with the term
"universal ground."

The essence is proclaimed to be the universal ground,
but those with weak minds do not understand.[85]

And:

The declaration of the universal ground
to be the essence is not an object of conceptual mind.

When the nature is examined,
it cannot be analyzed, and it is also
the fully established nature always seen
by those proficient in yoga.[86]

Here the dharmadhātu itself in which the ultimate levels are complete is taught to also be the universal ground, the sugata essence, and ultimate virtue. The ultimate levels are taught in detail in the *Tantra of the Ornament of the Vajra Essence*, "Establishing Sublimely Unchanging Primordial Awareness," and the *Great Commentary of Nāropa*, and are stated in concise form in *Chanting the Ultimate Names*, and so on.[87] These are only comprehensible through the uncommon esoteric instructions of an excellent master.

As for [that universal-ground primordial awareness] being ultimate virtue, the sūtra of Great Madhyamaka known as the *Journey to Laṅkā* says:

> The tathāgata essence is virtue,
> not a sophist's field of experience.[88]

And:

> [Ultimate] mind is naturally luminous,
> the tathāgata essence, virtue.[89]

And so on. The great Madhyamaka master, the honorable, noble Asaṅga also says:

> What is ultimate virtue? Thusness.[90]

The *Mahāparinirvāṇa* also says the sugata essence, the buddha nature, is virtue:

> Son of good family, I say this: even those who have damaged the four roots,[91] who are depraved, who denigrate the extremely detailed sūtras, and who have committed negative acts that bring immediate retribution have the buddha nature. Though attributes of virtue will not come to those sentient beings, the buddha nature is virtue.[92] {13}

And so on. [11] And:

> Son of good family, in this sūtra I say the buddha nature has six [unconditioned] properties: it is permanent, [the apex of] reality, true, virtue, pure, and seen.[93]

And so on in extreme detail. The Conqueror's Mother Sūtras also say:

> Whether [relative] tathāgatas appear or tathāgatas do not appear, that true nature of phenomena, dharmadhātu, constancy of phenomena, and flawlessness of phenomena abide [unchanging] in that way. To that the tathāgatas directly and completely awaken. They directly realize. And after directly and completely awakening and directly realizing, they speak, teach, express, comment, distinguish, clarify, and perfectly teach.[94]

And so on, it states extensively. The *Journey to Laṅkā* also says:

> Mahāmati, that true nature, constancy of phenomena, immutability of phenomena, thusness, reality itself, and truth itself, which I [Śākyamuni] and those [other] tathāgatas have realized, [always] exists.[95]

In many various sūtras of Great Madhyamaka this very approach is stated again and again. The *Sūtra of the Tathāgata Essence* also says:

> Sons of good family, this is the true nature of phenomena and, whether tathāgatas appear or tathāgatas do not appear, these sentient beings always have the tathāgata essence.[96]

And so on. That sugata essence having many synonyms such as "dharmadhātu" is thus said to be the ground and basis of all phenomena. Therefore, in the phase with the stains not removed, it is present as the ground with stains remaining; in the phase with them not removed and removed, as the ground being purified of stains; and in the phase when very pure, as the ground with stains removed. So it pervades all, ever present, like space. {14}

2. *How the characteristic of the result is stated in profound secret mantra*

Likewise, the *Glorious Hevajra* says:

> Sentient beings are buddhas,
> but obscured by incidental stains.
> If those are removed, they are buddhas.[97]

And:

> Once their own [nature] is realized,
> not one sentient being is not a buddha.
> The bliss of hell beings, hungry spirits,
> and animals, gods, anti-gods, and humans,
>
> and even of worms in feces,
> and so on, and of the gods
> and the anti-gods is unknown,
> yet their nature is always blissful.
>
> Buddha is not found anywhere else
> in the world. Mind is the perfect
> Buddha. Buddha is not taught to be
> anything else.[98] [12]

Such passages say the naturally luminous mind residing in all sentient beings is Buddha, and say just that is obtained by merely parting from all incidental stains. And:

> Great primordial awareness resides
> in the body, with all concepts fully abandoned.
> Pervader of all entities, residing in the body,
> but not born from the body.[99]

Thus it says that self-arisen primordial awareness, the sugata essence residing in the bodies of all sentient beings, is present like space pervading all entities, but not born from any entity. And the *Glorious Sampuṭa* also says:

> Buddha resides in one's body.
> Buddha exists nowhere else. Those
> obscured by the darkness of ignorance
> claim Buddha to be other than in the body. {15}
>
> Great primordial awareness, with all
> concepts abandoned, resides in the body.
> Pervading all entities, it resides in the body,
> but is not born from the body.[100]

And so on. And the *Vajra Garland*, an explanatory tantra of the *Glorious Guhyasamāja*, also states:

> In this body of the vajra master,
> the bodies of the conquerors reside
> in sequence. First, the body vajra
> perfectly resides in the aggregate of form.
>
> The vajra of subsequent passion
> resides in the aggregate of feeling.
> The bhagavān speech vajra resides
> in the aggregate of discrimination.
>
> The vajra of all actions resides
> in the aggregate of conditioning factors.
> The bhagavān mind vajra perfectly resides
> in the aggregate of consciousness.
>
> Also, in the flesh and so on of this one,
> the element of earth, bhagavatī mother
> Locanā resides. In the blood and so on,
> the element of water, bhagavatī mother
> Māmakī resides.
>
> In warmth and so on, the element of fire,
> bhagavatī mother Pāṇḍarā resides.
> In movement and so on, the element of wind,
> bhagavatī mother Tārā resides.
>
> In his two sense faculties of the eyes,
> tathāgata Kṣitigarbha.
> In his two sense faculties of the ears,
> sugata Vajrapāṇi.
>
> In his sense faculty of the nose,
> tathāgata Akaśagarbha.
> Residing in the sense faculty of his tongue,
> tathāgata Lokeśvara.

In the mass with the nature
of the four elements labeled "body,"
that tathāgata Sarvanīvaraṇaviṣkambhin
resides.

In his mental sense faculty,
tathāgata Mañjughoṣa resides.
In all the joints of the body,
tathāgata Samantabhadra.

In the body's veins and ligaments,
tathāgata Maitreya.
At the base of the right hand,
tathāgata Yamāri.

At the base of the left hand,
tathāgata Aparājita. [13]
Residing in the lotus of the mouth,
tathāgata Hayagrīva.

Residing in the secret place,
tathāgata Amṛtakuṇḍalī.
Residing in the right shoulder,
tathāgata Acala. {16}

Residing in the left shoulder,
tathāgata Ṭakkirāja.
Residing in the right knee,
tathāgata Nīladaṇḍa.

Residing in the left knee,
tathāgata Mahābala.
Residing at the top of his own head,
tathāgata Cakravartin.

Residing in the feet below,
tathāgata Śumbha.
Here in all this very body
all the tathāgatas reside.[101]

Such passages say all the deities of self-arisen primordial awareness, the ultimate father and mother conquerors, the children of the conquerors, the kings of the wrathful deities, and so on reside in the body.

B. *How just what is present in that way is all the ultimate Three Jewels of the true nature*

Here one must realize that the ultimate children of the conquerors, and so on, who appear as the Jewel of the Saṅgha, are also actual buddhas, and that all the ultimate Three Jewels have one essence. Referring to these points, the *Chapter of Firm Altruistic Intent* says:

> Ānanda, the [ultimate] Tathāgata is not demonstrable; eyes cannot look at him. Ānanda, the Dharma is not expressible; ears cannot hear it. Ānanda, the Saṅgha is unconditioned; body and mind cannot honor it.[102]

And the *Vajra Garland Tantra* also says:

> Stainless mind is the [ultimate] Buddha,
> the Dharma is perfectly stated to be speech.
> Body is called "Saṅgha," the place of
> the assembly of bodhisattvas.
>
> Buddha is explained as the syllable *hūṃ*.
> Speech is expressed as the syllable *āḥ*.
> Saṅgha is the syllable *oṃ*, the quintessence
> radiating everywhere.
>
> Buddha is the avadhūtī.
> Dharma is also expressed as the lalanā.
> Saṅgha is expressed as the rasanā.
> These are the characteristics of the three. {17}
>
> The [ultimate] formless realm is the [ultimate] Buddha.
> The form realm is the Dharma, and the desire realm,
> likewise, is the Saṅgha. In that way, the sublime
> [or other] characteristics of the three realms are

the [sugata] essence; [other than] its own [great]
lifeforce, nothing else exists in the three realms.
The three realms of illusory wind are seen to be
like dreams in a dream.

The quintessence of the [ultimate] three realms
is thusness, unique and quickly seen.
After one has been blessed, the attainment of
thusness is quickly achieved.

The Buddha is the sambhogakāya,
the excellent Dharma is the dharmakāya,
the Saṅgha is the nirmāṇakāya. [14]
Those have a quintessence of the three kāyas.

[Ultimate] appearance is the form of the Buddha,
The [ultimate] Dharma is the attainment of appearance.
The [ultimate] Saṅgha is the increase of appearance.
Those are the characteristics of the three appearances.[103]

And the *Glorious Tantra of the Arising of Saṃvara* also says:

The [ultimate] Buddha, and likewise the Dharma
and Saṅgha, are one, but designated as three.
That is the nature of the three refuges, the three
realities, the three kāyas, the three liberations,

the three faces, the three syllables,
the three gods, and the three realms.
It is taught to be the three maṇḍalas,
the three yogas, and the three paths.

It is the three sacred commitments,
the three virtues, and also body,
speech, and mind. It is also wisdom
and means, and their three unions.

It is the three secrets, however they are seen,
and the nature of the source of the attributes,

> through which, by the yoga without perception
> of the three spheres, it is the nature of the three
> mantras and the nature of the three channels.[104]

Such passages teach the ultimate sugata essence itself to be the three refuges, the three realities, the three kāyas, the three liberations, the three faces, the three gods, the three realms of the true nature, the three maṇḍalas, and so on. Therefore, the consummate Three Jewels are one, since the ultimate Three Jewels are dharmadhātu itself. {18}

In that way, if the division of the two truths regarding even the Three Jewels is understood, one will not be deluded about the Sage's word.

Likewise, the *Mahāparinirvāṇa* says:

> The buddha nature is unconditioned, so it is called "permanent." [The other] space is the buddha nature. The buddha nature is the Tathāgata. The Tathāgata is unconditioned. The unconditioned [Buddha] is permanent. The permanent [Buddha] is the Dharma. [That] Dharma is the Saṅgha. [That] Saṅgha is unconditioned. The unconditioned is permanent.[105]

And:

> Son of good family, furthermore, always remember and emphasize the [ultimate] Buddha, Dharma, and Saṅgha.
>
> These three aspects of the Dharma have the characteristic of not being different, the characteristic of not being impermanent, and the characteristic of immutability.
>
> If anyone perceives these three aspects of the Dharma to be different, that person is said to not abide in the three types of taking refuge, to not have moral discipline, and to not be able to obtain even the enlightenment of the śrāvaka and the pratyekabuddha.
>
> If anyone emphasizes that inconceivable [basic element] by perceiving it to be permanent, that is the source in which to take refuge.
>
> Son of good family, for example: because the tree exists the shadow exists.
>
> The Tathāgata is also like that. And because the permanent Dharma exists, a source of refuge exists; the impermanent is not [the sublime refuge]. [15]

> If anyone says "The Tathāgata is impermanent," the Tathāgata would also not be a source in which the gods and the world take refuge.[106]

And:

> Therefore, "utter peace" is perfect liberation. That perfect liberation is the Tathāgata. The [ultimate] Tathāgata is the [ultimate] Dharma.[107]

And:

> If anyone says "The Tathāgata is different than the Dharma and the Saṅgha," those would not be three sources in which to take refuge.[108]

And so on. And the *Uttaratantra* also says:

> Ultimately, the refuge for living beings
> is the Buddha alone, because the Sage
> has the kāya of the Dharma, and because
> the Assembly is also its consummation.[109]

That also has the same meaning as the previously presented. {19}

C. *Also, how just that is the sugata essence, presented with many examples and meanings*

Furthermore, condensing the meaning of the *Sūtra of the Tathāgata Essence* and so on, the *Uttaratantra* says:

> Like a buddha in a decaying lotus, honey amid bees,
> kernels in husks, gold in filth, a treasure in the earth,
> a sprout and so on from a small fruit, an image of
> the Conqueror within rags,
>
> a lord of human beings in the belly of a lowly woman,
> and a figure of precious substances inside clay,
> so too this basic element resides in sentient beings
> obscured by the stains of the incidental afflictions.

> The stains resemble the lotus, the creatures, the husks, the filth, the earth, the fruit, the rags, the woman tormented by burning suffering, and the element of clay. The buddha, the honey, the kernels, the gold, and the treasure, the banyan tree, the image of precious substances, the sublime lord of the continents, and the figure of precious substances resemble the sublime, stainless basic element.[110]

And:

> The husks of the afflictions over the basic
> element of sentient beings are not connected [to it],
> but are beginningless. The stainless nature
> of the mind is said to be beginningless.[111]

And so on. And:

> Manifesting differently as the thusness of
> ordinary beings, noble beings, and complete
> buddhas, this essence of the conquerors is taught
> to sentient beings by those who see reality.[112]

Also:

> Here, what is the meaning of the statement "All sentient beings have the tathāgata essence,"[113] made in the context of thusness with stains?
>
> > Since the kāya of a complete buddha
> > radiates, since thusness is indivisible,
> > and since they have the family, all embodied
> > beings always have the buddha essence.[114]

And so on. {20} And *One Hundred and Fifty Modes of the Perfection of Wisdom* also says:

> Since [the true nature] is the nature of all [phenomena], all sentient beings have the tathāgata essence. [16]

> Since all have been initiated by the vajra essence, all sentient beings have the vajra essence.
>
> Since all speech [of the true nature] is self-arisen, all sentient beings have the [ultimate] essence of Dharma.[115]

D. *Also, just that is shown to have the same meaning as the naturally abiding family*

And the Great Madhyamaka *Commentary on the "Uttaratantra"* also says:

> Referring to the utterly pure family, this basic element of a tathāgata, it is said:
>
> > Just as pure gold not seen
> > in gravel is seen when that
> > has been fully cleansed, so too
> > the Tathāgata [is seen] in the world.[116]

And:

> Since the naturally pure family exists [in all sentient beings], it is not appropriate that any will never be purified. Why? Having in mind that all sentient beings without difference are suitable to become pure, the Bhagavān said:
>
> > Beginningless, but having an end,
> > the beginningless husks [of the obscurations]
> > obscure the naturally pure permanent attribute
> > [of the sugata essence], unseen just like a figure
> > of gold that is obscured.[117]

The tathāgata essence is thus said to be the naturally, utterly pure family, and...

E. *Also, just that is shown to have the same meaning as the categories of the families stated in the tantras*

... that family is also said to consist of the three families, the five, and so on, the never-ceasing continuum of the natural true nature. The *Glorious Guhyasamāja* says:

The [natural] family is explained to be
the "continuum." [That] continuum is called
the "Ādi[buddha]," explained to be that protector
[Vajradhara], who is indestructible and unarisen.[118] {21}

And:

The [ultimate] continuum is said to be continuous.[119]

And:

The [natural] family is the five and the three
and the hundred families [established] by very essence.[120]

And so on. And the *Glorious Hevajra Tantra* also says:

The family is said to be the six and,
when condensed, becomes the five.
By the divisions of body, speech,
and mind, it later becomes the three.

The term "family" is used because, by family,
the families having the nature of the five elements
and the five aggregates are enumerated, or calculated,
and called "families."[121]

And:

Mind is great and just one,
but symbolized by the forms
of the five. From those five
families many thousands arise. [17]

Therefore, these are one nature,
great bliss, sublime benefit itself.
By division of the five minds
such as desire, that becomes the five.

> In the one family are as many tathāgata assemblies
> as the grains of sand found in ten Ganges Rivers.
> Those family assemblies become numerous families,
> and those families become hundreds of families.
>
> Those too become hundreds of thousands of great families,
> which become tens of millions of families, which become
> countless. Thus the family has countless families, which
> have come from the family of sublime joy.[122]

And *Chanting the Ultimate Names* also says:

> [Then Bhāgavan Śākyamuni] saw
> all the great families of secret mantra:
> the family of secret mantra and
> awareness holders, the three families,
>
> the mundane and the transcendent
> family, the great family that illuminates
> the world, the sublime family of mahāmudrā,
> and the great family of the great cranial dome.[123]

The meaning of that is stated in the *Glorious Kālacakra*:

> The cranial dome is the five emptinesses, and the three families
> also are likewise the vajras of body, speech, and mind. {22}
> *A* and so on are the family of [mahā]mudrā, and all the classes
> of *ka* and so on having *ha*, *ya*, *ra*, *va*, and *la* illuminate the world.
> Having *ha*, *ya*, *ra*, *va*, and *la* together with the vowel syllables
> is the mundane and the transcendent. The powerful holder of
> the mantras of awareness is the eight classes in which *ka* and so on
> all abide stacked up.[124]

And likewise:

> The six classes of *ka* and so on, the families fully arranged in series,
> are respectively those of vajra, sword, jewel, wheel, lotus, and,
> likewise, flaying knife, [the families] of the conquerors. And yet

> again each and all the classes are also divided by the five divisions of the sublime conquerors.[125]

Such passages mention many family divisions in that naturally pure family itself.

Likewise, to present the five families, it is said:

> Five faces having five hair-knots.[126]

And to present the six families:

> King of the wrathful, six-faced and fearful.[127]

And to present the one hundred families:

> Hundred-faced Halāhala.[128]

And the honorable, venerable lord Avalokiteśvara also says:

> Here, in a king of tantras [such as the *Guhyasamāja*] consisting of three families, the three-faced one consisting of body, speech, and mind is to be discussed.
>
> In [one like the *Kālacakra Tantra*] consisting of four families, the four-faced one consisting of body, speech, mind, and primordial awareness is to be discussed. Including the one natural family, the tantra consisting of four families is to be discussed.
>
> Likewise, one consisting of five families, together with the one natural family, becomes one consisting of six families.[129] [18]

And so on. And the *Tantra of the Glorious Sublime Primal* also says:

> That continuum holding
> the great vajra is the Tathāgata family.
> It is the great vajra family.
> It is the pure lotus family.
>
> It is explained to be the great gem family.
> Those are [ultimate] passionate desire,
> free of [relative] attachment.[130] {23}

And the *Vajra Garland Tantra* also states:

> It is clearly said in the root tantra
> that when the meaning of the family divisions
> is condensed, the family has five aspects.[131]

And so on. And the *Sublime Ādibuddha* also says:

> The three families and the five families themselves,
> the one natural and the one hundred families.[132]

And so on. All the categories of the families presented in the profound tantras should thus be understood to be categories of the natural family; they are not of the evolving family.

It might be asked, "The *Ornament of Direct Realization* says: 'Since the dharmadhātu is indivisible, difference in family is not appropriate.'[133] So are you not contradicting the explanation that different divisions are inappropriate for the natural family?"

No. That refers to no difference in essence, because in the profound tantras the essence is indivisible, but the divisions of family are stated by means of [different] aspects. Therefore, there is not even the slightest contradiction.

In *Lamp for the "Wisdom"* the teacher Bhāvaviveka quotes a passage of the *Stack of Jewels*:

> That which does not have karma and the result of karma is the family of the noble beings, and that family which is the family of the noble beings does not create physical karma, does not create vocal karma, and does not create mental karma.[134]

That also refers to the ground without karma and result, the true nature, the unconditioned basic element.

In that way, the meaning of the natural family itself stated in the profound sūtras and tantras is the same as thusness, natural luminosity, the tathāgata essence, and the primordial awareness of dharmadhātu itself. But since it is stated that there are differences of delusion and lack of delusion about the very many distinct attributes, such as its aspects and qualities, to soar into the sky of the profound intent of the tantras and look from a high point is the king of esoteric instructions.

F. *Also, how just that is present as the continuum of the profound true nature and as the vajra family*

Likewise, that natural family itself is also the consummate continuum of indivisible emptiness and compassion, and just that, always present as the ground of all phenomena, is the causal continuum, said to be the "vajra family." {24}

Furthermore, just as stated at the beginning of the *Glorious Hevajra Tantra*, in the "Chapter of the Vajra Family" [19]:

> The syllable *he* expresses great compassion,
> and also *vajra* expresses wisdom.
> That tantra with a quintessence of wisdom
> and means I will explain, so listen.[135]

And the *Root Tantra in Five Hundred Thousand Lines* also says:

> Compassion is for sentient beings, for phenomena,
> and nonreferential; these are explained to be the three.
> The term "great" indicates the nonreferential,
> directly expressed by the syllable *he*.
>
> Through union of body, speech, and mind,
> that same [*he*] is the previous syllable *vaṃ*.
> The term "vajra" is also the syllable *e*,
> emptiness having all aspects.
>
> The union of these is expressed
> by the term "yoga." The tantra with
> a quintessence of wisdom and means
> is called a "yogatantra."[136]

And:

> The union of all buddhas
> fully abides in the syllables *evaṃ*.
> Later, by division into three families,
> through separation into five families,
> by the division of six families, and

> likewise through separation into four,
> I will express the tantra with a quintessence
> of wisdom and means, so listen.[137]

And so on. In that way, the two families are the families of wisdom and means. The three families are the families of body, speech, and mind. The four families are the families of the four kāyas, the four vajras, and so on. Furthermore, this "Chapter of the Family" itself states:

> [The Bhagavān] said:
>
> The indivisible is called "vajra."
> Sattva is the three states of cyclic existence
> yet just one. By this wise reasoning,
> he is explained to be Vajrasattva.
>
> That sattva residing in enlightenment
> is called "bodhisattva." Filled with the taste
> of great primordial awareness, he is called
> "mahāsattva." Always abiding in samaya,
> he is called "samayasattva."[138] {25}

And the *Root Tantra in Five Hundred Thousand Lines* also says:

> The indivisible, explained as "vajra,"
> is that renowned as the syllable *vaṃ*.
> Indivisible body, speech, and mind
> is directly expressed by the syllable *vaṃ*.
>
> Sattva, the three states of cyclic existence
> yet just one, is expressed by the syllable *e*.
> United with wisdom (the syllable *e*), the syllable
> *vaṃ* has a quintessence of the three families.
>
> The hero residing at the middle of the **navel**,
> in the pistil, the secret field of experience,
> endowed with reflexive wisdom, is to be fully
> expressed as Vajrasattva.

Explained to be the two-armed Heruka,
he is the Mover of the Three Worlds;
he is called "the svābhāvika[kāya],"
the body of the buddhas; he is great bliss.

He is the primordial-awareness vajra.
He is connate joy; he is also explained
to be [the result] in accord with its cause,
expressed as a single-prong vajra.

He is also the extinguishing of the fourth state;
pure, sublime, and unchanging. He who resides
in enlightenment, residing in the middle of the lotus
of the **heart** center,

is the syllable *hūṃ* alone, explained
to be the sattva. He alone is Akṣobhya,
he is called "the mind vajra" and Viṣṇu himself,
the four-armed [Heruka];

he is Jvalajvala, he is explained to be
the dharmakāya. Vajra bearer residing
in the dharmacakra, holder of the mode
of the joy of exceptional joy,

he is also explained to be the ripened [result],
the extinguisher of the deep-sleep state.
Filled with the taste of great primordial awareness,
he is called "mahāsattva." [20]

Lord of the sambhogacakra at the **throat**,
he is called "Amitābha." He is explained to be
the speech vajra, the tathāgata with a lotus
in his hand.

He is explained to be sublime joy,
and called "the personally created" [result].
Relative and ultimate [indivisible],
he is also the extinguisher of the dream state.

He is the sambhogakāya,
teaching the Dharma of the buddhas.
He is fully expressed as Śaṃkara,
having three faces and six arms,

Kiṭikiṭivajra himself,
the third Heruka. {26}
Always residing in samaya,
the one who resides is to be called this:

Samaya, rabbit-bearer, seminal fluid,
great bliss residing at the **forehead**,
the sattva resides well in the nectar.
Fully explained as the syllable *oṃ*,

he is called "Vairocana,"
the body vajra is only him.
He is to be fully expressed
as Brahmā, holder of the body vajra.

Joy is the essence of Brahmā,
and he is called the "rūpakāya."
Explained to have a cakra in his hand,
his body has the characteristic of emanation.

By reversal [of the bodhicitta] he is also
the stainless [result]; the extinguishing of
the waking state. He is Picuvajra, explained
to be Heruka with eight faces,

the mahāsattva perfectly endowed
with four legs and sixteen arms.
In that way, by the distinctions of the bodies,
he is explained to be the fourth Heruka.

From the svābhāvika, there is the dharma.
From the dharma, the sambhoga itself.
From that, there is the nirmāṇakāya,
so in this way the kāyas are four.

Brahmā holds the body vajra,
Maheśvara the speech vajra.
Viṣṇu holds the mind vajra,
Vajrasattva is great bliss. [139]

Also, in the commentary on the "Chapter of the Family," the honorable, noble Vajragarbha says:

The families are to be expressed as three.
Together with the [family of] the very essence,
these are explained as the "four families."

By the divisions of the four activities,
that is the classification of the families.
It should be known by those yogins who
wish to actualize the path of the buddhas.[140]

And:

The syllables *evaṃ* are Vajrasattva.
the syllable *hūṃ* is the mind vajra.
The syllable *āḥ* is the speech vajra.
Oṃ is the body vajra.[141]

That ground continuum or causal continuum itself is thus said to be the ultimate deities such as the four Herukas, the quintessence of the four families.

Some may think, "This first chapter is renowned to be about the resultant continuum, so it is not the ground or causal continuum." {27}

Therefore, I should mention that it is established in our shared experience that the Omniscient One says "Chapter of the Vajra Family" but does not appear to say "Chapter of the Result." [21]

To state the ground or causal continuum at the beginning is also not unreasonable, just as is said:

Family, devotion to the Dharma,
and, likewise, arousing bodhicitta,
practicing generosity and so on,
entering the flawless,

fully ripening sentient beings,
purifying the realms, nonabiding
nirvāṇa, sublime enlightenment,
and the display.[142]

As stated, to begin by presenting ground or family first, leading to path and result, is also not inappropriate in the custom of the great, pure textual traditions. Furthermore, it says:

That thusness is no different in all,
yet when purified, it is a tathāgata.
Therefore, all living beings possess
its essence.[143]

As it says, referring to the essence of ground and result as one in thusness, it is not a fault if the ground or causal continuum is also expressed here as the resultant continuum, because the *Noble Eight Thousand Lines* also says:

That which is the thusness of a tathāgata is the thusness of all phenomena. The thusness of all phenomena is the thusness of a tathāgata.[144]

And so on. And because many such as the *Extensive Mother Sūtra* also say the thusness of a buddha and a sentient being are indivisible.

G. *Also, how just that is present as the continuum of the indivisible essence of ground and result, like space*

Likewise, the essence of the ground or family, that which is thusness, the dharmakāya, is stated to also pervade all phenomena, like space. Just as the *Ḍākinīvajrapañjara* says:

In every realm of space
and thousands of world systems,
excellent great bliss, mahāmudrā,
Buddha, is present like space.[145] {28}

Such passages show that vajra family, or naturally, utterly pure family itself, to be Buddha, mahāmudrā, the excellent great bliss of the indivisible essence of ground and result, and furthermore, to pervade all and to be the ground of all, like space. The *Mahāparinirvāṇa* also says:

> The buddha nature of sentient beings is like space. Space is not past, is also not future, is not present, is not inside, is not outside. As it is not comprised of form, sound, odor, taste, and tangible objects, so also the buddha nature is like that.[146]

And so on. [22] And:

> Son of good family, for example: space is not inside all sentient beings, also not outside, also not both inside and outside. Therefore, it is unimpeded, and the buddha nature of all sentient beings is also like that.[147]

And:

> The Tathāgata is unarisen and without [the conditioned] family and, because he is unarisen and without [the conditioned] family, he is permanent.
>
> The permanent attribute [thusness] pervades all and everything, just as space pervades all.[148]

And the *Sūtra Taught by Akṣayamati* also says:

> In any place where dharmadhātu is, in that place the basic element of sentient beings also is.
>
> In any place where the basic element of sentient beings is, there the element of space also is; therefore, all phenomena resemble space.[149]

Thus the buddha nature, the dharmakāya of the tathāgatas, and dharmadhātu are present pervading all, like space, and are also stated to be the ground and basis of all phenomena.

Likewise, the *Commentary on the "Uttaratantra"* also says:

> There is no sentient being whatsoever in the realm of sentient beings who is outside the dharmakāya of the tathāgatas, just as form [outside] the element of space [is impossible].[150]

And Vajragarbha's commentary also states:

> Just as a pot is broken, but the space
> is not destroyed, so too the body
> disintegrates, but primordial awareness
> is not destroyed.[151]

And the *Glorious Tantra* also says:

> Just as, even when the water inside a pot is taken out, the space does not go away, so too the ubiquitous Vajra Bearer of space, free of the sense objects, is in the center of the body.[152]

And the *Ornament of the Sūtras* also states:

> Just as space is accepted as always pervading all,
> so too this [true nature] is accepted as also pervading all.
> Just as space pervades all forms, so too this also pervades
> the entire multitude of sentient beings.[153] {29}

And the *Sūtra Teaching the Inconceivable Secrets of the Tathāgata* also says:

> Śāntamati, it is like this: for example, space pervades all that appear as form. Śāntamati, in a similar way, the [dharma]kāya of the Tathāgata also totally pervades all that appear as sentient beings.
>
> Śāntamati, it is like this: for example, all that appear as form are included within space. Śāntamati, in a similar way, all that appear as sentient beings are also included within the [dharma]kāya of the Tathāgata.[154]

And the *Uttaratantra* also states:

> Just as space with a nonconceptual
> quintessence permeates all, so too
> the nature of mind, the stainless basic
> element, is itself omnipresent.

> Since that is its general characteristic,
> it pervades the flawed, the qualified, and
> the consummated, and, like space, [pervades]
> inferior, middling, and sublime kinds of forms.[155]

And [23]:

> Just as all-permeating space
> is subtle and thus unsoiled, so too
> this basis in all sentient beings
> is unsoiled.
>
> Just as worlds in all [phases] arise
> and perish dependent on space,
> so too the sense faculties arise and perish
> dependent on the unconditioned basic element.[156]

And so on. And:

> The nature of the mind, like the element
> of space, has no causes, no conditions,
> no accumulation, and also does not arise,
> perish, or abide.
>
> That luminous nature of the mind
> is unchanging like space and not afflicted
> by incidental stains such as desire,
> which occur from concepts about the unreal.[157]

H. *Also, how just that is present as the three phases of the ultimate dharmakāya*

Also, that same source says:

> Impure, impure and pure,
> and very pure are called
> in sequence "sentient being,"
> "bodhisattva," and "tathāgata."[158] {30}

Thus the three phases of the dharmakāya are stated. And its commentary also says:

> In the impure phase it is called "the basic element of sentient beings," in the impure and pure phase it is called "bodhisattva," and in the very pure phase it is called "tathāgata." Just as [the Bhagavān said]:
>
> > Śāriputra, that dharmakāya itself, wrapped in ten million limitless husks of the afflictions, carried away by the stream of saṃsāra, circling through deaths and births in the cycle of beginningless and endless saṃsāra, is called "the basic element of sentient beings."
> >
> > Śāriputra, that dharmakāya itself, weary of the sufferings of the stream of saṃsāra, free of attachment to all objects of desire, engaging in conduct for the sake of enlightenment by means of the eighty-four thousand aggregates of the attributes contained in the ten perfections, is called "bodhisattva."
> >
> > Śāriputra, that dharmakāya itself, fully liberated from all the husks of the afflictions, beyond all suffering, free of all stains of the secondary afflictions, which has become pure and pristine and abides in the sublimely, utterly pure true nature, dwells at the level to be gazed upon by all sentient beings, has obtained the power of a person [at the level] of nonduality concerning all levels of knowable objects, has the attribute of being without obscurations, and has obtained the unimpeded strength of a lord of all phenomena, is called "Tathāgata, Arhat, perfectly complete Buddha."[159] [24]
>
> And:
>
> > Śāriputra, therefore the basic element of sentient beings is not other and the dharmakāya is also not other. The basic element itself of sentient beings is the dharmakāya; the dharmakāya itself is the basic element of sentient beings. In terms of their meaning, these are not two; they are different in letter only.[160]

I. *Also, how just that is present as the three phases of thusness and so on*
And the *Extensive Commentary on the "Sūtra in One Hundred Thousand Lines"* also states:

> The source texts say, "All sentient beings have the tathāgata essence,"[161] so all sentient beings have the nature of thusness. That thusness also has three phases: the impure phase, the pure and impure phase, and the very, utterly pure phase. {31}
>
> The impure phase is all ordinary beings. They do not have the phase of enlightenment; there is nothing but the phase of a being with sentience [sattva], so that thusness is referred to by the term "a being with sentience."
>
> The pure and impure phase is the noble beings. Because they have both the phase of enlightenment [bodhi] and the phase of a being with sentience, that pure and impure thusness is referred to by the term "bodhisattva."
>
> In the [very,] utterly pure phase, there is nothing but the phase of enlightenment, so that thusness is referred to by the term "tathāgata." As [the Buddha] says: "Subhūti, that 'tathāgata' is another word for perfect thusness."[162]

And the *Commentary on the "Extensive Mother Sūtra," the "Sūtra in Twenty-Five Thousand Lines," and the "Sūtra in Eighteen Thousand Lines"* also says:

> For that thusness called "tathāgata essence" there are also three phases: the impure phase at the level of an ordinary being, the pure and impure phase at the level of a bodhisattva, and the pure phase at the level of a tathāgata.
>
> The impure thusness is called "sentient being" and [concerning the essence of thusness] it is also called "the flawlessness of the defilements."
>
> In the pure and impure phase it is called "bodhisattva," because the phase of enlightenment is pure and the phase of a sentient being is impure. Just that is called "the flawlessness of a bodhisattva."
>
> In the pure phase it is called "tathāgata," because it is said, "Subhūti, tathāgata is another word for perfect thusness." Just that is called "the flawlessness of phenomena."[163] [25]

And:

> . . . because the thusness of all phenomena exists at all times. Because the thusness of the Tathāgata is also not other than that, it exists at all times.[164]

And {32}:

> "Wishing to be born in the family of the Buddha": here, take the [natural] family of the Tathāgata to be the fully established thusness.[165]

And:

> Take "a world as vast as the dharmadhātu" to be the world of sentient beings, and, because the world of sentient beings is also limitless, it is said "the tathāgata essence is vast."[166]

And:

> "Because of the utter purity of the field of sentient beings": because all sentient beings are just the tathāgata essence, the field of sentient beings is utterly purified.[167]

And so on, it states extensively. And the *Collection of Precious Qualities* also says:

> What is thusness in the past is thusness in the future.
> What is thusness now is the thusness of the arhats.
> What is the thusness of all phenomena is the thusness
> of the conquerors. This thusness of phenomena is
> no different in everything.[168]

And:

> The thusness of worldly beings, the thusness of the arhats,
> the thusness of the pratyekabuddhas, and the thusness
> of the children of the conquerors is just identical, thusness

free of entities, not something else, the perfection of wisdom
known by the buddhas.

Whether the expert [rūpakāya] reside in the world or are
in nirvāṇa, the flawless true nature, this [sugata essence]
empty of phenomena, resides, and bodhisattvas later realize
this thusness. So the buddhas bestow the name "Tathāgata."[169]

And:

This is the sublime treasure of [ultimate] attributes
and the excellent treasury of [ultimate] attributes.
It is the family of the Buddha and the treasury of bliss
and happiness for living beings. Those past and future
protectors in the worlds of the ten directions are born
from this, but the dharmadhātu is not exhausted.

Whatever trees, fruit, flowers, and forests there are,
they all perfectly arise and emerge from the earth.
The earth, however, is not exhausted, does not increase,
never deteriorates, does not conceptualize, and is not weary.

Whatever attributes of bliss and happiness the [relative]
buddhas, children of the conquerors, śrāvakas, pratyekabuddhas,
gods, and all living beings have, it all occurs from the sublime
perfection of wisdom, a wisdom that is never exhausted
and does not increase.[170] {33}

That which is the omnipresent dharmakāya, tathāgata essence, dharmadhātu, and thusness in the three phases is stated to exist at all times as that perfection of wisdom itself of the indivisible essence of ground and result, as the family of the Buddha, and as the ground of all phenomena. [26] Because just that is also the ultimate deities (such as the four Herukas), mantras, tantras, maṇḍalas, and so on, through depending on the sublime esoteric instructions of glorious beings on the tenth level[171] one should be confident that the intent of these profound scriptures is not contradictory and has just a single meaning.

Referring to this and points like this, the protector Avalokiteśvara says:

> Here, for just a single [meaning], there are various terms [used from the perspective] of the [existent] entity [of qualities] and the nonexistent entity [of faults]. Therefore, just one entity is indicated by various terms, but yogins should not conceptualize about the terms. With the esoteric instructions of excellent masters they fully examine well, as with gold, through depending on reliance on the meaning.[172]

J. *Also, how just that is present as the many mantra families, such as great affliction*

Likewise, referring to the naturally, utterly pure family, the basic element of a tathāgata, the *Glorious Guhyasamāja* also says:

> Vairocana is the sublime family of hatred,
> pride is the family of Ratneśvara,
> passionate desire is the family of Mahādharma,
> jealousy is Amoghasiddhi,
>
> and Akṣobhya is the great family of ignorance.
> The cause for this tantra, the creator,
> is Vajrasattva, the nonabiding essence,
> because he is in the family of Akṣobhya.[173]

Thus, ultimate hatred, pride, and so on are stated to be the five families of the conquerors. {34} And the *Glorious Sampuṭa* also says:

> This [Mahā]mudrā of various illusory [aspects]
> is known by the term *ḍākinī*. This is derived
> from the verbal root [*ḍai*], here meaning
> "she who goes through space."
>
> Accomplishing travel through all space,
> she is fully renowned as *ḍākinī*.
> Samanta[bhadrī], Viśva[mātā],
> [Mahā]mudrā, and Samanta[bhadra],
>
> Viśva[vajra], and [Cakra]saṃvara,
> are Vajra and Vajradhara [Varja Holder],
> Lotus and Padmadhara [Lotus Holder] and,

likewise, Gem and Maṇidhara [Gem Holder]—
this [ultimate *ḍākinī*] is their families.[174]

Thus the ground of emptiness, dharmadhātu itself, is said to be the ultimate ḍākinī having various forms, Mahāmudrā,[175] and she is said to be the families such as Vajra and Lotus. These are also the natural family.

The *Later Tantra of Direct Expression* also says:

[Dharmadhātu] is explained to be many
various families. If condensed, these are
renowned as three and five and also six.
These are the yoga and the master of union

totally surrounded by the ḍākinīs and so on.
All the [ultimate] three realms without exception
perfectly arise from the [natural] family.
All the kāyas arise individually [in the true nature],

and are other, the [true nature having] all [aspects],
the mātaraḥ family, joyful, pleasing, and attractive,
arising and occurring from [other] mind.[176] [27]

Thus such passages state extensively, beginning from the naturally, utterly pure family, the buddha nature. Likewise, the honorable, glorious Vajragarbha also says that naturally pure family itself is the ultimate deity consisting of the six families, and so on:

In that way, Heruka consisting of six families is Kālacakra, and he alone is also called "Ādibuddha." He has a garland of heads with one hundred faces, [representing] the hundred branches of the Veda; because of those severed heads he is known as the Bhagavān who is the Great Bearer of the Vajra Skulls of Brahmā. {35}

Thus united with a doubled court of ḍākinīs, he consists of six families. In various other tantras he consists of five families. Therefore:

The family is explained to be the six and,
when condensed, becomes the five.

> By the divisions of body, speech, and mind,
> it later becomes the three.[177]

In that way, according to the sequence of explanation:

> The term "family" is used because, by family,
> the families having the nature of the five elements
> and the five aggregates are enumerated, or calculated,
> and called "families."[178]

Thus the rule of the six families, five families, and three families.[179]

And so on. And likewise, the *Glorious Tantra of the Secret Drop of the Moon* also says:

> The [ultimate] family is taught in one hundred
> aspects and, if condensed, in five aspects.
> By union of [ultimate] body, speech, and mind,
> it also becomes three.[180]

And the *Glorious Tantra of the Drop of Primordial Awareness* also says:

> Body is the tathāgata who grants
> refuge [from all fears]; mind is remembered
> to be the Vajra Bearer. The bodies
> created from the [ultimate] five aggregates
>
> are the sublime quintessence of
> [the conquerors of] the five families.
> The sixth family is [Vajrasattva,]
> the vajra of mind, the lord of countless families.
>
> Those of wheel, jewel, and, likewise,
> lotus, sword, and vajra fifth, are likewise
> [ultimate] form, feeling, discrimination,
> conditioning factors, and consciousness.
>
> Form is renowned as Vairocana,
> the very essence of vajra ignorance.

Feeling is the king Ratna,
the very essence of vajra pride.

Discrimination is Amitābha,
fully renowned as vajra attachment.
Conditioning factors are Amoghasiddhi,
taught to be vajra jealousy.

Consciousness here is Akṣobhya,
meditated on as vajra hatred.
Space is renowned as Vajrasattva,
free of aspects, the established sovereign. {36}

Ignorance is mirrorlike primordial awareness,
pride is remembered as that of equanimity.
The discriminating is passionate desire,
and the all-accomplishing is jealousy.

Hatred is that of pure dharmadhātu.
From unique [ultimate] great bliss, here
it resides [in all] as five distinct [families].
From churned white bliss,

[Buddhalocanā] of fine face, who
is [the other] solidity; the one known
to be Vairocana has the characteristic
of the attribute of ignorance. [28]

The form of melting black bliss
is remembered to be Akṣobhya.
Because of the light of red bliss,
there is Amitābha tathāgata.

Because it is pervaded by wind,
bliss is blue; that is fully taught to be
Amoghasiddhi. From pride, bliss is yellow
here; that is Ratnasambhava.

Free of [ordinary] space, the established protector
is Vajrasattva, sovereign of all conquerors.
With wide eyes, the fine [mudrā is Prajñāpāramitā],
therefore the [dharma]kāya, the goddess having
[all] utterly sublime aspects.

She is to be energetically worshiped,
never scorned.[181]

Such passages teach ultimate form, feeling, and so on to be the families of the wheel, jewel, and so on, and teach ultimate ignorance and so on to be the families of the five self-arisen primordial awarenesses, such as mirrorlike primordial awareness. And they teach ultimate white bliss and so on to be the families of the buddhas Vairocana and so on.

Here, ultimate bliss is said to be the colors white and so on, but these are not the relative colors; these are what are stated to be "great color and majestic body,"[182] the colors of thusness, the other colors, the colors without the flaw of including contradiction.

Referring to these families of ultimate color, the *Glorious Hevajra Tantra* also says:

Bliss is black and bliss is yellow.
Bliss is red, bliss is white.
Bliss is green, bliss is blue.
Bliss is all that roam and do not roam. {37}

Bliss is wisdom, bliss is means.
Bliss arisen during sex is similar.
Bliss is existent, bliss is nonexistent.
Bliss is called "Vajrasattva."[183]

Since the Vajrasattva of the indivisible essence of ground and result has all aspects itself, it has all colors.

Therefore, because it abides as the indivisible essence of ultimate ground and result, that "Chapter of the Vajra Family" is also about the result.

K. *Also, how just that resides as the nirvāṇa, dharmakāya, and so on of the indivisible ground and result*

The *Mahāparinirvāṇa* also speaks of the indivisible essence of ground and result, because it says:

> Maudgalyāyana, "nirvāṇa" is a verbal articulation [of the ultimate ground of emptiness]. A footprint. Consummate abiding. Fearlessness. The great teacher. The great result. Consummate primordial awareness. Great patience. Unimpeded samādhi. Great dharmadhātu. The taste of sweetness. Difficult [for consciousness] to see.[184]

Thus it says that dharmadhātu itself, the ground of all, is also the great result, consummate primordial awareness, the great teacher, and so on.

Likewise, the *Sūtra of the Excellent Golden Light* also says that dharmakāya itself is the cause, the basis, the result, the ground, the Mahāyāna, [29] the very essence of a tathāgata, the tathāgata essence, and so on. Just as it states:

> That dharmakāya actualizes the various activities of a tathāgata.
>
> Sons of good family, this kāya is the inconceivable depended upon as the cause, the field of experience, the basis, the result, and the very ground. If that point is directly understood, that kāya is the Mahāyāna. It is the very essence of a tathāgata. It is the tathāgata essence. {38}
>
> Dependent on that kāya, bodhicitta is first aroused and the mind of the totally purified levels will manifest. The mind that will not fall back from the level [of a buddha] will also manifest, and the mind with only one rebirth remaining, the vajralike samādhi, and the intent of a tathāgata will also manifest. All the measureless and countless excellent attributes of a tathāgata will also manifest. Dependent on that dharmakāya, inconceivable great samādhis will also manifest. Dependent on this dharmakāya, all great primordial awarenesses will also appear. That being so, the two [rūpa]kāyas will also occur dependent on the samādhis and the primordial awarenesses.
>
> Because this [unconditioned] dharmakāya depends on its own [unchanging] essence, it is called "permanent." It is called "[the

> pure] self." Because it depends on the great samādhis, it is called "[ultimate] bliss." Because it depends on the great primordial awarenesses, it is called "pure." Therefore, a tathāgata permanently resides, having gained power over bliss and purity.[185]

L. *Also, how just that resides as the fully established true nature of the indivisible ground and result*

Likewise, the *Journey to Laṅkā* also says:

> Mahāmati, what is the fully established nature? It is like this: Thusness free of conceptualization having the characteristics of marks, names, and entities. Obtained through the realization of a noble being's primordial awareness, it is the field of experience of a noble being's personal, self-knowing primordial awareness. Mahāmati, this fully established nature is the essence and mind of the tathāgatas.[186]

Just that, which is the fully established true nature, is thus said to be the tathāgata essence and mind. Because just that is also the five self-arisen primordial awarenesses, this also refers to the fully established indivisible essence of ground and result. [30]

M. *Also, how just that resides as the ultimate dharmakāya and the collection of all its qualities*

In that way, this dharmadhātu itself, the ground of all phenomena, is also stated to be the dharmakāya. {39} Just as the *Sūtra Teaching the Nature without Decrease and without Increase* says:

> Śāriputra, the ultimate is to be realized through faith. Śāriputra, this "ultimate" is another term for the basic element of sentient beings. Śāriputra, this "basic element of sentient beings" is another term for tathāgata essence. Śāriputra, this "tathāgata essence" is another term for dharmakāya.[187]

It might be asked, "Does that not refer to just the seed of a buddha, or refer to emptiness in which all phenomena are just totally unestablished?"

No, because that [dharmakāya, the sugata essence,] is stated to be a buddha's measureless primordial awareness having limitless qualities. Just as the

Uttaratantra says: "Since indivisibly in the true nature,"[188] so the commentary explains:

> Here, since even at the level of a singularly defiled ordinary being the stainless qualities of a buddha exist indivisibly in the true nature without difference earlier and later, this point is inconceivable. Why? Among the types of sentient beings, there is no sentient being whatever who is not pervaded by the entire primordial awareness of a tathāgata. However, because of discriminating grasping, the primordial awareness of a tathāgata is not manifest. After becoming free of discriminating grasping, omniscient primordial awareness, which is self-arisen primordial awareness, fully occurs without impediment.
>
>> O son of the Conqueror, it is like this: Suppose there were a great silk cloth the size of the world system that is the largest chiliocosm in a trichiliocosm.[189] And on that great silk cloth the entire world system that is the largest chiliocosm in a trichiliocosm is also completely painted. It is like this: The great ring [of iron mountains] is painted the size of the great ring. The great [golden] ground is painted the size of the great ground. The world system of a dichiliocosm is the size of the world system of a dichiliocosm, the world system of a chiliocosm is the size of the world system of a chiliocosm, the four-continent world systems are the size of the four-continent world system, the great oceans are the size of the great ocean, the continents of Jambu are the size of the continent Jambu, {40} the eastern continents of Videha are the size of the continent of Videha, the western continents of Godāvarī are the size of the continent of Aparagodaniya, the northern continents of Kuru are the size of Kuru, the Mount Sumerus are the size of Mount Sumeru, the palaces of the gods living on the earth are the size of the palaces of the gods living on the earth, [31] the palaces of the gods living in the desire realm are the size of the palaces of the gods living in the desire realm, and the palaces of the gods

living in the form realm are painted the size of the palaces of the gods living in the form realm.

That great silk cloth would also be about the size of the expanse of the world system that is the largest chiliocosm in a trichiliocosm. Then that great silk cloth would also be inserted into a single particle of a tiny atom.

Just as the great silk cloth would be inserted into a single particle of a tiny atom, so also great silk cloths about that size would be inserted into all the particles of tiny atoms without exception.

Then a skillful, clever, clearly intelligent person with analytical ability applicable to that would be born. His divine eye would be utterly pure and luminous. Looking with that divine eye, he would think this: "Such a great silk cloth as this, yet it stays in just this small particle of a tiny atom and does not sustain any sentient being. Aha! With the power and strength of great effort, I will break open this particle of a tiny atom and make this great silk cloth into what will sustain all living beings."

With the power of great effort he would grow strong, break open that particle of a tiny atom with a miniature vajra, and, just as he intended, make that great silk cloth into what sustains all living beings. And, just as for that one, he would also do exactly that to each and every tiny atom without exception.

Likewise, O son of the Conqueror, the primordial awareness of a tathāgata, the measureless primordial awareness that is the primordial awareness sustaining all sentient beings, also entirely pervades the mindstreams of all sentient beings, and those mindstreams of all sentient beings are also as measureless as the primordial awareness of a tathāgata. {41}

Such is the case, but childish persons bound by discriminating grasping do not recognize, totally do not recognize, do not experience, and do not manifest the primordial awareness of the Tathāgata.

> Therefore, the Tathāgata, with unattached primordial awareness, sees the dharmadhātu of a tathāgata present in all sentient beings and resolves to be a teacher.
>
> [He thinks,] "Alas! These sentient beings do not understand the primordial awareness of a tathāgata exactly in accord with reality, even though they are pervaded by the primordial awareness of a tathāgata. By thoroughly teaching the noble path to these sentient beings, I will remove all the bonds created by discrimination, so that they themselves (removing the great knot of discrimination by awakening the power of the primordial awareness of a noble being) directly recognize the primordial awareness of a tathāgata and reach equality with the tathāgatas." [32]
>
> Likewise, through teaching the path of the Tathāgata, they eliminate all the bonds created by discrimination. In those who have eliminated all the bonds of discrimination, that measureless primordial awareness of a tathāgata becomes what sustains the entire world.[190]

The Buddha of the abiding state, with those measureless qualities and aspects of the dharmakāya, is thus said to be entirely present in all sentient beings. And the *Noble Sūtra of Śrīmālā* also teaches the possession of the indivisible, inconceivable attributes of a buddha exceeding the grains of sand found in the Ganges River to be the dharmakāya of a tathāgata:

> Bhagavān, this very dharmakāya of a tathāgata that is not released from the husks of the afflictions is called "tathāgata essence."[191]

That dharmakāya, the sugata essence itself, is thus said to be indivisible in nature with the qualities of a buddha, which are indivisible from the true nature and exceed even the grains of sand found in the Ganges River. The *Mahāparinirvāṇa* also says the sugata essence, that buddha nature or natural buddha itself, is the quintessence of the measureless qualities of the dharmakāya, such as the powers, types of fearlessness, and measureless samādhi. {42} Just as it says:

Son of good family, a tathāgata's ten powers, four types of fearlessness, great love, great compassion, three foundations of mindfulness, ten million eighty thousand enumerations of samādhi such as that of heroic progress, his thirty-two major marks, eighty fine minor marks, thirty-five thousand enumerations of samādhi such as that of the five mudrās of primordial awareness, and four thousand five hundred enumerations of samādhi such that of vajralike samādhi, his acquisition of measureless samādhis of means, and attributes such as those, are the buddha nature of a tathāgata.

In that way, that buddha nature has seven properties: it is permanent, the self [of thusness], bliss, utter purity, [the apex of] reality, true, and virtue. That is called "a reply through making distinctions."[192]

And:

Son of good family, for example: the moon of the third or fourth day may not be seen, but it is not correct to say it does not exist.

The buddha nature is also like that. All wicked infantile beings do not see it, but it is not correct to say the buddha nature does not exist in them.

Son of good family, [33] the buddha nature is like this: the ten powers, the four types of fearlessness, great compassion, and the three foundations of mindfulness. Even though the three aspects exist in all sentient beings, they will be seen to be primordial if the afflictions are utterly destroyed.

If depraved people utterly destroy depravity, they will obtain the primordial ten powers, four types of fearlessness, great compassion, and the three foundations of mindfulness.

Because of that truth, I say "The buddha nature always exists in all sentient beings."[193]

And:

Concerning the buddha nature of a tathāgata, there are two aspects: the existent [qualities] and the nonexistent [faults]. {43}

The existent are like this: the thirty-two major marks, the eighty fine minor marks, the ten powers, the four types of fearlessness, the three foundations of mindfulness, great love, great

> compassion, the acquisition of measureless samādhis such as the samādhi of heroic progress, the acquisition of measureless samādhis such as vajralike samādhi, the acquisition of measureless samādhis such as that of skillful means, and the acquisition of measureless samādhis such as that of the five primordial awarenesses are called "existent."
>
> The nonexistent are like this: a tathāgata's past virtues, nonvirtues, indeterminate [acts], karma, causes, results, ripenings, afflictions, five aggregates, and twelve links of dependent arising are called "nonexistent."[194]

Such passages state in detail how that in which something does not exist is empty of it, and how what remains permanently exists in that. Just this is also really the difference of naturally established abandonment and realization, the difference of nonimplicative negation and implicative negation, the difference of mere nonexistence and the ground of nonexistence, the difference of exclusion and positive determination, the difference of mere empty and isolated separation from conceptual elaboration, and the ground of those, and so on. Therefore, dependent on the esoteric instructions for relying on the meaning, these important, extremely profound, difficult to realize, and subtle points must be correctly realized.

The honorable, venerable lord Ajita also says:

> Luminosity, uncreated and
> manifesting indivisibly, bears all
> the attributes of a buddha, exceeding
> the grains of sand in the Ganges River.[195]

Such passages say that sugata essence, natural luminosity, the unconditioned basic element itself, indivisibly possesses the inseparable attributes of a buddha exceeding the grains of sand found in the Ganges River. [34] Likewise, the *Noble Sūtra to Benefit Aṅgulimāla*, rare as the udumvāra flower,[196] also says the flawed aspects such as birth and cessation are naturally nonexistent, and that basic element of a buddha (or that buddha of the basic element) with many naturally established qualities, such as the limitless major marks and minor marks of the true nature, exists in all sentient beings. Just as it says:

> Although all the buddhas completely, intently sought, they did not find a born tathāgata essence; the unborn basic element of a

buddha, the basic element adorned with the limitless major marks and fine minor marks, exists in all sentient beings. {44}

Although all the buddhas very intently sought, they did not find an arisen basic element; the unarisen basic element, the basic element of a buddha, the basic element adorned with the limitless major marks and fine minor marks, exists in all sentient beings.

Although all the buddhas themselves very intently sought, they did not find an impermanent basic element; the permanent basic element, the basic element of a buddha, the basic element adorned with the limitless major marks and fine minor marks, exists in all sentient beings.

Although all the buddhas very intently sought, they did not find a tathāgata essence that is not eternal; the eternal basic element, the basic element of a buddha, the basic element adorned with the limitless major marks and fine minor marks, exists in all sentient beings.

Although all the buddhas very intently sought, they did not find a tathāgata essence that is not everlasting; the everlasting basic element, the basic element of a buddha, the basic element adorned with the limitless major marks and fine minor marks, exists in all sentient beings.

Although all the buddhas very intently sought, they did not find illness in the tathāgata essence; the basic element without illness, the basic element of a buddha, the basic element adorned with the limitless major marks and fine minor marks, exists in all sentient beings.

Although all the buddhas very intently sought, they did not find aging and death in the tathāgata essence; the ageless, deathless basic element, the basic element of a buddha, the basic element adorned with the limitless major marks and fine minor marks, exists in all sentient beings.

Although all the buddhas very intently sought, they did not find a destructible tathāgata essence; the indestructible basic element, the basic element of a buddha, the basic element adorned with the limitless major marks and fine minor marks, exists in all sentient beings.

Although all the buddhas very intently sought, they did not find a perishable tathāgata essence; the imperishable basic element, the basic element of a buddha, the basic element adorned

> with the limitless major marks and fine minor marks, exists in all sentient beings. [35]
>
> Although all the buddhas very intently sought, they did not find stains in the tathāgata essence; the stainless basic element, the basic element of a buddha, the basic element adorned with the limitless major marks and fine minor marks, exists in all sentient beings.
>
> For example, water and mustard seed oil are not seen to mix. Likewise, the basic element of a buddha is indeed veiled by ten million afflictions, but there is no place where the afflictions and the basic element of a buddha are mixed. {45}
>
> The basic element is indeed within the ten million afflictions, but like a lamp within a pot. If the pot is broken, the lamp flame blazes and is beautiful. One who teaches the tathāgata essence will be a complete buddha.[197]

And so on, it says extensively. Here, if the division of the two truths is understood regarding even the major marks and minor marks, one will not be deluded about the Sage's word.

Furthermore, the major marks and minor marks stated to be naturally complete in the sugata essence, the dharmadhātu itself, are qualities of the ultimate dharmakāya, not of the relative rūpakāya. And since statements in the profound tantras about the consummate major marks and minor marks, such as "bearing the thirty-two major marks,"[198] are also to be understood only in that way through the esoteric instructions of excellent masters, they are not a sophist's field of experience.

The great Madhyamaka master, the honorable, noble Asaṅga also says:

> The basic element of a buddha is clarified through teaching the sixty types of qualities that fully purify its [natural] purity, because it is [only] if that object to be purified has the qualities that purifications of its purity are appropriate.[199]

Because the very mention of purifying antidotes also signifies a statement about the ground of purification (the sugata essence having many qualities), even though the sugata essence is not actually taught, all the scriptures that teach the purifying antidotes also implicitly teach the ground of purification, the sugata essence. This is the intent.

That being so, just as relative qualities exist for relative truth, ultimate qualities also exist for ultimate truth, and they are also indivisible from ultimate truth. Therefore, one should become expert in the meaning of the great intent of the repeated statement that it "bears inseparable qualities exceeding the grains of sand found in the Ganges River." {46} [36]

N. *Showing that the noble father Nāgārjuna and his spiritual sons also accepted that meaning*

It might be said, "Others accept the sugata essence to be of definitive meaning, but that is not accepted in the Madhyamaka tradition."

The honorable, noble Nāgārjuna does accept that, just as *In Praise of Dharmadhātu* says:

> I bow in homage to dharmadhātu,
> certainly present in all sentient beings.
> Yet if totally ignorant of it, they circle
> in the three states of cyclic existence.
>
> When that which has acted as
> the cause of saṃsāra is purified,
> that purity itself is nirvāṇa;
> dharmakāya is also just that.
>
> Just as the essence of butter
> is not apparent while mixed with milk,
> so too dharmadhātu is not seen
> while mixed with the afflictions.
>
> Just as the essence of butter
> becomes stainless when milk is purified,
> so too dharmadhātu becomes very
> stainless when the afflictions are purified.
>
> Just as a lamp sitting inside a pot
> does not illuminate at all,
> so too dharmadhātu is not seen
> dwelling inside the pot of the afflictions.
>
> From whichever sides holes
> are punched in a pot,

from just those same sides
the nature of light will emerge.

Whenever the vajra of samādhi
has shattered that pot, that
[dharmadhātu] will shine out
until the end of space.

Dharmadhātu never arises and
will never cease. Without afflictions
at all times, free of stains through
beginning, middle, and end.

Just as a beryl jewel
is luminous at all times,
but its light is not bright
if it remains within the rock,

so too dharmadhātu obscured
by the afflictions is stainless,
but its light is not bright in saṃsāra.
At nirvāṇa its luminosity [manifests].[200]

And:

Even the stainless sun and moon
become obscured by five obscurations:
clouds, mist, smoke, Rāhu's face, dust,
and so on.

So too the luminous mind
becomes obscured by five obscurations:
desire, malice, laziness, agitation,
and doubt. {47}

A cloth [of asbestos] to be cleansed
by fire may be soiled with various stains.
If put into a fire, the stains will burn,
but not the cloth.

So too, for the luminous mind
with stains such as passionate desire,
the fire of primordial awareness will burn
the stains, but not its luminosity.

However many sūtras the Conqueror
spoke that teach emptiness, they all
destroy the afflictions; they do not
damage that basic element.

As water dwelling in the depths
of the earth remains stainless,
so too primordial awareness remains
stainless within the afflictions.[201] [37]

And:

Just as a child exists in the belly
of a pregnant woman but is not seen,
so too dharmadhātu veiled by
the afflictions is not seen.[202]

And:

Water in the spring season
is called "warm."
Just that in the cold season
is called "cold."

Veiled by the web of the afflictions,
[dharmadhātu] is called "sentient being,"
but if separated from the afflictions
it is called "Buddha."[203]

By means of many examples, such passages speak in detail of the sugata essence that has the same meaning as dharmadhātu, dharmakāya, naturally luminous mind, self-arisen primordial awareness, and so on. And this teacher also says just that is the basis of all buddhas:

> This is ultimate truth,
> not appearing and signless.
> What is called "ultimate truth"
> is the basis of all the tathāgatas.[204]

And he also mentions further synonyms for this:

> It is also explained as consciousness,
> luminosity, nirvāṇa, emptiness of all [phenomena],
> and dharmakāya.[205]

Thus the teacher Bhāvaviveka quotes in the *Jewel Lamp of the Madhyamaka*. "Consciousness" in this context refers to consciousness of the true nature and pure consciousness, because it is stated to be a synonym of luminous dharmakāya.

The honorable, noble Āryadeva also accepts that; the *Lamp That Summarizes Conduct* says:

> Ultimate truth is without body, without example, free of all activity, and personal self-awareness, so it is not understood without teachings from the mouth of an excellent master. {48} Just as these words also say:
>
> > A lamp sitting inside
> > a pot will not shine outside;
> > but after that pot is shattered,
> > the light of the lamp will shine.
> >
> > So too, [the five aggregates of] one's body
> > are the pot, and reality is like the lamp; after
> > they are shattered by the speech of the master,
> > the primordial awareness of a buddha becomes clear.
> >
> > From the space [of great emptiness] emerges
> > the space [of great bliss]. That very space seeing
> > space is the [vajra] yoga well taught from the mouth
> > of the master.[206]

And so on. It might be asked, "In *[Explanation of] Entering the Madhaya-maka*, does the teacher Candrakīrti not refute the tathāgata essence as definitive in meaning?"[207]

In the *Illuminating Lamp*, the commentary on the *Guhyasamāja*, he teaches clearly. Just as it says:

> The syllable *oṃ* has the tathāgata essence; because that produces the unbreakable body of the yogin, it causes the obtainment of the vajrakāya.[208]

And [38]:

> The basis of all the conquerors is all sentient beings, because they have the tathāgata essence.[209]

And so on. *[Explanation of] "Entering the Madhyamaka"* also says:

> Whether buddhas appear or do not
> appear, in actuality the emptiness
> [that is the true nature] of all entities
> is renowned to be that of other entities.
>
> The apex of reality, and thusness,
> it is the emptiness of other entities.
>
> That of other entities [than this relative] is sublimely occurring reality. Its sublime occurrence [ultimate truth] always exists.[210]

Since this also occurs, it is reasonable to examine whether he spoke with internal contradictions. I also wonder if doubts of that type arose earlier during the time he was a dialectician, but later, because he had entered profound secret mantra, his comprehension improved and his philosophical tenet changed. {49}

III. *Advice to reject bad views fabricated by those not expert in scripture*
This has eleven topics.

A. *Rejecting the evil view that confuses [the teaching of the sugata essence] to be of provisional meaning because the purpose is presented*
This has two topics.

1. *Rejecting the evil view that confuses [the teaching of the sugata essence] to be of provisional meaning because the purpose is presented in the* Uttaratantra
The *Uttaratantra* says:

> Having said here and there that, like clouds, dreams,
> and illusions, "all knowable objects are empty in all
> aspects," why did the conquerors also say here that
> "the buddha essence exists in sentient beings"?
>
> They said that so those in whom they exist
> may abandon these five faults: despair, contempt
> for inferior sentient beings, grasping at the unreal,
> denigrating the real attribute, and excessive self-attachment.[211]

It might be asked, "Does that not state the sugata essence to be of provisional meaning?"

It does not. There are no words in that passage that teach the provisional meaning.

It might be said, "This 'said that so they may abandon these' establishes it to be of provisional meaning."

That presents the purpose, because the commentary before this very passage says:

> It might be asked, "This basic element is difficult to observe, so why does this presentation begin with childish, ordinary people?"
>
> Two verses summarize the purpose of the presentation: one presents the question and the second the reply.[212]

If it were of provisional meaning because the purpose is presented, that extremely absurd consequence would also occur for statements that are of definitive meaning.

As for the detailed explanation of those purposes:

> It is said that the apex of reality is isolated
> from all aspects of conditioned phenomena,
> with the entities of afflictions, karma, and their
> ripening resembling clouds and so on.
>
> The afflictions resemble clouds, actions done
> are like experiences in a dream, and the aggregates
> (the ripening of afflictions and karma) are like
> emanations and illusions. [39]
>
> It was presented in that way before,
> but once again in this latest text,
> in order to abandon the five defects,
> it is taught that "the basic element exists." {50}
>
> Not having heard about that
> in this way, for some who despair
> because of the defect of self-contempt,
> bodhicitta does not arise.
>
> When those in whom bodhicitta
> has arisen gloat, "I am superior,"
> they begin to consider those in whom
> bodhicitta has not arisen to be inferior.
>
> In that way, perfect understanding
> does not arise for those beings.
> Therefore, they grasp at the unreal
> and do not know the meaning of reality.
>
> Since they are just contrived and incidental,
> those faults of sentient beings are unreal.
> The [apex of] reality lacks the nature of those
> faults and is the naturally pure qualities.
>
> Grasping at unreal defects and denigrating
> the real qualities, even wise [bodhisattvas]

> will not attain the love that sees themselves
> and sentient beings as equal.
>
> Hearing of that [sugata essence] from this [text],
> enthusiasm, respect [for all beings] as for the Teacher,
> wisdom, primordial awareness, and great love arise.
> Since these five attributes arise, through that
>
> they come to have no flaws, regard [all] as equal,
> have no faults, possess the qualities, consider
> themselves and others equally, and quickly attain
> buddhahood.[213]

Thus the quick attainment of buddhahood after abandoning the five great defects and obtaining the five great qualities is stated to be the purpose for clearly presenting the sugata essence in the final wheel.

Therefore, claims that this passage that presents the purpose is presenting the provisional meaning are nonsense, because this same source text also says:

> In that way, the ten topics concerning
> the Conqueror's essence have been discussed.[214]

And so on. Thus the ten topics and nine examples extensively determine (by means of its many aspects) the sugata essence, thusness with stains, and repeatedly determine it to be the crucial point. {51}

It might be said, "Precisely those lines presented before are presented here to be of provisional meaning."

Such is not the case. After this, in the context of stainless thusness, it also says:

> The state of a conqueror is like the chief of sages,
> honey, a kernel, precious gold, a treasure, and a tree,
> similar to an image of the Sugata made from stainless
> precious substances, a lord of the earth, and a golden image.[215]

That statement about the nine examples for the sugata essence before in the context of thusness with stains also being stated here in the context of the result refers to no difference in the essence earlier and later, except for classification as ground and result due to the existence and nonexistence of the incidental stains. Therefore, if the essence of the ground, the sugata essence, were of provisional meaning, the essence of the result, the dharmakāya, would also be of provisional meaning, because it says:

> The changeless true nature
> is just the same before as after.[216]

And because there is no difference of essence in the thusness of the ground and the result. [40] Furthermore, in the context of enlightened activity it says:

> Having definitely accomplished the entire vehicle
> bearing the collection of the sublime jewels of the qualities
> and possessing the ocean of primordial awareness and
> the sunlight of merit and primordial awareness, and having
> seen buddhahood pervasive like the vast sky without limit
> and center to be a treasure of stainless qualities in all
> sentient beings without difference, the wind of the compassion
> of the buddhas scatters the web of the clouds [of the obscurations]
> of the afflictions and of the knowable.[217]

Thus it says buddhahood with the complete limitless qualities of the dharmakāya is seen to be present without difference in all sentient beings. And at the end it also states:

> Whatever virtue I have obtained from properly explaining
> the Three Jewels, the pure basic element, stainless enlightenment,
> the qualities, and the activity (the seven true points), by that may
> these living beings behold the seer Amitāyus endowed with
> infinite light and, after beholding him, may the stainless eye
> of Dharma arise [in them] and sublime enlightenment
> be obtained.[218]

Since that [implicitly] says the seven true points actually exist, thusness with stains is also established to actually exist.

Furthermore, if the sugata essence were of provisional meaning, dharmadhātu, thusness, would also be of provisional meaning. {52} If one accepted that, the ultimate unconditioned Buddha, the dharmakāya, would also be of provisional meaning. If one accepted even that, the extremely absurd consequence would be that Saṃvara, Hevajra, Kālacakra, Guhyasamāja, and so on, all the ultimate deities, mantras, tantras, mudrās, maṇḍalas, and so on that are ever present (partless, omnipresent, and pervading all) would also be of provisional meaning; such is also not the case.

Furthermore, internal contradiction earlier and later in the very same source text is impossible for the conqueror Maitreya. And if the sugata essence were actually nonexistent, that would contradict the profound sūtras and tantras, and also contradict the exceptional Bodhisattva Commentaries.[219]

2. *Rejecting the evil view that confuses [the teaching of the sugata essence] to be of provisional meaning because the purpose is presented in the* Journey to Laṅkā

Therefore, clearly presenting in that way the actually existent sugata essence, the basic element of thusness, has the purpose of abandoning the five great defects and obtaining the five great qualities and, likewise, also has the purpose of abandoning fear of selflessness.

Here, emptiness, and the apex of reality, and nirvāṇa, and birthlessness, and signlessness, and the ground of selflessness, and the sugata essence indeed have the same [meaning]. [41] But seeing that if it were presented by means of "emptiness" and "selflessness" and so on, some people would be frightened by just the terms, the uninterrupted ultimate quintessence is presented by means of "sugata essence," causing them to penetrate the meaning of emptiness and selflessness, which is natural luminosity, the nonconceptual basic element without the appearance of incidental stains. Just as the *Journey to Laṅkā* says:

> Mahāmati said, "In speaking other sūtras the Bhagavān taught the tathāgata essence. The Bhagavān said pure natural luminosity (pure from the beginning), having the thirty-two major marks, is within the bodies of all sentient beings. The Bhagavān said that, like a jewel of great value fully wrapped in stained cloth, it is fully wrapped in the cloth of the aggregates, elements, and sensory bases; overcome by passionate desire, hatred, and ignorance; soiled by imaginary stains; permanent, stable, and eternal. {53}
>
> "Bhagavān, how is this assertion of the tathāgata essence not like the assertion of a self by the non-Buddhists? Bhagavān, the

non-Buddhists also teach the assertion of a self that is called 'permanent, the agent, without qualities,[220] pervasive, and indestructible.'"

The Bhagavān replied, "Mahāmati, my teaching of the tathāgata essence is not the same as the non-Buddhist's assertion of a self. Mahāmati, the tathāgatas, arhats, and perfectly complete buddhas taught the meaning of terms such as 'emptiness,' 'the apex of reality,' 'nirvāṇa,' 'unarisen,' 'signlessness,' and 'wishlessness' to be the tathāgata essence. Then teaching by means of the tathāgata essence so that childish people might avoid the state of being frightened by selflessness, they teach the [ultimate] nonconceptual state [of great bliss], the [naturally luminous] field of experience without [all relative] appearances. Mahāmati, future and present bodhisattvas, mahāsattvas, should not fixate on this as the selves [of phenomena and persons].

"Mahāmati, for example, from a single heap of clay particles a potter creates vessels of various forms with his hands, craft, a stick, water, a string, and effort.

"Mahāmati, likewise, concerning the [ultimate] phenomenon that is without the [two] selves, that [natural luminosity] from which all conceptual characteristics have totally retreated, the tathāgatas also teach with various forms of wisdom and skillful means, teaching [with the terms] 'tathāgata essence' or 'selflessness,' teaching [natural luminosity] with various synonymous forms of words and phrases, [42] like the potter.

"Therefore, Mahāmati, the teaching of the tathāgata essence is not like the teaching of the non-Buddhists that asserts a self.

"Mahāmati, in that way the tathāgatas teach the tathāgata essence by teaching [with the term] 'tathāgata essence' for the purpose of attracting those who are fixated on the non-Buddhists assertion of a self. {54} And they consider, 'How can those whose minds have fallen into the view of conceptualizing an unreal self come to have minds that abide in the field of experience of the three liberations, and quickly awaken to direct, complete buddhahood in unsurpassable, perfectly complete enlightenment?' Mahāmati, for that purpose the tathāgatas, the arhats, the perfectly complete buddhas teach the tathāgata essence.

"That being so, that [sugata essence] is not the same as the non-Buddhist assertion of a self.

> "Mahāmati, that being so, in order to utterly repudiate the non-Buddhist view you should pursue the selfless tathāgata essence.
>
> "It is like this: this teaching about the emptiness [of all] phenomena, unarisen, nondual, and without the nature [of all entities], is the unsurpassable philosophical tenet of bodhisattvas.
>
> "By fully upholding this teaching of profound Dharma you fully uphold all the Mahāyāna sūtras."[221]

Concerning that, because the sugata essence is empty of both selves, it is not the same as the self of the non-Buddhists, and because the true nature is unconditioned and beyond the momentary, it is permanent, stable, and eternal, but not like space without buddha qualities, abilities, and aspects, or the same as the self of the person that the non-Buddhists imagine to be permanent.

Likewise, because the major marks and minor marks complete in the sugata essence are also the essence of the true nature having all aspects, all abilities, all sense faculties [in each one], and all qualities, these are not identical to the major marks and minor marks of the relative rūpakāya.

Here, this "for the purpose of attracting those who are fixated on the assertion of a self" presents the purpose, but it is not a statement of provisional meaning declaring that something exists even though it actually does not, like the words of a mother promising a sweet treat [to a child].

Why is that?

Because, referring to thusness, emptiness, and so on, there are statements of "tathāgata essence" and, referring to the tathāgata essence, {55} there are also statements by means of many synonyms such as "emptiness" and "thusness," but those all have the same meaning.

That being so, [43] since thusness and so on are actually existent, the sugata essence is also actually existent.

There is just one meaning, but the term agreeable to the thought of some people is not agreeable to the minds of some, and what is agreeable to their minds is not agreeable to the minds of others.

Because of that, the same ground empty of all phenomena, the true nature, the ultimate basic element, is spoken of in the profound sūtras and tantras by means of very many synonymous terms such as "emptiness" and "signlessness," and such as "natural nirvāṇa," "basic element of the self," and "buddha nature," and such as "Heruka" and "Vajrasattva," and the syllables *evaṃ* and *ahaṃ*, and "mahāmudrā," "source of the attributes," "bhaga," "vajra," and the syllable *a*. Of these, the meaning here is, "Seeing that if it were presented to some non-Buddhists by means of the terms 'emptiness' and 'selflessness,' it would not be beneficial, but if it were presented by means of the term 'sugata essence,' it would be greatly beneficial, he said that." That being so, these are the same in being actually existent, but it is also not the case that, for some people reliant on the terms and words, the style of teaching by means of the terms is no different.

Therefore, the *Mahāparinirvāṇa* translated by Lhai Dawa also says:

> If it is taught "The tathāgata essence is empty," childish people meditate on the terrifying extreme of annihilation.
>
> Those with wisdom know that permanent and eternal [basic element appears in various forms], just [like] an illusion, yet exists [in reality].[222]

And so on. Unlike that, if it were of provisional meaning just because of this "in order to lead," then the extremely absurd consequence would be that this "In order to lead some and . . ."[223] (stating the purpose of presenting one consummate vehicle) would also be a passage that teaches the provisional meaning. Furthermore, since all the profound paths of definitive meaning were stated in order to lead persons to be trained from the places of cyclic existence and the peace [of nirvāṇa] into the sublime city of great liberation, the extremely absurd consequence would be that they would all be just of provisional meaning.

So there is a great difference between provisional meaning and statements in order to lead persons to be trained, but some who do not realize that say the *Journey to Laṅkā* states the sugata essence to be of provisional meaning. That is the basis of the confusion, because there is no mention of "provisional meaning" in this passage. {56} [44]

B. *Establishing proof of the extremely absurd consequences that would occur if the sugata essence were actually nonexistent*

The *Journey to Laṅkā* itself says:

> Abiding in inner meditative absorption on the tathāgata essence, the level of a buddha, with a buddha's mind he heard a voice from space and from within: "Good, good, Lord of Laṅkā. Again, Lord of Laṅkā, you are good. Just as you train, so should yogins train.

Just as you see [the true nature], likewise they should view the [ultimate] tathāgatas and phenomena. If viewed in another way, they will abide in annihilation."[224]

And so on. And:

[Ultimate] mind is naturally luminous,
the tathāgata essence, virtue.
The appropriated [aggregates] of sentient beings
are limited, limitless, and abandoned.

Just as the color gold, pure gold,
and bronze are seen by cleaning, so too
the [ultimate] aggregates have no [relative]
sentient being, person, and aggregates.

Meditating on the taintless and
always peaceful primordial awareness
of the [ultimate] Buddha, I take refuge
in that.

Mind, naturally luminous, together
with the afflictions such as mentation,
and [grasping at] a self, has been
fully taught by the sublime speaker.[225]

And:

The tathāgata essence is virtue,
not a sophist's field of experience.[226]

If the sugata essence were actually nonexistent, that would contradict such passages, which refute that by saying the quintessence of the twelve ultimate levels, natural luminosity, mind beyond sophistry, the buddha essence, virtue by very nature, the ground free of all extremes, the consummate source of refuge, and the primordial awareness of a buddha is the sugata essence. {57}

Likewise, the *Vajraśekhara Tantra* also says:

The pure tathāgata essence,
the great mode of dharmadhātu
unsoiled by the mud of the afflictions,
is bestowal of the initiation of vajra and lotus.[227]

And:

A lotus is unsoiled by water
and not soiled by the defect of mud.
Likewise, in all sentient beings,
the primordially unarisen pure true nature,

this tathāgata essence, is the [ultimate]
phenomenon and true nature, emptiness.
The true nature of all [relative] phenomena
such as forms is held to be thusness.[228]

And:

Because all [ultimate] phenomena
are pure, they are free of all defects,
beginningless, the essence of phenomena.
Though incidental stains cause affliction,

I [the sugata essence] alone am
[unafflicted], the great phenomenon.
I am explained to be the essence
of phenomena. So I am the great king.[229]

And:

The pure tathāgata essence is explained
to be the essence of sentient beings.
I am the tathāgata essence, the same
as the self of all [ultimate] sentient beings.[230] [45]

[The claim that the sugata essence is actually nonexistent] also contradicts such passages, which say the primordially unarisen sugata essence, thusness, while also residing without difference in all sentient beings, is unsoiled by the defects of sentient beings.

Likewise, the *Glorious Tantra Determining the Intent* also says:

> The "essence" is this pure true nature
> of the buddhas, and the goal of the practice
> of mantra is, among practices, this sublime
> practice of enlightenment.[231]

The goal of the profound, sublime practice of mantra is thus stated to be the pure true nature, the buddha essence. And *Chanting the Ultimate Names* also says:

> Great essence of all buddhas.[232]

And:

> It is the essence of all tathāgatas.[233]

That kāya of ultimate primordial awareness is thus stated to be the sugata essence. And the honorable lord Avalokiteśvara also says:

> The yoga of the five changeless great emptinesses integrated as one
> is the essence of the tathāgatas, and . . .[234] {58}

And so on. And the *Glorious Kālacakra* also says:

> Sentient beings are buddhas; another great Buddha does not exist
> here in the cosmos.[235]

Thus it says a great Buddha other than the naturally luminous mind present in all sentient beings does not exist in the cosmos. And:

> That which dwells in the mind is not seen by sentient beings
> with negative karma, because of the power of the results of nonvirtue.
> That is not the fault of the wish-fulfilling gem; all sentient beings
> fully experience the results of their nonvirtue and virtue.

> If the mind is purified, even that person becomes a powerful
> conqueror; what would another conqueror do?[236]

Because the naturally original mind, luminosity, that essence like a wish-fulfilling gem abiding in the contrived incidental mind, is obtained by just stopping all the mass of incidental stains, [the claim that the sugata essence is actually nonexistent] also contradicts these statements that the sugata essence is actually existent.

Likewise, the *Ḍākinīvajrapañjara* also says:

> With grasping at self and other abandoned,
> self-knowing primordial awareness, the sublime
> quintessence of entities and nonentities, is equal
> to space, empty, and free of dust.
>
> Integrated passionate desire and freedom from desire,
> [the androgynous stage of] extremely integrated means
> and wisdom. Just that is the lifeforce of living creatures,
> just that is unchanging excellence,
>
> just that pervades everything. That [sugata essence]
> is here the primordial awareness of a buddha,
> called "glorious Heruka."[237]

And the *Glorious Two-Part Tantra* also says:

> That is the maṇḍalacakra and has
> a nature of the five primordial awarenesses.
>
> That is the form of mirrorlike primordial awareness,
> has the essence of the primordial awareness of
> equanimity, and is [the apex of] reality, [46]
> the discriminating. That is the all-accomplishing,
>
> and that of very pure dharmadhātu.
> That is the lord of the maṇḍala—me.
> That is Nairātmyā yoginī, having the nature
> of dharmadhātu.[238] {59}

And:

> This is great primordial awareness
> itself, present in the bodies of all.
> In dual and nondual mode, it is the primary
> quintessence of entities and nonentities.
>
> Present pervading the static and the mobile,
> it is held to have the form of an illusion.[239]

And:

> That [sugata essence] is the lifeforce
> of living creatures, that is the excellent
> syllable itself, that is the quintessence
> of living beings, that pervades all.
>
> Present in the bodies of all,
> entities and nonentities come from that.[240]

And so on. And the *Later Tantra of Direct Expression* also says:

> That [sugata essence] is the lifeforce
> of living creatures; just that is unchanging
> and excellent. It knows all and is present
> in the bodies of all.
>
> That is the primordial awareness of a buddha,
> explained to be glorious Heruka.[241]

And so on. And *Chanting the Ultimate Names* also says:

> The *a*, the most sublime of all phonemes,
> is of great meaning, changeless, and excellent.
>
> The great lifeforce, unarisen, inexpressible
> in words, yet the sublime cause of all
> expression.[242]

Such passages say that basic element of the five self-arisen primordial awarenesses, present pervading all that is static and mobile, is the nature of Heruka, the maṇḍalacakra, the lord of the maṇḍala, the syllable *a*, and so on, the great lifeforce of all living creatures. And the *Glorious Guhyasamāja* and so on say "the great mind of all sentient beings,"[243] stating with such passages that the sugata essence itself is also the great mind. And such passages as "the great offering, great passionate desire"[244] say that it is also the great afflictions such as passionate desire, hatred, and ignorance. And the *Glorious Kālacakra* says:

> That in which the form of the [conditioned] type has
> definitely deteriorated is called "the form of the great."
> That in which the sufferings of saṃsāra have deteriorated
> is called "the great feeling."[245] {60}

All such passages saying the aggregates and the elements and so on are *great* have the meaning of great self and great emptiness. And that is also the meaning of sugata essence, so if the sugata essence were actually nonexistent, the extremely absurd consequence would be that those would also be actually nonexistent.

It might be said, "If the 'sugata essence' and the 'basic element of the self' are synonyms, it would be no different than the self of the non-Buddhists, but if they are not synonyms, even by teaching with those terms one would not be able to lead non-Buddhists who are fixated on a self." [47]

That is not a fault because, even though they are synonyms, this is the ground empty of the two selves, which is the self of thusness, the pure self, and so on.

C. *Establishing proof of the extremely absurd consequences that would occur if the pure self and so on were actually nonexistent*

It might be said, "The basic element of the self, the great self, the pure self, and so on are themselves utterly impossible, because a self is not at all possible."

If that were so, the self of thusness, the pure self, would also be impossible, and, likewise, the vajra self born from a vajra; the unique solid vajra self; the sublime lord of knowing and knowable object; the unwavering, utterly clear self; the self of all buddhas, the sublime entity; the self of living beings immediately at birth; the lord of space, displaying a variety; the lord of the world, self of all; the pervasive lord, most sublime of all gems; the pervasive lord having excellent knowledge and sacred commitment; the great pervasive lord, jeweled parasol; the sublime lord of all tantras; the very wakened, wakened self; and the pure self of the afflicted elements would also be impossible.[246]

Likewise, the *Glorious Guhyasamāja* says:

> Sublimely fortunate Buddha, pure self.[247]

And:

> The attributes of the self that is not consciousness
> are ultimate [truth], the unchanging quintessence.[248]

And:

> It is explained to be "the lord of the vajrās,"
> the six such as Rūpavajrā.[249]

And:

> By this full cultivation of the vajra
> meditative state, the great self of a buddha,
> controlling all the world, is obtained
> in this very lifetime.[250] {61}

And the *Glorious Immaculate Tantra* also says:

> The self that includes all buddhas
> blesses quickly. The self that includes
> all buddhas, the self that is the union
> of all buddhas.[251]

Thus the meaning of such passages would also be impossible. The Omniscient One did not speak of a self with a different meaning than those, and we also do not accept one, but he did speak very many other names. So do not be confused by just the names; instead rely on the meaning.

Therefore, referring to the ground empty of the two selves, the quintessence of ultimate self-arisen primordial awareness never interrupted, the great Madhyamaka master, the honorable, noble Asaṅga also quotes a scripture:

> In that way, emptiness should be understood: the selves do not exist, but [the ground of] selflessness does exist.
>
> Referring to this, the Bhagavān said, "The existent is fully understood to be existent, and also the nonexistent to be nonexistent, exactly in accord with reality."[252] [48]

Furthermore, the ultimate Buddha is a perfection of self, but it is not the same as the self of worldly beings. Just as the *Sūtra of the Great Drum* says:

> In order to destroy those [ideas] of worldly beings about the "self," I taught selflessness. If it were not stated in that way in the Teacher's doctrine, how would I not be a villager? The Bhagavān Buddha is renowned for teaching selflessness.
>
> Thus [sentient beings] are amazed and, after that, guided into the doctrine by hundreds and thousands of causes and reasons.
>
> Guided in that way, at some point, when they also become faithful and enter the higher [doctrine of selflessness], they study the teachings of emptiness, are diligent, and are energetic.
>
> Then, after that, I teach them that [ultimate] liberation is peaceful, permanent, and having form.
>
> Furthermore, some worldly people say [conditioned] liberation exists, and to destroy those [ideas] I say this: "Liberation does not even slightly exist."
>
> If the Teacher did not teach in that way, similar to annihilating that view [of conditioned liberation], how would they believe in the doctrine of the Teacher? {62}
>
> That being so, by hundreds and thousands of causes and reasons I taught selflessness, [the means] of the very annihilation of [conditioned] liberation.
>
> Then, after that, since foolish people are ruined if they see a view that annihilates [ultimate] liberation, after that, by hundreds and thousands of causes and reasons, I also teach [ultimate] liberation to be just existent.[253]

And:

> If I also taught at the very beginning "The self exists," who would have faith?

If they did have faith in that, they would be grasping at a self with the view of the destructible collection[254] as generally agreed in the world, so my [doctrine] would also become that.

I also, like a person who lives in the region of Campaka,[255] first taught the selflessness [of persons and phenomena] and, after that, teach the existence of [the ultimate] self, also explaining that [pure self] and the reality of the self.

Kāśyapa, that being so, this should be taken as skill in means.

Kāśyapa, furthermore, suppose a person goes on a large path into a wilderness, where a brazen crow cries out. Then that person who has entered the path and is traveling hears that bird's call and thinks, "Have bandits not arrived?" He becomes terrified of bandits and strays [onto the wrong path]. Arriving where there are tigers in the wilderness, he suffers because of the mistake.

Kāśyapa, likewise, at a future time monks and nuns, laymen and laywomen, frightened by just the terms "self" and "my," will think no self exists in the worldly view of the destructible collection, and, with the nature of advocates of great emptiness, the view of annihilation, they will not have faith in sūtras such as these, which have the nature of the [ultimate] permanent Tathāgata and permanent Buddha.[256] [49]

And:

Wherever [profound] sūtras such as this are not explained, the teachers of what is beneficial will teach and explain other ordinary ones having chapters on emptiness. {63}

At that time, after those sentient beings see and hear many such sūtras, they will study them. And after they have studied, if at some point they hear [profound] sūtras such as these, which have the nature of the tathāgata essence, the permanent Tathāgata, they will become suspicious and doubtful and [countless] mistakes will occur in their minds.[257]

And:

Kāśyapa, when I teach sūtras of various intent to sentient beings of various inclinations, the lazy, the immoral, and those with unrestrained body, speech, and mind discard the [profound] sūtras such as these of the tathāgata essence, the permanence of the Buddha, and study the sūtras with chapters on emptiness. Here, some cite words and phrases. Some reject words and phrases, back and forth.

Why is that? They say, "All the Buddha's speech teaches emptiness and selflessness."

Foolish people who do not understand the meaning of emptiness and selflessness [that have the same meaning as ultimate thusness] go astray.[258]

And the *Mahāparinirvāṇa* also says:

In order to train non-Buddhists, I have said, "There is no self, no person, no sentient being, no lifeforce, no living being, no human, and no knower, observer, act, and agent."

Monks, the "self" that non-Buddhists speak of is like letters in the tracks of an insect.

Therefore, the Tathāgata says, "A self does not exist in the Buddha's Dharma," in order to train sentient beings and because he understands the moment. In that way, "a self does not exist" was said, but because of causes and conditions, "a self exists" is said, just as a skillful physician knows when milk is a suitable medicine and when it is unsuitable; it is not like the grasping at a self by vulgar children. {64}

The grasping at a self by vulgar children is grasping at [the self of a person], which is just the size of a thumb, or just a white mustard seed, or just a tiny particle.

The Tathāgata's mention of the [ultimate] "self" is not like that [imagined by non-Buddhists]. So, even though "no self exists in all phenomena" is said, in reality [the ultimate] self is not nonexistent. As for [the ultimate] "self": that attribute that is true, reality, permanent, abiding, sovereign, unchanging, and immutable is called [the ultimate] "self," just like that great physician skillful with milk as medicine.[259]

And:

> Selflessness is called "saṃsāra." [The ultimate] "self" is the Tathāgata.[260]

And [50]:

> [The ultimate] "self" means "Buddha."[261]

Such passages thus praise the pure self in many forms.

D. *Showing the reasons the existence and nonexistence of self, and so on, appear to be contradictory but are without flaw*

That appears to contradict the previous statement of selflessness, but is stated to be without flaw. The *Mahāparinirvāṇa* says:

> Son of good family, furthermore, when I previously turned the Dharma wheel in Vārāṇasī, I taught impermanence, suffering, emptiness, and selflessness [in regard to relative, incidental stains].
>
> When I now turn the Dharma wheel here in the village of Kuśinagara, I teach permanence, bliss, self, and utter purity [in regard to the ultimate sugata essence].[262]

And:

> Son of good family, having permanence, bliss, self, and utter purity is called "the meaning of the truth of reality."[263]

And:

> The unconditioned is great nirvāṇa, permanent nirvāṇa. [That] permanence is [the ultimate] self. The self is utter purity. Utter purity is called "bliss," and [the basic element of] permanence, bliss, self, and utter purity is the Tathāgata.[264]

And:

> Son of good family, [the ultimate] "self" means tathāgata essence. The existence of buddha nature in all sentient beings means [the ultimate] "self."[265] {65}

And:

> Buddha nature naturally cannot be made nonexistent; it is not a basis to be made nonexistent.
>
> The very nature of [the ultimate] "self" is the secret essence of the Tathāgata. In that way, that secret essence cannot be destroyed and made nonexistent by anything.[266]

And:

> The characteristic of the transcendent self is called "buddha nature." In that way, apprehending [the ultimate] self is called "very sublime."[267]

And:

> The one sense faculty of the [ultimate] Tathāgata sees [ultimate] form, hears sound, perceives odor, experiences taste, feels tangible objects, and knows phenomena, but the six sense faculties of the [ultimate] Tathāgata do not see [relative] form, do not hear sound, do not perceive odor, do not experience taste, do not feel tangible objects, and do not know phenomena [since they are not established in reality]. By that power, the sense faculty takes power, and such power is called the "great self" [of the great quintessence].[268]

And so on. The *Great Cloud Sūtra* also says:

> For the purpose of fully teaching sentient beings who express praise of impermanence, emptiness, the parinirvāṇa [of śravakas and pratyekabuddhas], and selflessness that the great qualities of the [ultimate] Buddha abide as [great] parinirvāṇa, the self of a permanent, eternal, stable, and peaceful nature, and . . .[269] [51]

And so on, it says extensively. In the *Mahāparinirvāṇa* translated by Lhai Dawa, when two strongmen compete in strength, the precious diamond on the forehead of one sinks into a wound, but he does not notice and believes it has been lost. When a physician extracts the diamond and shows it, he is amazed. Taking that as an example, [the Buddha] says, "The tathāgata essence exists in all sentient beings, but sentient beings do not know it."[270] And:

> Just as that strongman had a diamond in his own body but, because his perception had failed, believed it was lost, so too worldly sentient beings do not realize the reality of the self, fall under the power of nonvirtuous companions, do not understand intentionally ambiguous words, and so meditate on the nonexistence [of the ultimate] self while having [the ultimate] self.
>
> Those who do not meditate on the nonexistence of a self [in persons and phenomena] meditate on the worldly self. {66}
>
> Just as they do not realize the reality of the self while thinking "The worldly self exists," [they claim the reality of] even the transcendent one to be [nonexistent] like that [worldly self]. While relying on nonvirtuous companions, not understanding the limit of intentionally ambiguous words, and meditating, "The self does not exist, the self does not exist," they do not understand the reality of the [ground of the two] nonexistent selves. They think, "Where is the self? Where does it abide? Is it like a pot inside a pot? Or is it pervasive like moisture, or like the ornament between the eyes of the deluded strongman?"
>
> Like the physician, the Tathāgata tells them, "[The ultimate] self does not reside [apparent to all] everywhere, but is luminous like the precious diamond and obscured by aspects of the afflictions."
>
> Sentient beings believe what has been taught, that they merely have to extinguish the afflictions. Then, like the diamond, the tathāgata essence will be seen.
>
> Son of good family, that being so, the tathāgata essence has infinite [qualities].[271]

Also, this is just like the skilled royal physician earlier forbidding milk as medicine and later not forbidding it, so that earlier and later [actions] appear to be contradictory. But careful distinguishing and teaching later establishes that earlier and later were not contradictory. Taking that as an example, the Buddha, the king of physicians, because of the faculties of persons to be trained, earlier taught the nonexistence of the self and later said the basic element of the self exists. Just as is stated:

> After proclaiming the Dharma teaching "Selflessness is the word of the Buddha," and after knowing the faculties of persons to be trained and the time to benefit sentient beings, once again, in that very situation of teaching that all phenomena are without self, like a good physician [the Tathāgata] correctly teaches "[the ultimate] self exists." [52] But it is not like the self of worldly people, said to be "just the size of a thumb, just the size of a seed of wild millet."
>
> It is also not like those worldly people's view of a self. Here, all phenomena are said to be "without a self" [of persons or phenomena]. "But all [ultimate] phenomena are also not without a self; [the ultimate] self is reality. The self is permanence itself. The self is the qualities themselves. The self is eternity itself. The self is stability itself. The self is peace itself." {67}
>
> Thus, like the milk of the good physician, the Tathāgata also teaches what has the reality [of self]. The four followers must be diligent in meditating on that!"[272]

Also, an ointment of neem leaves is smeared on a mother's nipples and, until the infant's medicinal butter melts, he is not allowed to drink, but is allowed to drink when it melts. Taking that as an example, [the Buddha] says:

> Son of good family, so too, like letting the medicinal butter of a child melt, due to the faculties of persons to be trained I also said earlier (in order to destroy the worldly view of monks, to correctly show the greatness of transcendence, to correctly show the reality of the self of the worldly to be false, and to purify the body through meditation on selflessness): "Monks, meditate that all phenomena are without the [two] selves! Meditate in that way and the grasping at an 'I' will be abandoned. If grasping at an 'I' is utterly abandoned, nirvāṇa will be obtained."
>
> Just as the child's mother smeared an ointment of neem leaves on her nipples, likewise, I also said [earlier], "Meditate that all phenomena are selfless, emptiness!"
>
> That mother of the child later washes her nipples and says to the infant, "Earlier, to allow your medicinal butter to melt, I did not allow you to suck my nipples, but now suck!"
>
> Likewise, to turn you away from the worldly teaching [of the view of a self], I also taught in that way, saying, "The [two] selves

> do not exist." Now I teach "The tathāgata essence [the pure self] exists."
>
> Monks, without being frightened as the child was, if you examine just as that child who later sucked the mother's nipples did, likewise, monks, after you have also examined and thought, "The tathāgata essence exists in us," be diligent in meditation! Now I have taught.[273]

And [53]:

> Some phenomena are selfless, but some phenomena have self. {68} For example, because humans on the earth do not have the divine eye they do not see the trails of birds flying in the sky. Likewise, those abiding in the afflictions do not see the sublime [sugata] essence existing in themselves. Therefore, with intentionally ambiguous words I taught, "The self does not exist."
>
> "Human beings without the divine eye already have the self [of the true nature] in themselves," I say, "but do not see and are [obscured by] the afflictions."[274]

And so on. Due to the faculties of persons to be trained, such earlier statements that liberation and so on are all nonexistent and empty, selfless, and so on, refer to that which does not exist in something. But the later statements about nonempty, existence of self, and so on, refer to that which remains after the nonexistent. So earlier and later scriptures appear to be contradictory but, if carefully examined, are not contradictory, because implicative negation exists as the ground of nonimplicative negation, and because ubiquitous fully established primordial awareness with all original qualities complete is present as the ground with all faults primordially, naturally removed and abandoned.

Therefore, one must be expert in the meaning of the great intent and the meaning of intentionally ambiguous statements through perfectly relying on experience of the esoteric instructions of glorious beings of the tenth level, and on the four reliances.[275]

E. *Showing that the pure self,* aham̩, *and so on have the same meaning*
Likewise, the *Tantra of the Drop of Mahāmudrā* also says:

That self [of the fully established true nature]
exists pervading all entities, and if the self
did not exist, all living beings would be just like
a tree with severed roots.[276]

And the *Direct Expression of the Glorious Vajra Garland, Opening the Secret Essence of All Tantras* also says:

The *aham̩* [of the fully established true nature]
pervading all entities specially resides. A person
separated from *aham̩* would be like a tree whose
roots had been cut.[277] {69}

And the *Glorious Tantra of the Drop of Primordial Awareness* also says:

Not something else, but the self
[of the fully established true nature] itself;
it would be difficult for even a buddha
to find you nonexistent.

If you did not exist, the three realms would be
like a human being whose head was severed.[278]

Such passages say even a buddha cannot find the self of the ultimate true nature nonexistent, and, if it were nonexistent, how that would be a great defect.

In the *Ornament of the Sūtras*, the honorable conqueror Maitreya also says:

If emptiness is totally purified,
the sublime self of selflessness is obtained.
Since buddhas thus obtain pure self,
that is the self of the great quintessence.[279]

And the commentary on that says [54]:

> That taintless [ultimate] basic element is taught to be the sublime self of buddhas. Why? Because it is the quintessence of sublime selflessness. Sublime selflessness is totally pure thusness. That also, by the meaning of the svābhāvika[kāya], is the self of buddhas. If that [naturally pure basic element] is totally purified [of incidental stains], buddhas obtain the pure self of sublime selflessness. Therefore, because buddhas obtain pure self, that is the self of the great quintessence. This intent establishes the [ultimate] untainted basic element to be the sublime self of buddhas.[280]

And the *Uttaratantra* also says:

> The perfections of the qualities of purity,
> self, bliss, and permanence is the result.[281]

And:

> Since conceptual elaborations of self and selflessness
> have quieted, it is the excellent self.[282]

In his *In Praise of Tārā*, the honorable, great, accomplished teacher Sūryagupta also says:

> Obtaining purity, self, bliss, and permanence, you are
> the dharmakāya, without sickness, aging, birth, and death.[283]

Likewise, that which is stated to be the ground empty of the two selves, the fully established true nature, the buddha nature, the basic element of the self, is stated to be the consummate *ahaṃ*. Just as the *Glorious Tantra of the Drop of Mahāmudrā* says:

> Listen! I will explain the definitive meaning
> of the term "self" [*ahaṃ*], its reality. {70}
>
> *A* is the sublime phoneme and form existing
> within the bodies of all and everyone. Having
> all aspects, it is the supremely residing sublime
> existing in all, yet unarisen, all-knowing.

Always empty [of the relative], pervading all, having
all [aspects], in all [times], one [essence], lord of the
[other] elements. Appearing as [the other] cyclic existence
and lord of cyclic existence, it is the bliss of nirmāṇakāya.

Since the Tathāgata of the [ultimate] kāya grants
protection, it is able to benefit all. The phoneme *haṃ*,
without [relative] form, [is the sugata essence],
existing in the body, but not born from the body.

Having all aspects yet free [of their essence],
having the face and body and distinctive marks
of all, but without [their essence], liberated from
entity and nonentity, agent of creation and destruction.

With the characteristic that all entities have
disappeared, it has the nature of dharmakāya.
[Ultimate] mind is the vajra bestower of protection.
All [those are inexpressible], so it has no syllables.

The form of [ultimate] emptiness is nirvāṇa,
having the nature of the kāya of primordial awareness.
Stainless, inexpressible, peaceful, it is renowned
everywhere as *haṃ*.

Self [*ahaṃ*], in all [lands] and in all [times],
always resides as the quintessence of all [aspects].[284]

And:

The phoneme *haṃ* is at the end
of the compound, [the phoneme *a* at the tip
of its head].[285] The phoneme *a* is the pure [vajra]
moon, the phoneme *haṃ* the light of the [vajra] sun.

The phoneme *a* is the support, the phoneme
haṃ is explained to be the supported.

The phoneme *a* is explained to be the [other]
lifeforce, the phoneme *haṃ* remembered as effort.

What unites those in their place
illuminates the [ultimate] self itself.
Difficult to find in all tantras, that [*ahaṃ*]
is explained to be the term for the perfect self.[286] [55]

And the *Glorious Vajra Garland* also says:

[The other] *ahaṃ* is utterly liberated.

[The ultimate] *a* is the most sublime
of all entities, specially residing in all bodies.
Having the most sublime of all aspects,
it is all-pervasive, all-knowing, never extinguished.

Called "beginningless and endless," {71}
having all [aspects] yet arising as one [essence],
appearing and pervasive at all times, it is
the most sublime of nirmāṇakāyas,

and skillful at performing all functions.
Its qualities confirmed as those of the tathāgatas,
[the ultimate] *haṃ* is free of entities, residing
in the body, but not born from the body.

Beyond the sense faculties, unclear,
having all aspects yet with aspects
abandoned, liberated from entity and
nonentity, not specially residing anywhere,

it is [the ground] where all entities vanish.
It is the own-essence of the dharmakāya,
mind that is the confirmation of Vajradhara,
performing all functions yet free [of effort],

> the nature of emptiness, nirvāṇa,
> the very nature of the kāya of primordial
> awareness, liberated from expression
> and object of expression.
>
> It is also renowned as the syllable *haṃ*.
> All [ultimate attributes] are *ahaṃ*, omnipresent,
> pervasive, the quintessence of all [aspects],
> always residing.[287]

And the *Glorious Tantra of the Drop of Primordial Awareness* also says:

> Goddess, you do not arise. Birthless
> and deathless, supreme and sublime,
> own-essence free of the waves of concepts,
> luminous primordial awareness, sublime
> kāya of the primordial awareness of
> the quintessence, you are [Dharmadatv]īśvarī,
> [natural] luminosity.[288]

And:

> Countless world systems
> you light with primordial awareness.
>
> You are all, [have the aspects] of all
> entities, are the self of all, are all elements,
> and fully know all phenomena; that is
> renowned as omniscience.[289]

And so on. Identical in meaning, the *Glorious Two-Part Tantra* also says:

> All living beings come from me.
> The three places also come from me.
> I pervade all this and do not see
> another nature of living beings.[290]

And:

I am the instructor, I am also the Dharma.
I am the listener bearing my own assemblies.
I am the world's Teacher and what is to be achieved.
I am the mundane and the transcendent.

I am the nature of connate joy.[291] {72}

And the *Ḍākinīvajrapañjara* also says:

"What is this 'reality of a buddha' like?"
"It is awareness of all aspects."

"What is that? Does it have a body?"
"Likewise, that is true."

"Why is that?"
The Vajra Holder replied, "I [the ultimate Hevajra] am this [dharma]kāya adorned with the [ultimate] thirty-two major marks and the eighty fine minor marks."

"For what purpose?"
"Because knowledge of [ultimate] objects is to be achieved."

Vajrapāṇi also asked, "Is the Bhagavān inanimate?"
The Vajra Holder replied, "I [the ultimate Hevajra] am mirrorlike primordial awareness."

"What is mirrorlike primordial awareness like?" [56]
The Vajra Holder replied, "It is not [relatively] true. It is also not [ultimately] false. It is not to be acquired, yet also not to be discarded. Likewise, I [the ultimate Hevajra] am also the primordial awareness of equanimity. I am also discriminating primordial awareness. I am also all-accomplishing primordial awareness. Likewise, I am also primordial awareness of pure dharmadhātu. Therefore, great bodhisattva, do not say this enlightenment has no essence!"

I am nonexistence, I am existence,
the primordially liberated Tathāgata,

having the [other] sublime kāya,
having the profound and vast kāya.

I am Heruka, O mahāsattva,
united as one with Nairātmyā.
I am not inanimate, I am great bliss.
For the world to remain, I am inanimate [form].

I pervade women, men, the androgynous,
and the five types of living beings.[292]

And the *Glorious Vajraśekhara Tantra* also says:

I [*ahaṃ*, Vajraśekhara] alone am the great phenomenon.
I am explained to be the essence of phenomena.
So I am the great king. I am proclaimed to be
the [other] three states of cyclic existence.

I will tell what the [other] three worlds are.
The creatures of the desire world and,
likewise, those of the form and the formless,
are called "the [other] three worlds." {73}

They are self-arisen I myself alone.
To seek the pure [basic element], the [other]
phenomenon called "[great] desire,"
I reflect upon thusness, called "the [other]
phenomena of apprehended and apprehender."

Since I am indivisible from dharmadhātu,
I purify those [pure] phenomena.
So I am the great king, taught to be lord
of the three worlds.

Just as I am proclaimed to be the [other]
desire realm, likewise the form, and so too
the formless, since I am indivisible from emptiness,
I am explained to be the pure [sugata] essence.

What is the meaning of the [ultimate] three realms?
The desire realm, likewise, the form realm
and the formless, these good [other] three realms
are self-arisen I myself alone.

This [*ahaṃ*] is the basic element, the cause, the [other]
cause of the ultimate three realms, and the [other]
sentient being, explained to be emptiness and signlessness;
I myself am explained to be wishlessness.

What is the meaning of [relative] saṃsāra?
Childish beings, fully occurring [from karma
and the afflictions], in that way circle again
and again.

[The other] saṃsāra of pure self itself
is self-arisen I myself alone. Not even
a particle of the phenomena [relatively]
existing in saṃsāra exists [in reality].

Since [relative saṃsāra] is unreal
imagination, it is without beginning
and end, nonexistent. I am emptiness,
and those that are emptiness are I myself.

Therefore, that [other] saṃsāra
is conqueror Vajradhara; I myself
am said to be what the [other] nirvāṇa is.

In that thusness, purity, and emptiness
(the good nature itself of the Four Truths),
characteristics, entities, forms, and marks
have been abandoned.

It is not to be apprehended by words
and terms. Concepts do not exist.
So the term *nirvāṇa* should be fully
understood to be I myself alone.[293] [57]

And:

I am the [other] creator and producer,
I am lord of the [other] creatures.
I am the [other] lord of variety, creator,
producer, and ancestor.[294] {74}

And:

I [Vajraśekhara] am the king, the mind,
the [other] sovereign. Why am I called
"the creator"? Just as I am said to be
the other secret, I arose from myself.

And nirvāṇa, the [other] realm below the earth,
the realm above the earth, the three states of
cyclic existence, and the [other] three worlds
arose from mind, called "the basis [of all
phenomena]," which has no basis.[295]

And:

I am also the Vajra Bearer.
With all sufferings abandoned,
and all defects extinguished,
I am vajra bodhicitta.

I myself am self-arisen.
I myself am also [the other] Viṣṇu,
with all apprehended and so on abandoned,
pure thusness, and [the other] consciousness,
without the self and the afflictions.
So I am explained to be [the other] Viṣṇu.[296]

And:

Just as I have realized the profound
Dharma explained to be "reality,"

> so self-arisen I myself, [Vajraśekhara],
> am called "the [vajra] sun."
>
> I am called "the [vajra] moon,"
> and I am explained to be the realization
> of the peacefulness of all phenomena.[297]

And:

> I myself alone am the [other] ancestor.
> I am the [other] world of desire.
> I fully manifest the svābhāvika,
> sambhoga, and nirmāṇakāya.[298]

And:

> Severing the nooses of cyclic existence,
> I am the great king of cyclic existence.[299]

And:

> Since I hold the [other] three vehicles,
> I am explained to be the three realms [of the true nature].[300]

And:

> Just as the earth is the sublime holder,
> so too I [Vajraśekhara] hold the [other] Dharma.[301]

And:

> As [*ahaṃ*], called [the other] "above the earth"
> and "space," I naturally [pervade all] equally.
> Without the selves of phenomena and persons,
> I am explained to be the reality above the earth.[302]

And:

I am primordially unborn, unarisen. Not the selves,
selfless I am the [other] self of creatures. Bound
by the vines of cyclic existence, sentient beings
are tormented. I am the liberator, removing the vines.[303]

And:

The signless, unconditioned [basic element],
bodhicitta scatters the vines and nooses [of cyclic
existence], like wind. I am [the other] Maheśvara,
acting as [the other] lord of the vajra assembly. {75}

I am called "Buddha, the other Īśvara."
Great nectar, great city of liberation, I am
Maheśvara, granting the initiation of Īśvara.[304]

And:

I am explained to be [the other] "deliberate behavior,"
and I am explained to be the destruction of afflictions.
Definitely released from aging and death,
I am explained to be the Brahmā [of the true nature].

[The nature of] the desire, and [the other] hatred
and ignorance of the body of the [other] three worlds,
is the [other] three realms, the three worlds,
and I am the guardian and the servant.[305]

And:

The six of Buddha, Vajra, Jewel, Dharma,
and Karma, together with Holder of Secrets,
are the great wheel [of Dharma], so I am the great
sublime one with the six faces [of the six families].[306]

And:

I will explain the consummate intent
of the great city of the nature of liberation. [58]

I [Vajraśekhara] desire all [the other] sentient beings.
So I am explained to be the desire [of the true nature].[307]

And:

I myself am all liberated sentient beings.
I also liberate [sentient beings] individually.
Therefore, self-arisen I myself am the king
who holds liberation.[308]

And:

I am not the selves and phenomena.
I am totally free of attachment.
I present the path of immortality,
so I am the [other] hell being in the hells.[309]

And:

I achieve the desirable, ripening sentient
beings thirsty [for Dharma]. I have achieved
the place of joy, so I am [the other] hungry
spirit born [in the realm of] hungry spirits.[310]

And:

The river of saṃsāra is difficult to cross,
so all sentient beings remain.
Just as they are ignorant and deluded,
likewise, I [Vajraśekhara] liberate them.

Furthermore, I am [the other] attachment,
since I am attached to liberating sentient beings.
In order to eliminate cyclic existence, I am
[the other] hatred and, since I hold the treasury
of secrets, I am [the other] stinginess. {76}

I desire sentient beings, so I am [the other]
desire, and I am the sentient being who liberates

> sentient beings. That king who upholds the secrets
> is my fearless son,
>
> so I am the great secret. I am the holder
> of the treasury of Dharma, the great secret
> enlightenment of the buddhas. Therefore,
> I am the lord of secrets.[311]

And the *Hevajra Tantra* also says:

> As the primal being, Īśvara, self, lifeforce,
> sentient being, time, and person,
> this nature of all entities resides perfectly
> in the forms of illusion.[312]

And so on. By means of many names, words, phrases, and aspects, a great many profound tantras say the essence of the ground in which the entities of the two selves are primordially nonexistent—ultimate emptiness, naturally luminous, having all aspects, that naturally connate primordial awareness beyond the momentary—resides as the never interrupted self of thusness, the pure self. The meaning of that great intent should be seen through perfectly depending on the profound esoteric instructions for experiencing the meaning of the elegant statements by glorious beings on the tenth level, such as the Trilogy of Bodhisattva Commentaries.

F. *Showing that the basic element of the pure self and the perfection of wisdom have the same meaning*

Likewise, the *Great Mother Sūtra* also says the unarisen basic element, the dharmadhātu, the inconceivable basic element, the basic element of the self, and the basic element of the perfection of wisdom are not different. And the statements about purity—from the purity of the self and the purity of the sentient being, through that of the observer—also have the same meaning as the statements about the pure self, sentient being, and so on. [59] "That in which something does not exist is purified of it, and what remains after that, the ground of purification, permanently resides" is the esoteric instruction.

G. *Refuting those who are not expert about the abiding state, and then showing exactly how the ground is present*

Likewise, the sūtra rare as the udumvāra flower also states {77}:

> Then Aṅgulimāla also said this to Pūrṇa, son of Maitrī:
>
> "That which all the buddhas
> and śrāvakas do not find anywhere,
> that Dharma, after direct buddhahood,
> should be taught to living beings.
>
> "What is the meaning of that statement?"
>
> Pūrṇa replied, "Although past bhagavān buddhas very intently sought in all phenomena, they did not find a basic element of a sentient being, a self, a lifeforce, a person, Manu, or a descendent of Manu, and thinking 'Selflessness is the word of the buddhas,' passed away."[313]

Likewise, that is applied to present and future bhagavān buddhas, who also do not find and will not find those. Likewise, it is also applied to all śrāvakas and pratyekabuddhas:

> [Pūrṇa replied,] "In that way, a lifeforce, a person, Manu, a descendent of Manu, a sentient being, and a basic element of the self are taught to be nonexistent. In that way, the self is taught to be nonexistent. In that way, emptiness is taught. Such a Dharma discourse is taught."
>
> Aṅgulimāla again said this to Pūrṇa, son of Maitrī: "Alas! Venerable Pūrṇa, you act like a bug and do not know how to teach a Dharma discourse. Even a bug knows how to make a buzzing noise! You bug-like fool, don't say anything!
>
> "Pūrṇa, not understanding the enigmatic speech of the tathāgatas, thinking that [mere] selflessness is the Dharma, you fall like a moth into the lampflame of a Dharma of delusion.
>
> "As for that which 'buddhas do not find': past bhagavān buddhas did not find the tathāgata essence nonexistent in all sentient beings, and passed away.
>
> "Present bhagavān buddhas also do not find the basic element of [the ultimate] self nonexistent in all sentient beings.

"Future bhagavān buddhas also will not find the basic element of sentient beings nonexistent in all sentient beings.

"Pratyekabuddhas and śrāvakas also did not find, do not find, and will not find the tathāgata essence nonexistent in all sentient beings in the three times.

"This is the meaning of that verse. [60]

"Also, as for 'that which all buddhas do not find': past bhagavān buddhas also very intently sought but did not find in all phenomena a worldly self merely the size of a thumb, or merely the size of a millet seed, a grain of rice, a mustard seed, or a sesame seed, red, blue, yellow, or white, short, long, very long, and so on, said to be 'existing and blazing at the heart,' . . ."[314] {78}

Continuing through:

"All buddhas and all śrāvakas do not find those [worldly people's] permanent, stable, and eternal selves, said to be 'like this,' and, after direct buddhahood, explain that to living beings.

"This is the meaning of that verse. Since Pūrṇa's [explanation] is mistaken conceptualization, it is not the meaning [of that sūtra].

"As for 'that which buddhas do not find': past bhagavān buddhas did not find a created tathāgata essence, and passed away; the uncreated basic element of a buddha adorned with limitless major marks and fine minor marks exists in all sentient beings.

"Present bhagavān buddhas also intently seek but do not find a created tathāgata essence; the uncreated basic element of a buddha, adorned with limitless major marks and fine minor marks, exists in all sentient beings.

"It is known to śrāvakas and pratyekabuddhas in the three times, who are like bees, that 'the tathāgata essence exists,' but they question it, saying, 'The eyes cannot observe it.' I will show the reason for that.

"It is like this: Because Rāhulaśrī's[315] training and moral discipline was sincere, he very intently observed water that contained living creatures, thinking, 'Are these living creatures or are they not? If so, they are like dust particles, but they are all our mothers.' When he gradually investigated, he saw that they were tiny living creatures.

"In a similar way, tigerlike bodhisattvas who reach the tenth level themselves see that the basic element of the [ultimate] self exists in their own bodies, and see it to be an infinite basic element, such as this and like that.

"In that way, to penetrate the tathāgata essence is very difficult to do. Those who sacrifice even their own lives, becoming teachers in what seems to be a totally blazing and utterly blazing world, are teachers concerning what benefits beings having extreme difficulty.

"To those tigerlike bodhisattvas I teach the tathāgata essence, but I do not teach it to others [who are like foxes].

"Sentient beings are themselves tathāgatas.

"For example, of those having magical eyes, it is like Aniruddha.[316] A child with eyes of flesh traveled together with Aniruddha. When the child with eyes of flesh had looked for the trail of where a bird had gone in the sky, he said, 'Do you see the trail of the bird in the sky?' [61] The sthavira Aniruddha clearly saw it, and the person with eyes of flesh also fully believed the sthavira's description. {79}

"Likewise, śrāvakas and pratyekabuddhas, who are like the child with eyes of flesh, believe in the ways of all the sūtras and understand that the tathāgata essence exists. But how could they perfectly perceive the basic element that is the field [of experience] of the tathāgatas? Moreover, if even śrāvakas and pratyekabuddhas depend on the descriptions of others, how could blind human beings believe [in the sugata essence]?

"I have heard from the teachings of perfectly complete buddhas of the past, not spoken to others, that in the past this earth had four sweet tastes. Those sentient beings who experienced the four sweet tastes still eat earth even now when they are young, and those sentient beings who became habituated over a long time are even now still unable to give up that delicious taste.

"Likewise, those sentient beings who, in the presence of many perfectly complete buddhas of the past, meditated on the tathāgata essence and engaged in many [activities], even now still believe in the tathāgata essence. Those sentient beings who meditate for a long time and are grateful to the tathāgatas are not others.

"Even in future times, those sentient beings who teach the

> tathāgata essence, and those sentient beings who believe in it after hearing about it, will not be others. They will be like the children of the tathāgatas (or those who ate earth), who were grateful to the tathāgatas."[317]

And so on, it says extensively. So if one wants to understand the profound, consummate meaning of the great intent, one must also definitely hear and see that exceptional, sublime sūtra correctly, and carefully understand it according to the intent.

H. *Showing the intent of saying the sugata essence is the seed*

Some might think that if the sugata essence has the limitless qualities of the dharmakāya, that would contradict the statements that it is the seed, because this is said:

> That basic element, which is the seed,
> is held to be the support of all phenomena.
> Through its gradual purification, the enlightenment
> of a buddha will be attained.[318] {80}

And so on. Therefore, I should comment. Here, the "seed" is not a conditioned seed, as in planting the seed of liberation, because dharmadhātu itself is here said to be the seed, and because the sugata essence itself is said to be the seed. [62]

Moreover, the *Tantra of the Drop of Mahāmudrā* says:

> Furthermore, listen! I will explain
> that which is renowned as dharmadhātu.
> Space is dharmadhātu, and remember
> the basic element to be the seed.
>
> Existing within all phenomena,
> it is the sublime basis and the cause.
> Just as butter exists within sesame,
> just as fire exists in wood,
>
> likewise it exists in all phenomena.
> In that way, it exists in all phenomena,
> but is not seen [by consciousness].[319]

The space explained here to be dharmadhātu should be understood as ultimate space, because "element of space," "source of the attributes," "lotus," and so on are said to be synonyms for the true nature.

"Remember the basic element to be the seed" refers to the other seed, the ultimate seed, the seed beyond worldly examples, without the flaw of including contradiction.

"Existing within all phenomena," and so on, show (with examples) the sugata essence to be present but not seen, like the seed within all the phenomena of the incidental stains, which are like the husk. And the *Mahāparinirvāṇa* says:

> The seed that becomes a buddha, called "tathāgata essence," exists in me.[320]

This has the same meaning as the statement that the sugata essence itself is also the seed. Therefore, it is totally impossible for the sugata essence, which is the dharmadhātu yet also the seed, to be a relative, conditioned phenomenon, so this refers to the other, or sublime, or transcendent seed.

Likewise, the *Mahāparinirvāṇa* says:

> Son of good family, this "buddha nature" is the seed of the Middle Way, the path of the unsurpassable, foe-destroying, perfectly complete enlightenment of all buddhas.[321] {81}

And the *Mahāparinirvāṇa* translated by Lhai Dawa also says:

> Because those with wisdom know "Such a seed of the dharmakāya exists in my body," they do not grasp at everything.[322]

And so on. The intent of other scriptures like this must also be understood in that way. Otherwise, statements such as:

> Subtle, the seed, yet taintless.[323]

and:

> The limitless aggregate of the attributes
> is fully proclaimed to be my dharmakāya.[324]

and statements of dharmadhātu itself, the quintessence of the eighty-four thousand aggregates of the attributes (such as the powers and the types of fearlessness), and Mahāmudrā, to be the source of the attributes,[325] and furthermore, the scriptures presented before, would be mutually and internally contradictory. But such is not the case. [63]

I. *Therefore, briefly showing how the ultimate qualities are completely present*

Therefore, just as individual phenomena each have their own qualities, those that are its own qualities must also be complete in the true nature, the ultimate. And they are not partial, but all-pervasive and everywhere.

So those that are the indivisible, naturally complete qualities of the ultimate dharmakāya must also be complete in the sugata essence, because these are synonymous.

J. *Showing the reason [the sugata essence] is always present as the basic ground in that way, but does not appear to consciousness*

Even so, sentient beings do not see it, because they are obscured by incidental stains, because that [ultimate sugata essence] is not an object of consciousness, and because it is the field of experience of self-knowing primordial awareness.

Furthermore, the *Mahāparinirvāṇa* also says:

> Then the bodhisattva, the mahāsattva Siṃhanāda asked, "Bhagavān, if the buddha nature, like a powerful vajra, exists in all sentient beings, why do sentient beings not see it?" {82}
>
> The Bhagavān replied, "Son of good family, suppose different forms are blue, yellow, red, and white, long and short, but a blind person does not see them. In that way he does not see, but it is not correct to say the different blue, yellow, red, and white, and long and short shapes do not exist. Why is that? A blind person does not see them, but a sighted person does not fail to see them.
>
> "The buddha nature is similar to that. All sentient beings do not see it; a bodhisattva on the tenth level sees just a portion and a tathāgata sees all without exception. A bodhisattva on the tenth level sees the buddha nature like a form in the night. A tathāgata sees it like a form in the day.
>
> "Son of good family, for example, a person with impaired vision does not clearly see forms. But if a skilled physician treats his eyes, by the strength of the medicine he will see clearly. A bodhisattva

on the tenth level is similar to that; he sees the buddha nature, but not clearly. By the strength of the samādhi of heroic progress he will see it very clearly."[326]

And:

> Furthermore, there is knowing yet not seeing. [64] As for knowing, if one knows the buddha nature exists in all sentient beings, but does not see it because one is oppressed by the afflictions and obscured, that is called "knowing yet not seeing."
>
> Furthermore, there is knowing yet slightly seeing. Bodhisattvas residing on the tenth level know the buddha nature exists in all sentient beings yet do not clearly see it, like the moon being unclear in daytime.
>
> Furthermore, those who see what is to be seen and know what is to be known are the bhagavān buddhas. That is called "seeing and knowing."[327]

And:

> [Great] nirvāṇa itself is not nonexistent at the beginning yet existent now. If nirvāṇa itself were nonexistent at the beginning yet existent now, it would not be a taintless, always present phenomenon.
>
> Whether [relative] buddhas appear or [relative] buddhas do not appear, the [original] nature and [ultimate] characteristic are always present. Sentient beings obscured by the afflictions do not see nirvāṇa, so they think it does not exist. {83}
>
> Bodhisattvas, mahāsattvas who are accustomed to moral discipline, samādhi, and wisdom see [the sugata essence] after eliminating the afflictions. That being so, [great] nirvāṇa is an always present phenomenon, known to be not previously nonexistent yet now existent. That being so, it is called "permanent."[328]

And:

> Buddha nature exists in all sentient beings but is totally obscured by the afflictions, so it is not seen.[329]

And so on. And the *Sūtra of the Great Drum* also says:

> Kāśyapa, these four are similes of the causes and reasons for the obscurations on the basic element of sentient beings. What are the four? Like eyes that have become blurry because of yellow or blue cataracts, like the moon covered by clouds, like digging a well, and like a lamp within a pot.
>
> Kāśyapa, these four are causes and reasons that say the [sugata] essence exists. By those causes and reasons, the basic element of a buddha exists in all sentient beings and all living creatures, and appears adorned with limitless major marks and fine minor marks. Because of that basic element, all sentient beings will obtain nirvāṇa.
>
> Blurry eyes: When veiled by yellow and blue cataracts the eyes become blurry and need treatment. As long as a physician is not found they will be blind, but if a physician is found, they will quickly see. They become blurry when veiled by blue; this basic element covered by the husk of ten million afflictions is similar. As long as one is pleased with the śrāvakas and pratyekabuddhas, the [ultimate] self [seems] to not be [present as the ultimate] self, and there is [grasping] at the self of the self [of phenomena].
>
> Whenever one becomes pleased with the bhagavān buddhas, [65] at that point [the ultimate] self becomes [knowable] and, after that, one becomes a person capable of achieving [buddhahood].
>
> One should view the afflictions to be like that person's eye disease, the blurriness of the yellow and blue cataracts. The tathāgata essence definitely exists, like the eyes.
>
> The moon covered by clouds: Just as the sphere of the moon covered by dense clouds does not appear, so too the basic element covered by the husks of the afflictions does not appear. Whenever it becomes free of the mass of afflictions, like the clouds clearing, {84} the basic element will appear like the full moon.
>
> Digging a well: For example, when a person digs and digs a well, as long as dry soil appears, he thinks, "Because of that sign, water is far from here." Whenever mud appears, at that point he

> knows, "Because of that sign, water is near here." Whenever he reaches water, at that point the end of digging has been reached.
>
> Likewise, by pleasing the tathāgatas and relying on the performance of good conduct, śrāvakas and pratyekabuddhas dig out the afflictions and, after they have been dug out, find the tathāgata essence, like the water.
>
> A lamp within a pot: Just as the light a lamp has within a pot is not bright and sparkling and does not do anything for sentient beings, so too the statement that the tathāgata essence has limitless major marks and fine minor marks also does not benefit sentient beings.
>
> Whenever the pot has been broken, the lamp will shine on its own, benefiting living creatures. Likewise, the tathāgata essence present in the pot of saṃsāra (having the husk of ten million afflictions) will fiercely blaze like the lamp. So when the afflictions of saṃsāra are extinguished, the tathāgatas will benefit sentient beings, like the lamp in the broken pot.
>
> By these four reasons it should be known that, just as the basic element of sentient beings exists in me, so too it also exists in all sentient beings.[330]

And so on. And:

> Some, wishing to view the self, think this: "If we thought to seek the afflictions and the beginning and end of the self, would they be found?"
>
> [Kāśyapa] said, "Bhagavān, they would not. If the afflictions were purified, after that the self [of the true nature] would be found."[331] [66]

Such passages in a great many profound sūtras of definitive meaning state many examples and reasons why the naturally pure sugata essence is always present in all sentient beings but is not seen and not obtained if not separated from incidental stains.

The *Glorious Tantra* also says:

> Totally pure, unarisen, unceasing, producing sublime bliss,
> unsoiled, and to be realized by primordial awareness, yet not

> to be apprehended by anything else in the three realms, {85} and not to be realized by means of the sense faculties of all living beings.[332]

And:

> In the places of the three states of cyclic existence it is
> the agent of benefit to sentient beings and is the wish-fulfilling
> gem, yet without thoughts. That which dwells in the mind
> is not seen by sentient beings with negative karma, because
> of the power of the results of nonvirtue. That is not the fault
> of the wish-fulfilling gem; all sentient beings fully experience
> the results of their nonvirtue and virtue. If the mind is purified,
> even that person becomes a powerful conqueror; what would
> another conqueror do?[333]

And:

> It has all aspects yet is not seen, due to the stains on one's essence
> from the force of the afflictions and the māras.[334]

And the commentary on that says:

> It has all aspects, yet at all times is not seen by childish beings. Why is that? From the force of the afflictions and the māras, from the lifeforce wind fully circulating in the left and right channels. This is the rule.[335]

And so on, it says extensively. The incidental stains are unreal imagination. Their mount or root is the breath circulating to the left and the right, the winds of the afflictions and the māras.

Therefore, if those have not ceased, the incidental stains do not cease, and if they have not ceased, the sugata essence cannot be actualized or obtained. This is the rule.

That being so, if even bodhisattvas have not completely actualized or obtained the sugata essence because they still have residue of the breath, what need to mention other sentient beings?

Furthermore, in the *Mahāparinirvāṇa* translated by Lhai Dawa, taking as an example a physician who opens the eyes of many blind persons and shows them his fingers as many as two or three times, but they do not see anything, and then they finally see, [the Buddha] likewise says:

> Son of good family, even bodhisattvas, mahāsattvas who have reached the tenth level and to whom all the fully purifying examinations have been performed, are like that. Even though fully purified in that way, they are like those people, because I teach as many as two or three times that the tathāgata essence is present in them, but they do not see anything, and then they do see, and say this, "If you have fully turned the sole wheel of selflessness to even us for this long, it will be impossible for śrāvakas and pratyekabuddhas to perceive."
>
> Son of good family, in that way, the entrance to my treatises about the basic element is difficult to see.[336] [67]

And:

> If even bodhisattvas, mahāsattvas who have reached the tenth level, think, "We roughly see that the tathāgata essence exists in each of us," it will be impossible for all śrāvakas and pratyekabuddhas to perceive. {86} Suppose some people have taken a path but become ill with bile and lose their way. Then, if they carefully investigate, they roughly see the path and forms. Likewise, if bodhisattvas, mahāsattvas who have reached the tenth level, also carefully investigate, they will just roughly see that the uncreated basic element of the tathāgata essence exists in their own bodies.[337]

And so on, it says extensively, and finally also states:

> Son of good family, in that way the tathāgata essence is very difficult to see [with the consciousness]. It is the object of the tathāgatas, but not the object of the śrāvakas and pratyekabuddhas.
>
> Son of good family, in that way, my doctrine is to be known by experts; it does not agree with all the world.[338]

And so on. And the honorable Lord of Secrets, Vajrapāṇi, also says:

> This primordial awareness is the quintessence of the connate, the dharma, the sambhoga, and the nirmāṇa; it is primordial awareness, mind, speech, and body integrated as one, perfectly abiding in all phenomena in the three worlds (the higher realms, above the earth, and below the earth). It is difficult for those with inferior merit to discover.[339]

Thus he says the quintessence of the four kāyas and the four vajras, self-arisen primordial awareness, the sugata essence, exists pervading all, but is difficult for those with inferior merit to discover. Likewise, the *Sūtra of Śrīmālādevī* also states:

> Bhagavān, the tathāgata essence is also not the self, not a sentient being, not the lifeforce, not the person.
>
> Bhagavān, the tathāgata essence is not the field of experience of those who have fallen into the view of the destructible collection, those who have been ruined by mistakes, and those whose minds are distracted from emptiness.
>
> Bhagavān, this tathāgata essence is the essence of the excellent dharmadhātu. It is the essence of the dharmakāya. It is the essence of [naturally] transcendent phenomena. It is the essence of naturally, utterly pure phenomena.
>
> Bhagavān, this naturally, utterly pure tathāgata essence, unafflicted by incidental secondary afflictions, is the object of the tathāgatas, and I consider it to be inconceivable.[340] {87} [68]

And so on, it says extensively. Therefore, the sugata essence exists, but sentient beings do not see it because it is obscured by the faults of sentient beings.

K. *Refutation by means of the extremely absurd consequences that would occur if it were not present in that way, because the ultimate would also not exist*

If the sugata essence did not exist, the ultimate would also not exist, because these have the same meaning. That cannot be accepted, because the *Jewel Cloud Sūtra* says:

> Son of good family, whether tathāgatas arise or do not arise, the ultimate does not disintegrate. Son of good family, therefore

> bodhisattvas shave their hair and beards, wear saffron robes, and, with faith, go forth from their homes and become homeless.
>
> Even after going forth, in order to obtain this attribute alone, they become diligent and live as if their hair or their robes were on fire.
>
> Son of good family, if the ultimate were held to be nonexistent, pure conduct would be meaningless. The appearance of tathāgatas would also be meaningless.
>
> Because the ultimate does exist, however, bodhisattvas are known to be experts on the ultimate.[341]

Likewise, the *Sūtra to Benefit Aṅgulimāla* says:

> Furthermore, Mañjuśrī, knowing that butter exists in cow's milk, people churn it. Why do people not churn water? Because the substance [of butter] does not exist there.
>
> Likewise, Mañjuśrī, because the tathāgata essence exists, people guard moral discipline and practice pure conduct.
>
> Furthermore, Mañjuśrī, people with desire and thoughts of gold dig into rock. Why do they not dig into a tree? They dig into rock, where the element of gold exists, but they do not dig into a tree, where gold does not exist.
>
> Likewise, Mañjuśrī, people who consider the [ultimate] basic element to be existent think, "I will become a buddha," and guard moral discipline and are pure in conduct. {88}
>
> Furthermore, Mañjuśrī, if the basic element were nonexistent, pure conduct would be meaningless.
>
> Even if water has been churned for ten million years, oil will not emerge. Likewise, if the basic element of [the ultimate] self were nonexistent, the practices of pure and moral discipline with attachment to [the ultimate] self would be meaningless.[342]

And so on. The honorable, noble Nāgārjuna also says:

> If the basic element exists, by doing the work
> the pure gold will be seen. Without the basic
> element, even if the work is done, only misery
> will be produced.[343]

And the honorable conqueror Maitreya also states [69]:

> If the basic element of a buddha did not exist,
> there would be no weariness of suffering,
> and also no wish, striving, and aspiration
> for nirvāṇa.
>
> This seeing the faults of suffering in cyclic existence
> and the qualities of happiness in nirvāṇa is the activity
> of those having the [natural] family, since it does not
> exist in those without the [evolving] family.[344]

And the *Noble Sūtra of Śrīmālā* also says:

> Bhagavān, if the tathāgata essence did not exist, there would be no weariness of suffering, and also no wish, striving, and aspiration for nirvāṇa.[345]

Such passages state the many faults of claiming that the ultimate sugata essence does not exist, and the many qualities of realizing that it does exist. After consulting and listening extensively to the extremely profound, sublime sūtras of the final wheel, such as the *Mahāparinirvāṇa Sūtra*, the *Sūtra of the Great Drum*, and the *Sūtra to Benefit Aṅgulimāla*, and the profound tantras, one must definitely believe in the sugata essence.

IV. *Advice to avoid the disadvantages of not having faith in that [sugata essence]*
This has two topics.

A. *Advice to avoid the many disadvantages*
In order to teach the infinite great disadvantages that would occur if that were not so, the *Sūtra to Benefit Aṅgulimāla* says:

> Those sentient beings who were previously cattle and opposed their own mothers and became mad, even now still gnash their teeth while sleeping and do not believe in the Dharma of the tathāgata essence, reality. {89} Even in a future time, those sentient beings who gnash their teeth and do not believe in the tathā-

gata essence will not be others, venerable Pūrṇa, they will be the cattle who did not understand the true nature.

Those sentient beings who were previously born as pigeons and had extreme physical desire and fell under the power of fornication mostly do not believe in the tathāgata essence and engage in violent acts. Even in the future, those sentient beings who fall under the power of fornication will mostly not believe in the tathāgata essence. Those sentient beings will not be others, they will be the pigeons who were accustomed to the afflictions for a long time.

Those sentient beings who were previously shameless, extremely ungrateful crows who ate filth, even now are destitute and shameless and do not believe in the tathāgata essence. Even in the future, if they hear of the tathāgata essence in the presence of a teacher of what is beneficial to any sentient being, they will become agitated and leave. Those sentient beings who do not believe in the basic element of the self will not be others, venerable Pūrṇa, [70] they will be the shameless crows who ate filth.

Those sentient being who were previously ugly monkeys with minds shifting like the variegated sparkling waves of the sea, even now are disturbed if they hear of the tathāgata essence and do not believe in the tathāgata essence. Even in the future, they will be those sentient beings whose minds are disturbed when they hear of the tathāgata essence. And those sentient beings who do not believe in the tathāgata essence will not be others, venerable Pūrṇa, they will be agitated and lowly beings, like the monkeys.

Those sentient beings who were previously owls and could not see very much during the day but could see at night, and did not believe in the tathāgata essence, even now, if they see a master [teaching the sugata essence] in the world, do not want to even look. Even in a future time, those sentient beings who hear of the tathāgata essence in the presence of a teacher of what is beneficial to any sentient being, and who do not believe it is the teaching of the Buddha, venerable Pūrṇa, will be the owls who did not believe, [imagining it was] like the words of fortunetellers. {90}

Venerable Pūrṇa, those sentient beings who were previously born in marshes, were soiled by very meaningless treatises, and did not believe in the tathāgata essence, even now do not understand "selflessness" to be an intentionally ambiguous word. So those sentient beings of the marshes [who are afraid of the basic element of the self] do not believe in the tathāgata essence. Even in a future time, being attached to very meaningless treatises, they will not understand statements of enigmatic speech. Those marsh dwellers who do not believe in the tathāgata essence will not be others, venerable Pūrṇa, they will definitely be the marsh dwellers who did not believe in the tathāgata essence.

Those sentient beings who previously stayed at any doorway and were lowly thieves were said to be like dogs. And even in a future time, those sentient beings who roam around the homes of other sentient beings and do not believe in the tathāgata essence will not be others, venerable Pūrṇa, they will be the lowly beings who were like dogs.

Those sentient beings who were previously cats who were always attached to eating flesh and did not believe in the tathāgata essence, even now have become rākṣasa demons changed into the forms of cats who take lives and are attached to eating flesh. Even in the future, those sentient beings who are horrible rākṣasa demons changed into the forms of cats who take the lives of others, who eat flesh and have turned away from the tathāgata essence, will not be others, they will be the rākṣasa demons changed into the forms of cats who took the lives of others and ate flesh.

Those sentient beings who were mice and hermaphrodites, and turned away from the tathāgata essence, even now drink alcohol and have become mice and hermaphrodites, drinking very impure fluids. [71] Even in the future, those sentient beings who drink alcohol and are lowly like hermaphrodites will be satiated by the taste of worldly [sensory pleasure] and not accept the tathāgata essence. They will not be others; they will be those who were viewed as hermaphrodites and mice.

Those sentient beings who were shameless, cunning jackals who turned away from the tathāgata essence, even now do not understand explanations in enigmatic speech concerning the tathāgata essence and have become cunning sentient beings like jackals. Even in the future, those sentient beings who do not understand explanations in enigmatic speech concerning the tathāgata essence and misunderstand [the basic element of the self], saying, "[The teaching of selflessness] appears to be like this," will definitely be the jackals. {91}

Those sentient beings who were previously ugly insects, scorpions, sentient beings turned away from the tathāgata essence, even now blaze [with the fire of the afflictions] if they hear of the tathāgata essence. Those with hateful hearts definitely resemble scorpions. Even in the future, those sentient beings who, if they hear of the tathāgata essence, do not believe, saying, "It is not the explanation of the Buddha," will not be others, venerable Pūrṇa, they will definitely be those like scorpions, who engaged in hot actions.

Those sentient beings who were previously horrible poisonous snakes who spoke harshly about the tathāgata essence, even now have [been reborn] as arrogant, frightening, horrible poisonous snakes. Even in the future, those sentient beings who speak harshly about the beneficial doctrine of the tathāgata essence and perform negative acts will not be others, Pūrṇa, they will definitely be the horrible poisonous snakes.

Those sentient beings who were previously sheep, stupid and lethargic, with no known qualities, who did not value the tathāgata essence and condemned the sūtras, even now condemn the sūtras. Those sentient beings have definitely become sheep, stupid and lethargic. And even in the future, those sentient beings who sleep too much and, if they hear of the tathāgata essence, condemn it, will not be others, they will definitely be those who were lethargic and weak.

Those sentient beings who were previously lethargic water buffalos who turned away from the tathāgata essence, even now are definitely weak and thirsty, like water buffalos consumed by the three views [of the three poisons]. Even in the future, those sentient beings who are thirsty and angry, weak and lethargic, turned away from the tathāgata essence, will not be others, but will definitely be the water buffalos who were consumed by the three views. [72]

Those sentient beings who were previously bears, turned away from and not believing in the tathāgata essence, are even now sentient beings who declare unpleasant things, definitely having been [reborn as] beings like bears and jackals. Even in the future,

> those sentient beings who turn away from the tathāgata essence and declare unpleasant things will not be others, venerable Pūrṇa, {92} they will be those who were like bears and jackals.
>
> Those sentient beings who were previously sparrows, who turned away from and did not believe in the tathāgata essence, and even now are sentient beings with dull eyes, are definitely sparrows. Even in the future, those sentient beings who conceal knowledge of the tathāgata essence and perform malicious negative acts will not be others. Not teaching the tathāgata essence, they will definitely be the sparrows with dull eyes.
>
> Those sentient beings who were previously donkeys, who developed the attitude that the tathāgata essence was unnecessary, even now are poor and eat coarse food like donkeys. Even in the future, they will be reborn in bad families ordered around by other paupers. Those who do not believe in the tathāgata essence [the basic element of the self] and meditate on [mere] selflessness will not be others, venerable Pūrṇa, they will be those who were like prostitutes, outcastes, fowlers, and donkeys.
>
> Those who were previously anti-gods with short bodies like ugly turtles with long fangs, and slandered the tathāgata essence, and who even now have short bodies like turtles, are definitely anti-gods. Even in the future, those fierce sentient beings who are short like turtles, have long fangs, and slander the tathāgata essence will not be others, venerable Pūrṇa, they will be the sentient beings included in the family of anti-gods.
>
> Those sentient beings who were previously hungry spirits with flames coming from their mouths, who condemned and ridiculed the tathāgata essence, even now have dry lips and palates and have become hungry spirits, emaciated creatures with flames coming from their mouths. Even in the future, those sentient beings with extremely emaciated bodies, who condemn and ridicule the tathāgata essence, venerable Pūrṇa, will not be others, but will definitely be the feeble hungry spirits with fire coming from their mouths.[346]

And so on. The *Great Cloud Sūtra* also says:

> Mahāmeghagarbha, those whose minds are totally deluded and confused, who incorrectly say the Tathāgata is impermanent and

not eternal but unstable and will vanish, have fainted from bile. [73] Fallen asleep in their homes, where they are harmed by the darkness of the sleep of views that have burned them with painful poison, they have been burned by the views of horrible dreams, become crazed, and dream. For them, and all the frightened śrāvakas and pratyekabuddhas, and for the sentient beings who are like old arthritic cows, ignite the oil of the knowledge of the permanent nature of the greatness of the Buddha's qualities and the essence of the awareness of reality! {93}

For those sentient beings with many ignorant views, who have rejected the application of the lamp of the permanent nature of the qualities of the Tathāgata and spoken unflatteringly about the Śākya family, apply the eye medicine of the kataka fruit of the knowledge of reality!

Cut out and discard the tongues of those who have rejected the perfect primordial awareness of the greatness of the Tathāgata's [natural] family, but gone forth following the Tathāgata and disparage [the sugata essence]!

In order for those who have gone forth following the Tathāgata and become sons of the Buddha to wisely understand the enigmatic speech of the Tathāgata, give this magical key to all the views![347]

And so on. The *Sūtra to Benefit Aṅgulimāla* also says:

Those sentient beings who previously viewed the permanent kāya of the Tathāgata as impermanent became ill with leprosy and, even now, those sentient beings who are weak and become ill with leprosy have definitely condemned the kāya of the Tathāgata. Even in the future, those sentient beings who view the permanent kāya of the Tathāgata as impermanent and become ill with leprosy will not be others, venerable Pūrṇa, they will have condemned the permanent kāya of the Tathāgata.[348]

And:

Those many types of sentient beings with many illnesses, who previously deteriorated during an excellent time, viewed the everlasting kāya of the Tathāgata as not everlasting. Even now, those

> sentient beings who deteriorated during an excellent time view the everlasting kāya of the Tathāgata as not everlasting. Even in the future, those sentient beings who deteriorated during an excellent time will view the everlasting kāya of the Tathāgata as not everlasting and, venerable Pūrṇa, they will definitely not be others, but will have repudiated the luminous kāya of the Tathāgata by saying it is not luminous. {94}
>
> Those sentient beings who previously viewed the eternal kāya of the Tathāgata as not eternal died after taking birth in the womb of an excellent queen of a king, being impermanent. Even now, some of those sentient beings, after taking birth in the womb of an excellent queen of a king and dying, have definitely condemned the eternal and luminous kāya of the Tathāgata. [74] Even in the future, those sentient beings, being impermanent and having short lives, will condemn the eternal kāya. And, venerable Pūrṇa, they will not be others, but will have definitely condemned the eternal kāya of the Tathāgata.[349]

And the *Sūtra of the Great Drum* also says:

> When a discourse on the tathāgata essence is taught, by condemning it, a discourse on the permanence of the Buddha is rejected and, by just that, one will not pass into parinirvāṇa.[350]

And so on, it says extensively. If a natural buddhahood of reality beyond the momentary is established as actually, naturally permanent, the sugata essence has been established, because a previously nonexistent buddhahood that is newly arisen would not be suitable as the sugata essence.

Furthermore, the honorable, noble Lokeśvara says:

> The conquerors have said primordial awareness free of single or multiple moments is called "reality."[351]

Thus it is stated that primordial awareness of reality is beyond the momentary. And the honorable conqueror Maitreyanātha also says:

> In terms of nature, unbroken continuity,
> and continuity, those are indeed permanent.[352]

Thus the true nature, the svābhāvikakāya, is said to be naturally permanent. And:

> Unconditioned, spontaneous, . . .[353]

Such passages stating consummate buddhahood to be unconditioned also refer to being free of the momentary.

Therefore, those who claim that all statements that the dharmakāya or primordial awareness is permanent refer to a permanence of continuity, but that it is momentarily impermanent, and who claim that all statements that buddhahood or primordial awareness is unconditioned refer just to it being unconditioned by karma and the afflictions, have simply not understood these truths of the great intent and have also plainly not seen these profound passages.

Likewise, the *Mahāparinirvāṇa* translated by Lhai Dawa also says:

> By meditating on the selflessness of the tathāgata essence and constantly meditating on emptiness, sufferings do not cease; one becomes like a moth drawn into a lamp's flame. {95}
>
> Unlike that, sentient beings who meditate on the existence of the tathāgata essence stop the aspects of the afflictions while the afflictions still exist.
>
> Why is that?
>
> It is because of the catalyst of the tathāgata essence.[354]

And:

> For a monk with excellent moral discipline to say of the unconditioned Tathāgata "The Tathāgata is conditioned," it would be better to become a non-Buddhist, or even die. [75]
>
> Those who say "The Tathāgata is conditioned," while the Tathāgata is unconditioned, are lying.
>
> Those who say "The Tathāgata is conditioned" are sentient beings who will go to hell as if it were their own home.
>
> Venerable Mañjuśrī, do not view the Tathāgata to be [impermanent] like a conditioned phenomenon. From now on, having passed beyond ignorance while yet roaming in saṃsāra, you must realize only the knowledge of "The Tathāgata is unconditioned."

> Acting in that way, by the result of that meditation you will very quickly possess the thirty-two major marks, like the Tathāgata.[355]

And so on. And the *Noble Sūtra Taught by Vimalakīrti* also says:

> There are two reasons that beginner bodhisattvas hurt themselves and do not concentrate on the profound Dharma.
>
> What are the two? If they hear a profound sūtra not heard before, they become frightened and doubtful, do not rejoice, and reject it, thinking, "This has been taught, but if we have not heard such as this before, where has it come from now?" And, son of good family, they do not attend upon, do not associate with, and do not honor those who uphold the profound sūtras, become vessels of the profound Dharma, and teach the profound Dharma, and do not revere them. Sometimes they even speak unpleasantly about them.[356]

And so on. These passages teach that great defects will occur if one does not believe, is not respectful, repudiates, and so on, the sugata essence that has the same meaning as thusness, the perfection of wisdom, natural nirvāṇa, the pure self, the reality of the self, the buddha nature, the natural kāya, and so on. And the honorable, noble Lokeśvara also says:

> Sixth is to denigrate the philosophical tenets; the philosophical tenets are the sections on reality in the approach of the perfection of wisdom and in that of mantra. That which condemns those is the sixth.[357] {96}

And:

> If one finds faults in our own philosophical tenets and the philosophical tenet of others, it becomes the sixth root downfall.
>
> Therefore, knowing the relation between what comes earlier and later in the different tantras, one should understand the qualities and the faults.
>
> Otherwise, evil teachers attached to indulging the sense faculties in objects outside of the tathāgata essence, and who speak lies,

> finding faults in what they do not see, [76] will go to the Avīci Hell.[358]

Such passages teach that, finally, the meaning of mantra and the perfection of wisdom is the same in thusness, and, furthermore, that if these are held to be mutually exclusive and are disputed and denigrated without understanding the sugata essence, the perfection of wisdom, and so on to be synonymous, that becomes a root downfall for those who have entered mantra. And if fault is found in the faultless due to not seeing that many synonyms exist for one meaning, one will go to the Avīci Hell. Likewise, the *Extensive Mother Sūtra* also says:

> Venerable Śāradvatiputra, if this profound perfection of wisdom were explained in front of bodhisattvas, mahāsattvas who had newly entered the vehicle, what faults would occur?
>
> Śāradvatiputra replied, "Kauśika, if this profound perfection of wisdom were taught in front of bodhisattvas, mahāsattvas who had newly entered the vehicle, after hearing this profound perfection of wisdom, they would become frightened, fearful, scared, and turn away. They would reject it.
>
> They would also not respect it, and, Kauśika, because those bodhisattvas, mahāsattvas who had newly entered the vehicle, would have rejected this perfection of wisdom after hearing it, they would form and accumulate the karma of falling into error. And, also due to that creation and accumulation of karma, it would be difficult to directly, completely awaken to unsurpassable, perfectly complete enlightenment. A situation such as that would exist.[359]

And so on, it says in great detail, and the *Intermediate Mother Sūtra* and the *Condensed Mother Sūtra* also state extensively. {97} The *Collection of Precious Qualities* also says:

> Though in previous conduct they have honored
> a hundred billion buddhas, if they do not have faith
> in the Conqueror's perfection of wisdom, those of lesser
> intelligence will reject this after hearing it and, having
> rejected it, will have no protection and go to the Avīci Hell.

> That being the case, if you want to contact the sublime
> primordial awareness of the buddhas, have faith here
> in the Mother of the Conquerors![360]

Whatever disadvantages such passages mention concerning fear, rejection, disbelief, disrespect, and so on toward the perfection of wisdom are all disadvantages concerning rejection, disbelief, and so on from fear of the mere terms "sugata essence," "pure self," and so on, because that and those have the same meaning.

Likewise, the *Mahāparinirvāṇa* translated by Lhai Dawa also says:

> For example, as the milk of the cow is sweet, so too the taste of this sūtra is also like that. [77]
>
> Those who reject the doctrine of the tathāgata essence in this sūtra are like cattle. For example, just as ungrateful people thinking to kill themselves will create supreme misery, so too it should be known that those sentient beings who have rejected the tathāgata essence and then teach just selflessness will create supreme misery.[361]

The defects and faults of rejecting the sugata essence, pure self, and so on, and of disbelief in them, which such passages mention in detail, are also the defects and faults of rejection, and so on, of the profound perfection of wisdom, because that and those have just one meaning.

Likewise, the *Uttaratantra* also says:

> All denigration of the noble beings and blaming the Dharma
> they have spoken, which is done by those whose nature
> is afflicted and deluded, is created by fixated views.
> Therefore, the mind should not adhere to what is stained
> by fixated views; a clean cloth can be dyed, but not one soiled by oil.
>
> Because of lesser intelligence, because of lacking interest
> in what is good, because of relying on false pride, because of
> having a nature obscured by having lacked the excellent Dharma,
> because of grasping at the provisional meaning as being
> the definitive meaning of reality, because of craving gain,
> because of being under the power of views, because of relying

on those who repudiate Dharma, because of keeping at a distance from those who uphold the Dharma, and because of low interest, the Dharma of the arhats is rejected.

Experts should not be as terrified of fire, horrible poisonous snakes, murderers, or lightning as they should be of the loss of the profound Dharma. Fire, snakes, enemies, and lightning may just separate one from life, but through them one will not go to the terrifying realm of beings in Avīci Hell. {98}

Even persons who, again and again relying on bad friends, have evil intentions toward a buddha, kill their father, mother, or an arhat (doing what is never to be done), or divide the sublime assembly, will quickly be liberated from these [acts] if they have definitely reflected on the true nature; but how could liberation occur for those who hate the Dharma?[362]

And the *Ornament of the Mahāyāna Sūtras* also says:

Living beings, frightened though it is not a basis for that, become tormented, having accumulated a great mass of what is not merit for a long time. Lacking the [evolving] family, having bad companions, not having accumulated virtue in the past, and not training the mind, they are frightened by this Dharma and here fall from this great goal.[363]

And:

"I do not understand." "Buddhas do not know the profound."
"Why is the profound not an object for sophists?"
"Why should those who know the profound be liberated?"
Those are not suitable as bases for fear.[364]

And:

There are none other than those, but since they are very profound and in accord, they teach by means of various aspects, and constantly teach in many ways,

> yet the meaning is not just as explained, since the intent
> of the Bhagavān is very profound. If experts properly
> examine it, they will not be frightened by this Dharma.[365]

And [78]:

> If the meaning is totally thought to be literal,
> one becomes arrogant and one's intellect declines.
> Since even the careful statements are rejected,
> one will be destroyed, obscured by anger at the Dharma.[366]

And the *Abhidharma* of the Madhyamaka also says:

> Why do some sentient beings not believe the very extensive [sūtras] to be vast and profound and become frightened?
>
> Because they are separated from [the wisdom that realizes] the true nature, have not generated roots of virtue, and have been fully influenced by bad companions.[367] {99}

And:

> Why do some sentient beings believe the very extensive [sūtras], but are not definitely released?
>
> Because they continue to grasp at their own view as supreme and are fixated on the meaning as literal.
>
> Referring to this, in the *Dharma Discourse of the Great Mirror of Dharma* the Bhagavān says:
>
>> For bodhisattvas who incorrectly analyze the Dharma in a literal sense, twenty-eight bad views occur.
>>
>> What are the twenty-eight bad views? They are the view of characteristics, the view that denigrates the designated, the view that denigrates the imputed, the view that denigrates reality, the view of full adherence, the view of change, the view that no transgressions exist, the view of definite liberation, the view of humiliation, the view of hostility, the mistaken view, the view of increase, the view of no acceptance, the view of decep-

> tion, the view of adulation, the view of firm delusion, the root view, the view that the view is not the view, the view that undermines application, the view that is not conducive to definite liberation, the view of increasing obscurations, the view of demerit, the view without result, the view of ridicule, the view of denigration, the unspoken view, the great view, and the view of manifest pride.[368] {100}

Thus, to prevent the immense karma of rejecting Dharma (such as rejecting the sugata essence, pure self itself), which comes from taking some [statements] literally, not understanding the intentionally ambiguous meaning or the meaning stated with intentional ambiguity, and not realizing that a single profound meaning is taught with many synonyms, one must realize through the esoteric instructions of the profound sūtras of the final wheel (such as the *Mahāparinirvāṇa*) and of the profound tantras clarified by the Bodhisattva Commentaries, that statements about emptiness, selflessness, and so on refer to the sugata essence and pure self, and that statements about the sugata essence and the self of the true nature refer to the ground of emptiness and selflessness, and that their intentions are not contradictory but have the same meaning. [79]

B. *Advice to respect the means for that*

Moreover, the *Mahāparinirvāṇa* says:

> Furthermore, son of good family, it is like this: for example, if a great drought has occurred, flowers and fruit will not grow on palaśa, kanika, and aśoka trees. Furthermore, if there is no moisture, all lotuses will not grow to full size and all medicines will become less potent.
>
> Son of good family, this Mahāyāna sūtra, the *Mahāparinirvāṇa*, is also like that. After I have passed into nirvāṇa, sentient beings will not revere it. Its splendor will also lessen.
>
> Why is that? Because those sentient beings will not understand the intentionally ambiguous statements by the Tathāgata.
>
> And how is that? Because sentient beings will have little merit.
>
> Son of good family, furthermore, when the excellent Dharma of the Tathāgata is near destruction and extinction, at that point

> in time many monks will commit negative acts and, not understanding the [sugata] essence stated by the Tathāgata with intentional ambiguity, will act lazy and slothful and not be able to read and recite and distinguish and teach the perfect Dharma of the Tathāgata. {101}
>
> For example, like stupid thieves discarding perfect jewels and taking away chaff, they will not understand the [sugata] essence stated by the Tathāgata with intentional ambiguity and will act lazy and not develop diligence in regard to this sūtra.
>
> Alas! In a future time they will fall into a great terrifying abyss.
>
> Alas! Those sentient beings will not act diligently regarding this Mahāyāna sūtra, the *Mahāparinirvāṇa*. Only bodhisattvas, mahāsattvas, will penetrate the correct meaning of this sūtra just as it is and, unattached to the letters and the words, will follow its [profound meaning], not contradict it, and also teach it to sentient beings in that way.[369]

And so on. And:

> The sūtra sets come from the twelve [categories of] the sūtra sets. The very extensive set comes from the sūtra sets. The *Perfection of Wisdom* comes from the very extensive set. The *Mahāparinirvāṇa*, which is like the essence of butter, comes from the *Perfection of Wisdom*. "The essence of butter" is a metaphor for the buddha nature. The buddha nature is the Tathāgata.[370]

And:

> Son of good family, you asked, "In the past, did Tathāgata Kāśyapa have this sūtra?" [80]
>
> Son of good family, this *Mahāparinirvāṇa Sūtra* is the essence spoken with intentional ambiguity by all tathāgatas.
>
> Why is that?
>
> The tathāgatas have eleven of the [categories of] the sūtra sets, but the buddha nature, and the permanence, bliss, self, and utter purity of the Tathāgata, is not [clearly] explained in them. [The ultimate] bhagavān buddhas do not finally pass into nirvāṇa

> [because they are not impermanent]; therefore, this sūtra is "the [consummate] essence of the intent of the tathāgatas."[371]

And so on. And:

> Son of good family, you should know this *Mahāparinirvāṇa Sūtra* of the Mahāyāna to be a mass of measureless, infinite, inconceivable merit.
>
> Why is that? Because it [clearly] explains the secret essence of the Tathāgata.
>
> Therefore, if sons of good family or daughters of good family wish to quickly understand the secret essence of the Tathāgata, they should urgently and diligently apply themselves to this sūtra.[372] {102}

And so on. And the *Mahāparinirvāṇa* translated by Lhai Dawa also says:

> For example, if thunder rumbles from the sky, mushrooms will quickly and fully grow, but in the hot season even the name "mushroom" does not exist. Just as they are brought forth by thunder, so also that tathāgata essence, the [pure] self [exists yet] appears to be nonexistent because it has been obscured by aspects of the afflictions. But as soon as those [sentient beings] hear this great sūtra, hear this *Mahāparinirvāṇa*, understanding of the tathāgata essence will arise like mushrooms.
>
> All sūtras and all samādhis [in which the sugata essence is not clear] are like the hot season, and by hearing all [such] sūtras and all samādhis, one does not perfectly understand that the tathāgata essence exists. Just as mushrooms grow in summertime, all the secret words of intentional ambiguity come from this great *Mahāparinirvāṇa Sūtra*, and, just as mushrooms grow in summertime, as soon as all sentient beings hear this sūtra they will perfectly understand that the tathāgata essence exists.[373]

And:

> Son of good family, furthermore, for example, all rivers are collected within the ocean.

> Son of good family, likewise, all sūtras, all samādhis, and the Mahāyāna are collected within this great *Mahāparinirvāṇa Sūtra*.
>
> Why? Because the tathāgata essence is extremely, totally, consummately, clearly presented in this.[374] [81]

Such is extensively taught, so one should not condemn and denigrate the sugata essence, the pure self itself, and the buddha nature or natural Buddha, which have the same meaning as thusness, the Great Mother, the svābhāvikakāya, Mahāmudrā, great Vajradhara, Vajrasattva, and so on, . . . {103}

V. *Advice to take up the advantages of faith in that [sugata essence]*
This has two topics.

A. *The immense advantages to be obtained*
. . . but should be faithful, devoted, and believe, because if one acts in that way infinite great advantages will occur.

Furthermore, the *Sūtra to Benefit Aṅgulimāla* says:

> As a result of understanding that the permanent tathāgata essence exists in all sentient beings, the best forms of happiness and all and every excellence that exists in the world will be gained.
>
> By hearing of the permanent tathāgata essence, all the excellence in the three times (past, present, and future) and all the happiness in the higher realms and on the surface of the earth will always be obtained.[375]

And:

> Great wisdom arises from this immortal phrase that teaches "The Tathāgata is permanent," and the wise one who teaches in that way is the Buddha.[376]

And:

> Good. Good. I [Aṅgulimāla] will teach the tathāgata essence.
> I will speak elegantly and dance; the tathāgata essence will be heard.
>
> Pleasantly sounding like Nārada,[377] I recite
> the Mahāyāna sūtras. With the drums,

small drums, and cymbals of the kiṃnaras
and gandhārvas, I also worship the volumes.

Those sentient beings who always worship
in that way will constantly be [reborn as] human
beings in the world, and at a later time become
buddhas, so the Tathāgata says.[378]

And also:

Mañjuśrī, that is so, my doctrine will remain for many years in the southern regions.

Bodhisattvas such as you, who endure extreme austerities, sacrificing even their lives, will say, "The Tathāgata is permanent. The Tathāgata is eternal. The Tathāgata is everlasting," thus teaching the tathāgata essence to benefit all sentient beings.[379]

And:

Mañjuśrī, at the point when the excellent Dharma will remain for eighty years, those like you should carry the great load of the excellent Dharma and, thinking "I honor the excellent Dharma on my shoulders," sacrifice even your lives and fully teach the sentient beings of the Jambu continent and all the minor continents: "The tathāgata essence is permanent, eternal, peaceful, and everlasting." {104} [82]

Whether sentient beings believe or do not believe, whether my body is killed or chopped into pieces, my body is a primordial, permanent body; bodhisattvas who endure the extreme austerity of carrying the load will appear from the southern regions.[380]

And:

The Bhagavān said, "Aṅgulimāla, even the Tathāgata endured extreme austerities. In a future time, at the point when the excellent Dharma will remain for eighty years, those Mahāyāna sūtras teaching the tathāgata essence will be taught to benefit all sentient beings and will endure extreme austerity.

> It is taught that those sentient beings who hold that position will also endure extreme austerity.[381]

And:

> The Mahāyāna will be taught in southern regions, be emphasized as the essence, and the conduct of the Tathāgata will be practiced, free of the eight great concerns. It will be taught, "The Tathāgata is permanent, eternal, and peaceful, and the tathāgata essence is stable."
>
> My śrāvakas, monks, nuns, laymen, and laywomen will emphasize [that Dharma] as the essence. They will take up my doctrine as a load.[382]

And so on. And:

> As a result of the merit of hearing about the tathāgata essence, there will be no illnesses, no harm, long lives, and all living beings will be happy. Hearing that the Tathāgata is permanent, everlasting, and eternal, and that parinirvāṇa is also deathless, all will become prosperous, firm for a long time, and permanent.[383]

And:

> Those wishing to teach Dharma should teach in this way: the Tathāgata should be fully praised as permanent and real.
>
> Those who do not teach in that way, discarding the tathāgata essence, are, for example, not fit for a lion throne, as an outcaste is not fit for the mighty elephant of a king.[384]

And so on, it says extensively. And the *Mahāparinirvāṇa* also states:

> Therefore, Mañjuśrī, sons of good family who have modesty and shame do not view the [naturally original] bhagavān buddhas as comparable to conditioned phenomena.
>
> Mañjuśrī, non-Buddhists with bad views claim, "The [naturally original] Tathāgata is comparable to conditioned phenomena," but monks preserving moral discipline do not view the Tathāgata as being conditioned in that way. {105}

If one says, "The Tathāgata is conditioned," one is lying, and it should be known that, immediately after dying, that person will be born as a sentient being in the hells, [83] just like a person dwelling in his own home.

Mañjuśrī, the Tathāgata is in reality an unconditioned phenomenon, so do not say, "He is conditioned."

Mañjuśrī, from today on, while circling in saṃsāra, abandon unawareness [of the abiding state of reality] and seek perfect primordial awareness.

The Tathāgata is unconditioned, and if anyone views the Tathāgata in such a way, they will become endowed with the thirty-two major marks and quickly awaken to unsurpassable, perfectly complete enlightenment.

Then youthful Mañjuśrī said to Cundāla, "Good. Good. Son of good family, you have actualized the cause for a very long life, and it is good that you realize the Tathāgata to be an unconditioned phenomenon having the attribute of permanence, having unchanging, immutable attributes. It is good that you do not describe the Tathāgata in terms of conditioned characteristics.

"A person who has been burned and covers the body with clothing because of modesty and shame will, by the virtue of those thoughts, be born as a god in the Heaven of the Thirty-Three, will become Brahmārāja[385] and a universal monarch, and will always be born in a pleasant place and not be born in the lower realms.

"Likewise, by not describing the Tathāgata in terms of conditioned characteristics, you will also in a future lifetime undoubtedly have the thirty-two major marks, the eighty fine minor marks, the eighteen unshared attributes [of a buddha], unlimited lifespan, not remain in saṃsāra, have total bliss, and reach perfectly complete enlightenment before very long."[386]

And:

That person who believes in the Tathāgata as a permanent phenomenon is extremely rare, like the udumvāra flower.

After I have passed into nirvāṇa, if someone hears this extremely profound sūtra of the Mahāyāna, and a faithful mind arises, know that in the future that one will not fall into the lower realms for hundreds and thousands of eons.[387]

And:

> Here, the proclamation of the lion's roar does not explain that "all phenomena are impermanent, suffering, selfless, and utterly impure." It explains that the Tathāgata is only permanent, bliss, self, and utterly pure.[388] {106}

And the teacher Bhāvaviveka, citing the *Mahāparinirvāṇa* as proof in the *Lamp for the "Wisdom,"* a Madhyamaka commentary, also says:

> Those sentient beings of whom it is taught "The tathāgata essence exists in all sentient beings" have infinite qualities. And the countless negative acts those sons of good family who desire the excellent Dharma have committed will be purified merely by headaches, being struck by contagion, pains, [84] and denigration.[389]

The *Sūtra Teaching the Inconceivable Qualities and Primordial Awareness of the Tathāgata* also says:

> Some bodhisattva may practice the five perfections for eight billion eons, Mañjuśrī, but if another bodhisattva devotedly thinks "The Tathāgata is permanent," this produces countless merits greater than that.[390]

And the *Great Cloud Sūtra* also says:

> The bodhisattva, the mahāsattva Mahāmeghagarbha, said this to the Bhagavān: "Bhagavān, if they possess what sūtra will bodhisattvas also become oceans of samādhi . . ."[391]

And, continually applied in the same way:

> ". . . and also see the Tathāgata to be permanent; and also, after very clearly seeing the Tathāgata to be permanent and eternal, become kings who praise the self; and also come to advocate the eternal, saying the Tathāgata is the eternal kāya; and also come to the excellent view delighting in the peaceful nature of the Tathāgata; and also become all the oceans of the view in all aspects

that says the Tathāgata is permanent, {107} eternal, stable, and peaceful?"[392]

And:

For the purpose of fully teaching sentient beings who express praise of impermanence, emptiness, parinirvāṇa, and selflessness that the great qualities of the Buddha reside as parinirvāṇa, the self of a permanent, eternal, stable, and peaceful nature; and for the purpose of purifying the eye of the stable nature of the excellent Dharma for sentient beings who say the Dharma will vanish . . .[393]

And:

You asked the tathāgatas, the arhats, the perfectly complete buddhas about the meaning of teachings that are suitable for you, composed in subtle and profound words and phrases, and about the greatness of the qualities of a tathāgata having the characteristic of permanence in all sentient beings, the stable treasure of the doctrine of the excellent Dharma, the treasure of the peerless king of sūtras for those like you, the stable treasure of the doctrine of the excellent Dharma, the inexhaustible treasure of nectar for all sentient beings. It is good that you asked the tathāgatas. I will explain the stable placement of the treasure in all sentient beings.[394]

And:

Bhagavān buddhas are not created.
Tathāgatas are unborn, but with
bodies as solid as vajras, they also
display the nirmāṇakāya. [85]

Even relics the size of just
mustard seeds will never emerge.
Without bones, blood, and flesh,
how could there be relics?

In order to benefit sentient beings,
they skillfully leave relics.

The dharmakāya of the bhagavān buddhas,
the dharmadhātu of the tathāgatas, and
the bodies of the bhagavāns are like that;
teaching Dharma is also like that.[395]

And so on. And the *Uttaratantra* also says:

The basic element of a buddha, a buddha's
enlightenment, a buddha's attributes, and a buddha's
activity are not conceivable even by pure sentient beings;
these are the field of experience of the guides.

The wise who believe in these topics of the conquerors
become vessels for the collection of buddha qualities.
Their manifest delight in the collection of inconceivable
qualities outshines the merit of all sentient beings.

Suppose some who strive for enlightenment were always to offer golden realms adorned with gems, equal to the atoms in the buddha realms, to the kings of Dharma every day, while some others were to hear just one word from this [teaching of the sugata essence] and, upon hearing it, were also devoted—these latter ones would attain much more merit than that virtue arising from the generosity. {108}

Suppose some wise persons who desire unsurpassable enlightenment were to effortlessly maintain stainless moral discipline with body, speech, and mind for many eons, while some others were to hear just one word from this and, upon hearing it, were also devoted—these latter ones would attain much more merit than that virtue arising from the moral discipline.

Suppose some were to cultivate meditation as a means to extinguish the fires of the afflictions in the three states of cyclic existence here, arrive at the perfection of the states of the gods and Brahmā, and [reach] immutable complete enlightenment, while some others were to hear just one word from this and, after hearing it, were also devoted—these latter ones would attain much more merit than that virtue arising from the meditation.

> Why? Generosity accomplishes wealth, moral discipline the higher realms, and through meditation the afflictions are abandoned, but wisdom eliminates all [obscurations] of the afflictions and of the knowable, so this is the most sublime, and its cause is hearing about this [sugata essence].[396]

It is said that, when a past tathāgata called Sadāpramuktaraśmi[397] taught this Dharma of the tathāgata essence by means of many hundreds of thousands of examples for five hundred great eons while remaining on a single seat, it was also understood with little difficulty in world systems as numerous as the atoms of ten buddhafields in all the ten directions. And it is said that, at the least, the roots of virtue of all those who heard the term "tathāgata essence" also gradually ripened and they reached buddhahood, except for the four bodhisattvas Mahāsthāmaprāpta, Avalokiteśvara, Mañjuśrī, [86] and Vajramati.

The *Sūtra of the Tathāgata Essence* clearly and extensively states this meaning.[398] Then it also says:

> I, too, when previously engaged
> in the conduct, heard the name of
> this sūtra from the sugata Siṃhadhvaja.
> Devotedly I heard, and clasped my palms.
>
> By those well-done acts I quickly achieved
> excellent enlightenment. Therefore,
> expert bodhisattvas should always uphold
> this sublime sūtra.[399] {109}

Such passages teach the immense benefits of faith, devotion, and so on concerning the sugata essence.

B. *Advice to be diligent in the means for that*

In that way, if buddhahood will be reached even by hearing just the term "sugata essence," what need to mention what will happen with faith and devotion, and by actualizing it through meditation? So compassionate experts should teach it even if they may lose their lives, and so on, and those striving for liberation should seek it out, listen, and so forth, even if they must cross a great pit of fire. Just as the *Parinirvāṇa* says:

> Then the bodhisattva Kāśyapa also said this to the Bhagavān: "As the Bhagavān Tathāgata taught, I heard you say, 'The *Parinirvāṇa Sūtra* is sublime and superb, like ghee. If anyone drinks it, the aspects of an illness are cured, and it also goes into all medicines.' And I thought this: 'Anyone who does not listen to and does not want this sūtra is extremely ignorant and does not have a virtuous mind.'
>
> "Bhagavān, I could bear to flay my skin and use it as a base for writing the letters, extract my blood and use it for ink, extract my marrow and use it for water, whittle my bones and use them for pens, and write this *Parinirvāṇa Sūtra*.
>
> "Even after writing it, I could also bear to read, recite, master, and teach and explain it in detail to others.
>
> "Bhagavān, if any sentient being becomes attached to wealth, I will first give him wealth and, after that, urge him to read this *Mahāparinirvāṇa Sūtra*.
>
> "If he is a person with great wealth, I will first make pleasant conversation as he wishes, and after that urge him to read this *Parinirvāṇa Sūtra* of the Mahāyāna. {110} [87]
>
> "Even if he is a vulgar person, I will forcibly make him read.
>
> "Even if he is a proud person, I will first serve him as he wishes, delighting and pleasing him, and after that teach this *Parinirvāṇa Sūtra*.
>
> "If he is a person who denigrates the very extensive sūtras, I will subdue him with forceful power. When he has been subdued, after that I will have him read this *Parinirvāṇa Sūtra*.
>
> "If he is a person faithful and devoted to the sūtras of the Mahāyāna, I will stay in his presence and very respectfully serve, honor, worship, and praise him."
>
> Then the Bhagavān said to the bodhisattva Kāśyapa, "Good. Good."[400]

And so on. At the end of speaking, [the Bhagavān] says:

> "Soon you will teach and explain to many circles of followers the *Parinirvāṇa Sūtra*, in which the buddha nature of the Tathāgata, the [sugata] essence, is stated with intentional ambiguity."[401]

And:

"Son of good family, furthermore, it is like this: If any sentient being does not understand the Tathāgata to be permanent, you should know that person to be blind.

"If any sentient being does understand the Tathāgata to be permanent, I explain that that person, despite having eyes of flesh, will have the divine eye."[402]

And the *Sūtra to Benefit Aṅgulimāla* also says:

If one intently reveals the tathāgata essence and teaches the doctrine that benefits all sentient beings, one will obtain the divine eye and have the divine eye in the world.[403]

And:

Anyone who teaches the tathāgata essence, whether they have the afflictions or do not have the afflictions, will be called "a complete buddha."[404]

And:

One who teaches the tathāgata essence will be a complete buddha.[405]

And so on. And the *Sūtra of the Great Drum* also says:

Other than them, the Tathāgata will fasten the crown bestowing the Mahāyāna initiation of omniscient primordial awareness having the most sublime of all aspects upon those sentient beings who are specially intent on the vast, who desire the permanent, stable, peaceful, and eternal quintessence of the Tathāgata's greatness.[406] {111}

And:

The remaining qualities will be inconceivable for those who have taught "The permanent Buddha, the tathāgata essence, exists," proclaimed that to others, do not reject it, are firm, desire that eternal, sublime ground naturally empty of all conditioned phenomena (not the emptiness of the view of the destructible collection), [88] and whose [minds] are stable in qualities such as that.[407]

And:

At a future point in some future time I will have many disciples who uphold the excellent Dharma. He will be the very last of those hundred mentioned before in this sūtra, such as Bhadrapāla and Guhyagupta.

Kāśyapa, it might be asked, "Who is he?"

He is this very Licchavi youth, Sarvalokapriyadarśana. In a future time he will become an expert in the southern region and beat the great drum of the Dharma. He will blow the conch of the Dharma.[408]

And:

Then the Bhagavān also said this to Kāśyapa: "Kāśyapa, you cannot be like a guardian of the land. The youth skilled in means like a guardian of the land will listen to all of this sūtra and, having listened, will carry it on his body and directly reveal it to the world.

I will place him on the seventh level and, after blessing him as an ordinary human being, at the point when the doctrine will be lost in eighty years, he will be born in that family line called Kayori, in a town called Mahāmālā, near the city called Ayodhyā, sited on the banks of a river in the southern region known as Muruṇḍa.[409] He will become a monk bearing my name, and with skillful means [like] a guardian of the land, he will take ordination in the midst of my monks who are lazy, and gather them with the means of gathering. Finding this sūtra, he will hold it to his body and, after purifying the Saṅgha, first utterly reject the great bases of the unsuitable and proclaim the great Dharma. He will proclaim the conch of the Dharma and the victory banner of the Dharma spoken of in the *Great Drum*.

Second, he will speak the sūtras of the Mahāyāna, the discourses on emptiness.

Third, he will speak the discourse of the permanent basic element of sentient beings and the discourse of the *Sūtra of the*

> *Great Drum.* He will beat the great drum of the great Dharma. He will blow the conch of the great Dharma. He will hoist the victory banner of the great Dharma. {112} He will wear my manifest armor.[410]

And:

> If trainable sentient beings are also there, among such sentient beings it will be said, "Look at this Bhagavān Śākyamuni who appeared!" And it will be prophesied, "Look at a tathāgata such as him, who is permanent, stable, peaceful, and eternal. When I teach and explain the stable and the blissful, know it to be like that!"
>
> Then, from the sky in the ten directions, the bhagavān tathāgatas will each reveal their faces to him and say this: "He is like that." The entire world will also believe his teaching of the Dharma, saying, "Well taught."[411] [89]

And:

> [Sarvalokapriyadarśana] will also proclaim this secret of the Buddha to living beings in the manner of expressing words in praise of the [ultimate] Three Jewels: "The secret of the Buddha is like this—the Tathāgata is permanent, stable, peaceful, and eternal."[412]

And the *Great Cloud Sūtra* also says:

> Whatever the meaning of the name of a sūtra that explains the greatness of the qualities of the Tathāgata—profound, equanimous, permanent, eternal, and stable—and wherever it perfectly resides, there you should go, even into the center of a crossroad of paths of fire.
>
> Mahāmeghagarbha, furthermore, in order to listen to it, and for the purpose of honoring, painting, worshiping, and serving it, you should go and enter even into world systems totally filled with fire, as numerous as the grains of sand found in the Ganges River.[413]

And so on, [the Buddha] teaches eloquently, again and again, in great detail.

Therefore, have great diligence day and night, hearing, reflecting, and meditating with faith and devotion on the other, the inner awareness, the buddha nature, great nirvāṇa, the self of thusness, the pure self, the sugata essence, natural luminosity, the perfection of wisdom, the source of the attributes, Mahāmudrā, the syllable *a*, ultimate truth, the syllables *evaṃ*, Vajrasattva, the androgynous stage, the partless omnipresent pervader having the most sublime of all aspects, the vajra moon and sun, the sixteen aspects of reality, the twelve aspects of the meaning of the truth, the changeless fully established nature, the great Vajradhātu maṇḍala, the essence of the mantradhātu, the omnipresent dharmadhātu, having all aspects yet without aspect, beyond all to which worldly examples apply, the great wish-fulfilling gem, the sublime, expansive, great wish-granting tree!

Those are the ultimate Buddha always primordially present as the basic ground, the natural family, the ground with stains to be purified. {113}

The evolving family supported on that is the exceptional roots of virtue perfectly acquired through planting and growing the seeds of liberation, which is fully known to experts.

Therefore, fearing it would take too many words, I have not written about that here; for details, one must consult the *Ornament of the Sūtras*, the *Levels of the Bodhisattva*, and so on. [90]

VI. *Rejecting various deranged misconceptions about that*
This has three topics.

A. *Rejecting the absurd consequence that the abandonments and realizations would be complete in all sentient beings*
It might be said, "If the ultimate Buddha inherently exists in all sentient beings, the consummate abandonments and realizations would also inherently exist."

These must be distinguished and presented. There are two topics concerning abandonment: abandonment in which all stains are primordially, naturally unestablished, and the destruction and extinguishing of incidental stains by means of the antidotes. The first is complete in the true nature, in accord with the meaning of such passages as these:

> Extinguishing is not extinguishing by the antidotes; they are taught to be "extinguished" because they are extinguished from before.[414]

And:

> . . . because [the true nature] is naturally, utterly pure,
> and because the afflictions are primordially extinguished.[415]

And:

> Without afflictions at all times,
> free of stains through beginning, middle, and end.[416]

And:

> At all times free of all obscurations.[417]

And it is complete because that [ultimate] is "beyond the phenomena of consciousness,"[418] because it is "definitely liberated from all obscurations,"[419] because "the afflictions, the secondary afflictions, and the defilements, including habitual propensities, have been totally abandoned";[420] and because it is "dustless, free of dust, and stainless, flaws abandoned, faultless."[421]

This being the case, that natural abandonment is primordially complete in the Buddha of the ultimate true nature, because that true nature is the primordially liberated Tathāgata,[422] because it is the Buddha before all [rūpakāya] buddhas,[423] and because it is the nature of space, primordially liberated mind.[424] {114}

Therefore, wherever the true nature exists, that abandonment also exists, because that true nature is naturally pure.

The second abandonment does not exist in sentient beings who have not cultivated the path, but this is not a flaw in our philosophical tenet, because we do not claim that all sentient beings are buddhas or have reached buddhahood, and because we also do not claim that the relative buddha exists in all sentient beings.

Likewise, there are also two topics concerning the realization of a buddha: realization of the true nature primordially aware of itself, which is self-arisen primordial awareness, and realization born from cultivating the profound path, which is other-arisen primordial awareness.

The first is naturally complete in the ultimate true nature, because that is "aware of itself, aware of the other, having all [sense faculties in each one]";[425] because it is "excellent knowledge of all and awareness of all,"[426] because it is "unwavering, personal self-awareness,"[427] because it is "the pervasive lord, the self of the five primordial awarenesses,"[428] because it "holds the mode of nondual primordial awareness,"[429] because it is "the quintessence of the pure ten primordial awarenesses,"[430] and because it is "the holder of the pure ten primordial awarenesses."[431] [91]

That being the case, the natural, original abandonment and realization are complete in the ultimate true nature, because that also has the same meaning as:

> The basic element is empty of the incidental
> having the characteristic of separability,
> but not empty of the unsurpassable attributes
> having the characteristic of inseparability.[432]

And:

> In this there is nothing to be removed,
> and not the slightest to be added.[433]

And so on. Therefore, because the first realization is inseparably complete in the true nature, when that exists it also exists. But the second realization is not complete in sentient beings who have not entered the path, and they have not directly realized selflessness, yet this is not a flaw in our philosophical tenet; the reasons are as before. {115}

B. *Rejecting the absurd consequence that all sentient beings would have accumulated the two assemblies*

Also, it might be said, "If Buddha is inherently present in sentient beings, sentient beings would have accumulated the two assemblies and abandoned the two obscurations."

There is also no such logical entailment here; the reasons are as before.

Furthermore, the division of the two truths concerning the accumulation of the two assemblies must be understood. The accumulation of the ultimate two assemblies is primordially, naturally complete in ultimate truth, because ultimate truth:

> Has merit and is the assembly of merit,
> is primordial awareness and the great source

> of primordial awareness, has primordial awareness
> knowing existence and nonexistence, and is
> the accumulator of the assembly of the two assemblies.[434]

And because it is "Buddha, Great Vairocana, the Great Sage with great ability,"[435] because it is "Lord of Sages, the pervasive lord with ten powers,"[436] because it is "the sublime Ādi[buddha], the holder of the three kāyas, the Buddha with a quintessence of the five kāyas,"[437] and because it is "the complete Buddha, guide of the world."[438]

Sentient beings who have not entered the path have not accumulated the two relative assemblies, but this is not a flaw in our philosophical tenet; the reasons are as before.

Likewise, concerning abandonment of the two obscurations, there are also two modes, as explained earlier in the context of abandonment.

Therefore, some may say, "If Buddha existed in sentient beings, all karma, afflictions, and suffering would not exist in them." And so on. And they may say, "Sentient beings would know all knowable objects." And so on. These very many mistaken objections are ravings by those who do not understand the difference between having and being, because having does not establish being. [92] If it did establish it, since people have feces in them, are people feces, or what?

Therefore, realization, abandonment, and the two assemblies included in relative truth are the truth of the path, but realization, abandonment, and the two assemblies included in ultimate truth are the truth of cessation, so these are complete respectively in the relative rūpakāya and the ultimate dharmakāya. {116}

The first is fully known, but in the context of the second, it is stated: "conqueror, conqueror of the enemy, complete conqueror,"[439] and "lord of Dharma, king of Dharma,"[440] and "self of all buddhas, sublime entity,"[441] and "one passed into nonabiding nirvāṇa,"[442] and "holding the thirty-two major marks," [443] and "all-knowing, ocean of primordial awareness,"[444] and "holder of all the kāyas of primordial awareness without exception,"[445] and "kāya of primordial awareness, self-arisen,"[446] and "Tathāgata with the body of primordial awareness,"[447] and "grasping the treasury of omniscient primordial awareness,"[448] and "holder of the nature of all buddhas,"[449] and "unsurpassable enlightenment of the buddhas,"[450] and "complete Buddha arisen from *a*,"[451] and "complete Buddha in the vajrāsana,"[452] and "unique teacher, master of living beings,"[453] and "great essence of all buddhas,"[454] and "great mind of all buddhas."[455] And so on. The intent of these detailed statements is the meaning: "Ultimate truth itself is the naturally original Buddha of the profound abiding state." Because that which is present in sentient beings is thusness with stains, it is present as the ground with stains to be purified.

Extensive quotations and reasoning will also be explained in the context of its many synonyms, and so on.

C. *Rejecting confused misconceptions about the ground of purification, the object of purification, and so on*

It might be said, "If the ground of purification is like that, it contradicts what is renowned as 'the ground of purification, the aggregates, elements, and sensory bases.'"

True indeed, but it does not contradict scripture. The *Sūtra of the Tathāgata Essence* says:

> Just as if there were a beehive here,
> fully guarded and concealed by bees,
> but some person wanting honey were
> to see it and to fully drive away the bees,
>
> so too, here, all sentient beings of the three states
> of cyclic existence are like the beehive.
> They have many tens of millions of afflictions,
> but I see a tathāgata existing within the afflictions. {117}
>
> I too, in order to purify the Buddha, remove
> the afflictions, like driving away the bees.[456]

Here, the Buddha in "to purify the Buddha" is the Ādibuddha, "the Buddha before all buddhas,"[457] the sugata essence. [93]

To "purify" that refers to the ground of purification, not the stains that are the object of purification.

The appropriated aggregates and so on are not the Buddha, because they are the stains that are the object of purification.

Again, that same sūtra says:

> Sons of good family, this [ultimate sugata essence] is the true nature of phenomena and, whether tathāgatas appear or tathā-

> gatas do not appear, these sentient beings always have the tathāgata essence.
>
> Sons of good family, because it is obscured by the husks of the despised afflictions, in order to destroy their husks of the afflictions and to utterly purify the primordial awareness of a tathāgata, the Tathāgata, the Arhat, the perfectly complete Buddha teaches Dharma to the bodhisattvas, causing them to also be devoted to this activity.[458]

Here also, the primordial awareness of a tathāgata in "to utterly purify the primordial awareness of a tathāgata" is self-arisen primordial awareness, "the primordially liberated Tathāgata,"[459] the sugata essence.

To "utterly purify" that refers to the ground of purification, not the stains that are the object of purification.

Because the tainted aggregates and so on are the incidental stains, they are not the primordial awareness of a tathāgata.

Again, that same sūtra says:

> Sons of good family, again it is like this: for example, the kernels of winter rice, barley, millet, or monsoon rice are completely covered by husks. Until they emerge from their husks, they cannot serve the function of solid, soft, and tasty food. But, sons of good family, some men or women who want to eat and drink (solid food, soft food, and so on) reap them, thresh them, and remove the shells of the husks and the outer skins.
>
> Sons of good family, likewise, with the eye of a tathāgata the Tathāgata also sees the [ultimate] Tathāgata, the Buddha, the self-arisen itself wrapped in the skins of the husks of the afflictions and present in all sentient beings.
>
> Sons of good family, the Tathāgata also removes the skins of the husks of the afflictions, utterly purifies the Tathāgata in them, and teaches Dharma to sentient beings, thinking: "How will these sentient beings be released from all the skins of the husks of the afflictions and come to be counted among those called 'tathāgatas, arhats, perfectly complete buddhas' in the world?" {118}
>
> Then at that time the Bhagavān spoke these verses:

Whether monsoon rice or winter rice,
whether millet or else barley, as long as
they have husks, they do not serve
their function. [94]

If they are threshed and their husks removed,
they also serve many types of functions,
but those kernels having husks do not serve
their function for sentient beings.

Likewise, I see the Buddha level of all
sentient beings covered by the afflictions.
That they may purify those and quickly reach
buddhahood, I teach Dharma.

In order that, like mine, their true nature
(existing in all sentient beings wrapped in
hundreds of afflictions) be purified and they
all quickly become conquerors, I teach Dharma.[460]

That which is the level of the ultimate self-arisen Sugata Buddha, present in all sentient beings, is thus stated to be the ground of purification; the aggregates and afflictions are not that. "Removes the skins of the husks of the afflictions and," and so on, indicates the stains that are to be purified. In sequence, these are like the kernel and the skin of grain.

Again, that same sūtra says:

It is just like a person's gold nugget that,
fallen into some kind of filth, remains
there in that way for not a few years,
since it is an imperishable phenomenon.

A god, with the divine eye, sees it and,
to purify it, says to another, "The sublime
precious substance gold exists here.
Purify and use it."

So too, I see all sentient beings for
a long time always oppressed by the afflictions.
Knowing their afflictions to be incidental,

as a means to purify the nature, I teach Dharma.[461]

Here also, the nature in "to purify the nature" is the natural kāya:

The nature is uncontrived
and does not depend on another.

A nature that would change
into another would never be suitable.[462]

It is the sugata essence. To "purify" it refers to the ground of purification, not to the stains that are the object of purification, because the nature is luminosity.

Because the tainted aggregates are the incidental stains, they are not natural luminosity, since they are created by causes and conditions. Moreover:

A nature that occurred from causes
and conditions would be created.[463]

And so on. {119} And:

The nature of mind is luminosity;
the stains are incidental.[464]

And so on, state this extensively. Again, that same sūtra says:

Sons of good family, again it is like this: Suppose figures of horses or figures of elephants or figures of women or figures of men were made from wax, placed in clay, and encased. When that [wax] has melted and dripped out, gold is melted, poured, and fills [the cavities]. After it has gradually cooled, all those figures remain in a uniform state. The outer clay is black and ugly in color, but the inner forms are those made from gold. [95]

Then, if the smith or a smith's apprentice, seeing which of those figures have cooled, breaks away their outer layers of clay with a hammer, at that moment the figures made from gold that exist inside become completely clean.

Sons of good family, likewise, the Tathāgata also, with the eye of a tathāgata, sees that all sentient beings are like figures in clay;

> the cavities inside the husks of the outer afflictions and the secondary afflictions are filled with the attributes of a buddha and with precious, taintless primordial awareness; a beautiful tathāgata exists within.
>
> Sons of good family, seeing all sentient beings in that way, the Tathāgata goes among the bodhisattvas and perfectly, completely teaches such Dharma discourses as these.
>
> To utterly purify the precious primordial awareness of a tathāgata in those bodhisattvas, mahāsattvas who have become peaceful and cool, the Tathāgata smashes all the outer afflictions with the vajra hammer of the Dharma.[465]

Thus the precious primordial awareness of a tathāgata is said to be the ground of purification; the incidental aggregates are not that.

In that way, these passages stating the ground of purification, the sugata essence itself, to be Buddha, the Buddha level, and the primordial awareness of a tathāgata also refute the claim by some that the sugata essence is not Buddha.

Likewise, all the statements (by means of many kinds of different examples) about "teaching Dharma" in order to purify and remove the husks of the incidental stains {120} that obscure the sugata essence also show that the sugata essence is the ground of purification and the faults to be purified are the incidental stains. So one should consult that very sūtra for details.

Likewise, the *Uttaratantra* also states:

> As for what is to be realized, realization,
> its branches, and what causes realization,
> in sequence, one point is the cause to be cleansed;
> three are the conditions.[466]

Thus it says the sugata essence is the cause to be cleansed. Because it is not the stains to be cleansed, this establishes that it is unsuitable to be other than the ground itself that is the cause to be cleansed.

Furthermore, it says that which is thusness itself, when together with incidental stains, is the ground of purification and, when cleansed of those stains, is the result of purification. And it says those taught by the nine examples for the essence are the ground of purification, and those taught by the nine examples for the stains are the stains to be purified. [96] The stains are the appropriated aggregates and the sensory bases.

The *Noble Sūtra of the Purification of Infinite Gateways* also says self-arisen primordial awareness and omniscient primordial awareness, which have the same meaning as the sugata essence, are the ground to be cleansed and to be purified. Just as it says:

> That gateway is a sublime Dharma teaching and causes pure, omniscient, primordial awareness.
>
> Bodhisattvas purify their self-arisen primordial awareness through that gateway. Having gained self-arisen primordial awareness, they turn the wheel of Dharma and, in order for countless sentient beings to gradually purify the gateway of Dharma and utterly cleanse the gateway of nirvāṇa, they also incite them to seize the gateway of omniscient primordial awareness.[467]

And so on. Furthermore, because the sugata essence (thusness itself having many synonyms, such as "true nature") is the ground of all phenomena, it is the ground in which stains remain and also the ground of their purification.

Well, does the *Hevajra Tantra* not say the aggregates, elements, and so on are the ground of purification?

> The five aggregates, six sense faculties,
> six sensory bases, and five great elements are
> naturally pure. The obscurations of the afflictions
> and of the knowable are to be purified.[468]

That [first sentence] refers to the naturally pure aggregates, elements, and so on, which also have the same meaning as the ultimate sugata essence. But this "The obscurations of the afflictions and of the knowable are to be purified" shows that the impure aggregates, elements, and so on are the stains to be purified. {121}

Likewise:

> . . . the purification of hatred and so on.[469]

And:

> . . . the aggregates are to be purified by these.[470]

And:

> Likewise, the concept "entities"
> is also to be purified by certainty.[471]

And:

> One who purifies objects
> will gain the unsurpassable.[472]

After also understanding the division of the two truths concerning many such passages, one should know how the ground of purification and the stains to be purified are different. And the *Glorious Ādibuddha* also says:

> Mind having the stains of desire
> and so on is the cause of changeable
> saṃsāra. When separated from those
> it is pure; the nature is stainless purity.[473]

Therefore, the intent of statements in many scriptures that the aggregates, elements, and so on are the ground of purification should be understood in this way, because naturally pure phenomena are the ground of purification and impure phenomena are the stains to be purified.

It might be said, "In that case, since even the thusness of a tathāgata would be the ground of purification, even a buddha would have stains that must be purified."

That thusness itself present in a buddha as the result of purification is present in sentient beings as the ground of purification, [97] and that thusness itself present in sentient beings as the ground of purification is present in a buddha as the result of purification, because not even the slightest difference of essence exists in the thusness of sentient beings and buddhas, just as not even the slightest difference of essence exists in the sky that pervades everything, with or without clouds.

Therefore, depending on the person, naturally pure thusness is with stains, but is also without stains, and it is the ground of purification, but is also the result of purification, so one must be expert in the profound key point of being without the flaw of including contradiction.

VII. *Summarizing the meaning of those and offering praise and homage*

> The profound abiding state, the basic element of the universal-
> ground primordial awareness, is present in some as the ground

> with stains to be purified, and present in some as the ground
> free of stains. To indivisible thusness I bow in homage.

That is the section about the Buddha always present as the basic ground. {122}

Two:
Relying on the Sublime, Profound Path by Which That Can Be Obtained

This has three topics.

I. *General presentation of the classifications of the Mahāyāna path*
This has ten topics.

A. *Presenting the reasons a pure path is necessary*
In that way, the ultimate Buddha, the dharmakāya, the quintessence of limitless, inseparable qualities, is inherently present in all sentient beings, but the path (the two assemblies) is not unnecessary, because it is necessary to remove the incidental stains and it is necessary to produce the relative rūpakāya and act for the benefit of all sentient beings.

Here, (to be a pure, fine path,) pure and excellent view, meditation, and conduct are also necessary, with each of these also well present in both common and uncommon forms. [98]

B. *Presenting the pure view for realizing the emptiness of self-nature*
Here, to realize well the commonly known correct view, one must decisively conclude that in the abiding state all [relative] phenomena are like a sky-flower, because they are utterly nonexistent and totally unestablished, like the horn of a rabbit and the child of a barren woman. Since the proofs for that are fully known in the middle wheel of the Buddha's word, the Madhyamaka Collection of Reasoning,[474] and so on, and since it would take too many words here, I have not written about it.

C. *Presenting pure nonconceptual meditation free of elaborations*
Meditative absorption in that state should also be understood through the esoteric instructions of an excellent master, and scriptural passages of proof are also very extensively present in the Conqueror's Mother Sūtras and so on. Furthermore:

> Śāriputra, this is the excellent yoga of bodhisattvas, mahāsattvas.
> It is like this: the yoga of emptiness.[475] {123}

And:

> Śāriputra, bodhisattvas, mahāsattvas studying in that way, have no [thought of] studying any Dharma.[476]

And:

> Having no mindfulness and no mental engagement is subsequent mindfulness of the Buddha.[477]

And:

> If even [the thought of] Dharma is to be abandoned, what need to mention abandoning what is not Dharma?[478]

And so on. And:

> "Discrimination is this shore [saṃsāra],"
> the Guide has fully proclaimed. After
> discrimination has been destroyed and
> abandoned, one goes to the other shore.[479]

And so on. And:

> Not conceiving of both unarising and arising;
> this is the conduct of the sublime perfection of wisdom.[480]

And:

> If a bodhisattva even thinks "These aggregates are empty,"
> he is engaging in conceptual marks and has no faith in
> the unarisen basis.[481]

And:

> Free of various discriminations, and practicing peacefully,
> this is the conduct of the sublime perfection of wisdom.[482]

And so on. And likewise:

> Not conceiving and not thinking about any phenomena such as forms, and not conceiving and not thinking about their marks and nature.[483]

And so on. And:

> Not perceiving Dharma, what is not Dharma, the three times, the three realms, and the perfections, up to the knowledge of all aspects, to be real fully completes the meditation of the perfection of wisdom.[484]

And so on. And likewise:

> Meditate in such a way that mind and the phenomena of mental factors do not move at all.[485] [99]

The [Buddha's] comprehensive statements in many forms about not seeing and not focusing at all on any phenomena as happiness or suffering, permanent or impermanent, having or lacking a self, peaceful or not peaceful, empty or nonempty, having or lacking conceptual marks, having or lacking aspiration, conditioned or unconditioned, arisen or unarisen, ceasing or unceasing, isolated or not isolated, virtuous or nonvirtuous, having or lacking flaws, having or lacking taints, having or lacking afflictions, mundane or transcendent, afflicted or purified, diligent or not diligent, and so on, and about not grasping, not thinking, not meditating, not abiding, not combining, not desiring, not being attached, not engaging in mental activity, not joining, not dividing, and so on are widely known. But [those statements] should be consulted when one has the esoteric instructions of glorious beings on the tenth level. {124} Therefore, I have not written in detail here.

D. *Presenting the key points of esoteric instruction necessary for that*

In that way, when meditating in the manner of not meditating, for the many doors of the samādhi of integrated calm abiding and special insight (such as that called "the jewel lamp") to arise, the uncommon profound esoteric instructions to stop the breath, bind the channels, and so on are necessary. Those will be presented separately.

E. *Pure, common meditation and conduct, which will both be presented elsewhere*

Because the common conceptual meditations (such as love and compassion, equalizing and exchanging self for others, and creation-stage meditation) are also known elsewhere, and because I am afraid of too many words, I have not written of them here. The common and the uncommon conduct will also be presented elsewhere.

F. *Here, carefully distinguishing and recognizing existence, nonexistence, and so on*

In that way, when targeting the key points of body and mind has bound the channels and stopped the winds and mind, and when the samādhi of integrated calm abiding and special insight has arisen well, one must have the pure view that fully understands (exactly in accord with reality) the existent to be existent, and also fully understands (exactly in accord with reality) the nonexistent to be nonexistent. [100] This is because one must recognize those exactly as in the Dharma wheel that carefully distinguishes the natural and the contrived, the original and the incidental, the kernel and the husk, primordial awareness and consciousness, with appearance and without appearance, and so on, and exactly as in the profound secret mantra that carefully distinguishes the triad of outer, inner, and other, and so on. {125}

G. *Showing that understanding the meaning of the three wheels and mantra is necessary for that*

Why is that? Bringing into experience the meaning of the three wheels accords with cleansing the coarse, subtle, and extremely subtle stains on the sugata essence, which is like a wish-fulfilling gem. Furthermore, this is because the first wheel accords with the preliminaries for meditation on the profound definitive meaning of the Mahāyāna, while the second wheel accords with bringing into experience the exceptional samādhi of absorption in the profound meaning, and the third wheel (when exceptional samādhi has arisen and existence, nonexistence, and so on have been carefully distinguished and identified) accords with profound secret mantra.

H. *Showing through an example how the three wheels purify three layers of stains*

Concerning that, the gradual purifying of stains on the sugata essence by means of the three wheels is stated in the *Sūtra Teaching the Great Compassion of the Tathāgata*:

> Son of good family, it is like this: Suppose an expert jeweler knows well how to purify gems. He takes a totally unclean precious [beryl] gem from among the types of precious gems and fully

purifies it by soaking it in a strong soda solution. Then he fully polishes it with a coarse haircloth.

But he does not stop his efforts with just that. Next he totally purifies it by soaking it in a strong quicksilver solution and polishing it with a coarse woolen cloth.

But he does not stop his efforts with just that. Next he totally purifies it by soaking it in a great herbal liquid and polishing it with the finest cotton.

When fully purified and separated from stains, it is called "the great type of beryl."

Son of good family, likewise, when a tathāgata recognizes the totally unclean basic element of sentient beings, through discourses on impermanence, suffering, selflessness, impurity, and revulsion, he produces weariness in sentient beings who enjoy saṃsāra, causing them to enter the noble Dharma and the Vinaya [the first wheel]. {126}

But a tathāgata does not stop his efforts with just that. Next, through discourses on emptiness, signlessness, and wishlessness [he teaches the second wheel], causing sentient beings to understand the way of the Tathāgata. [101]

But a tathāgata does not stop his efforts with just that. Next, with discourses on the irreversible wheel of Dharma, and discourses on the purification of the three spheres, he causes those sentient beings, who have various natures, to enter the realm of the tathāgatas. If they enter and realize the true nature of the tathāgatas, they are called "unsurpassed recipients of generosity."[486]

I. *Carefully distinguishing and determining the differences of the three Dharma wheels*

Which of the three wheels are of provisional meaning and of definitive meaning, the differences of whether they are or are not carefully distinguished and clearly taught, and so on, are stated in the *Sūtra of Definitive Commentary on the Intent*:

Then the bodhisattva Paramārthasamudgata said this to the Bhagavān: "In the deer park of Ṛṣivadana in the Vārāṇasī region the Bhagavān first taught the four noble truths to those who had correctly entered the Śrāvakayāna. Thus you fully turned the wonderful wheel of Dharma that no god or human had turned before in accord with Dharma in the world. That turning of the wheel of Dharma by the Bhagavān was, however, surpassable and adapted to the circumstances. Of provisional meaning, it is a topic or grounds of dispute.

"Then, for those who had correctly entered the Mahāyāna, the Bhagavān turned the even more wonderful second wheel of Dharma in the form of a teaching on emptiness: 'Phenomena are without an essence, unarisen, unceasing, primordially at peace, and naturally parinirvāṇa itself.' That turning of the wheel of Dharma by the Bhagavān was, however, surpassable and adapted to the circumstances. Of provisional meaning, it is a topic or grounds of dispute. {127}

"But then, for those who had correctly entered all vehicles, the Bhagavān turned the extremely wonderful third wheel of Dharma having careful distinctions concerning the statement: 'Phenomena are without an essence, unarisen, unceasing, primordially at peace, and naturally parinirvāṇa itself.' This turning of the wheel of Dharma by the Bhagavān was unsurpassable and not adapted to the circumstances. Of definitive meaning, it is not a topic or grounds of dispute. [102]

"Referring to the Bhagavān's statement: 'Phenomena are without an essence, [unarisen, unceasing, primordially at peace, and] naturally parinirvāṇa itself,' the Bhagavān taught the definitive meaning. When any son of good family or daughter of good family hears this [third wheel of Dharma] and becomes devoted, commissions its transcription into writing, and, after it has been written, upholds, reads, venerates, correctly distributes it, expounds it, recites it, and engages in forms of reflection and meditation, how much merit will they produce?"

The Bhagavān said this to the bodhisattva Paramārthasamudgata: "Paramārthasamudgata, that son of good family or daughter of good family will produce incalculable, immeasurable merit. It is not easy to give examples for that. Nevertheless, I will briefly explain it to you.

"Paramārthasamudgata, it is like this: if the particles of earth on the tip of a fingernail are compared to the particles of earth on Earth, they do not come close to even a hundredth, they do not

> come close to even a thousandth, a hundred thousandth of it, or an approximation, a portion, an estimation, an illustration, or a comparison.
>
> "If the water in the hoofprint of an ox is compared to the water of the four great oceans, it does not come close to even a hundredth, . . . it does not come close to even a comparison.
>
> "Likewise, Paramārthasamudgata, if my explanation of the merit of devotion to the sūtras of provisional meaning (up to engaging in forms of meditation) is compared to this merit of perfect accomplishment through devotion to the teachings of definitive meaning (up to perfect accomplishment through engaging in forms of meditation), it does not come close to even a hundredth, . . . it does not come close to even a comparison.[487] {128}

And so on. When practicing the perfection of wisdom as yoga one must be free of all concepts, so all objects are refuted for the purpose of stopping the subjective apprehender. Therefore, by means of many aspects, such as all being nonexistent, unestablished, and isolated, [the Buddha] intently taught all to be emptiness, but did not intently distinguish existence, nonexistence, and so on. Therefore, the second wheel is said to be "through the aspect of asserting emptiness."

In that way, when the samādhi of united calm abiding and special insight has arisen through practicing the perfection of wisdom as yoga, existence and nonexistence, empty and nonempty, and so on, must be distinguished and taught, and must be recognized just as they abide and just as they are. [103] But all does not abide as nonexistent, unestablished, and so on, because (regarding nonexistence and emptiness and their grounds and so on) implicative negation exists as the ground of nonimplicative negation, because positive determination abides as the ground of exclusion, and because realization with all consummate qualities complete abides spontaneously as the ground in which all faults have been naturally abandoned. Therefore, the third wheel is said to "have careful distinctions."

Likewise, in the second wheel, for a purpose, [the Buddha] taught even what is not empty of self-nature to be empty of self-nature, and so on, and did not make careful distinctions without internal contradictions. For several such reasons, [the sūtra] says it "is surpassable and adapted to the circumstances. Of provisional meaning, it is a topic or grounds of dispute."

But in the third wheel, in contrast to those statements, because careful distinctions are made exactly in accord with the meaning, and so on, [the sūtra] says it "is unsurpassable and not adapted to the circumstances. Of definitive meaning, it is not a topic or grounds of dispute."

J. *Clearing away many confused misconceptions about that*

Here the claim by some that this sūtra is of provisional meaning is incorrect, because such is not stated, is not reasonable, and there is also nothing that refutes it being of definitive meaning.

It might be said, "That is refuted by the fact that, because the middle wheel is Madhyamaka and the final one is Cittamātra, the middle one is of definitive meaning and the final one is of provisional meaning." {129}

This is extremely, greatly incorrect, because there are absolutely no scriptures and reasons [proving] that the final wheel is the exclusive source texts of the Cittamātra, and because that [sūtra] teaches beyond Cittamātra, teaches the consummate meaning of Great Madhyamaka, and teaches in accord with the consummate meaning of the Vajrayāna.

This very scripture also says it is taught in the third wheel that phenomena are essenceless, unarisen, unceasing, primordially at peace, and naturally parinirvāṇa, which also establishes that it is not an exclusive source text of the Cittamātra. It might be said, "Because the perfection of wisdom is taught in the second wheel, that is of definitive meaning and unsurpassable, but this scripture is of provisional meaning and intentionally ambiguous, because it teaches the opposite of that."

These are the words of one who has not understood well, because [this sūtra] does not teach that [the second wheel] is of provisional meaning and surpassable by reason of teaching the perfection of wisdom, but teaches in that way for other reasons, such as [the second wheel] teaching what is not empty of self-nature to be empty of self-nature. [104]

Unarisen, unceasing, primordially at peace, and so on, and the perfection of wisdom are also taught in the third wheel, and in the Vajrayāna; but by reason of teaching unclearly, clearly, and utterly clearly, there are also great and extremely great differences, such as delusion and no delusion concerning the meaning of those.

Therefore, the stated differences of surpassable and unsurpassable, adapted to the circumstances and not adapted to the circumstances, and so on are also from the differences of teaching the consummate profound meaning unclearly and incompletely, clearly and completely, and so on in those textual traditions; they are not from [differences in] the essence of the meaning, because the essence of the consummate meaning is the same.

Likewise, the essence of the consummate meaning of the Vajrayāna and also of these two latter wheels is the same, because it is stated, "Although the meaning is the same, because they are free of delusion, . . ."[488] and so on.

Concerning what meaning are they the same?

They are the same as the perfection of wisdom, because all that are stated by means of many aspects—such as Vajrasattva, Vajradhara, Mahāmudrā, Viśvamātā, Vajranairātmyā, Vajravārāhī, *evaṃ*, *ahaṃ*, source of the attributes, bhaga, vajra, secret, great secret, lotus, and element of space, and such as sugata essence, {130} basic element of nirvāṇa, buddha nature, pure self, naturally luminous mind, naturally pure mind, ultimate bodhicitta, the real nature, emptiness, signlessness, the apex of reality, thusness, dharmakāya, dharmadhātu, svābhāvikakāya, and the naturally pure family—are ultimately the same in being the naturally pure basic element, ultimate truth itself, self-knowing primordial awareness.

It might be said, "Ultimate dharmadhātu is not the authentic perfection of wisdom; that is just designating the object by the name of the subject."

This is also greatly incompatible with the meaning, because nothing refutes that [ultimate] being the actual perfection of wisdom, and because there are absolutely no scripture and reasoning that show it to be the nominal.

It might be said, "The teacher Dignāga states:

> 'The "perfection of wisdom" is nondual
> primordial awareness; it is the Tathāgata.
> Since both the source texts and the paths
> have that meaning to be accomplished,
> it is also the term for them.'[489]

"Thus [it is just the nominal,] because the authentic perfection of wisdom is said to be the nondual primordial awareness of the Tathāgata, and because the ultimate true nature is not nondual primordial awareness and the total distinguishing of phenomena." [105]

Such is not the case, because much pure scripture and reasoning extensively teaches that ultimate true nature to be nondual primordial awareness, such as: "Since it is not inanimate, it is self-awareness itself."[490] Here, concerning "nondual primordial awareness," what are nondual? Dharmadhātu and self-arisen primordial awareness are nondually integrated as one and have the same taste. Just that is also consummate emptiness and compassion, means and wisdom, bliss and emptiness indivisible, united, and one taste. And it is also the knowing and knowable object of the consummate abiding state as one, and the one taste of the basic element and awareness indivisible.

The authentic perfection of wisdom such as that is the consummate perfection of wisdom as the ground and the perfection of wisdom as the result: thusness of indivisible essence. {131}

The paths that actualize that, and the source texts that present them, are just the nominal. And, likewise, of those also said to be included as synonyms of thusness—such as "Great Madhyamaka," "mahāmudrā," "union with the connate state," "equanimous union with all buddhas," "vajrayoga," "atiyoga," "Saṃvara," "Hevajra," "Guhyasamāja," and "Kālacakra"—all that are the source texts and paths are actually the nominal, and all that are the indivisible essence of ground and result are the authentic. This is a great general commentary on all profound, consummate sūtra and tantra, a great releaser of the knots of everything stated in vajra words, and a great commentary on the meaning of all the profound, intentionally ambiguous statements, or the great intent.

To correctly realize them in that way, however, one must abandon the habitual propensity of the notion that a claim is stronger just because it was made earlier, and then rely on the four reliances and the fine lamp of experiencing the profound esoteric instructions of beings on the tenth level.

II. *Explaining the uncommon view in particular*
This has two topics.

A. *The promise to explain the uncommon view in particular*
Therefore, even though the meaning of the last two wheels and the Vajrayāna is the same, if one brings that into experience during decisiveness when resting in meditative absorption in a nonconceptual state free of elaborations (the profound true nature of phenomena in accord with the middle wheel), and if during differentiation in postmeditation (when correctly discriminating phenomena) one carefully distinguishes and recognizes them as stated in the final wheel and the Vajrayāna, then the profound meaning of all the Mahāyāna scriptures will be brought into experience, complete, unmistaken, and utterly pure. [106]

Therefore, here I will carefully distinguish and present existence and nonexistence in the abiding state, empty and nonempty of own-essence, exclusion [of faults] and positive determination [of qualities], nonimplicative negation and implicative negation, abandonment and realization, and so on, just as they actually are in reality. {132}

B. *The actual meaning to be explained*
This has five topics.

1. *How statements about empty and nonempty, existent and nonexistent, and so on, establish the profound emptiness that is other than this emptiness of self-nature*
This has two topics.

a. *A brief presentation of the many divisions of the modes of emptiness*
This has four topics.

1) *Distinguishing phenomena and true nature as empty and nonempty of own-essence*
Furthermore, the *Noble Sūtra to Benefit Aṅgulimāla*, rare as the udumvāra flower, says:

> Aṅgulimāla asked Mañjuśrī, "Mañjuśrī, if you are the sublime one who sees great emptiness, what is seeing emptiness in the world? What is the meaning of 'empty, empty'? Having great knowledge, quickly speak and quickly eliminate my doubts!"
>
> Then youthful Mañjuśrī spoke in verse to Aṅgulimāla:
>
> > Buddha is like space;
> > space is without characteristic.
> > Buddha is like space;
> > space arose from signlessness.
> >
> > Buddha is like space;
> > space is without form.
> > Phenomena are like space;
> > the Tathāgata is the dharmakāya.
> >
> > Primordial awareness is like space;
> > the Tathāgata is the kāya of primordial awareness.

Nothing to grasp, nothing to contact;
unattached primordial awareness is the Tathāgata.

Liberation is like space;
space is also without characteristic.
Liberation, Buddha, and Tathāgata
are empty nothingness.

Aṅgulimāla, how could you understand?

Then Aṅgulimāla spoke again, saying this to youthful Mañjuśrī: "It is like this: Suppose rain pours down from a great cloud, and a person with a childish nature picks up a hailstone and, thinking it is a precious beryl gem, takes it home. But when it is too cold and he cannot hold it, he thinks, 'I should save it as a treasure,' and puts it carefully inside a pot. Seeing that piece of hail melt, he thinks, 'It is empty,' but does not say anything. Likewise, venerable Mañjuśrī, meditating on extreme emptiness [the emptiness of self-nature] and considering the empty to be profound, all phenomena are seen to not withstand destruction. [Ultimate] liberation is not empty [of own-essence], but is seen and conceived to be empty [of own-essence]. {133}

"It is like this: For example, after thinking the piece of hail was a gem, he meditates on the gem as empty. [107] Likewise, you also consider [ultimate] phenomena that are not empty [of own-essence] to be empty and, after seeing [relative] phenomena to be empty [of own-essence], also destroy as empty [of own-essence] the [ultimate] phenomena that are not empty [of own-essence].

"Phenomena that are empty [of own-essence] are other, phenomena that are not empty [of own-essence] are also other. Like the piece of hail, the ten million afflictions are empty [of own-essence]. Like the piece of hail, phenomena in the category of nonvirtue are quickly destroyed.

"Like the beryl gem, the [ultimate] Buddha is permanent; the apex of liberation is also like the beryl gem.

"[Ultimate] space is also the form of the buddhas; the liberation of all the śrāvakas and pratyekabuddhas is formless.

"If the liberation of the [ultimate] Buddha is also [other] form, and the liberation of the śrāvakas and pratyekabuddhas is form-

> less, do not perceive them to be inseparable by saying 'the characteristic of liberation is emptiness [of own-essence].'
>
> "Mañjuśrī, why is a built home in a village empty? It is empty because it lacks humans. A pot is empty because it lacks water. A ravine is empty because a stream does not flow.
>
> "Is a village called 'empty, empty,' because it lacks some homes or is empty of all homes? It is not empty of all; it is called 'empty' because it lacks humans.
>
> "Is a pot empty of all? It is not empty of all; it is called 'empty' because it lacks water.
>
> "Is a ravine empty of all? It is not empty of all; it is called 'empty' because a stream does not flow.
>
> "Likewise, [ultimate] liberation is not empty of all [ultimate qualities]; liberation is called 'empty' because it is free of all faults.
>
> "Bhagavān Buddha is not empty [of qualities]; he is called 'empty' because he is free of all faults and lacks the ten million afflictions of humans and gods.
>
> "Alas! Venerable Mañjuśrī, you act like a bug and do not understand the precise meaning of empty and nonempty.
>
> "The naked ascetics also meditate that all is empty; you bug of a naked ascetic, don't say anything!"[491]

Here, from "Buddha is like space," and so on, down to ". . . are empty nothingness. Aṅgulimāla, how could you understand?" (thus, teaching all to be nothingness empty of self-nature, in accord with the claims of some), is an introduction by noble Mañjuśrī for the purpose of determining the difference between empty of self-nature and empty of other, which he already knows. {134}

Then Aṅgulimāla uses the example of a piece of hail that melts and becomes nothing. This teaching of the afflictions and nonvirtuous phenomena to be empty shows everything included in the mundane relative to be each empty of own-essence. But, using the example of a beryl gem that does not melt and become nothing, this teaching of the consummate state of liberation, the [ultimate] Buddha, to be nonempty, shows that ultimate, transcendent truth, dharmakāya, is not empty of own-essence. [108]

Using the examples of an empty home, an empty pot, and an empty ravine, this teaching that it is empty of all faults shows consummate liberation to be empty of other.

All the explanations as nonempty—such as "liberation is not empty of all," "Bhagavān Buddha is not empty," "phenomena that are not empty are also other"—mean "the ultimate true nature is nonempty of itself." And those very many statements in many other sūtras and tantras of "is not empty" and "nonempty" are also likewise.

Even though noble Mañjuśrī indeed knows well both emptiness of self-nature and emptiness of other, to show that those inexpert people who claim "all is only empty of self-nature" resemble naked ascetics and (dependent on carefully distinguishing and asserting the differences of being and not being empty of self-nature) to show that those claiming that all is empty of self-nature are just bugs, [Aṅgulimāla] says:

> Venerable Mañjuśrī, you act like a bug and do not understand the precise meaning of empty and nonempty.
>
> The naked ascetics also meditate that all is empty; you bug of a naked ascetic, don't say anything![492]

And:

> Venerable Mañjuśrī, meditating on extreme emptiness and considering the empty profound, all phenomena are seen to not withstand destruction. Liberation is not empty, but is seen and conceived to be empty.[493]

And:

> You also consider phenomena that are not empty to be empty and, seeing phenomena to be empty, also destroy as empty the phenomena that are not empty.[494]

Such passages are advice and instructions to those who have unilaterally resolved that the emptiness of self-nature, in which phenomena are each empty of own-essence, unable to withstand analysis, and finally disintegrate, is the profound consummate state.

The meaning of "Buddha is permanent," "the liberation of the Buddha is form," "space is also the form of the Buddha," and so on will be understood at the point where I explain other form and so on, the purity of form and so on, {135} form and so on of the true nature, form and so on of thusness, form and so on beyond the three realms and the three times, and so on. The other passages are easy to understand.

Furthermore, because the mode of emptiness of the ultimate true nature is clearly stated again and again in this very sūtra, one certainly must consult this consummate sūtra of Madhyamaka. [109]

Do not think, "Aṅgulimāla was a great sinner, so what he says is not true," because he is a buddha. And, moreover, because this very sūtra explains that, to the south of this [buddha]field, beyond buddhafields as numerous as the grains of sand found in sixty-two Ganges Rivers, there is a field known as Adorned with All Gems, in which resides a buddha called Noble Great Diligence Whom All the World Is Pleased to See, and because this very sūtra says he emanated as Aṅgulimāla.[495]

2) *How just those are stated to be empty emptiness and nonempty emptiness*

Furthermore, if all were empty of self-nature, the dharmakāya of liberation would also be empty of self-nature and, if that were accepted, it would also be nothingness in accord with the tradition of the non-Buddhist naked ascetics and so on, because the *Mahāparinirvāṇa Sūtra* says:

> Furthermore, liberation is nonempty emptiness. "Empty emptiness" is nothingness. Nothingness is like the liberation of the non-Buddhist naked ascetics and so on. There is no perfect liberation for the naked ascetics, so that is called "empty emptiness." Perfect liberation is not like that, so it is nonempty emptiness. Nonempty emptiness is perfect liberation. Perfect liberation is the Tathāgata.
>
> Furthermore, liberation is nonempty. For example, an [empty] vessel, like a small clay pot for water, butter, yogurt, beer, or honey may be without water, butter, yogurt, beer, or honey, yet it is described as "a small clay pot for water and so on." But that small clay pot is not described as "empty" or "nonempty." Here, it is incorrect to describe what is called [relatively] "empty" as "the form, odor, taste, and tangible object [of the small clay pot]." What is called "nonempty" is without water and so on [but not empty of the small clay pot]. Liberation is also like that, not described as "form" or "not form," {136} or as "empty" or "nonempty."[496]

And:

> It is like this: Because it is without the twenty-five modes of cyclic existence, defilement, all suffering, all conceptual marks, and all conditioned phenomena, it is like a small clay pot without yogurt, and is called "empty."
>
> What is called "nonempty"—perfect form—is called "permanent, bliss, self, and pure," unfluctuating and immutable. For example, because a small clay pot has form, odor, taste, and is a tangible object, it is called "nonempty." Therefore, liberation is like that small clay pot.
>
> If that small clay pot encounters a cause, it will crack or break, but [ultimate] liberation is not like that and is indestructible [because it is unconditioned]. [110]
>
> The indestructible [ultimate] is perfect liberation.
> That perfect liberation is the Tathāgata.[497]

And so on, it says most extensively. Again, in that same sūtra, using the example of the nonexistence of a horse in a bull and the nonexistence of a bull in a horse, [the Buddha] teaches the ultimate true nature, great nirvāṇa, to be the emptiness of other that is not empty of itself:

> It is like this: Son of good family, in this way nirvāṇa is not previously nonexistent, as a clay pot is nonexistent when there is only mud. It also does not cease and become nonexistent, like a clay pot destroyed and nonexistent. It is also not totally nonexistent, like the hairs of a turtle and the horns of a rabbit. It is in accord with one not existing in the other.
>
> Son of good family, as you say, although no horse exists in a bull, it is incorrect to say, "The bull does not exist." Although no bull exists in a horse, it is incorrect to say, "The horse also does not exist."
>
> Nirvāṇa is also like that. Nirvāṇa is nonexistent in the afflictions; the afflictions are nonexistent in nirvāṇa. Therefore, it is said, "One does not exist in the other."[498]

And so on, it contains most extensive [statements]. {137}

3) *Also, that same source states the modes of emptiness for the incidental stains and the sugata essence*

Also, in that same sūtra [the Buddha] carefully distinguishes and explains empty forms and so on and nonempty forms and so on.

> It is like this: Kauṇḍinya, form [of the incidental stains] is empty [of own-essence]. By the catalyst of empty form having ceased, the liberation of form [of the sugata essence] that is not empty [of own-essence] is obtained. Up to feeling, discrimination, conditioning factors, and consciousness should also be known extensively in that way.[499]

Concerning those in sequence: form and so on of the incidental stains are the emptiness of nonentities, each empty of own-essence, and form and so on of the sugata essence are the emptiness that is the very essence of the nonexistence of entities, the ultimate emptiness of other.

4) *Other than those, a specific identification of the great emptiness of profound secret mantra*

Likewise, glorious, honorable Vajrapāṇi also says:

> In that way, having all aspects yet without aspect is the cause, the perfection of wisdom, great emptiness, having the most sublime of all aspects.[500] [111]

That being the case, "observable emptiness" and "emptiness having the most sublime of all aspects" also refer to the ultimate emptiness of other; form and so on empty of self-nature do not fit their definition, because their qualities, said to be infinite, are not complete in those.

Likewise, "the five syllables of the great emptinesses" and "the six syllables of the empty drops"[501] that are spoken of are also not empty of self-nature, because they are said to be primordially free of obscuration, the same taste, imperishable, of vajra nature, the pure other aggregates, other elements, other sense faculties, other objects, and so on, the great Vajradhātu maṇḍala, self-arisen primordial awareness, beyond dependent arising.

Furthermore, relying on the lamp of the profound esoteric instructions, one should understand that all descriptions of the consummate emptiness of definitive meaning in the profound tantras—such as "partless omnipresent pervader,"[502] {138} and "great one possessing the powerful ten aspects,"[503] and "vajra sun, great appearance,"[504] and "the *a*, the most sublime of all phonemes,"[505] and "sublime nature of all entities,"[506] and "excellent fine form without form"[507]—refer to the ultimate emptiness of other, the emptiness that is the very essence of the nonexistence of entities.

Likewise, all the emptinesses stated in the exceptional and stainless sūtras, tantras, and treatises to have the same meaning and be synonymous with many [terms]—such as "thusness," "the apex of reality," "the signless basic element," "ultimate truth," "dharmadhātu," "ultimate bodhicitta," the syllable *e*, "secret," "great secret," "element of space," "bhaga," "source of the attributes," "lotus," "vajra," "triangle," the syllable *a*, "lion throne," "basis of bliss," "Sukhāvatī," "Mahāmudrā," "Prajñāpāramitā," "Viśvamātā," "Vajravārāhī," "Vajranairātmyā," and "[goddess] having various forms"—are not just the emptiness of self-nature, the emptiness of nonentities, but refer to the ground of emptiness, the ultimate emptiness of other, the emptiness that is the very essence of the nonexistence of entities.

b. *Determining those [modes of emptiness] through extensive explanation of their meaning*
This has nine topics.

1) *Determining what the ground of emptiness is and what it is empty of*
This mode of carefully determining emptiness through distinguishing empty of self-nature and empty of other in that way is also stated by the great Madhyamaka master, the honorable, noble Asaṅga. [112] Just as the *Abhidharma* of consummate Madhyamaka says:

> What is the characteristic of emptiness?
>
> That in which something does not exist is correctly seen to be empty of it, and that which remains in this is fully understood exactly in accord with reality to exist in this. {139}
>
> This is called "the unmistaken approach to emptiness in accord with reality."
>
> What does not exist in what?
>
> A permanent, stable, eternal, and unchanging phenomenon [the self of a person], and the self [of phenomena] and mine, do not exist in the aggregates, elements, and sensory bases.
>
> That being the case, those are empty of those [two selves].

> What remainder exists there?
>
> That [ground of] selflessness itself. In that way, emptiness should be understood: the selves do not exist, but [the ground of] selflessness does exist.
>
> Referring to this, the Bhagavān said, "The existent is fully understood to be existent, and also the nonexistent to be nonexistent, exactly in accord with reality."[508]

This means the ground of emptiness in which some empty phenomenon does not exist is correctly seen to be empty of it. That which is the ground of emptiness, the fully established true nature, which remains in this after it is empty of that phenomenon, always exists in it. Thus it is fully understood exactly in accord with reality. In that way, this realization of empty phenomena to be empty of self-nature and the ground of emptiness to be empty of other is called "the unmistaken approach to emptiness in accord with reality." Otherwise, to claim that all is just empty of self-nature or to claim that all is just empty of other is not unmistaken.

Some might think, "Is it not here explaining the ground empty of self and mine to be the aggregates, elements, and sensory bases? Why claim here that the ground of emptiness is the fully established true nature?"

Therefore, I should comment. Here, the aggregates, elements, and sensory bases included in the dependent nature are temporarily said to be the ground empty of the imaginary self and mine, but since the ground of emptiness is finally the fully established true nature, the ground empty of even the dependent nature, the meaning is the same.

Because some elements and sensory bases included in the entirely unconditioned are also said to be thusness, they are said to be the ground empty of self and mine. Even so, since the ground of emptiness is finally established to be the fully established true nature, there is no flaw.

> What remainder exists there?
>
> That selflessness itself. In that way, emptiness should be understood.[509]

Also, with the imaginary nonexistent, the remainder (the selflessness of the dependent) tentatively exists. The selflessness of the fully established true nature (the remainder empty of even that dependent essence) exists in reality. {140} In sequence, these relatively exist and ultimately exist. [113]

> Referring to this, the Bhagavān said, "The existent is fully understood to be existent, and also the nonexistent to be nonexistent, exactly in accord with reality."[510]

In that way, the ground empty of the imaginary is the dependent. The ground empty of even the dependent is the fully established true nature. A ground empty of the fully established true nature is utterly impossible, because it is thusness spontaneously present forever and everywhere.

In that way, referring to these different modes of emptiness for the three essences, the consummate Madhyamaka *Ornament of the Sūtras* also says:

> If they know the emptiness of the nonexistent,
> and if they likewise know the emptiness
> of the existent and the natural emptiness,
> they are said to be "knowers of emptiness."[511]

The imaginary is the emptiness of the always nonexistent. The dependent temporarily exists, but is the emptiness of the nonexistent in reality. Those two are contrived, incidental.

Since it is the naturally original itself, the fully established true nature is the emptiness that is the very essence of the nonexistence of entities. Since it is not empty of own-essence, it is existent, but since it is empty of even the dependent it is also called "nonexistent," because the consummate Madhyamaka *Distinguishing the Middle and the Extremes* also says:

> Three essences—the always nonexistent,
> the existent but not real, and the existent
> and nonexistent reality—. . .[512]

The consummate Madhyamaka *Abhidharma* also says:

> Also, there are three aspects of emptiness: emptiness of very essence, likewise, emptiness of what is not existent, and natural emptiness.[513]

These also apply to the three essences.

2) *How those are stated to have the meaning of existent and nonexistent in reality*

Furthermore, the conqueror Maitreya says phenomena and true nature have the meaning of nonexistent and existent in reality. {141} The consummate Madhyamaka *Distinguishing Phenomena and True Nature* says:

> The two are not just one [in essence],
> but also not distinct [in essence], because
> [for phenomena] there is the difference of existence
> and nonexistence, but not [for the true nature].[514]

And the *Ornament of the Sūtras* also says:

> For the childish, [the apex of] reality itself
> is obscured, so the unreal appears everywhere.
> Bodhisattvas remove that, so [the apex of]
> reality itself appears everywhere.[515]

And:

> Know that what do not exist in reality and what
> does exist in reality do not appear and does appear.[516]

And [114]:

> Other than that [true nature], nothing even slightly exists
> in living beings, yet with minds utterly deluded about it,
> beings without exception totally abandon the existent and
> fixate on the nonexistent. What is this severe form of delusion
> in the world?[517]

Such passages show imaginary and dependent phenomena to be nonexistent in reality and the fully established true nature to be existent in reality; they also present the meaning of empty of self-nature and empty of other.

Referring to this, it is said:

> Possessing primordial awareness,
> knowing the existent and the nonexistent.[518]

Here also, what is existent in the abiding state is empty of other and what is nonexistent is empty of self-nature.

The chapter presenting reality in the *Ornament of the Sūtras* also speaks of the ultimate as empty of other, expressing in verse the characteristics of the ultimate in this way:

> Not existent, not nonexistent; not the same, not something else;
> not arising and not destroyed; it does not decrease or increase;
> without becoming pure, it still becomes pure—these are
> the characteristics of the ultimate.[519]

As for the meaning of this: It is "not existent" because the imaginary and the dependent are not existent in reality. It is "not nonexistent" because the fully established true nature is not nonexistent in reality.

It is "not the same" because those are not one in essence, yet "not something else" because they are also not different in essence, since an essence for the imaginary and the dependent is not established in reality.

In that way, because the fully established true nature, the ground empty of those two, is unconditioned, it is unarisen and indestructible, without increase or decrease. {142} And because it is naturally pure, its essence also does not have to be made pure, but to obtain it the incidental stains must be purified.

In that way, those complete five characteristics of nonduality are the characteristics of the ultimate.

That is thus the intent, explained according to [Vasubandhu's] commentary on that very text.

Therefore, because this also says the fully established true nature empty of the imaginary and dependent exists as the ultimate, the ultimate emptiness of other is well established.

3) *How exaggeration and denigration concerning existence and nonexistence as permanence and annihilation are transcended if understood in that way*

Here, in accord with the meaning of not existent and not nonexistent stated in that way, *Distinguishing the Middle and the Extremes* also says, "Not existent, also not nonexistent."[520] Furthermore, in the great many stainless textual traditions of the Madhyamaka the intent of all the statements about freedom from the extremes of existence and nonexistence is that the relative (all dependent arising) is not existent in reality, so if understood in that way one does not fall into the extreme of existence and is liberated from the extreme of exaggeration. [115] But the ultimate (the true nature beyond dependent arising) is never nonexistent, so if understood in that way one does not fall into the extreme of nonexistence and is liberated from the extreme of denigration. Other than that, according to some people's mode of assertion, "The ultimate itself is not existent in the ultimate; it is also not nonexistent in the ultimate." Such assertions of one phenomenon itself (not existent and also not nonexistent) to be the definitive meaning beyond extremes are not in accord with the meaning of the abiding state and contradict the intent of the buddhas and the great bodhisattvas.

4) *Showing just those modes of emptiness to be the intent of the Conqueror's Mother Sūtras*

The *Extensive Commentary on the "Sūtra in One Hundred Thousand Lines"* also says:

> The characteristic of the fully established [true nature] is empty of [all the relative having] the characteristic of the imaginary.[521]

And:

> That which is only just fully established thusness free of both imaginary and imputed [dependent] forms is called "the form of the true nature."[522]

And {143}:

> That characteristic of fully established thusness called "the form of the true nature," empty of imaginary and imputed forms, is not the very essence of [relative] form, since it is isolated from the aspects of [relative] form in all ways.[523]

And:

> Here, [the passage] "What is the emptiness of other entities?" and so on teaches the emptiness of other entities. "Constancy of phenomena," "the true nature," and so on—these are included among the synonyms for "thusness." Whether [relative] tathāgatas appear

> or tathāgatas do not appear in the world, the true nature of phenomena primordially resides in that way. The entities of other phenomena such as the aggregates do not exist in those; that is called "the emptiness of other entities."[524]

And so on, by means of many aspects it extensively states the mode of the ultimate emptiness of other. And the *Commentary on the "Extensive Mother Sūtra," the "Sūtra in Twenty-Five Thousand Lines," and the "Sūtra in Eighteen Thousand Lines"* also says:

> Empty is being free of other [the relative]; for example, as a pot is called "empty" because it is free of water.[525]

Such passages speak of the ultimate emptiness of other. And just that is also stated to be the nine fully established natures—thusness, unmistaken thusness, thusness that is not something else, true nature, dharmadhātu, constancy of phenomena, flawlessness of phenomena, the apex of reality, and inconceivable basic element—that are, in sequence, fully established as indestructible, [116] fully established as unmistaken, fully established as changeless, fully established as the very essence, fully established as the very cause of the attributes of purification, fully established as [present] at all times, fully established as irreversible, fully established as reality, and fully established as beyond the path of sophistry.[526]

5) *How just those modes of emptiness are stated to be the meaning of nothing to remove or add, and of empty and nonempty*

The root text and commentary of the *Uttaratantra* also say:

> Here, what is the tathāgata essence that is described as the mode of emptiness? {144}
>
> > In this there is nothing to be removed,
> > and not the slightest to be added.
> > View reality itself as reality.
> > If reality is seen, one is liberated.
> >
> > The basic element is empty of the incidental
> > having the characteristic of separability,
> > but not empty of the unsurpassable attributes
> > having the characteristic of inseparability.[527]

> What does this teach?
>
> In this naturally, utterly pure basic element of a tathāgata there is absolutely nothing to remove that is a characteristic of the afflictions, because freedom from incidental stains is the nature of this.
>
> In this there is not anything to add that has the characteristic of purity, because this has the nature of inseparable pure attributes.
>
> Therefore, it is stated:
>
>> The tathāgata essence is empty of all the husks of the afflictions that are divisible and can be realized as being separable [from it], but not empty of the inconceivable attributes of a buddha that are indivisible and cannot be realized as being separable [from it], which are more numerous than the grains of sand found in the Ganges River.[528]
>
> That being so, that in which something does not exist is correctly seen to be empty of it, but that which remains is understood exactly in accord with reality to permanently exist in that.
>
> These two verses present the unmistaken characteristic of emptiness, since it is free of the extremes of exaggeration and denigration.[529]

Thus the meaning of empty and nonempty of own-essence is stated.

6) *How just those modes of emptiness are stated to be the meaning of existent and nonexistent, the abandonments and realizations, and so on in the abiding state*

The *Mahāparinirvāṇa* also says:

> In that way, these four attributes—permanence, bliss, self, and utter purity—should not be called "emptiness [of own-essence]."[530] [117]

And so on, it speaks again and again of a profound emptiness not empty of itself. {145} And this very sūtra also says that which is empty of own-essence does not exist in the abiding state of reality, and that which remains after it does exist in the abiding state of reality. Just as it says:

Concerning the buddha nature of a tathāgata, there are two aspects: the existent [qualities] and the nonexistent [faults].

The existent are like this: the thirty-two major marks, the eighty fine minor marks, the ten powers, the four types of fearlessness, the three foundations of mindfulness, great love, great compassion, the acquisition of measureless samādhis such as the samādhi of heroic progress, the acquisition of measureless samādhis such as vajralike samādhi, the acquisition of measureless samādhis such as that of skillful means, and the acquisition of measureless samādhis such as that of the five primordial awarenesses are called "existent."

The nonexistent are like this: a tathāgata's past virtues, nonvirtues, indeterminate [acts], karma, causes, results, ripenings, afflictions, five aggregates, and twelve links of dependent arising are called "nonexistent."

Son of good family, just as with the existent and the nonexistent, [it also is and is not] virtue and nonvirtue, tainted and without taints, worldly and not worldly, noble and not noble, conditioned and unconditioned, perfect and not perfect, peace and not peace, disputable and not disputable, the basic element [of the true nature] and not the basic element, the afflictions and not the afflictions, appropriating and not appropriating, determinate [because it is virtue] and not determinate, existent and not existent, the three times and not the three times, time and not time, permanent and impermanent, self and selfless, bliss and without bliss, {146} utterly purified and not utterly purified, [ultimate] form and feeling and discrimination and conditioning factors and consciousness and not [relative] form and feeling and discrimination and conditioning factors and consciousness, the [ultimate] inner sensory bases and not the [relative] inner sensory bases, the [ultimate] outer sensory bases and not the [relative] outer sensory bases, the [ultimate] twelve links of dependent arising and not the [relative] twelve links of dependent arising. These are called "[what are and are not and,] the existent and the nonexistent buddha nature of a tathāgata." And it is like that down to the existent and the nonexistent buddha nature of a depraved being.[531]

And so on, it states extensively. [118] Relying on the profound esoteric instructions of being without the flaw of including contradiction, one must carefully distinguish the meaning of the existent and the nonexistent, the abandonments and the realizations, exclusion and positive determination, nonimplicative negation and implicative negation, and so on, and understand well the abiding state of the two truths, or the abiding state of the sugata essence and the incidental stains, just as it is. Otherwise, profound reality will not be seen, because it is said:

> Those who do not understand
> the division of those two truths
> do not see the profound reality
> of the Buddha's doctrine.[532]

7) *Clearing away misconceptions of a contradiction of scripture concerning the ground of emptiness, the ultimate emptiness of other*

Here it might be thought, "The *Journey to Laṅkā Sūtra* mentions seven emptinesses, of which the emptiness of one being empty of another is said to be the lowest of all seven, and it says emptiness such as that 'should be utterly rejected.'[533] So how is your ultimate emptiness of other different than that?"

It is not like that because the statement in the *Journey to Laṅkā Sūtra* that the emptiness of one being empty of another is the lowest is said in that very sūtra to refer to the emptiness of relative phenomena being mutually empty of one another,[534] such as a house being empty of people or a pot empty of a pillar, and because that type and the naturally ultimate that is empty of relative incidental phenomena {147} are so very much greater than even greatly different, and because that same sūtra says:

> Mahāmati, what is the primordial awareness of a noble being, great emptiness?
>
> It is like this: the primordial awareness of a noble being personally realized by oneself is empty of all views and habitual propensities for flaws. Therefore, the ultimate, the primordial awareness of a noble being, is called "great emptiness itself."[535]

Thus, of the seven emptinesses, the ultimate, that primordial awareness of a noble being, the emptiness of other that is empty of all views and habitual propensities for flaws, is stated to be "great emptiness."

Therefore, a house being empty of horses and elephants, and so on, are stated as examples of the ultimate emptiness of other, but are not stated to be the meaning of emptiness, because those are not relative emptiness and are also not ultimate emptiness.

That being so, just as emptiness of self-nature does not fit the definition of the ultimate emptiness of other, the emptiness of other also does not fit the definition of relative emptiness.

Therefore, referring to relative emptiness, it says one being empty of another should be rejected because it is the lowest type of emptiness. And we also maintain that in just the same way.

Therefore, there is no fault of contradicting scripture. [119]

8) *How just that ground of emptiness is stated to be the great emptiness of the profound abiding state*

Furthermore, because the ultimate emptiness of other is the quintessence of the infinite qualities of the dharmakāya, and since it is the exceptional emptiness that is not just totally unestablished emptiness, it is also great emptiness. This sūtra itself states the ultimate, the primordial awareness of a noble being, to be great emptiness. And the *Mahāparinirvāṇa* also says:

> Son of good family, "great emptiness" is like this: the perfection of wisdom, called "great emptiness."[536]

And the scriptures of profound secret mantra say "the five changeless great emptinesses" or "the five syllables of the great emptinesses,"[537] and glorious, honorable Vajrapāṇi also says:

> In that way, having all aspects yet without aspect is the cause, the perfection of wisdom, great emptiness, having the most sublime of all aspects.[538]

And:

> The attainment is great observable emptiness, because it is personally experienced by yogins.[539]

And the noble, honorable Lokeśvara also says:

> The great mind of all buddhas is the great emptiness at the end of the sixteenth phase of the moon.[540] {148}

And:

> Likewise, the great body of all buddhas is great emptiness.[541]

And:

> The stainless light of the vajra moon is the five changeless great emptinesses.[542]

And so on. One must be expert concerning the intent of the very many statements about the ground of emptiness, the ultimate emptiness of other, by the term "great emptiness," extensively in the *Stainless Light* and also in many other pure textual traditions.

The *Sūtra of Great Emptiness* also says:

> Ānanda, it is like this: for example, this fine house of the mother of Mṛgāra is empty of elephants, horses, cattle, sheep, chickens, and pigs, and empty of jewels, grain, cowrie shells, and gold, and empty of male and female servants doing work, laborers, men and women, and boys and girls, yet here it is like this: on the basis of only the Saṅgha of monks, or someone other than them, it is also nonempty.
>
> Ānanda, likewise, that in which something does not exist is correctly seen to be empty of it, but that which remains existing in that is fully understood exactly in accord with reality to exist in that.
>
> Ānanda, this approach to emptiness is exactly in accord with reality and unmistaken.[543] [120]

And so on. At the end of extensively speaking of the mode of the emptiness of other, [the Buddha] also states:

> Concerning that, bases of affliction dependent on the taints of desire and the taints of becoming and the taints of ignorance—those are nonexistent. Here, however, it is like this: bases of affliction merely dependent on only the body of the six sensory bases acting as the condition of life are existent.
>
> Ānanda, that being so, that in which something does not exist

> is correctly seen to be empty of it, but that which remains existing in that is fully understood exactly in accord with reality to exist in that.
>
> Ānanda, it is like this: because the taints have been extinguished, this taintless, directly unconditioned liberation is the unsurpassable approach to emptiness.
>
> Ānanda, because the taints had been extinguished, those bhagavān buddhas, tathāgatas, arhats, and perfectly complete buddhas who appeared in past times also in this way actualized with their bodies this taintless, directly unconditioned liberation, the unsurpassable approach to emptiness, and accomplished and resided in it.[544] {149}

At the end, [the Buddha] also applies and speaks of this concerning present and future tathāgatas.

Here, after using the example of the fine house of the mother of Mṛgāra being empty of horses, elephants, and so on, but nonempty of the Saṅgha and so on, [the Buddha] speaks of many modes of being empty of some phenomena yet nonempty of some. At the end, he says buddhas are empty of all taints yet nonempty of the unconditioned emptiness of liberation; this also clearly teaches the ground of emptiness, the ultimate emptiness of other.

This statement, "This approach to emptiness is exactly in accord with reality and unmistaken," actually shows that those approaches to emptiness in which all [phenomena are] each empty of own-essence are not correct.

9) *Rejecting exaggeration and denigration concerning textual traditions that teach in that way*

This has ten topics.

a) *Showing there are no proofs for and there are refutations of the claim that the third wheel is Cittamātra*

It might be said, "The third wheel of the Buddha's word, including the commentaries on its intent, are exclusive source texts of the Cittamātra, so to explain them as consummate Madhyamaka is incorrect."

There are absolutely no pure proofs that teach those to be exclusive source texts of the Cittamātra.

It might be said, "Because the three essences are taught in them, they are established to be exclusive source texts of the Cittamātra."

If that were so, the Conqueror's Mother Sūtras would also be exclusive source texts of the Cittamātra, because the three essences are taught in them. [121] Moreover, just as the *Intermediate Mother Sūtra* says:

> The Bhagavān Buddha spoke to the bodhisattva Maitreya: "Maitreya, bodhisattvas practicing the perfection of wisdom and abiding in expertise concerning the distinguishing of phenomena should know to designate distinctions of form by means of three aspects.
>
> "They should know to designate distinctions concerning feeling, discrimination, conditioning factors, and consciousness—up to the attributes of a buddha, in this way: this is imaginary form, this is imputed form, and this is the form of the true nature."[545]

Then it likewise teaches, applying this extensively to feeling, discrimination, and so on—up to the attributes of a buddha, which are in sequence imaginary, dependent, fully established form, and so on. {150}

Again that sūtra itself speaks of the basic element of the ultimate true nature, the ground empty of the imaginary and dependent, to be the fully established nature. Just as it says:

> Whether tathāgatas appear or tathāgatas do not appear, these basic elements of the true nature of phenomena and the constancy of phenomena just reside. That which is imaginary form is essenceless imputed form in permanent, permanent time, and in stable, stable time; this in which the self of [dependent] phenomena does not exist, and which is thusness and the apex of reality, is the form of the true nature.
>
> This is the feeling, discrimination, conditioning factors, and consciousness of the true nature—up to "these are the attributes of the Buddha of the true nature."[546]

And that source itself also states just what the three essences are:

> Maitreya, that which is imaginary form should be viewed as without substance.
>
> That which is imputed form is viewed as having substance because conceptualization has substance, but it does not function independently.
>
> That which is the form of the true nature is not without

> [ultimate] substance [i.e., essence], yet also does not have [relative] substance, and should be viewed as distinguished by the ultimate.[547]

And so on, it states, up to the attributes of a buddha.

b) *Showing the profound commentaries on the intent [of the third wheel] also agree with that*

The intent of those passages is also the same meaning as that carefully distinguished and stated by the great master of Madhyamaka, the conqueror Maitreya:

> Three essences—the always nonexistent,
> the existent but not real, and the existent
> and nonexistent reality—thus the essences
> are held to be three.[548] [122]

And:

> They [are included] in these in terms of
> the imaginary, the imputed, and the true nature.[549]

And:

> Unreal imagination exists.
> In it the two do not exist.
> Emptiness exists in it.
> And even in it, that exists. {151}
>
> Not empty, not nonempty.
> That being so, all is explained.
> Due to existence, due to nonexistence,
> there is existence—that is the Middle Way.[550]

That being so, a work does not become an exclusive source text of the Cittamātra by reason of teaching the three essences, because the classification of the three essences is also stated again and again in many various textual traditions of the Great Madhyamaka, such as the commentary on the *Extensive*

Mother Sūtra, the *Intermediate Sūtra*, and the *Sūtra in Eighteen Thousand Lines*, and the *Extensive Commentary on the "Sūtra in One Hundred Thousand Lines."* And because they say the ground empty of the imaginary is the dependent, the ground empty of even that is the fully established true nature, and a ground empty of that is impossible. And because, after also saying the first two are the imaginary, they say the ground empty of that is the ultimate, and a ground empty of that is impossible. And because the *Summary of the "Sūtra in Eight Thousand Lines"* also says this:

> The teaching in the perfection
> of wisdom correctly relies on three,
> which are only the imaginary,
> the dependent, and the fully established.
>
> Words such as "nonexistent"
> refute everything imaginary;
> the examples, such as an illusion,
> correctly teach the dependent.
>
> The four purifications
> proclaim the fully established.
> In the perfection of wisdom
> the Buddha teaches nothing else.[551]

And so on. So those who claim the three essences to be the uncommon Dharma language of the Cittamātra are very confused.

Furthermore, *Illuminating the Madhyamaka* says:

> It is not that advocates of the Madhyamaka also do not accept the classification of the three essences; otherwise, how would they abandon what contradicts sight and so on?[552]

And:

> By teaching the intent of the three essenceless aspects, he fully taught the Madhyamaka path to be free of the two extremes. Therefore, he established a textual system of definitive meaning alone.[553]

And the Great Madhyamaka source text called *Establishing All Phenomena to Be without Nature* also states:

> [The Bhagavān] said, "As for the three essences, when referring to the three essenceless aspects regarding all phenomena, I spoke of these as the three essences." This also does not contradict that teaching, because here also the classification of the three essences is not contradictory. {152}
>
> In this way, that which is the essence of the dependent arising of unexamined well-known entities is the dependent essence, and because it arises relatively by the force of conditions, as do illusions and so on, and [in reality] is essenceless, it is essencelessness regarding arising.[554] [123]

And so on, extensively. The *Entryway to the Three Kāyas*, composed by the great Madhyamaka master, the teacher Nāgamitra, also says:

> When the three essences are fully understood,
> abandoned, and purified, the three kāyas will
> be obtained. Therefore, they are summarized
> in that way.[555]

And the commentary on that composed by the great Madhyamaka master, the teacher Jñānacandra, also teaches with examples that the imaginary, the dependent, and the fully established essences are to be fully understood, abandoned, and actualized.[556] And so on, which also refutes those who claim there is no classification of the three essences in the Madhyamaka tradition. Those who speak in such a way simply have not seen or are uncertain about those source texts.

Furthermore, in reality the teaching of the three essences exists in many textual traditions that teach beyond Cittamātra, but some are confused to be Cittamātra and are proclaimed in that way. The *Sūtra of Definitive Commentary on the Intent* says it is like this: after the extreme of exaggeration and the extreme of denigration have been abandoned, that definite release by means of the Madhyamaka path is its wisdom. That wisdom also fully understands, exactly in accord with reality, the meaning of the gates of liberation (the three gates of liberation—emptiness, wishlessness, and signlessness). It also fully understands, exactly in accord with reality, the meaning of the essences (the three imaginary, dependent, and fully established essences).[557]

And so on. One must become very expert about the intent of the teachings of the three essences in the source texts that teach Madhyamaka free of extremes! {153}

c) *In particular, showing that those faults are also the same when claiming* Distinguishing the Middle and the Extremes *to be Cittamātra*

Likewise, claims that *Distinguishing the Middle and the Extremes* and so on are exclusive source texts of the Cittamātra by reason of teaching the three essences, the eight groups of consciousness, and so on are also confused, because those are also taught in the sūtras and tantras of consummate Madhyamaka.

Furthermore, *Distinguishing the Middle and the Extremes* says "all is just names only,"[558] the meaning of which also contradicts the Cittamātra view. And it says:

> Except for dharmadhātu,
> phenomena do not exist in this way . . .[559]

And [124]:

> Since dharmadhātu is
> naturally pure, it is like space.
> The two occur incidentally.[560]

And teaching the middle free of the fifteen extremes, with passages such as "The extremes of difference and oneness,"[561] also contradicts Cittamātra.

Likewise, the commentary on "that is the Middle Way"[562] says:

> In that way, this is taken to agree with what occurs in the Perfection of Wisdom and so on: "All this is not empty [of the ultimate], but also not nonempty [of the relative]."[563]

That also contradicts Cittamātra. And:

> Appearing as objects, sentient beings,
> self, and cognition, consciousness
> fully arises. Its objects do not exist.
> Since they do not exist, it also does not exist.[564]

The commentary states:

> It says "its objects do not exist" because appearances as objects and sentient beings are without aspect, and appearances as self and cognition are mistaken appearances.
>
> Since objects do not exist, that apprehending consciousness also does not exist.[565]

This teaching that mind, mentation, and consciousness exist relatively, but are simply nonexistent ultimately, also contradicts Cittamātra.

It might be said, "This establishes it to be a Cittamātra source text":

> Dependent on observation [of mere cognition],
> nonobservation [of objects] fully arises.
> Dependent on nonobservation, nonobservation
> fully arises.[566] {154}

Such is not the case, because [the commentary] says:

> Dependent on nonobservation of objects, nonobservation of even cognition arises.[567]

And because, commenting on being free of the fifteen extremes, it transcends Cittamātra:

> That knowledge of objects to be nonentities also eliminates that very knowledge of them to be mere cognition, because when objects are nonentities, cognition is not possible.[568]

Likewise, if one who has the uncommon esoteric instructions of the Trilogy of Bodhisattva Commentaries has observed carefully, it will be realized that [*Distinguishing the Middle and the Extremes*] completely presents the Mahāyāna path, including the ground and the result; it is not a source text just restricted to the Cittamātra.

d) *Showing that some are confused because they do not understand the division of the two truths in Cittamātra*

Likewise, while the *Journey to Laṅkā Sūtra* also temporarily teaches Cittamātra, finally, after perfectly transcending that, it teaches the Madhyamaka without appearance and, after transcending even that, the Madhyamaka with appearance,[569] and says that if one has not arrived at that, the profound meaning of the Mahāyāna is not seen. [125] Just as it says:

> Depending on Cittamātra,
> external objects are not imagined.
> Depending on no [relative] appearance,
> Cittamātra will be transcended.
>
> Depending on observation [of the apex]
> of reality, no appearance will be transcended.
> If abiding in no appearance, a yogin does not
> see the Mahāyāna.[570]

And so on. Likewise, it states:

> Free of conditioned objects
> and observation, without [relative] mind
> only [ultimate] mind is seen, which
> I explain to be Cittamātra [Mind Only].
>
> "Only" is the basic element of the very essence,
> with conditions and entities abandoned,
> the consummate svābhāvika[aya], sublime
> Brahmā [Vairocana]. That I explain with "only."[571]

Thus free of conditioned objects, subjects, and conditions, the ground without relative mind, the ultimate mind, the basic element of the very essence, and the body vajra, sublime Brahmā, is said to be Cittamātra. And, likewise, it says:

> All [bad] views eliminated,
> analysis and concepts abandoned,
> without object and unarisen,
> I explain to be Cittamātra. {155}

Not an entity, yet not a nonentity.
Thusness with entity and nonentity
abandoned is free of mind, which
I explain to be Cittamātra.

Emptiness, apex, and thusness,
nirvāṇa, dharmadhātu, and
the variegated body of mind,
I explain to be Cittamātra.[572]

The ground free of relative mind, thusness, the apex of reality, natural nirvāṇa, dharmadhātu, the luminous variegated body of totally good mind, the ground free of all extremes such as existence and nonexistence, is thus said to be Cittamātra. And that same source also states:

Without appearance of the external,
[ultimate] mind appearing in various forms,
like bodies, experiences, and places,
I explain to be Cittamātra.[573]

Thus the ground without the appearance of the external incidental stains, the sugata essence within, dharmadhātu itself, ultimate mind appearing in various forms such as bodies, experiences, and places is said to be Cittamātra. In that way, the meaning of the repeated statements about the ultimate Cittamātra that transcends the relative Cittamātra should be understood on the basis of the profound esoteric instructions of the Trilogy of Bodhisattva Commentaries.

That being so, do not be confused about the statements of ultimate Cittamātra in the *Journey to Laṅkā* and so on and assert that these are exclusive source texts of the Cittamātra that does not transcend consciousness, because there is a very great difference between transcending and not transcending consciousness. [126]

Also, the statements about the mundane Cittamātra in those source texts serve as doors and means for penetrating reality, but are not taking it to be the consummate. Here that sūtra itself speaks of the mundane Cittamātra:

Connected with the habitual propensities
of conceptuality, the various mental factors,

> external appearance to humans is the mundane
> Cittamātra.[574]

Thus it is identical to the Cittamātra known to sophists. That is unfit to be the consummate Cittamātra because, as that sūtra itself says:

> For as long as the mind engages,
> for that long one is [like] a mundane Cārvāka.[575]

And:

> If mind engages entities
> as apprehended and apprehender,
> it is mundane mind, also not suitable
> to be [ultimate] Cittamātra.[576]

And:

> Like clouds in space, likewise,
> [incidental] mind also does not appear.
>
> [Relative] mind also accumulates karma. {156}
> Primordial awareness removes it. Wisdom
> is without the appearance [of incidental
> phenomena] and also fully obtains the powers.[577]

And because such passages extensively state the difference between the two forms of mundane and transcendent Cittamātra.

e) *How the ultimate Cittamātra is presented in profound secret mantra sources*

In accord with that, the consummate source of Great Madhyamaka, the *Glorious Kālacakra Tantra*, also speaks in this way about the ultimate Cittamātra [Mind Only], the ground in which relative mind has primordially ceased:

> [The ultimate] Cittamātra, the essence of mantra, fully surrounded
> by deities, the nature of suffering and bliss.[578]

And so on. And:

> Merely an appearance of [ultimate] mind, arisen from one's mind,
> just like a reflected image in a mirror;
> that upon which all the Conqueror's children and the buddhas rely,
> a lord of yogins should rely.[579]

Such passages saying that the self-arisen ultimate basic element and awareness indivisible, Vajrasattva, and Mahāmudrā are Cittamātra also refer to the ultimate Cittamātra, which is identical to the ultimate Cittamātra stated in the profound textual traditions of the third wheel, such as the *Journey to Laṅkā*.

Likewise, the honorable, venerable lord Avalokiteśvara also says:

> That mind with a quintessence of observable emptiness and non-referential compassion.[580]

Such passages speaking of ultimate mind are likewise. The *Ḍākinīvajrapañjara* also says:

> This ordinary being with a mind
> just like space, through cultivating
> mind as sublime buddhahood, awakens.
>
> Outside the jewel mind,
> no Buddha exists and no sentient being.[581] [127]

And:

> As space is the ground of
> all elements and all phenomena,
> Saṃvara is the pure nature of mind,
> and the pure nature of mind is also like space. {157}
>
> The nature of objects and sense faculties
> is not outside the mind, but the individual
> appearances of [ultimate] forms and so on
> appear to the [ultimate] nature of mind alone.[582]

Such passages also clarify ultimate mind: by cultivating ultimate buddhahood as vast as space, unconditioned mind, one awakens; the jewel of ultimate mind is the ground of all saṃsāra and nirvāṇa; like space, the ground of all phenomena, [Cakra]saṃvara, pure mind itself, mind having all aspects such as objects and sense faculties, yet without aspect, is ultimate mind.

The honorable Saraha also says:

> The true nature of mind alone is the seed
> of all, radiating cyclic existence and nirvāṇa.
> I bow down to mind, like a wish-fulfilling gem,
> fully bestowing all desired results.[583]

Thus he speaks of the true nature that is the ground of all saṃsāra and nirvāṇa, ultimate mind, to be like a wish-fulfilling gem. Likewise, the *Glorious Vajra Garland Tantra* also says, "The basic element is said to be bodhicitta,"[584] stating dharmadhātu itself to be ultimate mind, and the *Tantra of the Drop of Mahāmudrā* also says, "Remember to know the basic element to be mind."[585] Such passages state dharmadhātu itself to be ultimate mind.

Likewise, the *Glorious Sampuṭa* also says:

> Partless, sublimely subtle, with the form
> of a drop, it is the essence of mind, having
> a light of great brilliance, always present
> in the center of the heart.[586]

And:

> With a light resembling stainless crystal,
> bodhicitta is luminous, the very essence
> of the five primordial awarenesses.[587]

Such passages also clarify ultimate mind, stating the natural luminosity always present in the center of the hearts of all beings, the partless, sublimely subtle drop, the five primordial awarenesses, and totally good ultimate mind to be ultimate bodhicitta.

Likewise, the *Glorious Ocean of Ḍākas* also says:

> Difficult to find in the three worlds,
> perfectly present at beginning, middle,

and end, that mind free of extremes,
[blissful yet empty] mind, has the same taste.[588]

Such passages also say ultimate mind, free of extremes, having the same taste, is always present at beginning, middle, and end, but difficult for worldly beings to find. {158}

Likewise, the *Glorious Ādibuddha* also says:

That unarisen and ceaseless knowable
object seen here is not other than one's
own mind.[589]

Such passages say [128] it is the ultimate knowable object yet also ultimate mind.

f) *Showing the intent of presenting the relative Cittamātra in some sources*

Also, it might be thought that [*Ornament of the Sūtras*] is established as an exclusive source text of the Cittamātra because it says:

Bodhisattvas, after accumulating well the limitless,
transcendent assemblies of merit and primordial awareness,
reflect on the Dharma and, with extreme certainty, realize
the forms of objects have [mental] expressions as their cause.

Knowing objects to be just [mental] expressions,
they perfectly reside there in appearances as mind only.
Then they directly realize dharmadhātu, free of
the characteristics of duality.

Mentally knowing there is nothing other than mind,
they then realize that even mind does not exist.
Knowing that the two do not exist, the wise reside
in dharmadhātu, which does not have them.

The force of the nonconceptual primordial awareness of
the wise always extends to everything equally, clearing the dense
thickets of accumulated faults based on that [universal-ground
consciousness], just as a great antidote removes poison.[590]

That [criticism] is not the case, because this line—"they then realize that even mind does not exist"—also shows that it transcends Cittamātra.

Furthermore, in this Mahāyāna there are also bodhisattvas who have accumulated the assemblies and, realizing everything included in the three states of cyclic existence to be empty of the two selves, penetrate reality by means of cognition only. In that context, it says:

> The wise, knowing both aspects of selflessness included
> in cyclic existence, and also equally understanding them,
> penetrate reality by means of apprehension. Then, since
> their minds reside in that [cognition], even those [objects]
> do not appear to them. That [cognition] not appearing is
> liberation, sublimely free of observation.[591]

And:

> If by means of the assemblies they have
> the ground and the development, they will see
> [all] to be just names. After seeing just names,
> [only cognition] there, later even that is not seen.[592] {159}

That being so, in the context of the aids to penetration,[593] bodhisattvas abide in mind only, but just after that they directly realize that even mind does not exist. From that point, they have perfectly transcended Cittamātra.

The commentary on *Distinguishing the Middle and the Extremes* also calls this approach "the means for penetrating the characteristic of the nonexistence [of unreal imagination]."[594] And the *Compendium of the Mahāyāna* also says "penetrating those and,"[595] stating that it is the means and door for penetrating reality. This is not restricted to just the Cittamātra. [129] That same source says:

> How do they penetrate the fully established essence? They penetrate it after even the discrimination of cognition only has been eliminated. At that point, for bodhisattvas who have destroyed the discrimination of objects, there is no occasion for those mental expressions that occur from the causes that are the habitual propensities of Dharma they have heard to occur as all the appearances of objects. Therefore, even appearance as cognition only does not occur.[596]

And:

> Because no objects at all appear
> to nonconceptual primordial awareness,
> it should be understood that objects do not exist.
> Since they do not exist, cognition does not exist.[597]

Such statements that cognition does not exist are extremely contrary to the Cittamātra claim that consciousness is ultimately true.

g) *Clearing away the faults of further denigration concerning other source texts such as the* Abhidharma

Likewise, to claim that the *Compendium of Abhidharma* and so on are exclusive source texts of the Cittamātra by reason of teaching the universal-ground consciousness is also confused, because the universal-ground consciousness is also taught again and again in the consummate textual traditions of the Madhyamaka, such as the profound tantras and the Trilogy of Bodhisattva Commentaries.

They also do not become exclusive source texts of the Cittamātra by teaching a classification of the aggregates, elements, and sensory bases, because those are also stated again and again in the profound sūtras and tantras of Great Madhyamaka and their commentaries. {160}

Furthermore, this source text says:

> Through meditative absorption, bodhisattvas
> see [all] to be mental images, so the discrimination
> of objects is eliminated. Then the discrimination
> of [mere cognition] itself is definitely apprehended.
>
> In that way, they reside in inner mind and
> will realize the nonexistence of the apprehended.
> After that, the apprehender becomes nonexistent,
> and then nonobservation will be known.[598]

Thus it quotes a sūtra that transcends Cittamātra. And:

> Where eyes and ears and, likewise,
> nose and tongue and body and mind

> and, likewise, name and form
> without exception cease.[599]

And:

> Where eyes cease and there is no discrimination of color, up to where phenomena cease and there is no discrimination of phenomena, that should be known as the basis.[600]

Thus it quotes scriptural passages that transcend Cittamātra. Furthermore, it refutes the occurrence of dependent arising from the four extremes, speaks of essencelessness regarding arising, and says all phenomena are unarisen and unceasing, primordially peaceful, naturally nirvāṇa, empty of the two selves, and so on. [130] Therefore, if one having the profound esoteric instructions of the Trilogy of Bodhisattva Commentaries has abandoned the habitual propensity [of establishing true and false] based on the greater or lesser numbers of advocates and the notion that a claim is stronger just because it was made earlier, and has carefully looked at it, [the *Compendium of Abhidharma*] is clearly a source text that temporarily teaches Cittamātra but finally transcends Cittamātra.

Furthermore, it also does not become an exclusive source text of the Cittamātra by saying the ground empty of the two selves, the ultimate true nature of phenomena, exists, because that extremely absurd consequence would occur for the Madhyamaka textual traditions that teach the ultimate emptiness of other.

Likewise, the claim that for those reasons the *Ornament of the Sūtras* is Cittamātra is also refuted.

It might be said that [the *Ornament of the Sūtras*] teaches the single vehicle to be of provisional meaning, therefore it is established as a Cittamātra source text:

> In order to lead some
> and perfectly keep others,
> the complete buddhas teach
> the uncertain a single vehicle.[601]

[Reply:] There is not even the slightest instance where this source text teaches the single vehicle to be of provisional meaning.

The lines "In order to lead some and perfectly keep others" show the purpose of teaching the consummate vehicle to be single; if it were of provisional meaning because it presents the purpose, extremely absurd consequences would occur. {161}

Also, it might be said that, by reason of describing those without the family, it is established as an exclusive source text of the Cittamātra:

> Some have certainty only in flawed conduct.
> Some have totally destroyed positive attributes.
> Some have no virtue as aids to liberation.
> Some have poor positive attributes, or lack the cause.[602]

Here also there is no such logical entailment. To be without the natural family is not possible for anyone, but many are without the evolving family. While that is actually the case, it is also carefully stated in the textual traditions of Madhyamaka, such as the *Mahāparinirvāṇa*, the *Noble Sūtra to Benefit Aṅgulimāla*, and the *Uttaratantra*.

Moreover, even though all sentient beings have the buddha essence, it should be understood that in many the seeds of liberation have not been planted and virtues have not developed.

As for the impossibility of being without the natural family, that same source text says:

> That thusness is no different in all,
> yet when purified, it is a tathāgata.
> Therefore, all living beings possess
> its essence.[603]

And so on, it states extensively. Furthermore, that source itself says:

> Primordial awareness observing
> thusness, abandoning dualistic grasping,
> and direct perception of the body of negative
> tendencies—thus it is held that the wise extinguish it.[604]

The commentary says [131]:

> This fully teaches just how the dependent essence is extinguished by fully understanding the three essences: through observing

> thusness the fully established essence is fully understood, through abandoning dualistic grasping the imaginary [is fully understood], through direct perception of the body of negative tendencies the dependent is fully understood, and through direct perception of the body of negative tendencies the universal-ground consciousness, which is that dependent [essence] itself, is extinguished.[605]

Thus the extinguishing of the dependent essence and the extinguishing of the universal-ground consciousness perfectly transcend Cittamātra.

Even so, notorious allegations have spread, such as "Cittamātra accepts being without the family, but Madhyamaka does not," and "Cittamātra accepts the single vehicle to be of provisional meaning," and "the three essences are the Dharma language of Cittamātra alone," and "teaching the eight groups of consciousness, such as the universal-ground consciousness, establishes [a source text] to be Cittamātra," but not the slightest pure proof has appeared, and there are very many great refutations. {162} Therefore, [these allegations] should be discarded like poison, because they are confusion upon confusion by those who have not encountered the profound esoteric instructions of the Bodhisattva Commentaries, and are thus based on not understanding the division of the two truths in Cittamātra and not scrutinizing the syntax of some texts.

Likewise, because ultimate mind itself is spoken of again and again in various profound tantras by means of many aspects, such as great mind, vajra mind, bodhicitta, blissful mind, great desire, great hatred, great ignorance, other mind and mental factors, and other consciousness, and absolutely no phenomena other than that exist in the abiding state of reality, it is identical in meaning to the statements that absolutely no phenomena except dharmadhātu exist.

Therefore, if the exceptional textual traditions that temporarily teach Cittamātra, but finally teach the profound and vast meaning of Great Madhyamaka that transcends that, were portrayed as exclusive source texts of the Cittamātra, that would be an act of rejecting the excellent Dharma.

h) *The extremely absurd consequences that would occur if, by temporarily teaching Cittamātra, a work became one of its exclusive source texts*

It might be said, "Temporarily teaching Cittamātra establishes a work to be a Cittamātra source text."

In that case, by the same reasoning, since the Mother Sūtras, the *Ornament of Direct Realization*, and so on also teach the Śrāvaka Vehicle, do they become śrāvaka source texts, or what? [132]

Therefore, do not denigrate the profound sūtras of the third wheel such as the *Sūtra of Definitive Commentary on the Intent*; the *Ornament of the Sūtras*, *Distinguishing the Middle and the Extremes*, and so on; and the *Yogācāra Levels*, the *Compendium of the Mahāyāna*, the *Compendium of Abhidharma*, and so on, which temporarily teach Cittamātra, but finally teach the meaning of Great Madhyamaka that totally transcends that and is one with secret mantra.

It might be said, "Concerning the *Treatise on the Levels*,[606] that name itself of the treatise *Yogācāra Levels* establishes it to be Cittamātra."

If that were so, the extremely absurd consequence would be that even the *Four Hundred Verses on Yogācāra*[607] would be a Cittamātra source text.

The *Main Treatise on the Levels* says:

> The Middle Way of no self in persons and no self in phenomena, which has fully excluded the two extremes, has fully excluded the extreme of exaggeration and fully excluded the extreme of denigration.[608] {163}

Such repeated statements about the middle free of extremes must also be seen and understood!

The *Thirty Verses* is also renowned to be a Cittamātra source text, but says:

> When objects of consciousness
> are not observed, at that point
> one abides in cognition only.[609]

Finally, it says cognition only is transcended, and, in this way, says immediately after that:

> No apprehended, no apprehender of it.

> That is without mind, nonobservation.
> That transcendent primordial awareness
> is transformation, because the two negative
> tendencies have been abandoned.

That is taintless, the basic element,
inconceivable, virtue, and stable.
That is bliss, the kāya of liberation,
called "the attributes of the Great Sage."[610]

Here, "without mind, nonobservation" also contradicts the Cittamātra claim that mind, consciousness, exists ultimately. And because the taintless basic element, the inconceivable basic element, ultimate virtue, the true nature unchanging and stable, bliss in the ultimate abiding state, the primordially liberated kāya, and the attributes of the qualities indivisible from the dharmakāya of the Great Sage exceeding the grains of sand found in the Ganges River are also totally beyond the phenomena of consciousness, they contradict the Cittamātra claim that consciousness is ultimately true.

Likewise, it says:

The established is before that.
It is what is always without it.[611]

Such passages state the fully established essence to be thusness that, because it is nondual primordial awareness itself, also perfectly transcends the phenomena of consciousness.

That being so, even though Cittamātra is taught in this source text, it finally teaches far beyond that. Therefore, if it were portrayed as just an exclusive source text of the Cittamātra, that would not agree with the author's intent. [133]

Furthermore, if primordial awareness, Buddha, dharmakāya, svābhāvikakāya, thusness, and so on beyond the phenomena of consciousness are carefully taught, the Cittamātra tradition has been transcended, because the *Glorious Stainless Light* says:

> Here, among the advocates of consciousness, there is no kāya of primordial awareness, the kāya of the sun, {164} the perfectly complete Buddha.
>
> Here, among the advocates of consciousness, why is there no kāya of primordial awareness, the kāya of the sun, the perfectly complete Buddha?
>
> I will discuss this. Because here [the view of] the advocates of consciousness abides in the phenomena of consciousness, and

because the perfectly complete Buddha is beyond the true nature of consciousness.

In that way also, the Tathāgata spoke the following in the twenty-third verse of the praise of discriminating primordial awareness in *Chanting the Names*:

> Beyond the true nature of consciousness,
> holding the mode of nondual primordial awareness,
> nonconceptual, spontaneous, holding the kāyas
> of the buddhas of the three times.[612]

Furthermore, statements that it is empty of the two selves and free of apprehended and apprehender also transcend Cittamātra, because the *Glorious Stainless Light* says:

> Now the Yogācāra advocates' fault of an apprehender is stated: "Those who advocate the entire three states of cyclic existence to be consciousness itself also accept consciousness [to be ultimately true]."[613]

And:

> For Yogācāra advocates an apprehender of consciousness also exists.[614]

And because, if an apprehender exists, it is not feasible to be free of the self of phenomena.

i) *Showing that, if even the tantras are claimed to be Cittamātra, their intent has not been understood*

Likewise, claiming that profound tantras such as the *Kālacakra* do not transcend Cittamātra is also extremely unreasonable, because the *Glorious Stainless Light* speaks of many profound and vast Dharma teachings that transcend Cittamātra, such as:

> Experts do not accept that even
> that consciousness ultimately exists,
> since it is free of one or many natures,
> like a sky lotus.

> Not existent, not nonexistent, not existent
> and nonexistent, also not a nature that
> is not either of those. Madhyamaka advocates
> know reality totally liberated from the four extremes.[615]

And:

> Therefore, "[Appearing as] one and many, yet one [taste in the true nature], the same and not the same, yet the same"; and so on, {165} [134] is the philosophical tenet of Madhyamaka advocates.[616]

And because all the consummate tantras, mantras, deities, and maṇḍalas of Kālacakra and so on are self-arisen primordial awareness beyond mind, mentation, and consciousness.

That being so, do not denigrate the profound scriptures that perfectly transcend Cittamātra, because that would be a great karmic act of rejecting the Dharma.

j) *Therefore, the benefits and disadvantages of having or lacking the differentiating esoteric instructions are presented*

Therefore, these careful divisions of existent and nonexistent in the abiding state, empty of self-nature and empty of other, nonimplicative negation and implicative negation, exclusion and positive determination, abandonment and primordial awareness, empty emptiness and nonempty emptiness, what does not exist and what remains after that, and so on, will also become clear through having the profound esoteric instructions of the final wheel and the profound tantras carefully clarified by the Bodhisattva Commentaries. And if one has those, the meaning of the middle wheel will also become totally clear, like viewing great mountains from high in the sky above.

If one lacks those, there will be many series of bad views, such as "Emptiness more than the emptiness of self-nature, a pure self, unconditioned primordial awareness, the basic element and awareness indivisible, ground and result indivisible, and so on are impossible and, because the sugata essence is of provisional meaning, it is not actually existent," which will stir up the dregs of the view. {166}

2. *How the true nature other than this emptiness of self-nature is established by reason of the many synonyms stated for the ground of emptiness*
This has two topics.

a. *The actual synonyms*
This has two topics.

1) *A brief presentation of great emptiness that has many synonyms*
Therefore, with the desire to abandon all bad views, the desire to have the excellent perfect view, the desire to see the meaning of the intentionally ambiguous statements or the great intent, and the desire to see the sublime meaning of reality, one must carefully determine the difference between empty of self-nature and empty of other, and so on, and gain unmistaken certainty. [135]

Moreover, the honorable conqueror Maitreya says:

> If briefly summarized, the synonyms
> for "emptiness" are "thusness," "the apex
> of reality," "signlessness," "the ultimate,"
> and "dharmadhātu."
>
> Since it is not something else, not mistaken,
> their cessation, the field of experience of noble beings,
> and the cause of the attributes of noble beings,
> these are, in sequence, the meanings of the synonyms.[617]

And the honorable, noble Nāgārjuna also says:

> That sublime bodhicitta
> is explained to be thusness,
> the apex of reality, signlessness,
> the ultimate, and emptiness.[618]

And the *Sublime Ādibuddha in Twelve Thousand Lines* also says:

> *E*, secret, element of space, bhaga,
> or source of the attributes, lotus, lion throne.[619]

And the honorable Bhagavān Lokeśvara also says:

> Likewise, of the names—syllable *e*, great secret, lotus, source of the attributes, element of space, basis of great bliss, lion throne, bhaga, and secret—syllable *e* alone is not the primary name, because all cause understanding of emptiness having all aspects.[620]

All aspects complete in one is impossible for any relative phenomenon. That being so, emptiness having all aspects (a single meaning having many synonyms, such as the syllable *e*) is ultimate emptiness; it is impossible for it to be relative emptiness. {167}

2) *Extensive explanations refuting the claim that "emptiness of self-nature," "the ultimate," and so on are synonyms*
This has thirteen topics.

a) *The extremely absurd consequences that would occur if "emptiness of self-nature" and "thusness" were synonyms*
It might be said, "The emptiness stated to have many synonyms, such as 'thusness,' is only the emptiness of self-nature in which all phenomena are each empty of own-essence."

If that were so, then even those stated to be "depraved beings having attributes that cause them to never reach parinirvāṇa"[621] would be thusness, because they are empty of own-essence.

If that were claimed, they would also be buddhas, because they would be thusness.

Do not think there is no logical entailment here, because the *Sūtra Teaching the Great Compassion of the Tathāgata* says:

> That which is the meaning of thusness is the meaning of the Tathāgata.[622]

And the honorable conqueror Maitreya also says:

> Thusness is accepted to be buddhahood.[623]

And the *Extensive Mother Sūtra* also says:

> Subhūti, the meaning of reality is called "Buddha."[624]

And the commentary on that also says:

> The meaning of "reality," "thusness," and "dharmakāya" is that they are terms for "Buddha."[625] [136]

And the *Commentary on the "Perfection of Wisdom in Seven Hundred Lines"* composed by the teacher Vimalamitra also says:

> Dharmadhātu itself is the Bhagavān.[626]

And it quotes a sūtra:

> That dharmadhātu itself is enlightenment.[627]

And the *Noble Eight Thousand Lines* also says:

> Thusness is without coming or going, and that thusness is the Tathāgata.[628]

And because there are very many pure scriptural passages such as those that teach that which is thusness to be Buddha.

Furthermore, if that [emptiness of self-nature] and that [thusness] were synonyms, incidental entities changing into something else and again into something else would also be thusness, because each is empty of own-essence. If that were accepted, the extremely absurd consequence would be that they do not change into something else and then again into something else, because the honorable, noble Asaṅga also says:

> Why is thusness called "thusness"? Because it simply does not change into something else.[629]

And because the honorable conqueror Maitreya also says, "not something else,"[630] stating the meaning of thusness to be that it does not change into something else.

Furthermore, because nonvirtues are also empty of self-nature, they would be thusness. But if that were accepted, they would be virtues, because they would be ultimate virtues, existent virtues, and unconditioned virtues, {168} because they would be thusness.

Because this reasoning has been accepted, and it is stated again and again in pure scriptures that if it is thusness it is ultimate virtue, existent virtue, and unconditioned virtue, those logical entailments also exist here.

That being so, although entities that are changeable phenomena are emptiness, they are not thusness.

That which is thusness is emptiness, but is not empty of self-nature and also not emptiness unaware of itself.

b) *The extremely absurd consequences that would occur if "emptiness of self-nature" and "the apex of reality" were synonyms*

Likewise, it should be known that the other [terms], such as "apex of reality," are simply not synonymous with "emptiness of self-nature."

If "emptiness of self-nature" and "the apex of reality" were synonyms, even what are mistaken [phenomena] would be the apex of reality. [137] If that were accepted, however, they would be unmistaken, because the honorable conqueror Maitreya states "not mistaken"[631] to be the meaning of the apex of reality, the unmistaken consummate state.

c) *The extremely absurd consequences that would occur if "emptiness of self-nature" and "the signless basic element" were synonyms*

Likewise, if "emptiness of self-nature" and "the signless basic element" were accepted as synonyms, even entities whose signs have not ceased would be the signless basic element, because they are empty of self-nature. If that were accepted, however, their signs would have ceased, because the honorable conqueror Maitreya says "their cessation"[632] has the meaning of the signless basic element, the ground in which those signs have ceased, and because the honorable, noble Asaṅga also says:

> Why is it called "signless"? Because signs are fully pacified.[633] {169}

d) *The extremely absurd consequences that would occur if "emptiness of self-nature" and "ultimate truth" were synonyms*

Likewise, if "emptiness of self-nature" and "ultimate truth" were accepted as synonyms, even the two obscurations would be ultimate truth, because they are empty of self-nature. If that were accepted, however, it would be inappropriate to abandon them by means of any remedy, and they would also be the field of experience of the self-knowledge of the excellent primordial awareness of noble beings, because the honorable, glorious Maitreyanātha says "the field of experience of noble beings,"[634] and because the esteemed, noble Asaṅga also says:

> Why is it called "ultimate"? Because it is the field of experience of the excellent primordial awareness of noble beings.[635]

e) *The extremely absurd consequences that would occur if "emptiness of self-nature" and "dharmadhātu" were synonyms*

Likewise, if "emptiness of self-nature" and "dharmadhātu" were accepted as synonyms, even the horrible actions and afflictions that are the causes of the lower realms would be dharmadhātu, since they are empty of self-nature. If that were accepted, however, they would be the cause of the attributes of noble beings, because it is said, "since it is the cause of the attributes of noble beings,"[636] and because it is said:

> Why is it called "dharmadhātu"? Because it is the cause of all the attributes of the śrāvakas, pratyekabuddhas, and buddhas.[637]

f) *The extremely absurd consequences that would occur if "emptiness of self-nature" and "ultimate bodhicitta" were synonyms*

Furthermore, if the emptiness in the statement that "ultimate bodhicitta," "emptiness," and so on are synonyms[638] referred to emptiness of self-nature, [138] the extremely absurd consequence would be that even minds of horrible negativity that are not ultimate bodhicitta would be ultimate bodhicitta, because they are empty of self-nature. {170}

g) *How to refute, exactly according to the context, replies that reject the faults in those [claims]*

It might be thought, "That which is the empty aspect of those previously mentioned entities such as negative acts is synonymous with 'ultimate bodhicitta,' 'dharmadhātu,' and so on, but such is not the case for that which is the apparent aspect, so those flaws do not exist."

If that were so, would that apparent aspect be empty or nonempty? If it were empty, it would also be thusness and so on. But a nonempty entity is impossible, because:

> The relative is explained to be emptiness,
> emptiness alone is the relative, since it is
> certain that, like being created and impermanent,
> one does not occur without the other.[639]

And because:

> Form is empty. Emptiness is form.[640]

And because the approach and reasoning of such lines would thus mean "Appearance is emptiness. Emptiness is appearance. That is not other than it, and it is also not other than that." This [claim that the empty aspect of the relative is the ultimate] is simply very unreasonable.[641]

Likewise, even if "the empty aspect of nonvirtue" were claimed to be synonymous with "thusness," it would need to be virtue. So one would also need to accept here that the apparent aspect is nonvirtue and the empty aspect is virtue, and since a nonempty apparent aspect is impossible, the extremely absurd consequence would be that even the apparent aspect of nonvirtue would be thusness and virtue, because it is empty of own-essence, and because the honorable, esteemed, noble Asaṅga says:

> What is ultimate virtue? Thusness.[642]

h) *The extremely absurd consequences that would occur if the "bhaga" of the abiding state and "emptiness of self-nature" were synonyms*

Furthermore, the many synonyms (such as "consummate bhaga") stated for "emptiness" are intended to be synonyms for "the ground of emptiness," "the ultimate emptiness of other," and not for "emptiness of self-nature."

If they were synonymous with "emptiness of self-nature," even horrible incidental stains in which the qualities of omniscience are not complete would be the consummate bhaga. {171} If that were accepted, however, they would be the jewel caskets of a buddha in whom the qualities of sovereignty and so on are complete, [139] because the *Tantra of the Drop of Mahāmudrā* says:

> Just as sesame butter in sesame seeds,
> and just as fire abiding in wood,
> likewise perfectly abiding in all phenomena,
> but unseen,
>
> dharmadhātu is explained as "bhaga."
> The bhaga is the jewel casket, because

it has the qualities of sovereignty and so on.
Therefore, it is explained as "bhaga."

[Ultimate] phenomena are renowned as "bhaga."
Remember to know the basic element to be mind.[643]

It should also be understood that this states the true nature abiding in all phenomena, the sugata essence, the bhaga, to be ultimate bodhicitta.

Furthermore, since one would have to accept even the great negative acts of bad sentient beings to be the consummate bhaga (because they are empty of self-nature), the extremely absurd consequence would be that all its qualities would be complete in them, because the *Great Commentary of Nāropa* quotes:

Since it eliminates passionate desires,
the afflictions are destroyed, and it is
invincible, it is called "bhaga."[644]

And because the *Root Tantra of the Sublime Ādibuddha* also says:

Sovereignty, fine form, and glory,
fame, primordial awareness,
and excellent diligence—these
six are explained as "bhaga."

Of the pure thirty-six elements,
earth and so on are the vajra queens;
their six qualities of sovereignty
and so on are famed as "bhaga."[645]

Likewise, a scriptural passage of the *Glorious Hevajra*, quoted by the teacher Acalagarbha in the *Combined Explanation*, also says:

The destroyer is called "bhaga" because
he has destroyed the māras and the afflictions,
the enemies. Prajñā destroys those afflictions,
therefore Prajñā is expressed as "bhaga."[646]

Prajñāpāramitā, primordially, naturally victorious over the māras and afflictions, is thus stated to be bhaga. And the *Glorious Vajraśekhara Tantra* also says:

> One who has destroyed the afflictions, karma,
> and, likewise, rebirth, the obscurations of the afflictions
> and the knowable, and, likewise, whatever are
> incompatible factors, is explained to be "Bhagavān."[647] {172}

Thus the ground in which all incompatible factors are primordially, naturally destroyed is stated to be bhaga. And the *Glorious Hevajra* also says:

> This Buddha possessing bhaga should
> be called "Bhagavān." Bhaga is expressed
> in six aspects, which are all the qualities,
> such as sovereignty. Or he is called
> "Bhagavān" because he destroys the māras
> of the afflictions and so on.[648]

Thus the Buddha of the consummate, naturally established qualities and abandonments is stated to be bhaga. And the *Glorious Vajra Garland Tantra* also says:

> Dharmadhātu is explained as "bhaga."
> Bhaga is the jewel casket, because
> it has the qualities of sovereignty
> and so on. Therefore, it is called "bhaga."
>
> Bhaga, the basic element in all phenomena,
> is stated to be bodhicitta.[649] [140]

Thus the basic element and awareness indivisible, bodhicitta in which all attributes of the ultimate qualities are complete, is said to be bhaga. And the *Tantra Determining the Intent* also says:

> That upon which all buddhas rely,
> that which is on the thirteenth level,

is correctly explained to be the queen,
the ultimate attribute also called "bhaga."[650]

Thus the ground having the twelve aspects of the meaning of the truth, the ultimate attribute, the queen of all buddhas, is stated to be bhaga. And the *Glorious Buddhakapāla Tantra* also says:

Precise primordial awareness of
sublime [bliss] resides in the middle
of the bhaga. All abides in just this,
which grants great bliss, but deluded
childish beings do not know.[651]

Thus the basic element that grants changeless sublime bliss and is its residence is stated to be bhaga. And the *Glorious Vajraḍāka Tantra* also says:

The lotus itself that attracts the beads,
the bhaga inside which they certainly penetrate,
should be considered the ocean of primordial awareness.[652]

Thus the lotus of the ultimate emptiness of other that attracts the beads of the primordial awareness of bliss is stated to be bhaga. And the *Illuminating Lamp*, the commentary on the *Guhyasamāja*, also quotes [an explanatory tantra]:

The queen, the well-purified mudrā,
is the well-purified bhaga, the lotus.[653]

Thus the queen of all buddhas, Mahāmudrā, is stated to be the bhaga and the lotus. And glorious Vajrapāṇi also quotes in the commentary on the *Cakrasaṃvara*:

Having the qualities of sovereignty and so on,
he is bhaga, or else because the māras have been destroyed.
Since he has those, this one is taught to be Bhagavān,
lord of the three realms.[654] {173}

Thus the basic element and awareness indivisible, in which the consummate abandonments and realizations are naturally complete, is stated to be bhaga.

And in the context of explaining *bhagavān* the honorable Bhagavān Lokeśvara also says:

> As for *bhagavān*: *bhaga* means "destroyed," because the māras and afflictions have been destroyed, or it means the "fortune" of the assembly of the qualities of an omniscient one, such as sovereignty. Because this one has [*vān*] that, he is *bhagavān*.[655]

Here, just as *bhagavān* translates as "destroyer," it also translates as "fortunate," so if the term is left as it is and explained, that is suitable and good.

The *Glorious Kālacakra, King of Tantras* also says:

> [Appearing as] one and many, yet one [taste in the true nature], the same and not the same, yet the same; everywhere right, left, front, back, above, and below; the image of great variegated color in which white and green [and so on] are one; [the sugata essence] without the qualities of short, long, and very long, yet having the qualities;[656] [the image of emptiness appearing as] man or woman, yet not woman or man; that which is the one support of all [bliss]—good bhaga, bhaga of the sublime, to you I bow, to you I bow.[657]

And the commentary on that also says [141]:

> The "good bhaga" is the quintessence of the qualities of sovereignty and so on. "Bhaga of the sublime" means the most sublime of three realms. For that reason, [Mañjuśrīyaśas] bows his head.[658]

And the *Later Tantra of Direct Expression* also says:

> Uniting the three secrets of [ultimate] sacred
> commitment, meditate in the middle of the bhaga.[659]

And:

> In the bhaga, meditate on Vajravārāhī [great bliss]
> as the [ultimate] three secrets.[660]

And:

> The [ultimate] maṇḍala is explained to be bhaga.[661]

Very many profound, consummate scriptures of Great Madhyamaka contain a huge number of such passages that speak of the ground of emptiness, thusness, the quintessence of the naturally, completely established, limitless qualities (such as sovereignty) of the true nature that has many names—such as the ultimate deity, mantra, mudrā, tantra, and maṇḍala—as bhaga. So consult those for details. {174}

i) *The extremely absurd consequences that would occur if the "vajra" of the abiding state and "emptiness of self-nature" were synonyms*

Furthermore, statements in the pure precious tantras about emptiness as "vajra" also refer to the ground of emptiness, the ultimate emptiness of other, not the emptiness of self-nature.

If it were accepted that emptiness of self-nature fits the definition of that vajra, then even vile things that are squashy, are not the essence, have a hollow core, are cuttable and divisible, burnable and destructible impure substances, such as the mushy, the filthy, and muck, would be the consummate vajra, because these are each empty of own-essence. But if that were accepted, one would have to accept that they are hard, are the essence, do not have a hollow core, and so on, because the *Glorious Vajraśekhara Tantra* says:

> "Vajra, vajra," it is said.
> Why is this called "vajra"?
>
> Having the characteristic of being hard,
> the essence, without a hollow core, uncuttable
> and indivisible, unburnable and indestructible,
> [ultimate] emptiness should be called "vajra."[662]

And:

> That which is [ultimately] true,
> actually existent, thusness, changeless,
> unarisen, ceaseless reality, such is
> [the ultimate] vajra.[663]

And:

Changeless thusness, dharmadhātu,
that which is stable, such as that
is here the vajra.[664]

And:

The wheel of the six realms creates defects,
but they are destroyed by the vajra.
That which is [ultimate] bodhicitta is the vajra,
which destroys all the afflictions.[665]

And:

The thusness of all phenomena,
emptiness, is called "vajra."[666]

And so on. And because the *Glorious Vajra Garland Tantra* also says:

The uncuttable, indivisible, unchanging,
unburnable, and sublimely penetrating
nature of the [ultimate] Buddha's sublime five
primordial awarenesses is called "vajra."[667] [142]

And:

Peaceful, nondual, free of aspects yet
the nature or self of all entities, this is called
[ultimate] "great bliss." Vajra, the very essence
of the five primordial awarenesses, having the self
or nature of the five buddhas.[668] {175}

And so on. And because the *Glorious Universal Secret Tantra* also says:

Naturally luminous mind
should be described as "vajra."[669]

And because the *Glorious Kālacakra* also says:

> ... and the vajra [symbolizes] the indivisible great kāya of primordial awareness.[670]

And so on. And because many tantras such as the *Glorious Hevajra* and the *Ādibuddha* also say "The indivisible is called 'vajra,'"[671] and so on. And because noble, honorable Lokeśvara also says:

> "Vajra" is indivisible primordial awareness, the inconceivable mind vajra. The one who has that is the Vajra Bearer.[672]

And:

> Vajra is the great indivisible and uncuttable; it is a vehicle, the Vajrayāna, where the way of mantra and the way of the perfections (having the nature of the result and the cause) are integrated as one.[673]

And:

> The Vajrayāna is the vehicle of perfectly complete buddhas. Because it is not divisible by the vehicles of the non-Buddhists, the śrāvakas, and the pratyekabuddhas, it is vajra; because one goes to liberation by means of this, it is the Vajrayāna.[674]

And so on. And because the *Vajravidāraṇā* says:

> Uncuttable, indestructible, true, hard, stable, and unimpeded everywhere.[675]

And so on, stating that which is the basic element—not cut and destroyed by anything, true, real, hard and stable, thusness without arising, ceasing, or change, the quintessence of the five self-arisen primordial awarenesses and the five buddhas, natural luminosity, bodhicitta—to be vajra.

Chanting the Ultimate Names also says:

> Unique, hard, and solid vajra self.[676]

And:

> Vajra force, creating fear,
> vajra fame, vajra heart,
> illusory great vajra belly,
> arisen from a vajra, vajra self,
> vajra essence like space.[677]

And:

> Vajrahāsa (the great proclamation).
>
> Vajrasattva, great being, Vajrarāja,
> great bliss, vajra violence, great joy,
> Vajrahūṃkāra, proclaiming *hūṃ*.
>
> Carrying a vajra arrow as a weapon,
> with a vajra sword he cuts all without exception,
> holding a crossed vajra, a vajra bearer,
> the unique vajra victorious in battle.
>
> Horrible eyes of blazing vajras,
> even his head hair blazing vajras, {176}
> Vajrāveśa, the great descent,
> with a hundred eyes, vajra eyes.
>
> Body bearing vajra body hair,
> vajra body hairs, a unique body,
> the nails arisen with vajra points,
> solid skin with vajra essence.
>
> Glorious carrying a vajra garland,
> adorned with vajra ornaments.[678] [143]

And:

> The six syllables, vajra sound.[679]

And:

> Vajraratna, glorious bestowal of initiation.[680]

And:

> Lord of all vajra holders.[681]

And:

> Vajra sun, great appearance;
> vajra moon, stainless light.[682]

And:

> Vajratīkṣṇa with a great sword.[683]

And:

> With the great weapon, the vajra Dharma,
> the profound vajra, conqueror of conquerors,
> vajra intelligence, aware of objects as they are.[684]

And:

> Having all the vajra seats without exception.[685]

Such passages say all the aspects of the other, the sugata essence—such as the force, fame, sound, laughter, illusion, heart, essence, self, bliss, joy, eyes, head hair, hair, body hair, nails, skin, belly, seats, garlands, ornaments, weapons such as arrow and sword, initiation, descent, intelligence, glory, sun and moon of the unique, hard, and solid ultimate, self-arisen primordial awareness—are themselves vajra.

Likewise, the seventy-second verse [of *Chanting the Ultimate Names*] also says—with terms such as "Vajrabhairava," "vajra assembly," "vajra body," "vajra eyes," "vajra ears," "vajra nose," "vajra tongue," "vajra teeth," "vajra nails," "vajra head hair," "vajra body hair," "vajra ornaments," "Vajrahāsa," "vajra song," "vajra dance," and "vajra weapons"—that all the sensory bases, limbs, song and dance, weapons, and so on of the deity of primordial awareness, the indivisible means and wisdom of ultimate thusness, are themselves vajra. The honorable Lord of Secrets, Vajrapāṇi, also says:

> The oneness of these dharma and connate kāyas is to be expressed as "Vajrasattva." "Vajra" is dharmakāya and emptiness and wisdom. "Sattva" is the connate kāya and compassion and means.
>
> In that way, the quintessence of the perfect union of wisdom and means is to be directly expressed as "Vajrasattva."[686]

Thus be confident that this vajra stated to be dharmakāya and Prajñāpāramitā, yet also to be emptiness, {177} cannot be anything but the ground of emptiness, the ultimate emptiness of other, the emptiness that is the very essence of the nonexistence of entities.

Likewise, the *Tantra That Utterly Purifies All Lower Realms* also says:

> The Buddha before all buddhas,
> with all stains of unknowing destroyed,
> is vajra and king of vajra holders,
> Vajra [Bearer], vajra [mantra], Vajra Holder.
>
> Vajrakāya, the great kāya,
> I bow down and praise Vajrapāṇi.
>
> Vajra limbs, sublime vajra;
> blazing [light of] the vajra [true nature],
> greatly blazing; force of the vajra [true nature],
> great force; vajra weapon, great weapon;
>
> vajra in hand, great hand; vajra arrow,
> utterly penetrating [all the three realms]; [144]
> vajra sharp [cutting through all], greatly sharp; . . .

And so on, ending with:

> . . . primary vajra quintessence of all.[687]

These lines state the basic element and awareness indivisible, all the deities of self-arisen primordial awareness, to be vajra. And *Compendium of the Reality of All Tathāgatas* also says:

> Vajrasattva, great being;
> vajra that is all [ultimate] tathāgatas;
> Vajra Ādi[buddha], totally
> good; I bow down to Vajrapāṇi.
>
> Vajrarāja, sublime Buddha;
> Vajrāṅkuśa, Tathāgata; definitive king,

Vajra Sublime; I bow down to you,
Vajra Summoner.

Vajra Attachment, great bliss;
Vajraśarī, controller; Great Vajra
desiring [to kill] the māras;
I bow down to you, Vajradhanuḥ.

And so on, down to:

"... Vajra Union, mahāmudrā, ..."[688]

And so on. These lines also state the sugata essence, the apex of reality, all the deities having all sense faculties [in each one] and having all aspects, to be vajra.

Likewise, the *Tantra of the Glorious Sublime Primal* also says:

All body, speech, and mind is vajra.[689]

And so on. And:

Because of vajra hardness, vajra equanimity (directly complete enlightenment) is great enlightenment.[690]

Such passages state the body, speech, and mind of great enlightenment to be vajra. And the *Glorious Vajraśekhara* also says:

Vajradhātu is very stable. Just that is
primordial awareness, direct buddhahood.[691]

Thus the very stable dharmadhātu itself is said to be primordial awareness, buddhahood, and vajra.

The *Tantra of the Glorious Sublime Primal* also says:

Great bliss, great vajra,
well adorned with all vajras.[692] {178}

And:

> Vajra Holder, basis of all,
> great bliss, great vajra.[693]

And:

> Then Bhagavān Vairocana, discovering the secret true nature of all tathāgatas (that all phenomena are free of conceptual elaboration), also spoke of the vajra of great bliss called "meaningful sacred commitment," the vajra true nature, the perfection of wisdom, the glorious sublime primal, this excellent [sugata essence] without beginning, end, and middle.[694]

The true nature free of conceptual elaboration, great bliss, the perfection of wisdom, is thus said to be vajra. And the *Glorious Stainless Light* also says:

> The conquerors state the five changeless great emptinesses, the quintessence of the thirty-six, to be vajra; because of holding that, they are the Vajra Holder.[695]

The basic element and awareness indivisible, the ultimate six aggregates and so on, the thirty-six deities, are thus said to be vajra.

Likewise, the *Glorious Guhyasamāja* of all buddhas also says:

> Here, the five paranormal abilities are the vajra eye, the vajra ear, the vajra mind, the vajra [memory] of past lives, and the vajra magical emanations.[696] [145]

And the commentary on that in the *Illuminating Lamp* also says:

> Vajra is nondual primordial awareness; because he holds its very essence, he is the Vajra Holder, the consummate state.[697]

Likewise, very many different tantras also speak of the body vajra, the speech vajra, the mind vajra, the primordial-awareness vajra, and so on; the vajra sensory bases such as vajra discrimination and vajra conditioning factors, and such as vajra eyes and vajra form; Vajradhara, Vajrāmṛita, Vajradhātu, Vajrahūṃkāra, Vajrabhairava, Vajreśvara, Vajraḍāka, Vajraśekhara, Vajracatuḥpīṭha, and so on; desire vajra, hatred vajra, ignorance vajra, jealousy vajra, and so on; vajra autumn, vajra winter, and so on; vajrayāna, vajramantra, vajrayoga, Vajravārāhī, Vajratārā, Vajranairātmyā, and so on; all having just the same meaning as the true nature, dharmadhātu, constancy of phenomena, flawlessness of phenomena, thusness, unmistaken thusness, thusness that is not something else, the apex of reality, and the inconceivable basic element, unarisen, {179} unceasing, primordially peaceful, natural nirvāṇa; the purity of form and so on stated extensively in the "Chapter on Purity";[698] the form of the true nature, and so on; and form beyond the three realms and the three times, and so on. Whether relative buddhas appear or do not appear in the world, whether persons understand or do not understand, believe or do not believe, whether the incidental stains have ceased or not ceased, these abide forever, pervading all like space.

j) *The extremely absurd consequences that would occur if "Mahāmudrā" and so on of the abiding state and "emptiness of self-nature" were synonyms*

Furthermore, if it were accepted that a profound emptiness other than the emptiness of self-nature did not exist, then Mahāmudrā of the indivisible essence of ground and result, emptiness having the most sublime of all aspects, and mother Prajñāpāramitā would also not exist, because emptiness of self-nature does not fit their definition.

If it did fit the definition, vile things such as poison and feces would also be those, because each is empty of own-essence.

That cannot be accepted. The honorable Bhagavān Avalokiteśvara says:

> Beyond the true nature of the particles of
> a tiny atom, having the nature of a prognostic
> image, she has the most sublime of all aspects;
> to that Mahāmudrā I bow.[699] [146]

And:

> [The true nature of] the object [seeming to have] the aggregates
> and so on, which totally destroys the obscurations, is like
> the eight prognostic images. Giving the bliss of omniscience,
> only that [ultimate observable emptiness] is the Mahāmudrā of
> the Vajra Holder, . . .[700]

And:

> Mahāmudrā, having the characteristics of all [ultimate] attributes without the nature [of all relative attributes], having the most sublime of all aspects, Prajñāpāramitā, produces the buddhas.[701]

And so on, it states extensively. And the *King of Tantras* also says:

> [Mahā]mudrā resembling an illusion, in the mind and in space like an image in a clean mirror, illuminating the [ultimate] three worlds, radiating many light rays similar to stainless lightning.[702]

And so on. And the *Ḍākinīvajrapañjara* also says:

> In every realm of space
> and thousands of world systems,
> excellent great bliss, mahāmudrā,
> Buddha, is present like space.[703] {180}

And *Compendium of the Reality of All Tathāgatas* also says:

> The [ultimate] Tathāgata is mahāmudrā.[704]

And:

> Just as the Vajra Holder is [spontaneously]
> established in the manner of mahāmudrā.[705]

And the honorable Lord of Secrets, Vajrapāṇi, also says:

> The attainment is mahāmudrā, the perfection of wisdom, having the most sublime of all aspects.[706]

And:

> Mahāmudrā, that desired attainment, is knowledge of all, knowledge of all aspects, knowledge of the path, knowledge of all

aspects of the path, she who gives all the qualities of a buddha, such as the ten powers and the four types of fearlessness . . .[707]

And [Sādhuputra says]:

Within, seeing the images of all the buddhas of the [ultimate] three realms without exception, which is seeing mahāmudrā . . .[708]

And [Vajrapāṇi says]:

Free of all obscurations, like a prognostic image, mahāmudrā, radiating endless clouds of the light rays of the buddhas, adorned with maṇḍalas of light.[709]

And:

That is Vajrayoginī, just the appearance of one's own mind, mahāmudrā, having the most sublime of all aspects, the perfection of wisdom, which is to be expressed as "emptiness" and "thusness" and "Kulikā" and "lotus."[710]

And so on. And the *Glorious Hevajra Tantra* also says:

The bliss of *bola* is mahāmudrā,
all the vajra sensory bases. This secret
meditative union does not teach that
of the two outer pairs.[711]

And so on. And:

Camphor itself, Nairātmyā,
bliss the nature of selflessness,
whose bliss is mahāmudrā,
abides in the navel maṇḍala itself,

with the nature of the first vowel,
which the buddhas label "intelligence."[712]

And [147]:

> Just that is Bhagavatī Prajñā.
>
> That is not long, not short,
> not square, not round, and
> beyond odor, taste, and flavor;
> creator of connate joy. {181}
>
> The yogin arisen from that
> consumes its bliss. Those together
> are mahāmudrā.[713]

And so on. And also:

> That is the form of the connate,
> the yoginī of good great bliss.
> That is the maṇḍalacakra and has
> a nature of five primordial awarenesses.
>
> That is the form of mirrorlike primordial awareness,
> has the essence of the primordial awareness of
> equanimity, and is [the apex of] reality,
> the discriminating. That is the all-accomplishing,
>
> and that of very pure dharmadhātu.
> That is the lord of the maṇḍala—me.
> That is Nairātmyā yoginī, having the nature
> of dharmadhātu.[714]

And:

> The attainment with the characteristics, [mahā]mudrā
> that is not divisible, is accomplished by the yogin.[715]

And the honorable, great paṇḍita, lord Nāropa, also says:

> To that very Mahāmudrā, whose essence
> is to be realized by means of the examples

> of an illusion and so on, I bow down with
> total devotion.[716]

And:

> "What is to be obtained," mahāmudrā, . . .[717]

Such passages state that dharmadhātu and self-arisen primordial awareness, one and indivisible itself, to be mahāmudrā, emptiness having the most sublime of all aspects, the nature of the definitive meaning, the bliss of the consummate *bola*, Nairātmyā, Prajñāpāramitā, the syllable *a*, lotus, thusness, emptiness, Vajrayoginī, Kulikā, and so on. And because that is also a profound emptiness that is not empty of self-nature, these exceptional proofs also say Mahāmudrā, the Great Mother, Nairātmyā, the syllable *a*, lotus, the connate kāya or joy, the maṇḍalacakra, the five primordial awarenesses, thusness, Vajrayoginī, Kulikā, and so on (the indivisible essence of the consummate ground and result) refer to the ground empty of all phenomena, the true nature, ultimate truth, the quintessence of the limitless inseparable qualities, the sugata essence, the buddha nature, the self of thusness, the pure self, the emptiness that is the very essence of the nonexistence of entities. If seen in that way, the correct meaning of the great intent is seen. {182}

If such is not the case, the mode of emptiness of Mahāmudrā and so on will not be discovered in accord with the intent of Vajradhara.

k) *The extremely absurd consequences that would occur if "the secret," "the great secret," and so on of the abiding state were synonyms for "emptiness of self-nature"*

Furthermore, statements in the precious tantras by glorious, great Vajradhara giving "the secret," "the great secret," [148] and so on as synonyms for "consummate emptiness" also refer to that which is the emptiness that is the very essence of the nonexistence of entities, the ground of emptiness, the ultimate emptiness of other; they do not refer to that which is just the emptiness of nonentities, the emptiness of self-nature, because that and this are not suitable as synonyms.

If "the secret" were a synonym for "emptiness of self-nature," the five appropriated aggregates would also be the secret of the consummate definitive meaning, because they are empty of self-nature. If that were accepted, however, the extremely absurd consequence would be that they would be the perfection of wisdom, because the honorable Lord of Secrets, Vajrapāṇi, says:

> In accord with the provisional meaning, the bhaga of the action mudrā is called "the secret." In accord with the definitive meaning, it is the perfection of wisdom, emptiness.[718]

Here, this perfection of wisdom, the indivisible essence of ground and result said to be emptiness, is also not the emptiness of self-nature; it is the ground of emptiness, the ultimate emptiness of other, the emptiness that is the very essence of the nonexistence of entities, because it is the perfection of wisdom and it is also the true nature.

Likewise, as synonyms for "the profound emptiness of the indivisible essence of the consummate ground and result," glorious Vajrapāṇi distinctly mentions "ḍākiṇī," "quintessence of all [aspects]," and so on:

> In the great secret place, the ḍākinī's secret, the quintessence of all [aspects], it always resides.[719]

And the *Glorious Little Tantra of Cakrasaṃvara* also says:

> In the great secret, the sublimely joyful, the quintessence of all [aspects], [great bliss] always resides.[720] {183}

Such passages state many synonyms for that which is the emptiness that is the very essence of the nonexistence of entities, the emptiness of other entities, the ground of emptiness, the ultimate emptiness of other.

l) *The extremely absurd consequences that would occur if "the triangle," "the source of the attributes," and so on of the abiding state and "emptiness of self-nature" were synonyms*

Furthermore, the many synonyms for emptiness stated by glorious Vajradhara, such as "the source of the attributes of the indivisible essence of consummate ground and result," "the triangle," the syllable *a*, "Vajrāralli," "bhaga of the queen," "perfection of wisdom," and "sugata essence," also refer to the ground of emptiness, the ultimate emptiness of other; emptiness of self-nature is not a synonym for those.

If it were, horrible great negative actions such as the five acts that bring immediate retribution would also be those, because each is empty of own-essence. If that were accepted, however, the extremely absurd consequence would be that they would also be what is to be relied upon by all buddhas, the delightful maṇḍala, and so on, [149] because the *Glorious Sampuṭa Tantra* says:

> This pure triangle, relied upon by all
> the buddhas, is adorned with a *vaṃ*
> in its center, and has a shape just like
> the [Sanskrit] syllable *e*.
>
> A delightful triangular maṇḍala in which
> Vajrāralli is mentioned, it is also called
> the "bhaga of the queen" and explained
> to be the "source of the attributes."[721]

And:

> Root of all tantras, triangle of vast
> form, common to all sentient beings,
> it is the basis of [them all], the demigods
> and the gods, Brahmā, and so on.[722]

And:

> That is Prajñāpāramitā,
> just that transcends sense objects
> and resides in the hearts of all living creatures.[723]

And so on. And because the *Ḍākinīvajrapañjara* also says:

> Blissful, triangle, dustless, and free of faults,
> free of dust, negative acts destroyed, and nature,
> waveless, bliss of the apex [of reality],
> awareness of the bliss, and sublime secret, joy, and . . .[724] {184}

And because such passages state those to be the quintessence of the many qualities of the naturally spontaneous abandonments and realizations.

Likewise, the honorable Bhagavān Mahākaruṇika Avalokiteśvara also states the meaning of "source of the attributes" as a synonym for "profound emptiness":

> The term "source of the attributes" also expresses that, because it is the source of the attributes from which all the [ultimate] attributes without [relative] nature occur.
>
> The [ultimate] attributes without [relative] nature are the eighty-four thousand aggregates of the attributes, such as the ten powers and the types of fearlessness. Those occur from the source of the attributes, the [ultimate] buddhafield.[725]

And:

> Therefore, the source of the attributes is Viśvamātā (who has the nature of dharmadhātu), embraced by Bhagavān Kālacakra, at all times free of all obscurations.[726]

Here also the division of the two truths must be recognized and, because the aggregates of the attributes such as the ultimate ten powers are indivisible from the source of the attributes itself, their "occurring without occurring" should be understood through the esoteric instructions of being without the flaw of including contradiction.

Likewise, the honorable Lord of Secrets, Vajrapāṇi, also says:

> As for "residing in the sublime great secret": the source of the attributes, the element of space, is the great secret. Residing in that is residing in the sublime great secret.[727]

And so on. The commentary on the *Glorious Cakrasaṃvara* also says:

> *E*, bhaga, and lotus; purity, basis
> of bliss, and blissful; lion throne,
> nonreferential [compassion], and
> thusness, the perfection [of wisdom].

And, likewise, in the *Ḍākinīvajrapañjara* the Bhagavān says [150]:

> The [other] element of space, not inanimate,
> clear, and vastness, utter luminosity, variegated

> vajra, and place, ground, and [dharma]dhātu of all,
> beautiful [goddess having various forms]. {185}

And so on, down to:

> In the great secret, the sublimely joyful, the quintessence of all [aspects], [great bliss] always resides.

Thus it says the place [of great bliss] is taught [to be ultimate great emptiness] through the nuances of the various names.[728]

Such passages state the synonyms for the ground of emptiness, the ultimate, by means of many aspects, such as dustless, free of dust, faultless, negative acts destroyed, waveless, consummate bliss, self-awareness of that, sublime secret, blissful, basis of bliss, pure nature, joyful, nonreferential [compassion], element of space, emptiness that is not inanimate, three states of cyclic existence totally clear, vastness, utter luminosity, variegated vajra, basis of the attributes, ground, basic element of all, beautiful consort, and nature.

Concerning that, it is said that the nature has not occurred from causes and conditions, is uncontrived, and not dependent on anything else. The honorable, esteemed, noble Nāgārjuna says:

> For the nature to occur from
> causes and conditions is not reasonable.
> A nature that occurred from causes
> and conditions would be created.
>
> "A nature that is created,"
> how could that be correct?
> The natural is uncontrived
> and does not depend on another.[729]

m) *Showing that many other synonyms stated for the ultimate are also other than the emptiness of self-nature*

This has three topics.

(1) *Showing that those stated in the* Lamp That Summarizes Conduct *are also other than the emptiness of self-nature*

Likewise, in the *Lamp That Summarizes Conduct*, the honorable, great teacher Āryadeva also says:

> That ultimate truth is also uncontrived, equal to space, the stainless svābhāvika[kāya]. To clarify this meaning, the *Sūtra Teaching the Single Mode* says:
>
> > This Dharma is taught with words and language,
> > but Dharma and language do not appear here.
> > Penetrating the true nature, the actual single mode,
> > one contacts unsurpassable, sublime patience.[730]

And:

> The name of the form of the very essence of the body of sublime joy, the quintessence of the form that will occur, is "Great Vajradhara." {186}
>
> Since it is definitely released from the bonds of saṃsāra, it is called "liberation."[731]

And so on. And:

> That which is indivisible is unarisen. That which is unarisen is held to be indestructible. That which is indestructible is clear. [151] That which is clear is pure. That which is pure is stainless. That which is stainless is luminous. That which is luminous is the nature of mind.[732]

And so on. Also, the "Chapter Eliminating Doubts, Which Summarizes Ultimate Truth" says:

> Now, in order to clear away the confusion of those who are fixated on names, some synonymous names for the ultimate will be introduced: first is luminosity, empty of all, primordial awareness of a buddha, vajra primordial awareness, unsurpassable primordial awareness, stainless, nonexistence of entities, not appearing [to consciousness], selflessness, beyond the selves, not a sentient

being, not a lifeforce, not a person, unsoiled, unarising, unceasing, without syllables, wordless, nonreferential [compassion], unsurpassable, inexpressible, inconceivable, infinite, countless, beyond the sense faculties, nonabiding, without characteristic, unconditioned, signless, unfluctuating, free of object, not consciousness, not to be examined, inextinguishable, wordless, unobscured, the single mode, peaceful, equal to space, naturally pure, beginningless, middleless, endless, without going, without coming, {187} not far, not near, not one, not distinct, difficult to contact, difficult to cultivate, meditation itself, reality, dharmakāya, the apex of reality, the apex of nonattachment, dharmadhātu, without body, dustless, limitless, established, established secret, purity of the perfections, purity of the view, purity of the cause, purity of the result, purity of the three realms, purity of merit, purity of negative acts, purity of the afflictions, purity of action, purity of birth, perfection of wisdom, mother of all buddhas, knowledge of all, knowledge of the aspects of the path, knowledge of all aspects, thusness, unmistaken thusness, equanimity, inexhaustible accumulation of the assemblies of merit and primordial awareness, descent of primordial awareness, producer of all bodhisattvas, [152] mother of all śrāvakas, creator of all pratyekabuddhas, provider of all worlds, purifier of the divine eye, bestower of the divine ear, knower of the minds of others, rememberer of previous states, performer of measureless miraculous displays, extinguisher of all afflictions.[733]

And:

Some synonymous names for this utterly perfect kāya of unity will be introduced: form of the person of great awareness, residing in the mode of the two truths, {188} having the quintessence of natural luminosity, having the quintessence of means and wisdom, having the quintessence of the three worlds, having the quintessence of the three vehicles, having the quintessence of the three maṇḍalas, having the quintessence of means; and, likewise, "excellent person, sublime person, great person, omniscient person, heroic person, stable person, tamed person, taming person, sublime person, ruling person, lion person, space person, person

> having the quintessence of all, person having a pure quintessence"; and, likewise, "one who has gone beyond saṃsāra, one who has gone to dry land, one who has obtained bliss, one who has obtained fearlessness, one who blazes from going beyond, one who has extracted the thorn, one who is free of conceptual elaborations, bhikṣu, arhat, one with taints extinguished, one without anything, śramaṇa, brahmin, kṣatriya, child of the buddhas, one without the afflictions, one in control, liberated mind, liberated wisdom, knowledge of all, great elephant, one who has done what was to be done, one who has done what is to be done, one who has discarded the burden, one who has achieved one's goals, one who has fully extinguished links with cyclic existence, one whose mind is liberated by the perfect word, one who has obtained power over all minds, one who is sublimely perfected, one who resides at the apex of saṃsāra, kāya of primordial awareness, self-arisen." Thus it is explained.[734]

Where are these explained? In the unsurpassable scriptures of the consummate definitive meaning, such as *Chanting the Ultimate Names*. {189} [153]

(2) *Showing that those stated in* Chanting the Ultimate Names *are also other than the emptiness of self-nature*
This has thirteen topics.

(a) *Those stated in the sections of the request and the reply*
Furthermore, [the ground of emptiness, emptiness of other itself] is the glorious syllable *śrī*, Vajradhara, sublime one who has tamed the difficult to tame, sublime sattva, conqueror of the three worlds, lord of the vajra, king of the secret, eyes [everywhere] like a wide white lotus, mouths [everywhere] like a wide lotus, Vajrapāṇi, pervasive lord, master of living beings, teacher of living beings, great sacred commitment, knowledge of reality, sublime knowledge of sense faculties and thoughts, kāya of primordial awareness, great cranial dome, lord of words, self-arisen primordial awareness, Mañjuśrī, primordial-awareness being, most sublime of profound and vast meaning, most sublime of great meaning, peerless sublime, utterly peaceful sublime, always virtuous sublime, great tantra, Māyājāla, sublime mantra holder, complete Buddha who is the most sublime of beings with two feet, Mañjuśrī who is the embodiment of primordial awareness, and . . .[735]

(b) *Those stated in the section of seeing the six mantra families*
. . . the great family of entire secret mantra: [the family of] sublime secret mantra and sublime awareness holders, the three natural families, the mundane and transcendent family, the great family illuminating the world, the sublime family of mahāmudrā, the great family of the great cranial dome, and . . .[736] {190}

(c) *Those stated as enlightenment by the* Māyājāla
. . . the six mantra kings, nondual arising, unarisen attribute, inexpressible *a ā* and *i ī* and *u ū* and *e ai* and *o au* and *aṃ aḥ*, the kāya of primordial awareness residing in the heart, I or self of a buddha, Buddha engaged in the three times, the syllable *oṃ*, Vajratīkṣṇa, cutter of suffering, kāya of primordial awareness from the prajñā,[737] assembly or kāya of primordial awareness, lord of speech, Arapacana, and . . .[738] [154]

(d) *Those stated as the great Vajradhātu maṇḍala*
. . . Buddha arisen from *a*, the syllable *a*, excellent changeless great meaning, great lifeforce, unarisen, inexpressible, sublime cause of all expression, all words of luminosity, the great offering, great passionate desire, great hatred, great ignorance, great wrath, great attachment, all afflictions primordially destroyed, great desire, great bliss, great joy, great delight, great form, great body, great color, great majestic body, great name, great width, vast great maṇḍala, sublime great wisdom, sublime holding weapons, great affliction, sublime iron hook, great renown, great fame, great appearance, great brilliance, great skill or great awareness, {191} upholding the great magical illusion, achieving the aim of the great magical illusion, joyful with the joy of the great magical illusion, conjurer of the great magical illusion, great benefactor, sublime lord, sublime holder of great moral discipline, sublime holder of great patience, sublime great stability, sublime great diligence, sublime suppressor of opponents, abiding in great meditation and sublime samādhi, holding the kāya of great wisdom, great force, great means, ocean of prayers, ocean of primordial awareness, great love, infinite nature, sublime great compassion, sublime intelligence, sublime great wisdom, sublime possession of great intelligence, sublime great means, sublime great performance, sublime great magic, sublime possession of force, sublime great strength, sublime great speed, sublime renown as great and greater magical illusion, sublime suppressor of forceful opponents, sublime destroyer of the mountain of cyclic existence, sublime solid, sublime holder of the great vajra, sublime

great ferocity, sublime great fury, frightener of even the most frightful, great sublime protector, great sublime awareness, sublime great master, sublime great secret mantra, sublime abiding or stability in the Mahāyāna way, sublime Mahāyāna way, [155] and . . .[739]

(e) *Those stated as the primordial awareness of dharmadhātu*

. . . great Buddha, great Vairocana, sublime great sage, sublime possessing great ability, arisen from the great way of secret mantra, self of the great way of secret mantra, {192} sublime attainment of the ten perfections, sublime abiding in the ten perfections, sublime purity of the ten perfections, sublime way of the ten perfections, sublime lord protector of the ten levels, sublime abiding on the ten levels, quintessence of the pure ten primordial awarenesses, holder of the pure ten primordial awarenesses, meaning of the aims of the ten aspects, pervasive lord of the lords of sages, pervasive lord of the ten powers, performer of benefit for all without exception, great one having the powerful ten aspects, beginningless self, self without conceptual elaborations, self of thusness, primordially pure self, sublime truthful speech, sublime unchanging speech, sublime doing as is said, sublime nonduality, sublime teaching nonduality, residing at the apex of reality, sublime proclaiming the sound of selflessness, sublime frightener of bad non-Buddhists, sublime omnipresence, sublime meaningful basis or force, Tathāgata, sublime quickness like the mind, sublime conqueror, sublime conqueror of enemies, sublime total conqueror, sublime universal monarch, sublime great force, sublime teacher of the assembly, sublime chief of the assembly, sublime lord of the assembly, sublime master of the assembly, sublime powerful, sublime great strength, sublime cherished one, sublime great way, sublime not reliant on others, sublime lord of words, sublime master of words, sublime skilled in speech, sublime power over words, sublime infinite words, sublime true words, sublime true speech, sublime teaching the four truths, sublime irreversible, sublime unreturning, sublime guide, {193} sublime pratyekabuddha, sublime like a rhinoceros, sublime definite release by means of various definite releases, great element or great existence or great truth or great reality, sole cause or support or basis of all, sublime monk, sublime arhat, sublime extinguishing of taints, sublime ground free of attachment, sublime taming of sense faculties, sublime gaining of bliss, sublime attaining fearlessness, [156] sublime coolness, sublime unsullied or unstained, sublime possessing awareness and legs, gone to bliss or abiding in bliss or realizing bliss, sublime awareness of the world, not grasping at the "I" as a self, abiding in the mode of the two truths, primordially gone to the end of saṃsāra, primordially having done what is to be done, primordially abiding on dry land, primordial awareness alone, sublime definite removal or definite release, sublime destruction with the weapon of wisdom, sublime excellent Dharma, sublime king of Dharma, sublime brilliance or appearance, sublime illuminating the world, lord of Dharma, king of Dharma, teacher of the fine path or the sublime path, sublime accomplishing aims, sublime accomplishing aspirations, all conceptualization abandoned, nonconceptual basic element, sublime inextinguishable, excellent basic element, sublime never extinguished, naturally possessing merit, primordially the assembly of merit, primordially self-arisen primordial awareness, great source of primordial awareness, sublime possessing primordial awareness, sublime knowing the existent to be existent and knowing the nonexistent to be nonexistent, the two assemblies primordially and naturally accumulated, sublime permanence, sublime conquering of all, primordially possessing yoga, primordially sublime meditation, sublime to be reflected upon, {194} sublime possessing intelligence, sublime self, sublime personal self-awareness, sublime unmovable, sublime primal, holding the three kāyas, self of the five kāyas of the Buddha, self pervading all, self of the five primordial awarenesses, crown of the self of the five buddhas, primordially holding the five eyes without attachment, producer of all buddhas, buddha son, excellent or other or transcendent or sublime, sublime wisdom, primordially released from cyclic existence, without birthplace or sublime birthplace, naturally occurring from the dharma[kāya] or the sublime source of the attributes, primordially removing cyclic existence or ending cyclic existence, unique self, hard and solid self, vajra self, always just born yet never aging, lord of living beings, sublime arisen from space, self-arisen, great fire of primordial awareness from the prajñā, great light of primordial awareness from the prajñā, illuminator of primordial awareness from the prajñā, bright appearance of primordial awareness, sublime clear appearance for living beings, lamp of primordial awareness, [157] primordially great splendor, natural luminosity, sovereign of sublime mantra, king of awareness, king of secret mantra, performing great benefit, great cranial dome, marvelous cranial dome, lord of space, sublime displaying variety, self of all buddhas, sublime entity, sublime living being, sublime joy for all, sublime possessing eyes, sublime producer of various forms, sublime worthy of worship and worthy of honor, sublime great seer, holding the three natural families, sublime possessing secret mantra, primordially great sacred commitment, primordially upholding secret mantra, sublime chief, Three Jewels of the true nature, holding those, {195} sublime teaching the sublime three vehicles, sublime Amoghapāśa, naturally victorious, great holder of the drop, sublime Vajrapāśa, sublime Vajrāṅkuśa, sublime great vajra noose, and . . .[740]

(f) *Those stated as mirrorlike primordial awareness*

. . . Vajrabhairava, frightening even the frightful, king of the wrathful, six-faced and frightening, six-eyed one having all sense faculties [in each one], six-armed one whose limbs are everywhere, having all powers, sublime skeleton, sublime baring fangs, great wrathful Halāhala, hundred-faced (or having mouths everywhere), Yamāntaka, sublime king of obstructions, vajra force, sublime Bhairava, vajra arrogance, vajra heart, vajra magical illusion, vajra great belly, born from a vajra or vajra birthplace, vajra self, vajra essence or vajra maṇḍala like space, Acala, great bliss with one braid (or Ekajaṭī), brandishing a vajra, wearing a wet elephant skin (the Lord of Death primordially destroyed), great ferocity, sublime frightening with roaring laughter, great laughter of the true nature, having the roaring laughter of thusness, Vajrahāsa (the great proclamation), Vajrasattva, mahāsattva, Vajrarāja, sublime great bliss, vajra ferocity or vajra fierceness, vajra great joy, vajra hūṃ, Vajrahūṃkāra, vajra arrow or bearing that, vajra sword, cutting all bonds, holding all vajras, Vajra Bearer, [158] unique vajra, victorious in battle or eliminating battle, horrible eyes of blazing vajras, hair of blazing vajras, {196} Vajrāveśa, great descent, a hundred wide eyes, vajra eyes, vajra body hairs or a body of them, vajra body hairs, kāya of the unique vajra, vajra nails, vajra skin, bearing a vajra garland, vajra glory, vajra ornaments or adorned with them, inexpressible roaring laughter, the six syllables or the six changeless, vajra sound, great Mañjuśrī, great sound without syllables (or great *nāda*), unique sound in the three worlds (or the other three worlds' many sounds that are one taste), ubiquitous soundless sound, most sublime of those possessing sound, and . . .[741]

(g) *Those stated as discriminating primordial awareness*

. . . meaning of reality, basic element of selflessness, thusness, the apex of reality, ground without syllables, sublime leader speaking of emptiness, proclaiming the sound of the profound and vast true nature, Dharma conch of spontaneous nature, gong of thusness, nonabiding nirvāṇa, great drum of the always ubiquitous fully established, fine form without form, excellent form without form, variegated body arisen from totally good [mind], glory in whom the forms of everything appear, dharmakāya holding all images without exception, invincible or unapprehendable by anything, renowned as great or great renown, other three realms, their great lord, extremely high noble path, sublime abiding there, sublime undeteriorating and greatly expansive, excellent pinnacle of Dharma, body uniquely youthful in the three worlds (the three worlds of the true nature), sublime sthavira, sublime elder, sublime lord of beings, holding the major marks and minor marks of the source of the attributes, {197} most sublime of what is desirable because lovely or attractive, beautiful in the three worlds of the great secret, sublime knowing the world, sublime that is totally fine, sublime teacher of all, sublime fearless teacher of the world, sublime protector of the world, sublime guardian of the world, basis of harmony for the world or pervading the three worlds, unsurpassable refuge, [159] unsurpassable guardian, enjoying the ends of other space or enjoying the pervading of space, ocean of omniscient primordial awareness, splitting the eggshell of ignorance, primordially destroying and having destroyed the web of cyclic existence, the afflictions primordially at peace and pacified, primordially gone naturally to the far shore of saṃsāra, primordially obtained bestowal of the initiation of primordial awareness, primordially having the crown of the five primordial awarenesses, naturally wearing or adorned by all buddhas as an ornament, naturally pacifying all suffering, sublime relieving the three [sufferings], sublime infinite, sublime attainment of the three liberations, definitely released from all obscurations by very nature, always abiding in equanimity like space, always passed beyond all stains of the afflictions, directly realizing the timeless three times, sublime great nāga of all sentient beings, the crown of those with crowns of qualities, primordially liberated from all afflictions or primordially liberated from all residues, fully abiding on the path of other space, other wish-fulfilling gem or holding that, sublime all-pervasive jewel, other wide great wish-granting tree, sublime other good vase, sublime agent, performer of benefit for all sentient beings, sublime benefit and affection for sentient beings, sublime knowing good and bad, sublime knowing timing, sublime knowing the sacred commitment of the pervasive lord, sublime knowing the good and bad of the pervasive lord, sublime possessing the sacred commitment of the pervasive lord, sublime knowing the time of the pervasive lord and knowing the sense faculties of sentient beings, expert in the three liberations, {198} possessing and knowing all the qualities of the good bhaga, sublime knowing all Dharma, sublime source of the good fortune of total peace, most sublime good fortune of all good fortune, fame of good fortune or excellent fame, sublime extensive renown, existent virtue or ultimate virtue or uncreated virtue, sublime great respite, sublime great celebration, sublime great music of great joy, basis of performing excellent honor and service, glory of sublime joy or utter joy, glory of the quintessence of great fame, chief of the sublime, chief giving the sublime, excellent refuge, sublime suitable to be the refuge, enemy of all great fears, utterly sublime enemy of great fears, reliever with all fears without exception primordially relieved, sublime topknot, sublime hair-tuft, [160] sublime with braids, sublime with twisted locks, sublime with a diadem of flax or a shaven head, sublime wearing a crown, sublime of the five families, sublime with a bald head, sublime holding great deliberate behavior, sublime deliberate behavior of celibate conduct, sublime perfection of austerity, sublime great austerity, sublime residing in purity, sublime Gautama, sublime brahmin, sublime Brahmā, sublime awareness or knowing of Brahmā, sublime having attained nirvāṇa as Brahmā, sublime body of liberation, sublime body of release, sublime body of total liberation, sublime peace of total liberation, conceptual elaborations primordially at peace, natural nirvāṇa, nirvāṇa in utter peace, definite release well finalized, basis removing or ending tainted pleasure and pain, sublime free of attachment, sublime beyond body or extinguishing labels or extinguishing appropriation, sublime invincible, sublime without example, sublime that is not manifest to and not apparent to and does not illuminate consciousness, sublime partless omnipresent all-pervasive, {199} sublime subtle and difficult to realize, sublime seed or ground of all phenomena, taintless basic element, sublime dustless free of dust and stainless, sublime with all faults primordially abandoned, sublime naturally flawless, sublime very wakened primordial awareness, fully wakened self of the true nature, sublime knowing all and aware of all, sublime beyond consciousness, mode of nondual primordial awareness, nonconceptual and spontaneous, sublime performing the actions of the buddhas of the three times, Buddha without beginning or end, Ādibuddha, integrated Buddha without [individual] continua [of means or wisdom] or partiality, unique eye of stainless primordial awareness, Tathāgata of embodied primordial awareness, lord of words, great speaker, sublime being of speech, king of speakers, excellent speaker, basis or ground of the sublime, sublime unharmable and invincible lion of speakers, sublime observed everywhere or seeing everywhere, primordially sublime joy, primordial garland of splendor, sublime beauty, naturally blazing good light, primordial endless knot, sublime bright and radiant illuminator, sublime great physician, chief of great physicians, unsurpassable remover of pain, sublime tree complete with all medicines without exception, sublime great enemy of all illnesses, [161] most sublime of the lovely three worlds (the other three states of cyclic existence), maṇḍala of the glorious constellations, ubiquitous victory banner of Dharma, encompassing all with a single wide sublime parasol of Dharma, sublime maṇḍala of love and compassion, glorious sovereign or lord of the lotus dance, pervasive lord who is the jeweled parasol of dharmakāya, great splendor or king of all buddhas, holding the essence of the self of all buddhas, great yoga of all buddhas, sole doctrine of all buddhas, sublime Vajraratna, sublime bestowal of glorious initiation, sublime quintessence of all jewels, {200} sublime lord of all jewels, sovereign of all lords of the world, lord of all vajra holders, great mind of all buddhas, abiding in the mind of all buddhas, great body of all buddhas, great speech of all buddhas, vajra sun (great appearance), vajra moon (stainless light), great desire that is the first freedom from desire, light blazing various colors, basis of vajra complete buddhahood, holding the Dharma of the speech of the buddhas, glorious Buddha born from a lotus, holding the treasury of omniscient primordial awareness, king holding various magical illusions, great holder of buddha awareness, sublime Vajratīkṣṇa, sublime great sword, sublime changeless purity, sublime Mahāyāna, sublime cutting off suffering, sublime great weapon, vajra Dharma, vajra profound, *jinajig* (or conqueror of conquerors), vajra intelligence, sublime awareness of objects as they are, all perfections primordially complete, all the levels of the true nature, possessing their ornaments, pure attribute, attribute without the selves, perfect primordial awareness, good moonlight of dharmadhātu, great diligence or great yoga of the true nature, Māyājāla of the true nature, sublime lord of all the tantras of the true nature, the consummation of all vajras or possessing all vajra seats or bases, holding all kāyas of primordial awareness without exception, Samantabhadra, good intelligence of the true nature, Kṣitigarbha with eyes everywhere, sublime holding living beings, buddha essence (sugata essence), sublime holding various wheels of emanation, sublime nature of all entities of the true nature, holding the nature of all entities of the true nature, unarisen true nature appearing as various objects, [162] holding the svābhāvika[kāya] of all phenomena, great wisdom comprehending all phenomena in just an instant, {201} sublime directly realizing all phenomena, sublime intelligence capable of the true nature, the apex of a being [of the true nature] or the apex of reality or the apex of existence or the apex of truth, excellent unfluctuating self, excellent utterly clear self, holding the enlightenment of a complete buddha, manifest to all buddhas, utterly bright flame of primordial awareness, and . . .[742]

(h) *Those stated as the primordial awareness of equanimity*

. . . excellent accomplisher of the desired goals, purifier of all lower realms or purifier of all faults, sublime protector of all sentient beings, utterly liberating all sentient beings, unique sattva victorious in battle over the afflictions, destroying the arrogance of the enemy that is unknowing or ignorance, possessing the intelligence of the true nature, sublime holding charm, sublime glorious, sublime or sattva of the stable true nature, sublime wrath bearing ugly forms, hands everywhere, feet everywhere, having all hands, sublime dancer, menses and sun naturally pure, semen and moon primordially pure, one meaning that is the meaning of the nondual dharma[kāya], indestructible ultimate, cognition of the true nature having sense objects of various forms, continuum of the mind of the true nature or existent mind, continuum of the consciousness of the true nature or existent consciousness, all meanings without exception of the actual entities of the true nature, all the joy of the true nature without exception, joy of the emptiness that is the very essence of the nonexistence of entities, passionate desire of the emptiness that is the very essence of the nonexistence of entities, intelligence of the emptiness that is the very essence of the nonexistence of entities, ground with the afflictions of cyclic existence primordially abandoned, great joy of the other three states of cyclic existence, white cloud of primordially pure semen, good autumn moonlight of the true nature, beautiful maṇḍala of the young sun of the true nature, {202} light of the nails of great passionate desire, sublime good azure hair locks of the true nature, bearing the great azure sublime hair of the true nature, glorious radiance of the great gem of the true nature, sublime having ornaments of the emanations of buddhas, sublime shaking all the hundreds of world systems, sublime possessing the great force of the bases for the miraculous, sublime bearing the great mindfulness of reality, sublime king of the four mindfulnesses, [163] king of all samādhis, fragrant flowers or joyous flowers of the limbs of enlightenment of dharmadhātu, ocean of qualities of the Tathāgata of the true nature, sublime awareness of the way of the eight limbs of the original path, sublime perfect awareness of the path of a buddha, sublime strongly attached to all sentient beings, sublime unattached like space, primordially penetrating the minds of all sentient beings, primordially quick other mind of all sentient beings, sublime knowing the objects of the sense faculties of all sentient beings, sublime captivating the minds of all sentient beings, sublime knowing the reality of the meaning of the five aggregates [of the true nature], sublime holding the pure five aggregates, sublime abiding at the end of all definite releases, sublime expert in all definite releases, sublime abiding on the path of all definite releases, sublime teaching all definite releases, sublime extracting the twelve limbs that are the root of cyclic existence, sublime bearing the twelve pure aspects, having the aspects of the four truths of the true nature, bearing realization of the eight knowledges of the true nature, having the twelve aspects of the meaning of the truth, knower of the sixteen aspects of [the joys of] reality, enlightened by means of the twenty aspects, sublime buddhahood aware of all, one who emits the infinite nirmāṇakāyas of all buddhas, sublime direct realization of all moments, sublime aware of all meanings in one mental moment, sublime benefiting all living beings by means of various vehicles, teaching definite release by means of the three vehicles yet primordially abiding in the single vehicle, self with karma and afflictions primordially extinguished, the river and the ocean and adherence [to cyclic existence] all primordially crossed over, {203} even the habitual propensities of the afflictions primordially abandoned, sublime great compassion, sublime wisdom and means, sublime actually existent, sublime performing benefit for living beings, meaning of the ground in which discrimination and consciousness have primordially ceased, object of the minds of all other sentient beings, sublime aware of the minds of all sentient beings, primordially residing in the minds of all sentient beings, engaging equally with their minds, satisfying the minds of all sentient beings, great joy abiding in the minds of all sentient beings, primordially established perfection without confusion, ground with all errors primordially abandoned, intelligence without doubt about the three benefits, self of three qualities beneficial to all, differentiating the aggregates and all the moments included in the three times, direct and complete buddhahood in one moment, holding the nature of all buddhas, [164] sublime body without body, primordially realizing the consummate body or emitting ten million kāyas, displaying everywhere all forms of the true nature without exception, jewel pinnacle of the great secret gem, and . . .[743]

(i) *Those stated as all-accomplishing primordial awareness*

. . . great secret to be realized by all buddhas, unsurpassable primordial enlightenment of the buddhas, ground without syllables that is the birthplace of secret mantra, the three families of great secret mantra, producer of all the meaning of secret mantra, great drop without [relative] syllables, the five syllables or five changeless great emptinesses, the six syllables or six changeless empty drops, having all aspects yet without aspect, primordially holding the four drops, partless beyond parts, primordially holding the peak or end of the fourth meditation of the true nature, knowing all limbs or parts of sublime meditation, sublime awareness of samādhis and awareness of their continuity, having a body of naturally established samādhi, {204} sublime body (body of thusness), king of all sambhogakāyas (sambhogakāya of thusness), sublime nirmāṇakāya (nirmāṇakāya of the true nature), bearing the continuity of emanations of the buddhas, emitting various emanations in the ten directions, exactly performing the benefit of living beings, god of gods (god of natural luminosity), sublime lord of gods (lord of the gods of the true nature), demigod lord of the true nature, generous lord of the true nature, immortal lord of the true nature, sublime master of gods (self-arisen primordial awareness), sublime destroyer (root destroying the incidental stains), lord of destroyers (nondual primordial awareness), or else that god of gods and so on who is the other Brahmā and Viṣṇu and Balavat and Rāhu and Śakra and Kilaka and Gaṇapati and Īśvara (Brahmā and so on of the true nature), naturally having crossed the wilderness of cyclic existence, unique teacher of living beings, unique master of living beings, sublime renowned in the ten directions of the world, sublime great patron of Dharma, sublime wearing the armor of love, sublime wearing the mail of compassion, bearing the sword and bow and arrow of wisdom, primordially removing the two obscurations in battle, enemy of the māras, sattva having primordially subdued the māras, removing fear of the four māras, defeating the armies of Māra, complete Buddha (guide of the world), [165] sublime worthy of worship and worthy of praise and object of homage, sublime always worthy of depiction, sublime worthy of honor and reverence, best master worthy of homage, traveling and covering the three worlds with one stride, sublime overcoming [worlds] limitless as space, sublime clean purity knowing the three,[744] possessing the most sublime of all qualities such as paranormal ability and subsequent mindfulness, self-arisen bodhisattva, mahāsattva of thusness, great magical emanation of the true nature, by very nature beyond the world, the apex of the perfection of wisdom, having obtained the reality of wisdom, aware of itself, aware of the other, having all [sense faculties in each one], {205} sublime being benefiting all, sublime beyond all exemplification or beyond worldly examples, sublime lord of other knowing and knowable objects, sublime chief patron of Dharma, sublime teacher of the meaning of the four mudrās,[745] sublime object of veneration for living beings, sublime [protector of] the three definite releases and those progressing, glorious pure excellent benefit, [glorious in] the three worlds of great good fortune, glorious creator of all wealth, sublime glorious Mañjuśrī, and . . .[746]

(j) *Those stated in homage to the five primordial awarenesses*
. . . sublime vajra giving the sublime, the apex of reality, arisen from emptiness or essence of emptiness, enlightenment of buddhas, attachment of buddhas, desire of buddhas, joy of buddhas, play of buddhas, smile of buddhas, laughter of buddhas, speech of buddhas, mind of buddhas, arisen from the true nature in which all phenomena do not exist, source of all buddhas, arisen from the space of the true nature, arisen from the primordial awareness of the true nature, Māyājāla of the true nature, displaying the play or performing the dance of the buddhas, present as the quintessence of all aspects in all places and times and situations, dharmakāya of self-arisen primordial awareness.[747] [166]

In that way, since it perfectly teaches the many synonymous names of the ultimate, this [tantra] is a witness and true authority for all tantras, perfectly expressing the very many, extremely many names of the ultimate that are synonymous, such as "ground empty of all phenomena," "true nature," and "thusness."

(k) *Showing that their meaning is identical to the emptiness of other*
Therefore, those who explain the meaning of this tantra to be a produced buddha and the truth of the path are not in accord with the intent of Vajradhara, {206} because those are relative, because this is the ultimate truth of cessation, and because it is not called *Chanting the "Relative" Names.*

Thus the meaning of these many synonyms (and many, so many similar to these also stated in other scriptures) is identical to the indivisible essence of the consummate ground and result with infinite taintless and inseparable qualities, the ubiquitous quintessence, the basic element of the ultimate great emptiness of other itself.

Therefore, in this context of teaching the profound consummate state, it is not appropriate to take a different meaning from merely a different name, and one should also not be confused by the notion that the intent of each different and distinct tantra is different and distinct, which is merely renowned to some.

(l) *Rejecting objections about that, and showing that it is actually existent*
It might be asked, "If the consummate ground and result are indivisible in essence, what use is the path?"

I will reply with a detailed explanation of this.

That which is self-arisen primordial awareness, ultimate truth always present pervading all, is no different in anyone as natural purity itself. Depending on the person, however, there is a difference of the incidental stains cleared or not cleared, like the single sky itself that is naturally clear and not the essence of the clouds, yet is not clear of clouds in some lands but clear in some.

Therefore, as there is no sky not clear of clouds in all lands, there is also no sky clear of clouds in all lands; depending on the land, however, it is not contradictory to say "not clear sky" and "clear sky."

Likewise, defining natural purity (the single ultimate basic element itself present in some persons as stained and present in some as unstained) as the ground or as the result depends on the stains existing or not existing in a person; a difference in the essence of the true nature does not exist.

Therefore, persons who have already abandoned all the incidental stains do not need to now again bring into experience the truth of the path, because they have completed the training, and because they have already obtained the kāya of ultimate primordial awareness. [167]

Persons other than those only need to correctly bring into experience the truth of the path, because that consummate Buddha is inherently present in them, but obscured by incidental stains and thus not obtained. {207}

In that way, cultivation of the path is also not to produce the dharmakāya as the result, because it is not appropriate for the naturally changeless and unconditioned basic element to be produced by any causes and conditions, and because it is always primordially, naturally, spontaneously present without having to be produced, and because if it existed yet had to be produced, the extremely absurd consequence would be that that would have to be done endlessly.

The *Mahāparinirvāṇa* also says:

> Son of good family, furthermore, there are two forms of causes: causes that create and causes that illuminate. Just as a potter's wheel is called a "cause that creates," so a lamp and so on that light a dark object are called "causes that illuminate" [what previously exists].
>
> Son of good family, great nirvāṇa is not established from a cause that creates, only a cause that illuminates.
>
> "Causes that illuminate" are like this: the thirty-seven factors conducive to enlightenment and the six perfections are called "causes that illuminate."[748]

And so on, it says extensively. That should be understood.

It might be said, "Well, if the path does not produce the dharmakāya, it is contradictory for that to be the result."

It is not contradictory, because obtaining the dharmakāya when the stains have been purified is the result of separation.

Even so, the two rūpakāyas are not primordially, inherently present, but must be produced by the assembly of merit. That being the case, in general, even the stated six causes and four conditions[749] are included in the two that separate the stains and that produce the entity, and even the stated five results[750] are included in the two of the result of separation and the result of production. Therefore, in particular, by means of the correct view one must carefully realize that the results of the path—the buddhas of the two truths, or the buddhas that exist and do not exist [in reality], or the buddhas of excellent benefit for oneself and benefit for others—also abide as two: the result of separation and the result of production.

Therefore, by means of the correct view one realizes that in which something does not exist and also realizes that which remains in that, because one realizes the difference between empty of self-nature and empty of other, because one realizes the difference between what is nonexistent and unestablished (merely isolated and ceased or cleared) and what is the ground of those, {208} because one realizes the difference between nonimplicative negation and implicative negation, exclusion and positive determination, and the natural abandonments and realizations, and because one realizes well the difference between the emptiness of own-entity and the emptiness of other entities, and empty emptiness and nonempty emptiness, and the emptiness of nonentities and the emptiness that is the very essence of the nonexistence of entities. [168]

(m) *A concluding summary by way of oral instruction*

That being so, after greatly compassionate experts striving for liberation have realized the ground of emptiness, the ultimate emptiness of other, they should also fully teach it to others, because if that is not realized, the primordial sublime Buddha will not be realized; and if that is not realized, *Chanting the Ultimate Names* will not be realized; and if that is not realized, Vajradhara's kāya of primordial awareness and the mantra vehicle will not be realized, so one will not be able to obtain the unsurpassable stage of a buddha bhagavān.

Referring to these points, the honorable Bhagavān Avalokiteśvara says:

> Taking *Chanting the Names* (by which sentient beings become without doubt) as authoritative, the Bhagavān thus perfectly taught the definitive meaning of all modes of mantra to Vajrapāṇi by means of the mantra vehicle in *Chanting the Names*.
>
> Therefore, one who does not know the *Sublime Ādibuddha* does not know *Chanting the Names*.
>
> One who does not know *Chanting the Names* does not know Vajradhara's kāya of primordial awareness.
>
> One who does not know Vajradhara's kāya of primordial awareness does not know the Mantra Vehicle.
>
> All those who do not know the Mantra Vehicle are saṃsāra beings and separated from the path of Bhagavān Vajradhara.
>
> That being so, excellent masters should teach the *Sublime Ādibuddha* and excellent disciples striving for liberation should listen.[751] {209}

And also summarizing the meaning of those many synonymous names, this same protector [Avalokiteśvara] says:

> Likewise, by means of one hundred and sixty-two verses (including the request) in *Chanting the Names*, the Tathāgata fully taught the sublimely unchanging primordial awareness of Bhagavān Vajradhara, which is the essence of buddhas and bodhisattvas.[752]

And so on, at the end of which he also states:

> These one hundred and sixty-two verses (drawing from all vehicles) perfectly summarize the essence of Bhagavān Vajradhara: totally good, sublimely unchanging great bliss, consummate element of space, totally illuminating, [169] accumulated assembly of pure primordial awareness, holding profound and vast form, naturally luminous, without beginning and end, free of the stains of concepts such as apprehended and apprehender of self and mine, [present] at all times, without defilement, knowing the nature of all phenomena, liberated from the habitual propensities of saṃsāra, free of going and coming, essence without conceptual elaborations, support of various samādhis and dhāraṇīs functioning and increasing by themselves, utterly fulfilling the aspirations

> of all sentient beings like the good vase and the wish-granting tree and the wish-fulfilling gem, not the field of experience of even the great sages, and sublimely pacifying sentient beings' great heap [of suffering] by means of [physical forms] like an illusion, like a dream, like a reflected image, like an echo. A yogin should not discard this sublimely unchanging bliss that is personally experienced through the yogin's primordial awareness and is to be worshiped by the three states of cyclic existence. This is the rule of the Tathāgata.[753] {210}

(3) *Showing that those stated in the* Mahāparinirvāṇa *and so on are also other than the emptiness of self-nature*

Likewise, the *Mahāparinirvāṇa* also states the synonyms of the ultimate ground of emptiness, because it says:

> Here, how are countless names explained from one name? As parinirvāṇa is also called "nirvāṇa," it is also called "unarisen," also called "without occurring," also called "without action," also called "unconditioned," also called "[consummate source of] taking refuge," also called "basis and support [of all phenomena]," also called "liberation," also called "illuminating light," also called "lamp," also called "culmination," also called "fearless," also called "irreversible," also called "basis of bliss," also called "peace," also called "without characteristic," also called "nondual," also called "sole activity," also called "utterly cool," also called "without darkness," also called "unimpeded," also called "indisputable," also called "great vastness," also called "elixir," and also called "auspicious." That is deriving countless names from [the meaning of] one name.[754]

And:

> Son of good family, the samādhi of heroic progress has five names. It is called "samādhi of heroic progress," also called "perfection of wisdom," also called "vajralike samādhi," also called "samādhi proclaiming the lion's roar," [170] and also called "buddha nature." Names are given in accord with what [faults do not exist] and

> what [qualities do exist] in this or that context, [so the names are limitless].[755]

Here also, the division of the two truths regarding samādhis must be understood. {211} The infinite, ultimate samādhis of heroic progress and so on are the buddha nature, the sugata essence itself. Moreover, that same sublime sūtra says:

> Furthermore, son of good family, "buddha nature" is the samādhi of heroic progress; with a nature like ghee, it is the mother of all buddhas.
>
> By the power of the samādhi of heroic progress the tathāgatas are permanent, bliss, self, and utter purity.
>
> All sentient beings also have the samādhi of heroic progress but do not see it because they have not meditated. Therefore, they have not become unsurpassingly, perfectly, completely enlightened.[756]

And so on, it says extensively. The *One Hundred and Eight Names of the Perfection of Wisdom* also states [the synonyms of the ultimate emptiness of other]:

> The mother of all past, future, and present
> conquerors (whoever they are) is you,
> virtuous lady. You are the [ultimate] goddess,
> the [true] child of the Conqueror,
>
> having the [ultimate] nature without the [relative]
> nature. The names of that mother of the buddhas,
> virtuous lady, I will express. One wishing to prosper
> [with the glory of the two assemblies] should listen:
>
> Perfection of wisdom, knowledge of all, knowledge of the aspects of the path, knowledge of all aspects, the apex of reality, thusness, unmistaken thusness, thusness that is not something else, truth, the real nature, reality, unmistakenness, emptiness, signlessness, wishlessness, the total nonexistence of entities, the very essence, the very essence of the nonexistence of entities, true nature, dharmadhātu, {212} constancy of phenomena, immutability

of phenomena, flawlessness of phenomena, characteristic of phenomena, selflessness of phenomena, without [relative] essence, without [relative] sentient being, without [relative] lifeforce, without [relative] nourishing being, without [relative] being, without [relative] person, [the ultimate] that is to be expressed, not [the relative] that is to be expressed, free of [relative] mind and mentation and consciousness, without equal, the same and not the same, nonexistence of self, without haughtiness, without conceptual elaboration, free of conceptual elaborations, free of all conceptual elaborations, very beyond all conceptual elaborations, mother of all buddhas, producing all bodhisattvas, gracing all śrāvakas, [171] creating all pratyekabuddhas, gracing all worlds, [natural] accumulation of an inexhaustible assembly of merit, descent of primordial awareness, performing magical emanations, cleansing the divine eyes, making the divine ears totally clear, knowing the minds of others, remembering previous places, remembering deaths and births, extinguishing all afflictions, noble, pure, accumulation, residing in the foundations of mindfulness, having the force of the perfect renunciations, having the feet of the four bases for the miraculous, cleansing the sense faculties, using the [five] powers, without flaws, beautified by the jewels of the seven limbs of enlightenment, granting the seven riches, {213} displaying the eight limbs of the noble path, displaying the nine sequential meditative absorptions, accomplishing the ten masteries, residing on the ten levels, utterly completing the ten powers, beautified by the ten sensory bases of totality, accomplishing the ten primordial awarenesses, destroying the enemy that is the ten tendencies, accomplishing the meditative states, perfectly beyond the formless realm, praised by all perfectly complete buddhas, using all knowledge, emptiness of the inner, emptiness of the outer, emptiness of the outer and the inner, emptiness of [the mind realizing] emptiness, emptiness of the great, emptiness of [what sees] the ultimate, emptiness of the conditioned, emptiness of the unconditioned, emptiness of the limitless, emptiness of beginningless and endless [saṃsāra], emptiness of what is not to be discarded, emptiness of the natural, emptiness of all attributes, emptiness of specific characteristics, emptiness of the unobservable, emptiness of nonentities, emptiness of very essence, emptiness that is the very essence of the nonexistence of entities, unoccurred, unarisen,

> unceasing, uninterrupted, without [impotent] permanence, not one thing, not a different thing, without coming, without going, [basis of] cultivation of [other] dependent arising, not to be totally analyzed, {214} not to be understood by consciousness, without the [universal-]ground [consciousness], without [conditioned] characteristics, not to be analyzed, not to be known [by consciousness], acting without destroying beginning and end, acting without fluctuation, without two [essences], [172] not without two [aspects], peace, abandonment of the mental engagement [of consciousness], without antidote, unsoiled, like the path of space, not expressed as [relatively] existent or [ultimately] nonexistent, the very essence of [the other] dream, true nature like an illusion, like a whirling firebrand, the one taste of all the [ultimate] attributes.[757]

And the *Jewel Lamp of the Madhyamaka* cites a quotation of the Bhagavān: "'Ultimate truth' is 'the eighteen emptinesses.'"[758] Those refer to the eighteen grounds of emptiness.

The *Little Text on the Perfection of Wisdom* also says:

> The ultimate, this perfection of wisdom producing all buddhas, is the mother of the bodhisattvas, instantly snatching away negativity, giving enlightenment.[759]

And so on. And the *One Hundred and Fifty Modes of the Perfection of Wisdom* also says:

> *Oṃ* vajra of bodhicitta, *oṃ* totally good conduct, *oṃ* wish-fulfilling gem, *oṃ* ceaselessness, *oṃ* eliminating birth, *oṃ* [other] consciousness [having all aspects], *oṃ* great true nature free of passionate desire, *oṃ* armor of diligence, *oṃ* omnipresence, *oṃ* vajra solid mind *hūṃ*, *oṃ* all [ultimate] tathāgatas, *oṃ* pure very essence, *oṃ* pure knowledge of the true nature.[760]

And it says, "*oṃ* perfection of wisdom" and "*oṃ* pure speech of all tathāgatas, *oṃ* vajra of the mind of all tathāgatas."[761] Such passages state the synonyms for the ground of emptiness, the ultimate sugata essence. And the *Jewel Cloud Sūtra* also says:

> Personally known by just those [noble ones], it is a stainless, unsoiled, pure, pristine, perfect, sublime, excellent, superb, permanent, stable, eternal, indestructible phenomenon. {215} And whether tathāgatas appear or do not appear, this dharmadhātu [the sugata essence] is simply there.[762]

And:

> Son of good family, that [sugata essence] is called "thusness," "the apex of reality," "knowledge of all," "knowledge of all aspects," "inconceivable basic element," "nondual basic element."[763]

And:

> Bhagavān, what is this called "reality"?
>
> "Son of good family," the Bhagavān replied, "that which is not deceptive is reality."
>
> Bhagavān, what is this called "not deceptive"?
>
> "It is thusness, unmistaken thusness, thusness that is not something else," the Bhagavān replied.[764] [173]

And so on. Likewise, the *Noble Sūtra on the Samādhi of the Miraculous Ascertainment of Utter Peace* also says:

> That which is not true is not thusness. That which is not thusness is not the Tathāgata. The Tathāgata is true, perfect thusness, unmistaken thusness, thusness that is not something else, a speaker of unmistaken truth, a speaker of reality, a speaker of knowledge, one who holds the weapon of primordial awareness, one who has limitless primordial awareness, an omniscient one, one who sees all, one having the ten powers, one who has attained the perfection of the excellent four types of fearlessness, one without thoughts and without concepts, one unsoiled [by consciousness], one who is similar to space, one who is unaccountable by calculations, one who is uncreated, unarisen, unceasing, without engagement [in the relative], limitless, not abiding [in the relative], not cognized [by consciousness], not an object of consciousness, totally without movement, utter purity, without afflictions,

> unarisen [from causes], without [conditioned] activity, not residing [in the relative].[765]

Thus it states synonyms for the ground of emptiness, thusness. And the *Mahāparinirvāṇa* translated by Lhai Dawa also says:

> That which is liberation is the [ultimate] Tathāgata, free of all [relative] forms and bonds, {216} unarisen, uncreated, without birth and death, without illness, unconditioned, without afflictions, taintless, peace, bliss, peerless, without misery, dustless, free of dust, not mushy, phenomenon without anything to be done, harmless, untroubled, not anything [tainted], amazing, miraculous, unarisen, infinite, sublime, superb, principal, best, highest, unsurpassable, certain, not a destructible phenomenon, limitless, not demonstrable, profound, difficult to view, without afflictions, flawless kāya, purity, liberation, peace, utter peace, transcendent, good, free of all faults, free of the three poisons, cessation, basis, refuge, defender, fearless, [ground] for the destruction of the basis [or universal-ground consciousness], without pride, abandonment of all that is an essence, [dharma]dhātu, virtue, ultimate, unfluctuating, very refined, consummate, uncontrived bliss, abandonment of the aggregates, annihilation of the path, [ultimate] emptiness, exhaustion of craving, the [ultimate] Buddha, inexhaustible nirvāṇa. All those are also that which is liberation, the Tathāgata.[766] [174]

After presenting these as synonyms, it states (with reliable reasons) that each also perfectly transcends conditioned phenomena, so that very sūtra should be consulted for details. {217}

The *Compendium of the Mahāyāna* also says:

> Natural purity is like this: thusness, emptiness, the apex of reality, signlessness, the ultimate, and also dharmadhātu.
>
> Since it is without stains, purity is like this: that very [natural purity] not having any obscurations.[767]

And the *Glorious Vajra Garland Tantra* also says:

[The true nature] pervading all phenomena,
utterly destroying all afflictions,
without stains, free of stains, pure, the sublime
stage of self-awareness,

having the nature of the Ādibuddha,
causes the five [natural] families to expand.[768]

And:

[The other] consciousness,
dharmadhātu, ultimate, great bliss,
liberated from apprehended and apprehender,
stainless bodhicitta,

Vajrasattva, great peace, nondual,
perfect, marvelous, bliss of the fourth
bestowal of initiation, sublime stage
of the joy of the fourth.

By specific names such as those,
the sublime [androgynous] stage is stated.[769]

And:

In the two syllables called *evaṃ*,
e is said to be emptiness [wisdom],
and, likewise, *vaṃ* to be compassion, means.
The drop arises from the union of those two.

That is the arisen marvelous, sublime yoga.

The buddhas speak the pair *e vaṃ*
at the beginning in tantras, to summarize
the great king [of Dharma], [mahā]mudrā
itself, by means of the mudrā of Dharma.[770]

And:

> *E* is the secret, the element of space,
> or bhaga, source of the attributes, lotus,
> and [vajra]yoga, residing on the lion seat,
> teaching the sublimely marvelous.
>
> Having names such as Vajrasattva,
> *vaṃ*, and vajra, Vajrabhairava,
> [Vajra] Īśvara, and Heruka, Kālacakra,
> and Ādibuddha,
>
> *evaṃ* is the mudrā of the tathāgatas,
> symbolizing nondual [means and wisdom],
> and in those [tantras] of indivisible emptiness
> and compassion, which directly express reality,
>
> the mudrā of the tathāgatas [is stated]. The symbols
> [*evaṃ*, *ahaṃ*, etc.] of nondual primordial awareness
> are stated in the settings of the discourses of all tantras.
> Where the summary of all tantras, {218}
>
> undivided emptiness and compassion,
> reality, is directly expressed is the
> two syllables called *evaṃ*. That which
> is without these two
>
> is without reality. By just that,
> one who fully knows these two
> will clearly recognize wrong explanations
> of tantra, like fake gold.
>
> Residing in the conduct of mantra, in that way
> the perfect sublime [meaning of *evaṃ*] is in this [tantra].[771] [175]

And the *Precept of Mañjuśrī* says:

> In that way, after the ritual of meditation
> for the perfect arising of the observation

of those infinite, superb, excellent [qualities]
of the thusness of all phenomena has been explained,

the synonyms will also be fully taught:
thusness, the apex of reality,
inconceivable basic element, true nature,
and flawless phenomenon,

emptiness, and signlessness, and
wishlessness, and also what rejects
the mechanism of the afflictions,
unarisen, luminous,

direct enlightenment, and
what knows the minds of others,
divine hearing, and what grants
the natural divine eye,

what radiates infinite magical
emanations, culmination of entities,
ultimate truth, [the other, natural]
completion stage,

utterly pure [naturally] clean kāya,
to be relied on by all [noble beings],
[naturally] pristine like space,
[essence] unsoiled by incidental stains,

primordially pure luminosity itself,
not destructible by anything. That
essence [of the true nature] is stated
and will be perfectly stated with

limitless [names] like those in the sūtras
and tantras; they do not refer to anything
other than this thusness.[772]

And:

The lord [true nature], sublime Vajra Holder,
[the other] yogin of the completion stage,
having done what was to be done, having done
what is to be done, [the other] Maheśvara

with mind untroubled by the great burden,
omniscient one, heroic being knowing
everything, the great elephant, the tamer,
[naturally] gone beyond the end of saṃsāra,

great yogin of the nonduality of the truths
of ultimate [essence] and relative [aspects],
wrath [naturally] abandoned or all paths complete,
totally good source of qualities, {219}

reality that includes everything,
filling all realms with bodies and so on,
the perfect base with nothing higher,
that [profound meaning] renowned by those

and other limitless names that symbolize
nondual primordial awareness in all
the sūtras and tantras, should be understood
by the wise.[773]

And the *Vast Commentary on the "Extensive Mother Sūtra"* also says:

"Thusness," "dharmadhātu," "the apex of reality," "equanimity," "inconceivable basic element," and "immovable" are included among the synonyms for the emptiness of dharmadhātu.[774]

And:

[Changeless] fully established phenomena are transcendent, unarisen, ceaseless, primordially peaceful, naturally parinirvāṇa, the very essence of the nonexistence of entities, [nonempty] emptiness, and so on.[775]

And the root text and commentary of the *Uttaratantra* also say:

> Beginning from the meaning of the indivisibility of the tathāgata essence that is the culmination of extreme purification in this phase of being extremely pure, a verse says [176]:
>
> > Since it is the dharmakāya, the Tathāgata,
> > the ultimate truth of noble beings, and nirvāṇa,
> > there is no nirvāṇa except buddhahood itself,
> > since its qualities are indivisible, like the sun
> > and its rays.[776]
>
> Here, what is taught by the first half of the verse?
>
> > In brief, since it is classified as
> > fourfold in meaning, the taintless
> > basic element should be known by
> > four synonyms, such as "dharmakāya."[777]
>
> In summary, in the context of four meanings for the taintless basic element, the tathāgata essence, four synonymous names should be known. What are the four meanings?
>
> > The indivisibility of the buddha attributes,
> > its [natural] family having been obtained just as it is,
> > the true nature without falsity and deception,
> > and being primordial, natural peace.[778]
>
> And the *Glorious Guhyasamāja* also says:
>
> > The three times are that which is vajra mind,
> > [the other] cyclic existence, and the apex
> > [of reality], peaceful and unobscured space,
> > the pure essence itself, vast buddhahood,
> > enlightenment, sovereignty, the Vajra Bearer,
> > to which I always bow down with body, speech,
> > and mind. {220}
> >
> > To that which is all form, feeling, discrimination,
> > conditioning factors, and consciousness, the six
> > sensory bases, the six sense faculties, earth, water,
> > fire, wind, and space, immense like bodhicitta,
> > I bow down.[779]

Just exactly as such passages say the ground of emptiness, the ultimate sugata essence, the pure self, the omnipresent dharmadhātu has very many synonymous names, so also does the noble, honorable Lokeśvara say:

> Nondual, unfluctuating, and without partiality,
> desirable, sublimely unchanging, and great passionate
> desire, without [relative] entity [existing] and
> [ultimate] entity not existing, primordial awareness,
>
> and sattva, totally good, without [relative] affliction,
> and [ultimate] great affliction, connate, glorious,
> and bodhicitta, holder of the drops, glorious Kālacakra,
> vajra, quintessence of means and wisdom, and yoga.[780]

And:

> In the mantra approach, *evaṃ* alone is not the name for this [ultimate truth]; even one entity has many names.
>
> Because of the many names, one name alone is not primary, since all the names cause understanding of one entity.
>
> For example, of woman, female, and girl, woman alone is not the primary name, since all cause understanding of an entity with breasts and hair.
>
> Likewise, of the names syllable *e*, [great] secret, lotus, source of the attributes, element of space, basis of great bliss, lion throne, bhaga, and secret—syllable *e* alone is not the primary name, since all cause understanding of emptiness having all aspects. [177]
>
> Likewise, of the names syllable *vaṃ*, great bliss, great desire, connate, sublimely unchanging, drop, reality, primordial awareness, {221} and pure mind—syllable *vaṃ* alone is not the primary name, since all also cause understanding of mahāmudrā, connate joy, changeless bliss.
>
> Likewise, since both syllable *e* and syllable *vaṃ* cause understanding of the entity of bodhicitta in which emptiness having the most sublime of all aspects and nonreferential compassion for all phenomena are indivisible, by many names such

as these—the syllables *evaṃ*, Vajrasattva, bodhicitta, Kālacakra, Ādibuddha, quintessence of wisdom and means, union, quintessence of knowing and knowable object, nondual, without beginning and end, peace, Samāja, and Saṃvara—a yogin should realize the quintessence of wisdom and means, the nondual yoga without partiality.[781]

And:

> Likewise, whatever entities the Tathāgata definitely presents in various tantras, and the compilers also write (with the terms of the treatises, regional terms, terms of the mantra syllables, and terms of the individual syllables), yogins should understand them all by means of provisional meaning and definitive meaning.
>
> Here, for just a single [meaning], there are various terms [used from the perspective] of the [existent] entity [of qualities] and the nonexistent entity [of faults]. Therefore, just one entity is indicated by various terms, but yogins should not conceptualize about the terms. With the esoteric instructions of excellent masters they fully examine well, as with gold, through depending on reliance on the meaning.[782]

And so on. Furthermore, fearing it would take too many words, I have not written here the various statements in many—a great many—very pure sūtras, tantras, and treatises, where that ground of emptiness, dharmadhātu penetrating all, the consummate profound abiding state itself, is called by the many different names of deities, maṇḍalas, syllables, hand implements, and so on, and by a very great many different names from the perspective of the complete infinite qualities of the abandonments and realizations. {222} These can also be understood through just the reasoning and esoteric instructions presented before. So one should also extensively consult other stainless textual traditions of definitive meaning and, comprehending the profound true nature in which the meaning of many names is one taste and the essence of many aspects is one taste, also correctly fully teach it to other worthy recipients. [178]

b. *The purpose of the synonyms*

Correctness of the Explanation says there are eight purposes for [the Buddha] to teach a single meaning through many synonymous names in that way:

> What are the purposes here? There are eight purposes, since statements of synonyms are for different persons to be trained: to cause some people to understand a certain meaning at that time or in a future life; to teach that meaning by way of a synonym because others would criticize it if that expression [were spoken] to people who are distracted at that time; to cause those who are not intelligent to not forget, by perfectly indicating that meaning again and again; to remove ideas about different meanings, because many names occur for one meaning; to perfectly establish that meaning by way of those names in other [contexts], like the correct formation of terms; to enable those who proclaim the Dharma to be expert in both explanation of the meaning and causing understanding; to demonstrate that [the Buddha] himself has the analytical perfect awareness of phenomena; and to produce the seeds for that in others.
>
> All acts of explanation also cause understanding in students through explanations of synonyms, so that which has such a nature does not entail the fault of repetition.[783] {223}

3. *How an ultimate other than the emptiness of self-nature is established by statements about the pure forms of the true nature, up to the knowledge of all aspects*

This has ten topics.

a. *A brief presentation of the pure forms and so on of the true nature*

In that way, the ground of emptiness, thusness having many synonyms, is the pure ground primordially isolated from and empty of all incidental phenomena. Therefore, it is also the phenomena of primordially pure forms, ending with the knowledge of all aspects. And of the three sets stated when dividing forms (up to the attributes of a buddha) into the three essences, it is the forms and so on of the fully established true nature, and the forms and so on beyond the three realms and the three times. And it is what the *Glorious Hevajra* mentions:

> Definitively, the purity of
> all entities is called "thusness."
> Later, by the divisions of each,
> that of the deities will be expressed.[784]

Likewise, it is what the venerable lord, honorable Maitreyanātha, also mentions [179]:

> The purity of the result is just the purity
> of form and so on. Why? Since those
> two are not different and are indivisible,
> they are called "pure."[785]

And the Conqueror's Mother Sūtras also say, "Subhūti, that which is the purity of form is the purity of the result,"[786] and so on, which is applied up to the knowledge of all aspects. And:

> That which is the purity of form is the utter purity of the perfection of wisdom; that which is the utter purity of the perfection of wisdom is the utter purity of form. And that being so, the utter purity of form and this utter purity of the perfection of wisdom are nondual, without dualistic activity, not individual, not different.[787] {224}

And so on, which is applied up to the knowledge of all aspects. And applied in a similar way, those that are the purity and utter purity of self, sentient being, lifeforce, nourishing being, being, person, Manu, human, agent, feeler, knower, and observer are "the purity and utter purity of form," and so on, which is applied individually up to the knowledge of all aspects.

And those that are the purity and utter purity of passionate desire, hatred, and ignorance are "the purity and utter purity of form," up to the knowledge of all aspects, which is extensively applied individually.

And because of the purity of unknowing, there is the purity of conditioning factors; because of the purity of conditioning factors, there is the purity of unknowing. With "and that being so," and so on, because of the purity of the former, there is the purity of the latter, and because of the purity of the latter, there is the purity of the former, is extensively applied up to the knowledge of all aspects.

Likewise, because of the purity of the perfection of wisdom, there is the purity of form, and because of the purity of form, there is the purity of the knowledge of all aspects. With "and that being so," and so on, this is applied up to feeling conditioned by contact that is mentally compounded.

Likewise, because of the purity of the perfection of meditation, and so on, up to the purity of the knowledge of all aspects, there is the purity of form, up to feeling conditioned by contact that is mentally compounded; because of the purity of feeling conditioned by contact that is mentally compounded, there is the purity of the knowledge of all aspects itself. With "and that being so," and so on, this is extensively applied individually.

Likewise, because of the purity of the knowledge of all aspects itself, there is the purity of form; because of the purity of form, there is the purity of the perfection of wisdom. With "and that being so," and so on, {225} this is extensively applied up to feeling conditioned by contact that is mentally compounded, and up to the perfection of generosity. [180]

Furthermore, "Because of the purity of conditioned phenomena, there is the purity of unconditioned phenomena. And, that being so, the purity of conditioned phenomena and the purity of these unconditioned phenomena is nondual, without dualistic activity, not individual, not different."

Likewise, "Because of the purity of the past, there is the purity of the future and the present, and that being so," and so on. And "Because of the purity of the future, there is the purity of the past and the present, and . . . ," and so on. "Because of the purity of the present, there is the purity of the past and the future, and that being so," and so on are applied. Likewise, "Because of the purity of form, purity is profound" is applied up to the knowledge of all aspects. And "Because of the purity of the perfection of wisdom, purity is light" is applied to the perfection of meditation and so on, up to the knowledge of all aspects. And "Form, without transference and without natal conception, is pure" is applied up to the knowledge of all aspects. And "Because form is naturally luminous, it is pure, without defilement" is applied up to the knowledge of all aspects. And "Form, not to be obtained and not to be directly realized, is pure" is applied up to the knowledge of all aspects. And "[The ground of relative] form that is not directly established is the purity of [form]" is applied up to the knowledge of all aspects. After teaching, again [the Buddha] states, "Subhūti, because of its extreme purity, and because of the nonexistence of the selves, [the ground of] the nonexistence of form is extremely pure," and so on, applying that very extensively.

Here there are two types of purity: primordially, naturally pure, and purified of the incidental stains. {226} Also, the primordially, naturally pure is purified of that which is imaginary and dependent (relative form and so on), because those phenomena are totally nonexistent and not established in the abiding state of reality, like the child of a barren woman. The ground, the forms and so on of the ultimate true nature that are purified of those, is never nonexistent, because—whether relative tathāgatas appear in the world or do not appear, and whether living beings are aware or are not aware—those are always present as the pure forms and so on, and furthermore, present as the assemblies of the ultimate deities of primordial awareness. [181]

b. *Extensive explanation applying those to mantra*
This has eighteen topics.

1) *How the pure five aggregates of the true nature always reside as the five conquerors and the five primordial awarenesses*
The pure ground—that which is the purity of the aggregate of form or the pure aggregate of form—is the ultimate deity of primordial awareness, Vairocana, who is mirrorlike primordial awareness. Likewise, the pure aggregates of feeling, discrimination, conditioning factors, and consciousness are also Ratnasambhava, Amitābha, Amoghasiddhi, and Akṣobhya, who are the primordial awareness of equanimity, that which is discriminating, that which is all-accomplishing, and that of the very pure dharmadhātu. Also concerning those:

> The aggregate of form is Vajrā,
> and feeling is also called Gaurī.
> Discrimination is Vāriyoginī,
> conditioning factors are Vajraḍākinī.
>
> The mode of the aggregate of
> consciousness resides as Nairātmyā yoginī.[788]

That statement also has the same meaning, {227} as does "holding the pure five aggregates."[789]

2) *How the pure sense faculties of the true nature reside as the ultimate children of the conquerors*
Likewise, the pure eyes, ears, nose, tongue, body, and mind are the ultimate deities Kṣitigarbha, Vajrapāṇi, Khagarbha, Lokeśvara, Nīvaraṇaviṣkambhin,

and Samantabhadra, and they are Mohavajrā, Dveṣavajrā, Mātsaryavajrā, Rāgavajrā, Īrṣyavajrā, and Nairātmyā yoginī.

3) *How the pure six objects of the true nature reside as the ultimate female bodhisattvas*

Likewise, pure form, sound, odor, taste, tangible objects, and the element of phenomena are Rūpavajrā, Śabdavajrā, Gandhavajrā, Rasavajrā, Sparśavajrā, and Dharmadhātuvajrā, and they are the six of vajra form and so on. Also, those have the same meaning as in this statement:

> Form is always explained as Gaurī.
> Sound is well known as Caurī.
> The aspect of odor is Vetālī.
> Taste is well known as Ghasmarī.
>
> Contact is explained as Bhūcarī.
> The element of phenomena is Khecarī.[790] [182]

4) *How the pure thirty-six aggregates of the true nature reside as the ultimate conquerors*

Likewise, the primordially pure six consciousnesses (such as eye consciousness) are Kṣitigarbha Akṣobhya, Vajrapāṇi Akṣobhya, Khagarbha Akṣobhya, Lokeśvara Akṣobhya, Nīvaraṇaviṣkambhin Akṣobhya, and Samantabhadra Akṣobhya—the other consciousnesses divided according to the six vajra sense faculties, the six vajra consciousnesses.

Likewise, the other six contacts, the pure six contacts such as that conditioned by contact that is visually compounded, are included in the ultimate aggregate of conditioning factors, just as the six relative contacts are included in the relative aggregate of conditioning factors. {228} The primordially pure six feelings, such as feeling conditioned by contact that is visually compounded, are Kṣitigarbha Ratnasambhava, Vajrapāṇi Ratnasambhava, Khagarbha Ratnasambhava, Lokeśvara Ratnasambhava, Nīvaraṇaviṣkambhin Ratnasambhava, and Samantabhadra Ratnasambhava—the other feelings, the six vajra feelings.

Likewise, the honorable Bhagavān Lokeśvara also says:

> The six aggregates, divided according to the six sense faculties, become thirty-six aggregates in this way: . . . the six consciousnesses (ear consciousness and so on) and, likewise, the six

> conditioning factors, the six feelings, the six discriminations, the six aggregates of form, and the six aggregates of primordial awareness are the manifestations of the aggregates.[791]

Because thirty-six ultimate aggregates of the true nature that are other than relative outer and inner phenomena are thus stated, the discrimination of the eyes (and the discriminations of the ears, nose, tongue, body, and mind) that are pure by very essence are Kṣitigarbha Amitābha, Vajrapāṇi Amitābha, Khagarbha Amitābha, Lokeśvara Amitābha, Nīvaraṇaviṣkambhin Amitābha, and Samantabhadra Amitābha—the other discriminations, the six vajra discriminations.

Likewise, the conditioning factors of the eyes (and the conditioning factors of the ears, nose, tongue, body, and mind) that are pure by very essence are Kṣitigarbha Amoghasiddhi, Vajrapāṇi Amoghasiddhi, Khagarbha Amoghasiddhi, Lokeśvara Amoghasiddhi, Nīvaraṇaviṣkambhin Amoghasiddhi, and Samantabhadra Amoghasiddhi—the other conditioning factors, the six vajra conditioning factors. [183]

Likewise, the naturally pure forms of the eyes, ears, nose, tongue, body, and mind are Kṣitigarbha Vairocana, Vajrapāṇi Vairocana, Khagarbha Vairocana, Lokeśvara Vairocana, Nīvaraṇaviṣkambhin Vairocana, and Samantabhadra Vairocana—the other aggregates of form, the six vajra aggregates of form.

Likewise, the primordially pure primordial awareness of the eyes (and the primordial awarenesses of the ears, of the nose, of the tongue, of the body, and of the mind) are Kṣitigarbha Vajrasattva, Vajrapāṇi Vajrasattva, Khagarbha Vajrasattva, Lokeśvara Vajrasattva, {229} Nīvaraṇaviṣkambhin Vajrasattva, and Samantabhadra Vajrasattva—the other primordial awarenesses, the six vajra aggregates of primordial awareness.

In that way, the primordially pure six discriminations, six conditioning factors, six forms, and six primordial awarenesses are stated in various scriptures; in this section I have discussed them in a digression.

5) *How the pure six elements of the true nature reside as the six ultimate female tathāgatas*

Now let us return to the point where the basic topics were being explained before. That which is the naturally pure element of earth is Buddhalocanā. Likewise, the elements of water, fire, wind, space, and consciousness are also

Māmakī, Pāṇḍarā, Tārā, Vajradhātvīśvarī, and Viśvamātā. Also, the first four have the same meaning as a statement in the *Hevajra Tantra*:

> Earth is explained as Pukkasī.
> The element of water is called Śavarī.
> Fire is known as Caṇḍālinī.
> Wind is well known as Ḍombī.[792]

In this way, that which is the ground empty of the imaginary and the dependent aggregates, elements, and so on, and which is the aggregates, elements, and so on of the fully established true nature, is the primordially pure and utterly pure aggregates, elements, and so on.

6) How the pure twelve limbs of the true nature reside as the ultimate levels, the twelve aspects of the meaning of the truth, and so on

Likewise, that which is the ground purified of the relative ignorance and so on included in the imaginary and the dependent, and which is the twelve, such as the ultimate ignorance of the true nature, is the twelve aspects of the meaning of the truth, {230} the twelve ultimate levels, the twelve sacred places and so on, the essence of the four kāyas, the qualities of the four vajras, the twelve faces, and so on. [184]

Furthermore, the *Glorious Stainless Light* says:

> The twelve truths are [the other] ignorance, conditioning factors, consciousness, name and form, the six sensory bases, contact, feeling, craving, appropriation, becoming, birth, and aging and death. The twelve truths of beings born from wombs include obscuration, but those of the buddhas are free of obscuration.
>
> Because the lifeforce wind circulates due to the divisions of the lifeforce of the twelve transits, [the twelve truths] of beings born from wombs include obscuration, but those of the buddhas are free of obscuration, because the twelve limbs [of cyclic existence] have ceased.[793]

Thus it is stated that the essence of the twelve aspects of the meaning of the truth is present without difference in buddhas and sentient beings, but due to having separated or not separated from the incidental obscurations through the winds of the twelve rising signs having ceased or not ceased, there is a difference of obtaining and not obtaining them.

Furthermore, this is the meaning of the statement in *Chanting the Ultimate Names*:

> With the twelve limbs, the root of cyclic existence,
> extracted, he bears the twelve pure aspects.[794]

And:

> Having the twelve aspects of the meaning of the truth.[795]

The *Stainless Light* also says:

> In that way, the three qualities for the primordial-awareness vajra are ignorance, conditioning factors, and consciousness. For the body vajra, they are name and form, the six sensory bases, and contact. For the speech vajra, they are feeling, craving, and appropriation. For the mind vajra, they are becoming, birth, and aging and death. These are due to the power of the form of the drops.
>
> In that way, ignorance and so on are produced, but "the primordial-awareness vajra that causes sublime bliss is the fourth"[796] indicates the womb of mantras, the body, speech, mind, and primordial-awareness vajras with the twelve aspects everywhere. This is the rule of the Bhagavān.[797] {231}

Thus ignorance and so on, the qualities of the four vajras, are said to be the twelve aspects of the meaning of the truth, the womb of ultimate mantras. Furthermore, these should be understood to be pure ignorance and so on; relative ignorance and so on are not pure, because they are incidental stains.

In [the section on] the glorious binding of the six cakras, it also says:

> By the cessation of the twelve limbs,
> due to the interruption of the flow of [the breaths
> of] the rising signs, the levels renowned as twelve,
> the sacred places and so on, are the ultimate.[798]

And so on, it states extensively. And the *Glorious Hevajra Tantra* also says:

> The sacred places and nearby sacred
> places, fields and nearby fields, Chandoha
> and nearby Chandoha, likewise areas
> and nearby areas for congregation,
> Pīlava and nearby Pīlava, charnel grounds
> and nearby charnel grounds;
> these are the twelve levels.[799] [185]

Here the reversal of the charnel grounds and the Pīlavas indicates [the need for] dependence on an excellent master who has the esoteric instructions of the root tantra.

The *Sublime Ādibuddha* also says:

> By the cessation of the twelve limbs,
> there are the twelve gates. Likewise,
> due to the [ultimate] twelve levels,
> there are the beautiful pediments.[800]

And so on. Therefore, after understanding the division of the two truths also for the twelve limbs, it should be known that that in which something does not exist is purified of it, and that which is the pure ground has the meaning of the purity and utter purity of the twelve limbs. {232}

7) *How the pure perfections of the true nature reside as the ultimate śaktīs, vidyās, ḍākinīs, and mudrās*

Likewise, if the divisions of the three essences and the two truths are also understood for the perfections of generosity and so on, one will not be deluded about the Sage's word.

Here the perfections included in the dependent ground empty of the imaginary, and in the truth of the path, are relative conditioned phenomena. Therefore, it is said that they are not established in the abiding state of reality. The perfections of generosity and so on included in the fully established true nature and the truth of cessation, that which is the ground primordially purified of those [relative phenomena], are said to be the ten śaktīs, the ten ḍākinīs, and so on, the ultimate deities of primordial awareness. Moreover, because these are also said to be the six mudrās, the three, and the one (the ten consummate mudrās), one should know the meaning of the purity and utter purity of the perfections of generosity and so on of the true nature to be the naturally spontaneous deities.

8) *How all the pure emptinesses of the true nature reside as the ultimate deities, compassion, and great bliss*
This has five topics.

a) *Carefully determining all emptinesses to be the two: emptiness of self-nature and emptiness of other*
Likewise, the eighteen and the twenty stated emptinesses are condensed into the sixteen. Moreover, the honorable conqueror Maitreya says:

> The emptiness of the consumer,
> of the consumed, of the body of those,
> and of the fundamental basis. Moreover,
> what sees, how, and for which, are also emptiness.
>
> In order to obtain the two virtues,
> in order to always benefit sentient beings,
> in order to not discard saṃsāra,
> in order to not exhaust virtue, [186]
>
> in order to also purify the family,
> in order to obtain the major marks and minor marks,
> and in order to purify the attributes of a buddha—
> bodhisattvas practice.[801] {233}

(1) The emptiness of the consumer is the inner sensory bases, which enjoy objects. (2) The emptiness of the consumed is the outer sensory bases, which are to be enjoyed. (3) The body of those is the basis or vessel of both the consumer and the consumed, and its emptiness is the emptiness of the outer and the inner. (4) The fundamental basis is the vast world of the environment, and its emptiness is the emptiness of the great. (5) In that way, *what sees* those inner sensory bases and so on to be empty? Knowledge of emptiness sees, and its emptiness is the emptiness of emptiness. Therefore, this teaches that knowledge realizing emptiness is also emptiness; assertions other than that are not the intent of the conquerors. (6) Likewise, *how* are they seen? They are seen to be aspects of the ultimate; its emptiness is emptiness of the ultimate. This also teaches that knowledge seeing the aspects of the ultimate

to be emptiness; it does not teach the ultimate to be the emptiness of self-nature. (7–8) Those *for which* bodhisattvas practice are also emptiness. Here there are eight aspects: Bodhisattvas practice in order to obtain the two virtues that are conditioned and unconditioned, which are the emptiness of the conditioned and the emptiness of the unconditioned. (9) Bodhisattvas practice in order to always benefit sentient beings, which is the emptiness of what transcends extremes. (10) Bodhisattvas practice in order to not discard saṃsāra, which is the emptiness of the beginningless and endless. (11) Bodhisattvas practice in order to never exhaust virtue, which is the emptiness of what is not to be discarded. (12) Bodhisattvas practice in order to purify even the natural family, which is the emptiness of the natural. (13) Bodhisattvas practice in order to obtain the major marks and minor marks of a buddha, which is the emptiness of specific characteristics. Explaining this to be the characteristics of conditioned phenomena is not in accord with the intent of the Conqueror, because the *Glorious Sampuṭa Tantra* also speaks in accord with this. (14) Bodhisattvas practice in order to purify the primordially pure attributes of a buddha, such as the powers and the types of fearlessness, which is the emptiness of all attributes.

In that way, the first four (of the consumer and so on) derive from knowable entities. {234} Moreover, *what sees* and *how* those are seen derive from the subject seeing emptiness and the aspects of the ultimate, which are the fifth and the sixth. [187] Those that derive from those *for which* bodhisattvas practice are the seventh and so on, ending with the fourteenth. In that way, having provisionally classified the fourteen emptinesses here, the meaning or characteristics of how they are empty is stated:

> Here the nonexistence of entities
> of persons and phenomena is emptiness.
> The existent entity of the nonexistence
> of entities is an emptiness other than that.[802]

Here, because all entities included among persons and phenomena are totally nonexistent and not established in the abiding state, they are each empty of own-essence, which is relative emptiness, and without appearance to the awareness of the abiding state. Because the ground empty of those phenomena, the essence of the true nature forever present, is not empty of itself but is empty of all incidental phenomena, it is the ultimate emptiness of other, with appearance to the awareness of the abiding state.

(15) In that way, the fifteenth, the emptiness of nonentities, is the meaning

of the repeated statement "That in which something does not exist is empty of it," which is the emptiness of own-entity, the relative emptiness of self-nature. (16) The sixteenth, the emptiness that is the very essence of the non-existence of entities, is the meaning of the repeated statement "That which remains in that permanently exists in this," which is the emptiness of other entities, the ultimate emptiness of other.

These meanings are also stated in the king of tantras, the *Later Tantra of the Glorious Sampuṭa*, and in the *Commentary on "Distinguishing the Middle and the Extremes."* Just as [that commentary] says:

> Here, emptiness of the consumer derives from the inner sensory bases. Emptiness of the consumed is that of the outer [objects]. The body of those, that which is the basis of both consumer and consumed, is the vessel. Its emptiness is called "the emptiness of the outer and the inner." The fundamental basis is the world of the environment; because that is vast, its emptiness is called "emptiness of the great." *What sees* those inner sensory bases and so on to also be empty? Knowledge of emptiness [sees], and its emptiness is the emptiness of emptiness. The emptiness of *how* they are seen to be aspects of the ultimate is the emptiness of the ultimate. Those [eight] *for which* bodhisattvas practice are also emptiness. {235} Why do they practice? It is said, "In order to obtain the two virtues." The two virtues are conditioned and unconditioned. "In order to always benefit sentient beings" means in order to permanently benefit sentient beings. "In order to not discard saṃsāra" means if beginningless and endless saṃsāra is not seen to be emptiness, one will become weary and utterly discard saṃsāra. [188] "In order to not exhaust virtue" means even in nirvāṇa without remaining aggregates, [virtue] is not to be discarded and not to be rejected. "In order to also purify the family" is said because the family is the natural [family], the svābhāvika[kāya]. "In order to obtain the major marks and minor marks" means in order to obtain the major marks of a great being, together with the fine minor marks. "Bodhisattvas practice in order to purify the attributes of a buddha" refers to the [ultimate] powers, the types of fearlessness, the unshared attributes, and so on. In that way, the classification of the fourteen emptinesses should be understood here. Here, what is [the meaning of] emptiness?

> Here the nonexistence of entities
> of persons or phenomena is emptiness.
> The existent entity of the nonexistence
> of entities is an emptiness other than that.[803]

The nonexistence of entities of persons or phenomena is the emptiness [of nonentities]. The existent entity [or essence of the ground] of that nonexistence of entities is the emptiness [that is the very essence of the nonexistence of entities]. In the statements about the emptiness of the consumer and so on mentioned above, in order to teach the characteristics of emptiness, two aspects of emptiness are finally defined: the emptiness of nonentities and the emptiness that is the very essence of the nonexistence of entities. These are, respectively, in order to clear away exaggeration about persons and phenomena and denigration of [the ground of] their emptiness. In that way, the divisions of emptiness should be understood.[804]

Just after this, that establishment of the divisions of emptiness (also clearly taught in the *Glorious Sampuṭa Tantra*) is stated by the conqueror Maitreya and the great expert, the honorable teacher Vasubandhu, in the root text and in the *Commentary on "Distinguishing the Middle and the Extremes."* This is exactly what it says:

How should the practice be understood?

> If it did not become afflicted,
> all embodied beings would be liberated.
> If it did not become pure, effort
> would be without result.[805] {236}

If the emptiness of phenomena did not become defiled by incidental secondary afflictions (even though the antidotes had not arisen), defilement would not exist, so all sentient beings would be liberated without effort. If it did not become pure even though the antidotes had arisen, diligence for the sake of liberation would be without result. That being so:

> Not afflicted, not unafflicted;
> it is not pure and not impure.[806]

> How can it be not afflicted and also not impure? Because the mind is naturally luminous.
>
> How can it be not unafflicted, yet also not pure? Because of the incidental afflictions.
>
> In that way, the presentation of the divisions of emptiness is established.[807] [189]

Because glorious great Vajradhara carefully teaches in that way in the profound unsurpassable yogatantras, which are the consummation of Great Madhyamaka, do not follow after the infamous confusion spread by some that *Distinguishing the Middle and the Extremes* is Cittamātra!

This is fully taught in very many textual traditions of the Madhyamaka, such as the *Noble Aṅgulimāla*, the *Mahāparinirvāṇa*, the root text and commentary on the *Uttaratantra*, and the *Vast Commentary on the Mother Sūtras*. And *Distinguishing the Middle and the Extremes* itself also states the characteristics of emptiness that has the same meaning as thusness and so on:

> The nonexistence of the entities of the two, and the entity that is the nonexistence of entities, are the characteristics of emptiness.[808]

That which is the very essence of the ground of the entities of the two (such as apprehended and apprehender) that are totally nonexistent and unestablished in the abiding state is thus presented as the characteristic of ultimate emptiness.

In that way, this emptiness that has the same meaning as dharmadhātu and so on is the meaning of "emptiness that is the very essence of the nonexistence of entities," "emptiness of other entities," and "nonempty emptiness," which are mentioned again and again in stainless scriptures; mere emptiness of self-nature does not fit the definition of those. Why? Because that which is ultimate emptiness, "Not existent, not nonexistent,"[809] not only clears away the extreme of existence but also clears away the extreme of nonexistence; {237} the emptiness of self-nature does not clear away the extreme of nonexistence.

Here, even though relative phenomena are totally nonexistent in the abiding state, the extreme of existence is their exaggeration as "existent." Even though the partless, omnipresent, primordial awareness of dharmadhātu always resides pervading all, the extreme of nonexistence is its denigration as "nonexistent and unestablished, empty of own-essence."

Because that which is the middle free of those extremes is the ground free of all extremes such as existence and nonexistence, exaggeration and denigration, and permanence and annihilation, it is the consummate Great Madhyamaka. And it is emptiness that is not inanimate, emptiness far from the emptiness of annihilation, great emptiness that is the ultimate primordial awareness of noble beings, the five changeless great emptinesses, the six changeless empty drops, the *a* that is the most sublime of all phonemes, the Buddha before all buddhas, primordially liberated Tathāgata, Ādibuddha without cause, having all aspects yet without aspect, and so on. Indestructible, unsuitable to abandon, and not to be denigrated, it is the inconceivable basic element beyond all the phenomena of consciousness, and not a sophist's field of experience, but to be personally known by the yogin himself. [190]

Therefore, those who only designate mere separation from all extremes to be "Madhyamaka," but resolve that "Madhyamaka is empty of Madhyamaka," and "even the ultimate is empty of the ultimate," and so on, are not in accord with the intent of the Conqueror, because it is stated that the mere emptiness of nonentities is not sufficient as the characteristic of the emptiness of the consummate abiding state, and that the emptiness that is the very essence of the nonexistence of entities is necessary.

Moreover, the root text and the commentary on *"Distinguishing the Middle and the Extremes"* say:

> In that way, the very essence [of the ground] of the nonexistence of entities is fully taught to be the characteristic of emptiness.
>
> That which is the very essence of the nonexistence of entities is not existent, not nonexistent.[810] How is it not existent? In this way: the entities of the two [selves] do not exist. How is it also not nonexistent? In this way: that entity [or essence of the ground] that is the nonexistence of the entities of the two is the characteristic of [ultimate] emptiness.[811]

And the *Commentary on the "Extensive Mother Sūtra," the "Sūtra in Twenty-Five Thousand Lines," and the "Sūtra in Eighteen Thousand Lines"* {238} also says:

> As for "the very essence of the nonexistence of entities": imaginary phenomena such as forms are referred to by the phrase "the

> nonexistence of entities." The [ultimate] very essence that is the opposite of those is also called "the very essence of the nonexistence of entities." After that, it teaches that [ultimate reality] is the perfection of wisdom, the very essence of the nonexistence of entities, and skillful means.[812]

After speaking of the ultimate very essence as the very essence of the nonexistence of entities (the opposite of the relative), empty of the incidental, imaginary relative, this says it is also the perfection of wisdom that is the indivisible essence of ground and result, thereby also establishing profound emptiness that is synonymous with the ultimate true nature to be the emptiness of other itself.

Likewise, the honorable, noble Nāgārjuna also says in the Madhyamaka *Stages of Meditation*:

> Emptiness of the unarisen is one,
> one is emptiness of the arisen.
> Emptiness of the unarisen is sublime,
> emptiness of the arisen disintegrates.[813]

Thus arising and disintegration are emptiness. Emptiness is arising and disintegration. They are not other than it, and it is also not other than them. Thereby, the emptiness of arising and disintegration here is the emptiness of self-nature, the emptiness of nonentities. The emptiness of other, the emptiness that is the very essence of the nonexistence of entities, is the emptiness of the unarisen. It is sublime, excellent, and other than the former. Moreover, that has the same meaning as the previously quoted lines:

> Here the nonexistence of entities
> of persons and phenomena is emptiness.
> The existent entity of the nonexistence
> of entities is an emptiness other than that.[814] [191]

In that way, by adding emptiness of the unobservable and emptiness of very essence to the sixteen, there are eighteen, and by adding emptiness of own-entity and emptiness of other entities, there are twenty. These last two also present emptiness of self-nature and emptiness of other. Emptiness of very essence also presents the very essence of the ground empty of phenomena, the ultimate true nature, the very essence of personal, self-knowing primordial awareness.

That being so, in the pure textual traditions that teach the profound abiding state—determining reality with statements such as "not existent, not nonexistent," or "beyond existence and nonexistence," {239} or "free of the extremes of existence and nonexistence"—the meaning of not existent, not nonexistent, and so on, should be understood as meaning those phenomena that are empty of self-nature are not existent, and that which is the ground of emptiness, the ultimate true nature, is not nonexistent. If seen in that way, the meaning of the great intent is seen.

The *Ornament of the Sūtras* also says:

> Not existent, not nonexistent; not the same, not something else; . . .[815]

And so on, it states the characteristics of reality. The commentary says:

> Because of the characteristics of the imaginary and the dependent, it is not existent. Because of the characteristics of the fully established [true nature], it is not nonexistent.

Down to:

> Since it does not naturally have the defilements, it does not become pure. Because it is free of incidental afflictions, it is also not impure.[816]

Thus the meaning of being without the flaw of including contradiction is stated. Likewise, the honorable, noble Nāgārjuna also says in the Madhyamaka *Stages of Meditation*:

> In that way, because pure wisdom
> [understands] this own-essence,
> the ultimate, to also be very established,
> other imaginary entities do not occur.[817]

The meaning is that, because the own-essence of the ultimate is also very established, it is not nonexistent, but imaginary entities other than that do not occur or exist. So one must have utterly pure wisdom to understand in that way the meaning of not existent, not nonexistent.

This also has the same meaning as the statement in the *Glorious Vajra Garland Tantra*:

> Mantra practitioners having
> the yoga of thusness see vividly.[818]

The meaning is: "the critical awareness of meditative absorption sees vividly." Therefore, these source texts also teach the ultimate to be not empty of self-nature.

Here, the own-essence of the ultimate is the self-arisen primordial awareness of a sugata, because the honorable, noble Vajragarbha says extensively:

> The essence is self-knowing, the primordial awareness of a tathāgata, and since that essence is free of apprehension, apprehended, and apprehender, which are manifestations of the eighteen elements, . . .

Down to:

> In that way, a yogin should meditate on precious reality free of the eighteen elements.[819] {240} [192]

In this way, that self-knowing ultimate truth, free of the extremes of existence and nonexistence, is beyond the phenomena of dependent arising, does not deteriorate from its own very essence, and is the nature not empty of own-essence. The teacher Jñānagarbha says in the *Path of Cultivating Yoga*:

> That which does not arise dependent on [causes and conditions] and does not deteriorate from its own very essence is called "the ultimate nature."[820]

And the *Sūtra on the Arising of Total Great Enthusiasm* also says:

> Not from other conditions, peaceful,
> not elaborated through conceptual elaboration,

nonconceptual, not various—these are
the characteristics of reality, thusness.[821]

The *Root Verses on Madhyamaka, Called "Wisdom"* also says:

Not known from another, peaceful,
not elaborated through conceptual elaboration,
without concepts, not of different meaning—
these are the characteristics of reality.[822]

Primordially, naturally peaceful and without conceptual elaborations, thusness of one taste with nonconceptual primordial awareness, reality beyond the phenomena of dependent arising, is thus perfectly presented.

That being the case, asserting that all twenty emptinesses are just the emptiness of self-nature is not the meaning of the great intent of the conquerors, because ultimate truth, the natural family, all the attributes of the qualities of the dharmakāya, and the emptiness of the very essence—that of the very essence of the nonexistence of entities and that of other entities—are emptiness, but are not the emptiness of self-nature.

Here, because [the emptinesses of] the consumer, the consumed, and so on are each empty of own-essence, they are what does not exist in something; they are totally unestablished and do not even slightly exist. The ground empty of those phenomena, dharmadhātu, is what remains; it exists in reality.

Closely considering these points, the great Madhyamaka master, the honorable, noble Asaṅga says:

How do they wrongly apprehend emptiness?

Those śramaṇas or brahmins who do not assert that [ground for the] emptiness of something, and who also do not assert what it is empty of, are said to "wrongly apprehend emptiness."

Why is that? Because it is reasonable that [the phenomena] it is empty of are the emptiness of the nonexistent, and [the ground] that is empty is the emptiness of the existent; if all were nonexistent, what would be empty of what where? It is not suitable for that [true nature] to be an emptiness of itself. Therefore, such [an assertion] wrongly apprehends emptiness.

> How does one accurately apprehend emptiness? {241}
>
> Correctly seeing that [ground] in which some [phenomena] do not exist to be empty of [those phenomena], but [the ground of emptiness] that is the remainder there to "perfectly exist in this" is to unmistakenly penetrate emptiness exactly in accord with reality.[823] [193]

And so on, it says extensively, so one must definitely also consult *Levels of the Bodhisattva*.

The *Stack of Jewels* also says:

> Kāśyapa, it is preferable to abide in a view like Mount Meru concerning persons; such is not the case with the view of emptiness by one with manifest pride. Why is that?
>
> I explain, Kāśyapa, that if what causes liberation from all views is emptiness, Kāśyapa, one who views [all] as only empty [of own-essence] is incurable.[824]

And so on, it states extensively, at the end of which it also says:

> For example, after a physician gives a purgative
> to a person in order to remove an illness, if the illness
> is not affected and purged, the illness will not be
> cured from its base.
>
> Likewise, the Conqueror says, "If emptiness
> is the sublime cause of liberation from dwelling
> in the darkness of views, one who views [all]
> as only empty [of own-essence] is incurable."[825]

The honorable, noble Nāgārjuna also says:

> The conquerors teach emptiness
> for definite liberation from all views.
> For those who view [all as] emptiness,
> they teach, nothing can be achieved.[826]

And:

> If emptiness is wrongly viewed,
> those with little wisdom will be ruined . . .[827]

Such passages say that to decisively conclude that all is just empty of self-nature is a great fault. {242}

b) *Of those, how all that are the ground of emptiness reside as the ultimate deities, compassion, and so on*

Statements in the precious tantras (presenting the sixteen emptinesses), such as "the sixteen emptinesses are the pillars,"[828] "the arms are the sixteen emptinesses themselves,"[829] and furthermore, "the sixteen lotus petals,"[830] "the sixteen charnel grounds,"[831] and "the sixteen outer sections of the maṇḍala,"[832] mean the syllable *e*, the source of the attributes, bhaga, the element of space, lion throne, and so on. Therefore, these do not refer to the emptiness of self-nature, the emptiness of nonentities, but distinguish the ultimate ground of emptiness, the natural family, the emptiness that is the very essence of the nonexistence of entities, the emptiness of other entities, and nonempty emptiness [into sixteen] by means of their aspects.

Moreover, the honorable Bhagavān Avalokiteśvara says:

> The "sixteen emptinesses" are the waning phase [of the moon] and the sun and wisdom.[833]

And:

> [Great] emptiness has three divisions: emptiness, emptiness of the great, and emptiness of the ultimate.
>
> Here, emptiness is the emptiness of the five aggregates, which is five days—the first day of waning and so on. [194]
>
> Emptiness of the great is the emptiness of the five elements, which is five days—the sixth day and so on.
>
> Emptiness of the ultimate is the emptiness of the five sense faculties, which is five days—the eleventh and so on.
>
> Therefore, the fifteen days ending with empty sky are fifteen emptinesses.
>
> In the middle, between the end of the empty sky and the beginning of the first day of waxing, is the sixteenth, emptiness having all aspects.[834]

To realize the meaning of these just as they are, one must carefully realize the meaning of the true nature having all aspects, {243} which is other than the relative outer and inner.

c) *If realized in that way, how these will be realized to be the middle, or the center devoid of the two extremes, the androgynous stage, beyond examples, a third category*

If that is realized, the profound meaning of the middle free of extremes will also be realized, because that is not extinguished in a mere nonimplicative negation or exclusion merely free of extremes; it is the middle or the center devoid of the two extremes, established through positive determination, which is a third category.

Moreover, the commentary on Āryadeva's *Compendium of the Essence of Primordial Awareness* says:

> It states, "Neither existent nor nonexistent," because it is a third category.[835]

Thus the great expert, the teacher Bodhibhadra, says. And the "Questions by Kāśyapa" in the *Stack of Jewels* also says:

> Kāśyapa, that "permanent" is one extreme. That "impermanent" is a second extreme. That [self-arisen primordial awareness] that is the middle between those two extremes is not analyzable, not demonstrable, not a support, without appearance, without cognition [i.e., consciousness], and nonabiding. Kāśyapa, this is the Middle Way, perfect discrimination of phenomena.
>
> Kāśyapa, that "self" is one extreme. That "selfless" is a second extreme. That [self-arisen primordial awareness] that is the middle between those two extremes is not analyzable, not demonstrable, not a support, without appearance, without cognition, and nonabiding. Kāśyapa, this is called "the Middle Way, perfect discrimination of phenomena."[836]

And:

> Kāśyapa, "existence" is one extreme. "Nonexistence" is a second extreme. That [self-arisen primordial awareness] that is the mid-

> dle between those two extremes is not analyzable, not demonstrable, not a support, without appearance, without cognition, and nonabiding. Kāśyapa, this is called "the Middle Way, perfect discrimination of phenomena."[837]

And {244}:

> Kāśyapa, "saṃsāra" is one extreme. "Nirvāṇa" is a second extreme. That [self-arisen primordial awareness] that is the middle between those two extremes is not analyzable, not demonstrable, not a support, without appearance, without cognition, and nonabiding. Kāśyapa, this is called "the Middle Way, perfect discrimination of phenomena."[838] [195]

Thus the meaning of that which is the middle devoid of the two extremes, the true nature, Madhyamaka, is stated to be the meaning of a third category. In *Distinguishing Phenomena and True Nature*, the honorable conqueror Maitreya states just that to be the characteristics of nonconceptual primordial awareness:

> Therefore, this is called "not examinable,
> not demonstrable, not a basis, without appearance,
> without cognition, and nonabiding," which
> expresses the characteristics of nonconceptual
> primordial awareness as in the *[Stack of Jewels] Sūtra*.[839]

Furthermore, the meaning of Madhyamaka free of extremes, that which is stated in the *Stack of Jewels*, is also clarified in *Commentary on "Distinguishing the Middle and the Extremes"*:

> That "those two, persons and phenomena, exist" is the extreme of permanence. That "[all] does not exist" is the extreme of annihilation. Because those are utterly excluded, it is the Middle Way, that which is the middle between those two extremes.[840]

This clears away the claim by some that the middle free of extremes is unestablished.

Likewise, others who accept Madhyamaka without accepting the middle are also confused. Here the meaning of the [Sanskrit] term *madhya* is "inner," "center," or "middle," which means the profound dharmadhātu is "not any extreme, but is the middle, or center." The meaning of statements about a third category is also that, the meaning of statements about the androgynous stage is also that, and the meaning of what is beyond worldly examples is also that, because being without the flaw of including contradiction, and a third category concerning direct contradiction, are impossible for relative truth.

The root text and commentary on *Distinguishing the Middle and the Extremes* also say:

> "It is a treatise distinguishing the middle," because it fully teaches the Middle Way. {245}
>
> This also distinguishes the middle and the extremes, because it fully teaches both the [ultimate] middle and the [relative] extremes.
>
> Or else, because it fully teaches the middle that is without beginning and end.[841]

And the honorable Bhagavān Lokeśvara also says:

> Having all aspects, arisen from space, totally good, having all sense faculties [in each one], abiding as the quintessence of all sentient beings, connate joy, eluding reasoning and example—an example for this would be something at once an entity yet a nonentity, since their attributes are incompatible.
>
> For example, since its attributes are incompatible with those of the worldly example of a pot, a sky-flower is nonexistent, completely nonexistent. Likewise, since its attributes are incompatible with those of a sky-flower, a pot is an entity; it is completely existent. [196]
>
> Since the attributes of these two are mutually incompatible, they are cited as an example.
>
> Likewise, since its attributes are incompatible with annihilation, cyclic existence is an entity; it is completely existent.
>
> Since its attributes are incompatible with cyclic existence, annihilation is nonexistent; it is completely nonexistent.
>
> The term "annihilation" refers to nirvāṇa [as maintained by

> śrāvakas and pratyekabuddhas], which has the characteristic of nonexistence.
>
> Likewise, an example of the transcendent would be these two—the pot and the sky-flower—being just one, since their attributes are incompatible.
>
> These two—the pot and the sky-flower—do not exist as just one in the relative world, since they are mutually contradictory.[842]

And:

> Since it is simply beyond worldly examples, that mind—existent mind—does not exist in [incidental] mind. Free of the characteristics of the attributes of permanence and annihilation, it is emptiness and compassion indivisible.[843]

Thus it should be known that [these passages] have the same meaning as statements that an example for profound reality is impossible in the world because it is the middle or third category between existence and nonexistence. {246}

d) *After rejecting many confused misconceptions about that, presenting the meaning in accord with the state of being*

It might be said, "If that were so, it would contradict the consensus that a third category is impossible concerning direct contradictions such as existent and nonexistent, existence and nonexistence of entities, existence and nonexistence of form."

That is indeed true, but those are in the context of the relative itself; the ultimate is not any of those single poles of direct contradiction, such as existent and nonexistent, because [the Buddha] carefully states:

> Beyond existence and nonexistence.[844]

And:

> Not existent, not nonexistent...[845]

And:

> Lord who has exhausted existent and nonexistent.[846]

And:

> Therefore, Buddha is not existence.
> It is also not a type of nonexistence.[847]

And:

> Liberated from form and nonform.[848]

And so on. That being so, those who assert the resolution that all knowable objects are either existent or nonexistent have simply not realized the abiding state of the ultimate true nature, because that is a knowable object but not at all existent or nonexistent. Therefore, it is also established as a third category and as the middle or center itself.

It might be said, "If the ultimate were a knowable object, that would contradict these statements":

> The ultimate is not the intellect's field of experience.[849]

And:

> Since the true nature is not to be known,
> it cannot be known.[850]

There is no fault, because those passages refer to it as not being the field of experience of an intellect of consciousness, and that it cannot be [directly] known by consciousness. [197] It is not that it is not an object of primordial awareness, because it is said:

> Field of experience for personal,
> self-knowing primordial awareness . . .[851]

And:

> The objects of those who see the ultimate.[852]

And:

> Since it is not inanimate, it is to be known by oneself.[853]

And:

> Since it is not inanimate, it is self-awareness itself.[854]

And:

> Aware of itself, aware of the other, having all
> [sense faculties in each one].[855]

And:

> Self-awareness, great bliss itself,
> knowing itself, becomes enlightened.[856]

And:

> Bodhisattvas later realize this thusness.
> So the buddhas bestow the name "Tathāgata."[857]

And because consummate emptiness is stated again and again to be the quintessence of compassion and to be bodhicitta. {247}

That being so, the middle devoid of the two extremes, profound dharmadhātu, is not to be directly known by consciousness, but is to be directly known by primordial awareness, because just that is the five types of self-arisen primordial awareness, and because it is also directly realized by other-arisen perfect primordial awareness.

In that way, the ground free of all extremes such as existence and nonexistence, omnipresent dharmadhātu, is the Buddha of the abiding state.

It might be said that if the Buddha is called "existent" or "nonexistent," that would be the fault of falling into the extremes of existence and nonexistence, because the *Ornament of the Sūtras* also states:

> Therefore, the Buddha is not existent,
> yet also not called "nonexistent."
> In that way, questions about the Buddha
> are held to be indeterminate.[858]

Here the meaning of "free of the extremes of existence and nonexistence" has two aspects. During full meditative absorption in the profound true nature, all conceptual elaborations (such as existent or nonexistent) are discarded, and there is nothing to say, think, or express. During postmeditation and so on, however, when determining how the abiding state is, if it is resolved (in accord with the abiding state) that the existent "exists" and the nonexistent "does not exist," there is no fault. But if the opposite of that [is resolved], there would be the fault of falling into extremes.

Here the meaning of "the Buddha is not existent, yet also not nonexistent" also states that it is not existent in the mind and not nonexistent in primordial awareness. That same source says:

> Just as heat in iron and blurriness
> in the eye fade, so too the Buddha
> is not called "existent in the mind"
> and "nonexistent in primordial awareness."[859]

The example is used that, when iron cools, the heat is not existent and the iron itself is not nonexistent, and when the eye is flawless, the blurriness is not existent and the eye itself is not nonexistent.

That being so, "not existent, not nonexistent" appears to include contradiction, but if well examined, the manner and reason it is without flaw of contradiction is like that. [198]

Unlike that, according to the claims of some persons, "the Buddha is not existent and also not nonexistent in the abiding state," and, "all relative phenomena are not existent and also not nonexistent," and so on, negating the existence of that single phenomenon itself but not establishing its nonexistence, and negating the nonexistence but not establishing the existence. {248} Such [claims] are not in accord with the intent of the conquerors and also contradict the meaning, because existence and nonexistence are mutually in direct contradiction, because negating a negation is the nature of establishing, because the authentic is understood by means of a double negation, and because the ground is also not unestablished.

It might be said, "Well, that contradicts the previous establishment that the Buddha of the abiding state is the middle and a third category, excluding existence and nonexistence."

There is no fault, because the previous was in the context of excluding the extremes of existence and nonexistence as entities such as forms, but here it is in the context of whether that freedom of extremes itself exists or does not exist in the abiding state.

If realized in that way, one will realize this does not contradict statements that it does not fall into any extremes such as existence and nonexistence, and statements that freedom of extremes itself exists forever in the abiding state, because that which is the ground free of all extremes such as existence and nonexistence is the Buddha of the profound abiding state.

It might be thought, "By reason of the true nature and the Buddha not being established as knowable objects, they are not existent and they are also not nonexistent."

If that were so, the extremely absurd consequence would also be that everything impossible as knowable objects, such as the horn of a rabbit, would not be nonexistent.

Furthermore, claiming that the Buddha of the true nature does not exist as a knowable object is a great evil among the views of annihilation, a great, horrible, negative view.

Referring to such as this, the Bhagavān says, "whether tathāgatas appear or do not appear,"[860] and so on, and:

> Do not say, "The Buddha does not exist."
> Buddha exists in meditative absorption.[861]

And so on, it states extensively. The honorable, noble Nāgārjuna also says:

> Sentient beings with afflictions
> do not see the Tathāgata.
>
> Just as hungry spirits see
> the ocean to be dry, so too
> those obscured by ignorance
> imagine that buddhas do not exist.
>
> What can the Bhagavān do for
> the lowly and those whose merit
> is low? It is just like a sublime jewel
> put in the hand of a blind person.
>
> For sentient beings who have
> performed merit, the Buddha resides
> in front of them, blazing with thirty-two
> major marks, bright and glorious with light.[862]

And [199]:

> "A plantain tree has no essence"
> is used as an example in the world,

> but its essence, its sweet fruit itself,
> is eaten.
>
> So too, if separated from saṃsāra
> (the cage of the afflictions) that has
> no essence, its essence, buddhahood,
> becomes nectar for all embodied beings.[863] {249}

And thus *In Praise of the Ultimate, In Praise of the Three Kāyas,*[864] and so on also state. The honorable lord Mahākaruṇika also says:

> When saṃsāra that has no essence is exhausted,
> from that the fruit is the buddhahood of the person,
> just as the ripened fruits of a plantain tree
> perfectly occur because the plantain tree withers.[865]

And so on. Many ways that Buddha exists in the abiding state are thus stated, so do not deny it.

Some might think that referring to buddhahood as not ultimately existent and not relatively nonexistent says it is not existent, not nonexistent.

Therefore, I should comment. Here, that ultimately nonexistent but relatively existent buddha is not the consummate Buddha, because that which is the consummate dharmakāya does not exist as any relative phenomenon and is always present as the essence of ultimate thusness.

That being so, because the consummate Buddha, the dharmakāya, is the apex of reality, it is the apex of existence and the apex of truth, because it ultimately exists and is ultimately true.

Moreover, it should be understood that the meaning of *bhūtakoṭi* [apex of reality] here applies to the apex of existence and the apex of truth. Just that is the consummate Buddha and, referring to this, the Bhagavān teaches extensively:

> That which is not true is not thusness. That which is not thusness is not the Tathāgata.[866]

And so on. It might be said, "Truth is nonexistent in any phenomenon, so an ultimately true [phenomenon] is impossible."

No. If not relatively true, it is unsuitable to be relative truth, so that which is relative truth is relatively true, not ultimately true. Just exactly like that, if not ultimately true, it is unsuitable to be ultimate truth, so that which is ultimate truth is ultimately true, not relatively true.

Moreover, the honorable, noble Nāgārjuna says in the autocommentary *Fearing Nothing*:

> Noble beings who unmistakenly understand ultimate truth see all phenomena to be unarisen; because that for them is ultimately true, it is the ultimate truth.[867] {250} [200]

And [a sūtra cited there] says:

> "Monks, it is like this: that undeceptive phenomenon, nirvāṇa, is the most sublime truth."[868]

And the explanatory commentary composed by the teacher Avalokitavrata to *Lamp for the "Wisdom"* (the commentary composed by the teacher Bhāvaviveka) also cites those very words.[869] And the commentary composed by the teacher Buddhapālita has those very words and, furthermore, says:

> Truth is one; there is no second.[870]

Sixty Verses on Reasoning also states:

> When the conquerors have said
> nirvāṇa is the one truth,
> what expert would imagine that
> the rest is not mistaken?[871]

And the *Sūtra of the Bodhisattva's Scriptural Collection* also says:

> The truth is just one, not two. It is like this: the truth of cessation.[872]

And:

> That which is the unarisen [ground] is definitive. That which is the definitive [true nature] is the definitive meaning. That which is the definitive meaning is the ultimate.[873]

And the *Sūtra of the Excellent Golden Light* also states:

> The dharmakāya of a tathāgata is that truth of reality itself, so it is called "nirvāṇa."[874]

And the *Sūtra of the Meeting of Father and Son* also says:

> This "enlightenment" is the apex of reality, and . . .[875]

And the *Sūtra of Śrīmālā* also states:

> The truth of the cessation of suffering is, in reality, true, permanent, and a refuge.[876]

And the Madhyamaka *Lucid Words* also says:

> The Bhagavān said, "Monks, this is the excellent truth, it is like this: the undeceptive phenomenon, nirvāṇa.[877]

And profound secret mantra sources also state extensively:

> Having the twelve aspects of the meaning of the truth.[878]

And:

> Residing in the mode of the two truths.[879]

And so on. Therefore, that which is ultimate truth is ultimately true.

Likewise, those relatively true [phenomena] are untrue and unarisen in reality, but if relative arising were refuted it would be a fault, because the Madhyamaka *Two Truths* refutes that with passages such as:

> Some renowned for bad arguments
> claim that entities not arisen in reality
> do not even relatively arise, like
> the child of a barren woman, and so on.[880]

It might be said that the consummate Buddha is actually existent, but if viewed as existent, one would fall into an extreme, {251} because the *Sūtra of the King of Samādhis* says:

> Both existence and nonexistence are extremes.
> Pure and impure—these are also extremes.
> Therefore, rejecting the two extremes,
> experts do not reside even in the middle.[881] [201]

And because the *Root Verses on Madhyamaka, Called "Wisdom"* also states:

> "Existence" is grasping at permanence.
> "Nonexistence" is a view of annihilation.
> Therefore, experts should not reside
> in existence or nonexistence.[882]

[Reply:] those passages are in the context of decisiveness, resting in profound meditative absorption free of all conceptual elaborations such as existence and nonexistence; here it is the context of differentiating existence and nonexistence, so there is no fault. Likewise, it says:

> Those with little intelligence,
> who view entities as existent or
> nonexistent, do not peacefully see
> what is to be viewed, the utterly peaceful.[883]

This also means that, if one views or grasps at existence, nonexistence, and so on, one will not see the utterly peaceful basic element; profound meditative absorption free of all conceptual elaborations is necessary to see that basic element.

Likewise, in the context of determining permanence and impermanence by means of differentiation, thusness and so on—partless, omnipresent, all-pervasive primordial awareness free of single or multiple moments—are classified as permanent, stable, eternal, everlasting, and unchanging; all phenomena not beyond the momentary are classified as impermanent and unstable, phenomena that are not eternal. But in the context of decisive, profound meditative absorption there must be no conceptual elaborations about permanence, impermanence, and so on. The *Root Verses on Madhyamaka, Called "Wisdom"* says:

> How could the four (permanence,
> impermanence, and so on) exist for this peace?

> How could the four (limited, limitless,
> and so on) exist for this peace?[884]

Such passages state how one must be free of all conceptual elaborations. And the *Sūtra Requested by Ratnacūḍa* in the *Stack of Jewels* also says:

> Son of good family, furthermore, both "self" and "selflessness" are also extremes; the pure very essence of self and selflessness is the Middle Way.
>
> Both "lifeforce" and "person" are also extremes; the pure very essence of lifeforce and person is the Middle Way.
>
> Both "sign" and "signlessness" are also extremes; signlessness and nonconceptuality is the Middle Way.
>
> Both "observation" and "nonobservation" are also extremes; {252} absence of conceptuality and disintegration is the Middle Way.
>
> Both "false" and "true" are also extremes; the inexpressible is the Middle Way.
>
> Both "this side" and "the other side" are also extremes; cessation of the destructible collection is the Middle Way.
>
> Both "conditioned" and "unconditioned" are also extremes; absence of analysis is also the Middle Way.
>
> Both "saṃsāra" and "nirvāṇa" are also extremes; [self-arisen primordial awareness] without cognition [i.e., consciousness] is the Middle Way.[885]

Such passages also refer to the context of absolutely no conceptuality in profound meditative absorption, but do not refer to the context of discrimination [in postmeditation]. [202] Statements also in various pure textual traditions that it is free of all conceptual elaborations—such as existence and nonexistence, pleasure and suffering, true and false, permanent and impermanent, empty and nonempty, pure and impure, peaceful and not peaceful, isolated and not isolated, with and without self, with and without arising and ceasing, with and without signs, with and without taints, virtue and nonvirtue, beyond and not beyond the world, beyond and not beyond consciousness and sophistry, beyond and not beyond the momentary and dependent arising—also refer to the context of decisive, profound, meditative absorption without any concepts. Those sources are thus not suitable as refutations in the context of differentiating and discriminating between existence and nonexistence, and so on.

That being so, those who desire expertise in the intent of the scriptures should not conflate and not mistake the intent of those individual contexts.

Likewise, "There is no permanent authority,"[886] and so on, also refer to a relative authority, and the teachings in some texts that whatever is knowledge is conditioned also refer to relative knowledge.

Likewise, resolutions that being without the flaw of including contradiction is impossible, that a third category is impossible concerning direct contradiction, and that whatever are knowable objects are the two (entity or nonentity, and so on), are also in the context of the relative; ultimate truth is not included in any of those. {253}

e) *Briefly presenting two modes of emptiness for all emptinesses that have been stated*

In that way, the meaning of the purity and utter purity of the eighteen emptinesses is the pure and utterly pure eighteen emptinesses, the eighteen emptinesses of the fully established true nature, which are the ground purified and utterly purified of the imaginary and the dependent emptinesses.

The emptinesses stated in the *Vajra Garland Tantra* are explained to be empty of conceptualization and apprehension as this or that. Fearing it would take too many words, however, [203] I have not written about them here.

9) *How the true nature's pure factors conducive to enlightenment reside as the ultimate deities, tantras, sacred places, and so on*

Likewise, the meaning of the purity and utter purity of the factors conducive to enlightenment is also the fully established true nature's factors conducive to enlightenment, which are the ground purified of the imaginary and the dependent factors conducive to enlightenment. These are also stated to be the thirty-seven syllables of the settings for the discourses in the profound kings of tantras, and also to be the ultimate deities of primordial awareness. As the honorable, noble Vajragarbha says:

> The syllable *e* is Locanā. The syllable *vaṃ* is Māmakī. The syllable *ma* is Pāṇḍarā. The syllable *yā* is Tāriṇī. The syllable *śru* is Vajradhātvīśvarī. The syllable *taṃ* is Prajñāpāramitā.
>
> Then the aggregates: the syllable *e* is Vajrasattva. The syllable *ka*

> is Akṣobhya. The syllable *smin* is Amoghasiddhi. The syllable *sa* is Ratneśa. The syllable *ma* is Amitābha. The syllable *ye* is Vairocana. The syllable *bha* is Gandhavajrā. The syllable *ga* is Rasavajrā. The syllable *vān* is Rūpavajrā. The syllable *sa* is Sparśavajrā. The syllable *rva* is Śabdavajrā. The syllable *ta* is Dharmadhātuvajrā. The syllable *thā* is Sarvanīvaraṇaviṣkambhin. {254} The syllable *ga* is Lokeśvara. The syllable *ta* is Kṣitigarbha. The syllable *kā* is Khagarbha. The syllable *ya* is Vajrapāṇi. The syllable *vāk* is Samantabhadra. In that way, these are the twelve sensory bases.
>
> The syllable *ci* is Stambhī. The syllable *tta* is Māninī. The syllable *va* is Jambhī. The syllable *jra* is Ativīryā. The syllable *yo* is Atinīlā. The syllable *ṣid* is Raudrākṣī. The syllable *bha* is Sumbha. The syllable *ge* is Uṣṇīṣa. The syllable *ṣu* is Vighnāntaka. The syllable *vi* is Prajñāntaka. The syllable *ja* is Padmāntaka. The syllable *hā* is Yamāntaka. The syllable *ra* is the lord Vajrasattva, the quintessence of wisdom and means, the thirty-seventh.
>
> In that way, the utter purities (in exact sequence) of the thirty-seven factors conducive to enlightenment, [the ultimate deities], are "the six elements, the six aggregates, the six objects, the six sense faculties, the six activities of the action faculties, the six action faculties, and great bliss," which are from extinguishing the fourth state.
>
> Therefore, these are the four foundations of mindfulness, the four perfect renunciations, the four bases for the miraculous, the five faculties, the five powers, the eight limbs of the noble path, and the seven limbs of enlightenment.[887] [204]

The *Glorious Stainless Light* also states the factors conducive to enlightenment (included in the fully established true nature and the truth of cessation) to be the ultimate yoginīs, sacred places, and so on. Just as it says:

> Now, "[The foundations of] mindfulness" and so on states the purity of the yoginīs by way of the thirty-seven factors conducive to enlightenment. Here are the four goddesses in sequence: The foundation of mindfulness of the body is Locanā and the foundation of mindfulness of feeling is Pāṇḍarā, who are behind and to the right. {255} The foundation of mindfulness of the mind is Māmakī and the foundation of mindfulness of phenomena is

Tārā, who are to the left and in front, and, by the divisions of the body, are the two sacred places and nearby sacred places. That this is "well known in the *Kālacakra*" means it is not well known in other tantras; it was hidden by the Bhagavān.

Likewise, of the seven limbs of enlightenment, one limb of enlightenment is the mother Vajradhātvīśvarī, the sacred place of family, the limb of enlightenment that is perfect equanimity. As for "the others are also the six such as Śabdavajrā": the limb of enlightenment that is perfect mindfulness is Śabdavajrā, the limb of enlightenment that is perfect distinguishing of phenomena is Sparśavajrā, and the limb of enlightenment that is perfect diligence is Rūpavajrā, who are, by the divisions of the body, the nearby fields. Likewise, the limb of enlightenment that is perfect joy is Gandhavajrā, the limb of enlightenment that is perfect refinement is Rasavajrā, and the limb of enlightenment that is perfect samādhi is Dharmadhātuvajrā, who are the two fields.

Likewise, concerning "the water-treasure perfect renunciations and . . .":[888] renunciation in order that unarisen negative acts are not produced is Carcikā, the root of virtue that renounces arisen negative acts is Vaiṣṇavī, producing the virtue of renouncing unarisen nonvirtues is Māheśvarī, renunciation through total dedication of arisen virtues to buddhahood is Mahālakṣmī, who are the four nearby Chandohas.

"The other water-treasuries"—the four goddesses—are the bases for the miraculous. Concerning them, the base for the miraculous that is aspiration is Brahmāṇī, the base for the miraculous that is diligence is Aindrī, the base for the miraculous that is mind is Vārāhī, the base for the miraculous that is analysis is Kaumārī. These are the divisions of Chandohas, and in that way there are eight.

Likewise, "the five wrathful females are the powers." Here, the power of faith is Atinīlā, the power of diligence is Atibalā, the power of mindfulness is Vajraśṛṅkhalā, the power of samādhi {256} is Mānī, and the power of wisdom is Cundā, [205] who are the nearby areas for congregation.

Likewise, "the utterly clear and definite faculties are five." Likewise, the faculty of faith is Stambhī, the faculty of diligence is Jambhī, the faculty of mindfulness is Mārīcī, the faculty of samādhi is

> Bhṛkuṭī, and the faculty of wisdom is Raudrākṣī, who are the areas for congregation. In that way, there are ten.
>
> "The correct path of eight limbs, O lord of human beings, is the eight born from demigods." Here, correct view is the dog-faced goddess Śvānāsyā, correct thought is the crow-faced goddess Kākāsyā, correct speech is the tiger-faced goddess Vyāghrāsyā, correct action is the owl-faced goddess Ulūkāsyā, correct livelihood is the jackal-faced goddess Jambukāsyā, correct effort is the garuḍa-faced goddess Garuḍāsyā, correct mindfulness is the pig-faced goddess Śūkarāsyā, and correct samādhi is the vulture-faced goddess Gṛdhrāsyā.
>
> That being so, "By way of the thirty-seven divisions a yogin should know that all those who are the thirty-seven factors conducive to enlightenment in the abodes of the [other] three states of cyclic existence are in the abodes on the surface of the earth as yoginīs who are [the other] outcaste women and so on."
>
> In that way, the sacred places and so on purified by the thirty-seven factors conducive to enlightenment are the characteristics of the dharmakāya, "O lord of human beings, likewise also in the outer and in the body"; this is the rule everywhere.[889]

If the division of the two truths is also understood here, one will not be deluded about the Sage's word.

Concerning that, the naturally original yoginīs are the factors conducive to enlightenment included in the ultimate truth of cessation, that which is the quintessence of the sugata essence also pervasively abiding like space in the outer and in the body.

The yoginīs included in the rūpakāya, and the factors conducive to enlightenment included in the truth of the path, are relative truth; conditioned, incidental phenomena.

In that way, if all incidental stains are purified by the relative truth of the path, its ground—the primordially, spontaneously present dharmakāya, {257} the quintessence of limitless qualities such as the naturally established sacred places, the twelve aspects of the meaning of the truth and so on—will be obtained, which is the correct meaning of the great intent.

Likewise, the glorious, honorable Vajrapāṇi also says:

> In accord with the definitive meaning, in "*ḍākinīcakrasaṃvara*" the *ḍākinī* are the thirty-seven factors conducive to en-

> lightenment. Their assembly is a *cakra*, the characteristics of the dharmakāya having a quintessence of [nonempty] emptiness. Those are united [*saṃvara*] with the svābhāvikakāya having a quintessence of nonreferential compassion; thus they are just one.[890] [206]

The mentioned factors conducive to enlightenment are also primordially, naturally pure, the ultimate truth of cessation, because they are the dharmakāya indivisible from the consummate svābhāvikakāya.

Likewise, *ka* vajra, *kha* vajra, and so on (the quintessence of the thirty-seven deities), all the assemblies of deities stated to be the factors conducive to enlightenment in very many scriptures such as the thirty-six kings of tantras, are also the attributes of the qualities isolated from and empty of imaginary and dependent phenomena, that which is the pure ground, the fully established true nature, naturally pure, naturally luminous, naturally spontaneous, naturally unarisen, naturally free of stains, the natural [kāya] or svābhāvikakāya, great bliss, great emptiness, having all aspects and having all qualities. The accumulation of these is called "dharmakāya" and their consolidation is called an "aggregate of the attributes."

Moreover, in *Brief Presentation of the Assertions of My Own View*, noble Mañjuśrī says:

> The limitless aggregate of the attributes
> is fully proclaimed to be my dharmakāya.[891]

And:

> The consolidation is the aggregate and, likewise,
> the kāya is proclaimed to be their perfect accumulation.[892]

Furthermore, the seventy-two goddesses of glorious, great Cakrasaṃvara are said to be the ultimate ten perfections, the five other aggregates, the five other elements, the twelve objects and subjects of the true nature, and the five sense faculties, five powers, ten levels, ten powers, and ten faculties of the truth of cessation. Just as the *King of Tantras* says:

> The goddesses are to be purified also by generosity and so on,
> [the other] aggregates, elements, objects, subjects and, furthermore,
> the five sense faculties, and so on, the levels [matching] the

directions and powers [matching] the directions, and the faculties of the glorious children of the conquerors.[893] {258}

Here, concerning "to be purified," those that are the ground of purification are included in the truth of cessation, those that are the stains to be purified are included in the [truths of] suffering and the origin, those that are the means of purification are included in the truth of the path, and those that are the result of purification are the attainment of the primordially established truth of cessation. This approach is to be understood by means of the exceptional, profound esoteric instructions.

Therefore, the difference between the truth of cessation and attainment of the truth of cessation must be understood here, exactly like the difference between the dharmakāya and the attainment of dharmakāya.

Likewise, [that difference must be understood] also for the natural family, the svābhāvikakāya, the sugata essence, the ultimate, thusness, the apex of reality, the buddha nature, great nirvāṇa, *ahaṃ, evaṃ*, [207] the syllable *a*, the Great Mother, Mahāmudrā, Hevajra, Cakrasaṃvara, Guhyasamāja, and so on, the ultimate deities, mantras, tantras, mudrās, maṇḍalas, and so on, which all have just the same meaning but are spoken of by many synonymous names.

10) *How all the pure attributes of the noble four truths of the true nature, and so on, reside as the ultimate deities*

Likewise, having understood the division of the two truths and so on concerning the Bhagavān's statements in the maṇḍala of the dharmadhātu lord of speech that the twelve levels, the twelve perfections, the twelve initiations, the twelve dhāraṇīs, and the four analytical perfect awarenesses are also the goddesses of self-arisen primordial awareness, and furthermore, the very many statements in many various profound mantra approaches such as the *Hevajra* and the *Kālacakra* that the other attributes of the qualities (such as the noble truths, meditations, and immeasurables) are the deities of the true nature—it should be known that the naturally pure attributes refer to the ultimate attributes. {259}

Here, the ultimate attributes, the attributes that are the ground of those without nature, are the eighty-four thousand aggregates of the attributes such as the ten powers, and Mahāmudrā of the indivisible essence of ground and result, the nature of Prajñāpāramitā, the source of the attributes, the field of the dharmakāya.

Moreover, the honorable Bhagavān Avalokiteśvara says:

> Mahāmudrā, having the characteristics of all the [ultimate] attributes without [relative] nature, having the most sublime of all aspects, Prajñāpāramitā, she who produces the buddhas.
>
> The term "source of the attributes" also expresses that, because it is the source of the attributes from which all the [ultimate] attributes without [relative] nature occur.
>
> The [ultimate] attributes without [relative] nature are the eighty-four thousand aggregates of the attributes such as the ten powers and the types of fearlessness. Those occur from the source of the attributes, the [ultimate] buddhafield.
>
> It is the basis of the buddhas and the bodhisattvas, the basis of bliss and the basis of birth.
>
> That from which blood, urine, and semen occur is not the source of the attributes.
>
> Here, the fields of desire and lack of desire for saṃsāra beings are not those of the tathāgatas.
>
> Therefore, the source of the attributes is Viśvamātā (who has the nature of dharmadhātu), embraced by Bhagavān Kālacakra, at all times free of all obscurations.[894] [208]

Concerning this, that the attributes without nature (such as the ultimate ten powers) "occur" is the self-arisen mode of occurrence without the flaw of including contradiction, beyond worldly example. Because other-arisen primordial awarenesses (the ten powers and so on occurring from the power of their blessing and meditation) are conditioned, they are not dharmadhātu, the nature of Viśvamātā, Kālacakra, and so on. In that way, the difference between self-arisen (concerning the source of the attributes, dharmadhātu) and other-arisen (concerning conditioned primordial awareness) must be understood.

In that way, fearing it would take too many words, I have not written here the statements in the profound secret mantra sources that the ground empty of relative truth (that which is the dependent, the ground empty of the imaginary), those primordially pure attributes such as the four noble truths of the fully established true nature, are the many aspects of the assemblies of the deities of self-arisen primordial awareness. {260} These are included in the statement "not empty of the attributes of the inconceivable qualities exceeding the grains of sand found in the Ganges River,"[895] and are what are mentioned here:

> Since it has incidental faults,
> and has qualities in its very nature,
> the changeless true nature
> is just the same before as after.[896]

11) *Showing that impure relative forms and so on are not the pure deities of the true nature*

That being so, the perfect view realizes the primordially, naturally pure to be pure, and realizes the impure to also be impure. Here, what are not pure are all forms and so on included in the incidental stains. The *Glorious Hevajra Tantra* says:

> "O Bhagavān, what are not pure?"
> The Bhagavān replied, "Forms and so on. If you ask why, it is because they are entities of apprehended and apprehender."[897]

And so on, it says extensively. This clears away the claims of some that the meaning of "pure" is that each are empty of own-essence, because it says all the entities of apprehended and apprehender (the quintessence of the two obscurations) are each empty of own-essence, but not pure.

That being so, one must carefully distinguish what are and are not primordially, naturally pure, and also realize the difference between the sugata essence and the incidental stains. And one must also carefully realize their modes of emptiness just as they are. [209]

12) *How great expert and accomplished beings have also taught in that way through applying sūtra and tantra*

This establishing of the intent of profound sūtra and tantra to be one, not contradictory, is also stated in that way by the honorable, glorious Nāropa, a teacher who accomplished mahāmudrā. The *Hevajra Tantra* states:

> Definitively, the purity of
> all entities is called "thusness."
> Later, by the divisions of each,
> that of the deities will be expressed.[898] {261}

[Nāropa's] commentary says:

> Now, "Other than that," and so on speak of pure reality and the divisions, first the purity of reality. The *Glorious Vajraśekhara* says:
>
> > What is purity?
> >
> > Not existent, also not nonexistent;
> > entities nonexistent and the entity
> > not nonexistent. Not speaker and also
> > not what is spoken. Pure nirvāṇa itself.[899]
>
> Concerning "of all entities" and so on [in the *Hevajra Tantra* lines], the equality of external and internal conceptual entities is pure thusness. Always abiding in only that way, that thusness is always pure and, because it is naturally stainless, it is explained to be the nature unconditioned like space. Because of its essence, that thusness should be meditated upon. And the "Chapter on Thusness" in the *Glorious Perfection of Wisdom* says:
>
> > Just as the thusness of the Tathāgata is changeless, unchanging, nonconceptual, nonconceptualizing, and indestructible in anything, likewise the thusness of all phenomena is changeless, unchanging, nonconceptual, nonconceptualizing, and indestructible in anything.
> >
> > Why is that?
> >
> > That which is the thusness of the Tathāgata and that which is the thusness of all phenomena is only one; thusness is nondual and without dualistic activity.[900]

Also, in that same text [Nāropa] says:

> By dividing the aggregates and so on, the purity of the deities is to be realized later, as in "The aggregate of form is Vajrā,"[901] and so on.
>
> Well, why are the sense faculties and so on called "pure"?
>
> It says, "Obscured by the afflictions and unknowing."[902] Unknowing is ignorance, grasping at thinking "I" and "mine." The afflictions are particulars of mind, the causes of desirable or

undesirable actions. Being obscured by them is to be veiled; those should be purified.

The *Glorious Stainless Light* also says:

> The assembly of entities in empty [space],
> devoid of imaginary forms, is seen to appear,
> just as by a young girl performing prognostic
> divination in a mirror.[903] {262} [210]

And it says,

> The purity of the aggregate of form included in transcendent truth is mirrorlike primordial awareness.[904]

And so on, he [Nāropa] quotes down to:

> The purity of the aggregate of consciousness is the primordial awareness of dharmadhātu.[905]

Once again, that same source [the *Stainless Light*] says:

> The primordial awareness of emptiness having all aspects has extinguished the bliss of emission, conceptual obscurations, and so on, and is the purity of the aggregates, elements, sensory bases, and so on.[906]

The *Glorious Perfection of Wisdom* also says in the "Chapter on Purity":

> Subhūti, that which is the purity of form is the purity of the result; that which is the purity of the result is the purity of form. And, Subhūti, that being so, this purity of form and purity of the result is nondual, without dualistic activity, not individual, not different.
>
> Subhūti, likewise for feeling, discrimination, and conditioning factors. Subhūti, that which is the purity of consciousness is the purity of the result; that which is the purity of the result is the purity of consciousness.[907]

Also, in that same work [Nāropa] quotes a passage of the *Vajrapañjara*:

That [true nature] is the Buddha [having all aspects],
just like the [aspects of] the world. Just as the

dharma[dhātu] is immaculate, so too is the basic element of sentient beings explained.

Though it is stainless like space, the [luminous] jewel of mind is stained by inferior discriminating concepts. If the mind is purified, it becomes pure, just like indestructible space.[908] {263}

And so on, it extensively explains, and . . .

13) *How all the pure phenomena of the true nature (desire and so on, and the three times and so on) reside as the ultimate deities*
. . . the *Tantra of the Glorious Sublime Primal* also says:

Then the Bhagavān, the Tathāgata, obtaining the true nature pure by its very essence, also spoke this mode of the perfection of wisdom, called "the equality of all phenomena, the mudrā of the primordial awareness of Avalokiteśvara": "Because of the purity of all desire [of the truth of cessation] itself, there is the purity of all hatred [of the truth of cessation] in the world [of the truth of cessation]. Because of the purity of all stains themselves, there is the purity of all negative acts in the world. Because of the purity of all phenomena themselves, there is the purity of all sentient beings in the world. Because of the purity of all knowledge, there is the purity of the perfection of wisdom in the world."[909] [211]

And so on. And the *Glorious Hevajra* says:

That explained as "hatred"
is Vajrā [Nairātmyā]. Desire is
Vāriyoginī. Jealousy is Vajraḍākinī.
Stinginess is secret Gaurī herself.

Ignorance, likewise, is explained as Vajrā.[910]

Thus the primordially pure hatred and so on of the true nature are said to be the goddesses of self-arisen primordial awareness. And various tantras also state "the great offering, great desire,"[911] and so on, and "hatred as Yamāri," and "ignorance as Yamāri," and so on, saying by means of many aspects that naturally pure ultimate hatred and so on are the self-arisen deities of primordial awareness. Likewise, the meaning of statements that conditioned phenomena, the three times, and so on are pure should also be understood through the meaning of "having all aspects yet without aspect,"[912] and "realizer of the timeless three times,"[913] and so on, and from the profound esoteric instructions of glorious beings on the tenth level. {264}

14) *How the pure self, sentient being, and so on of the true nature also reside as the ultimate deities*

Likewise, the meaning of the pure and utterly pure self and sentient being [of the truth of cessation]—down to the observer—can also be realized by means of the consummate self [of the truth of cessation], the self of thusness, the pure self, and so on presented before. And the *Mahāparinirvāṇa* translated by Lhai Dawa also says:

> That basic element of a tathāgata is the nature of the being [of the truth of cessation]. So taking the life [of a sentient being] does not kill that creature. If that [other] creature [of the truth of cessation] were killed, the [other] nourishing being [of the truth of cessation] would be made totally nonexistent, but it is impossible for that nourishing being to become totally nonexistent.
>
> Here, the [other] "nourishing being" [of the truth of cessation] is the tathāgata essence, and that basic element cannot be destroyed or killed or made totally nonexistent, and cannot also be seen as very pure until buddhahood is achieved.[914]

Thus it states the meaning of great lifeforce, vajra lifeforce or lifeforce of the true nature, other lifeforce or purity of the lifeforce, and so on.

15) *How naturally luminous forms and so on also have the same meaning as those presented before*

Likewise, it is stated, "Because form [of the truth of cessation] is naturally luminous, it is pure, without defilement,"[915] and so on. {265} [212] And...

16) *How forms and so on without transference, arising, and ceasing also have the same meaning as those presented before*

... it is said, "Form [of the truth of cessation], without transference and without natal conception, is pure,"[916] and so on, applied up to the knowledge of all aspects, has the same meaning as statements about the forms of the true nature, up to knowledge of all aspects of the true nature.

Fearing it would take extremely too many words, I have not written the others, but those who have the esoteric instructions for carefully distinguishing that of which something is purified and that which is the pure ground will easily understand.

17) *Showing that those meanings are the intent of the* Extensive Mother Sūtra, *the* Middle Length Sūtra, *and so on*

The commentary on the *Extensive Mother Sūtra*, the *Middle Length Sūtra*, and the *Sūtra in Eighteen Thousand Lines* also says:

> "Just that which is the purity of form is the purity of the result" means there is nothing other than purity that results from the phenomena of purification—the perfections, the factors conducive to enlightenment, and so on. Just that which is the purity of the fully established forms of the true nature, the always abiding svābhāvika[kāya], is purity in the form of the result.
>
> Likewise, this should also be applied to all phenomena.[917]

And:

> "Śāriputra, because it is extremely pure, purity is light." It is like this: for example, if there are no clouds, fog, mist, and so on, the extremely pure sun, moon, and so on fully shine. Likewise, because the forms and so on of the true nature are also extremely pure, they are called "light." Therefore, it says, "Because form is extremely pure, purity is light."
>
> "Bhagavān, purity is without natal conception." Because the stains of the afflictions and conceptual elaborations have been abandoned, {266} there is no further natal conception. Therefore, because it is stainless and pure, it is "without natal conception."
>
> "Śāriputra, because form [of the truth of cessation] is without transference, it is without natal conception, so it is pure." Therefore, the utterly abandoned imaginary forms and so on are without further transference.

> "Bhagavān, purity is without defilement." This is explained to mean that, like space, even if there have been clouds, fog, mist, and so on, it is naturally, utterly pure in all aspects. [213]
>
> "Bhagavān, there is no obtaining and direct realization of purity." If the two phenomena of the object to be obtained and the means of obtaining existed, obtaining would also exist; if the two of the object of direct realization and the means of direct realization existed, "direct realization" would exist. But since the mere nonexistence of [dependent] imagination and conceptualization about that is classified as "the purity of the fully established true nature," absolutely no "obtaining and direct realization" exist in that purity.
>
> "Bhagavān, purity is not directly established." Because phenomena such as imaginary and imputed forms not being directly established is classified as "purity," it has "the characteristic of [phenomena] not being directly established."
>
> "Purity does not arise in the desire, form, and formless realms." The desire, form, and formless realms are imaginary, and when not arising and occurring in them it is called "purity." So it says, "Because the nature of the desire realm is not observed."[918]

And:

> Likewise, during the phase of an ordinary being the tathāgata essence is naturally, utterly pure, so there is no defilement, and even when there is transformation there is no purification that has not occurred before, like space. So it says, "not as defilement, not as purification."[919] {267}

That which is the pure ground isolated from and empty of imaginary and dependent forms and so on is thus said to be the meaning of the forms and so on of the primordially, naturally pure, fully established true nature. For details, one must consult that great commentary itself.

18) *How those also reside as the mantras, tantras, maṇḍalas, mudrās, and so on of the abiding state*

In that way, just as all the primordially, naturally pure forms and so on of the true nature are the deities of the true nature, so too they all also reside primordially, naturally, and spontaneously as the mantras, tantras, maṇḍalas, [214] mudrās, and so on of the true nature.

c. *How form and so on beyond the three realms and the three times are also the same as those*

Also, those are stated in the Mother Sūtras to be the aggregates, elements, sensory bases, and so on beyond the three realms and the three times because, in the context of dedication [in the section on] knowledge of the path, it is said:

> Just as [ultimate] form is not included in the desire realm, the form realm, and the formless realm, those not included are not past, not future, and also not present.[920]

And so on. And because, after that is applied up to the knowledge of all aspects, and also applied to the true nature that never deteriorates and to always abiding in equanimity, it is also said that those are not to be dedicated:

> In that way, that form not included in the desire realm, the form realm, and the formless realm is not past, not future, and also not present. It cannot be fully dedicated by means of conceptual marks or by means of visualization. {268}
>
> Why is that?
>
> It is without nature. That which is without nature is a nonentity; because a nonentity is not an entity, it cannot be fully dedicated.[921]

And so on. And because such passages apply that up to the knowledge of all aspects, and also apply it to the true nature that never deteriorates and to always abiding in equanimity.

The protector Ajita summarizes these by saying, "is not included in the three realms, and . . ."[922] Because these are identical to the previously presented form and so on in the "Chapter on Purity,"[923] the form and so on of the true nature, and the infinite assemblies of the mantra deities of the abiding state, they are all stated to be profound emptiness far from emptiness of annihilation and inanimate emptiness.

d. *Showing that if not understood in that way, buddhahood is not obtained by meditating on the emptiness of self-nature*

That being so, those who claim there is no profound emptiness more, or other than, each [phenomenon] being empty of own-essence are far from the intent of the Conqueror, because the *King of Tantras* says:

> Buddhists teach the words "The three states of cyclic existence
> are not forms [comprised of atoms]. Here is just consciousness.
> Likewise, consciousness itself does not exist and the wisdom
> of a buddha does not abide anywhere."
> Human beings who, separated from the changeless, hold to
> that emptiness, view [all] as empty.
> So the lord teaches in the Mantra Vehicle that which is
> the connate without emission, the blisses of the body.[924] [215]

And:

> That which produces a lord of conquerors, from the power
> of [familiarity] each full day definitely releases one from
> [birth through] a womb. A single moment of that establishes
> total separation from the changes, causing the fluctuating
> to become unfluctuating. One who, abandoning that activity
> of a buddha, and separated from blissful equilibrium, meditating
> on other emptinesses through many tens of millions of eons of that,
> is far from buddhahood and the connate blisses. {269}
>
> Grapes do not come from the neem tree, nectar from poison,
> or lotuses from the fig tree. The bliss of nirvāṇa [is not gained]
> from the empty, bliss from the power of nonvirtue, or attainments
> from killing living creatures. Cattle from sacrifices [do not go to]
> the higher realms, and the stage of sublime peace [is not achieved]
> by blocking the sense faculties. The speech of an omniscient one
> [is not achieved] from the Vedas, nor unfluctuating changeless bliss
> by an impure mind with changes.[925]

And so on, and because Mañjuśrī's *Brief Presentation of the Assertions of My Own View* also says:

> The aggregates, fully examined,
> are empty, without essence, just like
> a plantain tree. Emptiness having the most
> sublime of all aspects is not like that.
>
> That which is the unarisen and unceasing
> [other] knowable object seen here is the emptiness
> of the [ground] entity empty [of phenomena],
> and not that of the examined aggregates.[926]

And because, by way of many aspects, such passages speak again and again of a profound emptiness other than the emptiness of self-nature.

e. *Rejecting many contradictions of scripture about those, and determining the state of being*

It might be asked, "If dharmadhātu, thusness, the apex of reality, and so on are not empty of self-nature, what is the intent of extensive statements such as these in the Conqueror's Mother Sūtras?"

> Dharmadhātu is empty of dharmadhātu. Thusness is empty of thusness. The apex of reality is empty of the apex of reality. The inconceivable basic element is empty of the inconceivable basic element.[927] {270}

And:

> The perfection of wisdom is empty of the perfection of wisdom, and that which is empty is not the perfection of wisdom; it is unarisen.

Up until it says, concerning knowledge of all aspects itself:

> . . . is empty of knowledge of all aspects itself, and that which is empty is not knowledge of all aspects itself; it is unarisen.[928]

And:

> If even the perfection of wisdom is itself totally nonexistent, how could going and coming exist in it?[929]

[Reply:] Those are stated in reference to the provisional meaning, because the *Sūtra of Definitive Commentary on the Intent* says [216]:

> Then, for those who had correctly entered the Mahāyāna, the Bhagavān turned the even more wonderful second wheel of Dharma in the form of a teaching on emptiness: "Phenomena are without an essence, unarisen, unceasing, primordially at peace, and naturally parinirvāṇa itself." That turning of the wheel of Dharma by the Bhagavān was, however, surpassable and adapted to the circumstances. Of provisional meaning, it is a topic or grounds of dispute.[930]

Likewise, in various scriptures of the middle turning of the wheel, all the statements about what is not empty of self-nature being empty of self-nature should also be understood (through relying on the lamp of the uncommon esoteric instructions of careful distinctions) to be of provisional meaning and intentionally ambiguous.

Here the purpose of speaking with intentional ambiguity in that way is to fully pacify grasping, discrimination, and conceptualization about dharmadhātu and so on as this or that.

That those [passages in the Mother Sūtras] are of definitive meaning is refuted because dharmadhātu, thusness, the apex of reality, and so on are stated to be the consummate Buddha, four kāyas, five primordial awarenesses, syllable *e*, bhaga, source of the attributes, lotus, secret, great secret, syllable *a*, Prajñāpāramitā, Viśvamātā, Vajravārāhī, and so on, and the syllable *vaṃ*, great bliss, drop, vajra, Heruka, reality, self-arisen Buddha, and so on, and Vajradhara, Vajrasattva, the syllables *evaṃ*, and Kālacakra, Vajrabhairava, Vajreśvara, Cakrasaṃvara, Guhyasamāja, Hevajra, and so on (all the ultimate deities, mantras, tantras, maṇḍalas, and mudrās), and because they are also stated to be the true nature, thusness, and so on, {271} and because they are stated to be the quintessence of the limitless attributes of the qualities that are not empty of self-nature, such as the powers and the types of fearlessness.

Concerning the basis of the intent here: such statements refer to grasping at those—dharmadhātu and so on, and all relative phenomena pervaded by them—as being empty of self-nature, because (of all phenomena such as forms stated in the three sets) those stated to be empty of self-nature refer to imaginary and dependent forms and so on.

Likewise:

> Since dharmadhātu is nonexistent, a bodhisattva does not observe a prior limit. [217]
>
> Since thusness, the apex of reality, and the inconceivable basic element are nonexistent, a bodhisattva does not observe a prior limit.[931]

This statement is also of provisional meaning and intentionally ambiguous, as before. Dharmadhātu, thusness, is not nonexistent; that is said referring to incidental phenomena not existing indivisibly in it, and for the purpose of pacifying discriminations and concepts about it as this or that.

Likewise:

> Since the very essence of dharmadhātu is nonexistent, a bodhisattva does not observe a prior limit.
>
> Since the very essence of thusness, the apex of reality, and the inconceivable basic element are nonexistent, a bodhisattva does not observe a prior limit.[932]

This statement also does not refer to the nonexistence of the essence of dharmadhātu, thusness itself; it refers to the nonexistence of the very essence of other incidental phenomena. Here also the purpose is as before.

That those passages are of definitive meaning is refuted by the same Mother Sūtras of the Conqueror:

> Whether tathāgatas appear or tathāgatas do not appear, the thusness, unmistaken thusness, thusness that is not something else, true nature, dharmadhātu, constancy of phenomena, flawlessness of phenomena, the apex of reality, and the inconceivable basic element of those phenomena abide in that way. If a [relative] self also does not exist there, and a [relative] sentient being, lifeforce, living being, nourishing being, being, person, Manu, human, agent, feeler, knower, and observer also do not exist, how could such as [relative] form exist there?[933] {272}

On through:

> ... how could such as [relative] aging and death exist? How could such as the phenomena of dependent arising exist? And if those phenomena are nonexistent, how could sentient beings who are to be liberated from the saṃsāra of the five types of living beings exist?[934]

And the *Bodhisattva's Scriptural Collection* in the *Stack of Jewels* also says:

> Furthermore, omnipresent [ultimate] emptiness exists [in reality]. In this, those called "the [relative] self," "sentient being," "life-force," "human being," and "person" do not exist [in reality].[935]

This shows that the ground of emptiness, thusness, is never nonexistent, and, because imaginary and dependent phenomena are primordially nonexistent in it, it is empty of them. Therefore, it is empty of other. This approach explains well the statement in the Mother Sūtras themselves [218]:

> Here, what is the emptiness of other entities? Whether tathāgatas appear or tathāgatas do not appear, constancy of phenomena, the true nature, dharmadhātu itself, the flawlessness of phenomena, thusness, unmistaken thusness, thusness that is not something else, and the apex of reality abide in that way. And, in that way, that which is empty of other entities than those phenomena is called "the emptiness of other entities."[936]

And also the statement in its commentary says:

> The entities of other phenomena such as the aggregates do not exist in those; that is called "the emptiness of other entities."[937]

In that way, the mode of emptiness for the true nature, thusness, is that it is not empty of itself, it is the ground empty of other phenomena.

Here, whether the rūpakāyas of a buddha appear in the world or do not appear in the world, whether persons realize it or do not realize it, see it or do not see it, the apex of reality (having many synonyms, such as "constancy of phenomena") is ever indestructible and unsuitable to be abandoned, present without change in thusness and without difference earlier and later, always partless, omnipresent, and all-pervasive. That is the meaning of being not empty of own-essence.

Here, empty of other entities means empty of imaginary phenomena such as the self, sentient being, lifeforce, living being, {273} nourishing being, and person, and primordially empty of dependent form and so on, the phenomena of the relative aggregates, elements, sensory bases, and dependent arising, and even the sentient beings who circle in the saṃsāra of the five types of living beings. That is the meaning of being empty of other entities. It is also the meaning of that in which something does not exist is empty of it, and that which is the remainder, or the ground of emptiness, always exists.

This approach also carefully explains the mode of emptiness stated in the Mother Sūtras themselves:

> Because dharmadhātu is emptiness, a bodhisattva does not observe a prior limit.
>
> Because thusness, the apex of reality, and the inconceivable basic element are emptiness, a bodhisattva does not observe a prior limit.[938]

Likewise:

> Because dharmadhātu is isolated, a bodhisattva does not observe a prior limit.
>
> Because thusness, the apex of reality, and the inconceivable basic element are isolated, a bodhisattva does not observe a prior limit.[939]

Concerning those statements also, the mode of not being isolated from itself but being isolated from other should be understood. And recalling again and again this uncommon, profound esoteric instruction (that also explains well the many contexts of "unestablished," "pure," "pristine," "utterly pure," "termination," "cessation," "exhaustion," "separation," "full separation," "purification," "abandonment," and so on), [219] one should understand well the meaning of emptiness of own-entity and emptiness of other entities; the meaning of empty emptiness and nonempty emptiness; the meaning of the emptiness of nonentities and the emptiness that is the very essence of the nonexistence of entities; merely being empty of the phenomenon that is to be negated; and the emptiness having many synonyms, such as "ground of emptiness," "true nature," and "thusness."

Likewise:

> Knowledge of all is empty of knowledge of all. Knowledge of the aspects of the path is empty of knowledge of the aspects of the path. Knowledge of all aspects is empty of knowledge of all aspects.[940]

And:

> If a tathāgata's ten powers, four types of fearlessness, and four analytical perfect awarenesses, and a buddha's eighteen unshared attributes are totally nonexistent and unobserved, how could such as the actual achievement of those exist?[941] {274}

And:

> If a tathāgata, an arhat, a perfectly complete buddha is totally nonexistent and unobserved, how could such as the actual achievement of that exist?[942]

And:

> A tathāgata's powers, types of fearlessness, and analytical perfect awarenesses, and a buddha's unshared attributes, are empty of a buddha's unshared attributes.
>
> Why is that?
>
> In emptiness the noble truths, up to a buddha's unshared attributes, do not exist; bodhisattvas do not exist.[943]

And so on. And:

> Because omniscience is nonexistent, a bodhisattva does not observe a prior limit.
>
> Because omniscience is emptiness, isolated, and without very essence, a bodhisattva does not observe a prior limit.[944]

Also concerning such passages, one must realize well the modes of the emptiness of self-nature (the emptiness of nonentities) and the emptiness of other (the emptiness that is the very essence of the nonexistence of entities).

Here, if the division of the two truths regarding knowledge of all, knowledge of the aspects of the path, knowledge of all aspects, the powers, the types of fearlessness, the analytical perfect awarenesses, a buddha's unshared attributes, buddha, enlightenment, bodhisattva, and so on is understood, one will not be deluded about the Sage's word.

Concerning that, because the ultimate ten powers and so on are the ground of emptiness, the true nature, the unconditioned basic element itself, they are the consummate truth of cessation. [220] Because the relative ten powers and so on are included in the conditioned, impermanent, truth of the path, it is accurate to say that they are empty of self-nature.

That being so, it should be known that teaching what abide as empty of self-nature to be empty of self-nature is without even the slightest contradiction, and that any statements about what is not empty of self-nature being empty of self-nature are just of provisional meaning and intentionally ambiguous, as presented before.

Referring to this, the *Noble Sūtra of the Great Drum* also says:

> "Bhagavān, in the Mahāyāna there are also many sūtras that teach the meaning of emptiness."
>
> The Bhagavān replied, "All those whatsoever that teach emptiness should be known to be intentionally ambiguous, but these like this unsurpassable sūtra should be known to not be intentionally ambiguous.[945]

And so on. {275} Here, the *Great Mother Sūtra* states what are included in conditioned, impermanent phenomena:

> Subhūti, concerning what are called "conditioned phenomena": the phenomena included in the desire realm, form realm, and formless realm, and furthermore, in the realms of conditioned phenomena that are not those, the four foundations of mindfulness, the four perfect renunciations, the four bases for the miraculous, the five faculties, the five powers, the seven limbs of enlightenment, the eight limbs of the noble path, the four noble truths, the four meditative states, the four immeasurables, the

> four formless meditative absorptions, the eight liberations, the nine sequential meditative absorptions, emptiness, signlessness, wishlessness, the five paranormal abilities, the six perfections, all emptinesses, all samādhis, all doors of dhāraṇīs, a tathāgata's ten powers, four types of fearlessness, four analytical perfect awarenesses, great love, great compassion, and the eighteen unshared attributes of a buddha are called "conditioned phenomena."[946]

Here, since the conditioned foundations of mindfulness, up to the unshared attributes of a buddha, are included in the truth of the path, they are empty of self-nature.

Likewise, the *Sūtra of the Meeting of Father and Son* in the *Stack of Jewels* also says:

> "Buddha" is only a term; likewise,
> the powers, the primordial awarenesses,
> and the four types of fearlessness
> are also called "relative," the Sage says.[947]

The Mother Sūtras also say:

> The perfection of wisdom is impermanent, but not because of separation from anything....[948]

On through:

> ... the eighteen unshared attributes of a buddha are impermanent, but not because of separation from anything.[949]

And so on. And:

> The perfection of generosity...[950]

On through:

> ... the eighteen unshared attributes of a buddha do not cause direct awakening in unsurpassable, perfectly complete enlightenment. [221]
>
> Subhūti, why is that?

> In this way, those phenomena [of the truth of the path] also are all conditioned, directly conditioned, but knowledge of all aspects [of the truth of cessation] cannot be achieved by means of conditioned and directly conditioned phenomena.
>
> Subhūti, those phenomena also, however, all become causes for practicing the paths and developing the paths, but not because they accomplish the result [of separation].[951] {276}

Here, the ten powers and so on included in the ultimate, unconditioned truth of cessation are discussed by the honorable Bhagavān Lokeśvara:

> Mahāmudrā, having the characteristics of all the [ultimate] attributes without [relative] nature, having the most sublime of all aspects, Prajñāpāramitā, she who produces the buddhas.
>
> The term "source of the attributes" also expresses that, because it is the source of the attributes from which all the [ultimate] attributes without [relative] nature occur.
>
> The [ultimate] attributes without [relative] nature are the eighty-four thousand aggregates of the attributes such as the ten powers and the types of fearlessness. Those occur from the source of the attributes, the [ultimate] buddhafield.
>
> It is the basis of the buddhas and the bodhisattvas, the basis of bliss and the basis of birth.
>
> That from which blood, urine, and semen arise is not the source of the attributes.
>
> Here, the fields of desire and lack of desire for saṃsāra beings are not those of the tathāgatas.
>
> Therefore, the source of the attributes is Viśvamātā (who has the nature of dharmadhātu), embraced by Bhagavān Kālacakra, at all times free of all obscurations.[952]

And so on. And the honorable conqueror Maitreya also says:

> The first kāya has the qualities
> of separation, such as the powers.[953]

Because all the qualities of the unconditioned dharmakāya are obtained by mere separation from the incidental stains, they are qualities of separation; the thirty-two here summarize the primary ones.

As for an extensive distinguishing of their aspects, they are stated to be innumerable and limitless.

> Luminosity, uncreated and
> manifesting indivisibly, bears all
> the attributes of a buddha, exceeding
> the grains of sand in the Ganges River.[954]

And:

> Not empty of the unsurpassable attributes
> having the characteristic of inseparability.[955]

The commentary on that also says:

> Therefore, it is said:
>
>> The tathāgata essence is empty of all the husks of the afflictions that are divisible and can be realized as being separable [from it], but not empty of the inconceivable attributes of a buddha that are indivisible and cannot be realized as being separable [from it], which are more numerous than the grains of sand found in the Ganges River.[956] [222]

Thus it quotes the *Sūtra of Śrīmālā*. And the commentary on "Since indivisibly in the true nature"[957] says:

> Here, since even at the level of a singularly defiled ordinary being the stainless qualities of a buddha exist indivisibly in the true nature without difference before and after, this point is inconceivable.[958] {277}

Thus the great Madhyamaka master, the honorable, noble Asaṅga also says. In that way, the source of the attributes, Mahāmudrā, Prajñāpāramitā, and Viśvamātā are indivisible from and cannot be realized as being separable from dharmadhātu, thusness, and the eighty-four thousand aggregates of the ultimate attributes such as the ten powers without nature, or the inconceivable attributes of a buddha exceeding the grains of sand found in the Ganges

River, which are the qualities of the unconditioned true nature, the apex of reality. Therefore, these are not empty of self-nature, but are the ground of emptiness, the emptiness that is the very essence of the nonexistence of entities, the emptiness of other entities, and nonempty emptiness.

The *Great Mother Sūtra* also says:

> Subhūti, what are called "unconditioned attributes" do not arise, are not destroyed, and do not change from abiding into something else; they are extinguished passionate desire, extinguished hatred, extinguished ignorance; they are thusness, unmistaken thusness, thusness that is not something else, the true nature, dharmadhātu, flawlessness of phenomena, the inconceivable basic element, and the apex of reality. Subhūti, those are called "unconditioned attributes."[959]

And:

> Venerable Śāradvatiputra, furthermore, all the [ultimate] attributes are virtuous, all the attributes are flawless, all the attributes are taintless, all the attributes are without the afflictions, all the attributes are pure, all the attributes are transcendent, all the attributes are unconditioned, but not because of separation from anything.[960]

Thus those that are stated to be naturally transcendent and pure, ultimate virtue, the attributes of the unconditioned qualities "exceeding the grains of sand found in the Ganges River" should be understood: these are not relative attributes. {278}

Likewise, in the *Stack of Jewels*, the *Sūtra Teaching the Inconceivable Sphere of a Buddha* also says:

> Monks, the unarisen, unoccurred, uncreated, directly unconditioned, and directly unconditioning exists. Monks, the unarisen, unoccurred, uncreated, directly unconditioned, and directly unconditioning is not nonexistent [in reality].[961] [223]

The meaning of such passages is explained well by just those previous explanations.

f. *Showing that to obtain those, these impure aggregates must cease*

In that way, it is stated that the quintessence in which the ten powers and so on without nature (the ultimate attributes of a buddha exceeding the grains of sand found in the Ganges River), and so on, naturally and spontaneously complete, which are the forms and so on of the true nature, are obtained when the forms and so on of the incidental stains have ceased. The *Mahāparinirvāṇa* says:

> The Bhagavān spoke this to the venerable all-knowing Kauṇḍinya: "Form [of the truths of suffering and the origin] is impermanent and, by form having ceased by means of the catalyst [of the truth of the path], [the truth of cessation's] form of constantly abiding liberation is obtained. Feeling, discrimination, conditioning factors, and consciousness are also impermanent and, by the catalyst of consciousness having ceased, the consciousness of constantly abiding liberation is obtained.
>
> "Kauṇḍinya, form is suffering and, by the catalyst of form having ceased, the blissful form of liberation is obtained. Feeling, discrimination, conditioning factors, and consciousness should also be known extensively in that way.
>
> "Kauṇḍinya, form is empty [of own-essence]. By the catalyst of empty form having ceased, the liberation of form that is not empty is obtained. Up to feeling, discrimination, conditioning factors, and consciousness should also be known extensively in that way. {279}
>
> "Kauṇḍinya, form is selfless. By the catalyst of form having ceased, the form of liberation, the perfect self, is obtained. Feeling, discrimination, conditioning factors, and consciousness should also be known extensively in that way.
>
> "Kauṇḍinya, form is utterly impure. By the catalyst of form having ceased, the utterly pure form of liberation is obtained. Feeling, discrimination, conditioning factors, and consciousness should also be known extensively in that way.
>
> "Kauṇḍinya, form is birth, aging, illness, and death. By the catalyst of form having ceased, the form of liberation that is not birth, aging, illness, and death is obtained. Feeling, discrimination, conditioning factors, and consciousness should also be known extensively in that way.

"Kauṇḍinya, form is unknowing. By the catalyst of form having ceased, the form of liberation that is not unknowing is obtained. Feeling, discrimination, conditioning factors, and consciousness should also be known extensively in that way.

"Kauṇḍinya, form becomes the cause of birth. By the catalyst of form having ceased, the form of liberation that is not born is obtained. Feeling, discrimination, conditioning factors, and consciousness should also be known extensively in that way. [224]

"Kauṇḍinya, form becomes the cause of the four mistakes.[962] By the catalyst of form having ceased, the form of liberation that is not the cause of the mistakes is obtained. Up to feeling, discrimination, conditioning factors, and consciousness should also be known extensively in that way.

"Kauṇḍinya, form is the cause of measureless nonvirtuous attributes. It is like this: from form come phenomena such as desire for bodies male, female, and so on, and for food; passionate desire, hatred, ignorance, stinginess, jealousy, nonvirtuous mind, and attached mind; food of the elements, food of consciousness, food of thought, and food of contact; {280} birth from an egg, birth from a womb, birth from heat and moisture, and miraculous birth; the five desires, and the five obscurations.[963] By the catalyst of form having ceased, the form of liberation (a body that has not acquired those measureless faulty defects) is obtained. Up to feeling, discrimination, conditioning factors, and consciousness should also be known extensively in that way.

"Kauṇḍinya, form is bound by bonds. By the catalyst of bound form having ceased, the unbound form of liberation is obtained. Up to feeling, discrimination, conditioning factors, and consciousness should also be known extensively in that way.

"Kauṇḍinya, form is the cause of an unbroken continuity [of suffering]. By the catalyst of the form of that continuity having ceased, the form of liberation that is not a continuity [of suffering but of bliss] is obtained. Up to feeling, discrimination, conditioning factors, and consciousness should also be known extensively in that way.

"Kauṇḍinya, form is not the cause [or source] of taking refuge. By the catalyst of form having ceased, the form of liberation that is [the source of] taking refuge is obtained. Up to feeling, discrimination, conditioning factors, and consciousness should also be known extensively in that way.

"Kauṇḍinya, form is like a wound. By the catalyst of form having ceased, the form of liberation that is without wounds is obtained. Up to feeling, discrimination, conditioning factors, and consciousness should also be known extensively in that way.

"Kauṇḍinya, form is not total peace. By the catalyst of form having ceased, the total peace of the form of parinirvāṇa is obtained. Up to feeling, discrimination, conditioning factors, and consciousness should also be known extensively in that way.

"Kauṇḍinya, if any person understands [the abiding state of the four truths] in such a way, he is called 'śramaṇa,' and also called 'brahmin.' He is also said to 'possess the Dharma of a śramaṇa and the Dharma of a brahmin.' {281}

"Kauṇḍinya, except for in the Dharma of the Buddha, there are no śramaṇas and no brahmins, and also no Dharma of śramaṇas and of brahmins. [225] All non-Buddhists just tell lies; they have no perfect conduct. They are conceited like those two types, but do not have the basis of those two types.

"Why is that?

"I say, 'Without the Dharma of śramaṇas and of brahmins, how could śramaṇas and brahmins exist?'

"I have also always proclaimed the lion's roar [of the ultimate sugata essence] in this circle of the retinue; you must also always proclaim the lion's roar in the great circle of the retinue."[964]

Here, because those forms and so on that are the objects of negation are the stains suitable to be abandoned, they are empty of self-nature. Because the forms and so on of the ultimate sugata essence (the objects to be obtained, always present as the basic ground in which those have ceased) are natural luminosity, unsuitable to be abandoned, they are empty of other.

g. *Showing that if those are obtained, all the profound abiding states such as the other* evaṃ *are obtained*

In that way, the forms and so on of the ultimate sugata essence—obtained when the continuity of the forms and so on of the incidental stains having a quintessence of impermanence, suffering, emptiness, selflessness, impurity, unknowing, and so on have ceased—are other than the outer and inner relative. These are also stated to be the quintessence of Vajrasattva, vajra and lotus, vajra semen and menses, vajra moon and sun, vajra knowing and knowable objects, the vajra vowels such as *a* and consonant-syllables such as *ka*, and so on, and to be the quintessence of the syllables *evaṃ*, in which the five changeless great emptinesses and the six changeless empty drops are primordially indivisible and integrated as the same taste. The great commentary on the tantra says:

> Here, these fourteen syllables—"Empty, also primordial awareness, drop, the sublime [and the sublime] and Vajra Holder, . . ."[965] —summarize this person who is a great being of the six elements by means of the terms "empty" and so on. It is like this: the aggregate of primordial awareness, the aggregate of consciousness, the element of primordial awareness, the element of space, mind, ears, {282} sound, the element of phenomena, the sublime sense faculties [the eyes], the bhaga, the flow of urine, and the emission of semen. These being free of obscuration, having the same taste, and integrated as one is called "empty." All are not nonentities, because they are personally experienced by the yogin. The conquerors say that is indestructible. The symbol of the term for this indestructible is just a drawing, unpronounceable, of the image of a flaying knife in the middle of south, north, east, and west. [226] This is the first changeless great emptiness.
>
> After that, the word "also" in this "also primordial awareness" is presented for the purpose of inclusion, because it causes an understanding of the meaning of inclusion. By this term "primordial awareness," "the third emptiness" should be understood, like this: the aggregate of feeling, the element of fire, the eyes, taste, the hands, and going. These being without obscuration, having the same taste, and integrated as one is primordial awareness, the third changeless great emptiness. The symbol of the term for this is two drops, unpronounceable, to the south of the symbol of the indestructible middle.
>
> By this term "drop," the fourth emptiness should be understood, because of the previous word "also." It is like this: the aggregate of discrimination, the element of water, the tongue, form, the feet, and taking. These being without obscuration, having the same taste, and integrated as one is the drop, the fourth changeless

great emptiness. The symbol of the term for this is one drop, unpronounceable, to the north of the symbol of the middle.

As for "the sublime [and the sublime] and Vajra Holder," the sublime and the sublime and Vajra Holder means "the sublime and Vajra Holder" because it is an *ekadvandva*.[966] Due to the previous word "also," these three become terms for [great] emptiness.[967] The first term "sublime" expresses "the second emptiness." {283} It is like this: the aggregate of conditioning factors, the element of wind, the nose, tangible objects, the sense faculty of speech, and the flow of feces. These being free of obscuration, having the same taste, and integrated as one is the sublime, the second changeless great emptiness. The symbol of the term for this is just a drawing of the image of a staff, unpronounceable, to the east of the indestructible middle.

The second term "sublime" expresses "the fifth emptiness" like this: the aggregate of form, the element of earth, the sense faculty of the body, odor, the anus, and expression. These being without obscuration, having the same taste, and integrated as one is the sublime, the fifth changeless great emptiness. The symbol of the term for this is the image of a plow, unpronounceable, to the west of the indestructible middle.

By the stated sequence in that way, all five integrated as one are said to be the five changeless great emptinesses, the syllable *vaṃ*, Vajrasattva, great bliss, vajra.[968]

And:

In that way, the syllable *vaṃ* is the five changeless great emptinesses, the quintessence of nonreferential compassion, beyond the true nature of tiny atoms, similar to the nature of a prognostic image, which the yogin should realize.[969]

And [227]:

The five changeless great emptinesses are the quintessence of the thirty-six [ultimate deities], and the conquerors state that to be vajra. Because of holding it, they are the Vajra Holder.

The six changeless empty drops are the syllable *e*, the source of the attributes, the images of emptiness having all aspects. It is like this: the aggregate of consciousness, the element of space, the ears, the element of phenomena, the bhaga, and the emission of semen; these free of obscuration are emptiness having all aspects. Above the indestructible middle, the symbol of the term for this is the syllable *ka*, the unpronounceable consonant consisting of the *ka* class,[970] which is the first empty drop. {284}

The aggregate of conditioning factors, the element of wind, the nose, tangible objects, speech, and the flow of feces; these free of obscuration are emptiness having all aspects. To the east of the eastern symbol, the symbol of the term for this is the syllable *ca*, the unpronounceable consonant consisting of the *ca* class,[971] which is the second empty drop.

The aggregate of feeling, the element of fire, the eyes, taste, the hands, and going; these free of obscuration are emptiness having all aspects. To the south of the southern symbol, the symbol of the term for this is the syllable *ṭa*, the unpronounceable consonant consisting of the *ṭa* class,[972] which is the third empty drop.

The aggregate of discrimination, the element of water, the tongue, form, the faculty of the feet, and taking; these free of obscuration are emptiness having all aspects. To the north of the northern symbol, the symbol of the term for this is the syllable *pa*, the unpronounceable consonant consisting of the *pa* class,[973] which is the fourth empty drop.

The aggregate of form, the element of earth, the faculty of the body, odor, the anus, and expression; these free of obscuration are emptiness having all aspects. To the west of the western symbol, the symbol of the term for this is the syllable *ta*,[974] the unpronounceable consonant consisting of the *ta* class, which is the fifth empty drop.

The aggregate of primordial awareness, the element of primordial awareness, mind, sound, the sublime sense faculties [the eyes], and the flow of urine; these free of obscuration are emptiness having all aspects. Below the symbol of the indestructible middle, the symbol of the term for this is the syllable *sa*, the unpronounceable consonant consisting of the *sa* class,[975] which is the sixth empty drop.

That being so, the six changeless empty drops are the source of

> the attributes, the Vajra Holder, the syllable *e*, which is observable emptiness having the nature of a prognostic image.[976]

And:

> Here, the five changeless great emptinesses are the group of vowels, called "semen and moon." {285} The six changeless empty drops are the group of consonants, called "menses and sun." Here, semen and moon are the syllable *vaṃ*—vajra. Menses and sun are the syllable *e*—lotus. The oneness of these two—vajra and lotus—is Vajrasattva. [228] Vajra is sublime bliss, knowing, and semen. Sattva is the form of wisdom having all aspects, knowable object, and sun; blessed by primordial awareness and consciousness, free of obscuration and integrated as one, reality, the one who performs the benefit of living beings.[977]

And:

> Likewise, the other inner awareness, Prajñāpāramitā, naturally luminous, Mahāmudrā, she who bears the form of connate joy, the state of completion in accord with dharmadhātu as its cause, mother of Vajrasattva and the buddhas, not the field of experience of the sense faculties of dependent arising, the field of experience of the sublime sense faculties [the eyes], the nature of sublimely unchanging bliss, beyond the true nature of tiny atoms, that which is similar to a prognostic image in a mirror and to a dream is stated by the conquerors to be the connate kāya, because of its sublimely unchanging nature.
>
> Here, the changeless are form, feeling, discrimination, conditioning factors, and consciousness without obscuration—the five changeless stated to be great emptiness. Likewise, the elements of earth, water, fire, wind, and space without obscuration are stated to be the five changeless.
>
> The six changeless are the eyes, ears, nose, tongue, body, and mind without obscuration, each of which have abandoned apprehending their individual objects. Likewise, form, sound, odor, taste, tangible objects, and the element of phenomena without obscuration are also stated to be the six changeless. The same taste

> in one, these aggregates, elements, and sensory bases are the empty drops. These drops, also being immutable, are called "sublimely unchanging." {286} The sublimely unchanging is also the syllable *a*, and what is arisen from the syllable *a* is the perfectly complete Buddha, the quintessence of wisdom and means, Vajrasattva, the androgynous stage, called "the connate kāya" because it is the quintessence of knowing and knowable objects, cause and result indivisible. That is also Bhagavān Kālacakra, the stage of sublimely unchanging bliss.[978]

And:

> Here the five changeless great emptinesses are vajra.[979]

And:

> The "six changeless empty drops" are the source of the attributes, the support of this [vajra], having the characteristics of the form of a buddha, manifesting in all the three realms and the three times.
>
> [The attributes] of these [six changeless empty drops] that have ceased are the six aggregates and so on, the thirty-six elements, and the thirty-seventh changeable primordial awareness [with obscurations]. These without obscurations are called "dharmakāya," source of the attributes. The four vajras [of body, speech, mind, and primordial awareness] are the five changeless [great emptinesses], and the emanations of these are the nirmāṇakāya, which displays various magical emanations. [229] The sound of the [dharmakāya] teacher of the Dharma is the [ultimate] sambhoga.[980]

h. *Showing that which is to be obtained to be other than, more sublime than, and beyond this relative outer and inner*

Those aggregates, elements, and so on—primordially free of obscuration, indivisible, having the same taste, the true nature having all aspects—are other than, or more sublime than, or beyond the aggregates, elements, and so on of the relative outer and inner.

Moreover, the *Root Tantra in Five Hundred Thousand Lines* says:

Through cessation of cause and result,
there is buddhahood, without doubt.

Dustless, free of dust, stainless,
flaws abandoned, faultless. Very
wakened, wakened self, excellent
one knowing all and aware of all.[981]

Through cessation of cause and result,
the kāya of the lord of conquerors is other.
Body, speech, mind, and bliss are other.
The collection of the aggregates is other,

the elements of earth and so on are other.
The objects and sense faculties and,
likewise, the action faculties and the activities
of the action faculties are other. {287}

Hands and feet and so on everywhere,
eyes and mouths and heads everywhere,
having ears everywhere, he resides
in the world pervading everything.[982]

This statement that—when these aggregates included in cause and result, abiding empty of self-nature, have ceased—other aggregates and so on are obtained, also states that aggregates, elements, and so on other than those empty of self-nature exist. Because they are also said to be emptiness, an emptiness other than the emptiness of self-nature is well established, and that is also the ultimate emptiness of other. "Hands and feet and so on everywhere," and so forth, shows just that to be the union of means and wisdom indivisible, the kāya of primordial awareness having all sense faculties [in each one], and also shows just that to reside pervading everything. And it is identical to the dharmakāya, great nirvāṇa, stated to be pure, self, blissful, and permanent.

Those points are also stated in the *Sūtra Taught by Akṣayamati*. Just as it says:

> Even though dharmadhātu is the [other] element of earth, dharmadhātu does not have the characteristic of solidity. Even though

> dharmadhātu is the element of water, dharmadhātu does not have the characteristic of wetness. Even though dharmadhātu is the element of fire, dharmadhātu does not have the characteristic of ripening. Even though dharmadhātu is the element of wind, dharmadhātu does not have the characteristic of movement. Even though dharmadhātu is the element of the eyes, dharmadhātu does not have the characteristic of vision. Even though dharmadhātu is the elements of the ears, nose, tongue, body, and mind, and those of eye consciousness, ear consciousness, nose consciousness, [230] tongue consciousness, body consciousness, and mental consciousness, dharmadhātu does not have the characteristics of hearing, smelling, feeling, tasting, and cognizing, and those of cognizing form, cognizing sound, cognizing odor, cognizing taste, cognizing tangible objects, and cognizing phenomena. Even though dharmadhātu is the element of form and the elements of sound, odor, taste, tangible objects, and phenomena, it does not have the characteristic to be cognized by means of eye consciousness, and by ear, nose, tongue, body, and mental consciousnesses.[983] {288}

And so on, which is applied individually in detail, so one must consult that very sūtra. Likewise, the *Glorious Immaculate Tantra* also says:

> Because the other aggregates and so on are seen,
> they are said to be "the maṇḍala of the assembly."[984]

And the "Chapter on Primordial Awareness" also says:

> This unique Vajrasattva appears as Heruka, equal to the cloud
> at the end of an eon, for the sake of ripening the malicious.
> He is also the conqueror of sacred commitment, for the sake of
> comfort to the deluded; the lord of jewels, for those who suffer;
> also the lotus holder, for the desire of those with desire; and for
> the sake of destroying obstructors he appears with a sword
> in his lotus hand as Amoghasiddhi.
>
> From hatred, she who is Viśvamātā, equal to the fire at the end
> of an eon, appears as ḍākinī. From ignorance, she who is called

> Locanā; and sublime compassion, Māmakī, from pride as the cause. From desire, she who is called Pāṇḍarā; and from jealousy, also Tārā, treasure of all qualities. These two, having various forms, also appear as all the other objects and subjects.[985]

The commentary says:

> This unique Vajrasattva himself, discussed before, appears as black Heruka, equal to the cloud at the end of an eon. By virtue of no emission, that other consciousness [appears as] Heruka. He is also emanated by Vajrasattva for the sake of ripening the malicious.
>
> That Vajrasattva also, the conqueror of sacred commitment, that other form, for the sake of ripening the deluded, appears as Vairocana.
>
> [That Vajrasattva] also, the lord of jewels, by virtue of no emission is that other feeling. For the sake of giving [bliss] to those in suffering, that appears as Ratnasambhava, who snatches away all suffering.
>
> [That Vajrasattva] also, the lotus holder, by virtue of no emission is that other discrimination. To [remove] the desire of those with desire, that appears as Amitābha, who bestows bliss without emission. [231]
>
> [That Vajrasattva] also, the one with a sword in his lotus hand for the sake of destroying obstructors, by virtue of no emission is the other conditioning factors. To eliminate obscurations in the mind and destroy the obscurations of the māras and so on, {289} that appears as Amoghasiddhi.
>
> Thus the purity of the five buddhas.
>
> Now the five elements are stated: "From hatred. . ." and so on. Here, from great hatred (ordinary hatred extinguished), Prajñāpāramitā, emptiness having all aspects, she who is Viśvamātā, appears as Vajradhātvīśvarī, Vajraḍākinī.
>
> Likewise, from great ignorance (ignorance extinguished), Locanā. Sublime compassion, Māmakī, appears from the cause of great pride (pride extinguished). From great desire (desire extinguished), she who is Pāṇḍarā. From great jealousy (jealousy extinguished), she who is a treasure of all qualities, Tārā, appears.
>
> In that way, the other element of space, the other element of

earth, the other element of water, the other element of fire, and the other element of wind.

Those characteristics of the elements are thus established to be "[emanated] from form without obscuration and the bliss of no emission."

Kālacakra and Viśvamātā, means and wisdom integrated as one, these two having various forms also appear as all the other objects and subjects—those other objects such as odor, those other subjects such as ears, the others such as speech and hands, and the others such as the activities of the action faculties. And, that being so:

> Hands and feet and so on everywhere,
> eyes and heads and mouths everywhere,
> having ears everywhere, Vajrasattva resides
> in the world pervading everything.[986]

In that way:

> Aware of itself, aware of the other, having
> all [sense faculties in each one], sublime being
> benefiting all, beyond worldly examples, sublime
> lord of other knowing and knowable objects.[987]

And the "Chapter on Sādhana" also says:

> Here, when relative phenomena have ceased, there are those other conditioning factors and so on. {290} Therefore, the purified conditioning factors are Amoghasiddhi, because the obscurations of the conditioning factors are extinguished. Feeling is "stainless gem in hand," Ratnasambhava; the word "and" [in the verse] has a conjunctive meaning. Likewise, discrimination is Amitābha. The aggregate of form is "cakra bearer," Vairocana. These [other aggregates], again, are Akṣobhya and so on—[the other] semen, called "rabbit-bearer";[988] flesh, called "power"; blood, urine, and feces. Because these are purified and without obscuration, they are the purified five aggregates of consciousness and so on. [232]
>
> Likewise, "by means of the [other] elements" (the "six goddesses" Viśvamātā, Vajradhātvīśvarī, Tārā, Pāṇḍarā, Māmakī, and

Locanā), the elements of [relative] primordial awareness, space, wind, fire, water, and earth have ceased, so those other elements are purified.

As for "by means of the objects and subjects": by the purified six objects such as form and subjects such as the eyes, that purified other form and so on and those other eyes and so on are Kṣitigarbha and so on together with Rūpavajrā and so on, the pure bodhisattvas with the mudrās.

Concerning the five wrathful beings, "by means of the powers" (the power of faith, the power of diligence, the power of mindfulness, the power of samādhi, and the power of wisdom), the obscurations of no faith, no diligence, no mindfulness, no samādhi, and no wisdom are extinguished. So there are the powers of faith and so on. Purified by those powers, the kings of the wrathful beings—Uṣṇīṣa, Vighnāntaka, Prajñāntaka, Padmāntaka, and Yamāntaka—are pure. {291}

"Definitely, again, the others"—Sumbharāja, Nīladaṇḍa, Ṭakkirāja, Acala, and Mahābala—are utterly purified by the five action faculties of the bhaga, speech, hands, feet, and anus, and by the activities of the action faculties, together with Raudrākṣī and so on.

Cāmuṇḍā and so on [are purified] by the eight units of time [in a day]. Bhīmā and so on residing on the petals of the lotus [are purified] by the rising signs and the sixty units of time. The four are purified by the empty petals. Because the obscurations of the nirmāṇacakra are extinguished, the other Cārcikā and so on, and the other Bhīmā and so on, are purified.

As for "the demigods and so on": Nairṛtya, Vāyu, Agni, Ṣaṇmukha, Samudra, Gaṇendra, Śakra, Brahmā, Rudra, Yakṣa, Viṣṇu, and Yama are pure because the obscurations of the twelve—the month of Caitra, the month of Vaiśākha, the month of Jyeṣṭha, the month of Āṣāḍha, the month of Śrāvaṇa, the month of Bhādra, the month of Āśvina, the month of Kārtika, the month of Mārgaśīrṣa, the month of Pauṣa, the month of Māgha, and the month of Phālguna—are extinguished.

Residing on the petals of their lotus, the three hundred and sixty associated with Lāsyā and so on are purified by the days having the number of breaths of the units of time and, because the obscurations of the three hundred and sixty days are extinguished, the other deities and other goddesses of the petals are purified. {292} [233]

"In the secret [cakra], the nāgas and the fierce females are also purified by sixteen units of time multiplied by two"; [sixteen] is multiplied by two because of the division of wisdom and means.

As for "Likewise, the passionate females and so on": here the thirty-six passionate females and the thirty-six outer passionate females[989] mentioned before are purified by means of the activities of the body due to the power of the qualities of the primary nature. And those other passionate females and so on are purified because the obscurations of the activities of the body are extinguished.

All the adepts [are purified] by means of the hairs of the head. The assemblies of elemental spirits in the charnel grounds are purified by the thirty-five million body hairs without obscuration. In that way, those other adepts and those other elemental spirits are purified.

The lord's weapons, the vajra and so on, are purified by the twenty-four aspects of reality without obscuration, because they are without the primary nature of the [relative] twenty-four aspects.

Concerning "by the power of the qualities of the primary nature": the primary nature is the collection of the elements of [relative] earth and so on. Their qualities are the [relative] six objects, and, from extinguishing their obscurations, the outer six mudrās [i.e., ornaments] are purified by the elements of the other [ultimate] odor and so on.

Concerning "by the vajras": because the vajras of body, speech, mind, and primordial awareness are without obscuration by means of the purified characteristics of the waking state, the dream state, the deep-sleep state, and the fourth state, the inner mudrās are purified, and those four mudrās of the other kāya [of ultimate primordial awareness] are purified. Concerning "at the heart of the Vajra Holder": these perfectly abide upon a moon at the heart of the lord of the maṇḍala.

The glorious Vajra Bearer is sublimely changeless connate joy. Viśvamātā is the primordial awareness of emptiness having all aspects and seeing the three times, because the obscurations of the

> bliss of emission and conceptualization are extinguished. Thus they are purified. {293}
>
> They "reside in threefold cyclic existence" everywhere and at all times with all aggregates and so on purified, because all the obscurations are extinguished. This is the rule of the Bhagavān.
>
> In that way, fully understanding [the other] cyclic existence is called "[great] nirvāṇa."[990]

Very many such passages say the aggregates, elements, and so on (that are other than the aggregates, elements, and so on abiding empty of self-nature) are the deities of primordial awareness, and are also emptiness. Therefore, a profound emptiness other than the emptiness of self-nature is established as existent.

Likewise, these statements that when the aggregates, elements, and so on of the incidental stains abiding empty of self-nature have ceased, the aggregates, elements, and so on of the sugata essence abiding as the deities of primordial awareness are obtained, also show that extinguishing the stains that are to be purified does not extinguish the ground of purification, the sugata essence. [234]

The noble, honorable Vajragarbha also says:

> Consciousness and the eyes, and so on, are bound by that binding of entities. Release through fully understanding that cessation of those objects and sense faculties is called "fully understanding." Therefore, release by means of the entity itself is release from the six consciousnesses by means of the divine eye and so on seeing past and future objects,[991] since the Bhagavān said that consciousness "is other." Likewise, form and so on are also called "other." Therefore, it says:
>
> > Hands and feet everywhere,
> > eyes and mouths and heads everywhere,
> > having ears in all the world, he resides
> > pervading everything.[992]

This shows that if the objects and sense faculties have not ceased, one is bound, but if they have ceased, one is released. And this kāya of primordial awareness having all sense faculties [in each one]—such as the other consciousness—that is stated to reside pervasively is also the profound emptiness other than the emptiness of self-nature. {294}

The *Glorious Stainless Light* also says:

> In the middle of these (earth and so on), the Vajra Bearer is not the [eight] primary natures and not the [sixteen] manifestations; the pervader is without the nature [of an entity]. Why? Because he is the [true] nature of mind released from the habitual propensities of saṃsāra. Therefore, "The mind that is [naturally luminous] existent mind [in reality], is not [relative] mind."[993] Thus the existence of the other mind of [great] nirvāṇa separate from the mind of saṃsāra is stated by the Bhagavān by means of the name Vajra Bearer.[994]

And:

> The ubiquitous Vajra Bearer of space, free of the sense objects, is without the [eight] qualities and without the nature [of an entity].[995]

This should be understood extensively from the esoteric instructions of a master. Furthermore, that same source says:

> Here, the purified four vajras of mind are the characteristics of the four kāyas. Mind without the entity of the mind of the fourth state consisting of [united] bhaga and male organ totally contaminated by the stains of passionate desire difficult to destroy is the svābhāvikakāya, the "Omniscient One."
>
> Mind without the entity of the mind of the deep-sleep state overwhelmed by darkness is the dharmakāya, the "kāya of primordial awareness."
>
> Mind without the entity of the mind of the dream state of existence and nonexistence produced by the lifeforce [wind] is the sambhogakāya, the "kāya of the sun."
>
> Mind without the entity of the mind of the waking state, the discrimination of the entities of many concepts, is the nirmāṇakāya, the "eyes wide like lotus petals."[996] [235]

These statements also show the relative to be empty of self-nature and the ultimate to be empty of other. How do they show that? Since the entity of the mind of the fourth state is incidental stain, it is empty of self-nature. Since the ground for its nonexistence (the ultimate sugata essence, the mind of changeless bliss) is the svābhāvikakāya, it is never nonexistent and is the consummation of purity, bliss, permanence, and self; it is not empty of self-nature. And since that is also great emptiness, this scripture also establishes the ultimate to be the emptiness of other.

Likewise, the entities of the minds of the deep-sleep state, the dream state, and the waking state are empty of self-nature. {295} The ground of their nonexistence (the minds of the mind, speech, and body of the sugata essence) are included in the ultimate dharmakāya, sambhogakāya, and nirmāṇakāya; those are also empty of other.

Here these statements four times about "mind without the entity of the mind" also totally agree with the previously mentioned passage:

> That in which something does not exist is empty of it. That which is the remainder permanently exists in that.[997]

And so on. That is also the way to understand existence and nonexistence.

These passages also show the stains to be purified and the ground of purification to be distinct. And they are not just conceptually distinct, because the difference of contrived incidental and naturally original exists, because the difference of relative and ultimate exists, because the difference of phenomena and true nature exists, because the difference of extreme and middle exists, because the difference of other-arisen and self-arisen exists, because the difference of imaginary or dependent and fully established true nature exists, because the difference of consciousness and primordial awareness exists, because the difference of worldly and transcendent exists, because the difference of conditioned and unconditioned exists, because the difference of suffering and bliss exists, because the difference of tainted and taintless exists, because the difference of incomplete and complete qualities of the dharmakāya exists, and because the difference of destructible and indestructible exists. And so on. Thus they differ by means of many great, great differences.

Likewise, the repeated statement of naturally luminous mind, "The mind that is existent mind; that does not exist in mind,"[998] should be understood to be speaking of the ultimate emptiness of other. Here ultimate mind is mind that exists in the abiding state. Relative mind is mind that does not exist in the abiding state.

Therefore, "the mind that is existent mind" is ultimate bodhicitta, naturally luminous. [236] And it is also said to be:

> The great mind of all sentient beings,
> naturally pure and stainless.[999]

"That does not exist in mind" means it does not exist as the own-essence of mind, mentation, and consciousness, because it is naturally pure. Therefore, the intent is that the natural mind of the ultimate emptiness of other is always present as the basic ground that is empty of the relative mind of the emptiness of self-nature. {296}

Likewise, the meaning of the phrase "vajra of mind without mind" should also be understood in accord with the previous. Here, the vajra of mind—the ground without relative mind—is vajra mind, great uncuttable and indestructible ultimate mind.

Likewise, many statements of being without the flaw of including contradiction—body without body, cyclic existence without cyclic existence, fine form without form, having all aspects yet without aspects, and so on—teach again and again the ground of emptiness, the profound ultimate emptiness of other, which is beyond worldly examples. The *Tantra Determining the Intent* also says:

> Ignorance, conditioning factors,
> consciousness, name, and form,
> the six sensory bases, contact,
> feeling, and craving,
>
> appropriation, becoming, birth,
> aging, and death are the vidyās.
> Pride, exalted pride, conceited pride,
> and manifest pride,
>
> furthermore, exaggerated pride,
> and slight pride, as well as mistaken
> pride—these with "vajra" at the end
> are sublime.[1000]

And the *Glorious Guhyasamāja* of all buddhas also says:

> In brief, the [ultimate] five aggregates
> are renowned to be the five buddhas.
> The vajra sensory bases themselves
> are also the sublime maṇḍala of bodhisattvas.[1001]

And:

> Earth is called Locanā.
> The element of water is Māmakī.
> Pāṇḍarā and Tārā are renowned to be
> fire and wind.
>
> The sacred commitment of the vajra element
> of space is that Vajra Holder himself.[1002]

Such passages also say extensively that the aggregates, elements, and so on of the naturally original true nature—the ground primordially empty of the contrived incidental aggregates, elements, and so on—are naturally pure; they are other and sublime and transcendent and excellent.

In that way, ultimate truth is beyond or other than this inferior outer and inner relative; it is excellent and sublime.

Moreover, the exceptional tantras say:

> Just as the outer, so the inner.
> Just as the inner, so the other.[1003]

Thus it is stated that, just as the outer husk of grain, the inner part, and the kernel of grain are not one in essence but abide in similar form, so too this outer world that is the environment, these inner sentient beings who are the inhabitants, {297} and the other sugata essence (thusness) are also not one in essence but have similar form. [237] This approach also has the same meaning as statements in other source texts of Great Madhyamaka:

> Only this just as it appears is the relative.
> The other is the alternative.[1004]

"This just as it appears" means this outer and inner that appear to consciousness, the relative. What is "other" than this is the ultimate true nature other than these relative phenomena, which is transcendent or sublime or excellent. Of the two truths, that is ultimate truth, the alternative to relative truth. Therefore, it "is the alternative." In that way, this statement that what is ultimate is other than the relative also clears away the claim by some that the two truths are indivisible.

Also, the claims by some that these entities appearing to consciousness are the relative, and their aspect empty of just that is ultimate truth, are very confused, because it is impossible for that which is empty of self-nature to be ultimate truth, and it is impossible for that which is ultimate truth to be empty of self-nature, and also because many pure proofs of those points have been explained and will be explained.

Likewise, the claim that what is apparent is the relative and what is empty is the ultimate is also foolish, because both appearance and emptiness are complete in the relative and both appearance and emptiness are also complete in the ultimate, and because it is refuted by the absurd consequence that the appearance of the true nature would be the relative, and the extremely absurd consequence that the emptiness of the relative would also be the ultimate. Other proofs of these points will also be presented as other esoteric instructions.

i. *Clearing away many major objections that those have the same meaning as the emptiness of self-nature*

It might be asked, "If 'emptiness of self-nature' and 'dharmadhātu' are not synonymous, how do you interpret this statement in the *Sūtra Teaching the Indivisible Nature of Dharmadhātu*, in the *Stack of Jewels*?"

> Venerable Śāradvatiputra, since even those [other] defilements are the very nature of dharmadhātu, that complete knowledge of the [other] defilements themselves to be the nature of dharmadhātu is called "purification."[1005]

As presented before, this is also said in reference to the thusness of the afflictions or the afflictions of thusness. {298} The purpose is as presented before.[1006]

Likewise, the *Sūtra Taught by Akṣayamati* says:

> [The bodhisattvas think,] "Because these [ultimate] afflictions [of the truth of cessation] are realized, that is enlightenment, and that which is the very essence of the afflictions is the very essence of enlightenment." Even though they directly rest in mindfulness in this way, they do not closely rest, do not totally rest, do not rest on anything. [238] They fully understand that true nature abides [in reality]. Therefore, it is said that dharmadhātu abides [in reality].[1007]

That statement also is said in reference to the thusness of the afflictions. The purpose is as presented before.

Likewise, the *Sūtra of the Meeting of Father and Son* also states:

> Bhagavān, this apex of reality comes after all [phenomena]; a phenomenon that is a phenomenon that is not the apex of reality does not exist [in reality].
>
> Bhagavān, this "enlightenment" is the apex of reality. What is enlightenment?
>
> Bhagavān, [the true nature] that does not have the nature of all [relative] phenomena is known to be enlightenment.
>
> At the worst, even acts that bring immediate retribution are enlightenment. How is that so?
>
> Bhagavān, enlightenment has no nature; the acts that bring immediate retribution are also its nature. How is that so?
>
> Bhagavān, all phenomena are the basic element of nirvāṇa without any remaining aggregates; the acts that bring immediate retribution are also its nature.[1008]

This is also said in reference to the thusness of the acts that bring immediate retribution, and so on, and the apex of reality of all phenomena or all the phenomena of the apex of reality. Here also the purpose is as presented before.

Likewise, the *Sūtra Teaching Relative and Ultimate Truth* also states:

> The divine being said, "Mañjuśrī, what is correct engagement?"
>
> Mañjuśrī replied, "Divine son, ultimately, whatever is equal to thusness, dharmadhātu, and what never arises is also ultimately equal to the five acts that bring immediate retribution.
>
> "Ultimately, whatever is equal to thusness, dharmadhātu, and what never arises is also ultimately equal to the views.

> "Ultimately, whatever is equal to thusness, dharmadhātu, and what never arises is also ultimately equal to the phenomena of ordinary beings."[1009] {299}

And:

> Mañjuśrī said, "Ultimately, all phenomena are equal in never occurring. Ultimately, all phenomena are equal in never arising. Ultimately, all phenomena are equal in being utterly unreal. So, divine son, ultimately all phenomena are equal.
>
> "Why is that? Divine son, because they ultimately never occur themselves, all phenomena cannot be differentiated. Divine son, it is like this example: the space within a clay vessel and the space within a precious vessel is the same element of space; ultimately, [239] not even the slightest differentiation can be made between them.
>
> "Divine son, in the very same way, the afflictions themselves ultimately never occur. Even purification itself ultimately never occurs. Ultimately, even saṃsāra itself never occurs. Ultimately, even up to nirvāṇa itself never occur. Ultimately, these cannot be even slightly differentiated.
>
> "Why is that? Because ultimately all phenomena themselves never occur."[1010]

This is also said in reference to the thusness of the phenomena of ordinary beings, affliction and purification, and all the phenomena of saṃsāra and nirvāṇa. Here also the purpose is as presented before.

It might be asked, "In *Primordial Awareness at the Moment of Death*, and so on, do the statements that if mind is realized it is primordial awareness[1011] not refer to the realization that mind is empty of mind?"

Just that will not cause it to be that. If it did, realizations that mind is empty of mind (while the passage of the breath has still not ceased) would also be primordial awareness. But if that were claimed, it would contradict the intent of the consummate profound tantras and of the beings on the tenth level, such as the Lords of the Three Families.[1012] Therefore, this passage also refers to ultimate mind. {300}

It might be asked, "The *Lamp That Summarizes Conduct* states:

> 'All the tathāgatas, having a quintessence of great compassion, after seeing all sentient beings who have fallen into the whirlpool of suffering and are without refuge and without defender, cause them to [first] purify the [coarse] afflictions by fully understanding the very essence of the afflictions by means of the mode of relative truth. After beings have also purified the relative truth by means of the ultimate truth, the tathāgatas cause them to correctly engage in samādhi having the quintessence of the mode of reality.'[1013]

"Do such passages not say the essence of the afflictions is purified by just understanding it to be empty of self-nature?"

That refers to the temporary dulling or suppression of the coarse afflictions, because even this very passage says that relative understanding of the afflictions to be empty of self-nature must finally also be purified by the nonconceptual samādhi that actualizes the ultimate.

Likewise:

> By the entity itself one is released,
> and by the bonds of the entity, bound.
> By fully understanding that, one is released.[1014]

The meaning of such passages is also not release by just understanding the entity to be empty of self-nature, but that (if released from the circulation of winds and mind) one is released from bonds, and that (after confusion, including confused appearances, fades) the own-appearance of primordial awareness will actualize. [240] This should be known extensively from the profound Bodhisattva Commentaries (the commentary of noble Vajragarbha and so on), including the esoteric instructions. And the intent of various teachings like release through recognition is also like that.

Therefore, if the main bond (the flow of breath that is the mount of self-grasping) has ceased, one is released from all bonds and, after obtaining the ground of emptiness (the ultimate emptiness of other, the quintessence of the limitless qualities), one will act for the benefit of all sentient beings. Therefore, whether the true nature (ultimate truth, the ground empty of all phenomena abiding as empty of self-nature) is actually taught clearly or taught through enigmatic speech, it is the consummate, definitive meaning of the profound scriptures.

Moreover, the *Journey to Laṅkā Sūtra* says:

> Mahāmati, my ultimate, permanent, and inconceivable [truth of cessation] has the characteristic of the ultimate cause. And because of the characteristic of a noble being's personal self-knowing free of the existence [of the imaginary and dependent] and the nonexistence [of the fully established true nature], it has the characteristic [of an object of awareness present in reality]. {301} Since it is the cause of ultimate primordial awareness, it has the cause. Since it is free of existence and nonexistence—and comparable to the examples of uncreated space, nirvāṇa, and cessation—it is permanent. Therefore, Mahāmati, this [ultimate sugata essence] is not in accord with the claims of permanent and inconceivable made by non-Buddhists.
>
> Mahāmati, this permanent and inconceivable [basic element] is the thusness to be realized by the tathāgatas through their personal, self-knowing primordial awareness of a noble being.[1015]

And so on. And furthermore, that is also the meaning of profound scriptures that have been explained and will be explained.

The *Noble Sūtra to Benefit Aṅgulimāla* also says:

> Mañjuśrī, likewise, how they will wrongly view the reality of the self to be "like this, like that" is as follows. Not understanding enigmatic speech about liberation, self, and the transcendent, they will say, "'Selflessness' is the word of the Buddha," thinking like non-Buddhists. Even the worldly who establish things through inference will fall under the power of a Dharma of delusion. Not understanding explanations in enigmatic speech also about the transcendent, their understanding will deteriorate. Therefore, the reality of phenomena and the thusness of the Tathāgata and the Saṅgha—devoid of the two extremes [of eternalism and annihilation] and included in [the ultimate] self—are taught to be the vehicle of the [ultimate] Tathāgata, the Middle Way. "Middle Way" is another term for Mahāyāna.[1016]

And so on, it says. [241]

j. *Showing the immense advantages of faith and so on in what is to be obtained*

The consummate Mahāyāna is the vehicle of the true nature and—because it is also the vehicle of the ground of emptiness, the ultimate emptiness of other, the sugata essence—if one develops confidence and devotion in that, many obscurations will be purified.

Moreover, the *Sūtra of Collecting and Crushing* says:

> Sarvaśūra, whoever develops total faith and devotion in the Mahāyāna will not go into the lower realms for a thousand eons. They will not be born in the wombs of animals for five thousand eons. Likewise also for the hungry spirits. They will be born in the worlds of the gods and the worlds of Brahmā for twenty-five thousand eons.[1017] {302}

The Madhyamaka *Four Hundred Verses* also says:

> One of little merit
> does not even doubt this Dharma.
> Even through just doubt,
> cyclic existence is torn apart.[1018]

This is also stated extensively in other sources, and many were also presented before.

It is said that to teach others by means of not denigrating it and by having confidence in it, and to bring it into experience by means of memorizing, upholding, reading, and so on, one must arouse bodhicitta in the presence of many buddhas. The *Mahāparinirvāṇa* says:

> Son of good family, if any sentient being arouses bodhicitta in the presence of buddhas as numerous as the grains of sand found in the Hiraṇyavatī River,[1019] during bad times he will hold and retain this sūtra, not denigrating it.
>
> Son of good family, if any sentient being arouses bodhicitta in the presence of buddhas as numerous as the grains of sand found in one Ganges River, during bad times he will not denigrate this Dharma and will be devoted to this sūtra, but will not be able to explicate and teach it to others.

Son of good family, if any sentient being arouses bodhicitta in the presence of buddhas as numerous as the grains of sand found in two Ganges Rivers, during bad times he will not denigrate this Dharma, will have faith and devotion, and will hold, retain, read, and recite it, but will not be able to extensively teach it to others.

If any sentient being arouses bodhicitta in the presence of buddhas as numerous as the grains of sand found in three Ganges Rivers, during bad times he will not denigrate this Dharma, and will hold, retain, read, recite, and write it in a volume, and teach it to others, but not understand the profound meaning.

If any sentient being arouses bodhicitta in the presence of buddhas as numerous as the grains of sand found in four Ganges Rivers, during bad times he will not denigrate this Dharma, and will hold, retain, read, recite, and write it in a volume. But he will teach just one-sixteenth of the profound meaning to others. He will teach and explain it, but even he will not completely understand. {303} [242]

If any sentient being arouses bodhicitta in the presence of buddhas as numerous as the grains of sand found in five Ganges Rivers, during bad times he will not denigrate this Dharma, and will hold, retain, read, recite, write it in a volume, and also be able to teach eight-sixteenths of the profound meaning to others.

If any sentient being arouses bodhicitta in the presence of buddhas as numerous as the grains of sand found in six Ganges Rivers, during bad times he will not denigrate this Dharma, and will hold, retain, read, recite, write it in a volume, and also be able to teach twelve-sixteenths of the profound meaning to others.

If any sentient being arouses bodhicitta in the presence of buddhas as numerous as the grains of sand found in seven Ganges Rivers, during bad times he will not denigrate this Dharma, and will hold, retain, recite, read, write it in a volume, and also be able to teach fourteen-sixteenths of the profound meaning to others.

If any sentient being arouses bodhicitta in the presence of buddhas as numerous as the grains of sand found in eight Ganges Rivers, during bad times he will not denigrate this Dharma, and will hold, retain, read, recite, and urge others also to write it in volumes, and will himself listen and retain it and urge others also to listen, retain, read, recite, and comprehend it. And because of compassionate love for the world, he will closely guard and worship the sūtra, and will likewise also urge others to worship, serve, honor, pay homage, read, and recite.

His complete understanding of even the profound meaning is like this: he will extensively explain that the [ultimate] Tathāgata has the attribute of always remaining unchanged, and is final bliss, and that the buddha nature exists in sentient beings. Very expert in the treasure of the Dharma of the Tathāgata, and having worshiped those buddhas, he will hold, retain, protect, and understand the classifications of these unsurpassable, perfect Dharma teachings.

If anyone arouses bodhicitta directed toward unsurpassable, perfectly complete enlightenment, in a future time that person will hold, retain, and protect this perfect Dharma, and will definitely know the classifications of the perfect Dharma. {304}

Therefore, you should understand that they will guard the excellent Dharma during future bad times. Why is that? Because those who have aroused bodhicitta will undoubtedly be able to guard and retain the unsurpassable, [243] perfect Dharma teachings.[1020]

4. *Clearing away various misconceptions about those and then establishing the meaning just as it is*

It might be said, "The Conqueror's Mother Sūtras state:

> 'Divine being, form itself is knowledge of all aspects, and knowledge of all aspects itself is also form. [. . .] The unshared attributes of a buddha are themselves knowledge of all aspects, and up to knowledge of all aspects itself are the unshared attributes of a buddha.'[1021]

"Therefore, are form and so on—those that are each empty of own-essence, or that recognition and realization of them to be that way—not thusness and knowledge of all aspects?"

No. It is clear in even that sūtra itself that such is said in reference to that which is the thusness of form being the primordial awareness of the knowledge of all aspects. Just as it says:

> Form itself is also knowledge of all aspects itself. Feeling itself, discrimination itself, conditioning factors themselves, and consciousness itself are also knowledge of all aspects itself.
>
> Up to the eighteen unshared attributes of a buddha are themselves also knowledge of all aspects itself.
>
> Why is that? Because it says, "In this way, that which is the thusness of form and that which is the thusness of the knowledge of all aspects is one thusness. From "feeling and" up to that which is the thusness of the eighteen unshared attributes of a buddha and the thusness of the knowledge of all aspects is itself one thusness."[1022]

Referring to these, it states extensively:

> If the thusness of form is understood, the core and extent of all phenomena are understood.[1023]

And so on. Some might think, "Well, the *Root Verses Called 'Wisdom'* says:

> 'No phenomena exist except
> what are dependently arisen.
> Therefore, no phenomena exist
> that are not emptiness.'[1024]

"Therefore, just as whatever is dependently arisen is emptiness, so too whatever is emptiness must also be dependently arisen, and, because whatever is dependently arisen is empty of self-nature, all emptiness is only the emptiness of self-nature." {305}

Therefore, I should comment. That passage says whatever is dependently arisen is emptiness, but it does not say whatever is emptiness is dependently arisen.

If one were to claim that all that are emptiness are dependently arisen, all the synonyms for the ground of emptiness (such as "the ultimate true nature" and "the apex of reality") would be dependently arisen, because they are emptiness; and one would also need to claim they are conditioned, impermanent, false, deceptive, and so on. But that is also not reasonable, because there would be the great defect of contradicting extensive statements in the Conqueror's Mother Sūtras [244]:

> Subhūti, it is taught that relative truth taken as valid creates results, but it cannot be taught that ultimate truth creates results.[1025]

And so on. And in the *Sūtra of Definitive Commentary on the Intent*:

> Subhūti, it is like this: Thusness, the ultimate, the selflessness of phenomena, is not dependently arisen from causes. It is not conditioned. Neither is it not the ultimate. Do not seek an ultimate other than that ultimate. In permanent, permanent time and in eternal, eternal time, whether tathāgatas appear or do not appear, the true nature of phenomena, that basic element of the constancy of phenomena, is existent; it does not change into another.[1026]

And so on. Furthermore, if ultimate truth were not beyond dependent arising, the consummate truth of cessation would also not be beyond dependent arising. And if that were claimed, it would not be beyond conditioned phenomena. That being so, there would be the extremely absurd consequence that it would be an impermanent, false, deceptive phenomenon, not the consummate source of refuge, because the *Sūtra of Śrīmālā* says:

> Bhagavān, of these four noble truths, three truths are impermanent. One truth is permanent. Why is that?
>
> Bhagavān, it is because three truths are included in the characteristics of conditioned phenomena and, Bhagavān, that which is included in the characteristics of conditioned phenomena is impermanent. That which is impermanent is a false, deceptive phenomenon.
>
> Bhagavān, that which is a false, deceptive phenomenon is untrue and impermanent, not a refuge.
>
> Bhagavān, that being so, the noble truth of suffering, the noble truth of the origin of suffering, and even the noble truth of the path leading to the cessation of suffering are, in reality, untrue and impermanent, {306} not a refuge.
>
> Bhagavān, here one truth is beyond objects with the characteristics of conditioned phenomena and, Bhagavān, that which is beyond objects with the characteristics of conditioned phenomena is permanent. That which is permanent is an undeceptive phenomenon.

> Bhagavān, that which is an undeceptive phenomenon is true, permanent, and a refuge.
>
> Bhagavān, that being so, here the truth of the cessation of suffering is in reality true, permanent, and a refuge.
>
> Bhagavān, the truth of the cessation of suffering, which is beyond the objects of the consciousness of all sentient beings, is inconceivable, not the field of experience of the consciousness of all śrāvakas and pratyekabuddhas.[1027] [245]

And because the *Root Verses on Madhyamaka, Called "Wisdom"* also says:

> The Bhagavān has said, "Whatever
> phenomenon is deceptive is false."
> All conditioned phenomena are deceptive
> phenomena, so they are false.[1028]

And because a passage quoted in the commentaries on that also extensively says, "All conditioned phenomena are false, deceptive phenomena."[1029] And so on.

Therefore, the logical entailment is that whatever are dependently arisen, conditioned phenomena are emptiness, but to accept that whatever are emptiness are all dependently arisen is mistaken, because ultimate emptiness is beyond dependent arising, yet is very consummate, profound emptiness.

It might be said, "Well, that contradicts this":

> The relative is explained to be emptiness;
> emptiness alone is the relative, since it is
> certain that, like being created and impermanent,
> one does not occur without the other.[1030]

There is no fault, because emptiness in that context is the dependently arisen emptiness of self-nature, taught to be mutually pervasive and identical in essence to dependent arising, which we also accept in that way.

It might be said, "If the ultimate true nature were not empty of own-essence, that would contradict the statement that all phenomena are essenceless."

There is no fault, because the intent of that and this [statement] are not contradictory. How are they not contradictory?

The imaginary, without essence, is without characteristics of its own, [just established as] the mere relative or the false relative, but not established even as relative truth or the correct relative. The dependent, without very essence, relatively exists as an essence arisen from another, but does not exist as an essence arisen from itself, and is totally unestablished in reality. In that way, because those two are empty of self-nature, {307} they are without own-essence.

Although the fully established true nature (the ground without those two) is not without own-essence, it is the ground of the nonexistence of the very essence of relative phenomena other than itself. Therefore, it is the essence of ultimate truth, and it is the svābhāvikakāya, or the natural kāya, naturally luminous, naturally connate primordial awareness, naturally pure, naturally spontaneous, the family residing as the nature.

It is stated that, if the tradition of essencelessness is understood in that way, the middle that does not fall into the extremes of existence and nonexistence, permanence and annihilation, and exaggeration and denigration is realized and one will not degenerate from the Madhyamaka path. And the *Definitive Commentary on the Intent* says:

> Phenomena are without an essence, phenomena
> are unarisen, phenomena are unceasing, phenomena
> are primordially at peace, all phenomena are naturally nirvāṇa;
> What expert would say this without intentional ambiguity?
>
> I have explained essencelessness regarding characteristics,
> essencelessness regarding arising, and essencelessness regarding
> the ultimate; any expert who understands the intent in that way
> will not travel a totally degenerate path.[1031] [246]

And the honorable, noble Asaṅga also says:

> What is the intent of those statements in the extremely extensive [sūtras] that "all phenomena are essenceless?"
>
> That is because they do not occur from themselves, have no quintessence of their own, do not abide in own-essence, and lack characteristics as apprehended by the childish.
>
> Also, it is because the imaginary essence is essencelessness regarding characteristics, the dependent is essencelessness regarding arising, and the fully established is essencelessness regarding the ultimate.[1032]

And making that same point, the honorable conqueror Maitreya also says:

> If they know the emptiness of the nonexistent,
> and if they likewise know the emptiness
> of the existent and the natural emptiness,
> they are said to be "knowers of emptiness."[1033]

Thus it teaches that, because the imaginary and the dependent are contrived and incidental, they are without own-essence and empty of self-nature, and because the fully established true nature is the naturally original, it is without other-essence and is empty of other.

That being so, saying all phenomena are essenceless does not mean the true nature lacks own-essence, because phenomena and true nature are different. As for the claim that they are indivisible, the refutations by means of scripture and reasoning are infinite.

Even if some works possibly say the true nature is essenceless, it should be known that this is said with the intent that it is without other-essence; for it to be without own-essence is totally impossible, because that would contradict infinite scriptures of the consummate definitive meaning. {308}

Likewise, statements that appropriated phenomena are impermanent, suffering, empty, selfless, and impure also do not refute statements that the ultimate dharmakāya is pure, self, bliss, and permanent, because the *Sūtra of Śrīmālā* says a view that accords with reality is faultless:

> Bhagavān, sentient beings who faithfully perceive the Tathāgata [of the state of reality] to be permanent also perceive him to be bliss, perceive him to be the self, and perceive him to be pure. Bhagavān, those sentient beings are not mistaken. Bhagavān, those sentient beings have the correct view. Why is that?
>
> Bhagavān, it is because the Tathāgata's dharmakāya itself is the perfection of permanence, the perfection of bliss, the perfection of self, and the perfection of purity.
>
> Bhagavān, those sentient beings who see the Tathāgata's dharmakāya in that way see reality. [247]
>
> Bhagavān, those who see reality are called sons of the Tathāgata (born from his mind, born from his mouth, and born from his Dharma), emanations of Dharma, and enjoy their share of Dharma.[1034]

Likewise, also concerning views of permanence and annihilation, that sūtra itself says they are faulty if they do not accord with reality, but faultless if they do accord:

> Bhagavān, these two are called "extreme views." Which two? The view of annihilation and the view of permanence.
>
> Bhagavān, if conditioned phenomena are viewed to be impermanent, that is not a view of annihilation concerning them; that is the correct view of them.
>
> Bhagavān, if [great] nirvāṇa is viewed to be permanent, that is not a view of permanence concerning it; that is the correct view of it.[1035]

It has already been explained that in the context of discrimination the view accords with the abiding state of reality, but in the context of meditative absorption free of conceptual elaborations there must be no view whatsoever. Yet there is no fault of contradiction between those, because these are separate contexts.

It might be said, "Because all that is awareness is conditioned, the perfection of wisdom and the primordial awareness of the knowledge of all aspects are also conditioned, and because the true nature, thusness, and so on are unconditioned, these are unsuitable as synonyms." {309}

They are not [unsuitable], because one must understand the division of the two truths also for wisdom and primordial awareness.

Here, the wisdom and primordial awareness included in the truth of the path are the conditioned relative, but the wisdom and primordial awareness included in the truth of cessation are the ultimate unconditioned; because those and the true nature and so on are synonyms, there is no fault.

It might be said, "Because the true nature is the object to be known and primordial awareness is the subject knowing that, it is improper for those two to be one thing, as it is with form and eye consciousness."

There is no fault, because knowing and knowable object that are not one are relative awareness of other, but knowing and knowable object that are ultimate self-awareness are one; because dharmadhātu itself is self-knowing primordial awareness, ultimate bodhicitta, indivisible emptiness and compassion, and indivisible means and wisdom and bliss and emptiness; because those united as one are the androgynous stage; and because the true nature's *evaṃ*, *ahaṃ*, *haṃkṣa*, vowels such as *a* and consonant-syllables such as *ka*, drop and triangle, vajra and bhaga, vajra and lotus, Vajrasattva, vajra moon and sun, vajra semen and menses, [248] vajra day and night, the two vajra phases, the two vajra transits, Kālacakra, Hevajra, Cakrasaṃvara, Guhyasamāja, Māyājāla, Vajracatuḥpīṭha, Vajrahūṃkāra, Vajraḍāka, Ḍākārṇava, and so on—all the ultimate father and mother deities and support and supported maṇḍalas—are indivisible, the same taste, identical.

It might be said, "If the ultimate true nature is empty of other but not empty of self-nature, that is a partial emptiness. So it would be a non-Buddhist tradition, because it is stated, '. . . of the non-Buddhists, [who advocate] partial emptiness.'"[1036]

It is not a partial emptiness, because it is empty of all phenomena.

It might be said, "If it is empty of all phenomena, it would be empty of even the true nature, because the true nature is also included within *all.*

Empty of *all* is impossible, because empty of the true nature is impossible. A ground empty of all phenomena is possible; that is the true nature. A ground empty of the true nature is impossible, because that is refuted by infinite absurd consequences.

Therefore, there is a very great difference between empty of *all* and empty of all phenomena, because the abiding state is empty of phenomena but not empty of the true nature. {310} This also clears away the claim that phenomena and true nature have one essence yet are conceptually distinct, and the claim that they are not at all distinct; those two are distinct because having one essence has been refuted.

It might be said, "Well, that contradicts the statement in the *Definitive Commentary on the Intent*, which says the two truths are neither one nor distinct":

> The characteristics of the realm of conditioned
> phenomena and that of the ultimate are characteristics
> free of being one or distinct; those who imagine
> them to be one or distinct are incorrect.[1037]

That passage refutes the two truths having one essence or distinct essences, because the essence of the ultimate is established in the abiding state but the essence of the relative is not established.

All explanations other than this are only the nocturnal ravings of those crazed by the poison of mixing the two truths together as one without distinguishing at all the distinction between the two modes of truth, the two modes of appearance, the two modes of emptiness, and (if those are claimed to be nonexistent) the two modes of the view of annihilation.

There are very many scriptural passages and reasons that prove this, but I have not written them here from fear that it would take too many words.

Some might think that thusness released from the husks of the afflictions is not the sugata essence, because it is said:

> Bhagavān, this very dharmakāya of a tathāgata that is not released from [249] the husks of the afflictions is called "tathāgata essence."[1038]

Therefore, I should comment. Here, although the thusness pervasively present during the three phases of each individual person is stated to be impure, impure and pure, and very pure, thusness is not solely pure and also not solely impure (like the sky pervading a land with or without masses of clouds), because it is pervasively present in all persons, with or without the stains.

That being so, depending on the person, precisely that which is thusness present with stains in some is present without stains in some, but there is no distinction in thusness, like the sky with or without clouds.

Referring to this, the *Sūtra of the Excellent Golden Light* says the very essence of a tathāgata and the tathāgata essence have one meaning; {311} the *Mahāparinirvāṇa* and so on say "buddha nature," "natural nirvāṇa," "basic element of the self," and so on are synonyms; the *Journey to Laṅkā* also says "sugata essence" and "fully established true nature" are synonyms; the tantra [*Chanting the Names of Mañjuśrī*] that expresses the many synonyms of the ultimate names also says "vajra essence," "essence of all buddhas," and "essence of all tathāgatas" are synonyms for "the ultimate"; the *Sūtra of the Tathāgata Essence* also says "conqueror," "tathāgata," "buddha," "self-arisen," "buddha level," "unspoiled true nature," "treasure of attributes," "true nature of a tathāgata," "body of a sugata," "body of a conqueror in meditative absorption," "tathāgata family," "true nature," "precious primordial awareness of a tathāgata," "nature," "and primordial awareness of a buddha" are synonyms for "sugata essence"; and the root text and commentary on the *Uttaratantra* also say "dharmakāya," "tathāgata," "ultimate truth," and "great nirvāṇa" are synonyms for "sugata essence." Because other sources also state this extensively, no matter how many synonymous names express the same meaning, there is no fault.

5. *In that way, how all mistakes are rejected by the correct view of realization in accord with reality*

In that way, after all mistakes have been rejected by means of the correct view, [thusness] will be realized just as it is [in reality]. The *Mahāparinirvāṇa* [250] says:

> Son of good family, if any sentient beings view the existent self as the nonexistent selves and view the nonexistent selves as the existent self, view the permanent as impermanent and view the impermanent as permanent, view bliss as not bliss and what is not bliss as bliss, view the utterly pure as utterly impure and view the utterly impure as utterly pure, view the unceasing as ceasing and view the ceasing as unceasing, {312} view negative acts as not negative acts and view what are not negative acts as negative acts, view light negative acts as heavy and view heavy negative acts as light, view what is the vehicle as not the vehicle and view what is not the vehicle as the vehicle, view the path as not the path and view what is not the path as the path, view perfect enlightenment as not enlightenment and view what is not enlightenment as enlightenment, view suffering as not suffering and view not suffering as suffering, view the origin as not the origin, view cessation as not cessation, view truth as not truth, view the relative as ultimate and view the ultimate as relative, view [the sources] of taking refuge as not [sources] of taking refuge and view what are not [sources] of taking refuge as [sources] of taking refuge, call the definite words of the Buddha "the words of Māra" and call the definite words of Māra "the words of the Buddha"—at such a time the tathāgatas speak this sūtra of primordial parinirvāṇa.[1039]

And:

> Son of good family, what is called "buddha nature" is ultimate emptiness. Ultimate emptiness is called "primordial awareness." Here, what is called "emptiness" [of own-essence] is not seeing both empty [of own-essence] and nonempty [of own-essence]. One with wisdom sees all—empty and nonempty, permanent and impermanent, suffering and bliss, self and selflessness. {313} What is called "empty" is all saṃsāra. What is called "nonempty"

> is parinirvāṇa. Selfless and so on are saṃsāra. What is called "self" is parinirvāṇa; seeing all to be empty but not seeing what is not empty is not called the "Middle Way." Seeing all to be selfless and so on but not seeing the self is not called the "Middle Way." What is called the "Middle Way" is the buddha nature.
>
> That being the case, the buddha nature is permanent, unchanging, and immutable—not seen by all sentient beings obscured by ignorance. Śrāvakas and pratyekabuddhas—seeing all to be empty but not seeing the nonempty—see all to be selfless and so on but do not see the self. [251] Therefore, they do not attain ultimate emptiness. Since they have not attained ultimate emptiness, they do not enjoy the Middle Way. Since they lack the Middle Way, they do not see the buddha nature.[1040]

And:

> Son of good family, whoever sees all phenomena to be without permanence, without self, without bliss, and utterly impure, and sees all [the ultimate true nature] that is not phenomena to be without permanence, without self, without bliss, and utterly impure, does not see the buddha nature.
>
> Here, what is called "all [phenomena]" is saṃsāra. What is not all [phenomena] is the [ultimate] Three Jewels. Śrāvakas and pratyekabuddhas see all phenomena to be impermanent, without self, without bliss, and utterly impure. They see all that is not phenomena to also be impermanent, without self, without bliss, and utterly impure. That being the case, they do not see the buddha nature. {314}
>
> Bodhisattvas on the tenth level see all phenomena to be impermanent, without self, without bliss, and utterly impure, but partially see all that is not phenomena to be permanent, self, bliss, and utter purity. That being the case, they see just one-tenth.
>
> Bhagavān buddhas see all phenomena to be impermanent, without self, without bliss, and utterly impure, but see all that is not phenomena to be permanent, self, bliss, and utter purity. That being so, they see the buddha nature like a myrobalan placed in the palm of the hand.
>
> That being the case, the samādhi of heroic progress is called "the consummate."[1041]

And:

> Perceiving what is without self to be the self and perceiving the self to be without self is also mistaken. Worldly people say the [relative] self exists. In the Dharma of the Buddha it is also said that [the ultimate] self exists. Worldly people may say the self exists, but since that is not [understanding] that the buddha nature [or pure self] exists, it is perceiving what is without self to be the self, which is called "mistaken."
>
> The existence of the self of the true nature of the Buddha is the buddha nature. Worldly people say the self does not exist in the Dharma of the Buddha. Therefore, it is said they "perceive the self [of the true nature] to be without self."[1042]

And:

> In the Dharma of non-Buddhists there is certainly no self [of the true nature]. That which is called the "self" [of the true nature] is the [ultimate] Tathāgata. Why is that? Because the kāya [of the true nature] is limitless, without the web of doubt, uncreated, and does not appropriate [cyclic existence], it is called "permanent."[1043]

And [252]:

> Here, what is called "wisdom" is like this: viewing the [ultimate] Tathāgata as permanent, bliss, self, and utterly pure; viewing all sentient beings as having buddha nature; viewing the characteristics of phenomena in pairs and, in this way, understanding empty [of own-essence] and not empty [of own-essence], permanent and impermanent, bliss and without bliss, self and without self, utterly pure and utterly impure, suitable to distinguish as different phenomena and unsuitable to distinguish as different phenomena, different phenomena that arise from conditions and different phenomena that do not arise from conditions, and different phenomena that are results from conditions and different phenomena that are not results from conditions—is called "having wisdom."[1044] {315}

And:

> At that time the Bhagavān spoke to the monks: "Listen well and keep this very much in mind! To use a drunken person as an example: you merely understand the words and syllables, but do not realize the meaning. What is called 'the meaning' here? For example, it is like a drunken person who perceives the sun, moon, and so on that are not spinning to be spinning. Ordinary people are also like that, utterly obscured by the ignorance of the defilements, so they develop mistaken minds, perceiving the self [of the true nature] to be selfless, perceiving permanent [ultimate emptiness] to be impermanent, perceiving utterly pure [ultimate emptiness] to be utterly impure, and perceiving bliss [ultimate emptiness] to be suffering. Utterly obscured by the ignorance of the defilements, they perceive in that way, but since they do not comprehend the meaning, they are like that drunken person who perceives what is not spinning to be spinning.
>
> "What is called [the pure] 'self' means 'buddha.' Permanent means what is called 'dharmakāya.' What is called 'bliss' means 'nirvāṇa.' Utterly pure means what is called [the ultimate] 'phenomenon.' So why do you monks say that one who perceives the self has pride and circles in saṃsāra? If, as you say, 'Even we insistently practice the perception of it as impermanent, suffering, and without self,' that is meaningless in reality. Because those three insistent practices are meaningless in reality, I will explain what is not those, what is more than the three teachings of insistent practice.
>
> "To hold suffering [saṃsāra] to be bliss and to hold bliss [nirvāṇa, the sugata essence,] to be suffering is a mistaken teaching. To hold the impermanent to be permanent and to hold the permanent to be impermanent is a mistaken teaching. To hold the selfless to be self and to hold the self to be selfless is a mistaken teaching. To hold the utterly impure to be utterly pure and to hold the utterly pure to be utterly impure is a mistaken teaching. These four mistaken teachings are not known by persons who insistently practice in accord with reality."[1045]

And [253]:

> In the world, the [merely imaginary] permanent, bliss, self, and utterly pure exist. {316} For the transcendent also, the [ultimate] permanent, bliss, self, and utterly pure exist. Worldly teachings are expressible but meaningless. The transcendent are expressible but also meaningful. Why is that? Because worldly teachings include the four mistakes, the meaning is not realized. How is that? With these three—mistaken perception, mistaken mind, and mistaken view—worldly people view bliss [nirvāṇa, the sugata essence,] as suffering, view the permanent as impermanent, view the self as selfless, and view the utterly pure as utterly impure, which is called "mistaken." Because they are mistaken, worldly people know to speak the words but do not know the meaning. What is the meaning here?
>
> What is selfless is called "saṃsāra." What is called "self" is the Tathāgata. What is impermanent is the śrāvakas and pratyekabuddhas. What is permanent is the dharmakāya of the Tathāgata. What is suffering is all non-Buddhists. What is bliss is parinirvāṇa. What is utterly impure is conditioned phenomena. What is utterly pure is the perfect true nature of buddhas and bodhisattvas, who are therefore called "unmistaken." Because they are unmistaken in that way, they know to speak the words but also know the meaning. If anyone wants to utterly abandon the four mistakes, they should know [nirvāṇa, the sugata essence,] to be permanent, bliss, self, and utterly pure in that way.[1046]

And so on. And the *Mahāparinirvāṇa* translated by Lhai Dawa says:

> Also, at that time all the laymen (such as the king famed as Vimalaprabha, a layman who had accepted the five basic points of training[1047] and had moral discipline, armor, and qualities) as numerous as the grains of sand found in two Ganges Rivers only wanted to know all as sets of pairs. They only wanted to know the differences and the exceptional natures of suffering [saṃsāra] and bliss [nirvāṇa, the sugata essence], permanent and impermanent, the existent self and the selfless, what is empty and not empty, what is reality and not reality, what is refuge and not refuge, what is a sentient being and not a sentient being, what is stable and not stable, what is peace and not peace, conditioned and

unconditioned, what is eternal and not eternal, what is parinirvāṇa and not parinirvāṇa, and so on.[1048] {317} [254]

And:

Whatever hesitations or qualms or doubts you have about what is empty [saṃsāra] and not empty [nirvāṇa, the sugata essence,] or permanent and impermanent, or what is refuge and not refuge, or what goes and does not go, or what is a support and not a support, or what is eternal and not eternal, or what is stable and not stable, or what is a sentient being and not a sentient being, or what is reality and not reality, or what is true and not true, or what is nirvāṇa and not nirvāṇa, or what is secret and not secret, and what is duality and without duality, and, likewise, the many aspects of phenomena—ask about them! And I will eliminate them all.

I will also teach you the sublime nectar [nirvāṇa, the sugata essence,] and after that pass into parinirvāṇa.[1049]

And so on. And the *Commentary on the "Uttaratantra"* says:

As for that, "Those who delight in the mistaken"[1050] refers to śrāvakas and pratyekabuddhas. Why is that? Because, in this way, they should also meditate on the tathāgata essence as just permanent. But after again reverting from cultivating the perception of it as permanent, they delight in cultivating the perception of [everything knowable] being impermanent. And they should meditate on the tathāgata essence as bliss. But after again reverting from cultivating the perception of it as bliss, they delight in cultivating the perception of [everything knowable] being suffering. And they should meditate on the tathāgata essence as a self. {318} But after again reverting from cultivating the perception of it as a self, they delight in cultivating the perception of [everything knowable] being selfless. And they should meditate on the tathāgata essence as pure. But after again reverting from cultivating the perception of it as pure, they delight in cultivating the perception of [everything knowable] being impure.

In that way, due to this [fourfold] sequence, they delight in the path that is contrary to attaining the dharmakāya. Therefore, it is explained that the basic element with the characteristics of sublime permanence, bliss, self, and beauty is "not even the field of experience of all śrāvakas and pratyekabuddhas."

That this [sugata essence] is not the field of experience of those delighting in the mistaken (those having the perceptions of impermanence, suffering, selflessness, and ugliness) was fully established by the Bhagavān extensively in the *Mahāparinirvāṇa Sūtra* through the example of a gem in the water of a pond, like this:

> Monks, suppose that when the hot season arrives people were to tie on bathing clothes and play in the water with their own ornaments and playthings. Then someone there were to put a genuine beryl gem in the water. And then they would all put down their ornaments and enter [the water to get] the beryl. [255] Through the power of the gem, even that water of the pond would appear like the light of the gem. Seeing the water appearing that way, they would think, "Aha! The gem!" with the perception of its quality fully engaged. Then, thinking the pebbles or gravel there were the gem, they would grab them, thinking, "I've found the gem," and take them out. But after taking them out, when observed on the shore of the pond, they would fully discern, "These are not the gem." Then someone there who is skilled and intelligent would actually find that gem.
>
> Monks, likewise, not knowing the reality of phenomena, like [mistaking the pebbles of the pond for] a gem, you have meditated and meditated, more and more, with all your grasping: "All is impermanent, all is suffering, all is selfless, all is ugly." All those foundations [of mindfulness] are meaningless.
>
> Monks, therefore, do not be like [those who mistake] the pebbles and gravel resting in the pond; be skilled in means!
>
> Monks, you have meditated and meditated, more and more, with all your grasping: "Everything

> [relative] and everything [ultimate] are all impermanent, all suffering, all selfless, and all impure." {319} There is that [relative], and there is that [ultimate dharmakāya] that is permanent, blissful, the self, and beauty itself.[1051]

Thus the teaching on those who are mistaken concerning the presentation of the ultimate reality of phenomena should be understood in detail just as it is in the sūtra.

As for that, "those whose minds are distracted from emptiness"[1052] refers to bodhisattvas who have newly, correctly entered the vehicle but have deviated from the mode of the meaning of emptiness, the tathāgata essence.[1053]

III. *Summarizing the meaning of the explanation, and offering advice and a prayer*

That being so, with the correct pure view one must well understand the abiding state of phenomena just as it is and just as it abides, because that must be understood in accord with reality.

Here, reality is the nature or characteristic of both truths, both saṃsāra and nirvāṇa, sugata essence and incidental stain, and so on, just as it abides. Some abide as impermanent, suffering, empty, selfless, impure, and so on, but some also abide as the opposite of those. [256]

Likewise, [one must well understand] the difference between empty of self-nature and empty of other, self-arisen and other-arisen, self-awareness and awareness of other; also for self-awareness, the difference between self-knowing consciousness and self-knowing primordial awareness; also for self-knowing primordial awareness, the difference between self-arisen and other-arisen, or primordial awareness of the truth of cessation and primordial awareness of the truth of the path, or self-awareness of perfect primordial awareness and that of thusness, or self-awareness of both the conditioned and the unconditioned fully established nature; the difference between knowing and knowable object that are one and not one; consciousness and primordial awareness that are one and not one; apprehended and apprehender that are one and not one; the three states of cyclic existence that are one and not one; the three states of cyclic existence having and not having arising and destruction; the three states of cyclic existence beyond and not beyond the momentary; the three worlds that are and are not totally clear;

the three realms that are and are not the Buddha or dharmakāya; and so on; the divisible and indivisible two truths; divisible and indivisible four truths; {320} divisible and indivisible three kāyas; divisible and indivisible saṃsāra and nirvāṇa; divisible and indivisible cause and result; divisible and indivisible ground and result; divisible and indivisible apprehended and apprehender; divisible and indivisible consciousness and primordial awareness; divisible and indivisible support and supported; divisible and indivisible expression and object of expression; divisible and indivisible vowels and consonants; divisible and indivisible aggregates and elements, and so on; having the flaw of including contradiction or being without the flaw of including contradiction; existence or nonexistence of a third category concerning direct contradiction; existence and nonexistence in the abiding state; beyond and not beyond dependently arisen phenomena; beyond and not beyond the phenomena of consciousness; beyond and not beyond momentary phenomena; beyond and not beyond the phenomena of sophists; beyond and not beyond worldly examples, and so on; the difference between naturally original and contrived incidental; in purity, the difference between naturally pure and purified by the antidotes; and likewise, also between the pairs for what are called separation, cleanliness, peace, isolation, cessation, abandonment, extinguishing, vanishing, and so on; also between the two modes of abandonment in that way and realization of the same key point; in statements about natural emptiness, the difference between that which does not exist and what remains after that; in statements about the nonexistence of self, sentient being, lifeforce, nourishing being, and so on, the difference between that which does not exist and what remains after that; likewise, also concerning unarisen, signless, without conceptual elaboration, free of extremes and so on, and free of purity and so on, the difference between what is unarisen—up to what it is free of—and what its ground or remainder is; [257] concerning Madhyamaka, the difference between with appearance and without appearance; concerning Cittamatrā, the difference between ultimate and relative, natural and contrived, and original and incidental; concerning nonexistence of very essence, the difference between modes of nonexistence; concerning transformation, the difference between modes of change; {321} concerning emptiness, the difference between the emptiness of nonentities and that of the very essence of the nonexistence of entities, or emptiness of own-entity and emptiness of other entities; concerning statements of similarity to dream, illusion, and so on, the difference between relative similarity and ultimate similarity; concerning statements of similarity to space, the difference between relative similarity and ultimate similarity; concerning statements of nothingness, the difference between the mode of nonexistence for the incidental stains and the mode of nonexistence in the sugata essence; and establish that the intent of these seemingly contradictory statements is not contradictory but in accord, statements about beyond existence and nonexistence, but also statements about being existent; statements about beyond permanence and annihilation, but also statements about being permanent; statements about having no nature, but also statements about spontaneous nature; statements about essencelessness, but also statements about the fully established svābhāvikakāya [i.e., essence kāya]; statements about unconditioned, but also statements about being beyond both conditioned and unconditioned; statements about the basis of all phenomena, but also statements about phenomena not abiding at all; statements about abiding in all phenomena, but also statements about not abiding at all in any phenomena; statements about support and supported, but also statements about the nonexistence of support and supported; statements about the nonexistence of self, but also statements about the existence of self; statements about empty, but also statements about nonempty; statements about existing, but also statements about not existing; statements about arising, but also statements about nonarising; statements about cessation, but also statements about unceasing; statements about change, but also statements about changeless; statements about conceptual elaboration, but also statements about no conceptual elaboration; statements about no collected and distracted thoughts, but also statements about collected and distracted thoughts; statements about no divisions, but also statements about many divisions; statements about observable, but also statements about unobservable; statements about appearing to primordial awareness or consciousness, but also statements about not appearing; statements about cognition, but also statements about no cognition; statements about no assertion and thesis, but also statements about having them; statements about nirvāṇa not existing or being untrue, but also statements about it existing or being true; statements about obtaining the result, but also statements about no obtaining; statements about Dharma to be done, but also statements about nothing to be done, and so on; {322} [258] the division of the universal ground into primordial awareness and consciousness, or the division into ground of purification and object of purification; concerning family, the difference between the existent, ultimate, natural family and the nonexistent, relative, evolving family; concerning the path, the difference between conceptual and nonconceptual, near and distant, meditative absorption and postmeditation, and so on; concerning the result, the difference between the result of separation and the result of production, beneficial to oneself and beneficial to others, and ultimate dharmakāya and relative rūpakāya; concerning the object of abandonment or object of purification, the difference between imaginary and connate, obscurations of the afflictions and obscurations of the knowable, and so on; what their roots and mounts are; concerning the antidotes, the difference between the wisdom of meditative absorption and the primordial awareness of postmeditation, and so on, and what their key points or roots are; the difference between the two, the four, and the twelve truths; the difference between the ground of purification, object of purification, means of purification, result of purification, agent of purification, and mode of purification; concerning ground, path, and result, and concerning view, meditation, and conduct, the difference between what is provisional meaning and what is definitive meaning, and what is common and what is uncommon; the three vehicles; the three trainings; the three wheels of the Buddha's word; the three essences; the three of outer, inner, and other; the differences that exist and the differences that do not exist in the modes of sūtra and mantra that have the nature of cause and of result, and so on.

If that which is the abiding mode of these is well understood just as it is, that will become the correct view; if otherwise, it will not become that.

That being so, never part from the pure view that correctly realizes the intent of the profound sūtras and tantras just as it is!

In that way, many aspects have been distinguished and well determined, but in the context of profound meditative absorption one must rest in equanimity, nonconceptual and free of elaborations. The pure accompanying conduct and group of sacred commitments must also be complete, which should be known from teachings elsewhere.

> After understanding well the abiding state and
> the confused state, just as they are, may I and
> all others quickly perfect very pure view, meditation,
> and conduct, the sublime means for destroying confusion.

That is the section about the pure fine path. {323} [259]

THREE:
Explanation of the Results of Separation and Production by Means of That Path

This has three topics.

I. *General presentation of the Mahāyāna results*

In that way, by means of correct view, meditation, and conduct, the path of the two assemblies is utterly completed and, through extinguishing the two obscurations that are to be abandoned, the result of buddhahood will be attained. The *Ornament of the Sūtras* says:

> Because of hundreds of immeasurable
> austerities, the accumulation of immeasurable
> virtue through immeasurable time, and extinguishing
> immeasurable obscurations,
>
> knowledge of all aspects will be attained,
> without the stains of all the obscurations.
> As when a chest of jewels is opened,
> buddhahood is perfectly revealed.
>
> Through amazing austerities with hundreds of difficulties,
> all virtues have been accumulated, all obscurations extinguished
> during the long time of a sublime eon, the subtle obscurations
> included on the levels have been destroyed, and buddhahood
> attained, as if a chest of powerful jewels were opened.[1054]

And:

> That in which the seeds of the obscurations of the afflictions
> and of the knowable (always possessed for long periods) have
> been utterly destroyed by all the very vast aspects of abandonment,
> and in which transformation and possession of the sublime best
> qualities of the positive attributes have been attained, is
> buddhahood. That is attained by means of the paths of
> the utterly pure nonconceptual and the very pure subjective
> primordial awarenesses.[1055]

And the *Uttaratantra* also says:

> Buddhahood, called "luminous by nature," yet having been obscured by the obscurations of the dense gathered clouds of the incidental afflictions and the knowable, like the sun and the sky, has all the stainless buddha qualities and is permanent, stable, and everlasting. It is attained on the basis of both the nonconceptual primordial awareness [of the true nature of] phenomena, and that which is discriminating. {324}
>
> Buddhahood, distinguished by its indivisible
> pure attributes, has the characteristics of
> both primordial awareness and abandonment,
> which are like the sun and the sky.[1056]

And:

> Without beginning, middle, or end; indivisible;
> without the two; free of the three;[1057] stainless and
> nonconceptual—that is the nature of dharmadhātu,
> seen in meditative absorption by yogins who realize it.
>
> Having immeasureable, inconceivable, and unequaled
> qualities exceeding the grains of sand in the Ganges River,
> that stainless basic element of a tathāgata has abandoned
> the flaws, including their habitual propensities.
>
> With its forms as various light rays of the excellent Dharma,
> it is energetic in achieving the goal of liberating living beings;
> with actions like the king of wish-fulfilling gems, it [appears]
> as various things, but without their nature.
>
> That which is the forms that cause the worldly
> to enter the path of peace, cause full ripening, and
> give prophecy, also always resides here, like the element
> of form in the element of space.[1058] [260]

And so on. That buddhahood—the quintessence of the immeasurable, unimaginable, infinite excellence of the wonderful, marvelous kāyas, primordial awarenesses, qualities, and activities—is vast like space and (like a wish-fulfilling gem, a wish-granting tree, and so on) is the excellent source of everything desirable to sentient beings. {325}

II. *Extensive explanation of those*
This has six topics.

A. *Explanation of the excellence of the wonderful kāyas*
This has six topics.

1. *Divisions of the kāyas renowned in the common Mahāyāna*
This has three topics.

a. *How these amount to the one kāya of the profound state of reality*
If the division of the two truths regarding any statements about the Bhagavān Buddha's kāyas as one, two, three, four, and so on is also understood, one will not be deluded about the Sage's word.

Here, the kāya of the consummate abiding state is only just one: the ultimate kāya:

> Nirvāṇa is the one truth.[1059]

And:

> A phenomenon that is not enlightenment does not exist.[1060]

And:

> Except for dharmadhātu,
> phenomena do not exist in this way . . .[1061]

Thus it is stated that all phenomena except the kāya of dharmadhātu do not exist in the abiding state of reality. And:

> Unique, hard, and solid vajra self.[1062]

And:

> Truth is one; there is no second.[1063]

And:

> The truth is just one, not two. It is like this: the truth of cessation.[1064]

What such passages say is that in the consummate abiding state there is just one truth, the ultimate truth, the kāya of the true nature, the incomparable and sole kāya in which the true nature and the many are one taste, and knowing and knowable object are one.

b. *Division into the two kāyas of the two truths*

Here the two kāyas are the ultimate dharmakāya and the relative rūpakāya, the sources of excellent benefit to oneself and to others. Moreover:

> Of benefit to oneself and benefit to others,
> the ultimate kāya and that relative kāya dependent
> on it have these sixty-four divisions of the qualities,
> the results of separation and ripening. {326}
>
> The source of one's own fulfillment
> is the ultimate kāya; the conventional
> kāya of the seers is the source of excellence
> for others.
>
> The first kāya has the qualities
> of separation, such as the powers.
> The second has the major marks of
> a great being, the qualities of ripening.[1065] [261]

Thus the qualities of separation (the powers and so on) are stated to be complete in that which is the result of separation, the dharmakāya, the changeless fully established nature, the kāya of thusness; and the qualities of production (the major marks and so on) are stated to exist in that which is the result of production, the rūpakāya, the unmistaken fully established nature, possessing perfect primordial awareness.

These points clear away the claim by some that even the dharmakāya is a relative result of production, and the claim by some that even the rūpakāya is an ultimate result of separation.

The *Entryway to the Three Kāyas* also says:

> Nirvāṇa with the aggregates is classified
> as the two [rūpa]kāyas of the Sage.
> Since it is separate from all aggregates,
> aggregates do not exist in the dharmakāya.[1066]

Likewise, the claim by some that even the dharmakāya does not exist at first in sentient beings and the claim by some that even the rūpakāya does exist at first in all sentient beings are also very confused, because it is extensively said: "Being like a treasure and a fruit tree,"[1067] and so on.

c. *Division into the three kāyas included in the two truths*

Here the three kāyas are the dharmakāya, sambhogakāya, and nirmāṇakāya, which are included in both truths. Moreover:

> Division of the kāyas of the buddhas
> is into the natural, the sambhoga,
> and another—the nirmāṇakāya;
> the first is the support of the two.[1068]

And:

> Know that the kāyas of the buddhas
> are included in the three kāyas. By means
> of the three kāyas, which benefit oneself
> and others, this [pair] with its support are taught.[1069]

Such passages in the *Ornament of the Sūtras*, the *Sūtra of the Excellent Golden Light*, and so on make it totally clear: one ultimate kāya and two relative kāyas.

The *Sūtra of Direct, Perfect Bodhicitta in the Palace of Akaniṣṭa* also says:

> The collection of a buddha's qualities, such as the powers, the types of fearlessness, and the unshared attributes—nondual with and not different than the perfection of wisdom—is the dharmakāya. {327}

> That which occurs from its blessings and is supported on its foundation is the sambhogakāya.
>
> Those that definitely occur from its blessings and occur in accord with the devotion of trainable beings are the nirmāṇakāya.[1070]

The *Ornament of Direct Realization* says:

> The svābhāvika, with the sambhoga,
> and likewise, another, which is the nirmāṇa,
> and the dharmakāya with its activity,
> are correctly said to be the four aspects.[1071]

Those such as noble Vimuktasena assert the meaning here to be the three kāyas, and others also assert it to be the four kāyas. [262] But it is obvious that also in the *Brief Presentation of the Assertions of My Own View* it is applied in the context of the four kāyas.[1072] These, however, are merely the difference of not dividing or dividing the ultimate kāya into the svābhāvikakāya and the dharmakāya, so whichever is done is clearly without fault. In that way, whether classified as three kāyas or four kāyas, this renowned [classification of] the two rūpakāyas as the relative conventional kāyas, together with the one or two ultimate kāyas to make three kāyas or four kāyas, is common in the Mahāyāna.

2. *Division of the kāyas in uncommon secret mantra*
This has two topics.

a. *Division of the kāyas from one to five*
In the uncommon mantra approach, that which is the vajrakāya or mantrakāya, the self of thusness, the pure self, is identical to Vajradhara or Vajrasattva, the kāya in which knowing and knowable object are one; that androgynous stage itself, in which emptiness and compassion, and means and wisdom, are integrated as one is also the one consummate kāya. But if divided by means and wisdom, emptiness and compassion, and so on, it is also two kāyas; if divided by mind, speech, and body, the Three Jewels, and so on, it is also three kāyas; if divided by the four vajras, the four knowledges,[1073] the four aspects of direct enlightenment, and so on, it is also four kāyas; and if divided (together with the kāya of primordial awareness) into five, it also becomes five kāyas:

Buddha having a quintessence of five kāyas,
pervasive lord, self of the five primordial awarenesses.[1074] {328}

b. *How those have the same meaning as the natural family*

In that way, those are the one naturally pure family, the two, the three, the four, and the five:

The three families and the five families themselves,
the one natural and the one hundred families.[1075]

And:

Mind is great and just one,
but symbolized by the forms
of the five. From those five
families many thousands arise.

Therefore, these are one nature,
great bliss, the sublime benefit itself.[1076]

And so on, as presented before. Likewise, as presented before in the section about the ground, the six families and so on should also be understood here in the section about the results, because every one of all the categories stated for the natural family are categories of the indivisible essence of ground and result. [263]

3. *Just how those are stated by noble Mañjuśrī*

Likewise, in the *Brief Presentation of the Assertions of My Own View*, noble Mañjuśrī says:

The Buddha, Lion of the Śākyas,
due to the inclinations of sentient beings,
states the kāyas to be one, two, three,
four, and five.

Buddha without beginning or end,
Ādibuddha without partiality, unique
eye of stainless primordial awareness,
the Tathāgata is the kāya of primordial awareness.[1077]

Just as the rūpakāya, so too the dharmakāya
of the Buddha, due to the inclinations of sentient
beings, are said by the treatises and the three sources
of refuge to be [the two kāyas].

By the divisions of mind, speech, and body,
the kāyas are fully proclaimed to be three:
the dharma, sambhoga, and nirmāṇa, accomplished
by human beings in the mantra approach.

The svābhāvika, with the sambhoga,
and likewise another, which is the nirmāṇa,
and the dharmakāya with its activity,
are correctly explained to be the four aspects.[1078]

Buddha having a quintessence of five kāyas,
pervasive lord, self of the five primordial awarenesses,
crown of the self of the five buddhas, having
the five eyes without attachment.[1079] {329}

The limitless aggregate of form
is my sublime nirmāṇakāya.
The limitless aggregate of sound
is my sublime sambhogakāya.

The limitless aggregate of the attributes
is fully proclaimed to be my dharmakāya.
The limitless aggregate of primordial awareness
is fully proclaimed to be my kāya of primordial awareness.

The limitless aggregate of bliss
is my sublime changeless kāya of bliss.[1080]

The consolidation is the aggregate and, likewise,
the [dharma]kāya is proclaimed to be their perfect accumulation.[1081]

4. *Division of the sambhogakāya and the nirmāṇakāya into the two truths*

If division into the two truths is also understood here regarding the sambhogakāya and the nirmāṇakāya, one will not be deluded about the Sage's word.

Here the two aspects of the rūpakāya are the relative sambhogakāya and the relative nirmāṇakāya, as commonly renowned.

The ultimate sambhogakāya and nirmāṇakāya are complete in the fully established true nature, thusness, because thusness is the consummate, ultimate four kāyas, four vajras, four joys, four knowledges, four aspects of direct enlightenment, four sattvas, four Herukas, four mothers, four *e vaṃ ma ya*, four *kā la ca kra*, four moments, four aspects of reality, four marks, four abodes of Brahmā, four liberations, four vajrayogas, four noble persons, four noble truths, four schools, four vajra seats or four bases, and so on, and because it is the knower of the sixteen aspects of reality. [264]

Moreover, since it is very clear in that way in the profound, consummate, secret mantra sources, there is no delusion, but wherever it is not clear in that way, there is delusion, yet the meaning is only the same: the fully established true nature, thusness.

Therefore, the ultimate sambhogakāya and nirmāṇakāya are renowned in the uncommon mantra approach. {330}

So if the sugata essence were of provisional meaning, those four ultimate kāyas and so on would also be of provisional meaning, and the fully established true nature, thusness, would also be of provisional meaning, because those all have one meaning.

A sugata essence with a meaning other than thusness has not been stated by noble, sublime beings, and we also do not accept that; but they have mentioned it by very many other names. Therefore, do not be confused by the names, rely instead on the meaning.

5. *How ultimate truth itself is present as the four kāyas of the abiding state*
This has three topics.

a. *The presentation*
This has two topics.

1) *Presentation of the four kāyas of the profound abiding state*
Therefore, the ultimate four kāyas of the ground of emptiness are the indivisible essence of ground and result, the four kāyas of the sugata essence. Moreover, the "Chapter on Primordial Awareness" says:

> Not wisdom, also not means, this [androgynous stage]
> is the connate kāya, and it is the dharmakāya, the nature
> of wisdom and means, definitely free of darkness, through

the divisions of primordial awareness and [other] consciousness.
This [ultimate] is also the sambhogakāya and, like a sweet sound,
the creator of benefit for many sentient beings. For the sake
of ripening sentient beings, again this [ultimate] becomes
the nirmāṇakāya of the buddhas.[1082]

Thus the four kāyas of ultimate primordial awareness are stated. They are also stated to be the four vajras. That same source says:

The body vajra of the Conqueror, which is not [to be realized]
by way of object and subject, has all aspects.
The speech vajra, by means of the languages in each heart,
causes all sentient beings to understand Dharma.
The mind vajra of the Vajra Bearer, which is the nature of the minds
of sentient beings, is present throughout the entire earth.
That which, like a [magical] stainless gem, apprehends entities
[as great bliss] is the primordial-awareness vajra.[1083]

And the honorable, venerable lord also says:

The kāya having the most sublime of all aspects,
seen from various perspectives by sentient beings
with their own inclinations, has the characteristic
of the nirmāṇa. {331} [265]

This which, through the speech of sentient beings,
clearly displays its miraculous quintessence in accord
with the inclinations of sentient beings, has the characteristic
of the sambhogakāya.

Not impermanent, yet not permanent,
not one, not having a characteristic of many,
not an entity, yet not a nonentity,
this is the dharmakāya, free of support.

Emptiness and compassion indivisible,
free of attachment and nonattachment,

> not wisdom, yet not means, this is
> the svābhāvikakāya, which is the other.
>
> To the one renowned as Kālacakra,
> the peaceful quintessence of the four kāyas,
> I bow down with my entire being.[1084]

And:

> Without cause and characteristic,
> without fluctuation and, likewise, stages,
> thus directly expressed as *kā la ca kra*,
> to that nondual [primordial awareness] I bow.
>
> And to that Tathāgata whom the syllables *kā* and so on
> state to be the four kāyas (nirmāṇa, sambhoga, good dharma,
> and the pure), the Ādibuddha without partiality,
> I fully bow the crown of my head.[1085]

Such passages state the fully established true nature itself to be the four kāyas of the consummate definitive meaning, because the conditioned rūpakāya is inappropriate for the Buddha of the consummate definitive meaning.

2) *Showing that is not the rūpakāya*
Moreover, this same honorable, venerable lord says:

> The Bhagavān Buddha [of the state of reality] is not the rūpakāya. Why? Because he arose from space, because he is self-arisen, because he has all aspects yet is without aspect, because he holds the four drops, because he is partless and beyond parts, because he holds the pinnacle of the fourth joy, because he is great attachment (the first of freedom from attachment), because he does not hold to "mine," because he does not hold to "I," because all his [unconditioned] elements are inexhaustible, {332} because he is the producer of all the meaning of secret mantra, because he is the great drop without syllables, because he is the five changeless great emptinesses, because he is the six changeless empty drops, and because he abides in equilibrium, like space.[1086]

These reasons also establish that he is beyond momentary conditioned phenomena, partial capacity, and dependent arising, and, in many other scriptures such as the Mother Sūtras and the *Mahāparinirvāṇa*, that which is the consummate Buddha is also fully renowned as not being the rūpakāya. [266]

b. *The extensive explanation*
This has ten topics.

1) *How that abiding state itself is present as the four kāyas, the sixteen, and so on*
Likewise:

> Embraced by Bhagavatī Prajñā[pāramitā] who has aspects
> yet is without aspect, possessing the changeless bliss of
> having abandoned arising and destruction, having abandoned
> the bliss of laughter and so on, the producer of the buddhas,
> having the three kāyas and perfectly aware of the three times—
> to the omniscient, sublime Ādibuddha, that Bhagavān nondual
> [primordial awareness] itself, I bow down.[1087]

That which is thusness, the changeless fully established nature, is the Ādibuddha, the svābhāvikakāya, and because it possesses the three remaining ultimate kāyas indivisibly as one taste, it is the omnipresent four kāyas of dharmadhātu. Moreover:

> Though not different earlier and later,
> we hold thusness without the stains
> of all the obscurations to be the Buddha,
> not pure, not impure.[1088]

And:

> That which is not thusness is not the Tathāgata.[1089]

And:

> Thusness with stains, the stainless one, . . .[1090]

In accord with such statements, although there is no difference in thusness, that which is present with stains in some beings has one purity and that which is present free of stains in some has two purities. Therefore, just that which is present as the essence of the ground in some beings is present as the essence of the result in some, and just that which is present in some beings as the essence of the result is also present in some as the essence of the ground, which is called "the indivisible essence of ground and result," just as the sky of indivisible essence pervades all lands, with or without masses of clouds. {333}

Therefore, that is the intent of statements that it is not solely pure, yet also not solely impure.

Likewise:

> The Omniscient One, the kāya of primordial awareness,
> the kāya of the sun, and the eyes wide like lotus petals,
> the Buddha . . .[1091]

That which is thus stated in the *Glorious Tantra* is also stated to be the primordially liberated four kāyas of the true nature:

> The Omniscient One and the kāya of primordial awareness
> are the connate [kāya] of the lord of conquerors and, likewise,
> the dharmakāya.
> The sambhogakāya and the nirmāṇakāya are also the kāya
> of the sun and the eyes wide like lotus petals.
> [These are] the pure yogas, the liberations, body, speech, mind,
> and [great] attachment residing in the cyclic existence free of
> cyclic existence, nondual wisdom and means.
> To that Ādibuddha, [the androgynous stage] praised by gods,
> humans, and demigods, I bow.[1092]

Although the four such as the Omniscient One are one taste in thusness with the quintessence of the four kāyas such as the connate, the four vajrayogas such as the pure yoga, the four gates of liberation such as emptiness, [267] and the four vajras such as the vajrakāyas, since these are different merely in name, that and those are synonyms. And since all are also primordial awareness with means and wisdom not divisible into two, indivisible cyclic existence and the peace [of nirvāṇa], present as cyclic existence without the flaw of including contradiction, they are beyond all that can be exemplified, the Buddha of the three realms.

Likewise:

> The Buddha seated on the lion throne is the pure vajrayoga
> worshiped by the three states of cyclic existence.
> Reality alone, by division into kāyas, has sixteen aspects, residing
> in cyclic existence without cyclic existence.
> Knowing and knowable object are one, the sacred commitment
> of the sublime Conqueror,
> the truths of the twelve limbs, bodhicitta, the vajra place of
> the Conqueror—to Kālacakra I bow down.[1093]

Reality alone—ultimate great bliss residing indivisibly in ultimate great emptiness—also resides as the four vajrayogas and the four vajrakāyas, and each kāya also always resides as ultimate body, speech, mind, and primordial awareness, or as the ultimate four joys. Therefore, it is the knower of the sixteen aspects of reality (the other knowing) and has the twelve aspects of the meaning of the truth (the other knowable object). {334} Those primordially, indivisibly integrated [the androgynous stage] are ultimate bodhicitta, the vajra place of the Conqueror, beyond worldly examples, the other three states of cyclic existence.

Likewise:

> Primordial awareness, well purified by the primordial
> awareness of emptiness, is pure, changeless. Mind,
> well purified by the primordial awareness of signlessness,
> is nonduality, the quintessence of phenomena.
>
> Speech, purified by the primordial awareness
> of wishlessness, is secret mantra, inexhaustible sound.
> Likewise, body purified by the primordial awareness
> of the directly unconditioned, and stainless,
>
> is shape, having miraculous motion.
> Those with a quintessence of wisdom
> and means united [as one] the Tathāgata
> calls "vajrasattva," "bodhisattva,"

"mahāsattva," and "samayasattva."
To that lord who has exhausted existent
and nonexistent, peaceful bodhicitta
without beginning or end, I bow down.[1094]

That previously presented ultimate Buddha, the fully established true nature itself, is thus primordially peaceful bodhicitta without beginning or end, which is the middle devoid of the two extremes of existent and nonexistent, the ultimate lord or other lord.

Moreover, the primordial awareness, mind, speech, and body of the omnipresent dharmadhātu, primordially purified by the primordial awarenesses of the four gates of ultimate liberation, are the quintessence of the four vajrayogas and the four sattvas; all are also the quintessence of wisdom and means primordially united as one. [268]

Likewise, after clarifying the previously presented sixteen aspects of reality, [Puṇḍarīka] speaks of mahāmudrā, *evaṃ*:

The body, speech, mind, and primordial awareness
of the nirmāṇa united as one binds [its drops];
the body, speech, mind, and primordial awareness
of the sambhoga united as one binds [its drops];

the body, speech, mind, and primordial awareness
of the glorious dharma united as one binds [its drops];
and body, speech, mind, and primordial awareness
of the connate united as one binds [its drops].

These are not the blisses arisen from the two organs
during the waking state, the dream state, the deep-sleep state,
and the fourth state, and [the drops of] primordial awareness,
mind, speech, and body do not perfectly abide in their four places.

Action mudrā totally discarded,
mudrā of primordial awareness abandoned,
perfectly arisen from Mahāmudrā,
the connate does not associate with others. {335}

> Beyond conceptual meditation,
> the unchanging bliss of mahāmudrā
> has abandoned apprehended, apprehender,
> shape, concepts, and repetitions.
>
> Having the aspect of a gandhārva village
> and the nature of a prognostic image,
> quintessence of means and wisdom united—
> to those syllables *evaṃ* I bow.[1095]

Because the naturally original true nature's sixteen aspects of reality are primordially, naturally beyond all relative, incidental phenomena, they are connate primordial awareness resembling a prognostic image and so on, the ground primordially free of the four worldly states,[1096] the four drops, and all conceptuality such as the meditations and repetitions of the creation stage. Since that is not united with other entities, even though the action mudrā and the mudrā of primordial awareness have been abandoned, its quintessence of means and wisdom, always primordially united, the androgynous stage, arisen from Mahāmudrā, is "the unarisen arisen," without the flaw of including contradiction, beyond worldly examples.

Therefore, although the other result (the ultimate result, changeless great bliss, nonreferential great compassion) has arisen from the other cause (observable emptiness, Mahāmudrā), it is not conditioned, because its cause—Mahāmudrā—has not arisen from anything. Referring to this, the *Root Tantra* also says:

> With mutual connections dissolved, it is the sublime androgynous stage.
>
> The prajñā [great emptiness] has not occurred from a cause,
> the result [great bliss] has occurred from the prajñā as its cause.
> Because the prajñā [great emptiness] has not arisen from a cause,
> [ultimate great bliss] arisen from the prajñā has not arisen from a cause.
>
> Because [self-arisen] primordial awareness has not arisen from a cause, it is the unsurpassable [ultimate] primordial awareness from the prajñā [of Mahāmudrā, the image of emptiness].[1097]

And so on. Likewise, the four knowledges, the four Herukas, the four aspects of direct enlightenment, the four moments, the four aspects of reality, and so on, which have the same meaning as the consummate, ultimate four kāyas (yet are mentioned by various different names) are all the four kāyas derived from the changeless fully established nature, thusness; they are not derived from perfect primordial awareness, from the unmistaken fully established nature, from the rūpakāya itself, or from a collection of the dharmakāya and the rūpakāya. {336} [269]

2) *How just that is present as the self of the five kāyas and the five primordial awarenesses pervading all*

Therefore, even though the self of the ultimate four kāyas, five kāyas, and five primordial awarenesses is indivisible in essence (like the sky pervading lands with or without clouds), because it is thusness always present in all sentient beings of the three realms and buddhas of the three times, it is well established as the indivisible essence of the consummate ground and result.

3) *How just that is present as reality, nirvāṇa free of sides*

This same honorable, venerable lord says:

> Therefore, the Bhagavān says the side without nature is without side. As for "side": those such as "entity" and "nonentity," "existence" and "nonexistence," "being" and "nonbeing," "one" and "not one," "permanence" and "annihilation," "cyclic existence" and "nirvāṇa," "form" and "not form," "sound" and "not sound," "momentary" and "not momentary," "attachment" and "not attachment," "hatred" and "not hatred," "ignorance" and "not ignorance," and so on, are sides because they are just mutually dependent.
>
> Freedom from these sides is the nonabiding nirvāṇa of the buddhas, [the ground of] no nature, and the conquerors have said primordial awareness free of single or multiple moments is called "reality."[1098]

4) *How just that is present also as the four and sixteen unconditioned joys*

> Just that also appears individually in four aspects and in sixteen aspects, in accord with the inclinations of the minds of sentient

beings themselves. By the divisions of joy, sublime joy, special joy, and the connate, there are four aspects. {337} [270]

Then, joy of body, joy of speech, joy of mind, and joy of primordial awareness; likewise, sublime joy of body, sublime joy of speech, sublime joy of mind, and sublime joy of primordial awareness; likewise, special joy of body, special joy of speech, special joy of mind, and special joy of primordial awareness; likewise, connate joy of body, connate joy of speech, connate joy of mind, and connate joy of primordial awareness. When a yogin knows the sixteen aspects of reality such as those, at that point the Bhagavān calls him "a knower of the sixteen aspects of reality."[1099]

5) *How just that is also present as the sixteen divisions of the kāya*

Just that alone is called the "connate kāya." After that is the dharmakāya, after that is the sambhogakāya, and after that is the nirmāṇakāya.

Likewise, connate speech, connate mind, and connate primordial awareness; likewise, dharma speech, dharma mind, and dharma primordial awareness; likewise, sambhoga speech, sambhoga mind, and sambhoga primordial awareness; likewise, nirmāṇa speech, nirmāṇa mind, and nirmāṇa primordial awareness. In that way, because of special aspirations in the minds of all sentient beings, it fully appears as the sixteen aspects of reality.[1100]

6) *How just that is also present as the four liberations, the four yogas, and so on*

Just that is the connate kāya, called "purified by the liberation of emptiness, primordial-awareness vajra, the Omniscient One, the quintessence of wisdom and means, the pure yoga." {338}

Just that is the dharmakāya, called "purified by the liberation of signlessness, mind vajra, kāya of primordial awareness, the quintessence of wisdom and means, the yoga of the quintessence of phenomena."

Just that is the sambhogakāya, called "purified by the liberation of wishlessness, speech vajra, kāya of the sun, the quintessence of wisdom and means, the yoga of mantra."

Just that is the nirmāṇakāya, called "purified by directly unconditioned liberation, body vajra, eyes wide like lotus petals, the quintessence of wisdom and means, the yoga of shape."

The four vajrayogas such as that were requested from the Buddha by Vajrapāṇi.[1101] [271]

7) *How just that is also present as the four synonyms (such as Omniscient One) for the four kāyas, and as the four knowledges*

The primordial-awareness vajra purified by the liberation of emptiness, the quintessence of wisdom and means, the connate kāya that has obtained omniscience itself, is the Omniscient One, because just that is all-seeing.

The mind vajra purified by the liberation of signlessness, the quintessence of wisdom and means, the dharmakāya that has obtained knowledge of the aspects of the path, is the kāya of primordial awareness, because it is present by means of sublimely unchanging bliss itself.

The speech vajra purified by the liberation of wishlessness, the quintessence of wisdom and means, the sambhogakāya that has obtained knowledge of the path, is the kāya of the sun, because it is the teacher of worldly and transcendent Dharma instantly in the languages of limitless, limitless sentient beings.

The body vajra purified by directly unconditioned liberation, the quintessence of wisdom and means, the nirmāṇakāya that has obtained knowledge of all aspects, is the eyes wide like lotus petals, because with limitless, limitless nirmāṇakāyas it instantly radiates the miraculous array of the kāya having all aspects.[1102] {339}

8) *How just that is also present as the four aspects of direct enlightenment and the four such as seeing all meanings*

Likewise, directly complete buddhahood by means of one instant is the primordial-awareness vajra, which sees all the [ultimate] truth.

Directly complete buddhahood by means of five aspects is the mind vajra, sublimely unchanging bliss.

Directly complete buddhahood by means of twenty aspects is the speech vajra, the twelve aspects of the meaning of the truth, the teacher of Dharma in the languages of all sentient beings.

> Directly complete buddhahood by means of Māyājāla is the body vajra, knowing the sixteen aspects of reality, the kāya radiated by limitless Māyājālas.[1103]

The division of the aspects is thus stated extensively by means of the names of many aspects (such as the ultimate four joys and the sixteen aspects of reality) of the indivisible essence of ground and result, that omnipresent dharmadhātu itself. [272]

9) *How all those are present in four cakras of the body*
This has seventeen topics.

a) *How those are present as the unpronounceable vowels such as* a *and consonant-syllables such as* ka, *and so on*
Likewise, the honorable, noble Vajragarbha also says:

> At the forehead, the vowels such as *a*. At the throat, the consonant-syllables such as *ka*. At the heart, wisdom. At the navel, means.[1104]

b) *How those are also present as the four kāyas of the changeless fully established nature*

> The connate kāya at the navel. The dharmakāya at the heart. The sambhogakāya at the throat. {340} The nirmāṇakāya at the forehead.[1105]

c) *How those are also present as the other states, the ultimate four states*

> At the navel, the fourth state. At the heart, the deep-sleep state. At the throat, the dream state. At the forehead, the waking state.[1106]

d) *How those are also present as the ground of emptiness, the four vajras of the emptiness of other*

> At the forehead, the body vajra. At the throat, the speech vajra. At the heart, the mind vajra. At the navel, the primordial-awareness vajra.[1107]

e) *How those are also present as the* e vaṃ ma yā *of the dharmakāya and as the four mothers*

At the navel, the syllable *e*. At the heart, the syllable *vaṃ*. At the throat, the syllable *ma*. At the forehead, the syllable *yā*. At the navel, Locanā. At the heart, Māmakī. At the throat, Pāṇḍarā. At the forehead, Tāriṇī. The four maṇḍalas.[1108]

f) *How those are also present as the other moments, the four moments of the middle beyond examples*

As for the four moments: variety, at the forehead. Ripening, at the throat. Rubbing, at the heart. Free of characteristics, at the navel.[1109] {341} [273]

g) *How those are also present as the other joys, the four naturally changeless four joys*

Likewise, joy, at the forehead. Sublime joy, at the throat. Joy of special joy, at the heart. Connate joy, at the navel.[1110]

h) *How those are also present as the other four truths, the four truths of the dharmakāya*

Likewise, the truth of suffering, at the forehead. The truth of origination, at the throat. The truth of cessation, at the heart. The truth of the path, at the navel.[1111]

i) *How those are also present as the four aspects of reality in the abiding state, the sugata essence*

The four aspects of reality: reality of self, at the forehead. Reality of mantra, at the throat. Reality of the deity, at the heart. Reality of primordial awareness, at the navel.[1112]

j) *How those are also present as the four of taking control, expressing the sound, and so on, of thusness*

At the forehead, taking control. At the throat, expressing the sound. At the heart, all thoughts. At the navel, experiencing bliss.[1113]

k) *How those are also present as the other schools, the four schools of the true nature*

The four schools: Sthāvira, at the navel. Sarvāstivāda, at the heart. Saṃmitīya, at the throat. {342} Mahāsāṃghika, at the forehead.[1114]

l) *How those are also present as the naturally original moon, sun, Rāhu, and so on*

The moon, at the forehead. The sun, at the throat. At the heart, Rāhu. At the navel, Kālāgni.[1115] [274]

m) *How those are also present as the other transits, the sixteen transits without the flaw of including contradiction, and so on*

At the forehead, the sixteen transits. At the throat, the thirty-two. At the heart, the eight. At the navel, the sixty-four transits.[1116]

n) *How those are also present as the other periods, the four solar periods of natural luminosity*

The previously explained four periods: the early period, at the forehead. The noon period, at the throat. The afternoon period, at the heart. The midnight period, at the navel.[1117]

o) *How those are also present as the other behaviors, the four naturally connate behaviors*

At the forehead, enjoyment. At the throat, control. At the heart, dissolution. At the navel, sovereignty.

In that way, all are fourfold.[1118] {343}

p) *How those are also present as the ultimate truth of cessation's factors conducive to enlightenment*

> After the thirty-six factors conducive to enlightenment and the thirty-six elements have been classified in parts, four [by four], as explained before, through the division of the families all should be applied four by four to the four cakras, in the usual order.[1119]

q) *Summary of the meaning of those points, and advice that the division of the two truths must be understood for all*
Here also, after understanding the division of the two truths for the phenomena of the four states, the four truths, the four schools, the sun, the moon, Rāhu, and Kālāgni, the four periods, the four behaviors, and so on, the yogin should know all the sets of four (such as the ultimate four states) to be the many divisions of the aspects stated in regard to the indivisible ground and result, the four kāyas of the sugata essence. [275]

10) *How those are obtained by the flow of breath ceasing in the four cakras*
Likewise, the *Later Kālacakra Tantra* also says:

> Because the lifeforce wind has ceased, he is the two-armed
> Hevajra, Śiva, here Vajrasattva, who has destroyed pride.
> Because the lifeforce wind has ceased, he is the four-armed
> Hevajra, Hutāśana,[1120] the bodhisattva who has destroyed hatred.
> He is Hevajra, the mahāsattva with three faces and six arms,
> who has destroyed desire.
> He is Brahmā, with eight faces, [sixteen arms], and four legs,
> the blissful samayasattva who has destroyed ignorance.
>
> Because the lifeforce wind has ceased at the navel, he is Vajrasattva
> free of the three stains, the Buddha himself.
> Because it has ceased at the heart, he is the bodhisattva free of
> the three stains, a pratyekabuddha, the Buddha himself.
> That sun at the throat is the mahāsattva, a sthavira free of the three
> stains. Because the lord of the winds has ceased at the forehead,
> he is the blissful samayasattva, the son of the Teacher.[1121] {344}

After understanding the division of the two truths also regarding Śiva, Hutāśana, Brahmā, and so on, and regarding buddha, pratyekabuddha, sthavira, and bodhisattva, one should understand all stated sets of four (ultimate Śiva and so on) to be synonyms of the four kāyas of indivisible ground and result, such as the four Herukas. And the other sets of four also extensively stated in the *Five Hundred Thousand Lines* are also like that; the scriptural passages are those cited before in the section on the basic ground.[1122]

c. Summary

Likewise, Mañjuśrī's *Brief Presentation of the Assertions of My Own View* as quoted by the great paṇḍita lord Nāropa and the teacher Acalagarbha also says:

> The limitless aggregate of form
> is my sublime nirmāṇakāya.
> The limitless aggregate of sound
> is my sublime sambhogakāya.
>
> The limitless aggregate of the attributes
> is fully proclaimed to be my dharmakāya.
> The limitless aggregate of bliss
> is my sublime changeless kāya of bliss.
>
> The consolidation is the aggregate and, likewise,
> the kāya is proclaimed to be their perfect accumulation.[1123]

Thus four kāyas that are the indivisible essence of ground and result are stated, which have the same meaning as the ultimate sets of four presented before. And all those are derived from changeless fully established thusness, dharmadhātu penetrating all, with nothing to remove or add, four kāyas like space, stated by means of many aspects. [276]

6. Showing the difference of delusion or no delusion about the five kāyas and the six families of the true nature

Likewise, that which is the fully established true nature, thusness, is also stated to be the quintessence of the five kāyas of the Buddha: the ultimate kāyas of nirmāṇa, sambhoga, dharma, primordial awareness, and bliss. {345}

Likewise, all statements that the six families of conquerors, the six mothers, and so on, are the deities of primordial awareness (the thirty-six manifestations of ultimate tastes and elements, the thirty-six ultimate aggregates, and so on) refer to the fully established true nature. Therefore, if the sugata essence were actually nonexistent, those would also be actually nonexistent, because that and those have just the same meaning.

That being the case, from the difference of understanding or not understanding them in that way because of the difference of textual traditions that are clear or not clear in that way, the difference of delusion or no delusion is stated: "Although the meaning is the same, . . ."[1124] and so on. This is just like the difference between looking at high mountains from high in the sky and looking at them from below or the same level.

B. *Explanation of the excellence of wonderful primordial awareness*
This has three topics.

1. *Brief presentation of self-arisen and other-arisen primordial awareness*

In that way, the ultimate Buddha is the five kāyas of self-arisen primordial awareness. Moreover, thusness, the changeless fully established nature itself, always resides as the five primordial awarenesses.

The relative rūpakāya has perfect primordial awareness, the unmistaken fully established nature, and has the primordial awareness of the Mahāyāna [path of] no more learning, which is not beyond the momentary.

2. *Individual division and extensive explanation of those*
This has two topics.

a. *Explanation of other-arisen primordial awareness and its causes*

Moreover, the *Ornament of the Sūtras* says:

> Mirrorlike primordial awareness is unwavering;
> three primordial awarenesses depend on it—
> those of equanimity, the discriminating, and
> the all-accomplishing. {346}
>
> Mirrorlike primordial awareness has no
> "mine," is totally unrestricted, always present,
> and not deluded about all knowable objects,
> yet never directed toward them.

Since it is the cause of all primordial awarenesses,
it is like the great source of primordial awareness.
It is the sambhogakāya buddha itself, because
reflections of primordial awareness occur in it. [277]

The primordial awareness of equanimity is said
to come from pure meditation on sentient beings.
To have entered nonabiding peace is accepted to be
the primordial awareness of equanimity.

At all times endowed with love and great
compassion, it definitely displays the kāyas
of a buddha to sentient beings in accord with
their inclinations.

Discriminating primordial awareness
is always unimpeded regarding all knowable
objects. It is just like a treasure of samādhi
and dhāraṇīs.

Within the circle of the retinue
it displays all the riches and rains down
the great Dharma that eliminates
all doubts.

All-accomplishing primordial awareness
accomplishes benefit for all sentient beings
through various, infinite, unimaginable
emanations in all realms.

Know those emanations of the buddhas,
always accomplishing their activities,
to be inconceivable in all aspects by means
of specifics, number, and realms.[1125]

The four primordial awarenesses that are mentioned are the relative, conditioned truth of the path, the unmistaken fully established nature, and, of the five topics,[1126] perfect primordial awareness. From what causes do the four primordial awarenesses such as those arise?

> Because of retention, equanimity of
> mind, fully teaching the perfect Dharma,
> and accomplishing activities, the four
> primordial awarenesses perfectly arise.[1127]

Referring to these primordial awarenesses of a buddha's rūpakāya, the extensive and intermediate Mother Sūtras and so on say a tathāgata's ten powers, four types of fearlessness, analytical perfect awarenesses, and so on, up to the eighteen unshared attributes of a buddha, are conditioned. {347}

b. *Explanation of self-arisen primordial awareness without causes and without conditions*
This has seven topics.

1) *How the other aggregates, the aggregates naturally beyond the world, reside as the five primordial awarenesses*
The five primordial awarenesses of the profound tantras are the ultimate, unconditioned truth of cessation, the changeless fully established nature, and, of the five topics, thusness. Moreover, "Establishing Sublimely Unchanging Primordial Awareness" says:

> [The Ādibuddha] Bhagavān Vajradhara—the sublimely unchanging essence of these approaches of the śrāvaka, the perfections, and mantra—is presented by the Tathāgata in *Chanting the Names.*
>
> Degenerate masters who do not understand the meaning of this, who are not excellent, and who have degenerated from sublimely unchanging primordial awareness will appear in a future time, and those who have degenerated will cause sentient beings to degenerate.
>
> Therefore, from the praise of the five types of primordial awareness in the *Root Tantra,* the Bhagavān speaks of the cultivation of the five types by means of five verses, like this [278]:
>
> > The assembly of entities in empty [space],
> > devoid of imaginary form, is not inanimate.
> > This is seen, as by a young girl performing
> > prognostic divination in a mirror.
>
> Thus the [other] aggregate of form in transcendent truth, mirror-like primordial awareness.

All entities [of the true nature] having become
equal, it resides unchanged as one entity.
Arisen from unchanging primordial awareness,
it is not annihilation, yet also not permanence.

Thus the [other] aggregate of feeling, the primordial awareness of equanimity.

All syllables, the quintessence of the [ultimate] names,
have perfectly arisen from the family of the syllable *a*.
The basis of the great unchanging obtained, there are no
[relative] names, also no bearers of names.

Thus the [other] aggregate of discrimination, discriminating primordial awareness.

Among attributes that have not arisen,
which are free of conditioning factors,
there is no buddhahood, no enlightenment,
no sentient being, no lifeforce itself.

Thus the [other] aggregate of conditioning factors, all-accomplishing primordial awareness.

Beyond the true nature of consciousness,
pure primordial awareness unsoiled,
the attributes of natural luminosity reside
on the path of dharmadhātu. {348}

Thus the [other] aggregate of consciousness, the primordial awareness of very pure dharmadhātu.[1128]

2) *How other form, great form, and so on reside as the conquerors*

Likewise, three verses (the one-hundred-first and so on) of the fifth chapter of the *Condensed Tantra* also state the symbols of the cakra and so on, and the characteristics of the aggregates of the Tathāgata, like this:

The cakra is "the three states of cyclic existence totally clear," bliss is the jewel, and the [great] attachment of this is the lotus. The extinguishing of the afflictions is the sword, the vajra is also the indivisible great kāya of primordial awareness, and the severance of unknowing is the flaying knife. Thus, the six families of the sublime [conquerors]. What these [symbols] produce are the aggregates, elements, sense faculties, and so on of the same taste, like space, and these also should likewise be known.

That in which the form of [the conditioned] type has definitely deteriorated is called "the form of the great." That in which the sufferings of saṃsāra have deteriorated is called "the great feeling," and that in which the discrimination of saṃsāra has deteriorated is "the great vajra discrimination." That in which the expansion of saṃsāra has deteriorated is "the vajra conditioning factors alone."

That in which the states of sleep and so on have deteriorated is also called [vajra] "consciousness." That in which the entity of ignorance has deteriorated is "the primordial awareness of the Sage." These are the excellent, sublime sixfold conquerors such as Vairocana, the six families.[1129] {349} [279]

3) *How the other elements, the elements of the original true nature, reside as the female sugatas*

The other [six mothers] are the divisions of the six elements—earth, water, fire, wind, space, and peace [i.e., primordial awareness].[1130]

4) *How* Chanting the Ultimate Names *extensively presents the five self-arisen primordial awarenesses*

> Likewise, in *Chanting the Names*, by means of one hundred and sixty-two verses (with supplications) the Tathāgata fully presents the sublimely unchanging primordial awareness of Bhagavān Vajradhara, the essence of buddhas and bodhisattvas.[1131]

And so on.

5) *How the five syllables of the great emptinesses also clearly present the five self-arisen primordial awarenesses*

And the *Glorious Tantra* also says:

> I bow down to that [Ādibuddha], without beginning,
> middle, and end; without abiding, dying, and cyclic existence,
> sound, odor, and taste, tangible objects, form, and the mind
> [of the four states]; without primary nature and person;
> without bondage, release, and creator; without seeds and clearly
> without time; without the nature of the very suffering and bliss
> of all cyclic existence; [great] nirvāṇa, without conceptual marks,
> free of conditioning, without the [eight] qualities.
>
> I bow down to Kālacakra, [having many names] such as Kāla
> and Viśva, the vajra, the peerless being, omnipresent, without
> conceptual elaborations, and eternally abiding, whose ears, noses,
> mouths, eyes, heads, hands, and feet are everywhere, the apex of
> a being, the lord of beings, apprehending the sublime three states
> of cyclic existence, the cause of causes, the [other] awareness and
> so on to be realized by yogins, the stage of sublime bliss. {350}
>
> I bow down to that *visarga*,[1132] having a form able to radiate,
> like the fire of lightning, having the splendor of the twelve suns,
> illuminating vajra primordial awareness, causing travel to
> the sublime stage. I bow down to the form of the drop, the white
> dripping from the lord of the three worlds, the [other] rabbit-
> bearer perfectly residing at the top of the heads of worldly beings,
> the nectar removing death and destroying the fears of
> cyclic existence. [280]

> I also bow down to Vajrasattva, [the ultimate] Cittamātra, the essence of mantra, fully surrounded by deities, the nature of suffering and bliss, experienced by excellent beings as a peaceful form, due to what they have done, but by horrible beings as a horrible one, due to what actions they have most done, producing the results of that in their own minds in accord with [previously performed] ritual, lord of cyclic existence, having various forms, producer of the [other] three states of cyclic existence.[1133]

6) *Showing that the six changeless empty drops are also indivisible from those*

> [Appearing as] one and many, yet one [taste in the true nature], the same and not the same, yet the same; everywhere right, left, front, back, above, and below; the image of great variegated color in which white and green [and so on] are one; [the sugata essence] without the qualities of short, long, and very long, yet having the qualities;[1134] [the image of emptiness appearing as] man or woman, yet not woman or man; that which is the one support of all [bliss]—good bhaga, bhaga of the sublime, to you I bow, to you I bow.[1135]

Thus the quintessence of the five self-arisen primordial awarenesses is the five-prong vajra, and its support is the lotus or bhaga; these are the five changeless great emptinesses and the six changeless empty drops.

7) *How those also reside as the maṇḍalacakra and so on*

The *Hevajra Tantra* also says:

> That is the form of the connate,
> the yoginī of good great bliss.
> That is the maṇḍalacakra and has
> a nature of five primordial awarenesses. {351}
>
> That is the form of mirrorlike primordial awareness,
> has the essence of the primordial awareness of
> equanimity, and is [the apex of] reality,
> the discriminating. That is the all-accomplishing,

and that of very pure dharmadhātu.
That is the lord of the maṇḍala—me.
That is Nairātmyā yoginī, having the nature
of dharmadhātu.[1136]

The changeless fully established nature, which is thusness, the spacious great maṇḍala of naturally connate great bliss itself, is thus stated to be the five unconditioned self-arisen primordial awarenesses.

3. *How their differences accord with scripture*
This has four topics.

a. *Showing that, as with a buddha, the division of the two truths must also be understood regarding the five primordial awarenesses*
That being so, just as the division of the two truths must be understood regarding a buddha, if the division of the two truths is also understood regarding the primordial awareness of a buddha, one will not be deluded about the Sage's word. [281] The *Sūtra about the Level of a Buddha* says:

> [The Buddha] spoke to the bodhisattva Sujāta: "Sujāta, the level of a buddha is comprised of five attributes. What are the five? They are like this: pure dharmadhātu, mirrorlike primordial awareness, primordial awareness of equanimity, discriminating primordial awareness, and all-accomplishing primordial awareness.[1137]

Thus [the Buddha] taught, including a detailed, extensive explanation of each. The four primordial awarenesses have the same meaning as those determined in the *Ornament of the Sūtras* and so on, and, because pure dharmadhātu is self-arisen primordial awareness itself, these are the five ultimate primordial awarenesses, the ultimate five aggregates or five elements clarified in the profound tantras.

Moreover, the honorable, noble Vajragarbha says:

The mirrorlike, the primordial awareness
of equanimity, the discriminating as the third,
the all-accomplishing as the other, and
that of pure dharmadhātu,

are [ultimate] form, feeling, discrimination,
conditioning factors, and consciousness itself;
[ultimate] earth, water, fire, wind, and emptiness
as the fifth;

the [ultimate] pure five primordial awarenesses,
the five aspects of direct enlightenment, the quintessence
of the [ultimate] pure ten primordial awarenesses,
holder of the pure ten primordial awarenesses.[1138] {352}

Therefore, concerning the statement "Although the meaning is the same, because they are free of delusion, . . ."[1139] the difference exists that, if pure dharmadhātu itself is realized to be the five self-arisen primordial awarenesses, there is no delusion, and if that is not realized, there is delusion. But the meaning is just the same, because that which is the five-prong vajra, the five primordial awarenesses or the five changeless great emptinesses clarified in the profound texts of secret mantra, is the dharmadhātu itself stated in unison in all profound sūtras and tantras.

b. *Showing that those primordial awarenesses included in the two truths have the same meaning as the two fully established natures*

Likewise, concerning the fully established (of the three essences): the changeless fully established nature stated to be unconditioned also has the same meaning as the five self-arisen primordial awarenesses clarified in the profound texts of secret mantra, [282] but the unmistaken fully established nature stated to be conditioned has the same meaning as the four primordial awarenesses determined in the *Ornament of the Sūtras* and so on.

c. *Also, how those abide as the meaning of thusness and perfect primordial awareness*

Likewise, of the five topics stated in the Mahāyāna (name, mark or reason, conceptuality, thusness, and perfect primordial awareness), thusness also has the same meaning as the five primordial awarenesses of profound secret mantra, but perfect primordial awareness has the same meaning as the four primordial awarenesses established in the *Sūtra of the Level of a Buddha* and so on. In sequence, these are the ultimate dharmakāya (unconditioned primordial awareness) and the relative rūpakāya (conditioned primordial awareness).

d. *Showing that a buddha therefore has nine or fourteen primordial awarenesses of the two truths*

The primordial awareness of very pure dharmadhātu is only ultimate. For the four primordial awarenesses, such as the mirrorlike, however, {353} there are the conditioned and there are also the unconditioned, so one must know there are the relative and there are also the ultimate. And by the division of the two truths, these also become eight primordial awarenesses. The four other-arisen primordial awarenesses and the five self-arisen primordial awarenesses are also nine primordial awarenesses, and the five self-arisen primordial awarenesses themselves (by division into means and wisdom) are the ten knowledges or primordial awarenesses of the abiding state. So, if combined with the four conditioned primordial awarenesses, there are also fourteen primordial awarenesses included in the two truths.

Therefore, if the sugata essence were not actually existent, thusness, the five changeless great emptinesses, and so on would also be actually nonexistent, because that and those have the same meaning.

C. *Explanation of the excellence of wonderful qualities*

This has five topics.

1. *The actual explanation, condensing the qualities of a buddha into the two truths*

This has two topics.

a. *Qualities of the ultimate dharmakāya*

In that way, statements that the ten powers, the four types of fearlessness, and the eighteen unshared attributes of a buddha (the thirty-two qualities of separation) are complete in the ultimate kāya is a condensing of the main qualities. By means of many aspects, extensive statements say the qualities are measureless—"the eighty-four thousand aggregates of the attributes,"[1140] and so on, "the attributes of the inconceivable qualities of a buddha exceeding the grains of sand found in the Ganges River,"[1141] and so on, "the basic element of a buddha, adorned with the limitless major marks and minor marks,"[1142] and so on. And several were also presented before. [283]

Likewise, in the *Ornament of the Sūtras* the conqueror Maitreya states the qualities of the true nature, the svābhāvikakāya, and the characteristics of having obtained them:

The natural kāya is held to be equanimous,
subtle, connected to that [sambhogakāya],
and to be the cause of the mastery of
the sambhoga in displaying all enjoyments.[1143] {354}

And the *Ornament of Direct Realization* says:

The svābhāvikakāya of the Sage
has attained the taintless attributes
and has the purity of all aspects and
the characteristic of their nature.

The factors conducive to enlightenment,
the immeasurables, the liberations, the quintessence
of the nine meditative sequential absorptions,
the quintessence of the ten totalities,

the overwhelming sensory bases divided
into eight types, absence of the afflictions,
knowledge through aspiration, the paranormal
abilities, the analytical perfect awarenesses,

the four purities in all aspects,
the ten masteries, the ten powers,
the four types of fearlessness,
the three ways of nothing to guard,

the three foundations of mindfulness,
the true nature of being without forgetfulness,
the perfect destruction of habitual propensities,
great compassion for beings,

the eighteen attributes explained
to be unique to a sage alone,
and the knowledge of all aspects
are described as "the dharmakāya."[1144]

And the "Chapter on Primordial Awareness" also says:

> Through the force of the lord's body, the sublime bodies of yogins have the divine eye. Through the force of his speech, they have the ear, and through his mind, they know what abides in the hearts of others. Through the force of the body of the prajñā, they remember previous lives abiding in threefold cyclic existence. Through the force of the speech of the prajñā, they fully have omnipresent magical emanations at all times equal to space.
>
> Through the nature of the mind of the prajñā, blissful equilibrium is indestructible at all times. Through the force of the divine eye, they see what eyes do not see, and also the three states of cyclic existence. Through the force of the divine ear, they hear what creatures say with their mouths, and the sound of the [ultimate] essence. Likewise, through the union of body, speech, and mind, O lord of human beings, all [ultimate] tangible objects and so on occur.[1145]

And so on. And the *Sūtra Perfectly Summarizing the Dharma* also says:

> Here, what is the Buddha of the very essence? The [ultimate] Buddha of the very essence is the transformation of negative tendencies, inconceivable and stainless, has various [ultimate] forms, is dharmadhātu with distinct aspects [yet one taste in essence], has various [ultimate] forms, proportions, and shapes, and appears [to primordial awareness] in the form of a buddha having the thirty-two major marks of a great being. This is called "the Buddha of the very essence."[1146] {355} [284]

Because such passages say all the qualities of the dharmakāya are primordially, naturally spontaneous and indivisibly complete in the ultimate true nature, those qualities also are not beyond ultimate truth itself.

b. *Qualities of the relative rūpakāya*

That statement about "the qualities, what are called the thirty-two major marks,"[1147] which ripen in the relative rūpakāya, is a summary of the main ones. Extensively, these are stated by means of many aspects, such as the eighty minor marks and the eighty design marks. Moreover, the *Ornament of the Sūtras* says:

> In all realms, the sambhoga differs
> with respect to fully gathered retinue,
> field, name, body, complete enjoyment
> of Dharma, and activities.[1148]

And the *Ornament of Direct Realization* says:

> This [kāya] consisting of the thirty-two
> major marks and eighty minor marks
> is held to be the sambhogakāya of the Sage
> because it fully enjoys the Mahāyāna.
>
> Hands and feet with the marks of cakras,
> tortoiselike feet, fingers and toes joined
> by webs, hands and feet soft and supple,
> his body has seven raised surfaces,
>
> long fingers, and broad heels. With body large and straight,
> ankles inconspicuous, body hairs standing up, calves
> like an antelope, arms long and beautiful, he is the most
> sublime of those whose sexual organ is covered by a sheath.
>
> Skin of gold color, skin that is delicate,
> well-grown body hairs each curling to the right,
> face adorned with a coil of hair between the eyebrows,
> upper body like a lion, his shoulders are round and broad. {356}
>
> Unpleasant tastes appear to him as sublime tastes,
> his body symmetrical like a banyan tree, a cranial
> dome on the head, he has a long and beautiful tongue,
> a melodious voice like Brahmā, jaws like a lion,
>
> teeth very white, equal in size,
> well arranged, and a full forty in number,

dark blue eyes, and eyelashes like a bull—
these are the thirty-two major marks.[1149]

And:

The Sage's nails are copper-colored,
glossy, and prominent, the fingers and toes
rounded, broad, and tapering, the veins
not obvious and without knots.

His ankles inconspicuous, the feet equal, he walks
with the stride of a lion, an elephant, a swan, and
a lord of bulls, turned to the right, walking elegantly
and upright. His body is slender and graceful,

smooth, well proportioned, clean, soft,
and pure. His genitals are fully developed,
his figure broad and good. [285]

His steps are equal, and both
eyes are pure, his skin youthful,
his body not gaunt, fully fleshed
and very firm.

His limbs are very attractive,
his vision unobscured and clear,
his abdomen round, smooth,
not sunken, and slender. His navel

is deep and coils to the right,
he is beautiful to behold in all ways,
his conduct pure, and his body without
black moles.

His hands are as soft as cotton wool,
the lines on his palms glossy, deep,
and long, his face is not too long, and
his lips are red like a bimba berry.

His tongue is supple, slender,
and red, his voice like thunder,
gentle and smooth, his eyeteeth
round, sharp, white, equal, and

tapering. His nose is prominent
and sublimely pure, his eyes wide
with thick eyelashes, and like the petals
of a lotus.

His eyebrows are long, soft, and shiny,
with hairs of equal length, his arms long
and muscular, his ears equal and fully
unimpaired,

his forehead well shaped and large,
his head broad. The hair of his head
is black as a bee, thick, smooth,
not tangled, {357}

not unruly, and has a fragrant aroma that captivates
the minds of people. [His hands and feet] are adorned
with endless knots and auspicious swastika spirals.
These are held to be the fine minor marks of a buddha.[1150]

And the *Sūtra of the Question by Mañjuśrī* says eighty design marks are on the palms of the Tathāgata's hands and the soles of his feet in this way:

> It is like this: a parasol, a victory banner, a *śrīvatsa*, a garland, a hook, a diadem, a staff, a vase, an elephant, a horse, a tiger, a makara, a fish, a turtle, a peacock, a kalaviṅka bird, a partridge, a cāṣa bird, a cakravāka shelduck, a parrot, a goose, a dove, barley, black aconite, bamboo, a gayal, a nāga, a goat, a bull, a mountain, a bilva fruit tree, a black antelope, a precious gem, a supreme sword, a vajra, a bow, an arrow, a lance, a trident, a plow, a mace, an axe, a lasso, a boat, a pearl ornament, a cloud, Brahmā, Indrā, Dhṛtarāṣṭra, Varuṇa, Virūḍhaka, Virūpākṣa, Dhanada, a great seer, Śrī, a sun, a moon, a fire, wind, a lotus, a *nandyāvarta*, a triangle, an excellent throne,

> a mirror, a tail whisk, dūrvā grass, [286] a *puroḍāśa* cake, a boy, a girl, a drum, a conch, an earthenware drum, a bracelet, an armband, an earring, a ring, a dangling earring, an excellent flower, a wish-granting tree, and a lion at the center of a wheel. These are the eighty design marks. They appear on the palms of the Tathāgata's hands and the soles of his feet.[1151]

Other statements about the many distinctions of the qualities have not been written here.

As for the relative nirmāṇakāya, the *Ornament of the Sūtras* says:

> The infinite emanations of the buddhas
> are held to be the nirmāṇakāya,
> and the excellent two benefits are based
> on the two in all aspects.
>
> Always displaying [the emanations] of artisans,
> birth, great enlightenment, and nirvāṇa,
> this nirmāṇakāya of the buddhas is the great
> means for liberation.[1152]

And the *Ornament of Direct Realization* also says:

> That kāya equally performing
> various benefits for living beings
> as long as saṃsāra exists is the
> continuous nirmāṇakāya of the Sage.[1153] {358}

2. *Distinguishing and presenting the profound intent by means of replies to objections stemming from that*
This has five topics.

a. *Explaining the intent of the inconceivability of the Buddha and the intent of no acceptance*
It might be asked, "Is the Buddha one or many?"

Not one, but also not many.

"How should the intent of that be viewed?"

The rūpakāya is not one, because there are very many attainments of kāyas that proceed from previous bodies. The dharmakāya is not many, because it has no conditioned bodies and is one taste with dharmadhātu.

Moreover, the Great Madhyamaka *Ornament of the Sūtras* says:

> In the taintless dhātu,
> buddhas are not many and not one,
> since they have no bodies—like space,
> and since they proceed from previous bodies.[1154]

The intent of the statement that it is inexpressible as one or many, and about no acceptance, is also only just that in the context of differentiation. In the context of decisiveness, the intent is beyond speech, thought, and expression.

It might be said, "If it is stated 'the Buddha exists,' one falls into the extreme of existence, but if it is stated '[the Buddha] does not exist,' one falls into the extreme of nonexistence."

There is no fault, because it is not stated to be existent or nonexistent.

"How should the intent of that be viewed?"

The ultimate dharmakāya is not nonexistent in the abiding state of reality, because the self of thusness, the pure self, the self of the great quintessence of a buddha is never interrupted. [287] The relative rūpakāya is not existent in the abiding state, because relative phenomena are totally unestablished.

Also, because that self of the great quintessence of a buddha is also not said to exist in mind, and not said to not exist in primordial awareness, it is not said to be existent or nonexistent.

Moreover, the *Ornament of the Sūtras* says:

> Though not different earlier and later,
> we hold thusness without the stains
> of all the obscurations to be the Buddha,
> not pure, not impure.
>
> If emptiness is totally purified,
> the sublime self of selflessness is obtained.
> Since buddhas thus obtain pure self,
> that is the self of the great quintessence.
>
> Therefore, the Buddha is not existent,
> yet also not called "nonexistent."

> In that way, questions about the Buddha
> are held to be indeterminate. {359}
>
> Just as heat in iron and blurriness
> in the eye fade, so too Buddha
> is not called "existent in the mind"
> and "nonexistent in primordial awareness."[1155]

The intent of the many statements about no acceptance is also only just that in the context of differentiation. In the context of decisiveness, the intent is beyond speech, thought, and expression.

It might be asked, "Does a buddha appear or not appear?"

He should be said to "not appear and also not not appear."

"What is the intent of that?"

It depends on having or not having the good fortune of seeing a buddha. Moreover, the *Ornament of the Sūtras* says:

> Just as somewhere a fire blazes
> and somewhere else dies out,
> so too know that buddhas appear
> and do not appear.[1156]

And:

> Just as it is held that the sun's rays
> are obscured by clouds and so on,
> so too the primordial awareness of buddhas
> is obscured by the faults of sentient beings.[1157]

And:

> Just as a reflection of the moon
> does not appear in a broken water vessel,
> so too the form of a buddha does not
> appear to bad sentient beings.[1158]

And the *Ornament of Direct Realization* also says:

Even though the king of gods sends down rain,
an unsuitable seed will not grow. Likewise,
even though buddhas appear, the unfortunate
do not experience the goodness.[1159]

And the honorable, noble Nāgārjuna also says:

Sentient beings with afflictions
do not see the Tathāgata.

Just as hungry spirits see
the ocean to be dry, so too
those obscured by ignorance
imagine that buddhas do not exist.

What can the Bhagavān do for
the lowly and those whose merit
is low? It is just like a sublime jewel
put in the hand of a blind person.

For sentient beings who have
performed merit, the Buddha resides
in front of them, blazing with thirty-two
major marks, bright and glorious with light.[1160] [288]

Likewise, because the indivisible essence of ground and result, the ultimate sugata essence, also "is not manifest to, is not apparent to, and does not illuminate"[1161] consciousness; it is not said to appear, yet because it is "a great appearance, a great brilliance"[1162] to primordial awareness, it is not said to not appear.

Likewise, the intent of "not pure, not impure,"[1163] and "not afflicted, not unafflicted,"[1164] and "not empty, not nonempty,"[1165] and so on, and the intent of statements about no acceptance in those [sources] is also as before. {360}

The *Root Verses on Madhyamaka, Called "Wisdom"* says:

Do not say "empty" and
also do not say "nonempty."

> Do not say "both" and do not
> say "neither."[1166]

This is intended for the context of profound meditative absorption, and "These are to be said for the purpose of designation"[1167] is intended for the context of postmeditation.

The *Refutation of Objections* says:

> If I had some theses,
> then I would have that fault.
> Because I have no theses,
> I am only without faults.[1168]

And the *Four Hundred Verses* also says:

> One who has no position of
> existence, nonexistence, or existence
> and nonexistence, cannot be criticized,
> even over a long period of time.[1169]

Also concerning the intent of such statements: the intent is a nonconceptual state free of elaborations during meditative absorption, and no acceptance during postmeditation that disagrees with reality, such as an acceptance of entities. The *Sixty Verses on Reasoning* also says:

> If acceptance of entities [as real] exists,
> horrible, malignant views will occur,
> from which desire and hatred will occur.
> Disputes arisen from that will occur.
>
> That is the cause of all [bad] views.
> Without it, afflictions do not arise.
> So if that is totally understood,
> views and afflictions are totally purged.[1170]

And so on. And the *Jewel Lamp of the Madhyamaka* also says:

> The honorable teacher [Nāgārjuna] says:

> If acceptance of entities exists,
> fear of annihilation and so on occur.
> For those with no acceptance of entities,
> how could fear of annihilation and so on occur?
>
> If entities do exist,
> the world would also have an end,
> not have an end, and so on.[1171]

And:

> [The teacher himself] says:
>
> > If an entity were to exist,
> > it would be necessary to accept it,
> > but since entities are unarisen,
> > how should it be accepted?[1172]

And:

> [The teacher] says:
>
> > An entity to be accepted, even as tiny
> > as an atom, does not exist [in reality],
> > because it is primordially unarisen,
> > like the child of a barren woman.
> >
> > For example, when a barren woman
> > is asked, "Who is your child?"
> > she cannot speak of it, because one
> > does not exist.[1173]

Therefore, if the intent of statements about no acceptance or thesis is seen in that way, the meaning of the great intent is correctly seen. But in accord with the claims of others, to explain that "Because the abiding state is totally unestablished there are absolutely no acceptance and theses" does not agree with the meaning, {361} [289] because all the qualities of the ultimate ground of emptiness stated before are always present in the abiding state.

b. *Rejecting the claim that in the abiding state there is no attribute to be established through positive determination*

Likewise, the claim that "in the abiding state, except for mere exclusion [of faults] and nonimplicative negation, there is no attribute to be established through positive determination [of qualities], and nothing established as an implicative negation" is also very confused. Again and again I have explained and will explain that in the profound abiding state all flaws are naturally nonexistent and unestablished, so natural exclusion, negation, and abandonment are complete and, as the ground for those, all the qualities of the true nature are naturally complete, so the natural realization of positive determination, establishment, and implicative negation is primordially complete. And also because the teacher, the great expert Jinaputra, says in the commentary on *In Praise of the Three Jewels* composed by the teacher Mātṛceṭa:

> Therefore, this negation "does not have" is an implicative negation, because those types of concepts do not exist [in the abiding state], but it does have naturally luminous primordial awareness isolated from them.[1174]

c. *Showing great nirvāṇa to be the meaning of the indivisibility of saṃsāra and nirvāṇa*

It might be asked, "If great nirvāṇa were established in the abiding state, would that not be an assertion that nirvāṇa is true, which is refuted in the chapter 'Analysis of Nirvāṇa' and so on?"

One must be very expert in its intent. The *Root Verses on Madhyamaka, Called "Wisdom"* says:

> That which is from abandonment
> and cessation is asserted to be nirvāṇa.
>
> No abandonment, no attainment,
> no annihilation, no permanence,
> no cessation, no arising—that is
> asserted to be nirvāṇa.[1175]

Of the two nirvāṇas mentioned, the first is refuted by ultimate reasoning and the latter [great nirvāṇa] is established by the reasoning of the true nature, so the honorable, noble Nāgārjuna also accepts it. {362} Moreover, he accepts it to be the meaning of the indivisibility of cyclic existence and the peace [of nirvāṇa], or the indivisibility of saṃsāra and nirvāṇa. The *Sixty Verses of Reasoning* says:

> These two, [relative] cyclic existence
> and nirvāṇa, do not exist; the full understanding
> itself of [the other] cyclic existence is called
> "[great] nirvāṇa."[1176]

And the *Stainless Light* also says:

> Total understanding of [the other] cyclic existence is called "[great] nirvāṇa."[1177] [290]

And the *Hevajra Tantra* also says:

> Having the nature of the form of *evaṃ*,
>
> it preserves bliss, so [dharmadhātu]
> is fully proclaimed to be "blissful."
> It is the place of buddhas, bodhisattvas,
> and vajra holders.
>
> [The form of] this [dharmadhātu] is called
> "saṃsāra," [the essence of] this [dharmadhātu]
> is nirvāṇa itself. After rejecting [the form of]
> saṃsāra, nirvāṇa will not be realized elsewhere.
>
> Saṃsāra is form, sound, and so on,
> saṃsāra is feeling and so on,
> saṃsāra is the sense faculties themselves,
> saṃsāra is hatred and so on.
>
> Their true nature is nirvāṇa. Because
> of delusion, it has the form of saṃsāra.
> Saṃsāra without delusion is pure,
> so [that form of] saṃsāra is nirvāṇa.

[That is ultimate] bodhicitta, nirvāṇa
in the mode of relative and ultimate [indivisible].[1178]

The *Root Verses on Madhyamaka, Called "Wisdom,"* and the autocommentary, *Fearing Nothing*, also say:

Saṃsāra is not even slightly
different than nirvāṇa.
Nirvāṇa is also not even slightly
different than saṃsāra.

That which is the apex of nirvāṇa
is the apex of saṃsāra; those two
also do not have even the slightest
very subtle difference.

Those that are the apex of reality, the apex of the unarisen, and the consummate state of reality for nirvāṇa and saṃsāra do not have even the slightest very subtle difference, because they are equally unobservable.[1179]

And the *Tantra of the Excellent Ādi[buddha]* also says:

Meditate on the form of the [dharmakāya] Buddha
[having the aspects] of all the three realms without exception.[1180]

And the *Commentary on the First Part of the "Cakrasaṃvara"* also says "the form of the Buddha of the three realms"[1181] and so on. And the many ultimate names sung in a song also says:

Lovely, most sublime of the three worlds.[1182]

And:

Lovely, beautiful in the three worlds.[1183] {363}

And others also say:

[Ultimate] cyclic existence is pure by very essence,
by very essence free of cyclic existence.

> One having a naturally pure mind will [obtain] the excellent [ultimate] cyclic existence.[1184]

As for the profound intent of such extensive statements, [the indivisibility of saṃsāra and nirvāṇa] should be understood through the esoteric instructions of an excellent master.

d. *Showing that also to be the meaning of the third category without the flaw of including contradiction*

Likewise, the intent of many statements of being without the flaw of including contradiction, such as cyclic existence without cyclic existence, and three states of cyclic existence yet just one, is also stated in the *Mahāparinirvāṇa*:

> The [dharma]kāya of the Tathāgata [of reality] is a kāya that is not a [conditioned] kāya, unarisen, unceasing.[1185]

And [291]:

> Free of [relative] mind, also not free of [ultimate] mind. Mind without equal, also not without. [Essence] without going and coming, also [aspects] not without going and coming.[1186]

And:

> Without [a relative] lord, also not without [the ultimate] lord. Not [relatively] existent, also not [ultimately] nonexistent.[1187]

And:

> Not [relative] syllables, also not without [ultimate] syllables. Not samādhi, yet also not without samādhi. Invisible [to consciousness], directly appearing [to primordial awareness]. Without basis, not without basis. Without support, also not without support. Not darkness, not [relative] appearance. Not the peace [of śrāvakas and pratyekabuddhas], not unpeaceful [saṃsāra]. Without any [faults], not without any [qualities].[1188]

And:

> Not [a relative] phenomenon, also not [ultimately] not a phenomenon. Not a [conditioned] field of merit, also not not a field of merit.[1189]

And:

> [Ultimate] emptiness, free of [relative] emptiness. [Essence] always abiding, [aspects] not always abiding.[1190]

And:

> The Tathāgata acts for the benefit of all sentient beings, yet without [the concept of] acting for the benefit of sentient beings, liberates sentient beings, yet without [the concept of] liberating, directly awakens sentient beings, yet without [the concept of] directly awakening.[1191]

And:

> Though always engaging in the single vehicle, sentient beings see it to be three. Not with [conditioned] characteristics, it abides in [unconditioned] characteristics.[1192] {364}

And:

> Not [the relative] aggregates and sensory bases and elements, also not not [the ultimate] aggregates and sensory bases and elements. Not increasing, not decreasing. Not [the relative] good, not the bad.
>
> The kāya of the Tathāgata in that way has measureless qualities, unknown [by consciousness] and also not unknown [by primordial awareness], [the relative] unseen and also [the ultimate] not unseen, not conditioned, not unconditioned [like space], [essence] not the world, [aspects] also not not the world, [essence] uncreated, [aspects] also not uncreated, not abiding, also not unabiding, not the four great [relative elements], also not not the four great [ultimate elements], not a [relative] cause, also not without [the other] cause, not a [relative] sentient being, also not without [the ultimate] sentient being, not [a conditioned] kāya, also not not [an unconditioned] kāya.[1193]

And:

> When [the rūpakāya] passes into nirvāṇa, [the dharmakāya] does not pass into nirvāṇa; the dharmakāya of the Tathāgata has excellent measureless qualities such as that.

> Kāśyapa, the Tathāgata alone knows that; śrāvakas and pratyekabuddhas do not know.[1194]

Such extensive statements should be understood in accord with the profound esoteric instructions.

Likewise, the *Great Cloud Sūtra* also says:

> There are what are called unequal and utterly unequal [forms], yet also not unequal [in essence]; and suffering and not blissful [forms], yet blissful [in essence]; [292] and empty [of the dependent] and utterly empty [of the imaginary], yet not empty [of the fully established true nature]; and impermanent and utterly impermanent [forms], yet utterly permanent [in essence], and without [relative] self, yet the utterly [ultimate] self itself; and ugly and utterly ugly [forms], yet utterly lovely [in essence].[1195]

And so on. And the *Ornament of the Sūtras* also says:

> That which is the nonexistence
> is the excellent existence.
> Nonobservation in all respects
> is held to be the sublime observation.
>
> Meditation that is nonconceptual
> is held to be the excellent meditation.
> The attainment of those not conceiving
> of attainment is also held to be excellent.[1196] {365}

And so on. The intent of that statement, and the very many, great many statements in other profound sūtras and tantras and the exceptional Bodhisattva Commentaries about that and similar states without the flaw of including contradiction should also be understood according to just how it actually is, and...

e. *Explaining that if understood in that way, it is a sign of seeing the great intent of the children of the conquerors*

... if seen in that way, the meaning of the great intent is also seen:

> Love, pleasant speech, stability,
> extending a hand, and definitive
> commentary on the profound intent—
> these are signs of the wise.[1197]

And of the mentioned five signs of a bodhisattva, this is in accord with the fifth.

3. *Presenting the proofs and qualities of the three kāyas commonly renowned in the Mahāyāna*

In that way, the three kāyas included in the two truths are also stated in the *Sūtra of the Excellent Golden Light*:

> Sons of good family, the nirmāṇakāya of all buddhas is in accord with the conduct of all buddhas. The sambhogakāya is in accord with the intent of all buddhas. The dharmakāya is in accord with the kāyas of all buddhas.[1198]

And:

> Sons of good family, the nirmāṇakāya depends on the sambhogakāya and manifestly appears. The sambhogakāya depends on the dharmakāya and manifestly appears. The dharmakāya is reality and is not based on anything.[1199]

And:

> Sons of good family, because of the three characteristics, childish ordinary people are bound and obscured, so they are far from the three kāyas. What are the three? The imaginary characteristic, the dependent characteristic, and the fully established characteristic. Because those characteristics have not been understood, have not ceased, and have not been purified, the three kāyas have not been obtained. [293]
>
> Because the three characteristics such as those have been understood, have ceased, and have been purified, the three kāyas are totally complete for bhagavān buddhas. {366}
>
> Sons of good family, because childish ordinary people have not abandoned the three consciousnesses, they are far from the three kāyas. What are the three? The [six groups of] consciousness that

engage entities, the [afflicted] mental [consciousness] abiding in the universal ground, and the universal-ground consciousness.

Those residing on the purifying paths purify the [six] engaging consciousnesses. Those residing on the path of severance purify the mental [consciousness] abiding in the universal ground. Those residing on the path of sublime conquest purify the universal-ground consciousness.

If the engaging consciousnesses have been purified, the nirmāṇakāya manifests. Because the mental [consciousness] abiding in the universal ground has been purified, the sambhogakāya is displayed. Because the universal-ground consciousness has been purified, the dharmakāya is obtained. That being so, the three kāyas of all tathāgatas are called "spontaneously accomplished."[1200]

And:

Furthermore, sons of good family, because the obscurations of the afflictions on the dharmakāya have been purified, the sambhogakāya appears. Because the obscurations of karma have been purified, the nirmāṇakāya appears. Because the obscurations of primordial awareness have been purified, the dharmakāya appears.

For example, dependent on the empty [sky], lightning occurs. Dependent on lightning, light appears. Likewise, dependent on the dharmakāya, the sambhogakāya appears. Dependent on the sambhogakāya, the nirmāṇakāya appears.

Concerning that, because the nature is purified, the dharmakāya appears. Because primordial awareness is purified, the sambhogakāya appears. Because samādhi is purified, the nirmāṇakāya appears.[1201]

And again, after teaching about the two rūpakāyas, [the Buddha] says:

Sons of good family, how should bodhisattvas, mahāsattvas, understand the dharmakāya?

Because it is free of all obscurations of the afflictions, and all virtuous attributes are complete, that which resides as just the real nature and the primordial awareness of reality is called "dharmakāya." Those two former [rūpa]kāyas are merely nominal. The dharmakāya is reality and acts as the ground of those two kāyas. Why is that? Because absolutely no attributes of the buddhas exist aside from the thusness of phenomena and nonconceptual primordial awareness.

Because tathāgatas have brought to completion the excellence of primordial awareness and the abandonment of all afflictions, they have reached the pure level of a buddha. By means of the real nature of phenomena and the primordial awareness of reality, they fully hold the attributes of a buddha. {367}

Furthermore, sons of good family, all buddhas bring to completion their own and others' benefits. By means of the thusness of phenomena, they perform their own benefit. [294] By means of the primordial awareness of thusness, they perform the benefit of others. Because they have gained control of actions to benefit themselves and others, a variety of limitless actions are spontaneously accomplished.[1202]

Concerning the statement here about the benefit of others performed by means of the primordial awareness of thusness: if that primordial awareness is self-arisen, it is the changeless fully established nature, so the meaning is the same as the statement in the *Kālacakra* that the dharmakāya performs benefit for others.[1203] And if that primordial awareness is other-arisen, the *Uttaratantra* says:

The dharmakāya should be known as twofold:
the very stainless dharmadhātu and the teaching
of its corresponding modes of profundity
and diversity.[1204]

Thus the authentic dharmakāya is the naturally pure dharmadhātu; the teaching of profound and vast Dharma by means of the perfect primordial awareness occurring from its blessing has the same meaning as the statement that it performs benefit.

4. *Further presentation of other marvelous distinctions of the qualities*
Levels of the Bodhisattva says extensively:

Further enumerations are the one hundred forty unshared attributes of a buddha, and a tathāgata's lack of the afflictions, knowledge through aspiration, and analytical perfect awarenesses, which are called "unsurpassable perfectly complete enlightenment."

Concerning those, these are the one hundred forty attributes of a buddha: the thirty-two major marks of a great being, the eighty fine minor marks, the four utter purities of all aspects, the ten powers, the four types of fearlessness, the three foundations of mindfulness, the three ways of nothing to guard, great compassion, a true nature without forgetfulness, the perfect destruction of habitual propensities, and knowledge of all aspects and the sublime.[1205]

The infinite mastery of the qualities of utter transformation is also stated in the *Ornament of the Sūtras*:

The mastery of the śrāvakas
overwhelms that of the worldly.
That of those on the pratyekabuddha
level overwhelms even that of the śrāvakas.

That does not compare to even
a fraction of the mastery of bodhisattvas.
That does not compare to even
a fraction of the mastery of tathāgatas. {368}

For whom it manifests, where, how,
to what extent, and for what length of time—
in these terms the mastery of the buddhas
is held to be inconceivable and infinite.

When the five sense faculties have
transformed, they [all] engage all objects,
and twelve hundred qualities occur
for them all. Excellent mastery is achieved. [295]

When the mind has transformed,
it engages consistently with that mastery
and, regarding very stainless nonconceptual
primordial awareness. Excellent mastery is achieved.

> When apprehending, including its objects,
> has transformed, one can display enjoyable things
> just as one wishes, and so, regarding the purification
> of realms. Excellent mastery is achieved.
>
> When conceptual thought has transformed,
> primordial awareness and all activities
> are unimpeded at all times. Excellent mastery
> is achieved.
>
> When the support has transformed,
> there is nonabiding nirvāṇa within
> the stainless abode of the buddhas.
> Excellent mastery is achieved.
>
> When sexual activity has transformed,
> one resides in the bliss of the buddhas and,
> when a woman is seen, no afflictions occur.
> Excellent mastery is achieved.
>
> When the perception of space has transformed,
> objects of thought are acquired, and movement,
> and the discernment of forms. Excellent mastery
> is achieved.
>
> In that way, within the stainless abode
> of the buddhas, there are infinite transformations,
> so infinite mastery accomplishing inconceivable
> activities is achieved.[1206]

And *[Explanation of] "Entering the Madhyamaka"* also says:

> Whether arisen from the dharmakāya or arisen from the power of a rūpakāya, those kāyas that are other than the kāya just explained, in accord with its cause, and arisen with the training of sentient beings as their cause, also have inconceivable special features of power. To express this, it is explained:

The lords of sages vividly display within one rūpakāya,
in accord with its cause, clearly and unmistakenly
in a single moment, all the ways their own situations
occurred in ceased past lives, without exception.[1207]

To display, without exception, the extent of the situations in their lifetimes that have already ceased in beginningless saṃsāra before the point of all-knowing primordial awareness, {369} they spontaneously display them all instantaneously, clearly and unmistakenly (vivid in the many ways they occurred without mutually combining them) within one body in accord with its cause, like the reflection of a face in the utterly pure circle of a mirror.

They also engage in displaying spontaneously within just one body all those ways they engaged in the practices of a bodhisattva—which, where, how, and for whom. To express this, it is explained:

What types of buddhafields, those lords of sages
there, their bodies, what types of powerful practices,
how many Saṅghas of śrāvakas, or what they were like,
the bodhisattvas there, what types of forms they had,

what kinds of Dharma, what they were like there,
the Dharma they heard, what practices they engaged in,
and what types of gifts they offered to [the buddhas]
are displayed without exception [296] within one body.[1208]

Those bhagavāns display within one body the bhagavān buddhas without exception whom they honored when previously engaged in the perfection of generosity; the buddhafields with the nature of beryl, ruby, sapphire, crystal, and so on, beautified with jeweled trees and so on, including their length, width, and circumference; and how those were beautified by the specific sentient beings living there when the bhagavān buddhas displayed birth and so on.

The bodies of those bhagavān buddhas; the excellent force of their practices; how many Saṅghas of their śrāvakas gathered, or what they were like, and through what kinds of practice in accord with Dharma were they in those Saṅghas of śrāvakas; in the buddhafields of those bhagavān buddhas, the bodhisattvas whose bodies were adorned with the major marks and minor marks, what their shapes, their full and complete enjoyment of Dharma robes, food, and residences were like; what types of Dharma were taught, whether based on one or three vehicles—all those are displayed within one body.

What they were like there, whether born in the caste of brahmins and so on; their forms, intelligence, and whether they were householders or gone forth [from households]; their acceptance of training with remainder after hearing the Dharma and without remainder, and what practices they engaged in; what and how many gifts they offered them, such as what, when, and what quantity of food and so on, and Dharma robes, jeweled ornaments, and so on they offered to those bhagavān buddhas with their Saṅgha of śrāvakas and bodhisattvas—all those without exception are displayed within one body. {370}

Just as this extent of their practices when engaging in the perfection of generosity is displayed:

> Likewise, all previous situations, without omission,
> of engaging in moral discipline, patience, samādhi,
> and wisdom are displayed without exception within
> one body.[1209]

This has been combined with the previous verse. Not only do they display all their situations simultaneously within one body, but all their own [previous] practices "are clearly displayed even in the pores of their body hairs."[1210] Nor do they display only their own practices. Furthermore:

> The practices of past, future, and present buddhas
> reaching to the ends of space, their teaching Dharma
> in a resounding tone to relieve living beings afflicted
> with suffering, their living in the world,
>
> their practices from first aspiration until the heart
> of enlightenment—all of those, as if they were their
> own, they clearly display simultaneously in the pores
> of their body hairs, while knowing these things to have
> the nature of optical illusions.[1211] [297]

If even ordinary people who temporarily understand the way of optical illusions are able to display various things in their own bodies just by the force of mantras, how could the lords of living beings—the bhagavān buddhas—and the bodhisattvas who know the nature of things is not different from the nature of optical illusions not do so? Therefore, what expert would have doubts? So, as clarified by this example, experts should have special conviction in this.

Just as they simultaneously display their own practices and the practices of other tathāgatas in the pores of their own body hairs:

> Likewise, all the practices of all bodhisattvas, pratyekabuddhas, and noble śrāvakas without exception throughout the three times and, moreover, all the situations of ordinary beings they display simultaneously in the pores of their body hairs.[1212]

Having expressed the excellence of body, that [root text] teaches the excellence of their control over wishing, even though they are already not under the control of conceptuality. To explain this, it says:

> By engaging in a wish, these pure beings display
> the worlds that fill space within the area of a particle,
> and display a particle that fills the directions of
> infinite worlds, yet the particle does not become
> larger or the worlds smaller.[1213] {371}

By means of wishing, the bhagavān buddhas display the worlds that fill the limits of space within the area of one atomic particle, yet the worlds do not become smaller and the atomic particle also does not become larger. By merely wishing, they perfectly display things just as they abide in essence. They also display a particle that fills the directions of infinite worlds. By means of just wishing, the bhagavān buddhas also display the directions of infinite worlds (the world of all worlds without exception) filled by one atomic particle.

Likewise:

> The amount of various acts displayed in every
> instant until the end of cyclic existence by you,
> who have no conceptuality, does not exist in
> the number of particles in the entire Jambu
> continent without exception.[1214]

The number of that measure of the various acts that you, who have no conceptuality, display instant to instant until the end of saṃsāra does not exist in that amount of atomic particles existing in the entire Jambu continent without exception.

This is praise of the bhagavān buddhas by means of expressing their uncommon, superb qualities.[1215] [298]

5. *Showing those all to be inconceivable and amazing*

The *Sūtra of the Mudrā of Engagement in Producing the Power of Faith* also says:

> Mañjuśrī, it is like this: Suppose there were a symmetrical lake of five hundred thousand leagues, suitable for crows to drink and covered with lotus petals. A person there has an iron chariot with wheels of a thousand spokes, drawn by a horse that is faster than the speed of a garuḍa. When such a fast chariot is drawn, the wheels do not touch the water and the horse's hooves also do not pierce the lotus petals. As such a chariot is drawn along, a poisonous serpent rises up through that great lake to the surface. During a single instant of the chariot's passage, that poisonous serpent circles the chariot ten times. {372}
>
> Mañjuśrī, in the single instant it takes the poisonous serpent to circle the chariot once, the monk Ānanda explains the teachings of ten topics of Dharma and causes the meaning to also be understood. In the single instant it takes the monk Ānanda to explain the teaching of one topic of Dharma, the monk Śāriputra explains the teachings of a thousand topics of Dharma and causes the meaning to also be understood. In the single instant it takes the monk Śāriputra to explain the teaching of one topic of Dharma, the sthavira Maudgalyāyana [magically] passes beyond eighty thousand world systems. In the single instant it takes the sthavira Maudgalyāyana to pass beyond one world system, the Tathāgata simultaneously displays on each continent of all the infinite world

> systems in the ten directions his departure from residing in the heaven of Tuṣita, being born, going forth, engaging in austerities, practicing yoga, going to the heart of enlightenment [at Bodhgayā], subduing Māra, reaching directly complete enlightenment, turning the wheel of Dharma, [displaying] mahāparinirvāṇa, the endurance of the Dharma, and the disappearance of the Dharma. He also simultaneously appears in all his lifetimes, including those where he practices in the places of non-Buddhists.[1216]

And so on, the wonderful and marvelous way of the inconceivable is stated.

D. *Explanation of the excellence of wonderful activities*
This has three topics.

1. *Brief presentation of the activities and their source*

In that way, while tathāgatas do not have conceptuality and effort, they do have uninterrupted activities spontaneously engaged in benefiting others in various ways in all myriad directions and times. [299] Furthermore, the *Uttaratantra* says:

> The pervasive lords always spontaneously
> engage the dispositions of persons to be trained,
> the means of training, the activities to train the dispositions
> of persons to be trained, and in going to their places and times.[1217]

And:

> Because of definite liberation for the sake of others,
> seeing themselves and sentient beings as equal, and
> not having fully completed their activities, their activity
> is uninterrupted for as long as saṃsāra exists.[1218] {373}

The *Ornament of Direct Realization* also says:

> Likewise, it is held that the activity of
> this [buddha] continues as long as saṃsāra.

And so on, down to:

> The activity of the dharmakāya
> is held to have twenty-seven aspects.[1219]

And the *Sūtra of the Excellent Golden Light* also says:

> Sons of good family, just how—while the thusness of phenomena and the primordial awareness of thusness are without conceptuality—does [a tathāgata] gain control of activities?
>
> Sons of good family, for example, even though a tathāgata has passed into nirvāṇa, because he has gained control of prayer he also performs all forms of activity; his control of accomplishing all goals by means of thusness and the primordial awareness of thusness are also similar to that.[1220]

And so on. And the *Ornament of the Sūtras* also says:

> Concerning the attributes of a buddha,
> such as the powers, enlightenment is like
> a source of jewels. For the crop of the virtues
> of living beings, it is also held to be like a great cloud.
>
> Since merit and primordial awareness
> are totally complete, it is held to be similar
> to the full moon. Since its primordial awareness
> illuminates, it is held to be like a great sun.
>
> Just as the infinite light rays of the orb
> of the sun merge together and always
> engage in the same functions, illuminating
> the world,
>
> likewise, it is also held that the infinite
> buddhas in the taintless dhātu merge
> together and perform the same activities,
> illuminating with their primordial awareness.
>
> For example, when a single light ray
> of the sun occurs, all the rays of light occur.

Know that the primordial awareness
of the buddhas also occurs in a similar way.

Just as the light rays of the sun have no sense
of "mine" when engaging, so too the primordial
awareness of the buddhas also does not have
a sense of "mine" when engaging.

As a single shining light ray of the sun
illuminates all living beings, so too
the primordial awareness of the buddhas
instantly illuminates all knowable objects.[1221]

And:

2. *Extensive explanation, together with examples*

At this point, in every direction of the world, the elegant
explications of the conquerors cause worldly beings
with enhanced virtue to advance to sublime purity,
while those who have not accumulated virtue are caused
to advance to the sublime enhancement of virtue.
Thus the unripened are always caused to ripen, but not
without exception. {374} [300]

Thus in every direction of the world, stable [bodhisattvas]
always at all times achieve the great enlightenment that
is difficult to achieve, has sublime qualities, and is marvelous,
permanent, stable, and the refuge of those without refuge.
That is so amazing, yet also not so amazing, since they
have practiced the good way.

Simultaneously, in some [realms] a [buddha] displays
[turning] the wheel of Dharma in many hundreds of ways,
in some taking birth and not appearing, in some the various
actions of [past] lives, in some all [three] enlightenments,
and in some nirvāṇa, yet all are done without straying from
that abode.

> Buddhas do not form thoughts, such as "I have ripened these beings," or "These I will fully ripen," or "I am ripening these now," yet through the three gateways always fully ripen beings in all and every direction by means of virtuous practices.
>
> Just as the sun effortlessly ripens crops with its many bright, infinite rays of light in all and every direction, so too the sun of the Dharma ripens sentient beings in all and every direction with its infinite, utterly pacifying light of Dharma.
>
> Just as a massive, immeasurable, countless group of lamps comes from a single lamp, yet it is not extinguished, so too a massive, countless, immeasurable group of ripened beings comes from one ripened being, yet that one is not extinguished.
>
> Just as this great ocean never has enough water and does not increase when many great rivers flow into it, so too the dhātu of the buddhas also never has enough of the constant, unceasing entry of purified beings and does not increase; it is the miraculous sublime state here.[1222]

And:

> Just as sounds fully occur without
> the drums [of the gods] being struck,
> so too explanations fully occur without
> the conquerors forming [thoughts].
>
> Just as a [wish-fulfilling] gem displays
> its own light without effort, so too the buddhas
> also definitely display their actions without
> forming [thoughts]. {375}
>
> Just as in space the activities
> of the world unceasingly appear,
> so too in the taintless dhātu the actions
> of the conquerors are also unceasing.[1223]

And:

> Rivers that have not gone underground
> have different locations, also different waters,
> little water, and perform different activities,
> providing for tiny creatures living in the water.
>
> Yet when they have gone into the ocean,
> they all have one location, their water is also large
> and one, and their activity is one, always greatly
> providing for the many creatures living in the water.
>
> The stable beings who have not entered buddhahood
> have different supports, different intelligence,
> little realization, and different activities of their own,
> always providing benefit for few sentient beings. [301]
>
> When they have entered buddhahood, they all have
> one support, their great realization is one, and their
> deeds merge together as one, always greatly providing
> for great multitudes of sentient beings.[1224]

And so on. And the "Chapter on Primordial Awareness" also says:

> By the force of the habitual propensities of things peaceful,
> desirous, and so on produced by their own hearts in previous
> lifetimes, the one residing in the [dharma]cakra is seen as many,
> by the power of the qualities of prayers. One in meaning,
> many languages fully enter the hearts of creatures through their
> own dispositions and, for the merit of householders, the one
> residing in the cakra goes to wander for alms.
>
> Speaking the three [teachings] that have occurred, will occur,
> and are occurring now, and the always true Dharma to animals,
> hungry spirits, and demigods, to kiṃnaras, gods, and humans
> in the Noble Land, Tibet, and so on perfectly establishes the three
> states of cyclic existence (without omission) on the path by means
> of their own different languages. This is the speech of an

omniscient one, giving the result of blissful equilibrium; it is not even the language of the gods. {376}

The illusory emanations of buddhas having infinite qualities not understandable even by buddhas display the quintessence [of primordial awareness] in the places of the three states of cyclic existence, exactly like a rainbow. Distinguished by various things, entering the individual minds of gods and humans, including the conquerors, these unarisen phenomena, like the sky [reflected] in water, here give the mistaken impression of arising.[1225]

And:

Those [who have obtained the dharmakāya] fully illuminate the magical emanations of Kālacakra. Many great nirmāṇakāya radiating vajra blazes [benefit] demigods and humans living in the desire realm, the sambhogakāya [benefits gods of] the form realm, and the dharmakāya [benefits] the children of the conquerors in the sky, and so on, and the arhats. The empty aspect [of the sugata essence] manifests in the entire three states of cyclic existence as the totality of emptiness; [its aspects of] wind, as the totality of wind;

its aspects of fire, as the totality of fire; its aspects of water, also emitting to living beings as water; its aspects of earth, as the totality of earth; its collective objects [other form and so on], as all the [other] nature of entities [such as form]; this quintessence of the one [dharmadhātu] equal to pure space everywhere manifests to those on the level of purity. In that way, since it is the kāya of a buddha, the nature of bliss alone, it also does not die.[1226]

And:

From the glorious moon and a moon-water crystal (by nature without conceptuality) water occurs. Likewise, dependent on the aggregates of [Vajrasattva,] the lord of conquerors in the world, the attributes of an omniscient one trickle down. Water, totally dependent on the elements of seeds, becomes one taste with them, and, just like that, the attributes [of a buddha]

> become many aspects because of the purified minds of sentient beings, due to the strength of their past actions.[1227]

And the *Stainless Light* also says {377} [302]:

> Therefore, by the force of the habitual propensities of other lifetimes of sentient beings, the appearances of the body and the appearances of the speech of a bhagavān occur, like unarisen bodies in dreams.
>
> Just as in dreams, students see a teacher, ask about topics of doubt, and the teacher also eliminates the students' doubts, yet no teacher is there; it is an appearance of the habitual propensities of the minds of the students.
>
> Likewise, [seeing a buddha] is an appearance of the minds of meritorious sentient beings themselves; a bhagavān has not arisen and has not ceased.[1228]

3. *Fully extensive explanation by means of very many examples*

The *Uttaratantra* also says:

> Suppose this surface of the earth
> became the nature of pure beryl and,
> because of its purity, in it were seen
> Śakra with groups of celestial nymphs
>
> and his palace Vaijayanta, celestial
> residences other than that, various
> palaces of those [gods], and many
> kinds of divine things.
>
> Then the groups of men and women
> dwelling on the surface of the earth
> would see those appearances and make
> such prayers as this:
>
> "Before too long, may we also
> become like this lord of gods!"
> and would live having perfectly
> adopted virtue in order to attain that.

They would not understand that this was
merely an appearance, yet through that
virtuous karma, after passing from the surface
of the earth they would be born as gods.

Though that appearance would be totally
without thought and without activity,
its abiding in the world in that way would
bring great benefit.

Likewise, when sentient beings with stainless
faith and so on have cultivated the qualities
of faith and so on, in their minds they see
the appearance of the complete Buddha,

who possesses the major marks and
minor marks, performs various types
of conduct (walking, standing, sitting,
laying down),

speaks the peaceful Dharma,
does not speak in meditative absorption,
performs various types of miraculous displays,
and possesses great splendor.

Having seen that, those who long for it
fully apply themselves to buddhahood
and, after perfectly adopting its causes,
attain the stage they wish for. {378}

Though that appearance is totally
without thought and without activity,
even so, its residing in the world brings
great benefit. [303]

Ordinary beings do not understand that
this is an appearance in their own minds.

Even so, to see the image will be beneficial
for them.

Gradually, based on seeing that,
those abiding in this vehicle will see
the inner ultimate dharmakāya through
the eye of primordial awareness.

Suppose all the earth became stainless beryl, free of other fearful places, with the qualities of a clear and beautiful gem free of stains and glorious, with a level surface. Because of its purity, an image of the various residences of the lord of gods, and Śakra together with the celestial [nymphs], would appear in it, but since the qualities of the earth would gradually be lost, that [reflection] would disappear again.

In order to attain that state, the groups of women and men devoted to the chosen conduct of temporary vows, to generosity, and so on, would scatter flowers and so on with aspiring minds. Likewise, in order to attain [the state of] the Lord of Sages, which appears in their minds that resemble pure beryl, the children of the conquerors fully arouse bodhicitta with a joyful mind.

Just as the reflection of the body of Śakra
appears in the pure ground of beryl, the reflection
of the body of the Lord of Sages manifests
in the pure ground of the minds of living beings.

The manifesting and vanishing of the reflection occurs
for living beings by the force of their own minds being
fully undisturbed or fully disturbed. As with the appearance
of a reflection in the worlds, [the Buddha] is not seen
to be existing or destroyed.

In the realm of the gods,
by the force of the previous virtue

of the gods, the drum of Dharma again
and again urges all the careless gods

with the sounds "impermanence,"
"suffering," "selflessness," and "peace,"
while free from effort, location, mind,
form, and conceptuality.

Likewise, the pervasive lords, though
free of effort and so on, with their buddha
speech pervade sentient beings without exception,
teaching the Dharma to the fortunate.

Just as the sound of the drum of the gods occurs in the realm of the gods from their own karma, likewise the sages speaking of the Dharma occurs in the world from [beings'] own karma. Just as that sound, free of effort, location, body, and mind accomplishes peace, likewise this Dharma free of those four accomplishes peace. {379}

Just as the sound of the drum in the cities of the gods occurs as the cause that gives them fearlessness and, when engaging in battle with the afflictions [i.e., the demigods], eliminates [carelessness] in their warplay and brings victory over the armies of the demigods, likewise, in the world [the speech of the Buddha] occurs as the cause for the meditations, formless [samādhis], and so on, totally vanquishing the afflictions and sufferings of sentient beings and explaining the mode of the path of unsurpassable peace.

Since it is universal, beneficial, pleasant,
and endowed with the three miraculous displays,
the voice of the Sage is more exceptional
than the divine cymbals.

The great sounds of the drum in the god realms
do not reach the ears of those living on earth.
But the sound of the drum of the Buddha reaches
into the worlds below the earth in saṃsāra.

The many tens of millions of divine cymbals
in the god realms resound to increase the fire of desire,
but the single voice of those whose quintessence is
compassion manifests to utterly pacify the fire of suffering. [304]

The beautiful and pleasant sounds of the cymbals in the god realms are the causes for increasing mental agitation, but the speech of tathāgatas whose quintessence is compassion just encourages the intention to entrust the mind to samādhi.

In brief, because that which is the cause of happiness for the gods and those on earth (and also in world systems without exception) appears pervasively in world systems without exception, it is stated that one should totally rely upon this voice.

Just as those who have no ears do not hear subtle sounds, likewise, all [sounds] do not reach even the ears of those with the divine ear. So too the sublime, subtle Dharma, the field of experience of acute primordial awareness, reaches the ears of some whose minds lack the afflictions.

Just as in summertime masses of water
that are the cause of excellent crops
continually fall from clouds without effort
onto the earth,

so too the rain of the water of the excellent
Dharma of the conquerors that is the cause
of the crop of the virtues of living beings falls
from clouds of compassion without conceptuality.

Just as, when those in the world enter the path of virtue, the wind rises and clouds pour down a rain of water, likewise, since the wind of love has increased the virtue of living beings, the rain of excellent Dharma falls from the cloud of the Buddha. {380}

With knowledge and great love for those in cyclic existence, residing in the center of the sky unsoiled by the changeable and the unchangeable, and bearing the essence of the stainless water of samādhi and dhāraṇīs, the cloud of the Lord of Sages is the cause of the crops of virtue.

Just as cool, sweet, soft, and light water emerges from those clouds, but assumes a great many tastes through contact with places on the earth that are salty and so on, so too the rain of the water of the eight limbs of the noble [path] that emerges from the essence of the vast cloud of compassion assumes many kinds of tastes due to the differences in the places that are the mindstreams of living beings.[1229]

And:

Just as Brahmā, without moving
from Brahmā's residence, effortlessly
displays that appearance in all the places
of the gods,

so too the sages, without stirring
from the dharmakāya, effortlessly
teach [the path] to the fortunate
through emanations in all realms.

Just as Brahmā, while never straying from his palace,
enters the desire realm and is seen by the gods, causing
the abandoning of joy in objects by those who see him,
so too the sugatas, while not stirring from the dharmakāya,
are seen by the fortunate in all worlds, causing the full removal
of all stains in those who see them.

Just as, by the force of his own
previous prayers and the virtue of the gods,
Brahma appears without effort,
so does the self-arisen [Buddha's] nirmāṇakāya. [305]

Descending [from Tuṣita], entering into a womb, being born,
arriving at his father's palace, amorous play, practicing in solitude,
vanquishing Māra, attaining great enlightenment, and teaching
the path to the city of peace—displaying [such acts], the sages
do not reach the sight of the unfortunate.

Just as lotuses and so on bloom and moon lilies close when struck
at the very same time by sunlight, but the sun has no thoughts
of the blooming and closing of water-born [flowers] being a quality
or a fault, so also the sun of the Noble One here [has no thoughts].

Just as the sun, without thoughts
and simultaneously radiating its own
light, causes lotuses to bloom and ripens
other [plants],

so too the sun of the Tathāgata
engages, without thoughts, the lotuses
of persons to be trained by its light rays
of the excellent Dharma.

The sun of the Omniscient One shining in the sky
of the essence of enlightenment, through the dharmakāya
and the rūpakāyas, radiates light rays of primordial awareness
for living beings. {381}

Therefore, infinite reflections of the sun
of the Sugata dawn simultaneously
in all the vessels of the water of purified
persons to be trained.

In the center of the sky of the dharmadhātu,
always pervading everywhere, the suns
of the buddhas shine on the mountains
of those to be trained, just as is appropriate.

Just as this sun, dawning with thousands of vast light rays,
fully illuminates the world and gradually shines on high,
medium, and low mountains, so too the suns of the conquerors
gradually shine on groups of sentient beings.

The sun cannot radiate to the ends of space in all [buddha]fields,
and also cannot reveal the meaning of knowable objects
to those shrouded by the darkness of ignorance. But those [suns
of the buddhas] having a quintessence of compassion remove it

with masses of light emanating the colors of the various [vehicles],
revealing to living beings the meaning of knowable objects.

When [the sun of] a buddha arrives in a city, people without eyes can see and, free of the masses of what are meaningless, see that which is meaningful, from which they experience [the true nature]. Those blinded by ignorance, fallen into the sea of cyclic existence and obscured by the darkness of views, are mentally illuminated by the light of the sun of the buddha and see the unseen abiding [true nature].

Just as a wish-fulfilling gem has
no thoughts, but simultaneously and
individually fulfills all intentions of those
abiding in its field of experience,

so too those with different intentions,
who rely on a wish-fulfilling buddha,
hear various Dharma teachings,
but he does not think about them.

Just as the precious gem without thoughts effortlessly
and fully grants others the wealth they desire, so too
the sages always effortlessly remain just as appropriate
for the benefit of others as long as cyclic existence exists.

Just as it is very hard in this world to find a desired fine gem
resting in the ocean or below the earth, so too it should be known
that the sight of a sugata is hard to find in these minds of very
unfortunate living beings seized by the afflictions.

Just as the sounds of echoes occur
through the cognition of others, [yet the cliffs
and so on] have no thoughts, make no effort,
[and the sounds] do not abide outside or inside,

so too the speech of tathāgatas occurs through
the cognition of others, [yet the tathāgatas]

have no thoughts, make no effort, and the [speech]
does not abide outside or inside. [306]

Though it is without the slightest [conditioning],
without appearance, unobservable, and without
support, utterly beyond the path of sight, formless,
and not demonstrable, {382}

highs and lows are seen in space,
but it is not like that. So too all see
[the rupakāyas] in [the dharmakāya of]
a buddha, but it is not like that.

Just as all that grows from
the earth increases, thrives,
and spreads through reliance
on the earth that is without thoughts,

so too all the roots of virtue of living
beings will increase without exception
through reliance on the earth of a complete
buddha who is without thoughts.[1230]

And the concise meaning of those:

That which is like Śakra, a drum, and clouds; like Brahmā,
the sun, and the precious king of wish-fulfilling gems;
like an echo, space, and the earth, effortlessly benefiting
others for as long as cyclic existence lasts, is known by yogins.

The displays like the reflections of the lord of gods in the jewel
[earth of beryl], the elegant instruction resembling the drum
of the gods, and the pervasive lords' knowledge and great love
[like] cloud banks, pervade limitless living beings, up to the Peak
of Cyclic Existence.

Like Brahmā, they fully display many kinds of emanations
without stirring from the taintless abode; like the sun, they fully

radiate the appearances of primordial awareness; their minds
resemble a pure, precious, wish-fulfilling gem.

Like an echo, the speech of the conquerors has no letters;
like space, their bodies are pervasive, formless, and permanent;
like the earth, the level of a buddha is in every way the ground
of all the medicinal virtuous attributes of living beings
without exception.

In minds that have become beryl-like
because of virtues, the cause of seeing
buddhas is the increase of the faculties
of irreversible faith in those [buddhas].

Since virtues arise and disintegrate,
the forms of buddhas arise and disintegrate.
But, like Śakra, the dharmakāya of
the Sage does not arise or disintegrate.

So too his activities, such as displays,
effortlessly manifest from the unarisen,
ceaseless dharmakāya for as long as
cyclic existence remains.[1231]

And:

Buddhas are like the reflections [of Śakra],
yet not alike, since those do not have a voice.
They are like the drum of the gods, yet not alike,
since that does not accomplish benefit everywhere.

They are similar to a great cloud, yet also not alike,
since that does not abandon worthless seeds.
They are like great Brahmā, yet also not alike,
since he does not completely ripen [beings].

They are like the form of the sun, yet also not alike,
since that does not totally destroy darkness.

> They are like a wish-fulfilling gem, yet also not alike,
> since its occurrence is not as difficult to find. {383}
>
> They are like an echo, yet also not alike,
> since that arises from conditions.
> They are like space, yet also not alike,
> since that is not the basis of virtues. [307]
>
> Since they are the support upon which
> all the worldly and transcendent excellence
> of living beings without exception rests,
> they are like the sphere of the earth.
>
> Since the transcendent path occurs on the basis
> of the enlightenment of the buddhas, the path of
> virtuous actions, the meditations, the immeasurables,
> and the formless [samādhis] occur.[1232]

And Śāntideva, the son of the conquerors, also says:

> Whenever entity and nonentity
> do not remain before the mind,
> at that point there are no other aspects,
> so it is utterly calm, with no objects.
>
> Just as a wish-fulfilling gem and
> a wish-granting tree fulfill all hopes, so too,
> due to the power of persons to be trained
> and to prayers, the body of a conqueror appears.
>
> For example, after building the garuḍa
> reliquary, [its builder] passed away.
> Though he passed away a long time ago,
> that [reliquary] still pacifies poison and so on.
>
> Likewise, the reliquary of a conqueror,
> built in accord with the bodhisattva's

> conduct, still accomplishes all benefits, even
> though the bodhisattva has passed into nirvāṇa.
>
> How could results come from offering
> worship to what has no mind? Because
> it is explained to be just the same, whether
> [a buddha] is living or passed into nirvāṇa.[1233]

E. *Presenting the distinctions of the fields and the settings of the discourses*

In that way, one must understand the division of the two truths also for the buddhafields, which have a quintessence of the wonderful, marvelous, and inconceivable excellences of body, primordial awareness, qualities, and activities. Because the ultimate Buddha is naturally connate great bliss (the syllable *vaṃ*), its field is the syllable *e* (the source of the attributes), emptiness having all aspects, the maṇḍala of the support, which is the other world of the environment; the field of the relative rūpakāya is that known to experts. {384} Moreover, because the utterly pure fields are included in the truth of the path but the impure fields are included in the truth of suffering, those that are the fields of the rūpakāya are included in relative truth and those that are the fields of the dharmakāya are included in ultimate truth.

Likewise, one must also understand the division of the two truths for the settings of the discourses in sūtras and tantras, and the divisions of lord and retinue, and so on, that are different and not different, in accord with the esoteric instructions of an excellent master. [308]

F. *Extensive presentation of other further distinctions*

This has sixteen topics.

1. *Rejecting an objection to the indivisible essence of ground and result, and showing how the two kāyas are obtained*

It might be asked, "If ground and result are indivisible in essence, what use is the path?"

Here, "indivisible essence of ground and result" is also in the context of the ultimate dharmakāya, not that of the relative rūpakāya. But the path is also not unnecessary, because the assembly of primordial awareness (that which is nonconceptual wisdom during meditative absorption) separates stains from the dharmakāya that is primordially present, and the assembly of merit (the possession of primordial awareness that realizes [phenomena] to be illusory during postmeditation) produces the conventional kāyas for the benefit of others.

Moreover, the *Uttaratantra* says:

> Like a lake of [stainless] water, and so on,
> the purification of the incidental afflictions
> of desire, and so on, is briefly stated to be
> the result of nonconceptual primordial awareness.
>
> That definite attainment of the kāya
> of a buddha having the most sublime
> of all aspects is taught to be the result
> of the primordial awareness of postmeditation.[1234]

And *Distinguishing the Middle and the Extremes* also says:

> Just as the element of water, gold,
> and space are pure, it is held to be pure.[1235]

And the honorable, noble Nāgārjuna says:

> The rūpakāya of the buddhas arise here
> from the assembly of merit; that dharmakāya,
> in brief, O king, arises from the assembly
> of primordial awareness.
>
> That being so, these two assemblies
> are the cause of obtaining buddhahood.[1236]

And:

> May they obtain the two excellent [kāyas]
> that occur from merit and primordial awareness.[1237] {385}

2\. *Brief presentation of how the stains are purified and how the levels and paths are traversed*

The *Sūtra of the Excellent Golden Light* also says:

Sons of good family, suppose someone who wants gold searches everywhere and finds a chunk of gold ore. After finely crushing that chunk, and smelting and purifying its essence, it becomes pure. That gold is transformed as wished into various ornaments such as bangles and used, but the nature of the gold does not change.

Sons of good family, furthermore, those sons of good family or daughters of good family who aspire to engage in worldly virtues may see tathāgatas or the retinues of tathāgatas, approach, and offer these questions: "Bhagavāns, what is virtue? What is nonvirtue? By performing what perfect practice is pure conduct achieved?" [309]

The bhagavān buddhas and their retinues will consider those questions, thinking this: "These sons of good family and daughters of good family aspire to listen to the excellent Dharma and want purification; we will teach them the perfect Dharma. After hearing it, they will correctly take it to mind and an emphatic intention will arise. Through the force of diligence, they will clear away the obscuration of laziness and all traits of negative nonvirtue. Living fully devoted to all the topics of training, they will clear away mental dullness and agitation and enter the first level.

"Dependent on the mind of the first level, through abandoning the obscurations to diligence for the benefit of many sentient beings, they will enter the second level. From that level, after they have abandoned the obscurations of the afflictions, they will enter the third level. From that level, after they have abandoned the obscurations to purifying the mind, they will enter the fourth level. From that level, after they have abandoned the obscurations to skillful means, they will enter the fifth level. From that level, after they have abandoned the obscurations to observing the ultimate and the relative, they will enter the sixth level. From that level, after they have abandoned the obscurations of observing conceptual marks and conduct, they will enter the seventh level. From that level, after they have abandoned the obscurations of not observing even the cessation of conceptual marks, they will enter the eighth level. From that level, after they have abandoned the obscurations of not observing even the arising of conceptual marks, they will enter the ninth level. From that level, after they have abandoned the obscurations of the six paranormal abilities, they will enter the tenth level. {386} From that level, because the obscurations of the knowable and the universal-ground consciousness have been purified, they will enter the level of a tathāgata.

"Because the level of a tathāgata is threefold purity, it is called 'totally pure.' What are the three? It is like this: purity of the afflictions, purity of suffering, and purity of conceptual marks. Fine gold, purified after smelting and refinement, is later not covered by dirt and stains, and appears as just naturally pure gold; the pure gold entity also does not become nonexistent.

"For example, after dirty water has become clean and pure, the very nature of the water becomes clear, but that water itself also does not become nonexistent.

"Likewise, after the dharmakāya has abandoned various accumulated afflictions and sufferings, all the habitual propensities without exception are removed and the pure buddha essence itself appears, but the entity itself does not become nonexistent.

"Again, for example, if the smoke, clouds, dust, and fog that obscure space become nonexistent, the element of space is purified, but that space itself does not become nonexistent.

"Likewise, the dharmakāya is called 'pure' because all the afflictions have been extinguished, but the kāya itself does not become nonexistent."[1238]

And [310]:

"Likewise, dharmadhātu is called 'pure' because all concepts do not arise, but the perfect kāya of the buddhas is not nonexistent."[1239]

And so on, it says. I have not written extensively here about how the levels and paths are traversed, because that is fully known.

3. *Showing that to traverse the levels and paths, the flow of breath must cease*

Profound secret mantra texts say that, to obtain the dharmakāya by extinguishing the stains, the breath must also definitely cease. The "Chapter on Primordial Awareness" says:

If the lifeforce wind and the downward-clearing wind have ceased, the form of the sun that moves the rabbit-bearer becomes fully [clear]. If the vajra is fully wakened by the lotus, again this is melted by tongues of fire from the sun's form. If the winds, moon, and sun have ceased, consciousness and primordial awareness become one. In that way, in that way, and likewise, in that way, it is threefold; another does not even slightly exist. {387}

If the forms of moon and sun have been consumed, day and night are never in space. Those periods abide at all times on the stage of nectar in the middle of the bodies of yogins. Just as, with phases extinguished, the moon abiding in space becomes the same taste as the form of the sun, so too if the lifeforce wind and the downward-clearing wind have been extinguished, those [sun and moon] clearly cease in the body at the time of attainment.

The passage of moon and sun deteriorates, and in both paths also the great lifeforce wind has ceased. With vajra totally awakened in the lotus, the rabbit-bearer melts and totally enters the great image of the sun. Indestructible [great bliss] abiding in [the form of] threefold cyclic existence in which entity and nonentity are one is well and totally realized. At that moment, that yogin goes to the sublime stage, [the sugata essence] in which duality does not even slightly exist.

The wrathful beings, the buddhas together with the goddesses, and Rasavajrā, Bhūmigarbha, and so on (with utterly joyful minds) certainly manifest in space to the yogin at the point of attainment. His desired attainment occurs at dawn or midnight of the day of the rabbit-bearer. At the appropriate time [of reaching] the sublime, a rain of jewels or flowers will fall upon the surface of the earth.

His body clear and its atomic particles deteriorated, the major marks and so on equal to space become totally complete. The [other] three variegated worlds themselves, clear and free of obscurations, appear like a dream. His voice, uninterrupted everywhere, enters the hearts of others by means of the other languages of many [living beings],

and his mind, filled with excellent bliss and unfluctuating,
is embraced by connate [great bliss] at all times.[1240] {388} [311]

And so on. The exceptional Bodhisattva Commentaries also state extensively how the [twelve] levels are reached after the four māras and the twelve limbs of dependent arising have ceased because the breaths have ceased, and how the levels are reached because the moments of bliss without emission are complete after the moments of emission have ceased. The *Glorious Guhyasamāja* also says:

Knowing reality, I will also explain
the cessation of all the winds.[1241]

And:

After eliminating the two winds of conceptuality
through that, one goes [to the city of great liberation].

If the great wind of nonconceptuality is eliminated
by the body, speech, [and mind] vajras,
the bestowal of nonconceptual bliss is obtained
through the reality of mantra.[1242]

And the *Glorious Vajra Garland Tantra* also says:

Through total application to vajra repetition,
the characteristics of the winds are known,
after which the winds of conceptuality are eliminated.
Observation of the mind is attained.
Also through the stages of self-blessing,
the eight attainments are achieved.[1243]

And glorious Saraha also says:

By gazing without blinking the eyes, and not thinking,
the winds will cease; [this] is the words of the excellent master.[1244]

Such passages say extensively, in many places, again and again, how the flow of the breath must cease for the continuity of what are to be abandoned to cease. Fearing it would take too many words, I have not written them here.

4. *How the profound, consummate transformation is achieved through its cessation*

In that way, the incidental stains have ceased because the winds have ceased, but the ultimate sugata essence does not cease, because the consummate transformation has been achieved.

> Here it is stated that the essence does not change, but the incidental stains do not appear and thusness alone does appear. The root text and commentary on *Ornament of the Sūtras* say:
>
> > Know that what do not exist in reality and what
> > does exist in reality do not appear and does appear.
> > And that is known to be transformation. Since one
> > can do as one pleases, that is liberation.
>
> Know the nonappearance of conceptual marks that do not exist in reality and the appearance of thusness that does exist to be transformation. Therefore, those do not appear and that does appear. Also know that [transformation] itself to be liberation.[1245] {389} [312]

And *Distinguishing Phenomena and True Nature* also says:

> Here, as for comprehending
> its essence, in terms of the incidental
> stains and thusness not appearing
> and appearing, thusness is that
> which is stainless.[1246]

Thus the nonappearance of the incidental stains and the appearance of thusness is stated to be the essence of transformation. And the root text and commentary on *Distinguishing the Middle and the Extremes* also says:

> Just as the element of water, gold,
> and space are pure, it is held to be pure.

> That refers to separation from the incidental stains; the very essence of that [thusness] does not change into something else.[1247]

The essence not changing, but the stained becoming stainless, is thus said to be the consummate transformation, like the cloudy sky becoming cloudless.

Therefore, the claim by some of a transformation in which the essence changes, such as "the five appropriated aggregates change into the five families of the conquerors," and the claim that a previously nonexistent [essence] arises anew, are inappropriate for the unconditioned true nature, because all the consummate deities, mantras, tantras, maṇḍalas, and mudrās that are the unconditioned true nature are permanently present as the fully established nature, never changeable anywhere by anything, whether the rūpakāyas of the buddhas appear or do not appear.

Likewise, the *Ornament of the Sūtras* also says:

> That which is always separate from duality, that which is the support of confusion, and that which is the utterly inexpressible quintessence free of conceptual elaborations—reality—should be understood, abandoned, and (though naturally stainless) purified. Like space, gold, and water, that [fully established nature] is held to be purified of the afflictions.[1248]

Thus it says the imaginary nature (that which is always separate from duality but appears as duality) should be understood, the dependent nature (that which is the support of confusion) should be abandoned, and the fully established nature (that which is naturally pure without conceptual elaborations) is the ground to be purified of stains. It also says that when the result of separation from stains is attained, transformation in which the essence does not change is attained, as shown by the three examples of space and so on.

It might be said, "Water and gold are conditioned phenomena, so they are not suitable examples for the unchanging nature."

Those both change moment by moment, but the examples are not applied from that perspective here; they refer to the unchanging continuity in situations with and without stains. Therefore, there is no fault, because that same source says:

> When muddy water becomes clear,
> the clearness has not arisen from that [muddiness],

> but simply because of a separation from stains. {390}
> That too is how it is with the purity of one's own mind.
>
> The mind is held to be always natural luminosity;
> it is made unfit by incidental faults. The other
> mind other than the mind of the true nature is not
> luminosity, which refers to the [true] nature.[1249]

And because the commentary on that also says:

> Just as water is naturally clear, yet muddied by incidental sediment, so too the mind is held to be natural luminosity, yet made unfit by incidental faults.
>
> Except for the mind of the true nature, the other mind (characteristic of the dependent nature) is not said to be natural luminosity itself. [313]
>
> That being so, know the mind [of natural luminosity] here to be the mind of the true nature alone.[1250]

It might be said, "If incidental faults make it unfit in that way, it is contradictory for that mind of natural luminosity to be unconditioned, hard like a vajra, uncuttable, indestructible, true, solid, stable, and so on."

There is no fault, because that is said in reference to the essence of natural luminosity not being harmed, yet being prevented from manifesting.

The *Uttaratantra* also says:

> Luminosity, uncreated . . .[1251]

And:

> That is not afflicted by incidental stains.[1252]

And so on, it states extensively.

5. *Showing that the stains to be purified are extinguished when that is achieved, but the essence that is the ground of purification is not extinguished*

Likewise, when a withered tree, the extinguishing of a lamp, the cooling of [glowing] iron, the orb of the moon, and so on, are used as examples in statements that the incidental stains are extinguished but the sugata essence is not extinguished, these are also dissimilar in being beyond or not beyond the momentary. Therefore, these are not applied as examples from that perspective, but are applied as examples from the perspective of having other similar attributes.

Moreover, the *Mahāparinirvāṇa* says:

> Bhagavān, suppose a tree in a grove of sāla trees outside a great city had previously grown and reached a hundred years. At that time the owner of the grove periodically brought water and did work. After the bark of that tree had rotted, all the bark, leaves, and limbs fell to the ground and only the inner essence remained. A tathāgata is also like that; after all [the stains that were like] the rot have been destroyed, {391} only the phenomenon of reality remains.[1253]

And:

> Son of good family, it is like this: for example, if a man or a woman sets up a lamp and fills it with butter from a large or small lamp container; that is the form. As long as there is butter, the light also exists. Whenever the butter is exhausted, the light also becomes nonexistent. The nonexistence of the light is like the extinguishing of the afflictions. The light is extinguished and becomes nonexistent, but the container of the lamp does not become nonexistent.
>
> A tathāgata is also like that; the afflictions are extinguished and nonexistent, but the dharmakāya always exists.[1254]

And:

> Ordinary people think a tathāgata is perfectly extinguished in cessation, but it should be known that, since a tathāgata is not finally extinguished, he is a permanently abiding phenomenon, an unchanging and immutable phenomenon. [314]
>
> Son of good family, what is called "mahāparinirvāṇa" is the dharmadhātu of bhagavān buddhas.[1255]

And the translation by Lhai Dawa also says:

> Just as the fire of iron cools, likewise, after the afflictions accumulated even by a tathāgata through many, countless, tens of millions of eons are extinguished, [the dharmakāya] is permanent, stable, and eternal. That being so, a perfectly released tathāgata is permanent, stable, and eternal.[1256]

And *Brief Presentation of Initiation* also says:

> Just as the waxing moon becomes gradually
> full through its phases, its fullness due to the receding
> of its shadow, not because the moon is annihilated
> and becomes full again,
>
> so too, the waxing primordial awareness becomes gradually
> full through the levels, its fullness due to the receding
> of the afflictions and so on, not because primordial awareness
> is annihilated and becomes full again.[1257]

And so on. From those statements by means of many examples and, furthermore, also from the presentation by means of the examples of the essence and the stains mentioned before, it should be understood that when transformation is achieved, in the wake of all the extinguished afflictions the sugata essence remains without ever being extinguished, so this is the consummate, profound transformation in which the essence does not change. {392}

6. *Showing that, of the examples of those that are extinguished and not extinguished, space itself is sublime*

And even of those, the example of space is exceptional because it is beyond the momentary, partless, omnipresent, all-pervasive, and so on. The *Sūtra of the Great Drum* says:

> Any buildings or mountains dependent on space disintegrate, but space is not destroyed; the basic element of nirvāṇa pervading all living beings is also similar to that.[1258]

All presentations by means of the example of space should also be remembered here, such as the previously cited "Just as a pot is broken, but . . ."[1259] and so on.

7. *Showing that, by establishing that the ground of purification is not extinguished, claims that the stream of primordial awareness is interrupted, and so on, are also refuted*

These scriptures eliminate the claim that consummate buddhahood is totally unestablished, the claim that the stream of the primordial awareness of a buddha is interrupted, and the claim that the ground of purification is also extinguished because the objects to be purified are extinguished. [315]

8. *Showing that this confused appearance does not arise to primordial awareness in which confusion has been extinguished*

Likewise, the claim that these incidental phenomena of the three realms appear to primordial awareness in which confusion has been extinguished is also not reasonable, because confused appearance is not possible for that which has extinguished confusion, and because this appearance of the three realms is also stated to be confused appearance itself.

Moreover, the honorable Āryadeva says:

> Confusing the existent to be nonexistent, and confusing
> it to be impermanent; confusing the nonexistent to be existent,
> and confusing it to be permanent; deceiving and having deceived
> the confused with confusion establishes confusion; the power
> of confusion confuses sentient beings about the meaning of reality;
>
> confusion about the causes, the result of which is confusion
> in the three lower realms; . . .[1260]

And *Establishing the Reasoning That Refutes Confusion* also says:

> Because of the power of confusion about that, confusion about the meaning of reality occurs: "The four concepts of all as permanent . . .[1261]

And so on. {393} And:

> [Hungry spirits] with mouths like the eye of a needle,
> throats like a hair from a horse's tail, stomachs the size
> of a mountain, and legs and arms as thin as twigs,
> creak like a cart, spreading smoke.

After looking at an arrangement of nice food
and drink, if they reach out a hand they see
a terrifying being in armor, carrying a sharp
weapon and a club,

who beats them to pieces, and, powerless
to take [the food and drink], they are tormented
by hunger. Some put food and drink in their
mouths, but spurts of flame blaze and burn them.

Some, not finding even stinky pus and blood,
squeeze and extract them from their bodies.
Some, not seeing and not hearing about food
and drink, race about in the ten directions.[1262]

And:

Until the ripened [results] of their bad activities
are extinguished, [hell beings] will not die.
Terror arises if even a drawing [of these sufferings]
is seen, an explanation heard, read, or remembered,
so what can be said of experiencing them?

Summarizing as one all the existing visible
phenomena of suffering in the world does not
slightly match nor equal a hundred-thousandth
of the smallest suffering of the hells.

Those have all arisen from ignorant views.
So beings are confused in the three lower realms.[1263]

And *Chapter the Length of a Forearm* also says:

Therefore, experts consider [these three realms]
to be mere confusion, nonexistent in reality;
from confusion [about the cause], that [result] is
also impure, so these do not exist just as they appear.

How could what appears, yet does not exist in reality,
have a quintessence of that [ultimate truth]?

One with an incisive mind knows all [the relative]
to be only imaginary. That wise person abandons
[thoughts that] desire and so on are happiness,
like being frightened by a snake.[1264]

Such passages state these three realms to be imaginary, occurring from ignorance, and confusion itself. The *Sixty Verses on Reasoning* also says:

Since the complete buddhas have said
the world is conditioned by ignorance,
why is it not correct that these worlds
are also conceptualization? [316]

If ignorance has ceased, what have
arisen cease; so why would it not become
clear that [these worlds] are imagined
by ignorance?[1265]

Since it states these worlds to be confused appearance imagined by ignorance, {394} it is not reasonable for them to appear to primordial awareness in which ignorance and the imaginary have been extinguished, just as floating hairs, a yellow conch, and so on do not appear to flawless eyes.

Āryadeva's *Madhyamaka Destruction of Confusion* also says:

Whenever the eye of intelligence has opened and one is free of the sleep of the habitual propensities of ignorance, the stainless primordial awareness of a sugata dawns, like waking up. At that point, [the three realms] are not seen at all, because a very essence of entities is not observed.[1266]

And:

After the sun of perfect primordial awareness knowing emptiness, signlessness, and wishlessness has dawned, all the habitual propensities of ignorance and the afflictions that lead to natal conception are cleared away. At that point, mind and mental factors (including their fields of experience) are not seen and not observed as entities and their very essence, because a great relief has been obtained when unsurpassable primordial awareness has dawned.

In that way, having taught through reasoning that all phenomena are relatively like a dream, floating hairs, and optical illusions, and having taught that, ultimately, those [relative] entities are nonexistent and that there is luminosity, no appearance [to consciousness], and freedom of elaborations, that is also taught to be the case by scriptural quotation. The honorable teacher says:

> Just as hairs, flies, double moons,
> and eyes of peacock feathers
> do not appear to pure, flawless eyes
> free of blurriness,
>
> likewise, there is also no appearance at all
> to an expert with flawless eyes of perfect knowledge
> free of the blurry darkness of the obscurations
> of the afflictions and of knowable objects.
>
> For example, just as when, fallen asleep,
> by the power of sleep one sees children,
> women, mansions, places, and so on,
> but does not see them after waking,
>
> likewise, the relative and consciousness
> are not seen when the eyes of intelligence
> have opened and one is awake and free
> of the sleep of ignorance.
>
> For example, just as an unreal spirit,
> seen in the midst of darkness at night,
> does not appear when the sun has dawned
> and one's eyes have opened,
>
> likewise, when the sun of perfect knowledge
> destroys all the habitual propensities of ignorance
> without exception, an expert does not see mind,
> mental factors, and objects.[1267] [317]

Just as the appearances of a dream fade when waking from sleep, and appearances as hairs and so on vanish when the eye is free of blurriness, it is stated that mind and mental factors, including objects and so on (the phenomena of the three realms), do not appear to primordial awareness awakened from the sleep of ignorance and free of the blurriness of consciousness, because for that, those (with their seeds) have ceased, {395} been extinguished, and vanished.

9. *Showing that the fault of the view of annihilation is also not entailed by merely that*

The fault of advocating annihilation is also not entailed by merely that, because the *Jewel Lamp of the Madhyamaka* says:

> Just because there is nothing [relative] in the presence of what is called "wisdom of the ultimate"—nonconceptual primordial awareness, the true nature, bodhicitta, great self-arisen primordial awareness—we also are not advocates of annihilation.[1268]

And because, even though the incidental stains (these three realms) are extinguished, we do not accept that the other three realms (the sugata essence) are extinguished.

10. *Showing that it is not contradictory for these [three realms] not to appear to those who have extinguished confusion, but to appear to those who have not extinguished it*

In that way, even though these appearances of the three realms have been extinguished for those who have obtained the true nature, it is also not contradictory for them to appear unextinguished to those who have not obtained that, as for persons to whom a conch appears to be white or to be yellow [due to jaundice].

Correctness of the Explanation also says:

> Since one has wakened from the sleep of ignorance,
> and the mind has also expanded concerning knowable objects . . .[1269]

Such passages also establish that the appearances of ignorance (these three realms) do not appear to primordial awareness awakened from the sleep of ignorance, because these three realms are the appearance of consciousness, and that which is consciousness is ignorance.

The *Vast Commentary on the "Sūtra in One Hundred Thousand Lines"* also says:

> Concerning "like a dream": phenomena seen in a dream do not appear in that way when one has awakened from sleep. Likewise, imaginary phenomena such as the five appropriated aggregates, which appear when fallen asleep in ignorance, also do not appear in that way when ignorance has been abandoned and the wisdom of a noble being has been obtained.[1270]

That says the appearances of a dream that arise in sleep vanish when awakened from sleep and, likewise, that these three realms that are like a dream do not appear to primordial awareness awakened from the sleep of ignorance. Again, that same source says:

> Concerning "all phenomena," there are two aspects to phenomena: imaginary phenomena and fully established phenomena. As for that, {396} imaginary phenomena are included in the three realms and included in the three times.[1271]

These say again and again that all the three realms and the three times are imaginary. [318] And the commentary on the *Extensive Mother Sūtra, the Middle Length Sūtra*, and so on also says:

> [A tathāgata] fully knows the desire realm, form realm, and formless realm that occur from unreal imagination.[1272]

And:

> Form does not appear. Why? Because imaginary form is nonexistent, like the horns of a rabbit, it does not appear.[1273]

And:

> The very pure wisdom of a tathāgata does not see the phenomena of mind, or passionate desire, or the phenomena of mental fac-

> tors, or those including passionate desire and so on, because those imaginary phenomena in the states including passionate desire and so on are totally nonexistent.[1274]

Such passages say these imaginary three realms are totally nonexistent in the abiding state, like the horns of a rabbit, so they do not appear to awareness of the abiding state, just as the horns of a rabbit do not appear to unconfused awareness.

Entering the Conduct of a Bodhisattva also states:

> Whenever entity and nonentity
> do not remain before the mind,
> at that point there are no other aspects,
> so it is utterly calm, with no objects.[1275]

Thus it says these entities of the three realms do not appear to utterly peaceful, consummate, primordial awareness.

11. *Showing that what appears to primordial awareness does not appear to consciousness, and what appears to consciousness does not appear to primordial awareness*

Distinguishing Phenomena and True Nature also says:

> When those appear, the true nature
> does not appear, and when those
> do not appear, the true nature appears.[1276]

Thus the true nature does not appear to that awareness to which phenomena appear, and phenomena do not appear to that awareness to which the true nature appears. Therefore, if these phenomena of the three realms did appear to self-arisen primordial awareness, the extremely absurd consequence would be that the ultimate true nature would not appear; but that is not the case.

Furthermore, if that primordial awareness did see these entities of the three realms, it would see confusion. And that is also not the case, as stated in the Madhyamaka *Stages of Meditation*:

> Noble beings do not see confusion, and . . .[1277]

Also, that same work says:

> Entities abiding [in reality], in that way
> are the field of experience of noble beings.
> What does not appear to the childish,
> in that way appears to experts.[1278] {397}

Thus it states that what appears to childish, ordinary people and to expert, sublime, noble beings is not the same, but different. And *Ornament of the Sūtras* also says:

> For the childish, [the apex of] reality itself
> is obscured, so the unreal appears everywhere.
> Bodhisattvas remove that, so [the apex of]
> reality itself appears everywhere.[1279]

And:

> Know that what do not exist in reality and what
> does exist in reality do not appear and does appear.[1280] [319]

Thus it says phenomena, these three realms that appear to consciousness, are actually nonexistent and unreal, and says the ultimate true nature that appears to primordial awareness is actually existent and reality itself.

12. *If that primordial awareness did see these actually nonexistent three realms, the extremely absurd consequence would be that it would not see the actually existent true nature*

Also, that same work says:

> Why can they not see the existent, yet see the nonexistent?
> What sort of dense darkness is this?[1281]

And:

> Other than that [true nature], nothing even slightly exists
> in living beings, yet with minds utterly deluded about it,
> beings without exception totally abandon the existent and
> fixate on the nonexistent. What is this severe form of delusion
> in the world?[1282]

Because it says the consciousness that sees nonexistent phenomena (the three realms) without seeing the actually existent true nature is like darkness and horrible delusion, it establishes that the appearance of those [phenomena] has ceased for a buddha for whom that [delusion] has ceased.

The *Buddhāvataṃsaka* also says:

> Eyes that engage in conceptuality
> are very confused. What confusion
> sees is mistaken; a buddha does not
> have mistakes.[1283]

Thus the appearance or the nonappearance of confused appearances (these three realms) are stated to be mistaken or unmistaken. And *In Praise of Dharmadhātu* also says:

> Without the appearance of the six objects,
> reality is known just as it is.[1284]

Thus there is no appearance of the six relative objects to primordial awareness that directly knows the apex of reality. And the Madhyamaka work *Illuminating Reality* also says:

> When the appearance of primordial awareness
> has occurred, that [confusion] is abandoned like darkness.[1285]

And:

> If it has not been abandoned, one is mistaken,
> and when abandoned, one becomes a yogin.[1286] {398}

And:

> The creator of delusion is like an illusionist.[1287]

Such passages say these mistaken phenomena of the three worlds, which are like darkness, do not appear to primordial awareness purified of delusion.

13. *If these three realms that are not beyond consciousness did appear [to primordial awareness], the extremely absurd consequence would be that it would not be beyond consciousness*
Furthermore, through [the Bhagavān's] elegant teaching "These three realms are consciousness only,"[1288] it is also established that these three realms do not appear to primordial awareness that is beyond consciousness. [320]

14. *If these unreal three realms did appear, the extremely absurd consequence would be that it would not be primordial awareness that sees reality*
If these did appear to that [self-arisen primordial awareness], it would be bound and also a cause of defilement, because Buddhapālita's commentary says:

> Those seeing the unreal are bound.
> Those seeing reality are liberated.[1289]

And *Distinguishing Phenomena and True Nature* also says:

> As for that, the characteristic
> of phenomena is appearance as
> duality and just how it is expressed,
> which is the unreal imagination, since
> the nonexistent appears. So it is not real.
>
> Furthermore, since all are nonexistent
> in reality, mere conception, they are imaginary.[1290]

And:

> Since the nonexistent appears, confusion
> is the cause of defilement because, as with
> the appearance of an illusory elephant and
> so on, the existent also does not appear.
>
> If either nonexistence or appearance
> were nonexistent, confusion and no confusion,
> and likewise defilement and purification,
> would not be feasible.[1291]

And:

> Illusions, dreams, and so on are examples
> of the appearance of nonexistent phenomena.
> Space, gold, water, and so on are used as
> examples for transformation.[1292]

Such passages show that because the relative three realms are imaginary, confusion, and not real, they do not appear to primordial awareness in which those have been extinguished. {399}

15. *If these sufferings and their origins did appear [to primordial awareness], the extremely absurd consequence would be that the seeds of cyclic existence, and dualistic appearances, would not have ceased*

Furthermore, it is stated that these three realms are not beyond the three and the eight sufferings. And the honorable, noble Asaṅga also says:

> What is the truth of suffering? That should be known also by means of the births and birthplaces of sentient beings.[1293]

And because he says their causes are the sources, it is reasonable for their appearance to also be extinguished for primordial awareness in which their seeds have been totally extinguished. The honorable, noble Nāgārjuna also says:

> If the two aspects of selflessness are seen,
> the seeds of existence cease.[1294]

And:

> . . . and because the childish imagine the two,
> rest in the yoga of their nonduality.[1295]

Such passages say dualistic phenomena and dualistic appearances have ceased for primordial awareness in which the seeds of existence have ceased, so it is also reasonable for this cyclic existence that is not beyond dualistic phenomena and dualistic appearances to not appear to that primordial awareness.

There appear to also be very many other pure scriptural passages and reasons for this approach, but fearing it would take too many words, I have not written them here. Some are also among those presented earlier, so their intent must be understood without any exception. [321]

16. *In regard to those, eliminating misconceptions in which the flawless is seen to be flawed*
This has thirteen topics.

a. *Describing a confused misconception that this contradicts scripture*
It might be said, "That being so, the primordial awareness of a buddha would not know the phenomena of the three realms, but that would contradict the extensive and middle length Mother Sūtras, and so on, which also say it knows minds, including collected thoughts, distracted thoughts, passionate desire, and so on just exactly as they are."

b. *Carefully establishing by means of scripture itself that there is no contradiction*
There is no fault, because there are countless instances of knowing [phenomena] while they do not appear; knowing does not imply appearance, like knowing the past, the future, selflessness, {400} and so on (separated by many eons) even though they do not appear.

Also concerning the intent of such statements in the Mother Sūtras: knowing that, since the mind is not established in reality, its distracted thoughts, collected thoughts, and so on are also not established in reality and are isolated is stated to be the meaning of knowing distracted thoughts, collected thoughts, and so on, because the commentary on those Mother Sūtras says:

> "Subhūti, by means of the true nature the tathāgatas perfectly, fully know the collected thoughts and distracted thoughts of those sentient beings just as they are" means that, because they see the true nature of mind, they know collected thoughts and distracted thoughts to be not real just as they are, and to be nonexistent. This is called "knowing collected thoughts and distracted thoughts."[1296]

And because it says:

> To know [the thoughts of] all sentient beings to be in their true nature extinguished, in their true nature free of passionate desire, in their true nature cessation, in their true nature abandonment, and by their very nature to be isolated, is explained to be "knowing those thoughts."[1297]

And so on.

Therefore, after the ground isolated from all phenomena—the fully established true nature—has actually appeared, that knowledge implicitly knows that phenomena are nonexistent. So that is said to be "knowing all phenomena." And if seen in that way, the correct meaning of the great intent is also seen.

c. *How those points also clarify the intent of the statement that nonseeing itself is seeing*

In that way, referring to these instances of knowing [phenomena] while they do not appear, it is said:

> Why? Because a buddha, after knowing,
> does not see phenomena.[1298]

This is the meaning of "knowing phenomena while they do not appear." Likewise, it is said [322]:

> Not seeing forms, also not seeing feelings, without seeing
> discriminations, not seeing intentions, and without seeing
> consciousness, mind, and thoughts, this is called "seeing
> phenomena," the Tathāgata teaches.
>
> Sentient beings say in words, "space is seen," but just how
> space is seen—this meaning must be examined. The Tathāgata
> teaches that seeing phenomena is also like that. The seeing
> cannot be conveyed by other examples.
>
> One who sees in that way sees all phenomena.[1299]

And the *Ornament of the Sūtras* also says:

> Nonobservation in all respects
> is held to be the sublime observation.[1300]

And the *Sūtra of the Bodhisattva Section* also says:

> What is seeing all phenomena just as they are? It is like this: without seeing.[1301] {401}

And the *Sūtra Perfectly Summarizing the Dharma* also says:

> Without seeing all phenomena is excellent seeing.[1302]

And so on. The intent of the teachings that nonseeing is itself seeing is stated to be that when seeing the phenomena to be negated, the true nature (the ground of negation) is seen, and that when knowing all phenomena that appear to confused perception to be unestablished in reality, all phenomena are known, which is inconceivable knowing.

In Praise of Mañjughoṣa, by the teacher Candragomin, also says:

> You are expert in teaching the path of Dharma, but do not see
> any of these phenomena. You delight in benefiting sentient beings,
> but do not observe any sentient beings themselves.[1303]

And so on. One must be very expert in the intent of the teachings that nonseeing is itself seeing, because otherwise the view will be mistaken and the intent of the profound scriptures will be denigrated.

d. *Showing that the mode of appearance to those with or without special insight is also not the same*

The *Buddhāvataṃsaka* also says:

> Seeing without special insight,
> one sees bad phenomena; if seeing
> [the true nature] with special insight,
> all [the three realms] are not seen.[1304]

Because that says there are good and bad appearances to those with or without special insight, and the appearances to those without special insight do not appear to special insight, and because the primordial awareness of a conqueror is the consummate special insight, it is established that these three realms do not appear to that, because these appear to those without special insight. [323]

e. *How harm by extremely absurd consequences would occur if those phenomena must appear to knowledge*

If those phenomena definitely must appear to knowledge, the extremely absurd consequence would be that very many nonimplicative negations (such as selflessness, no sentient being, no nourishing being, no lifeforce, and all past and future phenomena separated by long periods of time) would appear to omniscient primordial awareness, because it knows them.

Also, the extremely absurd consequence that it would not know them because they do not appear to it would occur. {402}

f. *Showing the basis of the confusion about the true nature not appearing to primordial awareness, and so on*

Therefore, because these statements that that primordial awareness knows negated phenomena while they do not appear, and knows the ground of negation (the true nature) after it does appear, are accurate, they also clear away the claim by some that the true nature does not appear to that primordial awareness, and the claim that its realization of the true nature is an implicit realization, because [the Buddha] states again and again (by means of "great appearance, great brilliance,"[1305] and so on, and examples such as the eight prognostic images) that the true nature actually appears to that primordial awareness, and because the true nature is the ground of emptiness and is an implicative negation, not just empty and a nonimplicative negation.

Therefore, these confusions come from the mistaken view that claims the true nature and the emptiness of self-nature have the same meaning and, likewise, the confusion that in the abiding state there is no attribute to be established through positive determination [of qualities] because, if all were empty of self-nature, and whatever is empty of self-nature is a nonimplicative negation, that [abiding state] would also be discarded by the mere attribute being established.

g. *How other misconceptions are cleared away by showing it to be actually existent*

That being so, because consummate primordial awareness that sees the ultimate is a valid cognition of actual realization concerning the knowledge that the true nature exists, and a valid cognition of implicit realization concerning the knowledge that phenomena do not exist, the statements of glorious masters (who are like an ocean of Dharma) that the assertion by some that there is no implicit realization concerning valid cognition is only nonsense appear to be very correct.

The claim that the second and following moments of a conqueror's primordial awareness are subsequent knowledge and not valid [cognition] is also similar [nonsense].

This existence of the true nature and nonexistence of phenomena in the abiding state is stated in many pure, exceptional, textual traditions such as *Distinguishing Phenomena and True Nature.* [324] Likewise, if one is expert in the intent of the extensive statements about the meaning of existence and nonexistence in the abiding state—such as the ultimate exists but the relative does not exist, [great] nirvāṇa exists but saṃsāra does not exist, {403} the truth of cessation exists but the three other truths do not exist, the fully established true nature exists but the other natures do not exist, thusness exists but other phenomena do not exist, the outer and inner incidental stains do not exist but the other, sublime, sugata essence does exist—one will have carefully distinguished and understood existence and nonexistence.

h. *Clearing away the confused misconception that a passage refutes that, although it does not*

It might be said, "If these three realms do not appear to the primordial awareness of a conqueror, that would contradict this":

> As a single shining light ray of the sun
> illuminates all living beings, so too
> the primordial awareness of the buddhas
> instantly illuminates all knowable objects.[1306]

There is no fault, because that is said in reference to simultaneously knowing all knowable objects; because that passage says the primordial awareness of a conqueror illuminates all knowable objects, but does not teach that all knowable objects appear to the primordial awareness of a conqueror; and because "illuminate" is also just used here in conjunction with the example of the sun as a poetical figure metaphor.

Moreover, it was already established before through scriptural passages that the meaning of knowing phenomena is knowing the true nature after it has appeared and knowing the nonexistence of phenomena that do not appear.

i. *Therefore, extremely absurd consequences would occur if [phenomena] appeared to a buddha as they appear to sentient beings*

If such were not the case, and these three realms also appeared to the primordial awareness of a conqueror just as they appear to sentient beings:

> Hell beings, hungry spirits, animals, and gods,
> according to their own types, are of different
> minds regarding a single entity. Therefore, ...[1307]

And:

> Sentient beings who do not see on earth a wish-granting tree,
> tastes, sublime tastes, medicines, and other lords of taste,
> which rob all disease and are totally produced by atomic particles,
> see those as common grass, trees, water, dust, stones, and iron.
> Hungry spirits [see] water as great fire; human beings who have
> gone to the hells [see] cutting and piercing everywhere.[1308] {404}

Because these say even just a single entity arises with many dissimilar appearances to many sentient beings with dissimilar karma, they would [absurdly] appear to the primordial awareness of a conqueror in accord with how they do to them. [325]

j. *Therefore, in the abiding state these three realms of karmic appearance are not established as even mere appearance*

Therefore, this confused karmic appearance of sentient beings is a specific attribute of the being itself that has a mind, because it is totally impossible in the abiding state, like the horns of a rabbit, the child of a barren woman, a sky-flower, and so on. These are not established as even mere appearance to awareness of the abiding state, and appearance to confused perception does not fit the definition of appearance in the abiding state.

Referring to these points, it is said again and again in many ways that all phenomena are unobserved, without appearance, nonobservable, and so on.

k. *Showing that it is not contradictory for these to not appear in the abiding state yet appear in the confused state*

It might be said, "If that were so, it would contradict the explanation in *Entering the Conduct of a Bodhisattva* that this appearance of apprehended and apprehender is not the object of refutation":

> What are seen, heard, and known are not
> to be refuted here; the concept that those
> are true, which is the cause of suffering,
> is just what is to be dismissed here.[1309]

There is no fault, because that means "since it is not contradictory for those to not be true in the abiding state yet appear to confused perception, we do not deny their appearance in just the relative sense," but does not say they appear to awareness of the abiding state; and because we also do not claim that confused appearance ceases while confusion has still not ceased.

l. *Showing that which appears to the critical awareness of meditative absorption to be the ultimate*

That being so, those phenomena do not have to appear for the primordial awareness of a conqueror to know them, because the honorable, noble Asaṅga says:

> Because no objects at all appear
> to nonconceptual primordial awareness,
> it should be understood that objects do not exist.
> Since they do not exist, cognition does not exist.[1310]

[Otherwise,] the extremely absurd consequence would be that that primordial awareness would not know objects, or else objects would appear to that primordial awareness. {405} If that were accepted, however, those external entities would be the true nature, thusness, [326] because they would appear to the consummate critical awareness of meditative absorption.

m. *Showing that a period without meditative absorption is impossible for a buddha*

It might be said, "Objects do not appear to the meditative absorption of the primordial awareness of a conqueror, but they do appear to his primordial awareness of postmeditation."

That primordial awareness [of a buddha] is simply meditative absorption alone, because passages such as "the Elephant arose but is in meditative absorption"[1311] say it is always meditative absorption itself, and because the honorable, noble Āryadeva also says:

> Buddhas are in meditative
> absorption on thusness at all times.
> There is no entering or departing
> in that ineffable state.
>
> How could that primordial awareness also
> be meditative absorption and postmeditation?
> If [buddhas] had that [postmeditation], how would
> they differ from those who have entered the levels?[1312]

That being so, the primordial awareness of a buddha is never without meditative absorption.

It might be said, "That contradicts '[The Bhāgavan] arose from absorption in the reality within,'[1313] '[The Bhāgavan] arose from that samādhi,'[1314] and so on."

In all ways, those are just total displays. Buddhas display the appearance of having arisen from samādhi, but they do not have minds that are not in meditative absorption, because [their minds] are primordial awareness in which the universal-ground consciousness together with its seeds are utterly extinguished, the circulation of all breath has ceased, and the two obscurations with the habitual propensities are utterly extinguished.

Therefore, one must be expert also in the intent of other similar scriptural passages, and must also be expert in the intent of others about postmeditation.

III. *Homage and a concise summary*

Now, to express a concise summary by means of praise and homage to those:

> The dharmakāya of the conquerors, the collection
> of white virtues, is [the apex of] reality and true; {406}
> from the dharma[kāya] there is the sambhogakāya, which
> is the collection of all languages; there is the nirmāṇakāya,
> which is the aggregate of the major marks and minor marks;
> and there is sublime unchanging bliss, which is [the svābhāvikakāya]

not the dharmakāya. Therefore, those that are the characteristics of the kāyas are [stated] here by the Sugata, noble Nāgārjuna, and also Tibetans:

That [dharmadhātu,] not one yet also not many, the ground for great, excellent benefit to oneself and others, not a nonentity yet not an entity, the same taste like space, having a nature difficult to realize, unsoiled and changeless, peaceful, pervading what are the same and not the same, utterly without conceptual elaborations, to be known through personal self-awareness—to that dharmakāya of the conquerors, for which no examples exist, I bow down. [327]

That which is the transcendent, inconceivable quintessence of hundreds of fine acts, the acquisition of the result greatly expanding in various ways the causes of joy for the wise within its circle, and fully spreading the unbroken stream of the vast sound of the excellent Dharma in all worlds—to that sambhogakāya of the buddhas, residing here as the great sovereign of Dharma, I bow down.

That which appears to blaze like fire to some for the purpose of ripening sentient beings, that which displays [turning] the Dharma wheel of complete enlightenment, also again displays the utter peace [of nirvāṇa] to some, and fully engages in many ways with various means that snatch away the fears of the three states of cyclic existence—to the nirmāṇakāya of the sages that extends in the ten directions for a great purpose, I bow down.

Liberated from the activities of the three worlds, equal to space, having the nature of all entities, pure, peaceful, and isolated, yet the sublimely peaceful nature to be realized by yogins, difficult to realize, difficult to examine, beneficial to oneself and others, pervasive, signless, and free of concepts—to the unique kāya, the conquerors' kāya of bliss in which not the same and the same [are indivisible], I bow down.[1315]

You who have love for sentient beings,
are intent on their meeting and their separating,

are intent on their not separating, and are intent
on their benefit and happiness—to you I bow down. {407}

Sage, definitely liberated from all obscurations,
dominating the entire world, your knowledge
pervades knowable objects—to you whose mind
is liberated, I bow down.

Taming all the afflictions of all
sentient beings without exception,
you destroy the afflictions yet have
love for the afflicted—to you I bow down.

Spontaneous, without attachment,
without impediment, always in meditative
absorption, and answering all questions—
to you I bow down.

As for the support and supported that are
to be explained, and the speech and knowledge
by which they are explained, your intelligence is
always unimpeded—elegant teacher, to you I bow down.

Having come, you know their conduct and,
in their languages, elegantly instruct sentient beings
about their coming, going, and definite release—
to you I bow down.

When all embodied beings see you,
they recognize you as an excellent being.
Just on sight, you inspire utter faith—
to you I bow down.

As the one who has mastered assuming,
residing, and releasing; emanation and total
transformation; samādhi; and primordial awareness—
to you I bow down. [328]

Vanquishing the māras who totally deceive
sentient beings about means, refuge, purity,
and definite release through the Mahāyāna—
to you I bow down.

You who, for the benefit of oneself and others,
show primordial awareness and abandonment,
definite release and the hindrances, undisturbed
by others who are non-Buddhists—to you I bow down.

Unguarded and not forgetful,
speaking openly among followers,
gathering followers by having abandoned
the two defilements—to you I bow down. {408}

Omniscient One, during all moving
or remaining, having no conduct that
is not of an omniscient one—to you
who really possess that meaning, I bow down.

By not delaying what is to be done
for all sentient beings, your actions
are always meaningful—to you who
are never forgetful, I bow down.

In all worlds, looking upon each and
every being six times during the day
and night, possessing great compassion
and intent on benefit—to you I bow down.

Through conduct, realization,
primordial awareness, and activities,
you are the master of all śrāvakas
and pratyekabuddhas—to you I bow down.

With the three kāyas, you have gained
all aspects of great enlightenment, and thus
[know] everything—to you who eliminate
the doubts of all sentient beings, I bow down.

Without grasping, having no faults,
unsullied, not abiding, never wavering,
and without conceptual elaborations
about all phenomena—to you I bow down.

Accomplishing ultimate truth, you are
definitely released from all the levels.
The most sublime of all sentient beings,
you act to liberate all sentient beings.

With inexhaustible, matchless
qualities, you appear in the worlds,
and also in maṇḍalas, yet are not
seen by gods and human beings.[1316]

. . .

At all times, may I diligently bow down to
all the conquerors, worship them with an ocean
of clouds of offerings, and single-mindedly practice
in accord with their words![1317] {409}

That is the section about the results of separation from stains and production of the entity by means of that path.

Part Three
A Concise Summary and Advice about Those

In that way, the ground and result of the ultimate dharmakāya are one in dharmadhātu itself, and the destroyer of the incidental stains is the assembly of purified primordial awareness (including associated factors) that is like the wind that scatters groups of clouds in the sky.

A statement about that by means of the example of purifying a wish-fulfilling gem was also explained above.[1318] Yet again, a sūtra quoted in *Commentary on the "Uttaratantra"* says:

> Sāgaramati, suppose a very cleansed, very pure, very stainless precious gem of priceless beryl were placed in mud and remained for a thousand years. After a thousand years have passed, it is taken from that mud, cleansed, wiped, and carefully washed. [329] When it has been carefully cleansed and carefully wiped, the very essence of the precious, stainless gem would not have been lost.
>
> Sāgaramati, so too bodhisattvas fully know the nature of the mind of sentient beings to be luminosity, but still see them afflicted by incidental stains.
>
> Concerning that, bodhisattvas think: "These afflictions do not penetrate the natural luminosity of the mind of sentient beings. These afflictions are incidental and produced by unreal imagination. We are able to teach the Dharma in order to pacify the afflictions of these sentient beings."
>
> In that way, a discouraged state of mind does not arise. An intention arises many times to go into the presence of sentient beings. And they think: "These afflictions also do not have power or strength. These afflictions have little strength or power. These have no real basis at all. {410} These afflictions are unreal imagination. When examined with proper mental engagement exactly

in accord with reality, we will not become upset. By all means, we should scrutinize them in such a way that they will not adhere to us. If the afflictions do not adhere, that is good, but if they do, that is not."[1319]

And so on, it says extensively. Concerning statements by means of many different examples of the essence and the stains, one should also understand how the ultimate ground and result are one essence in the truth of cessation, how the destroyer of the stains is the primordial awareness of the truth of the path, and, through the example of space, that even though transformation is achieved when that has cleansed all stains, the essence of the true nature does not change.

The ground of the relative rūpakāya is its first producer, the evolving family.

The paths are the perfections (beginning from the first arousing of bodhicitta) mostly included in the assembly of merit; the creation stage including associated factors; constructing and worshiping the three representations of the Three Jewels and so on, and restoring ruins and so on, which increases the crop of virtue from the field of the conquerors; accomplishing happiness and benefit in this and other [lifetimes] for the unprotected and the miserable, and so on; and [being energetic in] accomplishing immense prayers after increasing the crop of virtue also from the field of sentient beings. These are mainly the assembly of merit included in the paths of learning.

The result is the rūpakāya of the buddhas produced by those, the quintessence of the excellences of primordial awareness, qualities, and activities as presented before and, furthermore, extensively stated in the profound sūtras and tantras. [330]

The statements in *Levels of the Bodhisattva* that include in the category of the ground even the attributes of the paths of learning such as the initial arousing of bodhicitta and cultivating the factors conducive to enlightenment, and call those producers that are like "the root and seed of a turnip" the [causal] ground, are in the context of including them in the two [categories of] cause and result.[1320]

When these are divided into the three of ground, path, and result, the cause itself is divided into ground and path, so there is no contradiction in dividing them into three in that way or condensing them into the two [of cause and result]; the meaning is the same. Although the primordial awareness of the rūpakāya, and so on, included in the Mahāyāna path of no more learning, are the truth of the path, {411} they are not the path that is a member of the division into the three of ground, path, and result, because that is definitely [included among] the paths of learning.

What are to be known in teachings such as that are all the ground, paths, and results. What are to be brought into experience after understanding those are the pure paths included in the two assemblies. And the results are those focused upon to be attained, the sources of refuge, and those stated to be the objects of faithful and devoted activities such as prostrations and worship. Therefore, after understanding in that way, one should mainly be very diligent in accomplishing the two assemblies as the path.

Dedicating the Virtue of the Explanation

In that way, the consummate definitive meaning of all
the good, profound scriptures of the Conqueror, clarified
by the profound oral instructions of the sons of the Conqueror
(such as the Protectors of the Three Families), this which
has been realized by the kindness of venerable masters,
is a *Mountain Dharma* for those practicing profound yoga
in isolated mountain retreats.

Because all the streams without exception of the definitive meaning
of all the pure, exceptional sūtras, tantras, and treatises have been
gathered, this is also an *Ocean of Definitive Meaning*. Because it
presents all the *consummate, uncommon* grounds, paths, and results,
and also all the views, meditations, and conducts, the name of this
is meaningful.

Because it definitely comments on the profound intent,
this is a commentary on the intent of the Conqueror; because
it definitely comments on all the vajra words, it also releases
the knots of the vajra words; because it clearly presents
the profound true nature, it is a lamp on the sugata essence;
and because it gathers all the profound scriptural passages,
reasoning, and *esoteric instructions*, it is also a sublime
wish-fulfilling gem.

> Therefore, although it is difficult to agree here with people who call as witnesses the mere talk of the elders of their own line who (since they are attached to what they first heard) have fallen under the power of the notion that a claim is stronger just because it was made earlier, and for whom truth is established by many advocates separated from the four reliances—this does agree with the intent of the Conqueror, including his children, and agrees with the truth. [331]
>
> May those who again and again urged me with good intentions [to write] this, {412} agreeable companions, those who offered good resources, and so on—all living beings—see, realize, and quickly obtain the meaning of the profound, stainless sūtras, tantras, and esoteric instructions, and create immense benefit for others!
>
> May we always live with and never deteriorate from what pleases the buddhas in all situations—faith and diligence, wisdom and compassion, courage and intelligence, shame and modesty, the best livelihood and daring generosity, moral discipline and samādhi, and the good conduct of the four, six, eight, ten, and sixteen sacred commitments!

...

Urged again and again by the words of the crown jewel of excellent and great beings, Khenchen Jodenpa (the teacher and his students),[1321] and urged by the words of master Lotsāwa (expert in Sanskrit grammar and having many qualities of scripture and direct realization),[1322] and furthermore, urged by the words of master Choklé Namgyal[1323] and many other spiritual friends having the qualities of expertise, dignity, and goodness,[1324] and the words of the excellent lord of yogins, Samding Chokpupa[1325] and other good practitioners of the definitive meaning, and, in particular, by master Yeshé Gyaltsen (who supported me well with service and respect, including a fine hundredfold offering, and acted with great faith and devotion),[1326] the Wanderer[1327] wrote this at the glorious, great site of Jonang, exactly in accord with the scriptures, reasoning, and esoteric instructions of the consummate, profound, definitive meaning. This has a strict seal of secrecy, not being suitable to teach to those whose intelligence has not remained unbiased and who do not have experience meditating on the true nature of the definitive meaning. So I ask that you act in accord with only that. If that is transgressed, the sacred commitments are transgressed.

oṃ āḥ hūṃ hoḥ haṃ kṣaḥ

Appendix 1
Outline of *Mountain Dharma*

Appendix 2
Tibetan Transliteration

Barawa Gyaltsen Palsang	'Ba ra ba Rgyal mtshan dpal bzang
Bodong	Bo dong
Butön Rinchen Drup	Bu ston Rin chen grub
Chak Lotsāwa Rinchen Chögyal	Chag Lo tsā ba Rin chen chos rgyal
Chogyé Trichen Rinpoché	Bco brgyad Khri chen Rin po che
Choklé Namgyal	Phyogs las rnam rgyal
Chölung	Chos lung
Chukha	Chu kha
Dergé	Sde dge
Dewachen	Bde ba can
Dezhung Tulku Rinpoché	Sde gzhung Sprul sku Rin po che
Dilgo Khyentsé Rinpoché	Dil mgo Mkhyen brtse Rin po che
Dölpopa Sherab Gyaltsen	Dol po pa Shes rab rgyal mtshan
Dönyö Gyaltsen	Don yod rgyal mtshan
Drakpa Gyaltsen	Grags pa rgyal mtshan
Drigung Lotsāwa Maṇikaśrī	'Bri gung Lo tsā ba Ma ṇi ka shrī
Dro Lotsāwa Sherab Drak	'Bro Lo tsā ba Shes rab grags
Drokmi Shākya Yeshé	'Brog mi Shākya ye shes
Dzingkha	Rdzing kha
Geluk	Dge lugs
Gendun Chöphel	Dge 'dun chos 'phel
Geshé Thupten Jinpa	Dge bshes Thub bstan sbyin pa
Gharungwa Lhai Gyaltsen	Gha rung ba Lha'i rgyal mtshan
Gö Lotsāwa	'Gos Lo tsā ba
Gyalsé Thokmé	Rgyal sras thogs med

Gyantsé	Rgyal rtse
Gyedé	Rgyas sde
Jamgön Ameshab	’Jam mgon A mes zhabs
Jamyang Chögön	’Jam dbyangs chos mgon
Jangra	Lcang ra
Jangsem Sönam Drakpa	Byang sems Bsod nams grags pa
Jokhang	Jo khang
Jonang	Jo nang
Kadam	Bka’ gdams
Kagyü	Bka’ brgyud
Kangyur	bka’ ’gyur
Karmapa Rangjung Dorjé	Karma pa Rang byung rdo rje
Khachö Deden	Mkha’ spyod bde ldan
Khenchen Jodenpa	Mkhan chen Jo gdan pa
Khenchen Sönam Drakpa	Mkhan chen Bsod nams grags pa
Khön	’Khon
Kunga Drölchok	Kun dga’ grol mchog
Kunpang Chödrak Palsang	Kun spangs Chos grags dpal bzang
Kunpang Thukjé Tsöndrü	Kun spangs Thugs rje brtson ’grus
Kyitön Jamyang Drakpa	Skyi ston ’Jam dbyangs grags pa
Lama Dampa Sönam Gyaltsen	Bla ma dam pa Bsod nams rgyal mtshan
Lhai Dawa	Lha’i zla ba
Lhai Gyaltsen	Lha’i rgyal mtshan
Lhasa	Lha sa
Loburwa Chökyi Gyaltsen	Glo bur ba Chos kyi rgyal mtshan
Lochen Rinchen Sangpo	Lo chen Rin chen bzang po
Lopön Dawa Sangpo	Slob dpon Zla ba bzang po
Lotsāwa Lodrö Pal	Lo tsā ba Blo gros dpal
Manchukhawa Lodrö Gyaltsen	Sman chu kha ba Blo gros rgyal mtshan
Mati Paṇchen Lodrö Gyaltsen	Ma ti paṇ chen Blo gros rgyal mtshan

Nesar	Gnas gsar
Ngamring	Ngam ring
Ngawang Lodrö Drakpa	Ngag dbang blo gros grags pa
Nya Ön Kunga Pal	Nya dbon Kun dga' dpal
Nyang	Nyang
Nyangtö	Snyang stod
Nyenchung Dharma Trak	Gnyen chung Dharma grags
Nyingma	Rnying ma
Palden Wangchuk Sherab	Dpal ldan dbang phyug shes rab
Pang Lotsāwa Lodrö Tenpa	Dpang Lo tsā ba Blo gros brtan pa
Phakpa Palsang	'Phags pa dpal bzang
Phakpa Rinchen	'Phags pa rin chen
Phakmodru	Phag mo gru
Phuntsok Palsang	Phun tshogs dpal bzang
Pön Döndrup Sangpo	Dpon Don grub bzang po
Ramoché Khangsar	Ra mo che Khang gsar
rangtong	*rang stong*
Rinchen Gyaltsen	Rin chen rgyal mtshan
Rinchen Yeshé	Rin chen ye shes
Sakya	Sa skya
Samding	Bsam sdings
Samding Chokpupa	Bsam sdings Cog pu pa
Shalu	Zhwa lu
Sharpa	Shar pa
Sharpa Rinchen Gyaltsen	Shar pa Rin chen rgyal mtshan
shentong	*gzhan stong*
Shöl	Zhol
Shongtön Dorjé Gyaltsen	Shong ston Rdo rje rgyal mtshan
Shongtön Lodrö Tenpa	Shong ston Blo gros brtan pa
Sönam Drakpa	Bsod nams grags pa
Ta En Chökyi Gyaltsen	Ta dben Chos kyi rgyal mtshan
Ta En Lodrö Gyaltsen	Ta dben Blo gros rgyal mtshan

Tanak	Rta nag
Tāranātha	Tā ra nā tha
Tenga Rinpoché	Bstan dga' Rin po che
Thangtong Gyalpo	Thang stong rgyal po
Tishri Kunga Gyaltsen	Ti shri Kun dga' rgyal mtshan
Tokden Drakseng	Rtogs ldan Grags seng
Trophu	Khro phu
Trophu Lotsāwa Jampa Pal	Khro phu Lo tsā ba Byams pa dpal
Tsang	Gtsang
Tsangpo	Gtsang po
Tsechen	Rtse chen
Tsurphu	Mtshur phu
Yeshé Gyaltsen	Ye shes rgyal mtshan
Yönten Gyatso	Yon tan rgya mtsho

Notes

1. Dölpopa Sherab Gyaltsen, *Mountain Dharma*, Jo nang dpe tshogs edition, 109, Bod kyi gtsug lag gces btus edition, 86.
2. An episode that clearly illustrates the contrasting opinions about Dölpopa is found in Chak Lotsāwa Rinchen Chögyal, *Wish-Granting Sheaves*, 140–41. A scholar of the Sakya tradition once visited Jonang but was afraid to meet Dölpopa himself. When he went to circumambulate the great stūpa that Dölpopa had built, however, he unexpectedly met the master and could not help but prostrate to him. When this scholar later met the Kagyü master Tokden Drakseng (1283–1349, the first Red Hat Karmapa) at Tsurphu Monastery, he said, "You have unimpeded clairvoyance. Of what demon (*bdud*, *māra*) is the Omniscient Jonangpa an emanation?" Tokden Trakseng completely covered his head and said, "Are you done talking?" The scholar asked, "What did I say?" Tokden Trakseng replied, "Don't talk like that! He is an emanation of Kalkī [Puṇḍarīka]. If you listen to me, you will not condemn the Omniscient One but confess to him! He will grace you." The scholar immediately traveled to where Dölpopa was staying, offered him a maṇḍala of gold, confessed, and drank the water with which the master's feet had been washed. After requesting guiding instructions from Dölpopa, good meditative experiences and realization arose for him. The same story with very different phrasing and details is also found in Lhai Gyaltsen, *Biography of the Omniscient Dharma Lord of Jonang*, 35a–b, and Kunpang Chödrak Palsang, *Biography of the Omniscient Dharma Lord*, 361–62.
3. For example, see Dölpopa, *Instruction to Lhajé Tsultrim Ö*, 678–79, and Dölpopa, *Reply to the Questions of Lotsāwa Sherab Rinchen*, 774.
4. The following account of Dölpopa's life is largely summarized from the more detailed description in Stearns 2010, 9–40.
5. The Bodhisattva Trilogy (*Sems 'grel skor gsum*) is (1) *Vimalaprabhā*, or *Stainless Light* (Toh 1347), an immense commentary on the *Kālacakra Tantra* by Kalkī Puṇḍarīka; (2) *Hevajrapiṇḍārthaṭīkā*, or *Extensive Commentary on the Condensed Meaning of the Hevajra* (Toh 1180), a commentary on the *Hevajra Tantra* by Bodhisattva Vajragarbha; and (3) *Laghutantrapiṇḍārthavivaraṇa*, or *Brief Cakrasaṃvara Commentary* (Toh 1402), a commentary on the *Cakrasaṃvara Tantra* by Bodhisattva Vajrapāṇi.
6. According to Dölpopa, *Reply to Questions*, 344–45, the Ten Sūtras on the Essence (*Snying po'i mdo bcu*) are (1) *Sūtra of the Tathāgata Essence* (*De bzhin gshegs pa'i snying po'i mdo*), (2) *Dhāraṇī of Penetrating the Nonconceptual* (*Rnam par mi rtog pa la 'jug pa'i gzungs*), (3) *Sūtra of the Lion's Roar of Śrīmālādevī* (*Lha mo dpal phreng seng ge sgra'i mdo*), (4) *Sūtra of the Great Drum* (*Rnga bo che chen po'i mdo*),

(5) *Sūtra to Benefit Aṅgulimāla* (*Sor mo'i phreng ba la phan pa'i mdo*), (6) *Sūtra of Great Emptiness* (*Stong nyid chen po'i mdo*), (7) *Sūtra Teaching the Great Compassion of the Tathāgata* (*De bzhin gshegs pa'i thugs rje chen po bstan pa'i mdo*), (8) *Sūtra Teaching the Inconceivable Qualities and Primordial Awareness of the Tathāgata* (*De bzhin gshegs pa'i yon tan dang ye shes bsam gyis mi khyab pa'i bstan pa'i mdo*), (9) *Extensive Great Cloud Sūtra* (*Sprin chen po'i mdo rgyas pa*), and (10) the condensed and extensive versions of the *Mahāparinirvāṇa Sūtra* (*Myang 'das chen po'i mdo*), both counted together as one. The first five texts in this list are also called the Five Sūtras on the Essence (*Snying po'i mdo lnga*).

7. The Five Sūtras of Definitive Meaning (*Nges don mdo lnga*) are (1) *Perfection of Wisdom in Five Hundred Lines* (*Sher phyin lnga brgya pa*), (2) *Maitreya's Questions* (*Byang chub sems pa'i bslab pa rab tu dbye ba'i le'u cha gnyis gcig tu byas pa byams zhus su'ang grags pa*), (3) *Sūtra of the Dense Array* (*Rgyan btug po'i mdo*), (4) *Sūtra on the Samādhi of the Miraculous Attainment of Utter Peace* (*Rab tu zhi ba rnam par nges pa'i cho 'phrul gyi ting nge 'dzin kyi mdo*), and (5) *Jewel Cloud Sūtra* (*Dkon mchog sprin gyi mdo*). The two versions of *Maitreya's Questions* that Dölpopa mentions in his description of (2) are found in the eighteen-thousand-line and the twenty-five-thousand-line sūtras on the perfection of wisdom. A set of Ten Sūtras of Definitive Meaning (*Nges don mdo bcu*) is made by adding the following sūtras to the list: (6) the large *Excellent Golden Light* (*Gser 'od dam chen*), (7) *Definitive Commentary on the Intent* (*Dgongs pa nges par 'grel pa*), (8) *Journey to Laṅkā* (*Lang kar gshegs pa*), (9) *Sūtra Ornament of the Appearance of Primordial Awareness* (*Ye shes snang ba rgyan gyi mdo*), and (10) *Avataṃsaka* (*Sangs rgyas phal po che*). See Dölpopa, *Reply to Questions*, 344–45.
8. The Five Treatises of Maitreya (*Byams chos lnga*) are (1) *Uttaratantra*, (2) *Ornament of Direct Realization* (*Abhisamayālaṃkāra*), (3) *Distinguishing Phenomena and True Nature* (*Dharmadharmatāvibhāga*), (4) *Ornament of the Mahāyāna Sūtras* (*Mahāyānasūtrālaṃkāra*), and (5) *Distinguishing the Middle and the Extremes* (*Madhyāntavibhāga*).
9. The Six-Branch Yoga (*ṣaḍaṅgayoga*, *yan lag drug pa'i rnal 'byor/sbyor drug*), or Vajrayoga (*rdo rje'i rnal 'byor*), is the completion-stage practice taught in many tantras, especially the *Kālacakra* and the *Guhyasamāja*. For more information, see Newman 1987, and Wallace 2001 and 2010. Kongtrul 2007b, 289–330, is a clear summary of the six-branch yoga practices copied almost entirely from Jetsun Tāranātha's *Meaningful to Behold* (*Mthong ba don ldan*). Also see Lhai Gyaltsen, *Biography of the Omniscient Dharma Lord of Jonang*, 8b.
10. Dölpopa's studies with Rinchen Yeshé are mentioned in Tāranātha, *History of the Kālacakra Teachings*, 25, and Lhai Gyaltsen, *Biography of the Omniscient Dharma Lord of Jonang*, 6b. The Jonang master Kunga Drölchok (1507–66) later noted that Butön Rinchen Drup (1290–1364) thought Dölpopa had enhanced a previous philosophical tenet held by Rinchen Yeshé of Tanak. See Kunga Drölchok, *Lineage History of the "Hundred Guiding Instructions,"* 326. For important information about Rinchen Yeshé and how his views may have influenced Dölpopa, see Wangchuk 2011 (2012), 342–44.
11. Lhai Gyaltsen, *Biography of the Omniscient Dharma Lord of Jonang*, 6b, and Kunpang Chödrak Palsang, *Biography of the Omniscient Dharma Lord*, 299–300.

12. Tāranātha, *History of the Kālacakra Teachings*, 25.
13. Lhai Gyaltsen, *Biography of the Omniscient Dharma Lord of Jonang*, 8b. Kunpang Chödrak Palsang, *Biography of the Omniscient Dharma Lord*, 300, places this event earlier, before Dölpopa received full ordination.
14. Gyalwa Josang Palsangpo, *Brilliant Marvels*, 563: *sa skya'i gdan sa mdzad.* To my knowledge, this event is not mentioned in any literary work of the Sakya tradition.
15. See Tāranātha, *History of the Kālacakra Teachings*, 26.
16. Lhai Gyaltsen, *Biography of the Omniscient Dharma Lord of Jonang*, 9a, and Kunpang Chödrak Palsang, *Biography of the Omniscient Dharma Lord*, 304.
17. Kunpang Chödrak Palsang, *Biography of the Omniscient Dharma Lord*, 304–6. Dölpopa would later be famed as an emanation of Kalkī Puṇḍarīka.
18. Kunpang Chödrak Palsang, *Biography of the Omniscient Dharma Lord*, 308: *sor bsam gnyis la brten nas sangs rgyas kyi sku dang zhing khams dpag du med pa gzigs so/ srog rtsol dang 'dzin pa la brten nas bde drod 'bar bas nyams rtogs khyad par can 'khrungs so.* Tāranātha, however, says Dölpopa stayed in retreat for about two and a half years and realized the first three branches. Tāranātha, *Guidebook of Khyogpo Hermitage*, 2a: *chos rje kun mkhyen chen pos kyang lo gnyis ngo gsum bzhugs/ sor sdud bsam gtan srog rtsol gsum mthar phyin pa'i tshul ston sa yang 'di lags.*
19. Tāranātha, *History of the Kālacakra Teachings*, 27: *gzhan stong gi lta sgom khyad par can ni/ mkha' spyod bde ldan du bzhugs pa'i tshe thugs la 'khrungs pa yin kyang/ lo shas shig gzhan la ma gsungs.* "The exceptional *shentong* view and meditation arose in his mind while staying at Khachö Deden, but he did not speak of it to others for several years." As described below, Dölpopa would first openly teach the *shentong* view in 1330.
20. Lhai Gyaltsen, *Biography of the Omniscient Dharma Lord of Jonang*, 10a, says the request was made about two years before the death of Yönten Gyatso in 1327. Dölpopa's own words are quoted in describing these events and his feelings about them.
21. Lhai Gyaltsen, *Biography of the Omniscient Dharma Lord of Jonang*, 12a. Trophu Lotsāwa's stūpa was probably the model on which Dölpopa based his own monument. Trophu Lotsāwa began his stūpa in 1230 and completed the shrines on the third floor in 1234. It was built as a reliquary shrine for some of the remains and special relics of his master, Śākyaśrībhadra (d. 1225?). Chökyi Gyatso, *Pilgrimage Journal of Central Tibet and Tsang*, 481, says the Trophu structure was built of stone, with three stories of five temples on each of the four sides, totaling sixty.
22. Lhai Gyaltsen, *Biography of the Omniscient Dharma Lord of Jonang*, 13a and 15b. One of those who sent offerings was Tishri Kunga Gyaltsen (1310–58) of Sakya, who was a disciple of Dölpopa. On folio 20a, this same master of the Khön family is also said to have offered the materials for a large silk maṇḍala of Kālacakra after the completion of the stūpa.
23. The participation of these teachers in the construction work is mentioned by Lhai Gyaltsen, *Biography of the Omniscient Dharma Lord of Jonang*, 12b.
24. Kunpang Chödrak Palsang, *Biography of the Omniscient Dharma Lord*, 323: *chos rje'i thugs dgyes nas/ kun rdzob rang stong dang don dam gzhan stong gi phye bsal chen mo dang.* See also Tāranātha, *History of the Kālacakra Teachings*, 27.
25. Lhai Gyaltsen, *Biography of the Omniscient Dharma Lord of Jonang*, 15a–b.
26. Lhai Gyaltsen, *Biography of the Omniscient Dharma Lord of Jonang*, 21a: *sngar*

bod du ma grags pa don dam gzhan stong dang. This is from a long and significant list of topics that Dölpopa felt he had been the first in Tibet to realize and express correctly.

27. Both Dölpopa's comments and the opinions of Lhai Gyaltsen are found in Lhai Gyaltsen, *Biography of the Omniscient Dharma Lord of Jonang*, 22a.
28. See Tāranātha, *History of the Kālacakra Teachings*, 27, and Tāranātha, *Twenty-One Differences concerning the Profound Meaning*, 793–94.
29. Lhai Gyaltsen, *Biography of the Omniscient Dharma Lord of Jonang*, 45b, mentions these Sakya masters, with the exception of Dönyö Gyaltsen, in a list of Dölpopa's disciples.
30. See Tāranātha, *History of the Kālacakra Teachings*, 25.
31. See Barawa Gyaltsen Palsangpo, *Reply to Eight Major Disciples of the Omniscient Dölpopa*, 637–39. See especially 639, where Barawa quotes from Dölpopa's letter to him.
32. Dölpopa's collected writings contain a number of letters to different Buddhist teachers and students in which he replies to questions about the *shentong* view and other key elements of his theories. These are mostly included in *Kun mkhyen dol po pa shes rab rgyal mtshan gyi gsung 'bum*, vol. 8. 'Dzam thang: 'Dzam thang Bsam 'grub nor bu'i gling gi par khang, 1998. See also Tāranātha, *History of the Kālacakra Teachings*, 27.
33. Lhai Gyaltsen, *Biography of the Omniscient Dharma Lord of Jonang*, 17a, gives the exact date of the stūpa consecration as *dpal ldong gyi lo smin drug gi zla ba'i dkar phyogs kyi tshes bcu*. According to the online Tibetan Phugpa Calendar Calculator this corresponds to October 27, 1333.
34. Kunpang Chödrak Palsang, *Biography of the Omniscient Dharma Lord*, 333, 348. Dölpopa's visionary trip to Shambhala seems to have occurred in 1335.
35. Kunpang Chödrak Palsang, *Biography of the Omniscient Dharma Lord*, 349–50.
36. Lhai Gyaltsen, *Biography of the Omniscient Dharma Lord of Jonang*, 24a.
37. Lhai Gyaltsen, *Biography of the Omniscient Dharma Lord of Jonang*, 24b. For the invitation to Butön, see Seyfort Ruegg 1966, 122. Emperor Toghon Temür (Shun Di Emperor, reigned July 19, 1333–September 10, 1368) would have first heard of Dölpopa soon after the completion of the Jonang stūpa in October 1333, when Dölpopa's disciple Lopön Dawa Sangpo was sent to the imperial court to solicit offerings for the monument. Lavish offerings were sent to Jonang. See Lhai Gyaltsen, *Biography of the Omniscient Dharma Lord of Jonang*, 17b.
38. Lhai Gyaltsen, *Biography of the Omniscient Dharma Lord of Jonang*, 25a, and Tāranātha, *History of the Kālacakra Teachings*, 29. One modern Jonang source says Kunpang Chödrak Palsang went to China as Dölpopa's representative (*sku tshab*). See Ngawang Lodrö Drakpa, *History of the Jonang Tradition*, 33.
39. Lhai Gyaltsen, *Biography of the Omniscient Dharma Lord of Jonang*, 38a.
40. Lhai Gyaltsen, *Biography of the Omniscient Dharma Lord of Jonang*, 41a. Tāranātha, *History of the Kālacakra Teachings*, 31, says Dölpopa taught the Six-Branch Yoga seven times in Lhasa. At first he gave it to fifty, one hundred, or two hundred people, as the situation required. The last time he taught it was known as the "great guiding instruction" (*'khrid mo che*), to which more than eighteen hundred people came. He gave the great initiation of Kālacakra to many thousands of people. Lhai

Gyaltsen, *Biography of the Omniscient Dharma Lord of Jonang*, 42a, describes the scenes.

41. Dölpopa's *General Commentary on the Doctrine* is translated and studied in Stearns 2010.
42. See Tāranātha, *History of the Nyang Region*, 48, 90–91, and 93, and Lhai Gyaltsen, *Biography of the Omniscient Dharma Lord of Jonang*, 43b–44a. Phakpa Palsang was an important political figure in fourteenth-century Tibet and founded the great castle palace of Gyantsé in 1365. In fulfillment of Dölpopa's prophecy, he also laid the foundations for the monastery of Tsechen, which was founded in 1366 by Dölpopa's disciple Nya Ön Kunga Pal.
43. The procession back to Jonang is vividly described by Lhai Gyaltsen, who was present at the time. See Lhai Gyaltsen, *Biography of the Omniscient Dharma Lord of Jonang*, 44b.
44. Lhai Gyaltsen, *Biography of the Omniscient Dharma Lord of Jonang*, 50b, mentions that Dölpopa had often said, "I will make the stūpa my place to die" (*'chi sa sku 'bum du byed do*). At this point he knew he was going to die soon.
45. See Kunpang Chödrak Palsang, *Biography of the Omniscient Dharma Lord*, 425. The "powerful tenfold anagram" (*rnam bcu dbang ldan*) is the famous anagram in Lañtsa script of the ten syllables of the Kālacakra mantra. The entire Kālacakra system can be explained using this single emblem.
46. Lhai Gyaltsen, *Biography of the Omniscient Dharma Lord of Jonang*, 51a–b. Kunpang Chödrak Palsang, *Biography of the Omniscient Dharma Lord*, 439, says that on the eighth day Dölpopa's body was placed into a casket of white and red agarwood and white and red sandalwood. It was then taken onto the roof of his residence, where everyone was allowed to pay their respects.
47. Lhai Gyaltsen, *Biography of the Omniscient Dharma Lord of Jonang*, 52a–b. The master of the Sharpa family of Sakya was Sharpa Rinchen Gyaltsen, who is listed among Dölpopa's chief disciples. Lhai Gyaltsen, *Biography of the Omniscient Dharma Lord of Jonang*, 45b, 46a, says most of the teachers and Saṅgha members at Sakya were disciples of Dölpopa.
48. Kunpang Chödrak Palsang, *Biography of the Omniscient Dharma Lord*, 450.
49. Lhai Gyaltsen, *Biography of the Omniscient Dharma Lord of Jonang*, 27b.
50. Lhai Gyaltsen, *Biography of the Omniscient Dharma Lord of Jonang*, 28a: *'u cag jo mo nang pa ni/ gang gi yang phyogs su lhung ba med/ phyogs ris kyi chos kyis sangs rgyas mi thob pas/ don med sdig pa'i sgo skal ma len/ 'u cag ni nam mkha'i sprin dang 'dra bar gang gi'ang phyogs su lhung ba med do.*
51. See Kunpang Chödrak Palsang, *Biography of the Omniscient Dharma Lord*, 331: *de nas khyi lor bde ba can du bzhugs nas/ lo tsa blo gros rnam gnyis la dus kyi 'khor lo'i 'gyur gyi dag pa'i gzhi gyis gsungs nas/ chos rje dang kho bo gnyis dpang por bzhag nas/ slar legs pa'i nang nas legs pa yang dag par mdzad do/ de nas bdag gis bskul nas sa bcad dang mchan pu mdzad do.* Writing in the late fifteenth or early sixteenth century, the Kagyü author Chak Lotsāwa Rinchen Chögyal, *Wish-Granting Sheaves*, 131, says Dölpopa also proofread (*zhu chen mdzad*) the new translations at this time. See Stearns 2010, 24–29, for more information about these events. For brief accounts of the lives of Mati Panchen and Jonang Lotsāwa Lodrö Pal, see Gyalwa Josang Palsangpo, *Brilliant Marvels*, 577–82 and 573–77, and Stearns 2008d and

2008b. For the life of Kunpang Chödrak Palsang, see Gyalwa Josang Palsangpo, *Brilliant Marvels*, 566–73, and Stearns 2008c. The later Sakya author Jamgön Ameshab (1597–1659) simply copies Chak Lotsāwa's complete account of Dölpopa's life. See Jamgön Ameshab, *Chariot of Amazing Faith*, 148–57.

52. Kalāpa is the court of the Kalkī kings of the legendary land of Shambhala, where the Kālacakra teachings are believed to be preserved.

53. The three wisdoms arise from study, reflection, and meditation. This single couplet from Dölpopa's series of verses was also quoted later in Gö Lotsāwa's *Blue Annals* (completed in 1478), where the construction of the great stūpa is said to have caused a special realization for Dölpopa, and is linked to his composition of *Mountain Dharma* and its summary (*bsdus don*). Gö Lotsāwa also says Dölpopa's writings then spread throughout the regions of Tsang and Central Tibet (*dbus gtsang du khyab*). See Gö Lotsāwa Shönu Pal, *Blue Annals*, vol. 2, 910. See also Roerich 1976, 776–77, where an annotation by the Tibetan scholar Gendun Chöphel (1903–1951) specifically says that "the Ocean" in this line refers to Dölpopa's famous *Nges don rgya mtsho* (*Ocean of Definitive Meaning*). Mentioning *Ocean of Definitive Meaning* and Dölpopa's *Fourth Council* (*Bka' bsdus bzhi pa*), Gendun Chöphel also says that monks of the Geluk tradition "are forbidden to keep these books within the precincts of the monastery." In his history of the Kālacakra tradition Chak Lotsāwa Rinchen Chögyal further glosses the same line with the phrase "the secret treasury of Dharma gushed forth" (*chos kyi gsang mdzod brdol*). See Chak Lotsāwa Rinchen Chögyal, *Wish-Granting Sheaves*, 130–31. The terms "summary" (*bsdus don*) and "topical outline" (*sa bcad*) are used to refer to the same work by Dölpopa, for which see Dölpopa Sherab Gyaltsen, *Comprehensive Summary of the Commentary on the Glorious "Kālacakra Tantra."*

54. These lines are from a much longer series of verses by Dölpopa at the end of his annotations. See Puṇḍarīka, *Stainless Light* (Jonang trans.), chap. 5, Jo nang dpe tshogs, vol. 20, 456: *kye ma bdag ni skal ba rab dman yang/ 'di 'dra snyed pas skal ba bzang snyam byed/ le lo can gyi blun pos 'di rnyed pa/ rigs ldan rgyal pos byin gyis [b]rlabs min [yin] nam/ lus kyis ka la pā [lā pa] ru ma sleb kyang/ dad pa'i sems la rigs ldan zhugs sam ci/ shes rab gsum la blo gros sbyangs min yang/ lhun po bzhengs la [pas] rgya mtsho rdol ba snyam/ 'phags rnams kyis kyang rtogs par dka' ba'i gnas/ gang gi [gis] drin gyis ji bzhin rtogs mdzad pa/ bla ma sangs rgyas rigs ldan thams cad dang/ de yi mchod rten che la phyag 'tshal 'dud.* This edition of the *Stainless Light* includes annotations by both Dölpopa and his disciple Choklé Namgyal. For more information about the difficult task of distinguishing these annotations, see Stearns 2010, 324n91, and Reigle 2015. The variant spellings in brackets are from the same lines quoted in Lhai Gyaltsen, *Biography of the Omniscient Dharma Lord of Jonang*, 22a. The Kagyü master Chak Lotsāwa Rinchen Chögyal, *Wish-Granting Sheaves*, 131, places the writing of *Mountain Dharma* and many other works during a later period, sometime after Lotsāwa Lodrö Pal became abbot of Jonang in 1338. The sequence of events in such later works of other traditions does not always agree with the primary Jonang sources.

55. For example, see Kunpang Chödrak Palsang, *Biography of the Omniscient Dharma Lord*, 327, Tāranātha, *History of the Nyang Region*, 90, and Lhai Gyaltsen, *Biography of the Omniscient Dharma Lord of Jonang*, 35b. Anonymous verses at the end

of Dölpopa, *Distinguishing the Views*, 810, also refer to him as an emanation body (*nirmāṇakāya*) of Kalkī Puṇḍarīka. The modern Jonang master Ngawang Lodrö Drakpa (1920–75), discussing an exclamation Dölpopa made when reading his annotations to the *Stainless Light*, also says Dölpopa was stating his own belief that he was an actual emanation of Puṇḍarīka. See Ngawang Lodrö Drakpa, *History of the Jonang Tradition*, 542.

56. This is stated in the biography of Choklé Namgyal just before the beginning of the Earth Rabbit Year (1339) is mentioned, in a long description of his years of service to Dölpopa before that time. See Tenpai Gyaltsen, *Biography of the Dharma Lord Choklé Namgyal*, 422: *mdo rgyud zab mo rnams kyi lung bsdus pa dang/ phyogs snga ma bsu'i rtsod pa the tshom gyi gnas rnams la rtsod cing 'dri ba dang/ 'gal spong gi tshul du ma dang/ tshig don gyi zur gso ba'i sgo nas nges don rgya mtsho la sogs pa'i bstan bcos mang po rtsom pa'i zhabs tog mdzad/ dgongs pa yongs su skor ba'i slob mar mkhyen nas/ chos rje shin tu mnyes . . .*
57. Kunpang Chödrak Palsang, *Biography of the Omniscient Dharma Lord*, 352. On page 349 Kunpang mentions the fall of the Mouse Year (1336), after which Dölpopa traveled to Sakya to teach. At least another four months passed before he taught *Mountain Dharma* in Jonang.
58. Lhai Gyaltsen, *Biography of the Omniscient Dharma Lord of Jonang*, 20a
59. Lhai Gyaltsen, *Biography of the Omniscient Dharma Lord of Jonang*, 20b: *chos rje'i zhal nas/ nges don zab mo'i gnad thams cad dus kyi 'khor lo'i rgyud 'grel chen po nas rnyed pas khong shin tu bka' drin che/ ngas kyang gzhung la 'khrul pa 'gog pa la bsdus don dang chan bu khyad 'phags dang/ gzhan yang yig cha du ma byas.*
60. See Gyalwa Josang Palsangpo, *Brilliant Marvels*, 620.
61. See Dölpopa Sherab Gyaltsen, *Outline of "Mountain Dharma: An Ocean of Definitive Meaning."*
62. See notes 5–8.
63. For instance, see Dölpopa Sherab Gyaltsen, *Mountain Dharma*, Jo nang dpe tshogs edition, 69–71.
64. For example, see Dölpopa Sherab Gyaltsen, *Mountain Dharma*, Jo nang dpe tshogs edition, 114, Bod kyi gtsug lag gces btus edition, 90. And see *Chanting the Ultimate Names of Mañjuśrī*, v. 98d, Toh 360 Kangyur, rgyud 'bum *ka*, 6a1. The line in this Shong translation reads *thams cad ye shes kun rig mchog*, but Dölpopa quotes from the earlier Rinchen Sangpo translation of *kun shes kun rig dam pa po.*
65. See Dölpopa Sherab Gyaltsen, *Mountain Dharma*, Jo nang dpe tshogs edition, 156, Bod kyi gtsug lag gces btus edition, 126, and Lhai Gyaltsen, *Biography of the Omniscient Dharma Lord of Jonang*, 20b.
66. Dölpopa's major disciple Nya Ön Kunga Pal explains the meaning of this Sanskrit invocation, which Dölpopa used in several of his works. *Oṃ* is an opening expression of homage. In the context of definitive meaning, *oṃ* is the tathāgata essence (*de bzhin gshegs pa'i snying po*), and its position at the beginning of all mantras is to indicate that the sugata essence (*bde gshegs snying po*) pervades all sentient beings. *Guru* in Sanskrit means *heavy*, in the sense of being full of qualities. The main cause of liberation from saṃsāra is the practice of Dharma and the main reason the Buddha appeared in the world was to teach Dharma. A guru or master is considered *heavy* with kindness because such a person teaches Dharma and thus carries out

the enlightened activity of the Buddha. *Buddha* means both awakened from the sleep of ignorance and having a mind that has expanded to encompass everything knowable. A *bodhisattva* is a being (*sattva*) who is intently focused on the ultimate dharmakāya, or enlightenment (*bodhi*). *Bhyo* is the form of the Sanskrit dative plural indicator. Dölpopa intends the first *namo* as an expression of homage and the second *namaḥ* as an expression of offering or worship. See Nya Ön Kunga Pal, *Explanation of the "General Commentary on the Doctrine,"* 47–48.

67. That is, the dharmakāya.
68. *Sūtra of the Tathāgata Essence*, Toh 258 Kangyur, mdo sde *za*, 251a3. For lists of the ten powers, the four types of fearlessness, and the eighteen unshared attributes of a buddha or tathāgata, see Buswell and Lopez 2014, 1070, 1085, and 1092.
69. Maitreya, *Uttaratantra*, 1.112–14, Toh 4024 Tengyur, sems tsam *phi*, 59b6, and Asaṅga, *Commentary on the "Uttaratantra,"* Toh 4025 Tengyur, sems tsam *phi*, 107b2.
70. For the twenty-five modes of cyclic existence (*srid pa nyi shu rtsa lnga*), see Kongtrul 2012, 549–53. Kongtrul's explanation is based almost entirely on Tāranātha, *Ascertainment of the Great Madhyamaka*, 5–9, and the commentary on Tāranātha's verses by his student Khewang Yeshé Gyatso (d. 1632) in *Summarizing Notes of Explanation on "Ascertainment of the Great Madhyamaka,"* 76–87.
71. *Mahāparinirvāṇa Sūtra* (trans. by Lhai Dawa), Toh 120 Kangyur, mdo sde *tha*, 103a2.
72. *Mahāparinirvāṇa Sūtra* (trans. from Chinese), Toh 119 Kangyur, mdo sde *ta*, 209b7.
73. *Dhāraṇī of Penetrating the Nonconceptual*, Toh 142 Kangyur, mdo sde *pa*, 4a1.
74. Dölpopa's annotation in the Jo nang dpe tshogs edition of the Tibetan text identifies "that profound commentary on their intent" as the *Uttaratantra* and Asaṅga's commentary (Rgyud bla rtsa 'grel).
75. Maitreya, *Uttaratantra*, 1.149–50, Toh 4024 Tengyur, sems tsam *phi*, 61b3.
76. Maitreya, *Ornament of the Mahāyāna Sūtras*, 4.4a–c, Toh 4020 Tengyur, sems tsam *phi*, 4a2.
77. These lines are said to be from the lost *Abhidharma Mahāyāna Sūtra*.
78. *Sūtra of the Lion's Roar of Śrīmālā*, Toh 92 Kangyur, dkon brtsegs *cha*, 275a3. The passage in the Tengyur is somewhat different.
79. *Sūtra of the Lion's Roar of Śrīmālā*, Toh 92 Kangyur, dkon brtsegs *cha*, 274b2.
80. *Sūtra of the Lion's Roar of Śrīmālā*, Toh 92 Kangyur, dkon brtsegs *cha*, 274a6.
81. *Sūtra of the Lion's Roar of Śrīmālā*, Toh 92 Kangyur, dkon brtsegs *cha*, 274b5.
82. Asaṅga, *Commentary on the "Uttaratantra,"* Toh 4025 Tengyur, sems tsam *phi*, 111b6–112a5.
83. Maitreya, *Uttaratantra*, 1.53–57, Toh 4024 Tengyur, sems tsam *phi*, 57a3.
84. Asaṅga, *Commentary on the "Uttaratantra,"* Toh 4025 Tengyur, sems tsam *phi*, 98a7. The original source of this quote is *Sūtra Requested by Gaganagañja*, Toh 148 Kangyur, mdo sde *pa*, 321a3.
85. *Sūtra of the Dense Array*, Toh 110 Kangyur, mdo sde *cha*, 55b1.
86. *Sūtra of the Dense Array*, Toh 110 Kangyur, mdo sde *cha*, 55b6.
87. *Tantra of the Ornament of the Vajra Essence* (*Vajramaṇḍalāṃkāra*, *Rdo rje snying po rgyan gyi rgyud*), Toh 490; "Establishing Sublimely Unchanging Primordial Awareness" (*Mchog tu mi 'gyur ba'i ye shes grub pa*) is the third section in the fifth

chapter of Puṇḍarīka's *Stainless Light*, Toh 1327; *Great Commentary of Nāropa* (*Nā ro 'grel chen*) is the short title for *Vajrapādasārasaṃgrahapañjikā*, *Rdo rje'i tshig gi snying po bsdus pa'i dka' 'grel*, Toh 1186; *Chanting the Ultimate Names* is the short name for *Mañjuśrījñānasattvasyaparamārthanāmasaṃgīti*, *'Jam dpal ye shes sems dpa'i don dam pa'i mtshan yang dag par brjod pa*, Toh 360.

88. *Journey to Laṅkā Sūtra*, Toh 107 Kangyur, mdo sde *ca*, 186a6.
89. *Journey to Laṅkā Sūtra*, Toh 107 Kangyur, mdo sde *ca*, 186b1.
90. Asaṅga, *Compendium of Abhidharma*, Toh 4049 Tengyur, sems tsam *ri*, 61b2.
91. The four roots (*rtsa ba bzhi*) are the four basic vows of ordination: to abstain from killing, stealing, lying, and sexual misconduct.
92. *Mahāparinirvāṇa Sūtra* (trans. from Chinese), Toh 119 Kangyur, mdo sde *ta*, 210a2.
93. *Mahāparinirvāṇa Sūtra* (trans. from Chinese), Toh 119 Kangyur, mdo sde *ta*, 209b3.
94. *Sūtra on the Perfection of Wisdom in One Hundred Thousand Lines*, Toh 8 Kangyur, shes phyin *nya*, 339a7.
95. *Journey to Laṅkā Sūtra*, Toh 107 Kangyur, mdo sde *ca*, 112a7.
96. *Sūtra of the Tathāgata Essence*, Toh 258 Kangyur, mdo sde *za*, 248b6.
97. *Hevajra Tantra*, pt. 2, 4.69a–c, Toh 418 Kangyur, rgyud 'bum *nga*, 22a3. In this translation of *Mountain Dharma*, verse numbers in citations from the *Hevajra Tantra* almost always follow the numbering in Snellgrove 1959.
98. *Hevajra Tantra*, pt. 2, 4.73–75, Toh 418 Kangyur, rgyud 'bum *nga*, 22a5.
99. *Hevajra Tantra*, pt. 1, 1.12, Toh 417 Kangyur, rgyud 'bum *nga*, 2a6.
100. *Sampuṭa Tantra*, Toh 381 Kangyur, rgyud 'bum *ga*, 78b3.
101. *Vajra Garland Tantra*, chap. 64, Toh 445 Kangyur, rgyud 'bum *ca*, 270a2.
102. *Chapter of Firm Altruistic Intent*, Toh 224 Kangyur, mdo sde *dza*, 172b2.
103. *Vajra Garland Tantra*, chap. 65, Toh 445 Kangyur, rgyud 'bum *ca*, 271a3.
104. *Tantra of the Arising of Saṃvara*, Toh 373 Kangyur, rgyud 'bum *kha*, 268b3. All these sets of three are explained in Dölpopa's annotations to the verses in the Jo nang dpe tshogs edition of *Mountain Dharma*.
105. *Mahāparinirvāṇa Sūtra* (trans. from Chinese), Toh 119 Kangyur, mdo sde *nya*, 217b2.
106. *Mahāparinirvāṇa Sūtra* (trans. from Chinese), Toh 119 Kangyur, mdo sde *nya*, 48a1.
107. *Mahāparinirvāṇa Sūtra* (trans. from Chinese), Toh 119 Kangyur, mdo sde *nya*, 74a6. The Kangyur text is slightly different, reading *rab tu bde ba* (utter bliss) instead of *rab tu zhi ba* (utter peace), as in the *Mountain Dharma* citation.
108. *Mahāparinirvāṇa Sūtra* (trans. from Chinese), Toh 119 Kangyur, mdo sde *nya*, 48a7.
109. Maitreya, *Uttaratantra*, 1.21, Toh 4024 Tengyur, sems tsam *phi*, 55b6.
110. Maitreya, *Uttaratantra*, 1.96–98, Toh 4024 Tengyur, sems tsam *phi*, 58b7.
111. Maitreya, *Uttaratantra*, 1.129, Toh 4024 Tengyur, sems tsam *phi*, 60b5.
112. Maitreya, *Uttaratantra*, 1.45, Toh 4024 Tengyur, sems tsam *phi*, 56b5.
113. *Sūtra of the Tathāgata Essence*, Toh 258 Kangyur, mdo sde *za*, 248b6.
114. Asaṅga, *Commentary on the "Uttaratantra,"* Toh 4025 Tengyur, sems tsam *phi*, 88a4.

115. *One Hundred and Fifty Modes of the Perfection of Wisdom*, Toh 17 Kangyur, shes phyin *ka*, 137a6.
116. Asaṅga, *Commentary on the "Uttaratantra,"* Toh 4025 Tengyur, sems tsam *phi*, 77a3. See Brunnhölzl 2014, 1066n1144, about possible sūtra sources for this verse.
117. Asaṅga, *Commentary on the "Uttaratantra,"* Toh 4025 Tengyur, sems tsam *phi*, 94b3. The verse is said to be from the lost *Abhidharma Mahāyāna Sūtra*.
118. *Later Guhyasamāja Tantra*, Toh 443 Kangyur, rgyud 'bum *ca*, 150b1.
119. *Later Guhyasamāja Tantra*, Toh 443 Kangyur, rgyud 'bum *ca*, 150a1. The line is somewhat different in the Kangyur text.
120. *Later Guhyasamāja Tantra*, Toh 443 Kangyur, rgyud 'bum *ca*, 150a3. According to Dölpopa's annotations in the Jo nang dpe tshogs edition of *Mountain Dharma*, "five" refers to the five ultimate conquerors and "three" refers to the three vajras (of body, speech, and mind).
121. *Hevajra Tantra*, pt. 1, 5.9–10, Toh 417, Kangyur, rgyud 'bum *nga*, 6a6.
122. *Hevajra Tantra*, pt. 2, 2.58–61, Toh 418, Kangyur, rgyud 'bum *nga*, 16b1.
123. *Chanting the Ultimate Names of Mañjuśrī*, vv. 23–24, Toh 360 Kangyur, rgyud 'bum *ka*, 2b6. All verse numbering for this text follows the edition of Davidson 1981.
124. *Kālacakra Tantra* (Jonang trans.), 5.7, Jo nang dpe tshogs, vol. 17, 163. See also *Kālacakra Tantra* (Shong trans.), 5.7, Toh 362 Kangyur, rgyud 'bum *ka*, 102a4. The five emptinesses (*stong pa lnga*) are the five changeless great emptinesses (*stong pa chen po 'gyur med lnga*) explained in detail in Puṇḍarīka's *Stainless Light*. The key passages from Puṇḍarīka's work are cited later in the *Mountain Dharma*. See also the explanation of these topics (based on Puṇḍarīka's *Stainless Light*) in Kongtrul 2005, 188–97. Briefly, the five changeless great emptinesses are Kālacakra's five "other" aggregates, which are free of the obscurations of the relative five aggregates.
125. *Kālacakra Tantra* (Jonang trans.), 5.5a–c, Jo nang dpe tshogs, vol. 17, 163. See also *Kālacakra Tantra* (Shong trans.), 5.5a–c, Toh 362 Kangyur, rgyud 'bum *ka*, 102a2.
126. *Chanting the Ultimate Names of Mañjuśrī*, v. 93c, Toh 360 Kangyur, rgyud 'bum *ka*, 5b5.
127. *Chanting the Ultimate Names of Mañjuśrī*, v. 67a, Toh 360 Kangyur, rgyud 'bum *ka*, 4b4.
128. *Chanting the Ultimate Names of Mañjuśrī*, v. 67d, Toh 360 Kangyur, rgyud 'bum *ka*, 4b4.
129. Puṇḍarīka, *Stainless Light* (Jonang trans.), chap. 1, Jo nang dpe tshogs, vol. 18, 98. See also Puṇḍarīka, *Stainless Light* (Shong trans.), chap. 1, Toh 1347 Tengyur, rgyud *tha*, 137a7. The information in brackets is from the annotations in the Jonang translation.
130. *Fragment of the Mantra Section of the Glorious Sublime Primal*, Toh 488 Kangyur, rgyud 'bum *ta*, 186b5. The first line is very different in the Kangyur text.
131. *Vajra Garland Tantra*, chap. 43, Toh 445 Kangyur, rgyud 'bum *ca*, 248b2.
132. The *Kālacakra Root Tantra*, or *Sublime Ādibuddha*, is not extant. This quote is found in Puṇḍarīka, *Stainless Light* (Jonang trans.), chap. 1, Jo nang dpe tshogs, vol. 18, 139. See also Puṇḍarīka, *Stainless Light* (Shong trans.), chap. 1, Toh 1347 Tengyur, rgyud *tha*, 151b7.
133. Maitreya, *Ornament of Direct Realization*, 1.39ab, Toh 3786 Tengyur, shes phyin *ka*, 3b2.

134. Bhāvaviveka, *Lamp for the "Wisdom,"* Toh 3853 Tengyur, dbu ma *tsha*, 178a7.
135. *Hevajra Tantra*, pt. 1, 1.7, Toh 417, Kangyur, rgyud 'bum *nga*, 2a3.
136. The *[Hevajra] Root Tantra in Five Hundred Thousand Lines* is not extant. This quote is found in Vajragarbha, *Extensive Commentary on the Condensed Meaning of the Hevajra*, Toh 1180 Tengyur, rgyud *ka*, 9b2.
137. This quote from the lost *Hevajra Root Tantra* is found in Vajragarbha, *Extensive Commentary on the Condensed Meaning of the Hevajra*, Toh 1180 Tengyur, rgyud *ka*, 10a2.
138. Dölpopa has quoted these verses not directly from the *Hevajra Tantra* (translated into Tibetan by Drokmi Shākya Yeshé), but from (Dro Lotsāwa Sherab Drak's translation of) Vajragarbha, *Extensive Commentary on the Condensed Meaning of the Hevajra*, Toh 1180 Tengyur, rgyud *ka*, 8a5. Compare *Hevajra Tantra*, pt. 1, 1.4–5, Toh 417, Kangyur, rgyud 'bum *nga*, 2a1. The lines *byang chub la gnas sems dpa' de/ byang chub sems par brjod par bya*, translated as "That sattva residing in enlightenment is called *bodhisattva*," are not found in the Kangyur text, but they are in the Sanskrit. See Sferra 1999, 19, and Shendge 2004, 17. The remaining lines here are also quite different in the Kangyur text.
139. This quote from the lost *Hevajra Root Tantra* is found in Vajragarbha, *Extensive Commentary on the Condensed Meaning of the Hevajra*, Toh 1180 Tengyur, rgyud *ka*, 8a7.
140. Vajragarbha, *Extensive Commentary on the Condensed Meaning of the Hevajra*, Toh 1180 Tengyur, rgyud *ka*, 9a3.
141. Vajragarbha, *Extensive Commentary on the Condensed Meaning of the Hevajra*, Toh 1180 Tengyur, rgyud *ka*, 9a4.
142. Maitreya, *Ornament of the Mahāyāna Sūtras*, 20.61–62, Toh 4020 Tengyur, sems tsam *phi*, 35a4.
143. Maitreya, *Ornament of the Mahāyāna Sūtras*, 10.37, Toh 4020 Tengyur, sems tsam *phi*, 10a5.
144. *Sūtra on the Perfection of Wisdom in Eight Thousand Lines*, chap. 16, Toh 12 Kangyur, shes phyin *ka*, 170b2.
145. *Vajrapañjara Tantra*, chap. 6, Toh 419 Kangyur, rgyud 'bum *nga*, 43b7. The lines in the Kangyur text are very different than the passage quoted here in *Mountain Dharma.*
146. *Mahāparinirvāṇa Sūtra* (trans. from Chinese), Toh 119 Kangyur, mdo sde *ta*, 209b5.
147. *Mahāparinirvāṇa Sūtra* (trans. from Chinese), Toh 119 Kangyur, mdo sde *ta*, 171b1.
148. *Mahāparinirvāṇa Sūtra* (trans. from Chinese), Toh 119 Kangyur, mdo sde *ta*, 8b2.
149. *Sūtra Taught by Akṣayamati*, Toh 175 Kangyur, mdo sde *ma*, 160b2.
150. Asaṅga, *Commentary on the "Uttaratantra,"* Toh 4025 Tengyur, sems tsam *phi*, 111a1.
151. Vajragarbha, *Extensive Commentary on the Condensed Meaning of the Hevajra*, chap. 3, Toh 1180 Tengyur, rgyud *ka*, 11b4.
152. *Kālacakra Tantra* (Jonang trans.), 2.91cd, Jo nang dpe tshogs, vol. 17, 54. See also *Kālacakra Tantra* (Shong trans.), 2.91cd, Toh 362 Kangyur, rgyud 'bum *ka*, 49a7.

The term "ubiquitous Vajra Bearer of space" (*mkha' khyab mkha' yi rdo rje can*) refers to Vajradhara, or the Ādibuddha.

153. Maitreya, *Ornament of the Mahāyāna Sūtras*, 10.15, Toh 4020 Tengyur, sems tsam *phi*, 9a7.
154. *Sūtra Teaching the Inconceivable Secrets of the Tathāgata*, Toh 47 Kangyur, dkon brtsegs *ka*, 128b4.
155. Maitreya, *Uttaratantra*, 1.49–50, Toh 4024 Tengyur, sems tsam *phi*, 56b7.
156. Maitreya, *Uttaratantra*, 1.52–53, Toh 4024 Tengyur, sems tsam *phi*, 57a2.
157. Maitreya, *Uttaratantra*, 1.62–63, Toh 4024 Tengyur, sems tsam *phi*, 57a7.
158. Maitreya, *Uttaratantra*, 1.47, Toh 4024 Tengyur, sems tsam *phi*, 56b6.
159. Asaṅga, *Commentary on the "Uttaratantra,"* Toh 4025 Tengyur, sems tsam *phi*, 96a6. According to Brunnhölzl 2014, 372, 1088n1326, this quote is from the *Anūnatvāpūrṇatvanirdeśaparivarta* (Taishō 668, 467b). This sūtra was never translated into Tibetan and only survives in one Chinese translation. It is known in Tibetan literature from the various quotations in the *Commentary on the "Uttaratantra."*
160. Asaṅga, *Commentary on the "Uttaratantra,"* Toh 4025 Tengyur, sems tsam *phi*, 97a1. According to Brunnhölzl 2014, 373, 1088 n1327, this quote is also from the *Anūnatvāpūrṇatvanirdeśaparivarta* (Taishō 668, 467b).
161. For example, see *One Hundred and Fifty Modes of the Perfection of Wisdom*, Toh 17 Kangyur, shes phyin *ka*, 137a6.
162. Vasubandhu, *Extensive Commentary on the "Sūtra in One Hundred Thousand Lines,"* Toh 3807 Tengyur, shes phyin *na*, 24b7.
163. Vasubandhu, *Vast Explanation of the "Sūtra in One Hundred Thousand Lines," the "Sūtra in Twenty-Five Thousand Lines," and the "Sūtra in Eighteen Thousand Lines,"* Toh 3808 Tengyur, shes phyin *pha*, 52a3.
164. Vasubandhu, *Vast Explanation of the "Sūtra in One Hundred Thousand Lines," the "Sūtra in Twenty-Five Thousand Lines," and the "Sūtra in Eighteen Thousand Lines,"* Toh 3808 Tengyur, shes phyin *pha*, 219b7.
165. Vasubandhu, *Vast Explanation of the "Sūtra in One Hundred Thousand Lines," the "Sūtra in Twenty-Five Thousand Lines," and the "Sūtra in Eighteen Thousand Lines,"* Toh 3808 Tengyur, shes phyin *pha*, 53b2.
166. Vasubandhu, *Vast Explanation of the "Sūtra in One Hundred Thousand Lines," the "Sūtra in Twenty-Five Thousand Lines," and the "Sūtra in Eighteen Thousand Lines,"* Toh 3808 Tengyur, shes phyin *pha*, 53b4.
167. Vasubandhu, *Vast Explanation of the "Sūtra in One Hundred Thousand Lines," the "Sūtra in Twenty-Five Thousand Lines," and the "Sūtra in Eighteen Thousand Lines,"* Toh 3808 Tengyur, shes phyin *pha*, 151a6.
168. *Verse Summary of the Sūtras on the Perfection of Wisdom*, Toh 13 Kangyur, shes phyin *ka*, 9b6. Here Dölpopa uses the title *Collection of Precious Qualities* (*Yon tan rin chen sdud pa*), which is given as the name of this scripture on its last page.
169. *Verse Summary of the Sūtras on the Perfection of Wisdom*, Toh 13 Kangyur, shes phyin *ka*, 8a5.
170. *Verse Summary of the Sūtras on the Perfection of Wisdom*, Toh 13 Kangyur, shes phyin *ka*, 16a5.
171. According to Dölpopa's annotation in the Jo nang dpe tshogs edition of *Mountain*

Dharma, this refers to beings such as Puṇḍarīka, Vajragarbha, Vajrapāṇi, and Ajita (Maitreya).

172. Puṇḍarīka, *Stainless Light* (Jonang trans.), chap. 1, Jo nang dpe tshogs, vol. 18, 130. See also Puṇḍarīka, *Stainless Light* (Shong trans.), chap. 1, Toh 1347 Tengyur, rgyud *tha*, 148b5. The information in brackets is from Dölpopa's annotations in the Jo nang dpe tshogs edition of *Mountain Dharma*.
173. Quote not located.
174. *Sampuṭa Tantra*, Toh 381 Kangyur, rgyud 'bum *ga*, 79a7. The Tibetan translation in the Kangyur is extremely (sometimes totally) different than the quote here in *Mountain Dharma*. To make any sense of this quote, I have followed Dölpopa's annotations in the Jo nang dpe tshogs edition of *Mountain Dharma* and some of the Kangyur text readings, and have benefited from the translation at 84000 that follows the Sanskrit manuscripts and the Kangyur text.
175. Throughout this translation, the uppercase Sanskrit term "Mahāmudrā" (*phyag rgya chen mo*) refers to the great consort, and the lowercase "mahāmudrā" (*phyag rgya chen po*) refers to direct realization of the nature of reality. In one of his annotations to the *Stainless Light*, Dölpopa refers to Mahāmudrā as Vajradhara's queen (*rdo rje 'chang gi btsun mo*). See Dölpopa Sherab Gyaltsen, *[Annotations to] the First Summary of the Chapter on the Cosmos in the "Stainless Light,"* 3b.
176. *Later Tantra of Direct Expression*, chap. 24, Toh 369 Kangyur, rgyud 'bum *ka*, 304b4.
177. *Hevajra Tantra*, pt. 1, 5.9, Toh 417 Kangyur, rgyud 'bum *nga*, 6a6. The verse quoted here, and the one just below in Vajragarbha's commentary, and previously from the *Hevajra Tantra* itself, were translated by different Tibetan translators, so the Tibetan and the English are slightly different.
178. *Hevajra Tantra*, pt. 1, 5.10, Toh 417 Kangyur, rgyud 'bum *nga*, 6a6.
179. Vajragarbha, *Extensive Commentary on the Condensed Meaning of the Hevajra*, Toh 1180 Tengyur, rgyud *ka*, 43a3.
180. *Tantra of the Secret Drop of the Moon*, chap. 6, Toh 477 Kangyur, rgyud 'bum *ja*, 299a5.
181. *Tantra of the Drop of Primordial Awareness*, chap. 19, Toh 422 Kangyur, rgyud 'bum *nga*, 126a5.
182. *Chanting the Ultimate Names of Mañjuśrī*, v. 33b, Toh 360 Kangyur, rgyud 'bum *ka*, 3a5.
183. *Hevajra Tantra*, pt. 2, 2.32–33, Toh 418 Kangyur, rgyud 'bum *nga*, 15b1.
184. *Mahāparinirvāṇa Sūtra* (trans. from Chinese), Toh 119 Kangyur, mdo sde *ta*, 206b1.
185. *Sūtra of the Excellent Golden Light*, Toh 556 Kangyur, rgyud 'bum *pa*, 167b2.
186. *Journey to Laṅkā Sūtra*, Toh 107 Kangyur, mdo sde *ca*, 181a6.
187. This passage from the *Sūtra Teaching the Nature without Decrease and without Increase* (*'Grib pa med pa dang 'phel ba med pa nyid bstan pa'i mdo*) is quoted in Asaṅga, *Commentary on the "Uttaratantra,"* Toh 4025 Tengyur, sems tsam *phi*, 75a2. The Sanskrit title of the sūtra is *Anūnatvāpūrṇatvanirdeśaparivarta*. It only survives in one Chinese translation and was never translated into Tibetan. According to Brunnhölzl 2014, 1062n1115, the Chinese citation here is Taishō 668, 467a.
188. Maitreya, *Uttaratantra*, 1.25c, Toh 4024 Tengyur, sems tsam *phi*, 56a2.

189. A trichiliocosm is a universe comprised of a thousand groups of a thousand groups of a thousand world systems, each including a Mount Meru, the surrounding four continents, and so on.
190. Asaṅga, *Commentary on the "Uttaratantra,"* chap. 1, Toh 4025 Tengyur, sems tsam *phi*, 86a3. The original source of the long quotation is *Avataṃsaka Sūtra*, chap. 43, Toh 44 Kangyur, phal chen, *ga*, 116b5.
191. See Asaṅga, *Commentary on the "Uttaratantra,"* Toh 4025 Tengyur, sems tsam *phi*, 80b7. The original source is said to be *Sūtra of the Lion's Roar of Śrīmālā* (Toh 92), but these lines were not located in that scripture.
192. *Mahāparinirvāṇa Sūtra* (trans. from Chinese), Toh 119 Kangyur, mdo sde *ta*, 216b4.
193. *Mahāparinirvāṇa Sūtra* (trans. from Chinese), Toh 119 Kangyur, mdo sde *ta*, 89a4.
194. *Mahāparinirvāṇa Sūtra* (trans. from Chinese), Toh 119 Kangyur, mdo sde *ta*, 226a7.
195. Maitreya, *Uttaratantra*, 2.5, Toh 4024 Tengyur, sems tsam *phi*, 62b3. Ajita is another name for Maitreya.
196. The udumvāra lotus is said to blossom only when a buddha appears in the world.
197. *Sūtra to Benefit Aṅgulimāla*, Toh 213 Kangyur, mdo sde *tsha*, 157a4.
198. *Chanting the Ultimate Names of Mañjuśrī*, v. 81c, Toh 360 Kangyur, rgyud 'bum *ka*, 5a5.
199. Asaṅga, *Commentary on the "Uttaratantra,"* Toh 4025 Tengyur, sems tsam *phi*, 76b2. For the sixty types of qualities that purify the basic element of a buddha, which are briefly mentioned in this commentary, see Brunnhölzl 2014, 336. For a detailed explanation of them based on the original description in *Sūtra Requested by Dhāraṇīśvararāja*, see Brunnhölzl 2014, 1067–68nn1145–48.
200. Nāgārjuna, *In Praise of Dharmadhātu*, vv. 1–10, Toh 1118 Tengyur, bstod tshogs *ka*, 63b6.
201. Nāgārjuna, *In Praise of Dharmadhātu*, vv. 18–23, Toh 1118 Tengyur, bstod tshogs *ka*, 64a7.
202. Nāgārjuna, *In Praise of Dharmadhātu*, v. 27, Toh 1118 Tengyur, bstod tshogs *ka*, 64b5.
203. Nāgārjuna, *In Praise of Dharmadhātu*, vv. 36–37, Toh 1118 Tengyur, bstod tshogs *ka*, 65a3.
204. Nāgārjuna, *Condensed Sādhana*, Toh 1796 Tengyur, rgyud *ngi*, 3b4. The text in the Tengyur reads "the ultimate maṇḍala" (*don dam dkyil 'khor*) instead of "ultimate truth" (*don dam bden pa*). But another citation of the same passage in Bhāvaviveka, *Jewel Lamp of the Madhyamaka*, Toh 3854 Tengyur, dbu ma *tsha*, 272a5, says "ultimate truth" (*don dam bden pa*), as in *Mountain Dharma*.
205. These lines from Nāgārjuna, *Condensed Sādhana*, Toh 1796 Tengyur, rgyud *ngi*, 3b3, are cited in Bhāvaviveka, *Jewel Lamp of the Madhyamaka*, Toh 3854 Tengyur, dbu ma *tsha*, 272a4.
206. Āryadeva, *Lamp That Summarizes Conduct*, chap. 7, Toh 1803 Tengyur, rgyud *ngi*, 87a7. The original source of the three verses quoted by Āryadeva has not been identified. The honorific language used to introduce them (*ji skad du gsungs pa'i tshig*) clearly indicates they come from an exalted source and are not by Āryadeva himself. The first two verses are also found in another work attributed to Āryadeva:

Esoteric Instructions on the Stage of Direct Enlightenment, Toh 1806 Tengyur, rgyud *ngi*, 115a7. It seems doubtful, however, that this second work is even by Āryadeva. For a more detailed discussion of this issue, see Wedemeyer 2007, 57–58, 253n4.

207. See Candrakīrti, *Explanation of "Entering the Madhyamaka,"* Toh 3862 Tengyur, dbu ma *'a*, 281a6–282b5.
208. Candrakīrti, *Illuminating Lamp*, chap. 11, Toh 1785 Tengyur, rgyud *ha*, 77a5.
209. Candrakīrti, *Illuminating Lamp*, chap. 9, Toh 1785 Tengyur, rgyud *ha*, 66a1.
210. Candrakīrti, *Explanation of "Entering the Madhyamaka,"* Toh 3862 Tengyur, dbu ma *'a*, 324b2. The verses are originally from Candrakīrti, *Entering the Madhyamaka*, 6.222–23, Toh 3861 Tengyur, dbu ma *'a*, 215a1.
211. Maitreya, *Uttaratantra*, 1.156–57, Toh 4024 Tengyur, sems tsam *phi*, 61b6.
212. Asaṅga, *Commentary on the "Uttaratantra,"* Toh 4025 Tengyur, sems tsam *phi*, 114b6.
213. Maitreya, *Uttaratantra*, 1.158–67, Toh 4024 Tengyur, sems tsam *phi*, 62a1.
214. Maitreya, *Uttaratantra*, 1.95ab, Toh 4024 Tengyur, sems tsam *phi*, 58b6. The ten topics were summarized in an earlier verse in Maitreya, *Uttaratantra*, 1.29, Toh 4024 Tengyur, sems tsam *phi*, 56a4. These ten are: essence, cause, result, function, endowment, manifestation, phases, omnipresence, always unchanging qualities, and indivisibility. Also see Brunnhölzl 2014, 357.
215. Maitreya, *Uttaratantra*, 2.9, Toh 4024 Tengyur, sems tsam *phi*, 62b5.
216. Maitreya, *Uttaratantra*, 1.51cd, Toh 4024 Tengyur, sems tsam *phi*, 57a2.
217. Maitreya, *Uttaratantra*, 4.2, Toh 4024 Tengyur, sems tsam *phi*, 67a7.
218. Maitreya, *Uttaratantra*, 5.25, Toh 4024 Tengyur, sems tsam *phi*, 73a3.
219. See note 5.
220. The text here in *Mountain Dharma* reads *rtag pa byed pa yon tan med pa*, but *Journey to Laṅkā Sūtra*, chap. 2, Toh 107 Kangyur, mdo sde *ca*, 86a3, reads *rtag pa med pa byed pa med pa yon tan med pa*. I have translated according to the *Mountain Dharma* text.
221. *Journey to Laṅkā Sūtra*, chap. 2, Toh 107 Kangyur, mdo sde *ca*, 85b7.
222. *Mahāparinirvāṇa Sūtra* (trans. by Lhai Dawa), chap. 5, Toh 120 Kangyur, mdo sde *tha*, 110a7.
223. Maitreya, *Ornament of the Mahāyāna Sūtras*, 12.54a, Toh 4020 Tengyur, sems tsam *phi*, 15b1.
224. *Journey to Laṅkā Sūtra*, chap. 2, Toh 107 Kangyur, mdo sde *ca*, 58b7.
225. *Journey to Laṅkā Sūtra*, Toh 107 Kangyur, mdo sde *ca*, 186b1.
226. *Journey to Laṅkā Sūtra*, Toh 107 Kangyur, mdo sde *ca*, 186a6.
227. *Vajraśekhara Tantra*, Toh 480 Kangyur, rgyud 'bum *nya*, 148a3.
228. *Vajraśekhara Tantra*, Toh 480 Kangyur, rgyud 'bum *nya*, 161b5.
229. *Vajraśekhara Tantra*, Toh 480 Kangyur, rgyud 'bum *nya*, 154a5.
230. *Vajraśekhara Tantra*, Toh 480 Kangyur, rgyud 'bum *nya*, 189b4.
231. *Tantra Determining the Intent*, chap. 5, Toh 444 Kangyur, rgyud 'bum *ca*, 174b4.
232. *Chanting the Ultimate Names of Mañjuśrī*, v. 115c, Toh 360 Kangyur, rgyud 'bum *ka*, 6b3.
233. *Chanting the Ultimate Names of Mañjuśrī*, Toh 360 Kangyur, rgyud 'bum *ka*, 10a5. This line is not part of a verse.
234. Puṇḍarīka, *Stainless Light* (Jonang trans.), chap. 1, Jo nang dpe tshogs, vol. 18,

169. See also Puṇḍarīka, *Stainless Light* (Shong trans.), chap. 1, Toh 1347 Tengyur, rgyud *tha*, 162b5.
235. *Kālacakra Tantra* (Jonang trans.), 5.66a, Jo nang dpe tshogs, vol. 17, 78. See also *Kālacakra Tantra* (Shong trans.), 5.66a, Toh 362 Kangyur, rgyud 'bum *ka*, 108a3.
236. *Kālacakra Tantra* (Jonang trans.), 5.55b–d, Jo nang dpe tshogs, vol. 17, 174. See also *Kālacakra Tantra* (Shong trans.), 5.55b–d, Toh 362 Kangyur, rgyud 'bum *ka*, 107a2.
237. These lines were not located in *Vajrapañjara Tantra*, Toh 419 Kangyur, rgyud 'bum *nga*. But a very different version was located in *Hevajra Tantra*, pt. 1, 10.8c–10a, Toh 417 Kangyur, rgyud 'bum *nga*, 11b7. Clearly by a different Tibetan translator, but with much the same meaning, the lines are in different order and the last two are missing in the Kangyur text. My translation follows the text in *Mountain Dharma*.
238. *Hevajra Tantra*, pt. 2, 4.45cd–47, Toh 418 Kangyur, rgyud 'bum *nga*, 21a3.
239. *Hevajra Tantra*, pt. 2, 3.24–25ab, Toh 418 Kangyur, rgyud 'bum *nga*, 17b2.
240. *Hevajra Tantra*, pt. 1, 10.10–11b, Toh 417 Kangyur, rgyud 'bum *nga*, 11b7.
241. *Later Tantra of Direct Expression*, chap. 56, Toh 369 Kangyur, rgyud 'bum *ka*, 348b4.
242. *Chanting the Ultimate Names of Mañjuśrī*, vv. 28c–29c, Toh 360 Kangyur, rgyud 'bum *ka*, 3a3. Dölpopa is clearly consulting both the early Tibetan translation of Lochen Rinchen Sangpo and the later revised translation by Shongtön Lodrö Tenpa. In the second line here, the Sanskrit term *akṣara* is translated as *'gyur med* ("changeless"), as in Shongtön Lodrö Tenpa's translation, but the next line follows the earlier Rinchen Sangpo translation for another phrase.
243. *Guhyasamāja Tantra*, chap. 4, Toh 442 Kangyur, rgyud 'bum *ca*, 96b2.
244. *Chanting the Ultimate Names of Mañjuśrī*, v. 30a, Toh 360 Kangyur, rgyud 'bum *ka*, 3a3.
245. *Kālacakra Tantra* (Jonang trans.), 5.102ab, Jo nang dpe tshogs, vol. 17, 187. See also *Kālacakra Tantra* (Shong trans.), 5.102ab, Toh 362 Kangyur, rgyud 'bum *ka*, 111b5.
246. The list of phrases in this paragraph are taken from various places in *Chanting the Ultimate Names of Mañjuśrī*, Toh 360.
247. *Guhyasamāja Tantra*, chap. 8, Toh 442 Kangyur, rgyud 'bum *ca*, 101b7.
248. *Later Guhyasamāja Tantra*, Toh 443 Kangyur, rgyud 'bum *ca*, 150b6.
249. *Later Guhyasamāja Tantra*, Toh 443 Kangyur, rgyud 'bum *ca*, 151a5.
250. *Guhyasamāja Tantra*, chap. 13, Toh 442 Kangyur, rgyud 'bum *ca*, 117a2.
251. *Immaculate Tantra*, Toh 414 Kangyur, rgyud 'bum *ga*, 261a2.
252. Asaṅga, *Compendium of Abhidharma*, Toh 4049 Tengyur, sems tsam *ri*, 76b5. A scriptural source for the Bhagavān's statement has not been identified.
253. *Sūtra of the Great Drum*, Toh 222 Kangyur, mdo sde *dza*, 108b2.
254. The view of the destructible collection (*'jig tshogs lta ba*) is the belief in the five destructible aggregates as being a real "I" and "mine."
255. Campaka was an ancient Indian city. According to Dölpopa's annotation in the Jo nang dpe tshogs edition of *Mountain Dharma*, the residents of Campaka were known for speaking skillfully in ways that seemed contradictory at first, yet were beneficial in the end.
256. *Sūtra of the Great Drum*, Toh 222 Kangyur, mdo sde *dza*, 115b1. The spelling *rab*

gnod in this passage is a mistake for *rab gnon* (*praskandin*, a Sanskrit epithet for a crow). I thank David Reigle for this information.

257. *Sūtra of the Great Drum*, Toh 222 Kangyur, mdo sde *dza*, 104a5.
258. *Sūtra of the Great Drum*, Toh 222 Kangyur, mdo sde *dza*, 108a4.
259. *Mahāparinirvāṇa Sūtra* (trans. from Chinese), Toh 119 Kangyur, mdo sde *nya*, 38a1.
260. *Mahāparinirvāṇa Sūtra* (trans. from Chinese), Toh 119 Kangyur, mdo sde *nya*, 34b2.
261. *Mahāparinirvāṇa Sūtra* (trans. from Chinese), Toh 119 Kangyur, mdo sde *nya*, 33b7.
262. *Mahāparinirvāṇa Sūtra* (trans. from Chinese), Toh 119 Kangyur, mdo sde *nya*, 223b3.
263. *Mahāparinirvāṇa Sūtra* (trans. from Chinese), Toh 119 Kangyur, mdo sde *nya*, 211a4.
264. *Mahāparinirvāṇa Sūtra* (trans. from Chinese), Toh 119 Kangyur, mdo sde *ta*, 146a7.
265. *Mahāparinirvāṇa Sūtra* (trans. from Chinese), Toh 119 Kangyur, mdo sde *nya*, 115a3.
266. *Mahāparinirvāṇa Sūtra* (trans. from Chinese), Toh 119 Kangyur, mdo sde *nya*, 118b1.
267. *Mahāparinirvāṇa Sūtra* (trans. from Chinese), Toh 119 Kangyur, mdo sde *nya*, 118b7.
268. *Mahāparinirvāṇa Sūtra* (trans. from Chinese), Toh 119 Kangyur, mdo sde *ta*, 29a3.
269. *Great Cloud Sūtra*, Toh 232 Kangyur, mdo sde *wa*, 128b1.
270. *Mahāparinirvāṇa Sūtra* (trans. by Lhai Dawa), Toh 120 Kangyur, mdo sde *tha*, 105a5.
271. *Mahāparinirvāṇa Sūtra* (trans. by Lhai Dawa), Toh 120 Kangyur, mdo sde *tha*, 105b1.
272. *Mahāparinirvāṇa Sūtra* (trans. by Lhai Dawa), Toh 120 Kangyur, mdo sde *tha*, 35b5. The four followers (*'khor bzhi po*) are fully ordained monks, fully ordained nuns, male lay disciples, and female lay disciples.
273. *Mahāparinirvāṇa Sūtra* (trans. by Lhai Dawa), Toh 120 Kangyur, mdo sde *tha*, 104a2.
274. *Mahāparinirvāṇa Sūtra* (trans. by Lhai Dawa), Toh 120 Kangyur, mdo sde *tha*, 121b6.
275. The four reliances (*catuḥpratisaraṇa, rton pa bzhi*) are four guidelines or points to be relied on that are emphasized in various Buddhist scriptures and treatises: Rely on the teaching, not the teacher. Rely on the meaning, not the text. Rely on the definitive meaning, not the provisional meaning. Rely on primordial awareness, not consciousness. Dölpopa often signs his works with the pseudonym Possessor of the Four Reliances (Rton pa bzhi ldan).
276. *Tantra of the Drop of Mahāmudrā*, chap. 7, Toh 420 Kangyur, rgyud 'bum *nga*, 71b4.
277. *Vajra Garland Tantra*, chap. 48, Toh 445 Kangyur, rgyud 'bum *ca*, 251b1. The Sanskrit term *ahaṃ* means "I."
278. *Tantra of the Drop of Primordial Awareness*, chap. 21, Toh 422 Kangyur, rgyud 'bum *nga*, 128a2.

279. Maitreya, *Ornament of the Mahāyāna Sūtras*, 10.23, Toh 4020 Tengyur, sems tsam *phi*, 9b4.
280. Vasubandhu, *Explanation of the "Ornament of the Sūtras,"* Toh 4026 Tengyur, sems tsam *phi*, 155a6.
281. Maitreya, *Uttaratantra*, 1.35ab, Toh 4024 Tengyur, sems tsam *phi*, 56a7.
282. Maitreya, *Uttaratantra*, 1.37, Toh 4024 Tengyur, sems tsam *phi*, 56b1.
283. Sūryagupta, *In Praise of Noble Tārā*, Toh 1693 Tengyur, rgyud *sha*, 50b7.
284. *Tantra of the Drop of Mahāmudrā*, chap. 7, Toh 420 Kangyur, rgyud 'bum *nga*, 71a7. The text in the Kangyur is often quite different.
285. This bracketed line in the Kangyur text is missing in the *Mountain Dharma* quote: *a ni yig 'bru mgo bo'i rtser*. The translation of the first two lines here is uncertain.
286. *Tantra of the Drop of Mahāmudrā*, chap. 7, Toh 420 Kangyur, rgyud 'bum *nga*, 71b4. The text in the Kangyur is often very different.
287. *Vajra Garland Tantra*, chap. 48, Toh 445 Kangyur, rgyud 'bum *ca*, 251a5. The first line of this quote seems to include the meaning of two different lines in the Kangyur text. Dölpopa's annotations here in the Jo nang dpe tshogs edition of *Mountain Dharma* note this difference and many more throughout the quote, clearly showing that he was comparing two different Tibetan translations of this tantra.
288. *Tantra of the Drop of Primordial Awareness*, chap. 21, Toh 422 Kangyur, rgyud 'bum *nga*, 128a1.
289. *Tantra of the Drop of Primordial Awareness*, chap. 21, Toh 422 Kangyur, rgyud 'bum *nga*, 128a3.
290. *Hevajra Tantra*, pt. 1, 8.41, Toh 417 Kangyur, rgyud 'bum *nga*, 10a5.
291. *Hevajra Tantra*, pt. 2, 2.39–40a, Toh 418 Kangyur, rgyud 'bum *nga*, 15b5.
292. *Vajrapañjara Tantra*, chap. 14, Toh 419 Kangyur, rgyud 'bum *nga*, 58a1. The passage in the Kangyur is quite different than the quote here in *Mountain Dharma*, apparently from a different Tibetan translation of the tantra.
293. *Vajraśekhara Tantra*, Toh 480 Kangyur, rgyud 'bum *nya*, 154a6.
294. *Vajraśekhara Tantra*, Toh 480 Kangyur, rgyud 'bum *nya*, 189b3.
295. *Vajraśekhara Tantra*, Toh 480 Kangyur, rgyud 'bum *nya*, 189b5.
296. *Vajraśekhara Tantra*, Toh 480 Kangyur, rgyud 'bum *nya*, 189b5.
297. *Vajraśekhara Tantra*, Toh 480 Kangyur, rgyud 'bum *nya*, 189b7.
298. *Vajraśekhara Tantra*, Toh 480 Kangyur, rgyud 'bum *nya*, 190a5.
299. *Vajraśekhara Tantra*, Toh 480 Kangyur, rgyud 'bum *nya*, 190a6.
300. *Vajraśekhara Tantra*, Toh 480 Kangyur, rgyud 'bum *nya*, 190a6.
301. *Vajraśekhara Tantra*, Toh 480 Kangyur, rgyud 'bum *nya*, 190a7.
302. *Vajraśekhara Tantra*, Toh 480 Kangyur, rgyud 'bum *nya*, 190a7.
303. *Vajraśekhara Tantra*, Toh 480 Kangyur, rgyud 'bum *nya*, 190b1.
304. *Vajraśekhara Tantra*, Toh 480 Kangyur, rgyud 'bum *nya*, 190b2.
305. *Vajraśekhara Tantra*, Toh 480 Kangyur, rgyud 'bum *nya*, 190b3.
306. *Vajraśekhara Tantra*, Toh 480 Kangyur, rgyud 'bum *nya*, 190b4.
307. *Vajraśekhara Tantra*, Toh 480 Kangyur, rgyud 'bum *nya*, 190b6.
308. *Vajraśekhara Tantra*, Toh 480 Kangyur, rgyud 'bum *nya*, 190b6.
309. *Vajraśekhara Tantra*, Toh 480 Kangyur, rgyud 'bum *nya*, 190b7.
310. *Vajraśekhara Tantra*, Toh 480 Kangyur, rgyud 'bum *nya*, 190b7. The meaning of these lines remains obscure. The Kangyur text is very different. My translation uses readings from both texts.

311. *Vajraśekhara Tantra*, Toh 480 Kangyur, rgyud 'bum *nya*, 191a1.
312. *Hevajra Tantra*, pt. 1, 10.12, Toh 417 Kangyur, rgyud 'bum *nga*, 12a1.
313. *Sūtra to Benefit Aṅgulimāla*, Toh 213 Kangyur, mdo sde *tsha*, 150b6.
314. *Sūtra to Benefit Aṅgulimāla*, Toh 213 Kangyur, mdo sde *tsha*, 151a3.
315. Rāhulaśrī (Sgra gcan zin dpal) was the Buddha's physical son who later took full ordination and became his disciple. He is also frequently listed as one of the sixteen arhats.
316. Aniruddha (Ma 'gags pa) was the Buddha's first cousin and one of his ten great disciples. He is particularly renowned for having attained the divine eye.
317. *Sūtra to Benefit Aṅgulimāla*, Toh 213 Kangyur, mdo sde *tsha*, 151b4.
318. Nāgārjuna, *In Praise of Dharmadhātu*, v. 17, Toh 1118 Tengyur, bstod tshogs *ka*, 64a7.
319. *Tantra of the Drop of Mahāmudrā*, chap. 6, Toh 420 Kangyur, rgyud 'bum *nga*, 71a2. Some lines in the Kangyur text are very different and are noted by Dölpopa in his annotations in the Jo nang dpe tshogs edition of *Mountain Dharma*. The second to last line is missing in the Kangyur.
320. *Mahāparinirvāṇa Sūtra* (trans. by Lhai Dawa), Toh 120 Kangyur, mdo sde *tha*, 99a5.
321. *Mahāparinirvāṇa Sūtra* (trans. from Chinese), Toh 119 Kangyur, mdo sde *ta*, 83b6.
322. *Mahāparinirvāṇa Sūtra* (trans. by Lhai Dawa), Toh 120 Kangyur, mdo sde *tha*, 110a6.
323. *Chanting the Ultimate Names of Mañjuśrī*, v. 97d, Toh 360 Kangyur, rgyud 'bum *ka*, 5b7.
324. Mañjuśrīyaśas, *Brief Presentation of the Assertions of My Own View*, P 4610 Tengyur, rgyud 'grel *pu*, 22a6. As specifically noted in Chak Lotsāwa Rinchen Chögyal, *Wish-Granting Sheaves*, 389, this work is by Mañjuśrīyaśas, the first Kalkī king of Shambhala. It was translated from Sanskrit into Tibetan for the first time by Dölpopa's major disciple, Kunpang Chödrak Palsang.
325. For example, see Puṇḍarīka, *Stainless Light* (Jonang trans.), chap. 5, Jo nang dpe tshogs, vol. 20, 294. See also Puṇḍarīka, *Stainless Light* (Jonang trans.), chap. 5, Toh 1347 Tengyur, rgyud *da*, 237a2. See the passage from the *Stainless Light* translated on page 349.
326. *Mahāparinirvāṇa Sūtra* (trans. from Chinese), Toh 119 Kangyur, mdo sde *ta*, 88b1.
327. *Mahāparinirvāṇa Sūtra* (trans. from Chinese), Toh 119 Kangyur, mdo sde *nya*, 263b5.
328. *Mahāparinirvāṇa Sūtra* (trans. from Chinese), Toh 119 Kangyur, mdo sde *nya*, 341b3.
329. *Mahāparinirvāṇa Sūtra* (trans. from Chinese), Toh 119 Kangyur, mdo sde *ta*, 87b3.
330. *Sūtra of the Great Drum*, Toh 222 Kangyur, mdo sde *dza*, 110a7.
331. *Sūtra of the Great Drum*, Toh 222 Kangyur, mdo sde *dza*, 109b7.
332. *Kālacakra Tantra* (Jonang trans.), 5.107b–d, Jo nang dpe tshogs, vol. 17, 189. See also *Kālacakra Tantra* (Shong trans.), 5.107b–d, Toh 362 Kangyur, rgyud 'bum *ka*, 112a5.
333. *Kālacakra Tantra* (Jonang trans.), 5.55, Jo nang dpe tshogs, vol. 17, 174. See also *Kālacakra Tantra* (Shong trans.), 5.55, Toh 362 Kangyur, rgyud 'bum *ka*, 107a2.
334. *Kālacakra Tantra* (Jonang trans.), 5.119d, Jo nang dpe tshogs, vol. 17, 191. See also *Kālacakra Tantra* (Shong trans.), 5.119d, Toh 362 Kangyur, rgyud 'bum *ka*, 113b1.

335. Puṇḍarīka, *Stainless Light* (Jonang trans.), chap. 5, Jo nang dpe tshogs, vol. 20, 245. See also Puṇḍarīka, *Stainless Light* (Jonang trans.), chap. 5, Toh 1347 Tengyur, rgyud *da*, 218a2.
336. *Mahāparinirvāṇa Sūtra* (trans. by Lhai Dawa), Toh 120 Kangyur, mdo sde *tha*, 112b2.
337. *Mahāparinirvāṇa Sūtra* (trans. by Lhai Dawa), Toh 120 Kangyur, mdo sde *tha*, 112b6.
338. *Mahāparinirvāṇa Sūtra* (trans. by Lhai Dawa), Toh 120 Kangyur, mdo sde *tha*, 113b7.
339. Vajrapāṇi, *Brief Cakrasaṃvara Commentary*, Toh 1402 Tengyur, rgyud *ba*, 85b1.
340. *Sūtra of the Lion's Roar of Śrīmālā*, Toh 92 Kangyur, dkon brtsegs *cha*, 275a1.
341. *Jewel Cloud Sūtra*, Toh 231 Kangyur, mdo sde *wa*, 99a5.
342. *Sūtra to Benefit Aṅgulimāla*, Toh 213 Kangyur, mdo sde *tsha*, 195a4.
343. Nāgārjuna, *In Praise of Dharmadhātu*, v. 11, Toh 1118 Tengyur, bstod tshogs *ka*, 64a4.
344. Maitreya, *Uttaratantra*, 1.40–41, Toh 4024 Tengyur, sems tsam *phi*, 56b3.
345. *Sūtra of the Lion's Roar of Śrīmālā*, Toh 92 Kangyur, dkon brtsegs *cha*, 274b5.
346. *Sūtra to Benefit Aṅgulimāla*, Toh 213 Kangyur, mdo sde *tsha*, 152b4.
347. *Great Cloud Sūtra*, Toh 232 Kangyur, mdo sde *wa*, 132a7.
348. *Sūtra to Benefit Aṅgulimāla*, Toh 213 Kangyur, mdo sde *tsha*, 155a2.
349. *Sūtra to Benefit Aṅgulimāla*, Toh 213 Kangyur, mdo sde *tsha*, 155a5.
350. *Sūtra of the Great Drum*, Toh 222 Kangyur, mdo sde *dza*, 122a5.
351. Puṇḍarīka, *Stainless Light* (Jonang trans.), chap. 1, Jo nang dpe tshogs, vol. 18, 123. See also Puṇḍarīka, *Stainless Light* (Shong trans.), chap. 1, Toh 1347 Tengyur, rgyud *tha*, 145b7.
352. Maitreya, *Ornament of the Mahāyāna Sūtras*, 10.66cd, Toh 4020 Tengyur, sems tsam *phi*, 11b4.
353. Maitreya, *Uttaratantra*, 1.5a, Toh 4024 Tengyur, sems tsam *phi*, 55a1.
354. *Mahāparinirvāṇa Sūtra* (trans. by Lhai Dawa), Toh 120 Kangyur, mdo sde *tha*, 101b6.
355. *Mahāparinirvāṇa Sūtra* (trans. by Lhai Dawa), Toh 120 Kangyur, mdo sde *tha*, 25a7.
356. *Sūtra Taught by Vimalakīrti*, Toh 176 Kangyur, mdo sde *ma*, 238b3.
357. Puṇḍarīka, *Stainless Light* (Jonang trans.), chap. 3, Jo nang dpe tshogs, vol. 19, 390. See also Puṇḍarīka, *Stainless Light* (Jonang trans.), chap. 3, Toh 1347 Tengyur, rgyud *da*, 154a7.
358. Puṇḍarīka, *Stainless Light* (Jonang trans.), chap. 1, Jo nang dpe tshogs, vol. 18, 102. See also Puṇḍarīka, *Stainless Light* (Shong trans.), chap. 1, Toh 1347 Tengyur, rgyud *tha*, 138b5. The Avīci (Mnar med pa) Hell is the worst of the hell realms described in Buddhism.
359. *Sūtra on the Perfection of Wisdom in One Hundred Thousand Lines*, Toh 8 Kangyur, shes phyin *ta*, 4b7.
360. *Verse Summary of the Sūtras on the Perfection of Wisdom*, Toh 13 Kangyur, shes phyin *ka*, 6b2.
361. *Mahāparinirvāṇa Sūtra* (trans. by Lhai Dawa), Toh 120 Kangyur, mdo sde *tha*, 116a7.

362. Maitreya, *Uttaratantra*, 5.21–24, Toh 4024 Tengyur, sems tsam *phi*, 72b7.
363. Maitreya, *Ornament of the Mahāyāna Sūtras*, 2.8, Toh 4020 Tengyur, sems tsam *phi*, 2b3.
364. Maitreya, *Ornament of the Mahāyāna Sūtras*, 2.11, Toh 4020 Tengyur, sems tsam *phi*, 2b6.
365. Maitreya, *Ornament of the Mahāyāna Sūtras*, 2.9, Toh 4020 Tengyur, sems tsam *phi*, 2b4.
366. Maitreya, *Ornament of the Mahāyāna Sūtras*, 2.14, Toh 4020 Tengyur, sems tsam *phi*, 3a1.
367. Asaṅga, *Compendium of Abhidharma*, chap. 3, Toh 4049 Tengyur, sems tsam *ri*, 104b3.
368. Asaṅga, *Compendium of Abhidharma*, Toh 4049 Tengyur, sems tsam *ri*, 104b3. Asaṅga has quoted this last passage from *Sūtra of Cultivating Faith in the Mahāyāna*, chap. 2, Toh 144 Kangyur, mdo sde *pa*, 17b3. The passage quoted by Asaṅga is very different than in the Kangyur text of the sūtra. *Dharma Discourse of the Great Mirror of Dharma* (*Chos kyi me long chen po'i chos kyi rnam grangs*) is an alternate title for *Sūtra of Cultivating Faith in the Mahāyāna.*
369. *Mahāparinirvāṇa Sūtra* (trans. from Chinese), Toh 119 Kangyur, mdo sde *nya*, 151b4.
370. *Mahāparinirvāṇa Sūtra* (trans. from Chinese), Toh 119 Kangyur, mdo sde *nya*, 226b4.
371. *Mahāparinirvāṇa Sūtra* (trans. from Chinese), Toh 119 Kangyur, mdo sde *nya*, 291b1.
372. *Mahāparinirvāṇa Sūtra* (trans. from Chinese), Toh 119 Kangyur, mdo sde *nya*, 153a7.
373. *Mahāparinirvāṇa Sūtra* (trans. by Lhai Dawa), Toh 120 Kangyur, mdo sde *tha*, 112a1.
374. *Mahāparinirvāṇa Sūtra* (trans. by Lhai Dawa), Toh 120 Kangyur, mdo sde *tha*, 120a3.
375. *Sūtra to Benefit Aṅgulimāla*, Toh 213 Kangyur, mdo sde *tsha*, 156b5.
376. *Sūtra to Benefit Aṅgulimāla*, Toh 213 Kangyur, mdo sde *tsha*, 148b7.
377. Nārada (Mi sbyin) was a famous South Indian seer who appears in the *Rāmāyaṇa* and is said to have written the first judicial text.
378. *Sūtra to Benefit Aṅgulimāla*, Toh 213 Kangyur, mdo sde *tsha*, 167b4.
379. *Sūtra to Benefit Aṅgulimāla*, Toh 213 Kangyur, mdo sde *tsha*, 200a6.
380. *Sūtra to Benefit Aṅgulimāla*, Toh 213 Kangyur, mdo sde *tsha*, 200b2.
381. *Sūtra to Benefit Aṅgulimāla*, Toh 213 Kangyur, mdo sde *tsha*, 189a3.
382. *Sūtra to Benefit Aṅgulimāla*, Toh 213 Kangyur, mdo sde *tsha*, 200a3. The meaning of the phrase *dngos po chen po brgyad*, translated as "eight great concerns," remains obscure. Jeffrey Hopkins has speculated that it might refer to the eight worldly concerns (*'jig rten chos brgyad*): liking/disliking, gain/loss, praise/blame, fame/disgrace. See Döl-bo-ba Shay-rap-gyel-tsen 2006, 174na.
383. *Sūtra to Benefit Aṅgulimāla*, Toh 213 Kangyur, mdo sde *tsha*, 156b3.
384. *Sūtra to Benefit Aṅgulimāla*, Toh 213 Kangyur, mdo sde *tsha*, 157a2.
385. Trāyastriṃśa (Sum cu rtsa gsum pa), or the Heaven of the Thirty-Three, is the

second lowest of the six heavens of the desire realm. Brahmārāja (Tshangs pa'i rgyal po) is the chief deity in the Mahābrahmā realm.

386. *Mahāparinirvāṇa Sūtra* (trans. from Chinese), Toh 119 Kangyur, mdo sde *nya*, 25a4.
387. *Mahāparinirvāṇa Sūtra* (trans. from Chinese), Toh 119 Kangyur, mdo sde *nya*, 89b2.
388. *Mahāparinirvāṇa Sūtra* (trans. from Chinese), Toh 119 Kangyur, mdo sde *ta*, 140a4.
389. All the Tibetan texts of *Mountain Dharma* give the title here as Bhāvaviveka's *Lamp for the "Wisdom"* (*Shes rab sgon ma*), but the passage was actually located in Bhāvaviveka, *Jewel Lamp of the Madhyamaka*, Toh 3854 Tengyur, dbu ma *tsha*, 288b6.
390. *Sūtra Teaching the Inconceivable Qualities and Primordial Awareness of the Tathāgata*, Toh 185 Kangyur, mdo sde *tsa*, 143a3.
391. *Great Cloud Sūtra*, Toh 232 Kangyur, mdo sde *wa*, 124a3.
392. *Great Cloud Sūtra*, Toh 232 Kangyur, mdo sde *wa*, 124b3.
393. *Great Cloud Sūtra*, Toh 232 Kangyur, mdo sde *wa*, 128b1.
394. *Great Cloud Sūtra*, Toh 232 Kangyur, mdo sde *wa*, 131a5. The Kangyur text is somewhat different.
395. *Great Cloud Sūtra*, Toh 232 Kangyur, mdo sde *wa*, 179b5.
396. Maitreya, *Uttaratantra*, 5.1–6, Toh 4024 Tengyur, sems tsam *phi*, 71b7.
397. The conjectured Sanskrit name Sadāpramuktaraśmi has been taken from Zimmerman 2002, 156. The name in Tibetan is Rtag tu 'od zer gtong (Always Emitting Light).
398. *Sūtra of the Tathāgata Essence*, Toh 258 Kangyur, mdo sde *za*, 258a1. The previous paragraph closely summarizes the *Tathāgatagarbha Sūtra* passage translated in Zimmerman 2002, 156–57.
399. *Sūtra of the Tathāgata Essence*, Toh 258 Kangyur, mdo sde *za*, 258b5.
400. *Mahāparinirvāṇa Sūtra* (trans. from Chinese), Toh 119 Kangyur, mdo sde *nya*, 226b4.
401. *Mahāparinirvāṇa Sūtra* (trans. from Chinese), Toh 119 Kangyur, mdo sde *nya*, 227a7.
402. *Mahāparinirvāṇa Sūtra* (trans. from Chinese), Toh 119 Kangyur, mdo sde *nya*, 157a1.
403. *Sūtra to Benefit Aṅgulimāla*, Toh 213 Kangyur, mdo sde *tsha*, 150a3.
404. *Sūtra to Benefit Aṅgulimāla*, Toh 213 Kangyur, mdo sde *tsha*, 158a2.
405. *Sūtra to Benefit Aṅgulimāla*, Toh 213 Kangyur, mdo sde *tsha*, 158a1.
406. *Sūtra of the Great Drum*, Toh 222 Kangyur, mdo sde *dza*, 92a1.
407. *Sūtra of the Great Drum*, Toh 222 Kangyur, mdo sde *dza*, 89b7.
408. *Sūtra of the Great Drum*, Toh 222 Kangyur, mdo sde *dza*, 122b1.
409. *Sūtra of the Great Drum*, Toh 222 Kangyur, mdo sde *dza*, 122b4. The Sanskrit for two of these Indian names is uncertain. The Tibetan transcription of Kayori (spelled *ka yo ri* in the Kangyur text, instead of the *kar yo ri* in *Mountain Dharma*) has been used for the name of the family line. The name Mahāmālā has been tentatively used for the Tibetan *phreng ba chen po*, although it has not been found in any Sanskrit source.
410. *Sūtra of the Great Drum*, Toh 222 Kangyur, mdo sde *dza*, 122b4.

411. *Sūtra of the Great Drum*, Toh 222 Kangyur, mdo sde *dza*, 123a5.
412. *Sūtra of the Great Drum*, Toh 222 Kangyur, mdo sde *dza*, 121a3.
413. *Great Cloud Sūtra*, Toh 232 Kangyur, mdo sde *wa*, 136b5.
414. *Sūtra Teaching the Great Compassion of the Tathāgata*, Toh 147 Kangyur, mdo sde *pa*, 202a7.
415. Maitreya, *Uttaratantra*, 1.15cd, Toh 4024 Tengyur, sems tsam *phi*, 55b3.
416. Nāgārjuna, *In Praise of Dharmadhātu*, v. 8cd, Toh 1118 Tengyur, bstod tshogs *ka*, 64a2.
417. Puṇḍarīka, *Stainless Light* (Jonang trans.), chap. 5, Jo nang dpe tshogs, vol. 20, 294. See also Puṇḍarīka, *Stainless Light* (Jonang trans.), chap. 5, Toh 1347 Tengyur, rgyud *da*, 237a6.
418. *Chanting the Ultimate Names of Mañjuśrī*, v. 99a, Toh 360 Kangyur, rgyud 'bum *ka*, 6a1.
419. *Chanting the Ultimate Names of Mañjuśrī*, v. 85c, Toh 360 Kangyur, rgyud 'bum *ka*, 5a7.
420. *Chanting the Ultimate Names of Mañjuśrī*, v. 137ab, Toh 360 Kangyur, rgyud 'bum *ka*, 7b2.
421. *Chanting the Ultimate Names of Mañjuśrī*, v. 98ab, Toh 360 Kangyur, rgyud 'bum *ka*, 5b7.
422. *Vajrapañjara Tantra*, chap. 14, Toh 419 Kangyur, rgyud 'bum *nga*, 58a4. The line in the Kangyur is quite different. Dölpopa apparently used a different Tibetan translation of the tantra.
423. *Tantra That Utterly Purifies All Lower Realms*, Toh 483 Kangyur, rgyud 'bum *ta*, 95a7.
424. *Sūtra of the Ratnaketu Dhāraṇī*, Toh 138 Kangyur, mdo sde *na*, 195b4.
425. *Chanting the Ultimate Names of Mañjuśrī*, v. 155a, Toh 360 Kangyur, rgyud 'bum *ka*, 8a6. The words in brackets here and when quoted later are from the commentary by Dölpopa's disciple Manchukhawa Lodrö Gyaltsen, *Result of Stainless Light*, Jo nang dpe tshogs edition, 331.
426. *Chanting the Ultimate Names of Mañjuśrī*, v. 98d, Toh 360 Kangyur, rgyud 'bum *ka*, 6a1. The Shong translation in the Kangyur reads *thams cad ye shes kun rig mchog*, but Dölpopa quotes from the earlier Rinchen Sangpo translation of *kun shes kun rig dam pa po*.
427. *Chanting the Ultimate Names of Mañjuśrī*, v. 58c, Toh 360 Kangyur, rgyud 'bum *ka*, 4a6.
428. *Chanting the Ultimate Names of Mañjuśrī*, v. 59b, Toh 360 Kangyur, rgyud 'bum *ka*, 4a6.
429. *Chanting the Ultimate Names of Mañjuśrī*, v. 99b, Toh 360 Kangyur, rgyud 'bum *ka*, 6a1.
430. *Chanting the Ultimate Names of Mañjuśrī*, v. 44c, Toh 360 Kangyur, rgyud 'bum *ka*, 3b5.
431. *Chanting the Ultimate Names of Mañjuśrī*, v. 44d, Toh 360 Kangyur, rgyud 'bum *ka*, 3b5.
432. Maitreya, *Uttaratantra*, 1.155, Toh 4024 Tengyur, sems tsam *phi*, 61b6.
433. Maitreya, *Uttaratantra*, 1.154ab, Toh 4024 Tengyur, sems tsam *phi*, 61b5.
434. *Chanting the Ultimate Names of Mañjuśrī*, v. 57, Toh 360 Kangyur, rgyud 'bum *ka*, 4a5.

435. *Chanting the Ultimate Names of Mañjuśrī*, v. 42ab, Toh 360 Kangyur, rgyud 'bum *ka*, 3b3.
436. *Chanting the Ultimate Names of Mañjuśrī*, v. 45b, Toh 360 Kangyur, rgyud 'bum *ka*, 3b5.
437. *Chanting the Ultimate Names of Mañjuśrī*, vv. 58d–59a, Toh 360 Kangyur, rgyud 'bum *ka*, 4a6.
438. *Chanting the Ultimate Names of Mañjuśrī*, v. 151d, Toh 360 Kangyur, rgyud 'bum *ka*, 8a4.
439. *Chanting the Ultimate Names of Mañjuśrī*, v. 48c, Toh 360 Kangyur, rgyud 'bum *ka*, 3b7.
440. *Chanting the Ultimate Names of Mañjuśrī*, v. 55c, Toh 360 Kangyur, rgyud 'bum *ka*, 4a4.
441. *Chanting the Ultimate Names of Mañjuśrī*, v. 64a, Toh 360 Kangyur, rgyud 'bum *ka*, 4b2.
442. *Chanting the Ultimate Names of Mañjuśrī*, v. 78c, Toh 360 Kangyur, rgyud 'bum *ka*, 5a3.
443. *Chanting the Ultimate Names of Mañjuśrī*, v. 81c, Toh 360 Kangyur, rgyud 'bum *ka*, 5a5.
444. *Chanting the Ultimate Names of Mañjuśrī*, v. 83b, Toh 360 Kangyur, rgyud 'bum *ka*, 5a6.
445. *Chanting the Ultimate Names of Mañjuśrī*, v. 114d, Toh 360 Kangyur, rgyud 'bum *ka*, 6b3.
446. *Chanting the Ultimate Names of Mañjuśrī*, v. 10b, Toh 360 Kangyur, rgyud 'bum *ka*, 2a4.
447. *Chanting the Ultimate Names of Mañjuśrī*, v. 100d, Toh 360 Kangyur, rgyud 'bum *ka*, 6a2.
448. *Chanting the Ultimate Names of Mañjuśrī*, v. 110d, Toh 360 Kangyur, rgyud 'bum *ka*, 6b1.
449. *Chanting the Ultimate Names of Mañjuśrī*, v. 141d, Toh 360 Kangyur, rgyud 'bum *ka*, 7b5.
450. *Chanting the Ultimate Names of Mañjuśrī*, v. 143b, Toh 360 Kangyur, rgyud 'bum *ka*, 7b6.
451. *Chanting the Ultimate Names of Mañjuśrī*, v. 28b, Toh 360 Kangyur, rgyud 'bum *ka*, 3a2.
452. *Chanting the Ultimate Names of Mañjuśrī*, v. 110a, Toh 360 Kangyur, rgyud 'bum *ka*, 6a7.
453. *Chanting the Ultimate Names of Mañjuśrī*, v. 149b, Toh 360 Kangyur, rgyud 'bum *ka*, 8a2.
454. *Chanting the Ultimate Names of Mañjuśrī*, v. 115c, Toh 360 Kangyur, rgyud 'bum *ka*, 6b3.
455. *Chanting the Ultimate Names of Mañjuśrī*, v. 108a, Toh 360 Kangyur, rgyud 'bum *ka*, 6a6.
456. *Sūtra of the Tathāgata Essence*, Toh 258 Kangyur, mdo sde *za*, 249b6.
457. *Tantra That Utterly Purifies All Lower Realms*, Toh 483 Kangyur, rgyud 'bum *ta*, 95a7.
458. *Sūtra of the Tathāgata Essence*, Toh 258 Kangyur, mdo sde *za*, 248b6.
459. *Vajrapañjara Tantra*, chap. 14, Toh 419 Kangyur, rgyud 'bum *nga*, 58a4.

460. *Sūtra of the Tathāgata Essence*, Toh 258 Kangyur, mdo sde *za*, 250a2.
461. *Sūtra of the Tathāgata Essence*, Toh 258 Kangyur, mdo sde *za*, 251a1.
462. Nāgārjuna, *Root Verses on Madhyamaka, Called "Wisdom,"* 15.2cd and 8cd, Toh 3824 Tengyur, dbu ma *tsa*, 8b5.
463. Nāgārjuna, *Root Verses on Madhyamaka, Called "Wisdom,"* 15.1cd, Toh 3824 Tengyur, dbu ma *tsa*, 8b5.
464. Dharmakīrti, *Commentary on Valid Cognition*, chap. 2, v. 210, Toh 4210 Tengyur, tshad ma *ce*, 115b2.
465. *Sūtra of the Tathāgata Essence*, Toh 258 Kangyur, mdo sde *za*, 254a5.
466. Maitreya, *Uttaratantra*, 1.26, Toh 4024 Tengyur, sems tsam *phi*, 56a2.
467. *Sūtra Teaching the Purification of Infinite Gateways*, Toh 46 Kangyur, dkon brtsegs *ka*, 68b7.
468. *Hevajra Tantra*, pt. 1, 9.2, Toh 417 Kangyur, rgyud 'bum *nga*, 10b7. Dölpopa's annotation in the Jo nang dpe tshogs edition of *Mountain Dharma* specifies that the aggregates and so on mentioned in the first sentence are those of the ultimate Hevajra (*don dam kye'i rdo rje*).
469. *Hevajra Tantra*, pt. 1, 9.18b, Toh 417 Kangyur, rgyud 'bum *nga*, 11b1.
470. *Hevajra Tantra*, pt. 1, 9.18d, Toh 417 Kangyur, rgyud 'bum *nga*, 11b2.
471. *Hevajra Tantra*, pt. 2, 2.48cd, Toh 418 Kangyur, rgyud 'bum *nga*, 16a3.
472. *Hevajra Tantra*, pt. 2, 4.78cd, Toh 418 Kangyur, rgyud 'bum *nga*, 22a7.
473. These lines from the lost *Kālacakra Root Tantra* (also known as the *Glorious Ādibuddha*) are quoted in Puṇḍarīka, *Stainless Light* (Jonang trans.), chap. 5, Jo nang dpe tshogs, vol. 20, 339. See also Puṇḍarīka, *Stainless Light* (Jonang trans.), chap. 5, Toh 1347 Tengyur, rgyud *da*, 254a7.
474. The Mahāyāna Collection of Reasoning (*Dbu ma rigs pa'i tshogs*) is a set of six works by Nāgārjuna: *Root Verses on Madhyamaka, Called "Wisdom"* (Toh 3824), *Garland of Jewels* (Toh 4158), *Refutation of Objections* (Toh 3828), *Seventy Verses on Emptiness* (Toh 3827), *Treatise Called "The Finely Woven"* (Toh 95), and *Sixty Verses on Reasoning* (Toh 3825).
475. *Sūtra on the Perfection of Wisdom in One Hundred Thousand Lines*, Toh 8 Kangyur, shes phyin *ka*, 160a1.
476. *Sūtra on the Perfection of Wisdom in Twenty-Five Thousand Lines*, Toh 9 Kangyur, shes phyin *ka*, 156b4.
477. *Sūtra on the Perfection of Wisdom in Twenty-Five Thousand Lines*, Toh 9 Kangyur, shes phyin *ga*, 179b4.
478. *Diamond Cutter Sūtra on the Perfection of Wisdom*, Toh 16 Kangyur, shes phyin *ka*, 123a3.
479. *Verse Summary of the Sūtras on the Perfection of Wisdom*, chap. 1, Toh 13 Kangyur, shes phyin *ka*, 4a3.
480. *Verse Summary of the Sūtras on the Perfection of Wisdom*, chap. 1, Toh 13 Kangyur, shes phyin *ka*, 3a7.
481. *Verse Summary of the Sūtras on the Perfection of Wisdom*, chap. 1, Toh 13 Kangyur, shes phyin *ka*, 2a6.
482. *Verse Summary of the Sūtras on the Perfection of Wisdom*, chap. 1, Toh 13 Kangyur, shes phyin *ka*, 2b4.
483. *Sūtra on the Perfection of Wisdom in One Hundred Thousand Lines*, Toh 8 Kangyur,

shes phyin *ta*, 41b3. The passage here is actually Dölpopa's concise summary of a longer section in the Kangyur text.

484. The passage here also seems to be Dölpopa's concise summary of a longer section, but the exact source has not been located.
485. Vasubandhu, *Vast Explanation of the "Sūtra in One Hundred Thousand Lines," the "Sūtra in Twenty-Five Thousand Lines," and the "Sūtra in Eighteen Thousand Lines,"* Toh 3808 Tengyur, shes phyin *pha*, 252a1.
486. *Sūtra Teaching the Great Compassion of the Tathāgata*, Toh 147 Kangyur, mdo sde *pa*, 215b1. The text in the Kangyur is extremely different than the passage quoted here in *Mountain Dharma*. The translation follows the *Mountain Dharma* version, with some help from the Kangyur text.
487. *Sūtra of Definitive Commentary on the Intent*, chap. 7, Toh 106 Kangyur, mdo sde *ca*, 24b5.
488. Tripiṭakamāla, *Lamp of the Three Ways*, Toh 3707 Tengyur, rgyud *tsu*, 16b3. The full verse says: "Although the meaning is the same, because they are free of delusion, have many methods, no difficulties, and are for those with sharp faculties, the mantra treatises are exceptional."
489. Dignāga, *Verse Summary of the "Perfection of Wisdom,"* Toh 3809 Tengyur, shes phyin *pha*, 292b4.
490. Quote not located.
491. *Sūtra to Benefit Aṅgulimāla*, Toh 213 Kangyur, mdo sde *tsha*, 159b1. In Buddhist literature, the term *nirgrantha* (*gcer bu pa*) often refers to members of the Jain religion, but it can also refer to members of any other "naked ascetic" order.
492. *Sūtra to Benefit Aṅgulimāla*, Toh 213 Kangyur, mdo sde *tsha*, 160b1.
493. *Sūtra to Benefit Aṅgulimāla*, Toh 213 Kangyur, mdo sde *tsha*, 160a1.
494. *Sūtra to Benefit Aṅgulimāla*, Toh 213 Kangyur, mdo sde *tsha*, 160a2.
495. See *Sūtra to Benefit Aṅgulimāla*, Toh 213 Kangyur, mdo sde *tsha*, 204a1. Concerning this passage in the sūtra and possible Sanskrit names for the buddha and his buddhafield, see Jones 2021, 217.
496. *Mahāparinirvāṇa Sūtra* (trans. from Chinese), Toh 119 Kangyur, mdo sde *nya*, 82b4.
497. Quote not located.
498. *Mahāparinirvāṇa Sūtra* (trans. from Chinese), Toh 119 Kangyur, mdo sde *ta*, 280a7.
499. *Mahāparinirvāṇa Sūtra* (trans. from Chinese), Toh 119 Kangyur, mdo sde *ta*, 272a4.
500. Vajrapāṇi, *Brief Cakrasaṃvara Commentary*, Toh 1402 Tengyur, rgyud *ba*, 136b6.
501. *Chanting the Ultimate Names of Mañjuśrī*, v. 144cd, Toh 360 Kangyur, rgyud 'bum *ka*, 7b7.
502. *Chanting the Ultimate Names of Mañjuśrī*, v. 97c, Toh 360 Kangyur, rgyud 'bum *ka*, 5b7.
503. *Chanting the Ultimate Names of Mañjuśrī*, v. 45d, Toh 360 Kangyur, rgyud 'bum *ka*, 3b5.
504. *Chanting the Ultimate Names of Mañjuśrī*, v. 109a, Toh 360 Kangyur, rgyud 'bum *ka*, 6a7.
505. *Chanting the Ultimate Names of Mañjuśrī*, v. 28c, Toh 360 Kangyur, rgyud 'bum *ka*, 3a2.

506. *Chanting the Ultimate Names of Mañjuśrī*, v. 116a, Toh 360 Kangyur, rgyud 'bum *ka*, 6b3.
507. *Chanting the Ultimate Names of Mañjuśrī*, v. 79a, Toh 360 Kangyur, rgyud 'bum *ka*, 5a4.
508. Asaṅga, *Compendium of Abhidharma*, Toh 4049 Tengyur, sems tsam *ri*, 76b3.
509. Asaṅga, *Compendium of Abhidharma*, Toh 4049 Tengyur, sems tsam *ri*, 76b3.
510. Asaṅga, *Compendium of Abhidharma*, Toh 4049 Tengyur, sems tsam *ri*, 76b3.
511. Maitreya, *Ornament of the Mahāyāna Sūtras*, 15.34, Toh 4020 Tengyur, sems tsam *phi*, 20a2.
512. Maitreya, *Distinguishing the Middle and the Extremes*, 3.3a–c, Toh 4021 Tengyur, sems tsam *phi*, 42a4.
513. Asaṅga, *Compendium of Abhidharma*, Toh 4049 Tengyur, sems tsam *ri*, 76b6.
514. Maitreya, *Distinguishing Phenomena and True Nature*, Toh 4023 Tengyur, sems tsam *phi*, 50b6.
515. Maitreya, *Ornament of the Mahāyāna Sūtras*, 20.53, Toh 4020 Tengyur, sems tsam *phi*, 34b6.
516. Maitreya, *Ornament of the Mahāyāna Sūtras*, 20.54ab, Toh 4020 Tengyur, sems tsam *phi*, 34b7.
517. Maitreya, *Ornament of the Mahāyāna Sūtras*, 12.14, Toh 4020 Tengyur, sems tsam *phi*, 13b5.
518. *Chanting the Ultimate Names of Mañjuśrī*, v. 57c, Toh 360 Kangyur, rgyud 'bum *ka*, 4a5.
519. Maitreya, *Ornament of the Mahāyāna Sūtras*, 7.1, Toh 4020 Tengyur, sems tsam *phi*, 6a7.
520. Maitreya, *Distinguishing the Middle and the Extremes*, 1.13c, Toh 4021 Tengyur, sems tsam *phi*, 41a1.
521. Vasubandhu, *Extensive Commentary on the "Sūtra in One Hundred Thousand Lines,"* Toh 3807 Tengyur, shes phyin *na*, 32a3.
522. Vasubandhu, *Extensive Commentary on the "Sūtra in One Hundred Thousand Lines,"* Toh 3807 Tengyur, shes phyin *na*, 107a6.
523. Vasubandhu, *Extensive Commentary on the "Sūtra in One Hundred Thousand Lines,"* Toh 3807 Tengyur, shes phyin *na*, 107b3.
524. Vasubandhu, *Extensive Commentary on the "Sūtra in One Hundred Thousand Lines,"* Toh 3807 Tengyur, shes phyin *na*, 178b2.
525. Vasubandhu, *Vast Explanation of the "Sūtra in One Hundred Thousand Lines," the "Sūtra in Twenty-Five Thousand Lines," and the "Sūtra in Eighteen Thousand Lines,"* Toh 3808 Tengyur, shes phyin *pha*, 206a5.
526. See Vasubandhu, *Vast Explanation of the "Sūtra in One Hundred Thousand Lines," the "Sūtra in Twenty-Five Thousand Lines," and the "Sūtra in Eighteen Thousand Lines,"* Toh 3808 Tengyur, shes phyin *pha*, 95b7 and 96a4.
527. Maitreya, *Uttaratantra*, 1.154–55, Toh 4024 Tengyur, sems tsam *phi*, 61b6.
528. *Sūtra of the Lion's Roar of Śrīmālā*, Toh 92 Kangyur, dkon brtsegs *cha*, 272a7–272b1.
529. Asaṅga, *Commentary on the "Uttaratantra,"* Toh 4025 Tengyur, sems tsam *phi*, 113b6.
530. *Mahāparinirvāṇa Sūtra* (trans. from Chinese), Toh 119 Kangyur, mdo sde *nya*, 260a3.

531. *Mahāparinirvāṇa Sūtra* (trans. from Chinese), Toh 119 Kangyur, mdo sde *ta*, 226a7.
532. Nāgārjuna, *Root Verses on Madhyamaka, Called "Wisdom,"* 24.9, Toh 3824 Tengyur, dbu ma *tsa*, 15a1.
533. *Journey to Laṅkā Sūtra*, Toh 107 Kangyur, mdo sde *ca*, 85a5.
534. *Journey to Laṅkā Sūtra*, Toh 107 Kangyur, mdo sde *ca*, 85a.
535. *Journey to Laṅkā Sūtra*, Toh 107 Kangyur, mdo sde *ca*, 85a1.
536. *Mahāparinirvāṇa Sūtra* (trans. from Chinese), Toh 119 Kangyur, mdo sde *nya*, 261a6.
537. Here Dölpopa refers to an important difference between two Tibetan translations of Puṇḍarīka's *Stainless Light*. Dölpopa's disciples Jonang Lotsāwa Lodrö Pal and Mati Paṇchen Lodrö Gyaltsen often translated the Sanskrit term *akṣara* as *'gyur med* ("changeless"), but Shongtön Dorjé Gyaltsen had previously translated the same term as *yi ge* ("syllable"). The Sanskrit term has both meanings. For an example of Shongtön's translation as *stong pa chen po yi ge lnga* ("the five syllables of the great emptinesses"), see Puṇḍarīka, *Stainless Light* (Shong trans.), chap. 1, Toh 1347 Tengyur, rgyud *tha*, 150a5. For an example of the Jonang translation of the same Sanskrit phrase as *stong pa chen po 'gyur med lnga* ("the five changeless great emptinesses"), see Puṇḍarīka, *Stainless Light* (Jonang trans.), chap. 1, Jo nang dpe tshogs, vol. 18, 134.
538. Vajrapāṇi, *Brief Cakrasaṃvara Commentary*, Toh 1402 Tengyur, rgyud *ba*, 136b6.
539. Vajrapāṇi, *Brief Cakrasaṃvara Commentary*, Toh 1402 Tengyur, rgyud *ba*, 124b1.
540. Puṇḍarīka, *Stainless Light* (Jonang trans.), chap. 1, Jo nang dpe tshogs, vol. 18, 169. See also Puṇḍarīka, *Stainless Light* (Shong trans.), chap. 1, Toh 1347 Tengyur, rgyud *tha*, 162b6.
541. Puṇḍarīka, *Stainless Light* (Jonang trans.), chap. 1, Jo nang dpe tshogs, vol. 18, 170. See also Puṇḍarīka, *Stainless Light* (Shong trans.), chap. 1, Toh 1347 Tengyur, rgyud *tha*, 162b7.
542. Puṇḍarīka, *Stainless Light* (Jonang trans.), chap. 1, Jo nang dpe tshogs, vol. 18, 170. See also Puṇḍarīka, *Stainless Light* (Shong trans.), chap. 1, Toh 1347 Tengyur, rgyud *tha*, 162b7.
543. *Great Sūtra Called Emptiness*, Toh 290 Kangyur, mdo sde *sha*, 250a6.
544. *Great Sūtra Called Emptiness*, Toh 290 Kangyur, mdo sde *sha*, 252b7.
545. *Sūtra on the Perfection of Wisdom in Twenty-Five Thousand Lines*, Toh 9 Kangyur, shes phyin *ga*, 348a4.
546. *Sūtra on the Perfection of Wisdom in Twenty-Five Thousand Lines*, Toh 9 Kangyur, shes phyin *ga*, 349a3.
547. *Sūtra on the Perfection of Wisdom in Twenty-Five Thousand Lines*, Toh 9 Kangyur, shes phyin *ga*, 349b2.
548. Maitreya, *Distinguishing the Middle and the Extremes*, 3.3, Toh 4021 Tengyur, sems tsam *phi*, 42a4.
549. Maitreya, *Distinguishing the Middle and the Extremes*, 3.16cd, Toh 4021 Tengyur, sems tsam *phi*, 42b4.
550. Maitreya, *Distinguishing the Middle and the Extremes*, 1.1–2, Toh 4021 Tengyur, sems tsam *phi*, 40b2.
551. Dignāga, *Verse Summary of the "Perfection of Wisdom,"* Toh 3809 Tengyur, shes phyin *pha*, 293b4.

552. Kamalaśīla, *Illuminating the Madhyamaka*, Toh 3887 Tengyur, dbu ma *sa*, 150a3.
553. Kamalaśīla, *Illuminating the Madhyamaka*, Toh 3887 Tengyur, dbu ma *sa*, 150a2.
554. Kamalaśīla, *Establishing That All Phenomena Are without Nature*, Toh 3889 Tengyur, dbu ma *sa*, 287b3.
555. Nāgamitra, *Entryway to the Three Kāyas*, Toh 3890 Tengyur, dbu ma *ha*, 3a6.
556. See Jñānacandra, *Commentary on the "Three Kāyas,"* Toh 3891 Tengyur, dbu ma *ha*, 18a2. This statement in *Mountain Dharma* seems to be a summary of a much longer passage in Jñānacandra's work.
557. The last three sentences in this paragraph are a very close paraphrase of two lines in *Sūtra of Definitive Commentary on the Intent*, Toh 106 Kangyur, mdo sde *ca*, 45b6.
558. Maitreya, *Distinguishing the Middle and the Extremes*, 5.18b, Toh 4021 Tengyur, sems tsam *phi*, 44b2.
559. Maitreya, *Distinguishing the Middle and the Extremes*, 5.19ab, Toh 4021 Tengyur, sems tsam *phi*, 44b2.
560. Maitreya, *Distinguishing the Middle and the Extremes*, 5.21a–c, Toh 4021 Tengyur, sems tsam *phi*, 44b3. "The two" are apprehended object and apprehending subject.
561. Maitreya, *Distinguishing the Middle and the Extremes*, 5.23a, Toh 4021 Tengyur, sems tsam *phi*, 44b6.
562. Maitreya, *Distinguishing the Middle and the Extremes*, 1.2d, Toh 4021 Tengyur, sems tsam *phi*, 40a3.
563. Vasubandhu, *Commentary on "Distinguishing the Middle and the Extremes,"* Toh 4027 Tengyur, sems tsam *bi*, 2b1.
564. Maitreya, *Distinguishing the Middle and the Extremes*, 1.3, Toh 4021 Tengyur, sems tsam *phi*, 40b3.
565. Vasubandhu, *Commentary on "Distinguishing the Middle and the Extremes,"* Toh 4027 Tengyur, sems tsam *bi*, 2b4.
566. Maitreya, *Distinguishing the Middle and the Extremes*, 1.6, Toh 4021 Tengyur, sems tsam *phi*, 40b4.
567. Vasubandhu, *Commentary on "Distinguishing the Middle and the Extremes,"* Toh 4027 Tengyur, sems tsam *bi*, 3a2.
568. Vasubandhu, *Commentary on "Distinguishing the Middle and the Extremes,"* Toh 4027 Tengyur, sems tsam *bi*, 25b1.
569. The phrase "Madhyamaka without appearance" (*snang med dbu ma*) refers to teachings that nothing is established in ultimate reality, and even in the meditative equipoise of advanced bodhisattvas of the Mahāyāna nothing whatever appears; there is just an absence of conceptual elaboration (*spros bral tsam*). Seeing nothing is seeing reality. The phrase "Madhyamaka with appearance" (*snang bcas dbu ma*), however, refers to teachings that ultimate reality directly appears and is seen in the meditative equipoise of the Mahāyāna. This is the Madhyamaka of the appearance of reality (*yang dag snang ba'i dbu ma*), or the profound observable emptiness (*dmigs bcas stong nyid*).
570. *Journey to Laṅkā Sūtra*, Toh 107 Kangyur, mdo sde *ca*, 168b5.
571. *Journey to Laṅkā Sūtra*, Toh 107 Kangyur, mdo sde *ca*, 176b2.
572. *Journey to Laṅkā Sūtra*, Toh 107 Kangyur, mdo sde *ca*, 116a4.
573. *Journey to Laṅkā Sūtra*, Toh 107 Kangyur, mdo sde *ca*, 116a6.
574. *Journey to Laṅkā Sūtra*, Toh 107 Kangyur, mdo sde *ca*, 176b5.
575. *Journey to Laṅkā Sūtra*, Toh 107 Kangyur, mdo sde *ca*, 183a1. The Cārvāka (Rgyang

'phen pa) tradition was an ancient Indian school with a materialistic viewpoint. Adherents accepted only the evidence of the senses and rejected the existence of a creator deity or other lifetimes.

576. *Journey to Laṅkā Sūtra*, Toh 107 Kangyur, mdo sde *ca*, 179b3.
577. *Journey to Laṅkā Sūtra*, Toh 107 Kangyur, mdo sde *ca*, 169b5.
578. *Kālacakra Tantra* (Jonang trans.), 5.247a, Jo nang dpe tshogs, vol. 17, 221. See also *Kālacakra Tantra* (Shong trans.), 5.247a, Toh 362 Kangyur, rgyud 'bum *ka*, 127a2.
579. *Kālacakra Tantra* (Jonang trans.), 5.113ab, Jo nang dpe tshogs, vol. 17, 190. See also *Kālacakra Tantra* (Shong trans.), 5.113ab, Toh 362 Kangyur, rgyud 'bum *ka*, 112b6.
580. Puṇḍarīka, *Stainless Light* (Jonang trans.), chap. 2, Jo nang dpe tshogs, vol. 19, 12. See also Puṇḍarīka, *Stainless Light* (Shong trans.), chap. 2, Toh 1347 Tengyur, rgyud *tha*, 226a5.
581. *Vajrapañjara Tantra*, chap. 6, Toh 419 Kangyur, rgyud 'bum *nga*, 44a3. The text in the Kangyur is quite different than the passage quoted here in *Mountain Dharma*.
582. *Vajrapañjara Tantra*, chap. 14, Toh 419 Kangyur, rgyud 'bum *nga*, 56a2. The text in the Kangyur is quite different than the passage quoted here.
583. Saraha, *Treasury of Dohā Verses*, Toh 2224 Tengyur, rgyud *wi*, 72b5.
584. *Vajra Garland Tantra*, chap. 15, Toh 445 Kangyur, rgyud 'bum *ca*, 248a2.
585. *Tantra of the Drop of Mahāmudrā*, chap. 6, Toh 420 Kangyur, rgyud 'bum *nga*, 71a4.
586. *Sampuṭa Tantra*, Toh 381 Kangyur, rgyud 'bum *ga*, 74b4. The text in the Kangyur is quite different than the passage quoted here in *Mountain Dharma*.
587. *Sampuṭa Tantra*, Toh 381 Kangyur, rgyud 'bum *ga*, 74b3. The text in the Kangyur is slightly different than the passage quoted here in *Mountain Dharma*.
588. *Tantra of an Ocean of Ḍākas*, chap. 1, Toh 372 Tengyur, rgyud 'bum *kha*, 137b5.
589. *Brief Presentation of Initiation*, v. 156a–c, Toh 361 Kangyur, rgyud 'bum *ka*, 20a6. *Brief Presentation of Initiation* is the largest surviving section of the *Glorious Ādi-buddha* (*Dpal dang po'i sangs rgyas*), the lost Kālacakra root tantra.
590. Maitreya, *Ornament of the Mahāyāna Sūtras*, 7.6–9, Toh 4020 Tengyur, sems tsam *phi*, 6b3.
591. Maitreya, *Ornament of the Mahāyāna Sūtras*, 12.47, Toh 4020 Tengyur, sems tsam *phi*, 15a3.
592. Maitreya, *Ornament of the Mahāyāna Sūtras*, 12.48, Toh 4020 Tengyur, sems tsam *phi*, 15a4.
593. For more detail about the "aids to penetration" (*nges 'byed cha mthun*), see Buswell and Lopez 2014, 590.
594. Vasubandhu, *Commentary on "Distinguishing the Middle and the Extremes,"* Toh 4027 Tengyur, sems tsam *bi*, 3a1.
595. Asaṅga, *Compendium of the Mahāyāna*, Toh 4048 Tengyur, sems tsam *ri*, 2b6.
596. Asaṅga, *Compendium of the Mahāyāna*, Toh 4048 Tengyur, sems tsam *ri*, 24b7.
597. Asaṅga, *Compendium of the Mahāyāna*, Toh 4048 Tengyur, sems tsam *ri*, 35b4.
598. Asaṅga, *Compendium of Abhidharma*, Toh 4049 Tengyur, sems tsam *ri*, 104a1.
599. Asaṅga, *Compendium of Abhidharma*, Toh 4049 Tengyur, sems tsam *ri*, 90b4.
600. Asaṅga, *Compendium of Abhidharma*, Toh 4049 Tengyur, sems tsam *ri*, 90b5.
601. Maitreya, *Ornament of the Mahāyāna Sūtras*, 12.54, Toh 4020 Tengyur, sems tsam *phi*, 15b1.

602. Maitreya, *Ornament of the Mahāyāna Sūtras*, 4.11, Toh 4020 Tengyur, sems tsam *phi*, 4a6. According to Dölpopa's annotation in the Jo nang dpe tshogs edition of *Mountain Dharma*, the "cause" mentioned in the last line is the evolving family. For more detail about the "aids to liberation" (*thar pa'i cha mthun*), see Buswell and Lopez 2014, 547.
603. Maitreya, *Ornament of the Mahāyāna Sūtras*, 10.37, Toh 4020 Tengyur, sems tsam *phi*, 10a5.
604. Maitreya, *Ornament of the Mahāyāna Sūtras*, 20.51, Toh 4020 Tengyur, sems tsam *phi*, 34b5.
605. Vasubandhu, *Explanation of the "Ornament of the Sūtras,"* Toh 4026 Tengyur, sems tsam *phi*, 246a4.
606. The general title *Treatise on the Levels* (*Sa sde*) refers to Asaṅga's huge *Yogācāra Levels* (Toh 4035–4042).
607. Āryadeva's *Four Hundred Verses* (Toh 3846) is indisputably a fundamental Madhyamaka text.
608. Asaṅga, *Yogācāra Levels*, Toh 4035 Tengyur, sems tsam *tshi*, 162a1. *Main Treatise on the Levels* (*Sa'i dngos gzhi*) is the first and central work of the five sections in Asaṅga's *Yogācāra Levels*.
609. Vasubandhu, *Thirty Verses*, v. 28a–c, Toh 4055 Tengyur, sems tsam *shi*, 3a1.
610. Vasubandhu, *Thirty Verses*, vv. 28d–30, Toh 4055 Tengyur, sems tsam *shi*, 3a1.
611. Vasubandhu, *Thirty Verses*, v. 21cd, Toh 4055 Tengyur, sems tsam *shi*, 2b5.
612. Puṇḍarīka, *Stainless Light* (Jonang trans.), chap. 1, Jo nang dpe tshogs, vol. 18, 106. See also Puṇḍarīka, *Stainless Light* (Shong trans.), chap. 1, Toh 1347 Tengyur, rgyud *tha*, 140a2. The quoted verse is *Chanting the Ultimate Names of Mañjuśrī*, v. 99, Toh 360 Kangyur, rgyud 'bum *ka*, 6a1.
613. Puṇḍarīka, *Stainless Light* (Jonang trans.), chap. 2, Jo nang dpe tshogs, vol. 19, 204. See also Puṇḍarīka, *Stainless Light* (Shong trans.), chap. 2, Toh 1347 Tengyur, rgyud *da*, 25b7. The quoted line is *Kālacakra Tantra* (Jonang trans.), 2.167c, Jo nang dpe tshogs, vol. 17, 68. See also *Kālacakra Tantra* (Shong trans.), 2.167c, Toh 362 Kangyur, rgyud 'bum *ka*, 57a4.
614. Puṇḍarīka, *Stainless Light* (Jonang trans.), chap. 5, Jo nang dpe tshogs, vol. 20, 326. See also Puṇḍarīka, *Stainless Light* (Jonang trans.), chap. 5, Toh 1347 Tengyur, rgyud *da*, 249a5.
615. Puṇḍarīka, *Stainless Light* (Jonang trans.), chap. 2, Jo nang dpe tshogs, vol. 19, 207. See also Puṇḍarīka, *Stainless Light* (Shong trans.), chap. 2, Toh 1347 Tengyur, rgyud *da*, 26b4.
616. Puṇḍarīka, *Stainless Light* (Jonang trans.), chap. 5, Jo nang dpe tshogs, vol. 20, 453. See also Puṇḍarīka, *Stainless Light* (Jonang trans.), chap. 5, Toh 1347 Tengyur, rgyud *da*, 296b1. The quoted line is part of *Kālacakra Tantra* (Jonang trans.), 5.248a, Jo nang dpe tshogs, vol. 17, 221. See also *Kālacakra Tantra* (Shong trans.), 5.248a, Toh 362 Kangyur, rgyud 'bum *ka*, 127a3.
617. Maitreya, *Distinguishing the Middle and the Extremes*, 1.14–15, Toh 4021 Tengyur, sems tsam *phi*, 41a2.
618. Nāgārjuna, *Commentary on Bodhicitta*, v. 71, Toh 1800 Tengyur, rgyud *ngi*, 41a2. The lines in the Tengyur text are arranged in a different order than in the quotation here.

619. These lines from the lost *Sublime Ādibuddha in Twelve Thousand Lines* (*Mchog gi dang po'i sangs rgyas stong phrag bcu gnyis pa*) are quoted in Puṇḍarīka, *Stainless Light* (Jonang trans.), chap. 1, Jo nang dpe tshogs, vol. 18, 107. See also Puṇḍarīka, *Stainless Light* (Shong trans.), chap. 1, Toh 1347 Tengyur, rgyud *tha*, 140b4.
620. Puṇḍarīka, *Stainless Light* (Jonang trans.), chap. 1, Jo nang dpe tshogs, vol. 18, 93. See also Puṇḍarīka, *Stainless Light* (Shong trans.), chap. 1, Toh 1347 Tengyur, rgyud *tha*, 135b5.
621. Several Tibetan sources say this line is from a sūtra referred to as *Rnam par 'phrul pa'i mdo*. All sūtras with the phrase *rnam par 'phrul pa* in their titles have been searched, but the line has not been located.
622. *Sūtra Teaching the Great Compassion of the Tathāgata*, Toh 147 Kangyur, mdo sde *pa*, 181a4.
623. Maitreya, *Ornament of the Mahāyāna Sūtras*, 10.22c, Toh 4020 Tengyur, sems tsam *phi*, 9b4.
624. *Sūtra on the Perfection of Wisdom in One Hundred Thousand Lines*, Toh 8 Kangyur, shes phyin *da*, 213a6.
625. Vasubandhu, *Vast Explanation of the "Sūtra in One Hundred Thousand Lines," the "Sūtra in Twenty-Five Thousand Lines," and the "Sūtra in Eighteen Thousand Lines,"* Toh 3808 Tengyur, shes phyin *pha*, 260a2.
626. Vimalamitra, *Commentary on the "Perfection of Wisdom in Seven Hundred Lines,"* Toh 3814 Kangyur, shes phyin *ma*, 39b4.
627. Vimalamitra, *Commentary on the "Perfection of Wisdom in Seven Hundred Lines,"* Toh 3814 Kangyur, shes phyin *ma*, 39b6.
628. *Sūtra on the Perfection of Wisdom in Eight Thousand Lines*, chap. 31, Toh 12 Kangyur, shes phyin *ka*, 276b7. Only the second phrase here was located in the Kangyur, although the first phrase is repeated many times in the following lines.
629. Asaṅga, *Compendium of Abhidharma*, Toh 4049 Tengyur, sems tsam *ri*, 54a2.
630. Maitreya, *Distinguishing the Middle and the Extremes*, 1.15a, Toh 4021 Tengyur, sems tsam *phi*, 41a2.
631. Maitreya, *Distinguishing the Middle and the Extremes*, 1.15a, Toh 4021 Tengyur, sems tsam *phi*, 41a2.
632. Maitreya, *Distinguishing the Middle and the Extremes*, 1.15b, Toh 4021 Tengyur, sems tsam *phi*, 41a2.
633. Asaṅga, *Compendium of Abhidharma*, Toh 4049 Tengyur, sems tsam *ri*, 54a3.
634. Maitreya, *Distinguishing the Middle and the Extremes*, 1.15b, Toh 4021 Tengyur, sems tsam *phi*, 41a2.
635. Asaṅga, *Compendium of Abhidharma*, Toh 4049 Tengyur, sems tsam *ri*, 54a3.
636. Maitreya, *Distinguishing the Middle and the Extremes*, 1.15c, Toh 4021 Tengyur, sems tsam *phi*, 41a2.
637. Asaṅga, *Compendium of Abhidharma*, Toh 4049 Tengyur, sems tsam *ri*, 54a4.
638. Nāgārjuna, *Commentary on Bodhicitta*, v. 71, Toh 1800 Tengyur, rgyud *ngi*, 41a2.
639. Nāgārjuna, *Commentary on Bodhicitta*, v. 68, Toh 1800 Tengyur, rgyud *ngi*, 41a1. The lines are slightly different in the Tengyur text.
640. *Heart Sūtra on the Perfection of Wisdom*, Toh 21 Kangyur, shes phyin *ka*, 145a5.
641. An important annotation by Dölpopa in the Jo nang dpe tshogs edition of *Mountain Dharma* says: "The appearance of the ultimate does not transcend the ultimate

and the empty aspect of the relative also does not transcend the relative, so [the one making the claim] has not understood that the two truths apply to appearances and the two truths also apply to emptiness."

642. Asaṅga, *Compendium of Abhidharma*, Toh 4049 Tengyur, sems tsam *ri*, 61b2.
643. *Tantra of the Drop of Mahāmudrā*, chap. 6, Toh 420 Kangyur, rgyud 'bum *nga*, 71a3. The wording of the passage in the Kangyur text is quite different than the quotation here in *Mountain Dharma*.
644. Nāropa, *Great Commentary of Nāropa*, Toh 1186 Tengyur, rgyud *ga*, 66b4. These three lines are from *Vajraśekhara Tantra*, Toh 480 Kangyur, rgyud 'bum *nya*, 153b1. The text in the Kangyur is somewhat different than the passage quoted here in *Mountain Dharma*.
645. These lines from the lost *Root Tantra of the Sublime Ādibuddha* (*Rtsa rgyud mchog gi dang po'i sangs rgyas*) are quoted in Nāropa, *Commentary on "Brief Presentation of Initiation,"* Toh 1351 Tengyur, rgyud *na*, 221b7. The text in the Tengyur is slightly different than here in *Mountain Dharma*.
646. Acalagarbha, *Combined Explanation*, Toh 1349 Tengyur, rgyud *na*, 23b7. These lines have not been located in the Tibetan Kangyur text of the *Hevajra Tantra* itself.
647. *Vajraśekhara Tantra*, Toh 480 Kangyur, rgyud 'bum *nya*, 153b1. The text in the Kangyur is very different than the passage quoted here in *Mountain Dharma*.
648. *Hevajra Tantra*, pt. 1, 5.15, Toh 417 Kangyur, rgyud 'bum *nga*, 6b2.
649. *Vajra Garland Tantra*, chap. 42, Toh 445 Kangyur, rgyud 'bum *ca*, 248a1.
650. *Tantra Determining the Intent*, chap. 1, Toh 444 Kangyur, rgyud 'bum *ca*, 160a1.
651. *Buddhakapāla Tantra*, chap. 1, Toh 424 Kangyur, rgyud 'bum *nga*, 145a2.
652. *Vajraḍāka Tantra*, chap. 11, Toh 370 Kangyur, rgyud 'bum *kha*, 33b7. The passage in the Kangyur is quite different than the quotation here in *Mountain Dharma*.
653. Candrakīrti, *Illuminating Lamp*, chap. 1, Toh 1785 Tengyur, rgyud *ha*, 10a5.
654. Vajrapāṇi, *Brief Cakrasaṃvara Commentary*, Toh 1402 Tengyur, rgyud *ba*, 79b3.
655. Puṇḍarīka, *Stainless Light* (Jonang trans.), chap. 1, Jo nang dpe tshogs, vol. 18, 49. See also Puṇḍarīka, *Stainless Light* (Shong trans.), chap. 1, Toh 1347 Tengyur, rgyud *tha*, 119a7.
656. Dölpopa's annotations in the Jo nang dpe tshogs edition of *Mountain Dharma* say the source of the attributes, the syllable *e* (the prajñā that is emptiness having the most sublime of all attributes), has the inseparable qualities of a buddha, such as the ten powers, but not the three qualities of lightness (*sattva, snying stobs*), motility (*rajas, rdul*), and darkness (*tamas, mun pa*), referred to in the verse by the terms "short," "long," and "very long." Concerning the meaning of the three qualities in the Kālacakra tradition, see Wallace 2001, 36–37.
657. *Kālacakra Tantra* (Jonang trans.), 5.248, Jo nang dpe tshogs, vol. 17, 221. See also *Kālacakra Tantra* (Shong trans.), 5.248, Toh 362 Kangyur, rgyud 'bum *ka*, 127a3.
658. Puṇḍarīka, *Stainless Light* (Jonang trans.), chap. 5, Jo nang dpe tshogs, vol. 20, 454. See also Puṇḍarīka, *Stainless Light* (Jonang trans.), chap. 5, Toh 1347 Tengyur, rgyud *da*, 296b2.
659. *Later Tantra of Direct Expression*, chap. 31, Toh 369 Kangyur, rgyud 'bum *ka*, 317a6. The three secrets are those of body, speech, and mind.

660. *Later Tantra of Direct Expression*, chap. 31, Toh 369 Kangyur, rgyud 'bum *ka*, 317a7.
661. *Later Tantra of Direct Expression*, chap. 53, Toh 369 Kangyur, rgyud 'bum *ka*, 345a2.
662. *Vajraśekhara Tantra*, Toh 480 Kangyur, rgyud 'bum *nya*, 149a7. Some lines in the Kangyur text are very different than the passage here in *Mountain Dharma*.
663. *Vajraśekhara Tantra*, Toh 480 Kangyur, rgyud 'bum *nya*, 149b3.
664. *Vajraśekhara Tantra*, Toh 480 Kangyur, rgyud 'bum *nya*, 149b3.
665. *Vajraśekhara Tantra*, Toh 480 Kangyur, rgyud 'bum *nya*, 149b1. The lines in the Kangyur text are very different than the passage here in *Mountain Dharma*.
666. *Vajraśekhara Tantra*, Toh 480 Kangyur, rgyud 'bum *nya*, 149b2.
667. *Vajra Garland Tantra*, chap. 13, Toh 445 Kangyur, rgyud 'bum *ca*, 223b1. The first line is somewhat different in the Kangyur.
668. *Vajra Garland Tantra*, chap. 13, Toh 445 Kangyur, rgyud 'bum *ca*, 223a6.
669. *Universal Secret Tantra*, Toh 481 Kangyur, rgyud 'bum *ta*, 6a7. The first line in the Kangyur text is somewhat different and the second line is completely different.
670. *Kālacakra Tantra* (Jonang trans.), 5.101b, Jo nang dpe tshogs, vol. 17, 187. See also *Kālacakra Tantra* (Shong trans.), 5.101b, Toh 362 Kangyur, rgyud 'bum *ka*, 111b4. Only the last part of line 101b is quoted in *Mountain Dharma*.
671. See *Hevajra Tantra*, pt. 1, 1.4a, Toh 417 Kangyur, rgyud 'bum *nga*, 1b1. Also see the line from the lost *Hevajra Root Tantra* quoted in Vajragarbha, *Extensive Commentary on the Condensed Meaning of the Hevajra*, Toh 1180 Tengyur, rgyud *ka*, 8a7.
672. Puṇḍarīka, *Stainless Light* (Jonang trans.), chap. 5, Jo nang dpe tshogs, vol. 20, 450. See also Puṇḍarīka, *Stainless Light* (Jonang trans.), chap. 5, Toh 1347 Tengyur, rgyud *da*, 295a7.
673. Puṇḍarīka, *Stainless Light* (Jonang trans.), chap. 2, Jo nang dpe tshogs, vol. 19, 12. See also Puṇḍarīka, *Stainless Light* (Shong trans.), chap. 2, Toh 1347 Tengyur, rgyud *tha*, 226a4.
674. Puṇḍarīka, *Stainless Light* (Jonang trans.), chap. 3, Jo nang dpe tshogs, vol. 19, 218. See also Puṇḍarīka, *Stainless Light* (Jonang trans.), chap. 3, Toh 1347 Tengyur, rgyud *da*, 89b6.
675. *Dhāraṇī of Vajravidāraṇā*, Toh 750 Kangyur, rgyud 'bum *dza*, 265b6.
676. *Chanting the Ultimate Names of Mañjuśrī*, v. 61a, Toh 360 Kangyur, rgyud 'bum *ka*, 4a7.
677. *Chanting the Ultimate Names of Mañjuśrī*, vv. 68b–69b, Toh 360 Kangyur, rgyud 'bum *ka*, 4b5.
678. *Chanting the Ultimate Names of Mañjuśrī*, vv. 70d–75b, Toh 360 Kangyur, rgyud 'bum *ka*, 4b6.
679. *Chanting the Ultimate Names of Mañjuśrī*, v. 75d, Toh 360 Kangyur, rgyud 'bum *ka*, 5a2.
680. *Chanting the Ultimate Names of Mañjuśrī*, v. 107a, Toh 360 Kangyur, rgyud 'bum *ka*, 6a6.
681. *Chanting the Ultimate Names of Mañjuśrī*, v. 107d, Toh 360 Kangyur, rgyud 'bum *ka*, 6a6.
682. *Chanting the Ultimate Names of Mañjuśrī*, v. 109ab, Toh 360 Kangyur, rgyud 'bum *ka*, 6a6.

683. *Chanting the Ultimate Names of Mañjuśrī*, v. 111c, Toh 360 Kangyur, rgyud 'bum *ka*, 6b1.
684. *Chanting the Ultimate Names of Mañjuśrī*, v. 112b–d, Toh 360 Kangyur, rgyud 'bum *ka*, 6b1.
685. *Chanting the Ultimate Names of Mañjuśrī*, v. 114c, Toh 360 Kangyur, rgyud 'bum *ka*, 6b3.
686. Vajrapāṇi, *Brief Cakrasaṃvara Commentary*, Toh 1402 Tengyur, rgyud *ba*, 85a1.
687. *Tantra That Utterly Purifies All Lower Realms*, Toh 483 Kangyur, rgyud 'bum *ta*, 95a7.
688. *Compendium of the Reality of All Tathāgatas*, Toh 479 Kangyur, rgyud 'bum *nya*, 24b4.
689. *Mahāyāna Section of the Glorious Sublime Primal*, Toh 487 Kangyur, rgyud 'bum *ta*, 150b4.
690. *Mahāyāna Section of the Glorious Sublime Primal*, Toh 487 Kangyur, rgyud 'bum *ta*, 156b7.
691. *Vajraśekhara Tantra*, Toh 480 Kangyur, rgyud 'bum *nya*, 148a1.
692. *Fragment of the Mantra Section of the Glorious Sublime Primal*, Toh 488 Kangyur, rgyud 'bum *ta*, 202b3.
693. *Fragment of the Mantra Section of the Glorious Sublime Primal*, Toh 488 Kangyur, rgyud 'bum *ta*, 202b4.
694. *Fragment of the Mantra Section of the Glorious Sublime Primal*, Toh 488 Kangyur, rgyud 'bum *ta*, 173a5.
695. Puṇḍarīka, *Stainless Light* (Jonang trans.), chap. 1, Jo nang dpe tshogs, vol. 18, 134. See also Puṇḍarīka, *Stainless Light* (Shong trans.), chap. 1, Toh 1347 Tengyur, rgyud *tha*, 150a5.
696. *Guhyasamāja Tantra*, chap. 12, Toh 442 Kangyur, rgyud 'bum *ca*, 111a4.
697. Candrakīrti, *Illuminating Lamp*, chap. 6, Toh 1785 Tengyur, rgyud *ha*, 42b3.
698. The "Chapter on Purity" (Rnam dag le'u) is chapter 8 of the *Sūtra on the Perfection of Wisdom in Eight Thousand Lines*, Toh 12 Kangyur, shes phyin *ka*, 104a4–111b7.
699. Puṇḍarīka, *Stainless Light* (Jonang trans.), chap. 1, Jo nang dpe tshogs, vol. 18, 5. See also Puṇḍarīka, *Stainless Light* (Shong trans.), chap. 1, Toh 1347 Tengyur, rgyud *tha*, 108a5. Dölpopa's annotation to this line refers to Mahāmudrā (*phyag rgya chen mo*) as Vajradhara's queen (*rdo rje 'chang gi btsun mo*). See Dölpopa Sherab Gyaltsen, *[Annotations to] the First Summary of the Chapter on the Cosmos in the "Stainless Light,"* 3b.
700. Puṇḍarīka, *Stainless Light* (Jonang trans.), chap. 1, Jo nang dpe tshogs, vol. 18, 12. See also Puṇḍarīka, *Stainless Light* (Shong trans.), chap. 1, Toh 1347 Tengyur, rgyud *tha*, 109b2.
701. Puṇḍarīka, *Stainless Light* (Jonang trans.), chap. 5, Jo nang dpe tshogs, vol. 20, 294. See also Puṇḍarīka, *Stainless Light* (Jonang trans.), chap. 5, Toh 1347 Tengyur, rgyud *da*, 237a2.
702. *Kālacakra Tantra* (Jonang trans.), 4.198ab, Jo nang dpe tshogs, vol. 17, 151. See also *Kālacakra Tantra* (Shong trans.), 4.198ab, Toh 362 Kangyur, rgyud 'bum *ka*, 97b7.
703. *Vajrapañjara Tantra*, chap. 6, Toh 419 Kangyur, rgyud 'bum *nga*, 43b6. The lines in the Kangyur text are extremely different than the passage quoted here.
704. *Compendium of the Reality of All Tathāgatas*, Toh 479 Kangyur, rgyud 'bum *nya*, 106a6.

705. *Compendium of the Reality of All Tathāgatas*, Toh 479 Kangyur, rgyud 'bum *nya*, 106b5.
706. Vajrapāṇi, *Brief Cakrasaṃvara Commentary*, Toh 1402 Tengyur, rgyud *ba*, 124a7.
707. Vajrapāṇi, *Brief Cakrasaṃvara Commentary*, Toh 1402 Tengyur, rgyud *ba*, 124b2.
708. Sādhuputra, *Kālacakra Maṇḍala Ritual*, Toh 1359 Tengyur, rgyud 'grel *pa*, 129a5.
709. Vajrapāṇi, *Brief Cakrasaṃvara Commentary*, Toh 1402 Tengyur, rgyud *ba*, 133b2.
710. Vajrapāṇi, *Brief Cakrasaṃvara Commentary*, Toh 1402 Tengyur, rgyud *ba*, 87a5.
711. *Hevajra Tantra*, pt. 2, 4.50, Toh 418 Kangyur, rgyud 'bum *nga*, 21a6.
712. *Hevajra Tantra*, pt. 2, 4.40–41b, Toh 418 Kangyur, rgyud 'bum *nga*, 21a1.
713. *Hevajra Tantra*, pt. 2, 4.41d–43c, Toh 418 Kangyur, rgyud 'bum *nga*, 21a2.
714. *Hevajra Tantra*, pt. 2, 4.45–47, Toh 418 Kangyur, rgyud 'bum *nga*, 21a3.
715. *Hevajra Tantra*, pt. 1, 10.20ab, Toh 417 Kangyur, rgyud 'bum *nga*, 12a6.
716. Nāropa, *Great Commentary of Nāropa*, Toh 1186 Tengyur, rgyud *ga*, 58b5.
717. Nāropa, *Great Commentary of Nāropa*, Toh 1186 Tengyur, rgyud *ga*, 62b3.
718. Vajrapāṇi, *Brief Cakrasaṃvara Commentary*, Toh 1402 Tengyur, rgyud *ba*, 83a2.
719. Several other Tibetan sources say this quote is from Vajrapāṇi, *Brief Cakrasaṃvara Commentary* (Toh 1402), but it has not been found there.
720. *Little Tantra of Cakrasaṃvara*, chap. 1, Toh 368, rgyud 'bum *ka*, 213a2. The lines in the Kangyur are different than the quotation here, which closely matches the same lines quoted in Vajrapāṇi, *Brief Cakrasaṃvara Commentary*, Toh 1402 Tengyur, rgyud *ba*, 81b3. These lines (separated by several others) are also found in *Vajrapañjara Tantra*, chap. 1, Toh 419 Kangyur, rgyud 'bum *nga*, 30b1.
721. *Samputa Tantra*, Toh 381 Kangyur, rgyud 'bum *ga*, 80b4. The passage in the Kangyur text is extremely different than the lines quoted here in *Mountain Dharma*.
722. *Samputa Tantra*, Toh 381 Kangyur, rgyud 'bum *ga*, 80a3. The passage in the Kangyur text is extremely different than the lines quoted here.
723. *Samputa Tantra*, Toh 381 Kangyur, rgyud 'bum *ga*, 80a4. The passage in the Kangyur has four lines, the second of which is omitted in the quote here.
724. *Vajrapañjara Tantra*, chap. 1, Toh 419 Kangyur, rgyud 'bum *nga*, 30a7. The lines in the Kangyur are quite different than in this quotation.
725. Puṇḍarīka, *Stainless Light* (Jonang trans.), chap. 5, Jo nang dpe tshogs, vol. 20, 294. See also Puṇḍarīka, *Stainless Light* (Jonang trans.), chap. 5, Toh 1347 Tengyur, rgyud *da*, 237a3.
726. Puṇḍarīka, *Stainless Light* (Jonang trans.), chap. 5, Jo nang dpe tshogs, vol. 20, 294. See also Puṇḍarīka, *Stainless Light* (Jonang trans.), chap. 5, Toh 1347 Tengyur, rgyud *da*, 237a5.
727. Vajrapāṇi, *Brief Cakrasaṃvara Commentary*, Toh 1402 Tengyur, rgyud *ba*, 79a7.
728. Vajrapāṇi, *Brief Cakrasaṃvara Commentary*, Toh 1402 Tengyur, rgyud *ba*, 81b2. Also see *Vajrapañjara Tantra*, chap. 1, Toh 419 Kangyur, rgyud 'bum *nga*, 30a4–30b1. The *Vajrapañjara* text in the Kangyur is extremely different than the passage quoted here from the *Brief Cakrasaṃvara Commentary*, with many lines nearly unrecognizable and separated by other lines. The last two lines of verse in this quote are also found in *Little Tantra of Cakrasaṃvara*, chap. 1, Toh 368 Kangyur, rgyud 'bum *ka*, 213a2.
729. Nāgārjuna, *Root Verses on Madhyamaka, Called "Wisdom,"* 15.1–2, Toh 3824 Tengyur, dbu ma *tsa*, 8b4.

730. Āryadeva, *Lamp That Summarizes Conduct*, chap. 7, Toh 1803 Tengyur, rgyud *ngi*, 87b4. The *Sūtra Teaching the Single Mode* (*Tshul gcig par bstan pa'i mdo*) has not been identified.

731. Āryadeva, *Lamp That Summarizes Conduct*, chap. 8, Toh 1803 Tengyur, rgyud *ngi*, 91b4.

732. Āryadeva, *Lamp That Summarizes Conduct*, chap. 3, Toh 1803 Tengyur, rgyud *ngi*, 74a2.

733. Āryadeva, *Lamp That Summarizes Conduct*, chap. 7, Toh 1803 Tengyur, rgyud *ngi*, 88b5.

734. Āryadeva, *Lamp That Summarizes Conduct*, chap. 8, Toh 1803 Tengyur, rgyud *ngi*, 92b6.

735. For most of these names and phrases, see *Chanting the Ultimate Names of Mañjuśrī*, vv. 1–22, Toh 360 Kangyur, rgyud 'bum *ka*, 1a2–2b6. Here and in the following twelve sections Dölpopa is drawing these names from various Tibetan translations of *Chanting the Ultimate Names of Mañjuśrī*, not just the translation by Shongtön Lodrö Tenpa that is in the Dergé Kangyur. He is perhaps also including names and epithets found in the many Indian commentaries on this scripture in the Tengyur.

736. For these names and phrases, see *Chanting the Ultimate Names of Mañjuśrī*, vv. 23–24, Toh 360 Kangyur, rgyud 'bum *ka*, 2b6–2b7.

737. Throughout this translation, the lowercase Sanskrit terms *prajñā* and *mudrā* refer to a consort.

738. For most of these names and phrases, see *Chanting the Ultimate Names of Mañjuśrī*, vv. 25–27, Toh 360 Kangyur, rgyud 'bum *ka*, 2b7–3a2.

739. For most of these names and phrases, see *Chanting the Ultimate Names of Mañjuśrī*, vv. 28–41, Toh 360 Kangyur, rgyud 'bum *ka*, 3a2–3b3.

740. For most of these names and phrases, see *Chanting the Ultimate Names of Mañjuśrī*, vv. 42–66c, Toh 360 Kangyur, rgyud 'bum *ka*, 3b3–4b4.

741. For most of these names and phrases, see *Chanting the Ultimate Names of Mañjuśrī*, vv. 66d–76, Toh 360 Kangyur, rgyud 'bum *ka*, 4b4–5a2.

742. For most of these names and phrases, see *Chanting the Ultimate Names of Mañjuśrī*, vv. 77–118, Toh 360 Kangyur, rgyud 'bum *ka*, 5a3–6b5.

743. For most of these names and phrases, see *Chanting the Ultimate Names of Mañjuśrī*, vv. 119–42, Toh 360 Kangyur, rgyud 'bum *ka*, 6b5–7b6.

744. These three are the past, the future, and the extinguishing of taints.

745. These four are the action mudrā, dharmamudrā, mahāmudrā, and samayamudrā.

746. For most of these names and phrases, see *Chanting the Ultimate Names of Mañjuśrī*, vv. 143–57, Toh 360 Kangyur, rgyud 'bum *ka*, 7b6–8b1.

747. For most of these names and phrases, see *Chanting the Ultimate Names of Mañjuśrī*, vv. 158–62, Toh 360 Kangyur, rgyud 'bum *ka*, 8b1–4.

748. *Mahāparinirvāṇa Sūtra* (trans. from Chinese), Toh 119 Kangyur, mdo sde *nya*, 343a2.

749. The six causes are the enabling, the simultaneously occurring, the congruent, the concomitant, the omnipresent, and the ripened cause. The four conditions are the causal, the fundamental, the objective, and the immediate condition.

750. The five results are the result that resembles the cause, the ripened result, the result caused by the action of a being, the result of separation from stains, and the dominant result.

751. Puṇḍarīka, *Stainless Light* (Jonang trans.), chap. 1, Jo nang dpe tshogs, vol. 18, 144. See also Puṇḍarīka, *Stainless Light* (Shong trans.), chap. 1, Toh 1347 Tengyur, rgyud *tha*, 153b4.
752. Puṇḍarīka, *Stainless Light* (Jonang trans.), chap. 5, Jo nang dpe tshogs, vol. 20, 366. See also Puṇḍarīka, *Stainless Light* (Jonang trans.), chap. 5, Toh 1347 Tengyur, rgyud *da*, 264b5.
753. Puṇḍarīka, *Stainless Light* (Jonang trans.), chap. 5, Jo nang dpe tshogs, vol. 20, 368. See also Puṇḍarīka, *Stainless Light* (Jonang trans.), chap. 5, Toh 1347 Tengyur, rgyud *da*, 265a6.
754. *Mahāparinirvāṇa Sūtra* (trans. from Chinese), Toh 119 Kangyur, mdo sde *ta*, 195b6.
755. *Mahāparinirvāṇa Sūtra* (trans. from Chinese), Toh 119 Kangyur, mdo sde *ta*, 87a4.
756. *Mahāparinirvāṇa Sūtra* (trans. from Chinese), Toh 119 Kangyur, mdo sde *ta*, 87a2.
757. *One Hundred and Eight Names of the Perfection of Wisdom*, Toh 25 Kangyur, shes phyin *ka*, 174a3.
758. Bhāvaviveka, *Jewel Lamp of the Madhyamaka*, Toh 3854 Tengyur, dbu ma *tsha*, 260b5.
759. *Little Text on the Perfection of Wisdom*, Toh 22 Kangyur, shes phyin *ka*, 147a4.
760. *One Hundred and Fifty Modes of the Perfection of Wisdom*, Toh 17 Kangyur, shes phyin *ka*, 138b7.
761. *One Hundred and Fifty Modes of the Perfection of Wisdom*, Toh 17 Kangyur, shes phyin *ka*, 139a3.
762. *Jewel Cloud Sūtra*, Toh 231 Kangyur, mdo sde *wa*, 69a3.
763. *Jewel Cloud Sūtra*, Toh 231 Kangyur, mdo sde *wa*, 69a5.
764. *Jewel Cloud Sūtra*, Toh 231 Kangyur, mdo sde *wa*, 68b5.
765. *Sūtra on the Samādhi of the Miraculous Ascertainment of Utter Peace*, Toh 129 Kangyur, mdo sde *da*, 187a7.
766. *Mahāparinirvāṇa Sūtra* (trans. by Lhai Dawa), Toh 120 Kangyur, mdo sde *tha*, 68b6. This series of synonyms seems to be a summary (not a direct quotation) of a much longer and detailed passage on these topics in the Kangyur text.
767. Asaṅga, *Compendium of the Mahāyāna*, Toh 4048 Tengyur, sems tsam *ri*, 19a2.
768. *Vajra Garland Tantra*, chap. 15, Toh 445 Kangyur, rgyud 'bum *ca*, 225b6. The passage in the Kangyur text is extremely different.
769. *Vajra Garland Tantra*, chap. 18, Toh 445 Kangyur, rgyud 'bum *ca*, 231a3.
770. *Vajra Garland Tantra*, chap. 58, Toh 445 Kangyur, rgyud 'bum *ca*, 263b3.
771. *Vajra Garland Tantra*, chap. 58, Toh 445 Kangyur, rgyud 'bum *ca*, 263b5.
772. Buddhaśrījñāna, *Precept of Mañjuśrī*, Toh 1853 Tengyur, rgyud *di*, 12a6.
773. Buddhaśrījñāna, *Precept of Mañjuśrī*, Toh 1853 Tengyur, rgyud *di*, 13a3.
774. Vasubandhu, *Extensive Commentary on the "Sūtra in One Hundred Thousand Lines,"* Toh 3807 Tengyur, shes phyin *pa*, 137a4.
775. Vasubandhu, *Extensive Commentary on the "Sūtra in One Hundred Thousand Lines,"* Toh 3807 Tengyur, shes phyin *na*, 25b1.
776. Maitreya, *Uttaratantra*, 1.84, Toh 4024 Tengyur, sems tsam *phi*, 58a6.
777. Maitreya, *Uttaratantra*, 1.85, Toh 4024 Tengyur, sems tsam *phi*, 58a7.
778. Asaṅga, *Commentary on the "Uttaratantra,"* Toh 4025 Tengyur, sems tsam *phi*, 103b6. Maitreya, *Uttaratantra*, 1.86, Toh 4024 Tengyur, sems tsam *phi*, 58b1.

779. *Later Guhyasamāja Tantra*, Toh 443 Kangyur, rgyud 'bum *ca*, 157a3.
780. Puṇḍarīka, *Stainless Light* (Jonang trans.), chap. 1, Jo nang dpe tshogs, vol. 18, 20. See also Puṇḍarīka, *Stainless Light* (Shong trans.), chap. 1, Toh 1347 Tengyur, rgyud *tha*, 111a6. The words in brackets are mostly from the annotations in the Jonang translation; some are from Dölpopa's annotations in the Jo nang dpe tshogs edition of *Mountain Dharma*.
781. Puṇḍarīka, *Stainless Light* (Jonang trans.), chap. 1, Jo nang dpe tshogs, vol. 18, 93. See also Puṇḍarīka, *Stainless Light* (Shong trans.), chap. 1, Toh 1347 Tengyur, rgyud *tha*, 135b4.
782. Puṇḍarīka, *Stainless Light* (Jonang trans.), chap. 1, Jo nang dpe tshogs, vol. 18, 130. See also Puṇḍarīka, *Stainless Light* (Shong trans.), chap. 1, Toh 1347 Tengyur, rgyud *tha*, 148b3. The last paragraph was also cited earlier in *Mountain Dharma*, with Dölpopa's crucial annotations that I have also included here in the translation.
783. Vasubandhu, *Correctness of the Explanation*, Toh 4061 Tengyur, sems tsam *shi*, 31b7.
784. *Hevajra Tantra*, pt. 1, 9.1, Toh 417 Kangyur, rgyud 'bum *nga*, 10b6.
785. Maitreya, *Ornament of Direct Realization*, 2.28, Toh 3786 Tengyur, shes phyin *ka*, 6a1.
786. *Sūtra on the Perfection of Wisdom in One Hundred Thousand Lines*, Toh 8 Kangyur, shes phyin *cha*, 345b1.
787. *Sūtra on the Perfection of Wisdom in One Hundred Thousand Lines*, Toh 8 Kangyur, shes phyin *cha*, 348a2.
788. *Hevajra Tantra*, pt. 1, 9.8–9b, Toh 417 Kangyur, rgyud 'bum *nga*, 11a3.
789. *Chanting the Ultimate Names of Mañjuśrī*, v. 130d, Toh 360 Kangyur, rgyud 'bum *ka*, 7a5.
790. *Hevajra Tantra*, pt. 1, 9.13–14b, Toh 417 Kangyur, rgyud 'bum *nga*, 11a6.
791. Puṇḍarīka, *Stainless Light* (Jonang trans.), chap. 1, Jo nang dpe tshogs, vol. 18, 137. See also Puṇḍarīka, *Stainless Light* (Shong trans.), chap. 1, Toh 1347 Tengyur, rgyud *tha*, 151a1. As marked in the translation, Dölpopa omitted a phrase that applies to a different subject.
792. *Hevajra Tantra*, pt. 1, 9.16, Toh 417 Kangyur, rgyud 'bum *nga*, 11a7.
793. Puṇḍarīka, *Stainless Light* (Jonang trans.), chap. 1, Jo nang dpe tshogs, vol. 18, 60. See also Puṇḍarīka, *Stainless Light* (Shong trans.), chap. 1, Toh 1347 Tengyur, rgyud *tha*, 122b5.
794. *Chanting the Ultimate Names of Mañjuśrī*, v. 132ab, Toh 360 Kangyur, rgyud 'bum *ka*, 7a6.
795. *Chanting the Ultimate Names of Mañjuśrī*, v. 133a, Toh 360 Kangyur, rgyud 'bum *ka*, 7a7.
796. *Kālacakra Tantra* (Jonang trans.), 3.56d, Jo nang dpe tshogs, vol. 17, 80. See also *Kālacakra Tantra* (Shong trans.), 3.56d, Toh 362 Kangyur, rgyud 'bum *ka*, 63b4. Only the second half of line 56d is quoted.
797. Puṇḍarīka, *Stainless Light* (Jonang trans.), chap. 3, Jo nang dpe tshogs, vol. 19, 323. See also Puṇḍarīka, *Stainless Light* (Jonang trans.), chap. 3, Toh 1347 Tengyur, rgyud *da*, 128b4.
798. These lines from the lost Kālacakra root tantra are found in Puṇḍarīka, *Stainless Light* (Jonang trans.), chap. 5, Jo nang dpe tshogs, vol. 20, 185. See also Puṇḍarīka,

Stainless Light (Jonang trans.), chap. 5, Toh 1347 Tengyur, rgyud *da*, 197a2. The phrase "the glorious binding of the six cakras" (*dpal 'khor lo drug gi sdom pa*) refers to a teaching in the section of the *Stainless Light* in which these lines are found. In another annotation later in *Mountain Dharma* (page 242 in the Jo nang dpe tshogs edition) Dölpopa uses the phrase "the great binding of the cakras" (*'khor lo sdom chen*) when identifying the source of a few words from the same section of the *Stainless Light*.

799. *Hevajra Tantra*, pt. 1, 7.10–11a, Toh 417 Kangyur, rgyud 'bum *nga*, 8a3. This list of meeting places is discussed in the *Hevajra Tantra*, where they are said to correspond to the twelve levels of a bodhisattva. See also Snellgrove 1959, vol. 1, 68–70, and vol. 2, 22–23. The same topic is discussed in many other tantric scriptures and treatises, such as the *Stainless Light*.
800. These lines from the *Sublime Ādibuddha* (*Dang po mchog gi sangs rgyas*) are quoted in Puṇḍarīka, *Stainless Light* (Jonang trans.), chap. 4, Jo nang dpe tshogs, vol. 20, 15. See also Puṇḍarīka, *Stainless Light* (Jonang trans.), chap. 4, Toh 1347 Tengyur, rgyud *da*, 34a3.
801. Maitreya, *Distinguishing the Middle and the Extremes*, 1.17–19, Toh 4021 Tengyur, sems tsam *phi*, 41a3.
802. Maitreya, *Distinguishing the Middle and the Extremes*, 1.20, Toh 4021 Tengyur, sems tsam *phi*, 41a5.
803. Maitreya, *Distinguishing the Middle and the Extremes*, 1.20, Toh 4021 Tengyur, sems tsam *phi*, 41a5.
804. Vasubandhu, *Commentary on "Distinguishing the Middle and the Extremes,"* Toh 4027 Tengyur, sems tsam *bi*, 5a3.
805. Maitreya, *Distinguishing the Middle and the Extremes*, 1.21, Toh 4021 Tengyur, sems tsam *phi*, 41a5.
806. Maitreya, *Distinguishing the Middle and the Extremes*, 1.22ab, Toh 4021 Tengyur, sems tsam *phi*, 41a6.
807. Vasubandhu, *Commentary on "Distinguishing the Middle and the Extremes,"* Toh 4027 Tengyur, sems tsam *bi*, 5b3.
808. Maitreya, *Distinguishing the Middle and the Extremes*, 1.13ab, Toh 4021 Tengyur, sems tsam *phi*, 41a1.
809. For example, see Maitreya, *Distinguishing the Middle and the Extremes*, 1.13c, Toh 4021 Tengyur, sems tsam *phi*, 41a1.
810. Maitreya, *Distinguishing the Middle and the Extremes*, 1.13c, Toh 4021 Tengyur, sems tsam *phi*, 41a1.
811. Vasubandhu, *Commentary on "Distinguishing the Middle and the Extremes,"* Toh 4027 Tengyur, sems tsam *bi*, 4a5.
812. Vasubandhu, *Vast Explanation of the "Sūtra in One Hundred Thousand Lines," the "Sūtra in Twenty-Five Thousand Lines," and the "Sūtra in Eighteen Thousand Lines,"* Toh 3808 Tengyur, shes phyin *pha*, 259b3.
813. Nāgārjuna, *Stages of Meditation*, Toh 3908 Tengyur, dbu ma *ki*, 3a7.
814. Maitreya, *Distinguishing the Middle and the Extremes*, 1.20cd, Toh 4021 Tengyur, sems tsam *phi*, 41a5.
815. Maitreya, *Ornament of the Mahāyāna Sūtras*, 7.1a, Toh 4020 Tengyur, sems tsam *phi*, 6a7.

816. Vasubandhu, *Explanation of the "Ornament of the Sūtras,"* Toh 4026 Tengyur, sems tsam *phi*, 145a3.
817. Nāgārjuna, *Stages of Meditation*, Toh 3908 Tengyur, dbu ma *ki*, 4a2.
818. These lines are found in *Tantra Determining the Intent*, Toh 444 Kangyur, rgyud 'bum *ca*, 199b3. They were not located in the *Vajra Garland Tantra* (Toh 445).
819. Vajragarbha, *Extensive Commentary on the Condensed Meaning of the Hevajra*, Toh 1180 Tengyur, rgyud *ka*, 40a6 and 40b2.
820. Jñānagarbha, *Path of Cultivating Yoga*, Toh 3909 Tengyur, dbu ma *ki*, 4b3.
821. *Sūtra on the Arising of Total Great Enthusiasm* (*Rab tu dang ba chen po skyes pa'i mdo*) has not been identified. This is perhaps an obscure descriptive name for a sūtra usually known by another title.
822. Nāgārjuna, *Root Verses on Madhyamaka, Called "Wisdom,"* 18.9, Toh 3824 Tengyur, dbu ma *tsa*, 11a3.
823. Asaṅga, *Levels of the Bodhisattva*, Toh 4037 Tengyur, sems tsam *wi*, 26b3.
824. *Kāśyapa Chapter Sūtra*, Toh 87 Kangyur, dkon brtsegs *cha*, 132b1.
825. *Kāśyapa Chapter Sūtra*, Toh 87 Kangyur, dkon brtsegs *cha*, 132b5.
826. Nāgārjuna, *Root Verses on Madhyamaka, Called "Wisdom,"* 13.8, Toh 3824 Tengyur, dbu ma *tsa*, 8a6.
827. Nāgārjuna, *Root Verses on Madhyamaka, Called "Wisdom,"* 24.11ab, Toh 3824 Tengyur, dbu ma *tsa*, 15a2.
828. This line from the lost *Ādibuddha* is quoted in Puṇḍarīka, *Stainless Light* (Jonang trans.), chap. 4, Jo nang dpe tshogs, vol. 20, 15. Also see Puṇḍarīka, *Stainless Light* (Jonang trans.), chap. 4, Toh 1347 Tengyur, rgyud *da*, 34a4.
829. *Hevajra Tantra*, pt. 2, 9.12b, Toh 418 Kangyur, rgyud 'bum *nga*, 27b7.
830. See Puṇḍarīka, *Stainless Light* (Jonang trans.), chap. 5, Jo nang dpe tshogs, vol. 20, 180. See also Puṇḍarīka, *Stainless Light* (Jonang trans.), chap. 5, Toh 1347 Tengyur, rgyud *da*, 195a7, 195b1. Dölpopa's annotation here in the Jo nang dpe tshogs edition of *Mountain Dharma* locates these words in "the great binding of the cakras" (*'khor lo sdom chen*), which refers to a teaching in a section of the *Stainless Light*. Earlier in *Mountain Dharma* (page 231 of the Jo nang dpe tshogs edition) Dölpopa used the phrase "the glorious binding of the six cakras" (*dpal 'khor lo drug gi sdom pa*) when referring to the same section.
831. For example, see Puṇḍarīka, *Stainless Light* (Jonang trans.), chap. 5, Jo nang dpe tshogs, vol. 20, 181. See also Puṇḍarīka, *Stainless Light* (Jonang trans.), chap. 5, Toh 1347 Tengyur, rgyud *da*, 196a7.
832. For example, see Puṇḍarīka, *Stainless Light* (Jonang trans.), chap. 4, Jo nang dpe tshogs, vol. 20, 15. See also Puṇḍarīka, *Stainless Light* (Jonang trans.), chap. 4, Toh 1347 Tengyur, rgyud *da*, 34a1.
833. Puṇḍarīka, *Stainless Light* (Jonang trans.), chap. 1, Jo nang dpe tshogs, vol. 18, 61. See also Puṇḍarīka, *Stainless Light* (Shong trans.), chap. 1, Toh 1347 Tengyur, rgyud *tha*, 123a3.
834. Puṇḍarīka, *Stainless Light* (Jonang trans.), chap. 1, Jo nang dpe tshogs, vol. 18, 61. See also Puṇḍarīka, *Stainless Light* (Shong trans.), chap. 1, Toh 1347 Tengyur, rgyud *tha*, 123a4.
835. Bodhibhadra, *Combined Explanation of the "Compendium of the Essence of Primordial Awareness,"* Toh 3852, Tengyur, dbu ma *tsha*, 44a4. The quoted line is from the

basic verses by Āryadeva in his *Compendium of the Essence of Primordial Awareness*, Toh 3851 Tengyur, dbu ma *tsha*, 27b3.

836. *Kāśyapa Chapter Sūtra*, Toh 87 Kangyur, dkon brtsegs *cha*, 131a1.
837. *Kāśyapa Chapter Sūtra*, Toh 87 Kangyur, dkon brtsegs *cha*, 131a7.
838. *Kāśyapa Chapter Sūtra*, Toh 87 Kangyur, dkon brtsegs *cha*, 131b1.
839. Maitreya, *Distinguishing Phenomena and True Nature*, Toh 4023 Tengyur, sems tsam *phi*, 52a5.
840. Vasubandhu, *Commentary on "Distinguishing the Middle and the Extremes,"* Toh 4027 Tengyur, sems tsam *bi*, 24b1.
841. Vasubandhu, *Commentary on "Distinguishing the Middle and the Extremes,"* Toh 4027 Tengyur, sems tsam *bi*, 26b5.
842. Puṇḍarīka, *Stainless Light* (Jonang trans.), chap. 1, Jo nang dpe tshogs, vol. 18, 117. See also Puṇḍarīka, *Stainless Light* (Shong trans.), chap. 1, Toh 1347 Tengyur, rgyud *tha*, 144a2.
843. Puṇḍarīka, *Stainless Light* (Jonang trans.), chap. 1, Jo nang dpe tshogs, vol. 18, 119. Puṇḍarīka, *Stainless Light* (Shong trans.), chap. 1, Toh 1347 Tengyur, rgyud *tha*, 144b2.
844. These lines from the lost *Kālacakra Root Tantra* are quoted in Puṇḍarīka, *Stainless Light* (Jonang trans.), chap. 1, Jo nang dpe tshogs, vol. 18, 119. See also Puṇḍarīka, *Stainless Light* (Shong trans.), chap. 1, Toh 1347 Tengyur, rgyud *tha,* 144b4.
845. Maitreya, *Ornament of the Mahāyāna Sūtras*, 7.1a, Toh 4020 Tengyur, sems tsam *phi*, 6a7. This same statement is found in many other tantras and treatises.
846. Puṇḍarīka, *Stainless Light* (Jonang trans.), chap. 1, Jo nang dpe tshogs, vol. 18, 4. See also Puṇḍarīka, *Stainless Light* (Shong trans.), chap. 1, Toh 1347 Tengyur, rgyud *tha*, 108a1.
847. *Hevajra Tantra*, pt. 2, 2.43ab, Toh 418 Kangyur, rgyud 'bum *nga*, 15b4.
848. *Brief Presentation of Initiation*, v. 150c, Toh 361 Kangyur, rgyud 'bum *ka*, 20a3.
849. Śāntideva, *Entering the Conduct of a Bodhisattva*, 9.2, Toh 3871 Tengyur, dbu ma *la*, 31a1.
850. *Diamond Cutter Sūtra on the Perfection of Wisdom*, Toh 16 Kangyur, shes phyin *ka*, 131b1.
851. Ratnakīrti, *In Praise of the Deities of the Four Yogas*, Toh 1170 Tengyur, bstod tshogs *ka*, 247b5.
852. Maitreya, *Uttaratantra*, 1.23d, Toh 4024 Tengyur, sems tsam *phi*, 56a1.
853. *Tantra of the Arising of Saṃvara*, Toh 373 Kangyur, rgyud 'bum *kha*, 310a2.
854. The source of this line has not been located.
855. *Chanting the Ultimate Names of Mañjuśrī*, v. 155a, Toh 360 Kangyur, rgyud 'bum *ka*, 8a6.
856. *Hevajra Tantra*, pt. 1, 8.46bc, Toh 417 Kangyur, rgyud 'bum *nga*, 10a7.
857. *Verse Summary of the Sūtras on the Perfection of Wisdom*, chap. 4, Toh 13 Kangyur, shes phyin *ka*, 8a6.
858. Maitreya, *Ornament of the Mahāyāna Sūtras*, 10.24, Toh 4020 Tengyur, sems tsam *phi*, 9b5.
859. Maitreya, *Ornament of the Mahāyāna Sūtras*, 10.25, Toh 4020 Tengyur, sems tsam *phi*, 9b5.

860. This line is found in many scriptures, such as the *Sūtra on the Perfection of Wisdom in One Hundred Thousand Lines*, Toh 8 Kangyur, shes phyin *ta*, 122b5.
861. *Sūtra of the Dense Array*, Toh 110 Kangyur, mdo sde *cha*, 7b3.
862. Nāgārjuna, *In Praise of Dharmadhātu*, vv. 51cd–54, Toh 1118 Tengyur, bstod tshogs *ka*, 65b4.
863. Nāgārjuna, *In Praise of Dharmadhātu*, vv. 14–15, Toh 1118 Tengyur, bstod tshogs *ka*, 64a5.
864. Nāgārjuna, *In Praise of the Ultimate*, Toh 1122, Tengyur, bstod tshogs *ka*, 70a–b, and Nāgārjuna, *In Praise of the Three Kāyas*, Toh 1123 Tengyur, bstod tshogs *ka*, 70b–71a.
865. Puṇḍarīka, *Stainless Light* (Jonang trans.), chap. 1, Jo nang dpe tshogs, vol. 18, 21. See also Puṇḍarīka, *Stainless Light* (Shong trans.), chap. 1, Toh 1347 Tengyur, rgyud *tha*, 111a5.
866. *Sūtra on the Samādhi of the Miraculous Ascertainment of Utter Peace*, Toh 129 Kangyur, mdo sde *da*, 187a7.
867. Nāgārjuna, *Fearing Nothing*, Toh 3829 Tengyur, dbu ma *tsa*, 89a2.
868. Nāgārjuna, *Fearing Nothing*, Toh 3829 Tengyur, dbu ma *tsa*, 58a3.
869. Avalokitavrata, *Extensive Commentary on "Lamp for the 'Wisdom,'"* Toh 3859 Tengyur, dbu ma *zha*, 278b2.
870. Buddhapālita, *Buddhapālita's Commentary on the "Root Verses on Madhyamaka,"* Toh 3842 Tengyur, dbu ma *tsa*, 217b4 (for previous words from Nāgārjuna's *Fearing Nothing*), and 217b5 for the line here.
871. Nāgārjuna, *Sixty Verses on Reasoning*, v. 35, Toh 3825 Tengyur, dbu ma *tsa*, 21b5.
872. *Sūtra of the Bodhisattva's Scriptural Collection*, Toh 56 Kangyur, dkon brtsegs *ga*, 167b1.
873. *Sūtra of the Bodhisattva's Scriptural Collection*, Toh 56 Kangyur, dkon brtsegs *ga*, 38a6.
874. *Sūtra of the Excellent Golden Light*, Toh 556 Kangyur, rgyud 'bum *pa*, 161b4.
875. *Sūtra of the Meeting of Father and Son*, Toh 60 Kangyur, dkon brtsegs *nga*, 66b7.
876. *Sūtra of the Lion's Roar of Śrīmālā*, Toh 92 Kangyur, dkon brtsegs *cha*, 273a1.
877. Candrakīrti, *Lucid Words*, Toh 3860 Tengyur, dbu ma *'a*, 13a4.
878. *Chanting the Ultimate Names of Mañjuśrī*, v. 133a, Toh 360 Kangyur, rgyud 'bum *ka*, 7a7.
879. *Chanting the Ultimate Names of Mañjuśrī*, v. 53d, Toh 360 Kangyur, rgyud 'bum *ka*, 4a3.
880. Jñānagarbha, *Distinguishing the Two Truths*, Toh 3881 Tengyur, dbu ma *sa*, 2b5.
881. *Sūtra of the King of Samādhis*, chap. 9, Toh 127 Kangyur, mdo sde *da*, 27a1. The passage in the Kangyur has quite different wording, but the same meaning.
882. Nāgārjuna, *Root Verses on Madhyamaka, Called "Wisdom,"* 15.10, Toh 3824 Tengyur, dbu ma *tsa*, 9a2.
883. Nāgārjuna, *Root Verses on Madhyamaka, Called "Wisdom,"* 5.8, Toh 3824 Tengyur, dbu ma *tsa*, 4a5.
884. Nāgārjuna, *Root Verses on Madhyamaka, Called "Wisdom,"* 22.12, Toh 3824 Tengyur, dbu ma *tsa*, 13b2.
885. *Sūtra Requested by Ratnacūḍa*, Toh 91 Kangyur, dkon brtsegs *cha*, 229b5.

886. Dharmakīrti, *Commentary on Valid Cognition*, chap. 2, v. 8, Toh 4210 Tengyur, tshad ma *ce*, 107b7.

887. Vajragarbha, *Extensive Commentary on the Condensed Meaning of the Hevajra*, Toh 1180 Tengyur, rgyud *ka*, 7a6. I am grateful to David Reigle for comparing the two extant Sanskrit versions of this passage and determining the correct names for all the deities. Here each of the thirty-seven factors conducive to enlightenment (*byang chub kyi phyogs kyi chos*) is stated to also be one of the thirty-seven syllables that specify the settings for the discourses (*gleng gzhi'i yi ge sum bcu rtsa bdun*) at the beginning of the kings of tantras, and to also be individual deities of ultimate primordial awareness. The original Sanskrit sentence here is *evaṃ mayā śrutam ekasmin samaye bhagavān sarvatathāgatakāyavākcittavajrayoṣidbhageṣu vijahāra* (Thus have I heard, at one time the Bhagavān dwelt in the bhagas of the vajra queens, the body, speech, and mind of all tathāgatas). For a translation of Vajragarbha's original explanation, see Sferra 1999, 125–26, and Shendge 2004, 163–65. See also Newman 1987, 325n11, for a translation of Butön's summary of Vajragarbha's explanation of the definitive meaning of these thirty-seven syllables. For the seven sets of the thirty-seven topics listed in the final paragraph, see the List of Lists in Buswell and Lopez 2014, 1065–1102.

888. *Kālacakra Tantra* (Jonang trans.), 3.167c, Jo nang dpe tshogs, vol. 17, 102. See also *Kālacakra Tantra* (Shong trans.), 3.167c, Toh 362 Kangyur, rgyud 'bum *ka*, 74a7. Only the first half of line 167c is quoted. "Water treasure" (*chu gter*), a poetic term for ocean, is used here as a symbolic term for the number four, since four great oceans surround Mount Meru.

889. Puṇḍarīka, *Stainless Light* (Jonang trans.), chap. 3, Jo nang dpe tshogs, vol. 19, 439. See also Puṇḍarīka, *Stainless Light* (Jonang trans.), chap. 3, Toh 1347 Tengyur, rgyud *da*, 172a1. This passage comments on and quotes much of *Kālacakra Tantra* (Jonang trans.), 3.167–68, Jo nang dpe tshogs, vol. 17, 102–3. See also *Kālacakra Tantra* (Shong trans.), 3.167–68, Toh 362 Kangyur, rgyud 'bum *ka*, 74a6. I am grateful to David Reigle for checking and correcting the Sanskrit names in this passage.

890. Vajrapāṇi, *Brief Cakrasaṃvara Commentary*, Toh 1402 Tengyur, rgyud *ba*, 84b2.

891. Mañjuśrīyaśas, *Brief Presentation of the Assertions of My Own View*, P 4610 Tengyur, rgyud 'grel *pu*, 22a6.

892. Mañjuśrīyaśas, *Brief Presentation of the Assertions of My Own View*, P 4610 Tengyur, rgyud 'grel *pu*, 22a7.

893. *Kālacakra Tantra* (Jonang trans.), 5.34cd, Jo nang dpe tshogs, vol. 17, 169. See also *Kālacakra Tantra* (Shong trans.), 5.34cd, Toh 362 Kangyur, rgyud 'bum *ka*, 104b7. The term "direction" (*phyogs*) is used here as a code word for the number ten, since there are ten directions.

894. Puṇḍarīka, *Stainless Light* (Jonang trans.), chap. 5, Jo nang dpe tshogs, vol. 20, 294. See also Puṇḍarīka, *Stainless Light* (Jonang trans.), chap. 5, Toh 1347 Tengyur, rgyud *da*, 237a2.

895. Asaṅga, *Commentary on the "Uttaratantra,"* Toh 4025 Tengyur, sems tsam *phi*, 114a3. The text in the Tengyur is somewhat different, and quoted there from *Sūtra of the Lion's Roar of Śrīmālā*, Toh 92 Kangyur, dkon brtsegs *cha*, 272a7–272b1.

896. Maitreya, *Uttaratantra*, 1.51, Toh 4024 Tengyur, sems tsam *phi*, 57a2.

897. *Hevajra Tantra*, pt. 1, 9.5, Toh 417 Kangyur, rgyud 'bum *nga*, 11a1. This is not in verse and is only part of the prose numbered as verse 5 in Snellgrove 1959, vol. 2, 30.
898. *Hevajra Tantra*, pt. 1, 9.1, Toh 417 Kangyur, rgyud 'bum *nga*, 10b6.
899. This verse was not located in *Vajraśekhara Tantra*, Toh 480, which was translated into Tibetan by a different translator than the one for the *Great Commentary of Nāropa*.
900. Nāropa, *Great Commentary of Nāropa*, Toh 1186 Tengyur, rgyud *ga*, 105b1. The passage in the Kangyur is quite different than the quote in Nāropa's work. See *Sūtra on the Perfection of Wisdom in Eight Thousand Lines*, Toh 12 Kangyur, shes phyin *ka*, 170b6.
901. *Hevajra Tantra*, pt. 1, 9.8a, Toh 417 Kangyur, rgyud 'bum *nga*, 11a3.
902. Original source of line not located.
903. Puṇḍarīka, *Stainless Light* (Jonang trans.), chap. 5, Jo nang dpe tshogs, vol. 20, 364. See also Puṇḍarīka, *Stainless Light* (Jonang trans.), chap. 5, Toh 1347 Tengyur, rgyud *da*, 264a3. The Tibetan translations here in the *Great Commentary of Nāropa* are slightly different than in the *Stainless Light* itself because the same passages were translated by different Tibetan translators.
904. Nāropa, *Great Commentary of Nāropa*, Toh 1186 Tengyur, rgyud *ga*, 105b6. Quote not located in the *Stainless Light* itself.
905. Quote not located in the *Stainless Light* itself.
906. Puṇḍarīka, *Stainless Light* (Jonang trans.), chap. 4, Jo nang dpe tshogs, vol. 20, 79. See also Puṇḍarīka, *Stainless Light* (Jonang trans.), chap. 4, Toh 1347 Tengyur, rgyud *da*, 60b6.
907. Nāropa, *Great Commentary of Nāropa*, Toh 1186 Tengyur, rgyud *ga*, 106a5. See also *Sūtra on the Perfection of Wisdom in Eight Thousand Lines*, Toh 12 Kangyur, shes phyin *ka*, 105a1.
908. Nāropa, *Great Commentary of Nāropa*, Toh 1186 Tengyur, rgyud *ga*, 106b1. Also see *Vajrapañjara Tantra*, chap. 6, Toh 419 Kangyur, rgyud 'bum *nga*, 44a2.
909. *Mahāyāna Section of the Glorious Sublime Primal*, Toh 487 Kangyur, rgyud 'bum *ta*, 161a4.
910. *Hevajra Tantra*, pt. 1, 9.17–18a, Toh 417 Kangyur, rgyud 'bum *nga*, 11b1.
911. *Chanting the Ultimate Names of Mañjuśrī*, v. 30a, Toh 360 Kangyur, rgyud 'bum *ka*, 3a3.
912. *Chanting the Ultimate Names of Mañjuśrī*, v. 145a, Toh 360 Kangyur, rgyud 'bum *ka*, 7b7.
913. *Chanting the Ultimate Names of Mañjuśrī*, v. 86b, Toh 360 Kangyur, rgyud 'bum *ka*, 5b1.
914. *Mahāparinirvāṇa Sūtra* (trans. by Lhai Dawa), Toh 120 Kangyur, mdo sde *tha*, 106a5.
915. *Sūtra on the Perfection of Wisdom in One Hundred Thousand Lines*, Toh 8 Kangyur, shes phyin *nya*, 129b1.
916. *Sūtra on the Perfection of Wisdom in One Hundred Thousand Lines*, Toh 8 Kangyur, shes phyin *nya*, 126b1.
917. Vasubandhu, *Vast Explanation of the "Sūtra in One Hundred Thousand Lines," the "Sūtra in Twenty-Five Thousand Lines," and the "Sūtra in Eighteen Thousand Lines,"* Toh 3808 Tengyur, shes phyin *pha*, 196b6.

918. Vasubandhu, *Vast Explanation of the "Sūtra in One Hundred Thousand Lines," the "Sūtra in Twenty-Five Thousand Lines," and the "Sūtra in Eighteen Thousand Lines,"* Toh 3808 Tengyur, shes phyin *pha*, 199a3.
919. Vasubandhu, *Vast Explanation of the "Sūtra in One Hundred Thousand Lines," the "Sūtra in Twenty-Five Thousand Lines," and the "Sūtra in Eighteen Thousand Lines,"* Toh 3808 Tengyur, shes phyin *pha*, 187b4.
920. *Sūtra on the Perfection of Wisdom in Twenty-Five Thousand Lines*, Toh 9 Kangyur, shes phyin *kha*, 152a1.
921. *Sūtra on the Perfection of Wisdom in One Hundred Thousand Lines*, Toh 8 Kangyur, shes phyin *cha*, 150a5.
922. Maitreya, *Ornament of Direct Realization*, 2.23a, Toh 3786 Tengyur, shes phyin *ka*, 5b5.
923. The "Chapter on Purity" (Rnam dag le'u) is chapter 8 of the *Sūtra on the Perfection of Wisdom in Eight Thousand Lines*, Toh 12 Kangyur, shes phyin *ka*, 104a4–111b7.
924. *Kālacakra Tantra* (Jonang trans.), 4.200, Jo nang dpe tshogs, vol. 17, 151. See also *Kālacakra Tantra* (Shong trans.), 4.200, Toh 362 Kangyur, rgyud 'bum *ka*, 98a3.
925. *Kālacakra Tantra* (Jonang trans.), 5.70–71, Jo nang dpe tshogs, vol. 17, 179. See also *Kālacakra Tantra* (Shong trans.), 5.70–71, Toh 362 Kangyur, rgyud 'bum *ka*, 108b2.
926. Mañjuśrīyaśas, *Brief Presentation of the Assertions of My Own View*, P 4610 Tengyur, rgyud 'grel *pu*, 23a8. Some lines in the Tengyur text are very different.
927. *Sūtra on the Perfection of Wisdom in One Hundred Thousand Lines*, Toh 8 Kangyur, shes phyin *nga*, 56a2. These lines quoted in *Mountain Dharma* are each separated by several phrases in the Kangyur text. This seems to be Dölpopa's style in many quotations from such huge scriptures.
928. *Sūtra on the Perfection of Wisdom in One Hundred Thousand Lines*, Toh 8 Kangyur, shes phyin *nga*, 207b2.
929. *Sūtra on the Perfection of Wisdom in Twenty-Five Thousand Lines*, Toh 9 Kangyur, shes phyin *kha*, 317a6. The Kangyur text is slightly different, reading *ma dmigs na* instead of the *med na* quoted in *Mountain Dharma*.
930. *Sūtra of Definitive Commentary on the Intent*, chap. 7, Toh 106 Kangyur, mdo sde *ca*, 24b7.
931. *Sūtra on the Perfection of Wisdom in One Hundred Thousand Lines*, Toh 8 Kangyur, shes phyin *nga*, 18b7. The first sentence is exactly as in the Kangyur. The next paragraph summarizes a series of similar phrases about different terms.
932. *Sūtra on the Perfection of Wisdom in One Hundred Thousand Lines*, Toh 8 Kangyur, shes phyin *nga*, 19a1. The first sentence is exactly as in the Kangyur. The next paragraph summarizes a series of similar phrases about different terms.
933. *Sūtra on the Perfection of Wisdom in One Hundred Thousand Lines*, Toh 8 Kangyur, shes phyin *a*, 228b4.
934. *Sūtra on the Perfection of Wisdom in One Hundred Thousand Lines*, Toh 8 Kangyur, shes phyin *a*, 228b7.
935. *Sūtra of the Bodhisattva's Scriptural Collection*, Toh 56 Kangyur, dkon brtsegs *kha*, 287a7. The text in the Kangyur is slightly different.
936. *Sūtra on the Perfection of Wisdom in One Hundred Thousand Lines*, Toh 8 Kangyur, shes phyin *ga*, 164b1.

937. Vasubandhu, *Extensive Commentary on the "Sūtra in One Hundred Thousand Lines,"* Toh 3807 Tengyur, shes phyin *na*, 178b3.
938. *Sūtra on the Perfection of Wisdom in One Hundred Thousand Lines*, Toh 8 Kangyur, shes phyin *nga*, 19a1. The first sentence is exactly as in the Kangyur. The next paragraph summarizes a series of similar phrases about different terms.
939. *Sūtra on the Perfection of Wisdom in One Hundred Thousand Lines*, Toh 8 Kangyur, shes phyin *nga*, 19a1. The first sentence is exactly as in the Kangyur. The next paragraph summarizes a series of similar phrases about different terms.
940. *Sūtra on the Perfection of Wisdom in Twenty-Five Thousand Lines*, Toh 9 Kangyur, shes phyin *kha*, 326b1.
941. *Sūtra on the Perfection of Wisdom in One Hundred Thousand Lines*, Toh 8 Kangyur, shes phyin *nga*, 80a6. Dölpopa has summarized this passage in the Kangyur text, which has a full sentence for each of the topics listed.
942. *Sūtra on the Perfection of Wisdom in One Hundred Thousand Lines*, Toh 8 Kangyur, shes phyin *nga*, 80b3.
943. This seems to be a summary of a longer unidentified passage in the *Sūtra on the Perfection of Wisdom in One Hundred Thousand Lines*.
944. *Sūtra on the Perfection of Wisdom in One Hundred Thousand Lines*, Toh 8 Kangyur, shes phyin *nga*, 23b3. The first sentence is exactly as in the Kangyur. The next paragraph summarizes a series of similar phrases about different terms.
945. *Sūtra of the Great Drum*, Toh 222 Kangyur, mdo sde *dza*, 107b6.
946. *Sūtra on the Perfection of Wisdom in One Hundred Thousand Lines*, Toh 8 Kangyur, shes phyin *ga*, 63b5. For most of these topics, see the List of Lists in Buswell and Lopez 2014, 1065–1102.
947. *Sūtra of the Meeting of Father and Son*, Toh 60 Kangyur, dkon brtsegs *nga*, 106a1.
948. *Sūtra on the Perfection of Wisdom in One Hundred Thousand Lines*, Toh 8 Kangyur, shes phyin *nga*, 83b5.
949. *Sūtra on the Perfection of Wisdom in One Hundred Thousand Lines*, Toh 8 Kangyur, shes phyin *nga*, 84b3.
950. *Sūtra on the Perfection of Wisdom in One Hundred Thousand Lines*, Toh 8 Kangyur, shes phyin *a*, 365b4.
951. *Sūtra on the Perfection of Wisdom in One Hundred Thousand Lines*, Toh 8 Kangyur, shes phyin *a*, 367b1.
952. Puṇḍarīka, *Stainless Light* (Jonang trans.), chap. 5, Jo nang dpe tshogs, vol. 20, 294. See also Puṇḍarīka, *Stainless Light* (Jonang trans.), chap. 5, Toh 1347 Tengyur, rgyud *da*, 237a2.
953. Maitreya, *Uttaratantra*, 3.3ab, Toh 4024 Tengyur, sems tsam *phi*, 65b2.
954. Maitreya, *Uttaratantra*, 2.5, Toh 4024 Tengyur, sems tsam *phi*, 62b3.
955. Maitreya, *Uttaratantra*, 1.155cd, Toh 4024 Tengyur, sems tsam *phi*, 61b6.
956. *Sūtra of the Lion's Roar of Śrīmālā*, Toh 92 Kangyur, dkon brtsegs *cha*, 272a7–b1.
957. Maitreya, *Uttaratantra*, 1.25c, Toh 4024 Tengyur, sems tsam *phi*, 56a2.
958. Asaṅga, *Commentary on the "Uttaratantra,"* Toh 4025 Tengyur, sems tsam *phi*, 86a3.
959. *Sūtra on the Perfection of Wisdom in One Hundred Thousand Lines*, Toh 8 Kangyur, shes phyin *ga*, 64a3.
960. *Sūtra on the Perfection of Wisdom in Twenty-Five Thousand Lines*, Toh 9 Kangyur, shes phyin *ka*, 336a7.

961. *Sūtra Teaching the Inconceivable Sphere of a Buddha*, Toh 79 Kangyur, dkon brtsegs *ca*, 268b2.
962. The four mistakes are to take the impure to be pure, the selfless to be self, suffering to be happiness, and the impermanent to be permanent.
963. The five desires are for the objects of the five senses. The five obscurations are sensual desire, malice, lethargy and sleep, agitation and worry, and doubt.
964. *Mahāparinirvāṇa Sūtra* (trans. from Chinese), Toh 119 Kangyur, mdo sde *ta*, 272a1.
965. That is, the first fourteen syllables in the Sanskrit and the Tibetan translation of *Kālacakra Tantra* (Jonang trans.), 1.2a, Jo nang dpe tshogs, vol. 17, 1. See also *Kālacakra Tantra* (Shong trans.), 1.2a, Toh 362 Kangyur, rgyud 'bum *ka*, 22a3.
966. An *ekadvandva* in Sanskrit is a rare type of dual compound in which one of the members is not stated, but only implied, and the other one remains. Shongtön Dorjé Gyaltsen and earlier Tibetan translators unpacked the Sanskrit compound with the inherent duplication of *vara* (*mchog, sublime*), but Jonang Lotsāwa Lodrö Pal and Mati Paṇchen Lodrö Gyaltsen kept just one *mchog*, as in the Sanskrit. For a detailed explanation of this issue, see Reigle 2018, 3, and Newman 1987, 390n5.
967. The annotations to this phrase by Jamyang Chögön (a student of Dölpopa and Choklé Namgyal), 61a, identifies these three as "the flaying knife of the middle, the *visarga* of the south, and the drop of the north" (*dbus kyi gri gug lho'i tsheg drag byang gi thig le*). See Jamyang Chögön, *[Annotations to] the "Extensive Commentary on the Chapter on the Cosmos,"* 61a3. As mentioned above, these are the symbols of the terms "empty," "primordial awareness," and "drop." The *visarga* is the last in the series of Sanskrit vowels and looks like two drops, one on top of the other. Cf. Newman 1987, 390, who identifies the three as "gnosis," "drop," and "best."
968. Puṇḍarīka, *Stainless Light* (Jonang trans.), chap. 1, Jo nang dpe tshogs, vol. 18, 131. See also Puṇḍarīka, *Stainless Light* (Shong trans.), chap. 1, Toh 1347 Tengyur, rgyud *tha*, 148b6.
969. Puṇḍarīka, *Stainless Light* (Jonang trans.), chap. 1, Jo nang dpe tshogs, vol. 18, 133. See also Puṇḍarīka, *Stainless Light* (Shong trans.), chap. 1, Toh 1347 Tengyur, rgyud *tha*, 149b5.
970. The consonants of the *ka* class (*ka sde*) in Sanskrit are *ka kha ga gha ṅa*.
971. The consonants of the *ca* class (*ca sde*) in Sanskrit are *ca cha ja jha ña*.
972. The consonants of the *ṭa* class (*ṭa sde*) in Sanskrit are *ṭa ṭha ḍa ḍha ṇa*.
973. The consonants of the *pa* class (*pa sde*) in Sanskrit are *pa pha ba bha ma*.
974. The consonants of the *ta* class (*ta sde*) in Sanskrit are *ta tha da dha na*.
975. The consonants of the *sa* class (*sa sde*) in Sanskrit are *sa ḫpa ṣa śa ḫka*.
976. Puṇḍarīka, *Stainless Light* (Jonang trans.), chap. 1, Jo nang dpe tshogs, vol. 18, 134. See also Puṇḍarīka, *Stainless Light* (Shong trans.), chap. 1, Toh 1347 Tengyur, rgyud *tha*, 150a5.
977. Puṇḍarīka, *Stainless Light* (Jonang trans.), chap. 1, Jo nang dpe tshogs, vol. 18, 137. See also Puṇḍarīka, *Stainless Light* (Shong trans.), chap. 1, Toh 1347 Tengyur, rgyud *tha*, 151a4.
978. Puṇḍarīka, *Stainless Light* (Jonang trans.), chap. 5, Jo nang dpe tshogs, vol. 20, 255. See also Puṇḍarīka, *Stainless Light* (Jonang trans.), chap. 5, Toh 1347 Tengyur, rgyud *da*, 221b1.
979. Puṇḍarīka, *Stainless Light* (Jonang trans.), chap. 5, Jo nang dpe tshogs, vol. 20, 451.

See also Puṇḍarīka, *Stainless Light* (Jonang trans.), chap. 5, Toh 1347 Tengyur, rgyud *da*, 295b5.

980. Puṇḍarīka, *Stainless Light* (Jonang trans.), chap. 5, Jo nang dpe tshogs, vol. 20, 453. Some crucial information in brackets in the translation is from this edition. See also Puṇḍarīka, *Stainless Light* (Jonang trans.), chap. 5, Toh 1347 Tengyur, rgyud *da*, 296a6.

981. This verse is identical to *Chanting the Ultimate Names of Mañjuśrī*, v. 98, Toh 360 Kangyur, rgyud 'bum *ka*, 5b7.

982. These lines from the lost *Hevajra Root Tantra in Five Hundred Thousand Lines* are quoted in Vajragarbha, *Extensive Commentary on the Condensed Meaning of the Hevajra*, Toh 1180 Tengyur, rgyud *ka*, 41a4. The Tibetan translation in the Tengyur is slightly different. The last verse here is quite famous and is found in many different tantric scriptures and commentaries. It corresponds to *Bhagavadgītā* 13.13, from where it was apparently absorbed into Buddhist scriptures such as the *Hevajra Root Tantra* and the *Cakrasaṃvara Tantra*, and then into important commentaries and treatises such as the Bodhisattva Trilogy. See Sferra 2009, 95, and Sferra 2000, 303n182.

983. *Sūtra Taught by Akṣayamati*, Toh 175 Kangyur, mdo sde *ma*, 121a1.

984. *Immaculate Tantra*, Toh 414 Kangyur, rgyud 'bum *ga*, 260a3.

985. *Kālacakra Tantra* (Jonang trans.), 5.90–91, Jo nang dpe tshogs, vol. 17, 183. See also *Kālacakra Tantra* (Shong trans.), 5.90–91, Toh 362 Kangyur, rgyud 'bum *ka*, 110b2.

986. As mentioned in a previous note, this verse corresponds to *Bhagavadgītā* 13.13, from where it was apparently absorbed into Buddhist scriptures such as the *Hevajra Root Tantra* and the *Cakrasaṃvara Tantra*, and then into important commentaries and treatises such as the Bodhisattva Trilogy. Here it is somewhat different than in the earlier quote by Vajragarbha.

987. Puṇḍarīka, *Stainless Light* (Jonang trans.), chap. 5, Jo nang dpe tshogs, vol. 20, 230. See also Puṇḍarīka, *Stainless Light* (Jonang trans.), chap. 5, Toh 1347 Tengyur, rgyud *da*, 213a6. The last verse quoted here is *Chanting the Ultimate Names of Mañjuśrī*, v. 155, Toh 360 Kangyur, rgyud 'bum *ka*, 8a6.

988. That is, the moon, which bears the image of a rabbit.

989. The passionate females (*icchā*, *'dod ma*) and the outer passionate females (*pratīcchā*, *phyir 'dod ma*).

990. Puṇḍarīka, *Stainless Light* (Jonang trans.), chap. 4, Jo nang dpe tshogs, vol. 20, 76. See also Puṇḍarīka, *Stainless Light* (Jonang trans.), chap. 4, Toh 1347 Tengyur, rgyud *da*, 59b4. This section comments on, and quotes passages from, *Kālacakra Tantra* (Jonang trans.), 4.104–6, Jo nang dpe tshogs, vol. 17, 130. See also *Kālacakra Tantra* (Shong trans.), 4.104–6, Toh 362 Kangyur, rgyud 'bum *ka*, 88a6. For the astrological terms in this section I have relied on Henning 2007, and for the spelling of Sanskrit names I have relied on Wallace 2010, 128–32.

991. The previous lines include and explain *Hevajra Tantra*, pt. 1, 1.10d–11b, Toh 417 Kangyur, rgyud 'bum *nga*, 2a5.

992. Vajragarbha, *Extensive Commentary on the Condensed Meaning of the Hevajra*, Toh 1180 Tengyur, rgyud *ka*, 10a7.

993. This is perhaps a different wording of a well-known phrase in *Sūtra on the Perfection of Wisdom in Eight Thousand Lines*, chap. 1, Toh 12 Kangyur, shes phyin *ka*, 3a3.

994. Puṇḍarīka, *Stainless Light* (Jonang trans.), chap. 2, Jo nang dpe tshogs, vol. 19, 120. See also Puṇḍarīka, *Stainless Light* (Shong trans.), chap. 2, Toh 1347 Tengyur, rgyud *tha*, 269a6. According to the *Stainless Light*, the eight primary natures (*prakṛti, rang bzhin*) are the five elements, mind, intellect, and self-grasping. The sixteen manifestations (*vikāra, rnam 'gyur*) of the primary nature are the five sense faculties, the five sense objects in the body, the five action faculties, and the mind. For two slightly different lists, see Wallace 2001, 64–65, and Wallace 2004, 135. The words in brackets in the translation are from Dölpopa's annotations in the Jo nang dpe tshogs edition of *Mountain Dharma* and the annotations in the Jonang translation of the *Stainless Light*.
995. Puṇḍarīka, *Stainless Light* (Jonang trans.), chap. 2, Jo nang dpe tshogs, vol. 19, 116. See also Puṇḍarīka, *Stainless Light* (Shong trans.), chap. 2, Toh 1347 Tengyur, rgyud *tha*, 267b6. This line, repeated when explained in the *Stainless Light*, is *Kālacakra Tantra* (Jonang trans.), 2.83d, Jo nang dpe tshogs, vol. 17, 53. See also *Kālacakra Tantra* (Shong trans.), 2.83d, Toh 362 Kangyur, rgyud 'bum *ka*, 48b3. The words in brackets are from Dölpopa's annotations in the Jo nang dpe tshogs edition of *Mountain Dharma*. The eight qualities (*yon tan, guṇa*) are the five subtle elements (*pañcatanmātra, de tsam lnga*) of sound, contact, form, taste, and smell, together with the three qualities of motility (*rajas, rdul*), darkness (*tamas, mun pa*), and (*sattva, snying stobs*) lightness. See Wallace 2001, 36–37, and Wallace 2004, 131.
996. Puṇḍarīka, *Stainless Light* (Jonang trans.), chap. 1, Jo nang dpe tshogs, vol. 18, 126. See also Puṇḍarīka, *Stainless Light* (Shong trans.), chap. 1, Toh 1347 Tengyur, rgyud *tha*, 147a2.
997. This is a paraphrase of the famous passage in Asaṅga, *Commentary on the "Uttaratantra,"* Toh 4025 Tengyur, sems tsam *phi*, 114a3.
998. This would seem to be yet another different wording of a well-known phrase in *Sūtra on the Perfection of Wisdom in Eight Thousand Lines*, chap. 1, Toh 12 Kangyur, shes phyin *ka*, 3a3. The same phrase was quoted just above in a passage from the *Stainless Light*.
999. *Guhyasamāja Tantra*, chap. 4, Toh 442 Kangyur, rgyud 'bum *ca*, 96b2.
1000. *Tantra Determining the Intent*, chap. 5, Toh 444 Kangyur, rgyud 'bum *ca*, 158a3.
1001. *Guhyasamāja Tantra*, chap. 17, Toh 442 Kangyur, rgyud 'bum *ca*, 142b5.
1002. *Guhyasamāja Tantra*, chap. 17, Toh 442 Kangyur, rgyud 'bum *ca*, 142b7.
1003. These two lines are a very close paraphrase of the famous formula of the Kālacakra system, the only difference being the word "inner" (*nang*) instead of the word "body" (*lus*) in each line. For the original verse, see Puṇḍarīka, *Stainless Light* (Jonang trans.), chap. 3, Jo nang dpe tshogs, vol. 19, 316. See also Puṇḍarīka, *Stainless Light* (Jonang trans.), chap. 3, Toh 1347 Tengyur, rgyud *da*, 125b7. The first line alone (identical to that in the *Mountain Dharma*) is also found in Vajragarbha, *Extensive Commentary on the Condensed Meaning of the Hevajra*, Toh 1180 Tengyur, rgyud *ka*, 100a1.
1004. Jñānagarbha, *Distinguishing the Two Truths*, Toh 3881 Tengyur, dbu ma *sa*, 1a4.
1005. *Sūtra Teaching the Indivisible Nature of Dharmadhātu*, Toh 52 Kangyur, dkon brtsegs *kha*, 141b2.
1006. As explained before, the purpose of speaking with intentional ambiguity in that

way is to fully pacify grasping, discrimination, and conceptualization about dharmadhātu and so on.

1007. *Sūtra Taught by Akṣayamati*, Toh 175 Kangyur, mdo sde *ma*, 160b1.

1008. *Sūtra of the Meeting of Father and Son*, chap. 18, Toh 60 Kangyur, dkon brtsegs *nga*, 66b7.

1009. *Sūtra Teaching Relative and Ultimate Truth*, Toh 179 Kangyur, mdo sde *ma*, 248a6.

1010. *Sūtra Teaching Relative and Ultimate Truth*, Toh 179 Kangyur, mdo sde *ma*, 248b7.

1011. *Sūtra on Primordial Awareness at the Moment of Death*, Toh 122 Kangyur, mdo sde *tha*, 153a5.

1012. The Lords of the Three Families (Rigs gsum mgon po) are Avalokiteśvara, Mañjuśrī, and Vajrapāṇi. Dölpopa often refers in this way to Puṇḍarīka, Vajragarbha, and Vajrapāṇi, the three authors of the Bodhisattva Commentaries (Sems 'grel), or Bodhisattva Trilogy (Sems 'grel skor gsum).

1013. Āryadeva, *Lamp That Summarizes Conduct*, chap. 5, Toh 1803 Tengyur, rgyud *ngi*, 84a2.

1014. *Hevajra Tantra*, pt. 1, 1.10d–11b, Toh 417 Kangyur, rgyud 'bum *nga*, 2a5.

1015. *Journey to Laṅkā Sūtra*, Toh 107 Kangyur, mdo sde *ca*, 78b5.

1016. *Sūtra to Benefit Aṅgulimāla*, Toh 213 Kangyur, mdo sde *tsha*, 199b1.

1017. *Sūtra of Collecting and Crushing* (*Bsdus 'joms kyi mdo*) has not been identified.

1018. Āryadeva, *Four Hundred Verses*, chap. 8, v. 5, Toh 3846 Tengyur, dbu ma *tsha*, 9a7.

1019. I thank David Reigle for informing me that the Tibetan translation *dga' bskyed* here for the Sanskrit name of the Hiraṇyavatī River is difficult to explain. In the other Tibetan translation of the *Mahāparinirvāṇa Sūtra*, by Lhai Dawa, the expected term *gser ldan*, meaning "golden," is used. The name Hiraṇyavatī River is also found in several extant Sanskrit fragments of this sūtra and in English translations of the Chinese translation of the original Sanskrit work.

1020. *Mahāparinirvāṇa Sūtra* (trans. from Chinese), Toh 119 Kangyur, mdo sde *nya*, 91a5.

1021. Quote not located.

1022. This seems to be Dölpopa's summary of a very long passage in the sūtra itself. See *Sūtra on the Perfection of Wisdom in One Hundred Thousand Lines*, Toh 8 Kangyur, shes phyin *ta*, 363b3–370a3.

1023. *Sūtra on the Perfection of Wisdom in One Hundred Thousand Lines*, Toh 8 Kangyur, shes phyin *da*, 92a2.

1024. Nāgārjuna, *Root Verses on Madhyamaka, Called "Wisdom,"* 24.19, Toh 3824 Tengyur, dbu ma *tsa*, 15a6.

1025. *Sūtra on the Perfection of Wisdom in One Hundred Thousand Lines*, Toh 8 Kangyur, shes phyin *a*, 85b3.

1026. *Sūtra of Definitive Commentary on the Intent*, chap. 4, Toh 106 Kangyur, mdo sde *ca*, 11b5. This passage is extremely different in the Kangyur.

1027. *Sūtra of the Lion's Roar of Śrīmālā*, Toh 92 Kangyur, dkon brtsegs *cha*, 272b4.

1028. Nāgārjuna, *Root Verses on Madhyamaka, Called "Wisdom,"* 13.1, Toh 3824 Tengyur, dbu ma *tsa*, 8a3.

1029. For example, see Buddhapālita, *Buddhapālita's Commentary on the "Root Verses on*

Madhyamaka," Toh 3842 Tengyur, dbu ma *tsa*, 217b5. The word "false" (*brdzun pa*) is missing in the Tengyur text.

1030. Nāgārjuna, *Commentary on Bodhicitta*, v. 68, Toh 1800 Tengyur, rgyud *ngi*, 41a1. The passage is slightly different in the Tengyur text and the final two lines of Tibetan are reversed.
1031. *Sūtra of Definitive Commentary on the Intent*, chap. 7, Toh 106 Kangyur, mdo sde *ca*, 22a4.
1032. Asaṅga, *Compendium of Abhidharma*, Toh 4049 Tengyur, sems tsam *ri*, 105a2.
1033. Maitreya, *Ornament of the Mahāyāna Sūtras*, 15.34, Toh 4020 Tengyur, sems tsam *phi*, 20a2.
1034. *Sūtra of the Lion's Roar of Śrīmālā*, Toh 92 Kangyur, dkon brtsegs *cha*, 273b5.
1035. *Sūtra of the Lion's Roar of Śrīmālā*, Toh 92 Kangyur, dkon brtsegs *cha*, 273a6.
1036. *Sūtra of the King of Samādhis*, chap. 9, Toh 127 Kangyur, mdo sde *da*, 27b7.
1037. *Sūtra of Definitive Commentary on the Intent*, chap. 3, Toh 106 Kangyur, mdo sde *ca*, 9b1.
1038. See Asaṅga, *Commentary on the "Uttaratantra,"* Toh 4025 Tengyur, sems tsam *phi*, 80b7. The original source is said to be *Sūtra of the Lion's Roar of Śrīmālā* (Toh 92), but these lines were not located in that scripture.
1039. *Mahāparinirvāṇa Sūtra* (trans. from Chinese), Toh 119 Kangyur, mdo sde *nya*, 292a6.
1040. *Mahāparinirvāṇa Sūtra* (trans. from Chinese), Toh 119 Kangyur, mdo sde *ta*, 83a5.
1041. *Mahāparinirvāṇa Sūtra* (trans. from Chinese), Toh 119 Kangyur, mdo sde *ta*, 88b6. The Tibetan term *skyu ru ra* (*āmalakī*) indicates emblic myrobalan (the Indian gooseberry, or amla).
1042. *Mahāparinirvāṇa Sūtra* (trans. from Chinese), Toh 119 Kangyur, mdo sde *nya*, 114b2.
1043. *Mahāparinirvāṇa Sūtra* (trans. from Chinese), Toh 119 Kangyur, mdo sde *ta*, 142a2.
1044. *Mahāparinirvāṇa Sūtra* (trans. from Chinese), Toh 119 Kangyur, mdo sde *ta*, 154b7.
1045. *Mahāparinirvāṇa Sūtra* (trans. from Chinese), Toh 119 Kangyur, mdo sde *nya*, 33b4.
1046. *Mahāparinirvāṇa Sūtra* (trans. from Chinese), Toh 119 Kangyur, mdo sde *nya*, 34a6.
1047. The five basic points of training for a layperson (*bslab pa'i gzhi lnga*) are to abstain from taking life, taking what is not given, lying, sexual misconduct, and intoxicants.
1048. *Mahāparinirvāṇa Sūtra* (trans. by Lhai Dawa), Toh 120 Kangyur, mdo sde *tha*, 6b5.
1049. *Mahāparinirvāṇa Sūtra* (trans. by Lhai Dawa), Toh 120 Kangyur, mdo sde *tha*, 29b4.
1050. This phrase is from a sūtra passage quoted by Asaṅga just before the following section in his commentary. See *Sūtra of the Lion's Roar of Śrīmālā*, Toh 92 Kangyur, dkon brtsegs *cha*, 275a3.
1051. See *Mahāparinirvāṇa Sūtra* (trans. by Lhai Dawa), Toh 120 Kangyur, mdo sde *tha*, 33a4–b2.
1052. This phrase is also from a sūtra passage quoted by Asaṅga just before the following

section in his commentary. See *Sūtra of the Lion's Roar of Śrīmālā*, Toh 92 Kangyur, dkon brtsegs *cha*, 275a3.

1053. Asaṅga, *Commentary on the "Uttaratantra,"* Toh 4025 Tengyur, sems tsam *phi*, 112b6. The information in brackets has been condensed from Dölpopa's annotations in the Jo nang dpe tshogs edition of *Mountain Dharma* and from his *Annotations to Asaṅga's "Commentary on the 'Uttaratantra,'"* 88–90.

1054. Maitreya, *Ornament of the Mahāyāna Sūtras*, 10.1–3, Toh 4020 Tengyur, sems tsam *phi*, 8b3.

1055. Maitreya, *Ornament of the Mahāyāna Sūtras*, 10.12, Toh 4020 Tengyur, sems tsam *phi*, 9a4.

1056. Maitreya, *Uttaratantra*, 2.3–4, Toh 4024 Tengyur, sems tsam *phi*, 62b1.

1057. According to Dölpopa's annotations in the Jo nang dpe tshogs edition of *Mountain Dharma*, this means without the two extremes and free of the three obscurations of the afflictions, the knowable, and meditative absorption.

1058. Maitreya, *Uttaratantra*, 2.38–41, Toh 4024 Tengyur, sems tsam *phi*, 63b7.

1059. Nāgārjuna, *Sixty Verses on Reasoning*, v. 35a, Toh 3825 Tengyur, dbu ma *tsa*, 21b5.

1060. *Sūtra on the Perfection of Wisdom in Seven Hundred Lines*, Toh 24 Kangyur, shes phyin *ka*, 166b1.

1061. Maitreya, *Distinguishing the Middle and the Extremes*, 5.19ab, Toh 4021 Tengyur, sems tsam *phi*, 44b2.

1062. *Chanting the Ultimate Names of Mañjuśrī*, v. 61a, Toh 360 Kangyur, rgyud 'bum *ka*, 4a7.

1063. Buddhapālita, *Buddhapālita's Commentary on the "Root Verses on Madhyamaka,"* Toh 3842 Tengyur, dbu ma *tsa*, 217b5.

1064. *Sūtra of the Bodhisattva's Scriptural Collection*, Toh 56 Kangyur, dkon brtsegs *ga*, 167b1.

1065. Maitreya, *Uttaratantra*, 3.1–3, Toh 4024 Tengyur, sems tsam *phi*, 65b1.

1066. Nāgamitra, *Entryway to the Three Kāyas*, Toh 3890 Tengyur, dbu ma *ha*, 3a3.

1067. Maitreya, *Uttaratantra*, 1.149, Toh 4024 Tengyur, sems tsam *phi*, 61b3. For the full verses and context, see page 34.

1068. Maitreya, *Ornament of the Mahāyāna Sūtras*, 10.60, Toh 4020 Tengyur, sems tsam *phi*, 11a7.

1069. Maitreya, *Ornament of the Mahāyāna Sūtras*, 10.65, Toh 4020 Tengyur, sems tsam *phi*, 11b3.

1070. *Sūtra of Direct, Perfect Bodhicitta in the Palace of Akaniṣṭa* (*'Og min gyi pho brang du mngon par rdzogs par byang chub pa'i sems kyi mdo*) has not been identified.

1071. Maitreya, *Ornament of Direct Realization*, 1.17, Toh 3786 Tengyur, shes phyin *ka*, 2b4.

1072. See Mañjuśrīyaśas, *Brief Presentation of the Assertions of My Own View*, P 4610 Tengyur, rgyud 'grel *pu*, 22a4, where the previous verse 1.17 in the *Ornament of Direct Realization* is repeated almost exactly.

1073. The four knowledges (*mkhyen pa bzhi*) are of the dispositions of sentient beings, their nature, their thoughts, and their tendencies.

1074. *Chanting the Ultimate Names of Mañjuśrī*, v. 59ab, Toh 360 Kangyur, rgyud 'bum *ka*, 4a6.

1075. This passage from the lost *Sublime Ādibuddha* (*Mchog gi dang po'i sangs rgyas*) is quoted in Puṇḍarīka, *Stainless Light* (Jonang trans.), chap. 1, Jo nang dpe tshogs, vol. 18, 139. See also Puṇḍarīka, *Stainless Light* (Shong trans.), chap. 1, Toh 1347 Tengyur, rgyud *tha*, 151b7.

1076. *Hevajra Tantra*, pt. 2, 2.58–59b, Toh 418 Kangyur, rgyud 'bum *nga*, 16b1.

1077. With very slight differences, this verse is also found in *Chanting the Ultimate Names of Mañjuśrī*, v. 100, Toh 360 Kangyur, rgyud 'bum *ka*, 6a2.

1078. These four lines are the same as Maitreya, *Ornament of Direct Realization*, 1.17, Toh 3786 Tengyur, shes phyin *ka*, 2b4.

1079. This exact verse is also found in *Chanting the Ultimate Names of Mañjuśrī*, v. 59, Toh 360 Kangyur, rgyud 'bum *ka*, 4a6.

1080. According to Dölpopa's annotations in the Jo nang dpe tshogs edition of *Mountain Dharma*, these last five kāyas are the ultimate five kāyas.

1081. Mañjuśrīyaśas, *Brief Presentation of the Assertions of My Own View*, P 4610 Tengyur, rgyud 'grel *pu*, 22b1.

1082. *Kālacakra Tantra* (Jonang trans.), 5.89, Jo nang dpe tshogs, vol. 17, 183. See also *Kālacakra Tantra* (Shong trans.), 5.89, Toh 362 Kangyur, rgyud 'bum *ka*, 110b1.

1083. *Kālacakra Tantra* (Jonang trans.), 5.99, Jo nang dpe tshogs, vol. 17, 186. See also *Kālacakra Tantra* (Shong trans.), 5.99, Toh 362 Kangyur, rgyud 'bum *ka*, 111b1. A magical gem transforms anything it touches into a gem.

1084. Puṇḍarīka, *Stainless Light* (Jonang trans.), chap. 4, Jo nang dpe tshogs, vol. 20, 1. See also Puṇḍarīka, *Stainless Light* (Jonang trans.), chap. 4, Toh 1347 Tengyur, rgyud *da*, 29a2.

1085. Puṇḍarīka, *Stainless Light* (Jonang trans.), chap. 5, Jo nang dpe tshogs, vol. 20, 149. See also Puṇḍarīka, *Stainless Light* (Jonang trans.), chap. 5, Toh 1347 Tengyur, rgyud *da*, 183b2.

1086. Puṇḍarīka, *Stainless Light* (Jonang trans.), chap. 5, Jo nang dpe tshogs, vol. 20, 283. See also Puṇḍarīka, *Stainless Light* (Jonang trans.), chap. 5, Toh 1347 Tengyur, rgyud *da*, 232b5. Many of these phrases are taken from different verses in *Chanting the Ultimate Names of Mañjuśrī*.

1087. Puṇḍarīka, *Stainless Light* (Jonang trans.), chap. 1, Jo nang dpe tshogs, vol. 18, 2. See also Puṇḍarīka, *Stainless Light* (Shong trans.), chap. 1, Toh 1347 Tengyur, rgyud *tha*, 107b2.

1088. Maitreya, *Ornament of the Mahāyāna Sūtras*, 10.22, Toh 4020 Tengyur, sems tsam *phi*, 9b3.

1089. *Sūtra on the Samādhi of the Miraculous Ascertainment of Utter Peace*, Toh 129 Kangyur, mdo sde *da*, 187b1.

1090. Maitreya, *Uttaratantra*, 1.23a, Toh 4024 Tengyur, sems tsam *phi*, 55b7.

1091. *Kālacakra Tantra* (Jonang trans.), 1.1ab, Jo nang dpe tshogs, vol. 17, 1. See also *Kālacakra Tantra* (Shong trans.), 1.1ab, Toh 362 Kangyur, rgyud 'bum *ka*, 22b2.

1092. Puṇḍarīka, *Stainless Light* (Jonang trans.), chap. 1, Jo nang dpe tshogs, vol. 18, 3. See also Puṇḍarīka, *Stainless Light* (Shong trans.), chap. 1, Toh 1347 Tengyur, rgyud *tha*, 107b5.

1093. Puṇḍarīka, *Stainless Light* (Jonang trans.), chap. 1, Jo nang dpe tshogs, vol. 18, 2. See also Puṇḍarīka, *Stainless Light* (Shong trans.), chap. 1, Toh 1347 Tengyur, rgyud *tha*, 107b4.

1094. Puṇḍarīka, *Stainless Light* (Jonang trans.), chap. 1, Jo nang dpe tshogs, vol. 18, 3. See also Puṇḍarīka, *Stainless Light* (Shong trans.), chap. 1, Toh 1347 Tengyur, rgyud *tha*, 107b6.

1095. Puṇḍarīka, *Stainless Light* (Jonang trans.), chap. 1, Jo nang dpe tshogs, vol. 18, 4. Puṇḍarīka, *Stainless Light* (Shong trans.), chap. 1, Toh 1347 Tengyur, rgyud *tha*, 108a2.

1096. The four worldly states (*'jig rten pa'i gnas skabs bzhi*) are the waking state, the dream state, the deep-sleep state, and the fourth state.

1097. *Brief Presentation of Initiation*, vv. 151c–153b, Toh 361 Kangyur, rgyud 'bum *ka*, 20a4. *Brief Presentation of Initiation* is the largest surviving section of the lost *Kālacakra Root Tantra*. The information in brackets is from Dölpopa's annotations in the Jo nang dpe tshogs edition of *Mountain Dharma*, except in the last line, which is from an explanation of this verse by Jonang Tāranātha. See Tāranātha, *Sun Illuminating the Entire Profound Meaning*, 301.

1098. Puṇḍarīka, *Stainless Light* (Jonang trans.), chap. 1, Jo nang dpe tshogs, vol. 18, 122. Puṇḍarīka, *Stainless Light* (Shong trans.), chap. 1, Toh 1347 Tengyur, rgyud *tha*, 145b4.

1099. Puṇḍarīka, *Stainless Light* (Jonang trans.), chap. 1, Jo nang dpe tshogs, vol. 18, 123. See also Puṇḍarīka, *Stainless Light* (Shong trans.), chap. 1, Toh 1347 Tengyur, rgyud *tha*, 146a1. The last phrase is a line from *Chanting the Ultimate Names of Mañjuśrī*, v. 133b, Toh 360 Kangyur, rgyud 'bum *ka*, 7a7.

1100. Puṇḍarīka, *Stainless Light* (Jonang trans.), chap. 1, Jo nang dpe tshogs, vol. 18, 124. See also Puṇḍarīka, *Stainless Light* (Shong trans.), chap. 1, Toh 1347 Tengyur, rgyud *tha*, 146a4.

1101. Puṇḍarīka, *Stainless Light* (Jonang trans.), chap. 1, Jo nang dpe tshogs, vol. 18, 124. See also Puṇḍarīka, *Stainless Light* (Shong trans.), chap. 1, Toh 1347 Tengyur, rgyud *tha*, 146a7.

1102. Puṇḍarīka, *Stainless Light* (Jonang trans.), chap. 1, Jo nang dpe tshogs, vol. 18, 125. See also Puṇḍarīka, *Stainless Light* (Shong trans.), chap. 1, Toh 1347 Tengyur, rgyud *tha*, 146b3.

1103. Puṇḍarīka, *Stainless Light* (Jonang trans.), chap. 1, Jo nang dpe tshogs, vol. 18, 125. See also Puṇḍarīka, *Stainless Light* (Shong trans.), chap. 1, Toh 1347 Tengyur, rgyud *tha*, 146b7.

1104. Vajragarbha, *Extensive Commentary on the Condensed Meaning of the Hevajra*, Toh 1180 Tengyur, rgyud *ka*, 15b3. This and the following sixteen sections are one passage in Vajragarbha's text: 15b3–16a5.

1105. Vajragarbha, *Extensive Commentary on the Condensed Meaning of the Hevajra*, Toh 1180 Tengyur, rgyud *ka*, 15b4.

1106. Vajragarbha, *Extensive Commentary on the Condensed Meaning of the Hevajra*, Toh 1180 Tengyur, rgyud *ka*, 15b4.

1107. Vajragarbha, *Extensive Commentary on the Condensed Meaning of the Hevajra*, Toh 1180 Tengyur, rgyud *ka*, 15b5.

1108. Vajragarbha, *Extensive Commentary on the Condensed Meaning of the Hevajra*, Toh 1180 Tengyur, rgyud *ka*, 15b5.

1109. Vajragarbha, *Extensive Commentary on the Condensed Meaning of the Hevajra*, Toh 1180 Tengyur, rgyud *ka*, 15b6.

1110. Vajragarbha, *Extensive Commentary on the Condensed Meaning of the Hevajra*, Toh 1180 Tengyur, rgyud *ka*, 15b6.
1111. Vajragarbha, *Extensive Commentary on the Condensed Meaning of the Hevajra*, Toh 1180 Tengyur, rgyud *ka*, 15b7.
1112. Vajragarbha, *Extensive Commentary on the Condensed Meaning of the Hevajra*, Toh 1180 Tengyur, rgyud *ka*, 16a1.
1113. Vajragarbha, *Extensive Commentary on the Condensed Meaning of the Hevajra*, Toh 1180 Tengyur, rgyud *ka*, 16a1.
1114. Vajragarbha, *Extensive Commentary on the Condensed Meaning of the Hevajra*, Toh 1180 Tengyur, rgyud *ka*, 16a2.
1115. Vajragarbha, *Extensive Commentary on the Condensed Meaning of the Hevajra*, Toh 1180 Tengyur, rgyud *ka*, 16a2.
1116. Vajragarbha, *Extensive Commentary on the Condensed Meaning of the Hevajra*, Toh 1180 Tengyur, rgyud *ka*, 16a3.
1117. Vajragarbha, *Extensive Commentary on the Condensed Meaning of the Hevajra*, Toh 1180 Tengyur, rgyud *ka*, 16a3.
1118. Vajragarbha, *Extensive Commentary on the Condensed Meaning of the Hevajra*, Toh 1180 Tengyur, rgyud *ka*, 16a4.
1119. Vajragarbha, *Extensive Commentary on the Condensed Meaning of the Hevajra*, Toh 1180 Tengyur, rgyud *ka*, 16a5.
1120. Hutāśana (Byin za) is the fire god, in this context probably a name for Agni.
1121. *Later Kālacakra Tantra*, Toh 363 Kangyur, rgyud 'bum *ka*, 133a5.
1122. The *Five Hundred Thousand Lines* (*'Bum phrag lnga pa*) is the lost *Hevajra Root Tantra*. See the lines translated on pp. 60–63.
1123. See Nāropa, *Commentary on "Brief Presentation of Initiation,"* Toh 1351 Tengyur, rgyud *na*, 277a6. Also see Acalagarbha, *Combined Explanation*, Toh 1349 Tengyur, rgyud *na*, 29a2. The original source of these lines is Mañjuśrīyaśas, *Brief Presentation of the Assertions of My Own View*, P 4610 Tengyur, rgyud 'grel *pu*, 22a5.
1124. Tripiṭakamāla, *Lamp of the Three Ways*, Toh 3707 Tengyur, rgyud *tsu*, 16b3. The full verse says: "Although the meaning is the same, because they are free of delusion, have many methods, no difficulties, and are for those with sharp faculties, the mantra treatises are exceptional."
1125. Maitreya, *Ornament of the Mahāyāna Sūtras*, 10.67–75, Toh 4020 Tengyur, sems tsam *phi*, 11b4.
1126. The "five topics" (*chos lnga*) are name, mark or reason, conceptuality, thusness, and perfect primordial awareness.
1127. Maitreya, *Ornament of the Mahāyāna Sūtras*, 10.76, Toh 4020 Tengyur, sems tsam *phi*, 12a2.
1128. Puṇḍarīka, *Stainless Light* (Jonang trans.), chap. 5, Jo nang dpe tshogs, vol. 20, 364. See also Puṇḍarīka, *Stainless Light* (Jonang trans.), chap. 5, Toh 1347 Tengyur, rgyud *da*, 264a1. "Establishing Sublimely Unchanging Primordial Awareness" (Mchog tu mi 'gyur ba'i ye shes grub pa) is the title of the third section in the fifth chapter of the *Stainless Light*.
1129. Puṇḍarīka, *Stainless Light* (Jonang trans.), chap. 5, Jo nang dpe tshogs, vol. 20, 365. See also Puṇḍarīka, *Stainless Light* (Jonang trans.), chap. 5, Toh 1347 Tengyur, rgyud *da*, 264a7. This continues from the previous passage in the *Stainless Light*. The verse lines here are *Kālacakra Tantra* (Jonang trans.), 5.101–103c, Jo nang dpe

tshogs, vol. 17, 187. See also *Kālacakra Tantra* (Shong trans.), 5.101–103c, Toh 362 Kangyur, rgyud 'bum *ka*, 111b3.

1130. Puṇḍarīka, *Stainless Light* (Jonang trans.), chap. 5, Jo nang dpe tshogs, vol. 20, 366. Puṇḍarīka, *Stainless Light* (Jonang trans.), chap. 5, Toh 1347 Tengyur, rgyud *da*, 264b5. This continues from the previous passage in the *Stainless Light*. The verse line is *Kālacakra Tantra* (Jonang trans.), 5.103d, Jo nang dpe tshogs, vol. 17, 188. See also *Kālacakra Tantra* (Shong trans.), 5.103d, Toh 362 Kangyur, rgyud 'bum *ka*, 111b7.

1131. Puṇḍarīka, *Stainless Light* (Jonang trans.), chap. 5, Jo nang dpe tshogs, vol. 20, 366. See also Puṇḍarīka, *Stainless Light* (Jonang trans.), chap. 5, Toh 1347 Tengyur, rgyud *da*, 264b5.

1132. The *visarga* is the last in the series of Sanskrit vowels and looks like two drops, one on top of the other. It is the symbol for primordial awareness.

1133. *Kālacakra Tantra* (Jonang trans.), 5.244–47, Jo nang dpe tshogs, vol. 17, 220. See also *Kālacakra Tantra* (Shong trans.), 5.244–47, Toh 362 Kangyur, rgyud 'bum *ka*, 126b4. Verses 244 and 245 concern the first and second of the five changeless great emptinesses (*stong pa chen po 'gyur med lnga*), verse 246 concerns both the third and the fourth, and verse 247 concerns the fifth. Curiously, the heading from Dölpopa's outline inserted into *Mountain Dharma* before these verses refers to "the five syllables of the great emptinesses" (*stong pa chen po yi ge lnga*), but the sentence at the end of the next set of verses identifies the topic of the earlier verses as "the five changeless great emptinesses" (*stong pa chen po 'gyur med lnga*). This slim piece of evidence perhaps indicates Dölpopa wrote the separate outline for *Mountain Dharma* before the Jonang revised translation of *Stainless Light* in 1334, after which he wrote *Mountain Dharma*. As previously mentioned, the quotations in *Mountain Dharma* are all from the revised Jonang translations. In the earlier thirteen-century revised translation by Shongtön, the Sanskrit term *akṣara* is translated as *yi ge* ("syllable"), but the revised Jonang translation often uses *'gyur med* ("changeless"). The Sanskrit term has both meanings. Could Dölpopa have been working on his outline before the new revised Jonang translation, and thus used the earlier translation of this term?

1134. Dölpopa's annotations in the Jo nang dpe tshogs edition of *Mountain Dharma* say the source of the attributes, the syllable *e* (the prajñā that is emptiness having the most sublime of all attributes), has the inseparable qualities of a buddha, such as the ten powers, but not the three qualities of lightness (*sattva*, *snying stobs*), motility (*rajas*, *rdul*), and darkness (*tamas*, *mun pa*), referred to in the verse by the terms "short," "long," and "very long." Concerning the meaning of the three qualities in the Kālacakra tradition, see Wallace 2001, 36–37.

1135. *Kālacakra Tantra* (Jonang trans.), 5.248, Jo nang dpe tshogs, vol. 17, 221. See also *Kālacakra Tantra* (Shong trans.), 5.248, Toh 362 Kangyur, rgyud 'bum *ka*, 127a3.

1136. *Hevajra Tantra*, pt. 2, 4.45–47, Toh 418 Kangyur, rgyud 'bum *nga*, 21a3.

1137. *Sūtra about the Level of a Buddha*, Toh 275 Kangyur, mdo sde *ya*, 37a4. This sūtra has not survived in Sanskrit. The Tibetan translation *shin tu 'dus* for the bodhisattva's name here is difficult to explain. The English translation of the name in this exact quotation in the Chinese translation of this sūtra from Sanskrit, and the English translation for the same name in a Chinese translation of another sūtra for which the Sanskrit does survive, are the same. In the sūtra for which the Sanskrit does survive, the original name is Sujāta. I am grateful to David Reigle for a detailed explanation of this issue, which I have tried to briefly summarize here.

1138. Vajragarbha, *Extensive Commentary on the Condensed Meaning of the Hevajra*, Toh 1180 Tengyur, rgyud *ka*, 37b7.

1139. Tripiṭakamāla, *Lamp of the Three Ways*, Toh 3707 Tengyur, rgyud *tsu*, 16b3. The full verse says: "Although the meaning is the same, because they are free of delusion, have many methods, no difficulties, and are for those with sharp faculties, the mantra treatises are exceptional."

1140. Mentioned in various works, such as Puṇḍarīka, *Stainless Light* (Jonang trans.), chap. 5, Jo nang dpe tshogs, vol. 20, 294. See also Puṇḍarīka, *Stainless Light* (Jonang trans.), chap. 5, Toh 1347 Tengyur, rgyud *da*, 237a4.

1141. Mentioned in various works, such as Asaṅga, *Commentary on the "Uttaratantra,"* Toh 4025 Tengyur, sems tsam *phi*, 114a2.

1142. *Sūtra to Benefit Aṅgulimāla*, Toh 213 Kangyur, mdo sde *tsha*, 157a4.

1143. Maitreya, *Ornament of the Mahāyāna Sūtras*, 10.62, Toh 4020 Tengyur, sems tsam *phi*, 11b1.

1144. Maitreya, *Ornament of Direct Realization*, 8.1–6, Toh 3786 Tengyur, shes phyin *ka*, 11a7.

1145. *Kālacakra Tantra* (Jonang trans.), 5.157–58, Jo nang dpe tshogs, vol. 17, 200. See also *Kālacakra Tantra* (Shong trans.), 5.157–58, Toh 362 Kangyur, rgyud 'bum *ka*, 117a7.

1146. *Sūtra Perfectly Summarizing the Dharma*, Toh 238 Kangyur, mdo sde *zha*, 10b6.

1147. Maitreya, *Uttaratantra*, 3.38ab, Toh 4024 Tengyur, sems tsam *phi*, 67a4.

1148. Maitreya, *Ornament of the Mahāyāna Sūtras*, 10.61, Toh 4020 Tengyur, sems tsam *phi*, 11a7.

1149. Maitreya, *Ornament of Direct Realization*, 8.12–17, Toh 3786 Tengyur, shes phyin *ka*, 11b7.

1150. Maitreya, *Ornament of Direct Realization*, 8.21–32, Toh 3786 Tengyur, shes phyin *ka*, 12a6.

1151. *Sūtra of Question by Mañjuśrī*, Toh 172 Kangyur, mdo sde *ma*, 3b4.

1152. Maitreya, *Ornament of the Mahāyāna Sūtras*, 10.63–64, Toh 4020 Tengyur, sems tsam *phi*, 11b2. Dölpopa's annotation in the Jo nang dpe tshogs edition of *Mountain Dharma* says the phrase "two in all aspects" refers to the natural kāya and the sambhogakāya.

1153. Maitreya, *Ornament of Direct Realization*, 8.33, Toh 3786 Tengyur, shes phyin *ka*, 12b6.

1154. Maitreya, *Ornament of the Mahāyāna Sūtras*, 10.26, Toh 4020 Tengyur, sems tsam *phi*, 9b6.

1155. Maitreya, *Ornament of the Mahāyāna Sūtras*, 10.22–25, Toh 4020 Tengyur, sems tsam *phi*, 9b3.

1156. Maitreya, *Ornament of the Mahāyāna Sūtras*, 10.17, Toh 4020 Tengyur, sems tsam *phi*, 9b1.

1157. Maitreya, *Ornament of the Mahāyāna Sūtras*, 10.34, Toh 4020 Tengyur, sems tsam *phi*, 10a3.

1158. Maitreya, *Ornament of the Mahāyāna Sūtras*, 10.16, Toh 4020 Tengyur, sems tsam *phi*, 9a7.

1159. Maitreya, *Ornament of Direct Realization*, 8.10, Toh 3786 Tengyur, shes phyin *ka*, 11b5.

1160. Nāgārjuna, *In Praise of Dharmadhātu*, vv. 51cd–54, Toh 1118 Tengyur, bstod tshogs *ka*, 65b4.

1161. *Chanting the Ultimate Names of Mañjuśrī*, v. 97b, Toh 360 Kangyur, rgyud 'bum *ka*, 5b7. The quote in *Mountain Dharma* (*mi mngon mi snang gsal byed min*) is from the old Tibetan translation by Lochen Rinchen Sangpo, not the revised translation (*gsal min mi snang gos pa med*) by Shongtön Lodrö Tenpa that is in the Tengyur.

1162. *Chanting the Ultimate Names of Mañjuśrī*, v. 34d, Toh 360 Kangyur, rgyud 'bum *ka*, 3a6.

1163. Maitreya, *Ornament of the Mahāyāna Sūtras*, 10.22d, Toh 4020 Tengyur, sems tsam *phi*, 9b4.

1164. Maitreya, *Distinguishing the Middle and the Extremes*, 1.22ab, Toh 4021 Tengyur, sems tsam *phi*, 41a6.

1165. Maitreya, *Distinguishing the Middle and the Extremes*, 1.2a, Toh 4021 Tengyur, sems tsam *phi*, 40b2.

1166. Nāgārjuna, *Root Verses on Madhyamaka, Called "Wisdom,"* 22.11a–c, Toh 3824 Tengyur, dbu ma *tsa*, 13b1.

1167. Nāgārjuna, *Root Verses on Madhyamaka, Called "Wisdom,"* 22.11d, Toh 3824 Tengyur, dbu ma *tsa*, 13b2.

1168. Nāgārjuna, *Refutation of Objections*, Toh 3828 Tengyur, dbu ma *tsa*, 28a1.

1169. Āryadeva, *Four Hundred Verses*, chap. 16, v. 25, Toh 3846 Tengyur, dbu ma *tsha*, 18a5.

1170. Nāgārjuna, *Sixty Verses on Reasoning*, vv. 46–47, Toh 3825 Tengyur, dbu ma *tsa*, 22a3.

1171. Bhāvaviveka, *Jewel Lamp of the Madhyamaka*, Toh 3854 Tengyur, dbu ma *tsha*, 276a1. These lines, and those in the next two quotes, have not been identified in any of Nāgārjuna's works.

1172. Bhāvaviveka, *Jewel Lamp of the Madhyamaka*, Toh 3854 Tengyur, dbu ma *tsha*, 273b5.

1173. Bhāvaviveka, *Jewel Lamp of the Madhyamaka*, Toh 3854 Tengyur, dbu ma *tsha*, 273b6.

1174. Jinaputra, *Commentary on "In Praise of the Three Jewels,"* Toh 1145 Tengyur, bstod tshogs *ka*, 107a2.

1175. Nāgārjuna, *Root Verses on Madhyamaka, Called "Wisdom,"* chap. 25, vv. 2cd–3, Toh 3824 Tengyur, dbu ma *tsa*, 16a6. As referred to just above, this chapter 25 is entitled "Analysis of Nirvāṇa."

1176. Nāgārjuna, *Sixty Verses on Reasoning*, v. 6, Toh 3825 Tengyur, dbu ma *tsa*, 20b4.

1177. Puṇḍarīka, *Stainless Light* (Jonang trans.), chap. 4, Jo nang dpe tshogs, vol. 20, 79. See also Puṇḍarīka, *Stainless Light* (Jonang trans.), chap. 4, Toh 1347 Tengyur, rgyud *da*, 61a1.

1178. *Hevajra Tantra*, pt. 2, 4.30d–35b, Toh 418 Kangyur, rgyud 'bum *nga*, 20b3.

1179. Nāgārjuna, *Root Verses on Madhyamaka, Called "Wisdom,"* 25.19–20, Toh 3824 Tengyur, dbu ma *tsa*, 17a1; cited in Nāgārjuna, *Fearing Nothing*, Toh 3829 Tengyur, dbu ma *tsa*, 94a2.

1180. This passage from the lost *Kālacakra Root Tantra*, here called the *Tantra of the*

Excellent Ādi[buddha] (*Dam pa dang po'i rgyud*) is quoted in Puṇḍarīka, *Stainless Light* (Jonang trans.), chap. 4, Jo nang dpe tshogs, vol. 20, 85. See also Puṇḍarīka, *Stainless Light* (Jonang trans.), chap. 4, Toh 1347 Tengyur, rgyud *da*, 62b4.

1181. Vajrapāṇi, *Brief Cakrasaṃvara Commentary*, Toh 1402 Tengyur, rgyud *ba*, 130b2.
1182. *Chanting the Ultimate Names of Mañjuśrī*, v. 104a, Toh 360 Kangyur, rgyud 'bum *ka*, 6a4.
1183. *Chanting the Ultimate Names of Mañjuśrī*, v. 81d, Toh 360 Kangyur, rgyud 'bum *ka*, 5a5.
1184. See Nāgārjuna, *Guhyasamāja Maṇḍala Ritual*, Toh 1798 Tengyur, rgyud *ngi*, 27a6. The first two lines in the Kangyur text are the same, but the second two lines are very different.
1185. *Mahāparinirvāṇa Sūtra* (trans. from Chinese), Toh 119 Kangyur, mdo sde *nya*, 49a2.
1186. *Mahāparinirvāṇa Sūtra* (trans. from Chinese), Toh 119 Kangyur, mdo sde *nya*, 49a4.
1187. *Mahāparinirvāṇa Sūtra* (trans. from Chinese), Toh 119 Kangyur, mdo sde *nya*, 49a5.
1188. *Mahāparinirvāṇa Sūtra* (trans. from Chinese), Toh 119 Kangyur, mdo sde *nya*, 49a6.
1189. *Mahāparinirvāṇa Sūtra* (trans. from Chinese), Toh 119 Kangyur, mdo sde *nya*, 49a7.
1190. *Mahāparinirvāṇa Sūtra* (trans. from Chinese), Toh 119 Kangyur, mdo sde *nya*, 49b1.
1191. *Mahāparinirvāṇa Sūtra* (trans. from Chinese), Toh 119 Kangyur, mdo sde *nya*, 49b3.
1192. *Mahāparinirvāṇa Sūtra* (trans. from Chinese), Toh 119 Kangyur, mdo sde *nya*, 49b5.
1193. *Mahāparinirvāṇa Sūtra* (trans. from Chinese), Toh 119 Kangyur, mdo sde *nya*, 49b6.
1194. *Mahāparinirvāṇa Sūtra* (trans. from Chinese), Toh 119 Kangyur, mdo sde *nya*, 50a2.
1195. *Great Cloud Sūtra*, Toh 232 Kangyur, mdo sde *wa*, 159b7. These are the last six of the twenty-three examples of enigmatic speech (*ldem po ngag*) listed by the Buddha in this sūtra.
1196. Maitreya, *Ornament of the Mahāyāna Sūtras*, 10.78–79, Toh 4020 Tengyur, sems tsam *phi*, 12a3.
1197. Maitreya, *Ornament of the Mahāyāna Sūtras*, 21.1, Toh 4020 Tengyur, sems tsam *phi*, 36a4.
1198. *Sūtra of the Excellent Golden Light*, Toh 556 Kangyur, rgyud 'bum *pa*, 166b1.
1199. *Sūtra of the Excellent Golden Light*, Toh 556 Kangyur, rgyud 'bum *pa*, 166b4.
1200. *Sūtra of the Excellent Golden Light*, Toh 556 Kangyur, rgyud 'bum *pa*, 166a3.
1201. *Sūtra of the Excellent Golden Light*, Toh 556 Kangyur, rgyud 'bum *pa*, 169b1.
1202. *Sūtra of the Excellent Golden Light*, Toh 556 Kangyur, rgyud 'bum *pa*, 164b7.
1203. For example, *Kālacakra Tantra* (Jonang trans.), 5.55a, Jo nang dpe tshogs, vol. 17, 174. See also *Kālacakra Tantra* (Shong trans.), 5.55a, Toh 362 Kangyur, rgyud 'bum *ka*, 107a2.

1204. Maitreya, *Uttaratantra*, 1.145, Toh 4024 Tengyur, sems tsam *phi*, 61a7.
1205. Asaṅga, *Levels of the Bodhisattva*, Toh 4037 Tengyur, sems tsam *wi*, 48a6.
1206. Maitreya, *Ornament of the Mahāyāna Sūtras*, 10.38–48, Toh 4020 Tengyur, sems tsam *phi*, 10a5.
1207. Candrakīrti, *Entering the Madhyamaka*, 11.19, Toh 3861 Tengyur, dbu ma *'a*, 216b4.
1208. Candrakīrti, *Entering the Madhyamaka*, 11.20–21, Toh 3861 Tengyur, dbu ma *'a*, 216b5.
1209. Candrakīrti, *Entering the Madhyamaka*, 11.22a–c, Toh 3861 Tengyur, dbu ma *'a*, 216b6. Here the last seven syllables of 21d have been joined to the first five syllables of 22c to make a new third line in Tibetan.
1210. Candrakīrti, *Entering the Madhyamaka*, 11.22d, Toh 3861 Tengyur, dbu ma *'a*, 216b6.
1211. Candrakīrti, *Entering the Madhyamaka*, 11.23–24, Toh 3861 Tengyur, dbu ma *'a*, 216b7.
1212. Candrakīrti, *Entering the Madhyamaka*, 11.25, Toh 3861 Tengyur, dbu ma *'a*, 217a2.
1213. Candrakīrti, *Entering the Madhyamaka*, 11.26, Toh 3861 Tengyur, dbu ma *'a*, 217a2.
1214. Candrakīrti, *Entering the Madhyamaka*, 11.27, Toh 3861 Tengyur, dbu ma *'a*, 217a3.
1215. Candrakīrti, *Explanation of "Entering the Madhyamaka,"* Toh 3862 Tengyur, dbu ma *'a*, 332a7–334a3.
1216. *Sūtra of the Mudrā of Engagement in Producing the Power of Faith*, Toh 201 Kangyur, mdo sde *tsha*, 49a6.
1217. Maitreya, *Uttaratantra*, 4.1, Toh 4024 Tengyur, sems tsam *phi*, 67a6.
1218. Maitreya, *Uttaratantra*, 4.12, Toh 4024 Tengyur, sems tsam *phi*, 67b6.
1219. Maitreya, *Ornament of Direct Realization*, 8.34ab–40cd, Toh 3786 Tengyur, shes phyin *ka*, 13a4.
1220. *Sūtra of the Excellent Golden Light*, Toh 556 Kangyur, rgyud 'bum *pa*, 165a7.
1221. Maitreya, *Ornament of the Mahāyāna Sūtras*, 10.27–33, Toh 4020 Tengyur, sems tsam *phi*, 9b6.
1222. Maitreya, *Ornament of the Mahāyāna Sūtras*, 10.49–55, Toh 4020 Tengyur, sems tsam *phi*, 10b5. According to Dölpopa's student Mati Panchen, *Brilliant Illumination of the Mahāyāna*, 187, the "dhātu of the buddhas" in the last verse refers to the taintless dharmadhātu of the buddhas (*sangs rgyas rnams kyi zag pa med pa'i chos kyi dbyings*).
1223. Maitreya, *Ornament of the Mahāyāna Sūtras*, 10.18–20, Toh 4020 Tengyur, sems tsam *phi*, 9b1.
1224. Maitreya, *Ornament of the Mahāyāna Sūtras*, 10.82–85, Toh 4020 Tengyur, sems tsam *phi*, 12a5.
1225. *Kālacakra Tantra* (Jonang trans.), Jo nang dpe tshogs, vol. 17, 185. See also *Kālacakra Tantra* (Shong trans.), 5.96–98, Toh 362 Kangyur, rgyud 'bum *ka*, 111a3.
1226. *Kālacakra Tantra* (Jonang trans.), 5.60–61, Jo nang dpe tshogs, vol. 17, 176. See also *Kālacakra Tantra* (Shong trans.), 5.60–61, Toh 362 Kangyur, rgyud 'bum *ka*, 107b1.
1227. *Kālacakra Tantra* (Jonang trans.), Jo nang dpe tshogs, vol. 17, 174. See also *Kālacakra Tantra* (Shong trans.), 5.54, Toh 362 Kangyur, rgyud 'bum *ka*, 106b7.
1228. Puṇḍarīka, *Stainless Light* (Jonang trans.), chap. 5, Jo nang dpe tshogs, vol. 20, 328.

Puṇḍarīka, *Stainless Light* (Jonang trans.), chap. 5, Toh 1347 Tengyur, rgyud *da*, 249b7.

1229. Maitreya, *Uttaratantra*, 4.14–46, Toh 4024 Tengyur, sems tsam *phi*, 67b7.
1230. Maitreya, *Uttaratantra*, 4.53–76, Toh 4024 Tengyur, sems tsam *phi*, 69b7.
1231. Maitreya, *Uttaratantra*, 4.85–91, Toh 4024 Tengyur, sems tsam *phi*, 71a5.
1232. Maitreya, *Uttaratantra*, 4.93–8, Toh 4024 Tengyur, sems tsam *phi*, 71b3.
1233. Śāntideva, *Entering the Conduct of a Bodhisattva*, 9.34–38, Toh 3871 Tengyur, dbu ma *la*, 32a4.
1234. Maitreya, *Uttaratantra*, 2.10–11, Toh 4024 Tengyur, sems tsam *phi*, 62b6.
1235. Maitreya, *Distinguishing the Middle and the Extremes*, 1.16cd, Toh 4021 Tengyur, sems tsam *phi*, 41a3.
1236. Nāgārjuna, *Garland of Jewels*, chap. 3, vv. 12–13ab, Toh 4158 Tengyur, spring yig *ge*, 115a1.
1237. Nāgārjuna, *Sixty Verses on Reasoning*, v. 60cd, Toh 3825 Tengyur, dbu ma *tsa*, 22b4.
1238. *Sūtra of the Excellent Golden Light*, chap. 3, Toh 556 Kangyur, rgyud 'bum *pa*, 168a7.
1239. *Sūtra of the Excellent Golden Light*, chap. 3, Toh 556 Kangyur, rgyud 'bum *pa*, 169a7.
1240. *Kālacakra Tantra* (Jonang trans.), 5.160–64, Jo nang dpe tshogs, vol. 17, 201. See also *Kālacakra Tantra* (Shong trans.), 5.160–64, Toh 362 Kangyur, rgyud 'bum *ka*, 117b4.
1241. These lines were not located in the *Guhyasamāja Tantra* itself, but were found in the *Vajra Garland Tantra*, chap. 22, Toh 445 Kangyur, rgyud 'bum *ca*, 234a5. The *Vajra Garland* is an explanatory tantra of the *Guhyasamāja*.
1242. *Vajra Garland Tantra*, chap. 22, Toh 445 Kangyur, rgyud 'bum *ca*, 234b3.
1243. *Vajra Garland Tantra*, chap. 68, Toh 445 Kangyur, rgyud 'bum *ca*, 274b6. The eight attainments are those of eye medicine, swift-footedness, the enchanted sword, going beneath the earth, pills, traveling through the sky, invisibility, and subsisting on elixirs. This list varies somewhat according to the source.
1244. Saraha, *Treasury of Dohā Verses*, Toh 2224 Tengyur, rgyud *wi*, 74b1. The text in the Tengyur is very different.
1245. Maitreya, *Ornament of the Mahāyāna Sūtras*, 20.54, Toh 4020 Tengyur, sems tsam *phi*, 34b7, and Vasubandhu, *Explanation of the "Ornament of the Sūtras,"* Toh 4026 Tengyur, sems tsam *phi*, 246b4.
1246. Maitreya, *Distinguishing Phenomena and True Nature*, Toh 4023 Tengyur, sems tsam *phi*, 51b3.
1247. Maitreya, *Distinguishing the Middle and the Extremes*, 1.16cd, Toh 4021 Tengyur, sems tsam *phi*, 41a3, and Vasubandhu, *Commentary on "Distinguishing the Middle and the Extremes,"* Toh 4027 Tengyur, sems tsam *bi*, 4b6.
1248. Maitreya, *Ornament of the Mahāyāna Sūtras*, 12.13, Toh 4020 Tengyur, sems tsam *phi*, 13b4.
1249. Maitreya, *Ornament of the Mahāyāna Sūtras*, 14.18–19, Toh 4020 Tengyur, sems tsam *phi*, 18a7.
1250. Vasubandhu, *Explanation of the "Ornament of the Sūtras,"* Toh 4026 Tengyur, sems tsam *phi*, 188b6.
1251. Maitreya, *Uttaratantra*, 2.5a, Toh 4024 Tengyur, sems tsam *phi*, 62b3.

1252. Maitreya, *Uttaratantra*, 1.63d, Toh 4024 Tengyur, sems tsam *phi*, 57b1.
1253. *Mahāparinirvāṇa Sūtra* (trans. from Chinese), Toh 119 Kangyur, mdo sde *ta*, 290b7.
1254. *Mahāparinirvāṇa Sūtra* (trans. from Chinese), Toh 119 Kangyur, mdo sde *nya*, 68a3.
1255. *Mahāparinirvāṇa Sūtra* (trans. from Chinese), Toh 119 Kangyur, mdo sde *nya*, 66a3.
1256. *Mahāparinirvāṇa Sūtra* (trans. by Lhai Dawa), Toh 120 Kangyur, mdo sde *tha*, 58a5.
1257. *Brief Presentation of Initiation*, vv. 102–103, Toh 361 Kangyur, rgyud 'bum *ka*, 18a3.
1258. *Sūtra of the Great Drum*, Toh 222 Kangyur, mdo sde *dza*, 97b1.
1259. Vajragarbha, *Extensive Commentary on the Condensed Meaning of the Hevajra*, chap. 3, Toh 1180 Tengyur, rgyud *ka*, 11b4. The full verse says: "Just as a pot is broken, but the space/ is not destroyed, so too the body/ disintegrates, but primordial awareness/ is not destroyed."
1260. Āryadeva, *Establishing the Reasoning That Refutes Confusion*, Toh 3847 Tengyur, dbu ma *tsha*, 19b3. These lines in the Tengyur are somewhat different.
1261. Āryadeva, *Establishing the Reasoning That Refutes Confusion*, Toh 3847 Tengyur, dbu ma *tsha*, 21a6.
1262. Āryadeva, *Establishing the Reasoning That Refutes Confusion*, Toh 3847 Tengyur, dbu ma *tsha*, 22a1.
1263. Āryadeva, *Establishing the Reasoning That Refutes Confusion*, Toh 3847 Tengyur, dbu ma *tsha*, 22a4.
1264. Āryadeva, *Chapter the Length of a Forearm*, Toh 3848 Tengyur, dbu ma *tsha*, 22b3.
1265. Nāgārjuna, *Sixty Verses on Reasoning*, vv. 37–38, Toh 3825 Tengyur, dbu ma *tsa*, 21b6. This passage in the Tengyur text is quite different.
1266. Āryadeva, *Madhyamaka Destruction of Confusion*, Toh 3850 Tengyur, dbu ma *tsha*, 25b4.
1267. Āryadeva, *Madhyamaka Destruction of Confusion*, Toh 3850 Tengyur, dbu ma *tsha*, 26a1. Dölpopa's annotation in the Jo nang dpe tshogs edition of *Mountain Dharma* identifies the author of the quoted verses to be Nāgārjuna, but they were not found in any of his works. The verses were located, however, in Bhāvaviveka, *Essence of Madhyamaka*, chap. 2, Toh 3855 Tengyur, dbu ma *dza*, 12b7.
1268. Bhāvaviveka, *Jewel Lamp of the Madhyamaka*, Toh 3854 Tengyur, dbu ma *tsha*, 262a1.
1269. Vasubandhu, *Correctness of the Explanation*, Toh 4061 Tengyur, sems tsam *shi*, 29a3. These lines in the Tengyur text are extremely different.
1270. Vasubandhu, *Extensive Commentary on the "Sūtra in One Hundred Thousand Lines,"* Toh 3807 Tengyur, shes phyin *na*, 102b5.
1271. Vasubandhu, *Extensive Commentary on the "Sūtra in One Hundred Thousand Lines,"* Toh 3807 Tengyur, shes phyin *na*, 25b1.
1272. Vasubandhu, *Vast Explanation of the "Sūtra in One Hundred Thousand Lines," the "Sūtra in Twenty-Five Thousand Lines," and the "Sūtra in Eighteen Thousand Lines,"* Toh 3808 Tengyur, shes phyin *pha*, 137a3.
1273. Vasubandhu, *Vast Explanation of the "Sūtra in One Hundred Thousand Lines,"*

the "Sūtra in Twenty-Five Thousand Lines," and the "Sūtra in Eighteen Thousand Lines," Toh 3808 Tengyur, shes phyin *pha*, 214a4.

1274. Vasubandhu, *Vast Explanation of the "Sūtra in One Hundred Thousand Lines," the "Sūtra in Twenty-Five Thousand Lines," and the "Sūtra in Eighteen Thousand Lines,"* Toh 3808 Tengyur, shes phyin *pha*, 210a5.
1275. Śāntideva, *Entering the Conduct of a Bodhisattva*, 9.34, Toh 3871 Tengyur, dbu ma *la*, 32a4.
1276. Maitreya, *Distinguishing Phenomena and True Nature*, Toh 4023 Tengyur, sems tsam *phi*, 52b6.
1277. Nāgārjuna, *Stages of Meditation*, Toh 3908 Tengyur, dbu ma *ki*, 3a1.
1278. Nāgārjuna, *Stages of Meditation*, Toh 3908 Tengyur, dbu ma *ki*, 3a6.
1279. Maitreya, *Ornament of the Mahāyāna Sūtras*, 20.53, Toh 4020 Tengyur, sems tsam *phi*, 34b6.
1280. Maitreya, *Ornament of the Mahāyāna Sūtras*, 20.54ab, Toh 4020 Tengyur, sems tsam *phi*, 34b7.
1281. Maitreya, *Ornament of the Mahāyāna Sūtras*, 7.4cd, Toh 4020 Tengyur, sems tsam *phi*, 6b2.
1282. Maitreya, *Ornament of the Mahāyāna Sūtras*, 12.14, Toh 4020 Tengyur, sems tsam *phi*, 13b5.
1283. *Avataṃsaka Sūtra*, Toh 44 Kangyur, phal chen *ka*, 242b1.
1284. Nāgārjuna, *In Praise of Dharmadhātu*, v. 61cd, Toh 1118 Tengyur, bstod tshogs *ka*, 66a2.
1285. Kamalaśīla, *Illuminating Reality*, Toh 3888 Tengyur, dbu ma *sa*, 244b4.
1286. Kamalaśīla, *Illuminating Reality*, Toh 3888 Tengyur, dbu ma *sa*, 251b5.
1287. Kamalaśīla, *Illuminating Reality*, Toh 3888 Tengyur, dbu ma *sa*, 252a7.
1288. This exact quote has not been located, but Dölpopa may be referring to a statement in the *Avataṃsaka Sūtra*, Toh 44 Kangyur, phal chen *ka*, 220b4. Another possibility is the *Journey to Laṅkā Sūtra*, Toh 107 Kangyur, mdo sde *ca*, 87a3. The phrase in the *Mountain Dharma* says the three realms are "consciousness only" (*rnam par shes pa tsam*), but the phrase in the *Avataṃsaka* says "mind only" (*sems tsam*), and the *Journey to Laṅkā* reads "one's own mind only" (*rang gi sems tsam*).
1289. Buddhapālita, *Buddhapālita's Commentary on the "Root Verses on Madhyamaka,* Toh 3842 Tengyur, dbu ma *tsa*, 159a4.
1290. Maitreya, *Distinguishing Phenomena and True Nature*, Toh 4023 Tengyur, sems tsam *phi*, 50b3.
1291. Maitreya, *Distinguishing Phenomena and True Nature*, Toh 4023 Tengyur, sems tsam *phi*, 50b4.
1292. Maitreya, *Distinguishing Phenomena and True Nature*, Toh 4023 Tengyur, sems tsam *phi*, 53a5.
1293. Asaṅga, *Compendium of Abhidharma*, Toh 4049 Tengyur, sems tsam *ri*, 73b2.
1294. Nāgārjuna, *In Praise of Dharmadhātu*, v. 64cd, Toh 1118 Tengyur, bstod tshogs *ka*, 66a4.
1295. Nāgārjuna, *In Praise of Dharmadhātu*, v. 65cd, Toh 1118 Tengyur, bstod tshogs *ka*, 66a4.
1296. Vasubandhu, *Vast Explanation of the "Sūtra in One Hundred Thousand Lines," the "Sūtra in Twenty-Five Thousand Lines," and the "Sūtra in Eighteen Thousand Lines,"* Toh 3808 Tengyur, shes phyin *pha*, 209b6.

1297. Vasubandhu, *Vast Explanation of the "Sūtra in One Hundred Thousand Lines," the "Sūtra in Twenty-Five Thousand Lines," and the "Sūtra in Eighteen Thousand Lines,"* Toh 3808 Tengyur, shes phyin *pha*, 210a1.
1298. Maitreya, *Ornament of Direct Realization*, 2.5cd, Toh 3786 Tengyur, shes phyin *ka*, 5a3.
1299. *Verse Summary of the Sūtras on the Perfection of Wisdom*, Toh 13 Kangyur, shes phyin *ka*, 8b2.
1300. Maitreya, *Ornament of the Mahāyāna Sūtras*, 10.78cd, Toh 4020 Tengyur, sems tsam *phi*, 12a3.
1301. *Sūtra of the Bodhisattva's Scriptural Collection*, Toh 56 Kangyur, dkon brtsegs *ga*, 164a3.
1302. *Sūtra Perfectly Summarizing the Dharma*, Toh 238 Kangyur, mdo sde *zha*, 68b6. The wording in the Kangyur text is somewhat different, but the meaning is the same.
1303. Candragomin, *In Praise of Mañjuśrī*, Toh 2710 Tengyur, rgyud *nu*, 77b4. The *Mountain Dharma* text here uses the name Mañjughoṣa instead of Mañjuśrī, which is found in the Kangyur text.
1304. *Avataṃsaka Sūtra*, Toh 44 Kangyur, phal chen *ka*, 242a6.
1305. *Chanting the Ultimate Names of Mañjuśrī*, v. 34d, Toh 360 Kangyur, rgyud 'bum *ka*, 3a6.
1306. Maitreya, *Ornament of the Mahāyāna Sūtras*, 10.33, Toh 4020 Tengyur, sems tsam *phi*, 10a3.
1307. Asaṅga, *Compendium of the Mahāyāna*, Toh 4048 Tengyur, sems tsam *ri*, 16a1. The lines here are very different than the passage in the Tengyur.
1308. *Kālacakra Tantra* (Jonang trans.), 5.192, Jo nang dpe tshogs, vol. 17, 208. See also *Kālacakra Tantra* (Shong trans.), 5.192, Toh 362 Kangyur, rgyud 'bum *ka*, 121a2.
1309. Śāntideva, *Entering the Conduct of a Bodhisattva*, 9.26, Toh 3871 Tengyur, dbu ma *la*, 31b6.
1310. Asaṅga, *Compendium of the Mahāyāna*, Toh 4048 Tengyur, sems tsam *ri*, 35b4.
1311. Vasubandhu, *Explanation of the "Treasury of Abhidharma,"* Toh 4090 Tengyur, mngon pa *ku*, 175b4. When quoted in Vasubandhu's work this passage is identified as "from a sūtra" (*mdo las*). Dölpopa's annotation in the Jo nang dpe tshogs edition of *Mountain Dharma* says it is from a Vinaya scripture ('Dul ba lung), but it has not been located. "The Elephant" is an epithet for the Buddha.
1312. This passage by Āryadeva is quoted in Bhāvaviveka, *Jewel Lamp of the Madhyamaka*, Toh 3854 Tengyur, dbu ma *tsha*, 83b4. It has not been located in any independent work by Āryadeva.
1313. *Basis of Monastic Discipline*, Toh 1 Kangyur, 'dul ba *ga*, 88a4.
1314. *Heart Sūtra on the Perfection of Wisdom*, Toh 21 Kangyur, shes phyin *ka*, 145b5.
1315. Dölpopa has chosen to quote these five long verses of the *Later Kālacakra Tantra* from Nāropa, *Commentary on "Brief Presentation of Initiation,"* Toh 1351 Tengyur, rgyud *na*, 274b2, instead of from the basic source, *Later Kālacakra Tantra*, Toh 363 Kangyur, rgyud 'bum *ka*, 130b3. The Tibetan translations of the same verses in these two works are extremely different. The *Later Kālacakra Tantra* was translated by Nyenchung Dharma Drak, but Nāropa's commentary was later translated by Drakpa Gyaltsen in Nepal and then revised by Rinchen Gyaltsen in Sakya. Of the five verses, verses two, three, and four are also found in Nāgārjuna, *In Praise of*

the Three Kāyas, Toh 1123 Tengyur, bstod tshogs *ka*, 70b3, translated into Tibetan by Lochen Rinchen Sangpo, which is also very different than the translation in Nāropa's commentary and *Mountain Dharma*. The fifth verse from the tantra is also the same as the first verse in Nāgārjuna, *Condensed Sādhana*, Toh 1796 Tengyur, rgyud *ngi*, 1a1, translated by Lochen Rinchen Sangpo, which is again very different than the version in *Mountain Dharma* cited from Nāropa's work. Dölpopa's annotations in the Jo nang dpe tshogs edition of *Mountain Dharma* say the first of the five verses is from the *Later Kālacakra Tantra*, verses two, three, and four are from Nāgārjuna's *In Praise of the Three Kāyas*, and the fifth verse is the word of the Buddha (i.e., from the tantra). It is certainly surprising that four verses by Nāgārjuna are quoted here, and also very odd that both Nāgārjuna and Tibetans are specifically mentioned in the first verse from the tantra.

1316. Maitreya, *Ornament of the Mahāyāna Sūtras*, 21.43–61, Toh 4020 Tengyur, sems tsam *phi*, 38a3.

1317. This verse is by Dölpopa himself. A crucial annotation here in the Jo nang dpe tshogs edition of *Mountain Dharma* says "This last verse is my own prayer" (*ces pa tshigs bcad phyi ma 'di ni rang gi smon lam mo*). This is the only direct evidence that the annotations were written by Dölpopa, although there are many other reasons indicating that to be the case.

1318. See the sūtra passage translated on pp. 186–87.

1319. Asaṅga, *Commentary on the "Uttaratantra,"* Toh 4025 Tengyur, sems tsam *phi*, 100b7. The original source of the quote is *Sūtra Requested by Sāgaramati*, Toh 152 Kangyur, mdo sde *pha*, 85a4.

1320. For example, see Asaṅga, *Levels of the Bodhisattva*, Toh 4037 Tengyur, sems tsam *wi*, 1a4. I am grateful to Artemus Engle for helping me understand this paragraph.

1321. As identified in Dölpopa's annotations in the Jo nang dpe tshogs edition of *Mountain Dharma*, Khenchen Jodenpa is Khenchen Sönam Drakpa (1273–1353), the great abbot of Chölung Monastery. The term *jodenpa* (*jo gdan pa*) does not refer to the Jonang tradition in any way, but to an ascetic monk who maintains strict disciplined conduct according to the monastic code of the Vinaya. This master, also known as Jangsem Sönam Drakpa, was one of Dölpopa's teachers, who gave him the vows of full monastic ordination. He also told Dölpopa to write other texts, including the *Exceptional Esoteric Instructions on Madhyamaka* (*Dbu ma'i man ngag khyad 'phags*), an early work that does not contain Dölpopa's later special Dharma language, such as "emptiness of other" (*gzhan stong*). Sönam Drakpa later received many transmissions from Dölpopa, such as the great Kālacakra initiation and the instructions of the Six-Branch Yoga. He was also a Kālacakra master, and an important teacher of the Sakya master Lama Dampa Sönam Gyaltsen, the Kadam master Gyalsé Thokmé (1295–1369), to whom he transmitted the Mind Training (*blo sbyong*) and other teachings, and many other masters. For more information, see Chak Lotsāwa Rinchen Chögyal, *Wish-Granting Sheaves*, 117–18, 131. Also see Stearns 2010, 14.

1322. Master Lotsāwa is Jonang Lotsāwa Lodrö Pal (1299–1354), who was one of Dölpopa's fourteen major disciples. As a young man Lodrö Pal studied with many teachers in various monasteries. He mastered Sanskrit grammar and language under the instruction of the famous translator Pang Lotsāwa Lodrö Tenpa (1276–1342), who then sent him to Jonang to receive the profound inner Dharma teachings from Dölpopa. From that point on, Lodrö Pal stayed with Dölpopa, receiving from him full monastic ordination and all the tantric initiations, scriptures, and commentaries, as well as all the teachings of the Vehicle of the Perfections, epistemology, abhidharma, and the monastic code. In 1334 Dölpopa ordered Lodrö Pal and another of his major disciples, Mati Panchen (1294–1376), to begin a revised Tibetan translation of the *Kālacakra Tantra* and the *Stainless Light*, which came to be known as the "new Jonang translation" (*jo nang 'gyur gsar*). In 1338 Dölpopa appointed Lodrö Pal as his successor and enthroned him as the fifth occupant of the monastic seat of Jonang. For more information, see Gyalwa Josang Palsangpo, *Brilliant Marvels*, 573–77, Stearns 2008b, and Stearns 2010.

1323. Master Choklé Namgyal (1306–86), one of Dölpopa's fourteen major disciples, also studied as a young man with many teachers at various monasteries. In 1333, when he heard how Dölpopa had built an amazing stūpa at Jonang and was giving Dharma teachings that did not agree with most previous philosophical tenets, Choklé Namgyal traveled to Jonang, where he was overwhelmed by Dölpopa's presence and teachings. For the next twenty years, he received all of Dölpopa's teachings on esoteric subjects, and also many transmissions from several of Dölpopa's other major disciples. When he was thirty-nine years old he was appointed to the monastic seat at Ngamring. After Jonang Lotsāwa died in 1354, Dölpopa invited Choklé Namgyal back to Jonang. There he was enthroned as the sixth holder of the monastic seat, a position he held for the next four or six years, before retiring to a hermitage. When Dölpopa passed away in 1361, Choklé Namgyal returned to Jonang and again held the monastic seat for the next fifteen years. He was the only person to hold the monastic seat of Jonang twice, for a total of about twenty years. He wrote many important works, especially a set of texts on the Six-Branch Yoga of Kālacakra based on the teachings of Dölpopa, and crucial annotations to the *Kālacakra Tantra* and the *Stainless Light*. For more information, see Tenpai Gyaltsen, *Biography of Dharma Lord Choklé Namgyal*, Gyalwa Josang Palsangpo, *Brilliant Marvels*, 582–88, Stearns 2008a, and Stearns 2010.

1324. Dölpopa's annotations here in the Jo nang dpe tshogs edition of *Mountain Dharma* also mention a certain Loburwa Chökyi Gyaltsen, who has not been identified.

1325. According to Dölpopa's annotation in the Jo nang dpe tshogs edition of *Mountain Dharma*, the personal name of Samding Chokpupa was Palden Wangchuk Sherab. The biography of Dölpopa by his major disciple Gharungwa Lhai Gyaltsen (1311–1401) describes Samding Chokpupa as a great ordained yogin from Samding in the Nyangtö region who meditated in the same crossed-leg posture for twelve years, which resulted in excellent samādhi and paranormal abilities. Chokpupa came to Jonang and offered Dölpopa a letter of questions, mentioning he had been his disciple for many lifetimes. The first few lines of this letter are quoted in the biography. See Lhai Gyaltsen, *Biography of the Omniscient Dharma Lord of Jonang*, 35a. The complete text of Dölpopa's reply has survived. It begins with exactly the same three lines that begin *Mountain Dharma*, and is full of personal advice on the practice, experiences, and results of concentrated Vajrayoga meditation. Dölpopa says Chokpupa (a term referring to a specific meditation posture) had asked him to send a portion of Dharma (*chos skal*) that "must be adorned with scriptural quotations" (*lung gis brgyan dgos*). In what could be a direct reference to his composition of *Mountain Dharma*, Dölpopa also says, "I am not writing what have been commonly known before; I am writing some unknown, uncommon, very profound key points, but I am not yet finished. When I am finished, it will be offered for Pön Döndrup Sangpo to see." See Dölpopa Sherab Gyaltsen, *Reply to the Questions of Samtengpa Chokpupa*, 845: *sngar thun mong du grags pa rnams ni 'bri mi 'tshal gda' zhing/ ma grags pa thun mong ma yin pa'i gnad zab zab 'ga' zhig 'bri zhing bdog na'ang da dung ma tshang bas nam tshar ba na dpon don grub bzang pos gzigs pa 'phul bar bdog/.*

1326. Master Yeshé Gyaltsen has not been identified, but might be the master of the same name who later requested Dölpopa's major disciple Drigung Lotsāwa Maṇikaśrī (1313–87) to write a biography of Dölpopa. See Drigung Lotsāwa Maṇikaśrī, *Bright Lamp of Great Bliss*, 14.

1327. The Wanderer (Rgyal khams pa) is one of Dölpopa's pseudonyms.

Bibliography

The following works in the Kangyur and Tengyur are quoted or mentioned in *Mountain Dharma*.

Kangyur (Canonical Scriptures)

Avataṃsaka Sūtra. Buddhāvataṃsakanāmamahāvaipūlyasūtra. Sangs rgyas phal po che zhes bya ba shin tu rgyas pa chen po'i mdo. Toh 44, phal chen *ka, kha, ga, a.*

Basis of Monastic Discipline. Vinayavastu. 'Dul ba gzhi. Toh 1, 'dul ba *ga,* 1b–293a.

Brief Presentation of Initiation. Sekoddeśa. Dbang mdor bstan pa. Toh 361, rgyud 'bum *ka,* 14a–21a.

Buddhakapāla Tantra. Śrībuddhakapālanāmayoginītantrarāja. Dpal sangs rgyas thod pa zhes bya ba rnal 'byor ma'i rgyud kyi rgyal po. Toh 424, rgyud 'bum *nga,* 143a–167a.

Chanting the Ultimate Names of Mañjuśrī, the Embodiment of Primordial Awareness. Mañjuśrījñānasattvasyaparamārthanāmasaṃgīti. 'Jam dpal ye shes sems dpa'i don dam pa'i mtshan yang dag par brjod pa. Toh 360, rgyud 'bum *ka,* 1b–13b.

Chapter of Firm Altruistic Intent. Āryasthirādhyāśayaparivartanāma-mahāyānasūtra. 'Phags pa lhag pa'i bsam pa brtan pa'i le'u zhes bya ba theg pa chen po'i mdo. Toh 224, mdo sde *dza,* 164a–173b.

Compendium of the Reality of All Tathāgatas. Sarvatathāgatatattva-saṃgrahanāmamahāyānasūtra. De bzhin gshegs pa thams cad kyi de kho na nyid bsdus pa. Toh 479, rgyud 'bum *nya,* 1b–142a.

Dhāraṇī of Penetrating the Nonconceptual. Āryāvikalpapraveśanāmadhāraṇī. 'Phags pa rnam par mi rtog par 'jug pa shes bya ba'i gzungs. Toh 142, mdo sde *pa,* 1b–6b.

Dhāraṇī of Vajravidāraṇā. Vajravidāraṇānāmadhāraṇī. Rdo rje rnam par 'joms pa zhes bya ba'i gzungs. Toh 750, rgyud 'bum *dza,* 265b–266b.

Diamond Cutter Sūtra on the Perfection of Wisdom. Āryavajracchedikānāmaprajñāpāramitāmahāyānasūtra. 'Phags pa shes rab kyi pha rol tu phyin pa rdo rje gcod pa zhes bya ba theg pa chen po'i mdo. Toh 16, shes phyin *ka*, 121a–132b.

Extensive Mother Sūtra. Yum rgyas pa. Short title for *Sūtra on the Perfection of Wisdom in One Hundred Thousand Lines.*

Fragment of the Mantra Section of the Glorious Sublime Primal. Śrīparamādyamantrakalpakhaṇḍa. Dpal mchog dang po'i sngags kyi rtog pa'i dum bu. Toh 488, rgyud 'bum *ta*, 173a–265b.

Great Cloud Sūtra. Āryamahāmeghanāmamahāyānasūtra. 'Phags pa sprin chen po zhes bya ba theg pa chen po'i mdo. Toh 232, mdo sde *wa*, 113a–214b.

Great Sūtra Called "Emptiness." Śūnyatānāmamahāsūtra. Mdo chen po stong pa nyid. Toh 290, mdo sde *śa*, 250a1–253b2.

Guhyasamāja Tantra. Sarvatathāgatakāyavākcittarahasyaguhyasamājanāmamahākalparāja. De bzhin gshegs pa thams cad kyi sku gsung thugs kyi gsang chen gsang ba 'dus pa zhes bya ba brtag pa'i rgyal po chen po. Toh 442, rgyud 'bum *ca*, 90a–148a.

Heart Sūtra on the Perfection of Wisdom. Bhagavatīprajñāpāramitāhṛdaya. Bcom ldan 'das ma shes rab kyi pha ro tu phyin pa'i snying po. Toh 21, shes phyin *ka*, 144b–146a.

Hevajra Tantra (The King of Tantras, Called "Hevajra"). Hevajratantrarājanāma. Kye'i rdo rje zhes bya ba rgyud kyi rgyal po/ Kye'i rdo rje mkha' 'gro ma dra ba'i sdom pa'i rgyud kyi rgyal po. Toh 417/418, rgyud 'bum *nga*, 1b–13b/13b–30a.

Immaculate Tantra. Anāvilatantrarāja. Rgyud kyi rgyal po rnyog pa med pa. Toh 414, rgyud 'bum *ga*, 259b–261b.

Jewel Cloud Sūtra. Āryaratnameghanāmamahāyānasūtra. 'Phags pa dkon mchog sprin zhes bya ba theg pa chen po'i mdo. Toh 231, mdo sde *wa*, 1b–112b.

Journey to Laṅkā Sūtra. Āryalaṅkāvatāramahāyānasūtra. 'Phags pa lang kar gshegs pa'i theg pa chen po'i mdo. Toh 107, mdo sde *ca*, 56a–191b.

Kālacakra Tantra (Jonang trans.). *Paramādibuddhoddhṛtaśrīkālacakranāmatantrarāja. Jo nang phyogs las rnam rgyal gyis mchan gyis gsal bar mdzad pa'i bsdus pa'i rgyud kyi rgyal po dpal dus kyi 'khor lo.* This edition contains annotations by Jonang Choklé Namgyal. In *Dus 'khor rgyud mchan*, Jo nang dpe tshogs (Jonang Publication Series), vol. 17: 1–226. Beijing: Mi rigs dpe skrun khang, 2008. See also *Kālacakra Tantra* (Shong trans.). *Mchog gi dang po'i sangs rgyas las phyung ba rgyud kyi rgyal po dpal dus kyi 'khor lo zhes bya ba.* Toh 362, rgyud 'bum *ka,* 22b–128b.

Kāśyapa Chapter Sūtra. Āryakāśyapaparivartanāmamahāyānasūtra. 'Phags pa 'od srung gi le'u shes bya ba theg pa chen po'i mdo. Toh 87, dkon brtsegs *cha,* 119b–151b.

Later Guhyasamāja Tantra. [Guhyasamāja] Uttaratantra. Rgyud phyi ma. Toh 443, rgyud 'bum *ca,* 90a–157b.

Later Kālacakra Tantra. Śrīkālacakratantrottaratantrahṛdaya. Dpal dus kyi 'khor lo'i rgyud phyi ma rgyud kyi snying po. Toh 363, rgyud 'bum *ka,* 129a–144a.

Later Tantra of Direct Expression. Abhidhānottaratantra. Mngon par brjod pa'i rgyud bla ma. Toh 369, rgyud 'bum *ka,* 247a–370a.

Little Tantra of Cakrasaṃvara. Tantrarājaśrīlaghusaṃvara. Rgyud kyi rgyal po dpal bde mchog nyung ngu. Toh 368, rgyud 'bum *ka,* 213b–246b.

Little Text on the Perfection of Wisdom. Āryasvalpākṣaraprajñāpāramitānāmamahāyānasūtra. 'Phags pa shes rab kyi pha rol tu phyin pa yi ge nyung ngu zhes bya ba theg pa chen po'i mdo. Toh 22, shes phyin *ka,* 146a–147b.

Mahāparinirvāṇa Sūtra (trans. from Chinese). *'Phags pa yongs su mya ngan las 'das pa chen po'i mdo.* Toh 119, mdo sde *nya,* 1b–343a, and mdo sde *ta,* 1b–339a.

Mahāparinirvāṇa Sūtra (trans. by Lhai Dawa). *Āryamahāparinirvāṇanāmamahāyānasūtra. 'Phags pa yongs su mya ngan las 'das pa chen po theg pa chen po'i mdo.* Toh 120, mdo sde *tha,* 1b–151a. Lhai Dawa (Lha'i zla ba) was a Tibetan monk who worked with two Indian scholars on the translation of this sūtra from Sanskrit. In the colophon to the translation he uses the Sanskrit form of his name, Devacandra.

Mahāyāna Section of the Glorious Sublime Primal. Śriparamādyanāmamahāyānakalparāja. Dpal mchog dang po zhes bya ba theg pa chen po'i rtog pa'i rgyal po. Toh 487, rgyud 'bum *ta,* 150b–173a.

One Hundred and Eight Names of the Perfection of Wisdom. Āryaprajñāpāramitānāmāṣṭaśataka. 'Phags pa shes rab kyi pha rol tu phyin pa'i mtshan brgya rtsa brgyad pa. Toh 25, shes phyin *ka,* 174a–175b.

One Hundred and Fifty Modes of the Perfection of Wisdom. Āryaprajñāpāramitānayaśatapañcaśatikā. 'Phags pa shes rab kyi pha rol tu phyin pa'i tshul brgya lnga bcu pa. Toh 17, shes phyin *ka,* 133a–139b.

Sampuṭa Tantra. Sampuṭanāmamahātantra. Yang dag par sbyor ba zhes bya ba'i rgyud chen po. Toh 381, rgyud 'bum *ga,* 73b–158b.

Sūtra to Benefit Aṅgulimāla. Āryāṅgulimālīyanāmamahāyānasūtra. 'Phags pa sor mo'i phreng ba la phan pa zhes bya ba theg pa chen po'i mdo. Toh 213, mdo sde *tsha*, 126a–206b.

Sūtra of the Bodhisattva's Scriptural Collection. Āryabodhisattvapiṭakanāmamahāyānasūtra. 'Phags pa byang chub sems dpa'i sde snod ces bya ba theg pa chen po'i mdo. Toh 56, dkon brtsegs *kha*, 255b–94a, and dkon brtsegs *ga*, 1b–205b.

Sūtra of Cultivating Faith in the Mahāyāna. Āryamahāyānaprasādaprabhāvananāmamahāyānasūtra. 'Phags pa theg pa chen po la rab tu sgom pa shes bya ba theg pa chen po'i mdo. Toh 144, mdo sde *pa*, 6b–34a.

Sūtra of Definitive Commentary on the Intent. Āryasaṃdhinirmocananāmamahāyānasūtra. 'Phags pa dgongs pa nges par 'grel pa zhes bya ba theg pa chen po'i mdo. Toh 106, mdo sde *ca*, 1b–55b.

Sūtra of the Dense Array. Āryaghanavyūhanāmamahāyānasūtra. 'Phags pa rgyan stug po bkod pa zhes bya ba theg pa chen po'i mdo. Toh 110, mdo sde *cha*, 1b–55b.

Sūtra of the Excellent Golden Light. Āryasuvarṇaprabhāsottamasūtrendrarājanāmamahāyānasūtra. 'Phags pa gser 'od dam pa mdo sde'i dbang po'i rgyal po zhes bya ba theg pa chen po'i mdo. Toh 556, rgyud 'bum *pa*, 151b–273a.

Sūtra of the Great Drum. Āryamahābherīhārakaparivartanāmamahāyānasūtra. 'Phags pa rnga bo che chen po'i le'u zhes bya ba theg pa chen po'i mdo. Toh 222, mdo sde *dza*, 84b–126b.

Sūtra of the King of Samādhis. Āryasarvadharmasvabhāvasamatāvipañcitasamādhirājanāmamahāyānasūtra. 'Phags pa chos thams cad kyi rang bzhin mnyam pa nyid rnam par spros pa ting nge 'dzin gyi rgyal po zhes bya ba theg pa chen po'i mdo. Toh 127, mdo sde *da*, 1b–170b.

Sūtra about the Level of a Buddha. Āryabuddhabhūminămamahāyānasūtra. 'Phags pa sangs rgyas kyi sa shes bya ba theg pa chen po'i mdo. Toh 275, mdo sde *ya*, 36a–44b.

Sūtra of the Lion's Roar of Śrīmālā. Āryaśrīmālādevīsiṃhanādanāmamahāyānasūtra. 'Phags pa lha mo dpal phreng gi seng ge'i sgra zhes bya ba theg pa chen po'i mdo. Toh 92, dkon brtsegs *cha*, 255a–277b.

Sūtra of the Meeting of Father and Son. Āryapitāputrasamāgamananāmamahāyānasūtra. 'Phags pa yab dang sras mjal ba zhes bya ba theg pa chen po'i mdo. Toh 60, dkon brtsegs *nga*, 1b–168a.

Sūtra of the Mudrā of Engagement in Producing the Power of Faith. Āryaśrāddhābalādhānāvatāramudrānāmamahāyānasūtra. 'Phags pa dad pa'i stobs bskyed pa la 'jug pa'i phyag rgya zhes bya ba theg pa chen po'i mdo. Toh 201, mdo sde *tsha*, 1b–63a.

Sūtra on the Perfection of Wisdom in Eight Thousand Lines. Āryāṣṭasāhasrikāprajñāpāramitā. 'Phags pa shes rab kyi pha rol tu phyin pa brgyad stong pa. Toh 12, shes phyin *ka*, 1b–286a.

Sūtra on the Perfection of Wisdom in Eighteen Thousand Lines. Āryāṣṭādaśasāhasrikāprajñāpāramitānāmamahāyānasūtra. 'Phags pa shes rab kyi pha rol tu phyin pa khri brgyad stong pa zhes bya ba theg pa chen po'i mdo. Toh 10, shes phyin *ka–ga*.

Sūtra on the Perfection of Wisdom in Five Hundred Lines. Āryapañcaśatikāprajñāpāramitā. 'Phags pa shes rab kyi pha rol tu phyin pa lnga brgya pa. Toh 15, shes phyin *ka*, 104a–120b.

Sūtra on the Perfection of Wisdom in One Hundred Thousand Lines. Śatasāhasrikāprajñāpāramitā. Shes rab kyi pha rol tu phyin pa stong phrag brgya pa. Toh 8, shes phyin *ka–da*, and *a*. This massive sūtra fills the first twelve volumes of the *shes phyin* section of the Kangyur.

Sūtra on the Perfection of Wisdom in Seven Hundred Lines. Āryasapaśatikānāmaprajñāpāramitāmahāyānasūtra. 'Phags pa shes rab kyi pha rol tu phyin pa bdun brgya pa zhes bya ba theg pa chen po'i mdo. Toh 24, shes phyin *ka*, 148a–174a.

Sūtra on the Perfection of Wisdom in Twenty-Five Thousand Lines. Pañcaviṃśatisāhasrikāprajñāpāramitā. Shes rab kyi pha rol tu phyin pa stong phrag nyi shu lnga pa. Toh 9, shes phyin *ka–ga*.

Sūtra Perfectly Summarizing the Dharma. Āryadharmasaṃgītināmamahāyānasūtra. 'Phags pa chos yang dag par sdud pa zhes bya ba theg pa chen po'i mdo. Toh 238, mdo sde *zha*, 1b–99b.

Sūtra on Primordial Awareness at the Moment of Death. Āryātajñānanāmamahāyānasūtra. 'Phags pa 'da' ka ye shes zhes bya ba theg pa chen po'i mdo. Toh 122, mdo sde *tha*, 153a–153b.

Sūtra of the Question by Mañjuśrī. Āryamañjuśrīparipṛcchānāmamahāyānasūtra. 'Phags pa 'jam dpal gyis dris pa zhes bya ba theg pa chen po'i mdo. Toh 172, mdo sde *ma*, 1b–5a.

Sūtra of the Ratnaketu Dhāraṇī. Āryamahāsannipātaratnaketudhāraṇīnāmamahāyānasūtra. 'Phags pa 'dus pa chen po rin po che tog gi gzungs zhes bya ba theg pa chen po'i mdo. Toh 138, mdo sde *na*, 187b–277b.

Sūtra Requested by Gaganagañja. Āryagaganagañjaparipṛcchānāmamahāyānasūtra. 'Phags pa nam mkha' mdzod kyis zhus pa zhes bya ba theg pa chen po'i mdo. Toh 148, mdo sde *pa*, 243a–330a.

Sūtra Requested by Ratnacūḍa. Āryaratnacūḍaparipṛcchānāmamahāyāna-sūtra. 'Phags pa gtsug na rin po ches zhus pa zhes bya ba theg pa chen po'i mdo. Toh 91, dkon brtsegs *cha,* 210a–254b.

Sūtra Requested by Sāgaramati. Āryasāgaramatiparipṛcchānāmamahāyāna-sūtra. 'Phags pa blo gros rgya mtshos zhus pa zhes bya ba theg pa chen po'i mdo. Toh 152, mdo sde *pha,* 1b–115b.

Sūtra on the Samādhi of the Miraculous Ascertainment of Utter Peace. Āryapraśāntaviniścayaprātihāryasamādhināmamahāyānasūtra. 'Phags pa rab tu zhi ba rnam par nges pa'i cho 'phrul gyi ting nge 'dzin zhes bya ba theg pa chen po'i mdo. Toh 129, mdo sde *da,* 174b–210b.

Sūtra of the Tathāgata Essence. Āryatathāgatagarbhanāmamahāyānasūtra. 'Phags pa de bzhin gshegs pa'i snying po shes bya ba theg pa chen po'i mdo. Toh 258, mdo sde *za,* 245b–259b.

Sūtra Taught by Akṣayamati. Aryākṣayamatinirdeśanāmamahāyānasūtra. 'Phags pa blo gros mi zad pas bstan pa zhes bya ba theg pa chen po'i mdo. Toh 175, mdo sde *ma,* 79a–174b.

Sūtra Taught by Vimalakīrti. Āryavimalakīrtinirdeśanāmamahāyānasūtra. 'Phags pa dri ma med par grags pa'i bstan pa shes bya ba theg pa chen po'i mdo. Toh 176, mdo sde *ma,* 175a–239b.

Sūtra Teaching the Great Compassion of the Tathāgata. Āryatathāgatamahā-karuṇānirdeśanāmamahāyānasūtra. 'Phags pa de bzhin gshegs pa'i snying rje chen po nges par bstan pa zhes bya ba theg pa chen po'i mdo. Toh 147, mdo sde *pa,* 142a–242b. This sūtra is often known by the name *Sūtra Requested by Dhāraṇīśvararāja. Dhāraṇīśvararājaparipṛcchā. Gzungs kyi dbang phyug rgyal pos zhus pa.*

Sūtra Teaching the Inconceivable Qualities and Primordial Awareness of the Tathāgata. Āryatathāgataguṇajñānācintyaviṣayāvatāranirdeśanāma-mahāyānasūtra. 'Phags pa de bzhin gshegs pa'i yon tan dang ye shes bsam gyis mi khyab pa'i yul la 'jug pa bstan pa shes bya ba theg pa chen po'i mdo. Toh 185, mdo sde *tsa,* 106a–143b.

Sūtra Teaching the Inconceivable Secrets of the Tathāgata. Āryatathāgat-ācintyaguhyanirdeśanāmamahāyānasūtra. 'Phags pa de bzhin gshegs pa'i gsang ba bsam gyis mi khyab pa bstan pa shes bya ba theg pa chen po'i mdo. Toh 47, dkon brtsegs *ka,* 100a–203a.

Sūtra Teaching the Inconceivable Sphere of a Buddha. Āryācintyabuddhaviṣaya-nirdeśanāmamahāyānasūtra. 'Phags pa sangs rgyas kyi yul bsam gyis mi khyab pa bstan pa zhes bya ba theg pa chen po'i mdo. Toh 79, dkon brtsegs *ca,* 266b–284b.

Sūtra Teaching the Indivisible Nature of Dharmadhātu. Āryadharmadhātuprakṛtyasaṃbhedanirdeśanāmamahāyānasūtra. 'Phags pa chos kyi dbyings kyi rang bzhin dbyer med pa bstan pa zhes bya ba theg pa chen po'i mdo. Toh 52, dkon brtsegs *kha*, 140b–164a.

Sūtra Teaching the Purification of Infinite Gateways. Āryānantamukhapariśodhananirdeśaparivartanāmamahāyānasūtra. 'Phags pa sgo mtha' yas pa rnam par sbyong ba bstan pa'i le'u zhes bya ba theg pa chen po'i mdo. Toh 46, dkon brtsegs *ka*, 45b–99b.

Sūtra Teaching Relative and Ultimate Truth. Āryasamvṛtiparamārthasatyanirdeśanāmamahāyānasūtra. 'Phags pa kun rdzob dang don dam pa'i bden pa bstan pa zhes bya ba theg pa chen po'i mdo. Toh 179, mdo sde *ma*, 244b–266b.

Tantra of the Arising of Saṃvara. Śrīmahāsamvarodayatantrarājanāma. Dpal bde mchog 'byung ba shes bya ba'i rgyud kyi rgyal po chen po. Toh 373, rgyud 'bum *kha*, 265a–311a.

Tantra Determining the Intent. Sandhiviyākaraṇanāmatantra. Dgongs pa lung bstan pa zhes bya ba'i rgyud. Toh 444, rgyud 'bum *ca*, 158a–207b.

Tantra of the Drop of Mahāmudrā. Śrīmahāmudrātilakanāmamahāyoginītantrarājādhipati. Dpal phyag rgya chen po'i thig le shes bya ba rnal 'byor ma chen mo'i rgyud kyi rgyal po'i mnga' bdag. Toh 420, rgyud 'bum *nga*, 66a–90b.

Tantra of the Drop of Primordial Awareness. Śrījñānatilakayoginītantrarājaparamamahādbhuta. Dpal ye shes thig le rnal 'byor ma'i rgyud kyi rgyal po chen po mchog tu rmad du byung ba. Toh 422, rgyud 'bum *nga*, 96b–136b.

Tantra of an Ocean of Ḍākas. Śrīḍākārṇavamahāyoginītantrarāja. Dpal mkha' 'gro rgya mtsho rnal 'byor ma'i rgyud kyi rgyal po chen po. Toh 372, rgyud 'bum *kha*, 137a–264b.

Tantra of the Ornament of the Vajra Essence. Śrīvajramaṇḍalāṃkāranāmamahātantrarāja. Dpal rdo rje snying po rgyan zhes bya ba'i rgyud kyi rgyal po. Toh 490, rgyud 'bum *tha*, 1b–82a.

Tantra of the Secret Drop of the Moon. Śrīcandraguhyatilakanāmamahātantrarāja. Dpal zla gsang thig le zhes bya ba rgyud kyi rgyal po chen po. Toh 477, rgyud 'bum *ja*, 247b–303a.

Tantra That Utterly Purifies All Lower Realms. Sarvadurgatipariśodhanatejorājasya-tathāgatasyārhatosamyaksambuddhasyakalpa. De bzhin gshegs pa dgra bcom pa yang dag par rdzogs pa'i sangs rgyas ngan song thams cad yongs su sbyong ba gzi brjid kyi rgyal po'i brtag pa. Toh 483, rgyud 'bum *ta*, 58b–96a.

Universal Secret Tantra. Sarvarahasyanāmatantrarāja. Thams cad gsang ba zhes bya ba rgyud kyi rgyal po. Toh 481, rgyud 'bum *ta,* 1b–10a.

Vajra Garland Tantra. Śrīvajramālābhidhanamahāyogatantrasarvatantrahṛdayarahasyavibhaṅga. Rnal 'byor chen po'i rgyud dpal rdo rje phreng ba mngon par brjod pa rgyud thams cad kyi snying po gsang ba rnam par phye pa. Toh 445, rgyud 'bum *ca,* 208a–277b.

Vajraḍāka Tantra. Śrīvajraḍākanāmamahātantrarāja. Rgyud kyi rgyal po chen po dpal rdo rje mkha' 'gro. Toh 370, rgyud 'bum *kha,* 1b–125a.

Vajrapañjara Tantra. Āryaḍākinīvajrapañjaramahātantrarājakalpanāma. 'Phags pa mkha' 'gro ma rdo rje gur zhes bya ba'i rgyud kyi rgyal po chen po'i brtag pa. Toh 419, rgyud 'bum *nga,* 30a–65b.

Vajraśekhara Tantra. Vajraśekharamahāguhyayogatantra. Gsang ba rnal 'byor chen po'i rgyud rdo rje rtse mo. Toh 480, rgyud 'bum *nya,* 142b–274a.

Verse Summary of the Sūtras on the Perfection of Wisdom. Āryaprajñāpāramitāsañcayagātha. 'Phags pa shes rab kyi pha rol tu phyin pa sdud pa tshigs su bcad pa. Toh 13, shes phyin *ka,* 1b–19b.

Tengyur (Canonical Treatises)

Acalagarbha. *Combined Explanation. Bshad sbyar.* Short title for *Śrīmanvimalaprabhātantrāvatāraṇīvādācalahṛdayāloka. Dpal ldan dri ma dang bral ba'i 'od kyi rgyud la 'jug pa'i bshad sbyar mi g.yo snying po snang ba.* Toh 1349, rgyud *na,* 20a–72b.

Āryadeva. *Chapter the Length of a Forearm. Hastavālaprakāraṇakārikā. Rab tu byed pa lag pa'i tshad kyi tshig le'ur byas pa.* Toh 3848, dbu ma *tsha,* 22b.

———. *Compendium of the Essence of Primordial Awareness. Jñānasārasamuccaya. Ye shes snying po kun las btus pa.* Toh 3851, dbu ma *tsha,* 26b–28a.

———. *Esoteric Instructions on the Stage of Direct Enlightenment. Abhibodhikramopadeśa. Mngon par byang chub pa'i rim pa'i man ngag.* Toh 1806, rgyud *ngi,* 114b–117a.

———. *Establishing the Reasoning That Refutes Confusion. Skhalitapramardanayuktihetusiddhi. 'Khrul pa bzlog pa'i rigs pa gtan tshigs grub pa.* Toh 3847, dbu ma *tsha,* 19b–22b.

———. *Four Hundred Verses. Catuḥśatakaśāstrakārikā. Bstan bcos bzhi brgya pa zhes bya ba'i tshig le'ur byas pa.* Toh 3846, dbu ma *tsha*, 1b–18a.

———. *Lamp That Summarizes Conduct. Caryāmelāpakapradīpa. Spyod pa bsdus pa'i sgron ma.* Toh 1803, rgyud *ngi*, 57a–106b.

———. *Madhyamaka Destruction of Confusion. Madhyamakabramaghāta. Dbu ma 'khrul pa 'joms pa.* Toh 3850, dbu ma *tsha*, 24a–26b.

Asaṅga. *Commentary on the "Uttaratantra." Mahāyānottaratantraśāstra-vyākhyā. Theg pa chen po rgyud bla ma'i bstan bcos rnam par bshad pa.* Toh 4025, sems tsam *phi*, 74b–129a.

———. *Compendium of Abhidharma. Abhidharmasamuccaya. Chos mngon pa kun las btus pa.* Toh 4049, sems tsam *ri*, 44b–120a.

———. *Compendium of the Mahāyāna. Mahāyānasaṃgraha. Theg pa chen po bsdus pa.* Toh 4048, sems tsam *ri*, 1b–43a.

———. *Levels of the Bodhisattva [Yogācārabhūmaubodhisattvabhūmi]. Rnal 'byor spyod pa'i sa las byang chub sems dpa'i sa.* Toh 4037, sems tsam *wi*, 1b–213a.

———. *Yogācāra Levels. Yogācārabhūmi. Rnal 'byor spyod pa'i sa.* Toh 4035, sems tsam *tshi*, 1b–283a. This is only the first section of the huge collection that is also known by the same name.

Avalokitavrata. *Extensive Commentary on "Lamp for the 'Wisdom.'" Prajñāpradīpaṭīkā. Shes rab sgron ma rgya cher 'grel pa.* Toh 3859, dbu ma *zha*, 1b–338a.

Bhāvaviveka. *Essence of Madhyamaka. Madhyamakahṛdayakārikā. Dbu ma'i snying po'i tshig le'ur byas pa.* Toh 3855, dbu ma *dza*, 1b–40b.

———. *Jewel Lamp of the Madhyamaka. Madhyamakaratnapradīpa. Dbu ma rin po che'i sgron ma.* Toh 3854, dbu ma *tsha*, 259b–289a.

———. *Lamp for the "Wisdom." Prajñāpradīpamūlamadhyamakavṛtti. Dbu ma'i rtsa ba'i 'grel pa shes rab sgron ma.* Toh 3853, dbu ma *tsha*, 45b–259b.

Bodhibhadra. *Combined Explanation of the "Compendium of the Essence of Primordial Awareness." Jñānasārasamuccayanāmanibandhana. Ye shes snying po kun las btus kyi bshad sbyar.* Toh 3852, dbu ma *tsha*, 28a–45b.

Buddhapālita. *Buddhapālita's Commentary on the "Root Verses on Madhyamaka." Buddhapālitamūlamadhyamakavṛtti. Dbu ma rtsa ba'i 'grel pa buddha pā li ta.* Toh 3842, dbu ma *tsa*, 158b–281a.

Buddhaśrījñāna. *Precept of Mañjuśrī. 'Jam dpal zhal gyi lung.* Title in Tengyur: *A Precept Known as "Cultivating the Reality of the Two Stages." Dvikramatattvabhāvanānāmamukhāgama. Rim pa gnyis pa'i de kho na nyid bsgom pa zhes bya ba'i zhal gyi lung.* Toh 1853, rgyud *di*, 1a–17b.

Candragomin. *In Praise of Mañjuśrī. Bhagavadāryamañjuśrīsādhiṣṭāna-stuti. Bcom ldan 'das 'phags pa 'jam dpal gyi bstod pa byin rlabs dang bcas pa.* Toh 2710, rgyud *nu*, 77a–78b.

Candrakīrti. *Entering the Madhyamaka. Madhyamakāvatāra. Dbu ma la 'jug pa.* Toh 3861, dbu ma *'a*, 201b–219a.

———. *Explanation of "Entering the Madhyamaka." Madhyamakāvatāra-bhāṣya. Dbu ma la 'jug pa'i bshad pa.* Toh 3862, dbu ma *'a*, 220b–348a.

———. *Illuminating Lamp. Pradīpodyotanaṭīkā. Sgron ma gsal bar byed pa zhes bya ba'i rgya cher bshad pa.* Toh 1785, rgyud *ha*, 1–201b.

———. *Lucid Words: A Commentary on the "Root Verses on Madhyamaka." Mūlamadhyamakavṛttiprasannapadā. Dbu ma rtsa ba'i 'grel pa tshig gsal ba.* Toh 3860, dbu ma *'a*, 1b–200a.

Dharmakīrti. *Commentary on Valid Cognition. Pramāṇavārttikakārikā. Tshad ma rnam 'grel gyi tshig le'ur byas pa.* Toh 4210, tshad ma *ce*, 94b–151a.

Dignāga. *Verse Summary of the "Perfection of Wisdom." Āryaprajñāpāra-mitāsaṃgrahakārikā. 'Phags pa shes rab gyi pha rol tu phyin ma bsdus pa'i tshig le'ur byas pa.* Toh 3809, shes phyin *pha*, 292b–294b.

Jinaputra. *Commentary on "In Praise of the Three Jewels." Triratnastotra-vṛtti. Dkon mchog gsum la bstod pa'i 'grel pa.* Toh 1145, bstod tshogs *ka*, 105a–109b.

Jñānacandra. *Commentary on the "Three Kāyas." Kāyatrayavṛtti. Sku gsum 'grel pa.* Toh 3891, dbu ma *ha*, 8a–39b.

Jñānagarbha. *Distinguishing the Two Truths. Satyadvayavibhāgakārikā. Bden pa gnyis rnam par 'byed pa'i tshig le'ur byas pa.* Toh 3881, dbu ma *sa*, 1b–3b.

———. *Path of Cultivating Yoga. Yogabhāvanāmārga. Rnal 'byor bsgom pa'i lam.* Toh 3909, dbu ma *ki*, 4a–6a.

Kamalaśīla. *Establishing That All Phenomena Are without Nature. Sarvadharmāsvabhāvasiddhi. Chos thams cad rang bzhin med par grub pa.* Toh 3889, dbu ma *sa*, 273a–291a.

———. *Illuminating the Madhyamaka. Madhyamakāloka. Dbu ma snang ba.* Toh 3887, dbu ma *sa*, 133b–244a.

———. *Illuminating Reality. Tattvālokanāmaprakaraṇa. De kho na nyid snang ba zhes bya ba'i rab tu byed pa.* Toh 3888, dbu ma *sa*, 244b–273a.

Maitreya. *Distinguishing the Middle and the Extremes. Madhyāntavibhāga-kārikā. Dbus dang mtha' rnam par 'byed pa'i tshig le'ur byas pa.* Toh 4021, sems tsam *phi*, 40b–45a.

———. *Distinguishing Phenomena and True Nature. Dharmadharmatāvibhaṅgakārikā. Chos dang chos nyid rnam par 'byed pa'i tshig le'ur byas pa.* Toh 4023, sems tsam *phi,* 50b–53a.

———. *Ornament of Direct Realization. Abhisamayālaṃkāranāmaprajñāpāramitopadeśaśāstrakārikā. Shes rab kyi pha rol tu phyin pa'i man ngag gi bstan bcos mngon par rtogs pa'i rgyan zhes bya ba'i tshig le'ur byas pa.* Toh 3786, shes phyin *ka,* 1b–13a.

———. *Ornament of the Mahāyāna Sūtras. Mahāyānasūtrālaṃkāranāmakārikā. Theg pa chen po mdo sde'i rgyan zhes bya ba'i tshig le'ur byas pa.* Toh 4020, sems tsam *phi,* 1b–39a.

———. *Uttaratantra. Mahāyānottaratantraśāstra. Theg pa chen po rgyud bla ma'i bstan bcos.* Toh 4024, sems tsam *phi,* 54b–73a.

Mañjuśrīyaśas, Kalkī. *Brief Presentation of the Assertions of My Own View. Pradarśanānumatoddeśaparikṣā. Rang gi lta ba'i 'dod pa mdor bstan pa yongs su brtag pa.* P 4610, rgyud 'grel *pu,* 21a–50b. Since this work is not found in the Dergé edition of the Tengyur it is cited from the Peking edition.

Nāgamitra. *Entryway to the Three Kāyas. Kāyatrayāvatāramukhanāmaśāstra. Sku gsum la 'jug pa'i sgo shes bya ba'i bstan bcos.* Toh 3890, dbu ma *ha,* 1b–8a.

Nāgārjuna. *Commentary on Bodhicitta. Bodhicittavivaraṇa. Byang chub sems kyi 'grel pa.* Toh 1800, rgyud *ngi,* 38a–42b.

———. *Condensed Sādhana. Piṇḍīkramasādhana. Sgrub pa'i thabs mdor byas pa.* Toh 1796, rgyud *ngi,* 1b–11a.

———. *Fearing Nothing: A Commentary on the "Root Verses on Madhyamaka." Mūlamadhyamakavṛttyakutobhayā. Dbu ma rtsa ba'i 'grel pa ga las 'jigs med.* Toh 3829, dbu ma *tsa,* 29b–99a.

———. *Garland of Jewels. Rājaparikathāratnāvalī. Rgyal po la gtam bya ba rin po che'i phreng ba.* Toh 4158, spring yig *ge,* 107a–126a.

———. *Guhyasamāja Maṇḍala Ritual. Śrīguhyasamājamaṇḍalavidhi. Dpal gsang ba 'dus pa'i dkyil 'khor gyi cho ga.* Toh 1798, rgyud *ngi,* 15b–35a.

———. *In Praise of Dharmadhātu. Dharmadhātustava. Chos kyi dbyings su bstod pa.* Toh 1118, bstod tshogs *ka,* 63b–67b.

———. *In Praise of the Three Kāyas. Kāyatrayastotra. Sku gsum la bstod pa.* Toh 1123, bstod tshogs *ka,* 70b–71a.

———. *In Praise of the Ultimate. Paramārthastava. Don dam par bstod pa.* Toh 1122, 70a–b.

———. *Refutation of Objections. Vigrahavyāvartanīkārikā. Rtsod pa bzlog pa'i tshig le'ur byas pa.* Toh 3828, dbu ma *tsa,* 27a–29a.

———. *Root Verses on Madhyamaka, Called "Wisdom." Prajñānāmamūlamadhyamakakārikā. Dbu ma rtsa ba'i tshig le'ur byas pa shes rab ces bya ba.* Toh 3824, dbu ma *tsa*, 1b–19a.

———. *Sixty Verses on Reasoning. Yuktiṣaṣṭhikākārikā. Rigs pa drug cu pa'i tshig le'ur byas pa.* Toh 3825, dbu ma *tsa*, 20a–22b.

———. *Stages of Meditation. Bhāvanākrama. Bsgom pa'i rim pa.* Toh 3908, dbu ma *ki*, 1b–4a.

Nāropa. *Commentary on "Brief Presentation of Initiation." Paramārthasaṃgrahanāmasekoddeśaṭīkā. Dbang mdor bstan pa'i 'grel bshad don dam pa bsdus pa.* Toh 1351, rgyud *na*, 220b–289a.

———. *Great Commentary of Nāropa. Nā ro 'grel chen.* Short title for *A Commentary on Difficult Points That Summarizes the Essence of the Vajra Words. Vajrapādasārasaṃgrahapañjikā. Rdo rje'i tshig gi snying po bsdus pa'i dka' 'grel.* Toh 1186, rgyud *ga*, 58b–146b.

Puṇḍarīka, Kalkī. *Stainless Light* (Jonang trans.). *Vimalaprabhā. Dri med 'od.* Short title for *Vimalaprabhānāmamūlatantrānusāriṇīdvādaśasāhasrikālagukālacakratantrarājaṭīkā. Bsdus pa'i rgyud kyi rgyal po dus kyi 'khor lo'i 'grel bshad/ rtsa ba'i rgyud kyi rjes su 'jug pa stong phrag bcu gnyis pa dri ma med pa'i 'od. Jo nang phyogs las rnam rgyal gyis mchan gyis gsal bar mdzad pa'i bsdus pa'i rgyud kyi rgyal po dpal dus kyi 'khor lo'i rgyas 'grel rtsa ba'i rgyud kyi rjes su 'jug pa stong phrag bcu gnyis pa dri ma med pa'i 'od.* This edition contains annotations by Dölpopa Sherab Gyaltsen and Jonang Choklé Namgyal. In *Dus 'khor mchan 'grel,* Jo nang dpe tshogs (Jonang Publication Series), vols. 18–20. Beijing: Mi rigs dpe skrun khang, 2008. See also Kalkī Puṇḍarīka, *Stainless Light* (Shong and Jonang trans.), Toh 1347, rgyud *tha*, 107b–277a, rgyud *da* 1b–297a. The first two chapters of this Tibetan translation in the Dergé edition are the "Shong translation" (*shong 'gyur*) of Shongtön Dorjé Gyaltsen. The last three chapters are the "new Jonang translation" (*jo nang gsar 'gyur*) of Jonang Lotsāwa Lodrö Pal and Mati Paṇchen Lodrö Gyaltsen. In this edition, the fourth chapter has mistakenly been placed before the third chapter.

Ratnakīrti. *In Praise of the Deities of the Four Yogas. Yogacaturdevastotra. Sbyor ba bzhi'i lha la bstod pa.* Toh 1170, bstod tshogs *ka*, 246b–249a.

Sādhuputra. *Kālacakra Maṇḍala Ritual. Śrīkālacakramaṇḍalavidhi. Dpal dus kyi 'khor lo'i dkyil 'khor gyi cho ga.* Toh 1359, rgyud 'grel *pa*, 118a–156a.

Śāntideva. *Entering the Conduct of a Bodhisattva. Bodhisattvacaryāvatāra. Byang chub sems pa'i spyod pa la 'jug pa.* Toh 3871, dbu ma *la*, 1b–40a.

Saraha. *Treasury of Dohā Verses. Dohākoṣagīti. Do ha mdzod kyi glu.* Toh 2224, rgyud *wi*, 70b–77a.

Sūryagupta. *In Praise of Noble Tārā. Āryatārāstotra. 'Phags ma sgrol ma la bstod pa.* Toh 1693, rgyud *śa*, 49b–51a.

Tripiṭakamāla. *Lamp of the Three Ways. Nayatrayapradīpa. Tshul gsum gyi sgron ma.* Toh 3707, rgyud *tsu*, 6b–26b.

Vajragarbha. *Extensive Commentary on the Condensed Meaning of the Hevajra. Hevajrapiṇḍārthaṭīkā. Kye'i rdo rje'i bsdus pa'i don gyi rgya cher 'grel pa.* Toh 1180, rgyud *ka*, 1a–126a.

Vajrapāṇi. *Brief Cakrasaṃvara Commentary. Lakṣābhidhānāduddhṛtalaghutantrapiṇḍārthavivaraṇa. Mngon par brjod pa 'bum pa las phyung ba nyung ngu'i rgyud kyi bsdus pa'i don rnam par bshad pa.* Toh 1402, rgyud *ba*, 78b–141a.

Vasubandhu. *Commentary on "Distinguishing the Middle and the Extremes." Madhyāntavibhaṅgaṭīkā. Dbus dang mtha' rnam par 'byed pa'i 'grel pa.* Toh 4027, sems tsam *bi*, 1b–27a.

———. *Correctness of the Explanation. Vyākhyāyukti. Rnam par bshad pa'i rigs pa.* Toh 4061, sems tsam *shi*, 29a–134b.

———. *Explanation of the "Ornament of the Sūtras." Sūtrālaṃkāravyākhyā. Mdo sde'i rgyan gyi bshad pa.* Toh 4026, sems tsam *phi*, 129b–260a.

———. *Explanation of the "Treasury of Abhidharma." Abhidharmakośabhāṣya. Chos mngon pa'i mdzod kyi bshad pa.* Toh 4090, mngon pa *ku*, 26b–258a.

———. *Extensive Commentary on the "Sūtra in One Hundred Thousand Lines." Śatasāhasrikāprajñāpāramitābṛhaṭṭīkā. Shes rab kyi pha rol tu phyin pa 'bum pa rgya cher 'grel pa.* Toh 3807, shes phyin *na*, 1b–331a, and shes phyin *pa*, 1b–252a.

———. *Thirty Verses. Triṃśikākārikā. Sum cu pa'i tshig le'ur byas pa.* Toh 4055, sems tsam *shi*, 1b–3a.

———. *Vast Explanation of the "Sūtra in One Hundred Thousand Lines," the "Sūtra in Twenty-Five Thousand Lines," and the "Sūtra in Eighteen Thousand Lines." Āryaśatasāhasrikāpañcaviṃśatisāhasrikāṣṭādaśasāhasrikāprajñāpāramitābṛhaṭṭīkā. 'Phags pa shes rab kyi pha rol tu phyin pa 'bum pa dang nyi khri lnga stong pa dang khri brgyad stong pa'i rgya cher bshad pa.* Toh 3808, shes phyin *pha*, 1b–292b.

Vimalamitra. *Commentary on the "Perfection of Wisdom in Seven Hundred Lines." Āryasapaśatikāprajñāpāramitāṭīkā. 'Phags pa shes rab kyi pha rol tu phyin pa bdun brgya pa'i rgya cher 'grel pa.* Toh 3814, shes phyin *ma*, 6b–89a.

Tibetan Works Consulted by the Translator

Barawa Gyaltsen Palsangpo ('Ba' ra ba Rgyal mtshan dpal bzang po). *Reply to Eight Major Disciples of the Omniscient Dölpopa. Skyes mchog chen po 'ba' ra bas/ kun mkhyen dol bu'i bu chen brgyad la lan phyogs cig du btab pa nyi ma'i 'od zer*. In *A Tibetan Encyclopedia of Buddhist Scholasticism*, vol. 11: 637–709. Dehradun, 1970.

Butön Rinchen Drup (Bu ston Rin chen grub). *Annotations to the Chapter on the Cosmos in the "Stainless Light." 'Jig rten khams kyi le'u'i 'grel bshad dri ma med pa'i 'od mchan bcas*. In *The Collected Works of Bu-ston*, pt. 2: 301–603. New Delhi: International Academy of Indian Culture, 1965.

———. *Annotations to the "Kālacakra Tantra." Mchog gi dang po'i sangs rgyas las phyung ba rgyud kyi rgyal po chen po dpal dus kyi 'khor lo'i bsdus pa'i rgyud go sla'i mchan bcas*. In *The Collected Works of Bu-ston*, pt. 1: 1–299. New Delhi: International Academy of Indian Culture, 1965.

Chak Lotsāwa Rinchen Chögyal (Chag Lo tsā ba Rin chen chos rgyal). *Wish-Granting Sheaves: Biographies in the Precious Lineage of Glorious Kālacakra. Dpal dus kyi 'khor lo'i brgyud pa rin po che'i rtogs pa brjod pa dpag bsam gyi snye ma*. Lhasa: Bod ljongs bod yig dpe rnying dpe skrun khang, 2014.

Choklé Namgyal, Jonang (Phyogs las rnam rgyal, Jo nang). *Illumination of the Definitive Meaning: Combined Explanation of the First Brief Summary in the "Stainless Light," the Vast Commentary on the "Glorious Kālacakra, King of Tantras." Dpal dus kyi 'khor lo'i rgyud kyi rgyal po'i rgya cher 'grel pa 'dri ma med pa'i 'od kyi mdor bsdus dang po'i bshad sbyar nges don snang ba*. In *Gzhi lam 'bras bu'i ngo sprod*, Jo nang dpe tshogs (Jonang Publication Series), vol. 21: 61–139. Beijing: Mi rigs dpe skrun khang, 2008.

———. *Introductory Treatise for Teaching the Commentary on the "Kālacakra Tantra." Dpal dus kyi 'khor lo'i rgyud 'grel bshad pa la 'jug pa'i yan lag rnam par bzhag pa ngo mtshar rtogs brjod*. In *Gzhi lam 'bras bu'i ngo sprod*, Jo nang dpe tshogs (Jonang Publication Series), vol. 21: 1–60.

———. *Ornament of Shambhala: Clarifying the Landscape of Glorious Shambhala. Dpal sham bha la'i bkod pa gsal bar byed pa sham bha la'i rgyan*. In *Gzhi lam 'bras bu'i ngo sprod*, Jo nang dpe tshogs (Jonang Publication Series), vol. 21: 349–58.

Chökyi Gyatso, Katok Situ (Chos kyi rgya mtsho, Kaḥ thog Si tu). *Pilgrimage Journal of Central Tibet and Tsang. Gangs ljongs dbus gtsang gnas *bskor lam yig nor bu zla shel gyi se mo do*. Tashijong: Sungrab Nyamso Gyunphel Parkhang, 1972.

Dölpopa Sherab Gyaltsen (Dol po pa Shes rab rgyal mtshan). *Analysis of Dharma for the Ruler of Jang. Dpon byang ba'i phyag tu phul ba'i chos kyi shan 'byed*. In *The 'Dzam-thang Edition of the Collected Works (Gsung-'bum) of Kun-mkhyen Dol-po-pa Shes-rab rgyal-mtshan*, vol. 5: 473–702. Delhi: Shedrup Books, 1992.

———. *[Annotations to] Asaṅga's "Commentary on the 'Uttaratantra.'" Theg pa chen po rgyud bla ma'i 'grel pa 'phags pa thogs med kyis mdzad pa*. In *Rgyud bla'i ṭikka*, Jo nang dpe tshogs (Jonang Publication Series), vol. 2: 1–128. Beijing: Mi rigs dpe skrun khang, 2007.

———. *[Annotations to] the Chapter on Initiation in the "Stainless Light." Dbang gi le'u rgyas 'grel*. In *Dus 'khor phyogs bsgrigs chen mo*, vol. 20: 1–287. Lhasa: Bod ljongs bod yig dpe rnying dpe skrun khang, 2012.

———. *[Annotations to] the Chapter on Primordial Awareness in the "Stainless Light." Ye shes le'u rgyas 'grel*. In *Dus 'khor phyogs bsgrigs chen mo*, vol. 21: 1–345. Lhasa: Bod ljongs bod yig dpe rnying dpe skrun khang, 2014.

———. *[Annotations to] the Chapter on Sādhana in the "Stainless Light." Sgrub thabs le'u rgyas 'grel*. In *Dus 'khor phyogs bsgrigs chen mo*, vol. 20: 289–471. Lhasa: Bod ljongs bod yig dpe rnying dpe skrun khang, 2012.

———. *[Annotations to] the First Summary of the Chapter on the Cosmos in the "Stainless Light." Bsdus pa'i rgyud kyi rgyal po dpal dus kyi 'khor lo'i rgyas 'grel rtsa ba'i rgyud kyi rjes su 'jug pa stong phrag bcu gnyis pa dri ma med pa'i 'od las 'jig rten khams kyi leu'i mdor dang po*. Dbus med ms., 14 fols. Tibetan Buddhist Resource Center, Work: W3PD987, Image group: I3PD1216. This manuscript has been inserted (out of order) between manuscripts of the *Ye shes le'u* of the *Kālacakra Tantra* and the *Sgrub thabs le'u* of the *Stainless Light*. The authorship of Dölpopa is verified in an annotation at the end of the *Ye shes le'u* of the *Stainless Light*: "The annotations to the First Summary were composed by the Great Omniscient One" (*mdor bsdus dang po'i mchan sbyar kun mkhyen chen pos mdzad*).

———. *[Annotations to] "In Praise of Dharmadhātu," Composed by Noble Nāgārjuna. 'Phags pa klu sgrub kyis mdzad pa'i chos dbyings bstod pa*. In *Kun mkhyen dol po pa shes rab rgyal mtshan gyi gsung 'bum*, vol. 3: 137–57. 'Dzam thang: 'Dzam thang Bsam 'grub nor bu'i gling gi par khang, 1998.

———. *Autocommentary on the "Fourth Council." Bka' bsdu bzhi pa'i rang 'grel*. In *The Collected Works (Gsung 'bum) of Kun-mkhyen Dol-po-pa Shes-rab rgyal-mtshan (1292–1361): Reproduced from the copies of prints from the Rgyal-rtse Rdzong blocks preserved at the Kyichu Monastery in the Paro Valley, Bhutan*, vol. 1: 585–665. Paro/Delhi: Lama Ngodrup and Sherab Drimay, 1984.

———. *Brief Analysis Composed by the Great Omniscient One. Kun mkhyen chen pos mdzad pa'i gshag 'byed bsdus pa*. In *The 'Dzam-thang Edition of the Collected Works (Gsung-'bum) of Kun-mkhyen Dol-po-pa Shes-rab rgyal-mtshan*, vol. 5: 435–71. Delhi: Shedrup Books, 1992.

———. *Commentary on the First Verse. Tshigs bcad dang po'i ṭī ka*. In *The 'Dzam-thang Edition of the Collected Works (Gsung-'bum) of Kun-mkhyen Dol-po-pa Shes-rab rgyal-mtshan*, vol. 6: 65–76. Delhi: Shedrup Books, 1992.

———. *Comprehensive Summary of the Commentary on the Glorious "Kālacakra Tantra." Dpal ldan dus 'khor rgyud 'grel gyi/ bsdus don yongs 'du lta bu bzhugs*. In *Dus 'khor rgyud mchan*, Jo nang dpe tshogs (Jonang Publication Series), vol. 17: 227–83. Beijing: Mi rigs dpe skrun khang, 2008. Also in *Dus 'khor 'grel mchan phyogs bsgrigs*, vol. 1: 487–539. Beijing: Krung go'i bod rig pa dpe skrun khang, 2007.

———. *Distinguishing the Views. Lta ba shan 'byed yid kyi mun sel*. In *The 'Dzam-thang Edition of the Collected Works (Gsung-'bum) of Kun-mkhyen Dol-po-pa Shes-rab rgyal-mtshan*, vol. 5: 789–810. Delhi: Shedrup Books, 1992.

———. *Exceptional Esoteric Instructions on Madhyamaka. Dbu ma'i man ngag khyad 'phags*. In *The 'Dzam-thang Edition of the Collected Works (Gsung-'bum) of Kun-mkhyen Dol-po-pa Shes-rab rgyal-mtshan*, vol. 7, pt. 2: 1171–81. Delhi: Shedrup Books, 1992.

———. *Explanation of the Nine Fully Established Natures. Dpal yongs grub dgu'i bshad pa khyad 'phags g.yu rnying lta bu*. In *The 'Dzam-thang Edition of the Collected Works (Gsung-'bum) of Kun-mkhyen Dol-po-pa Shes-rab rgyal-mtshan*, vol. 4, pt. 1: 111–40. Delhi: Shedrup Books, 1992.

———. *Fourth Council*. Short title for *Great Reasoning That Has the Significance of a Fourth Council. Bka' bsdu bzhi pa'i don gtan tshigs chen po*. In *The Collected Works (Gsung 'bum) of Kun-mkhyen Dol-po-pa Shes-rab rgyal-mtshan (1292–1361): Reproduced from the copies of prints from the Rgyal-rtse Rdzong blocks preserved at the Kyichu Monastery in the Paro Valley, Bhutan*, vol. 1: 363–417. Paro/Delhi: Lama Ngodrup and Sherab Drimay, 1984.

———. *General Commentary on the Doctrine.* Short title for *Supplication Entitled "General Commentary on the Doctrine." Bsṭan pa spyi 'grel zhes bya ba'i gsol 'debs.* In *The Collected Works* (*Gsung 'bum*) *of Kun-mkhyen Dol-po-pa Shes-rab rgyal-mtshan (1292–1361): Reproduced from the copies of prints from the Rgyal-rtse Rdzong blocks preserved at the Kyichu Monastery in the Paro Valley, Bhutan*, vol. 1: 686–94. Paro/Delhi: Lama Ngodrup and Sherab Drimay, 1984.

———. *Instruction to Lhajé Tsultrim Ö. Lha rje tshul khrims 'od la gdams pa.* In *The 'Dzam-thang Edition of the Collected Works (Gsung-'bum) of Kun-mkhyen Dol-po-pa Shes-rab rgyal-mtshan*, vol. 7, pt. 2: 668–79. Delhi: Shedrup Books, 1992.

———. *Mountain Dharma: An Ocean of Definitive Meaning: Consummate, Uncommon Esoteric Instructions. Ri chos nges don rgya mtsho zhes bya ba mthar thug thun mong ma yin pa'i man ngag.* In Jo nang dpe tshogs (Jonang Publication Series), vol. 1: 1–412. Beijing: Mi rigs dpe skrun khang, 2007. See also the critical Tibetan edition, *Ri chos nges don rgya mtsho zhes bya ba mthar thug thun mong ma yin pa'i man ngag.* In *Ri chos nges don rgya mtsho*, Bod kyi gtsug lag gces btus, vol. 7. New Delhi: Institute of Tibetan Classics, 2013. See also *Ri chos nges don rgya mtsho zhes bya ba mthar thug thun mong ma yin pa'i man ngag.* In *Kun mkhyen dol po pa shes rab rgyal mtshan gyi gsung 'bum*, vol. 3: 189–741. 'Dzam thang: 'Dzam thang Bsam 'grub nor bu'i gling gi par khang, 1998. See also *Ri chos nges don rgya mtsho zhes bya ba mthar thug thun mong ma yin pa'i man ngag.* Jonang dpe rnying thor bu, bdr:W00KG0638, vol: 5: 1–739. See also *Ri chos nges don rgya mtsho zhes bya ba mthar thug thun mong ma yin pa'i man ngag.* In *Ri chos nges don rgya mtsho zhes bya ba'i bstan bcos dang bsdus don*, 19–598. Bir: D. Tsondu Senghe, The Bir Tibetan Society, 1984. See also *Ri chos nges don rgya mtsho.* In Rin chen shing par dpe rnying dpe dkon phyogs bsdus, bdr:W2PD19644, vol. 15: 247 fols.

———. *Outline of "Mountain Dharma: An Ocean of Definitive Meaning." Ri chos nges don rgya mtsho'i sa bcad.* In Jo nang dpe tshogs (Jonang Publication Series), vol. 1: 413–24. Beijing: Mi rigs dpe skrun khang, 2007. See also *Ri chos nges don rgya mtsho'i sa bcad.* In *Kun mkhyen dol po pa shes rab rgyal mtshan gyi gsung 'bum*, vol. 3: 171–88. 'Dzam thang: 'Dzam thang Bsam 'grub nor bu'i gling gi par khang, 1998. See also *Ri chos nges don rgya mtsho'i bsdus don.* In *Ri chos nges don rgya mtsho zhes bya ba'i bstan bcos dang bsdus don*, 1–18. Bir: D. Tsondu Senghe, The Bir Tibetan

Society, 1984. See also *Ri chos nges don rgya mtsho'i sa bcad*. In Rin chen shing par dpe rnying dpe dkon phyogs bsdus, bdr:W2PD19644, vol. 15: 8 fols.

———. *In Praise of the Sublime Land of Shambhala. Zhing mchog sham bha la'i bstod pa*. In *The 'Dzam-thang Edition of the Collected Works (Gsung-'bum) of Kun-mkhyen Dol-po-pa Shes-rab rgyal-mtshan*, vol. 7, pt. 2: 853–61. Delhi: Shedrup Books, 1992.

———. *Reply to Questions. Zhu don gnang ba*. In *The 'Dzam-thang Edition of the Collected Works (Gsung-'bum) of Kun-mkhyen Dol-po-pa Shes-rab rgyal-mtshan*, vol. 5: 343–46. Delhi: Shedrup Books, 1992.

———. *Reply to the Questions of Lotsāwa Sherab Rinchen. Lo tsā ba shes rab rin chen gyi zhus lan*. In *The 'Dzam-thang Edition of the Collected Works (Gsung-'bum) of Kun-mkhyen Dol-po-pa Shes-rab rgyal-mtshan*, vol. 7, pt. 2: 771–74. Delhi: Shedrup Books, 1992.

———. *Reply to the Questions of Samtengpa Chokpupa. Bsam steng pa cog bu pa'i zhus len*. In *The Collected Works (Gsung-'bum) of Kun-mkhyen Dol-po-pa Shes-rab rgyal-mtshan (1292–1361): Reproduced from the copies of prints from the Rgyal-rtse Rdzong blocks preserved at the Kyichu Monastery in the Paro Valley, Bhutan*, vol. 1: 839–46. Paro/Delhi: Lama Ngodrup and Sherab Drimay, 1984. Also in *Kun mkhyen chen po dol po pa shes rab rgyal mtshan gyi gsung 'bum*, vol. 8 (Taṃ): 561–66. 'Dzam thang, 1998. Also in *The 'Dzam-thang Edition of the Collected Works (Gsung-'bum) of Kun-mkhyen Dol-po-pa Shes-rab rgyal-mtshan*, vol. 7, pt. 2: 763–71. Delhi: Shedrup Books, 1992.

———. *Sunbeams: An Elegant Explanation of the Commentary on the Treatise of the "Uttaratantra." Theg pa chen po rgyud bla ma'i bstan bcos kyi 'grel pa legs bshad nyi ma'i 'od zer*. In *Rgyud bla'i ṭikka*, Jo nang dpe tshogs (Jonang Publication Series), vol. 2: 129–281. Beijing: Mi rigs dpe skrun khang, 2007.

Drigung Lotsāwa Maṇikaśrī ('Bri gung Lo tsā ba Ma ṇi ka shrī). *Bright Lamp of Great Bliss: A Biography of the Peerless Protector. Mtshungs med mgon po'i rnam thar bde chen gsal sgron*. In *Kun mkhyen jo nang pa yab sras kyi rnam thar dad pa'i khrus rdzing*, 1–14. Shang kang: Shang kang then mā dpe skrun khang, 2005(?).

Ga Rabjampa Kunga Yeshé (Sga Rab 'byams pa Kun dga' ye shes). *The Jewel Lamp: An Elegant Explanation to Fully Clarify the Meaning of the Tantra, A Commentary on "Chanting the Names of Noble Mañjuśrī." 'Phags pa 'jam dpal gyi mtshan yang dag par brjod pa'i 'grel pa rgyud don rab tu gsal bar byed pa legs bshad nor bu'i sgron ma*. In *'Phags pa 'jam dpal gyi don dam pa'i mtshan yang dag par brjod pa'i 'grel rnying gces btus*, 371–502. Lhasa: Bod ljongs bod yig dpe rnying dpe skrun khang, 2018. This commentary includes and follows Rinchen Sangpo's translation of *Chanting the Names of Mañjuśrī*.

Gö Lotsāwa Shönu Pal ('Gos Lo tsā ba Gzhon nu dpal). *Blue Annals. Deb ther sngon po*. 2 vols. Chengdu: Mi rigs dpe skrun khang, 1984.

Gyalwa Josang Palsangpo (Rgyal ba Jo bzang dpal bzang po). *Brilliant Marvels: Abbreviated Biographies of the Great Omniscient Dharma Lord, the Father, and His Fourteen Spiritual Sons. Chos kyi rje kun mkhyen chen po yab sras bco lnga'i rnam thar nye bar bsdus pa ngo mtshar rab gsal*. In *Kun mkhyen dol po pa shes rab rgyal mtshan gyi gsung 'bum*, vol. 1: 559–629. 'Dzam thang: 'Dzam thang Bsam 'grub nor bu'i gling gi par khang, 1998. Also in Jangsem Gyalwa Yeshé (Byang sems Rgyal ba ye shes), *Biographies of the Masters in the Lineage of the Jonangpa Tradition of Glorious Kālacakra. Dpal ldan dus kyi 'khor lo jo nang pa'i lugs kyi bla ma brgyud pa'i rnam thar*, 143–209. Beijing: Mi rigs dpe skrun khang, 2004.

Jamgön Ameshab Ngawang Kunga Sönam ('Jam mgon A mes zhabs Ngag dbang kun dga' bsod nams). *Chariot of Amazing Faith: An Elegant Explanation of the History of the Excellent Teachings of the Profound and Vast Glorious Kālacakra. Dpal dus kyi 'khor lo'i zab pa dang rgya che ba'i dam pa'i chos byung ba'i tshul legs par bshad pa ngo mtshar dad pa'i shing rta*. In *The Collected Works of A mes zhabs Ngag dbang kun dga' bsod nams*, vol. 19: 1–532. Kathmandu: Sa skya rgyal yongs gsung rab slob gnyer khang, 2000.

Jamyang Chögön ('Jam dbyangs Chos mgon). *[Annotations to] the "Extensive Commentary on the Chapter on the Cosmos." 'Jig rten khams kyi le'u'i rgya cher 'grel pa*, 1a–167a. Tibetan Buddhist Resource Center, Work: W3PD987, Image group: I3PD1215.

Khewang Yeshé Gyatso (Mkhas dbang Ye shes rgya mtsho). *Summarizing Notes of Explanation on "Ascertainment of the Great Madhyamaka of the Very Extensive Sublime Vehicle." Theg mchog shin tu rgyas pa'i dbu ma chen po rnam par nges pa'i rnam bshad zin bris*. In *Dbu ma theg mchog*, Jo nang dpe tshogs (Jonang Publication Series), vol. 17: 55–399. Beijing: Mi rigs dpe skrun khang, 2007.

Krang Yi Sun (Krang dbyi sun), ed. *Great Dictionary of Tibetan and Chinese. Bod rgya tshig mdzod chen mo*. 2 vols. Beijing: Mi rigs dpe skrun khang, 1993.

Kunga Drölchok, Jonang (Kun dga' grol mchog, Jo nang). *Lineage History of the "Hundred Guiding Instructions." Khrid brgya'i brgyud pa'i lo rgyus*. In *Gdams ngag mdzod*, vol. 12: 309–40. Delhi: N. Lungtok and N. Gyaltsan, 1972.

Kunga Palden Gyatso, Drokgé Khenpo (Kun dga' dpal ldan rgya mtsho, 'Brog dge mkhan po). *Introduction. Sngon gleng ngo sprod*. In *Ri chos nges don rgya mtsho*, Bod kyi gtsug lag gces btus, vol. 7: xxiii–xxxiii. New Delhi: Institute of Tibetan Classics, 2013.

Kunpang Chödrak Palsang (Kun spangs Chos grags dpal bzang). *Biography of the Omniscient Dharma Lord. Chos rje kun mkhyen chen po'i rnam thar gsal sgron gyi rnam grangs dge legs chen po nor bu'i 'phreng ba*. In *The 'Dzam-thang Edition of the Collected Works (Gsung-'bum) of Kun-mkhyen Dol-po-pa Shes-rab rgyal-mtshan*, vol. 1. Delhi: Shedrup Books, 1992.

Lhai Gyaltsen, Gharungwa (Gha rung ba Lha'i rgyal mtshan). *Biography of the Omniscient Dharma Lord of Jonang. Chos rje jo nang pa kun mkhyen chen po'i rnam thar. Dbu med* ms., 57 fols. Beijing: Cultural Palace of Nationalities.

———. *Illumination of Reality: An Explanation of the Treatise of the "Uttaratantra." Theg pa chen po rgyud bla ma'i bstan bcos kyi rnam par bshad pa de nyid snang ba*. In *Bstan pa spyi 'grel gyi 'grel pa*, Jo nang dpe tshogs (Jonang Publication Series), vol. 30: 65–249. Beijing: Mi rigs dpe skrun khang, 2010.

Manchukhawa Lodrö Gyaltsen (Sman chu kha ba Blo gros rgyal mtshan). *Result of Stainless Light: Explication of "Chanting the Names of Mañjuśrī, the Embodiment of Primordial Awareness." 'Jam dpal ye shes sems dpa'i mtshan yang dag par brjod pa'i 'grel bshad dri ma med pa'i 'od kyi 'bras bu*. This commentary includes and follows Rinchen Sangpo's translation of *Chanting the Names of Mañjuśrī*. All modern editions mistakenly attribute Manchukhawa's commentary to Mati Paṇchen Lodrö Gyaltsen. In Mati Paṇchen Lodrö Gyaltsen, *Blang dor rab gsal*, Jo nang dpe tshogs (Jonang Publication Series), vol. 8: 261–341. Beijing: Mi rigs dpe skrun khang, 2007. Also in *'Phags pa 'jam dpal gyi don dam pa'i mtshan yang dag par brjod pa'i 'grel rnying gces btus*, 253–370. Lhasa: Bod ljongs bod yig dpe rnying dpe skrun khang, 2018.

Mati Paṇchen Lodrö Gyaltsen (Ma ti Paṇ chen Blo gros rgyal mtshan). *Brilliant Illumination of the Definitive Meaning: An Explanation of the Treatise of the "Uttaratantra." Theg pa chen po rgyud bla ma'i bstan bcos kyi rnam par bshad pa nges don rab gsal snang ba*. Jo nang dpe tshogs (Jonang Publication Series), vol. 13. Beijing: Mi rigs dpe skrun khang, 2008.

———. *Brilliant Illumination of the Mahāyāna: An Explanation of the "Ornament of the Mahāyāna Sūtras." Theg pa chen po mdo sde'i rgyan gyi rnam par bshad pa theg chen rab gsal snang ba*. Jo nang dpe tshogs, vol. 26. Beijing: Mi rigs dpe skrun khang, 2010.

———. *Brilliant Illumination of the Meaning of the Treatise: An Explanation of "Entering the Conduct of a Bodhisattva." Byang chub sems dpa'i spyod pa la 'jug pa'i rnam par bshad pa gzhung don rab gsal snang ba*. Jo nang dpe tshogs, vol. 12. Beijing: Mi rigs dpe skrun khang, 2008.

Ngawang Lodrö Drakpa (Ngag dbang blo gros grags pa). *History of the Jonang Tradition. Dpal ldan jo nang pa'i chos 'byung rgyal ba'i chos tshul gsal byed zla ba'i sgron me*. Koko Nor: Krung go'i bod kyi shes rig dpe skrun khang, 1992.

Nya Ön Kunga Pal (Nya dbon Kun dga' dpal). *Explanation of the "General Commentary on the Doctrine." Bstan pa spyi 'grel zhes bya ba'i gsol 'debs kyi rnam bshad dgongs pa rnam gsal yid kyi mun sel*. In *'Od gsal rgyan gyi bshad pa*, Jo nang dpe tshogs (Jonang Publication Series), vol. 32: 45–133. Beijing: Mi rigs dpe skrun khang, 2010.

Shong Lotsāwa Lodrö Tenpa (Shong Lo tsā ba Blo gros brtan pa). *Illumination of the Definitive Meaning: An Explication of "Chanting the Names of Noble Mañjuśrī." 'Phags pa 'jam dpal gyi mtshan yang dag par brjod pa'i 'grel bshad nges pa'i don gyi snang ba*. In *'Phags pa 'jam dpal gyi don dam pa'i mtshan yang dag par brjod pa'i 'grel rnying gces btus*, 43–252. Lhasa: Bod ljongs bod yig dpe rnying dpe skrun khang, 2018. This commentary includes and follows Shong's own translation of *Chanting the Names of Mañjuśrī*, which is the translation in the Dergé Kangyur.

Tāranātha, Jonang (Tā ra nā tha, Jo nang). *Ascertainment of the Great Madhyamaka of the Very Extensive Sublime Vehicle. Theg mchog shin tu rgyas pa'i dbu ma chen po rnam par nges pa*. In *Dbu ma theg mchog*, Jo nang dpe tshogs (Jonang Publication Series), vol. 17: 1–53. Beijing: Mi rigs dpe skrun khang, 2007.

———. *Guidebook of Khyogpo Hermitage. 'Khyog po ri khrod kyi gnas bshad*. Xylograph, 3 fols. Kathmandu: National Archives.

———. *History of the Kālacakra Teachings. Dpal dus kyi 'khor lo'i chos bskor gyi byung khungs nyer mkho*. In *The Collected Works of Jo-nang rje-btsun Tāranātha*, vol. 2: 1–43. Leh: Smanrtsis Shesrig Dpemdzod, 1983.

———. *History of the Nyang Region. Myang yul stod smad bar gsum gyi ngo mtshar gtam gyi legs bshad mkhas pa'i 'jug ngogs*. Lhasa: Bod ljongs mi dmangs dpe skrun khang, 1983.

———. *Meaningful to Behold: Guiding Instructions for the Profound Path of the Vajrayoga. Zab lam rdo rje'i rnal 'byor gyi 'khrid yig mthong ba don ldan*. In *The Collected Works of Jo-nang rje-btsun Tāranātha*, vol. 3: 345–446. Leh: Smanrtsis Shesrig Dpemdzod, 1983.

———. *Sun Illuminating the Entire Profound Meaning, a Commentary on the "Brief Presentation of Initiation." Dbang mdor bstan gyi 'grel pa zab mo'i don mtha' dag gsal bar byed pa'i nyi* ma. In *Jo nang rje btsun tā ra nā tha'i gsung 'bum dpe bsdur ma*, vol. 45: 128–325. Beijing: Krung go'i bod rig pa dpe skrun khang, 2008.

———. *Twenty-One Differences concerning the Profound Meaning. Zab don nyer gcig pa*. In *The Collected Works of Jo-nang rje-btsun Tāranātha*, vol. 4: 781–95. Leh: Smanrtsis Shesrig Dpemdzod, 1983. The colophon title is *Zab don khyad par nyer gcig pa*.

Tenpai Gyaltsen (Bstan pa'i rgyal mtshan). *Biography of the Dharma Lord Choklé Namgyal. Chos rje phyogs las rnam par rgyal ba'i rnam par thar pa*. In *Bod kyi lo rgyus rnam thar phyogs bsgigs*, vol. 50: 391–459. Xining: Mtsho sngon mi rigs dpe skrun khang, 2011.

Sources in English Consulted by the Translator

The Absorption of the Miraculous Ascertainment of Peace. Praśāntaviniścaya-prātihāryasamādhi (Toh 129). Translated by the Dharmachakra Translation Committee. 2020. 84000: Translating the Words of the Buddha. Current version (2021): https://read.84000.co/translation/toh129.html.

Anacker, Stefan. 1984. *Seven Works of Vasubandhu*. Delhi: Motilal Banarsidass.

The Application of Mindfulness of the Sacred Dharma. Saddharmasmṛyupasthāna (Toh 287). Translated by the Dharmachakra Translation Committee. 2021. 84000: Translating the Words of the Buddha. Current version (2023): https://read.84000.co/translation/toh287.html.

Arnold, Edward A., ed. 2009. *As Long as Space Endures: Essays on the Kālacakra Tantra in Honor of H. H. the Dalai Lama*. Ithaca, NY: Snow Lion Publications.

Ārya Asaṅga. 2016. *The Bodhisattva Path to Unsurpassed Enlightenment: A*

Complete Translation of the Bodhisattvabhūmi. Translated by Artemus B. Engle. Boulder, CO: Snow Lion Publications.

Brambilla, Filippo. 2018. "A Late Proponent of the Jo nang gZhan stong Doctrine: Ngag dbang tshogs gnyis rgya mtsho (1880–1940)." *Revue d'Etudes Tibétaines* 45: 5–55.

———. 2021. "The Jo nang pas and the Others: Intersectarian Relations in Nineteenth- and Early Twentieth-Century A mdo and Khams." In *Nonsectarianism (ris med) in 19th- and 20th-Century Eastern Tibet: Religious Diffusion and Cross-Fertilization beyond the Reach of the Central Tibetan Government*, edited by Klaus-Dieter Mathes and Gabriele Coura, 117–64. Leiden: Brill.

———. 2022. "Empty of True Essence, Yet Full of Qualities: Tsoknyi Gyatso (1880–1940) on Buddha Nature." In *Buddha Nature across Asia*, edited by Klaus-Dieter Mathes and Casey A. Kemp, 377–422. Weiner Studien zur Tibetologie und Buddhismuskunde. Vienna: Arbeitskreis für Tibetische und Buddhistische Studien, Universität Wien.

Brunnhölzl, Karl, trans. 2007. *In Praise of Dharmadhātu, by Nāgārjuna, Commentary by the IIIrd Karmapa*. Ithaca, NY: Snow Lion Publications.

———. 2010–11. *Gone Beyond: The Prajñāpāramitā Sūtras,* The Ornament of Clear Realization, *and Its Commentaries in the Tibetan Kagyü Tradition*. 2 vols. Ithaca, NY: Snow Lion Publications.

———. 2011b. *Prajñāpāramitā, Indian "gzhan stong pas," and the Beginning of Tibetan gzhan stong*. Vienna: Arbeitskreis für Tibetische und Buddhistische Studien, Universität Wien.

———. 2012a. *Groundless Paths: The Prajñāpāramitā Sūtras,* The Ornament of Clear Realization, *and Its Commentaries in the Tibetan Kagyü Tradition*. Ithaca, NY: Snow Lion Publications.

———. 2012b. *Mining for Wisdom within Delusion: Maitreya's* Distinction between Phenomena and the Nature of Phenomena *and Its Indian and Tibetan Commentaries*. Boston: Snow Lion Publications.

———. 2014. *When the Clouds Part: The Uttaratantra and Its Meditative Tradition as a Bridge between Sūtra and Tantra*. Boston: Snow Lion Publications.

———. 2018. *A Compendium of the Mahāyāna: Asaṅga's* Mahāyānasaṃgraha *and Its Indian and Tibetan Commentaries*. 3 vols. Boulder, CO: Snow Lion Publications.

Buswell Jr., Robert E., and Donald S. Lopez Jr., eds. 2014. *The Princeton Dictionary of Buddhism*. Princeton, NJ: Princeton University Press.

Cabezón, José Ignacio, and Geshe Lobsang Dargyay. 2007. *Freedom from Extremes: Gorampa's "Distinguishing the Views" and the Polemics of Emptiness*. Boston: Wisdom Publications.

The Chapter on Going Forth. Pravrajyāvastu (Toh 1–1). Translated by Robert Miller and team. 2018. 84000: Translating the Words of the Buddha. Current version (2023): https://read.84000.co/translation/toh1-1.html.

The Chapter Teaching the Purification of Boundless Gateways. Anantamukhapariśodhananirdeśaparivarta (Toh 46). Translated by the Dharmachakra Translation Committee. 2020. 84000: Translating the Words of the Buddha. Current version (2021): https://read.84000.co/translation/toh46.html.

Chim Jampaiyang. 2018. *Ornament of Abhidharma: A Commentary on Vasubandhu's* Abhidharmakośa. Translated by Ian James Coghlan. The Library of Tibetan Classics 23. Boston: Wisdom Publications, in association with the Institute of Tibetan Classics.

Conze, Edward. 1973. *The Perfection of Wisdom in Eight Thousand Lines & Its Verse Summary*. Bolinas: Four Seasons Foundation.

Cultivating Trust in the Great Vehicle. Mahāyānaprasādaprabhāva (Toh 144). Translated by the Dharmachakra Translation Committee. 2020. 84000: Translating the Words of the Buddha. Current version (2023): https://read.84000.co/translation/toh144.html.

Dakpo Tashi Namgyal. 2019. *Moonbeams of Mahāmudrā*. With *Dispelling the Darkness of Ignorance* by Wangchuk Dorje, the Ninth Karmapa. Translated, annotated, and introduced by Elizabeth M. Callahan. Boulder, CO: Snow Lion Publications.

Daṃṣṭrasena (Diṣṭasena)? Vasubandhu? *The Long Explanation of the Noble Perfection of Wisdom in One Hundred Thousand, Twenty-Five Thousand, and Eighteen Thousand Lines. *Āryaśatasāhasrikāpañcaviṃśatisāhasrikāṣṭādaśasāhasrikāprajñāpāramitābṛhaṭṭīkā* (Toh 3808). Translated by Gareth Sparham. 2022. 84000: Translating the Words of the Buddha. Current version (2023): https://read.84000.co/translation/toh3808.html.

Davidson, Ronald. 1981. "The *Litany of Names of Mañjuśrī*: Text and Translation of the *Mañjuśrīnāmasaṃgīti*." In *Tantric and Taoist Studies in Honour of R. A. Stein*, ed. Michel Strickmann, vol. 1, 1–69. Brussels: Institut Belge des Hautes Études Chinoises.

The Dhāraṇī "Entering into Nonconceptuality." Avikalpapraveśadhāraṇī (Toh 142). Translated by the Dharmachakra Translation Committee.

2020. 84000: Translating the Words of the Buddha. Current version (2021): https://read.84000.co/translation/toh142.html.

Dharmachakra Translation Committee. 2006. *Middle Beyond Extremes. Maitreya's* Madhyāntavibhāga, *with Commentary by Khenpo Shenga and Ju Mipham*. Ithaca, NY: Snow Lion Publications.

———. 2011. *Ornament of Reason: The Great Commentary on Nāgārjuna's* Root of the Middle Way, *by Mabja Jangchub Tsöndrü*. Ithaca, NY: Snow Lion Publications.

———. 2013. *Distinguishing Phenomena from Their Intrinsic Nature: Maitreya's* Dharmadharmatāvibhaṅga *with Commentaries by Khenpo Shenga and Ju Mipham*. Boston: Snow Lion Publications.

———. 2014. *Ornament of the Great Vehicle Sūtras: Maitreya's* Mahāyānasūtrālaṃkāra *with Commentaries by Khenpo Shenga and Ju Mipham*. Boston: Snow Lion Publications.

Döl-bo-ba Shay-rap-gyel-tsen. 2006. *Mountain Doctrine: Tibet's Fundamental Treatise on Other-Emptiness and the Buddha Matrix*. Translated and introduced by Jeffrey Hopkins. Ithaca, NY: Snow Lion Publications.

Dorje, Gyurme, and Tudeng Nyima, trans. 2001. *An Encyclopaedic Tibetan-English Dictionary: A Revised Version of* Bod rgya tshig mdzod chen mo. Beijing: The Nationalities Publishing House and the School of Oriental and African Studies.

Duoji, Nyingcha. 2014. "Gha rung pa Lha'i rgyal mtshan as a Scholar and Defender of the Jo naṅg Tradition: A Study of His *Lamp That Illuminates the Expanse of Reality* with an Annotated Translation and Critical Edition of the Text." PhD dissertation. Harvard University.

Emergence from Samputa. Samputodbhavaḥ. Translated by the Dharmachakra Translation Committee. 2020. 84000: Translating the Words of the Buddha. Restricted tantric text, current version (2023): https://read.84000.co/translation/toh381.html.

Farrow, G. W., and I. Menon, trans. 1992. *The Concealed Essence of the Hevajra Tantra*. Delhi: Motilal Banarsidass.

Goldstein, Melvyn C., ed. 2001. *The New Tibetan-English Dictionary of Modern Tibetan*. Berkeley: University of California Press.

Gorampa Sönam Senge. 2014. *Distinguishing the Views: Moon Rays Illuminating the Crucial Points of the Excellent Vehicle*. Translated by Khenpo Jamyang Tenzin and Pauline Westwood. Kathmandu: Vajra Books.

Gray, David B. 2007. *The Cakrasaṃvara Tantra: (The Discourse of Śrī Heruka) Śrīherukābhidhāna*. A Study and Annotated Translation. New York: American Institute of Buddhist Studies, Columbia University.

———. 2009. "The Influence of the Kālacakra: Vajrapāṇi on Consort Meditation." In Arnold, *As Long as Space Endures*, 193–202.

Hackett, Paul G. 2019. *A Tibetan Verb Lexicon*. 2d ed., updated and expanded. Boulder, CO: Snow Lion Publications.

Hammar, Urban. 2005. "Studies in the *Kālacakra Tantra*: A History of the *Kālacakra Tantra* in Tibet and a Study of the Concept of Ādibuddha, the Fourth Body of the Buddha and the Supreme Unchanging." PhD dissertation, Stockholm University.

Hartzell, James Francis. 1997. "Tantric Yoga: A Study of the Vedic Precursors, Historical Evolution, Literatures, Cultures, Doctrines, and Practices of the 11th Century Kaśmīri Śaivite and Buddhist Unexcelled Tantric Yogas." PhD dissertation, Columbia University.

Hatchell, Christopher. 2014. *Naked Seeing: The Great Perfection, the Wheel of Time, and Visionary Buddhism in Renaissance Tibet*. New York: Oxford University Press.

The Heart of the Perfection of Wisdom, the Blessed Mother. Bhagavatīprajñāpāramitāhṛdaya (Toh 21). Translated by the Dharmachakra Translation Committee. 2022. 84000: Translating the Words of the Buddha. Current version (2023): https://read.84000.co/translation/toh21.html.

Henning, Edward. 2007. *Kālacakra and the Tibetan Calendar*. New York: American Institute of Buddhist Studies, Columbia University.

Higgins, David, and Marina Draszczyk. 2016. *Mahāmudrā and the Middle Way: Post-classical Kagyü Discourses on Mind, Emptiness and Buddha-Nature*. Weiner Studien zur Tibetologie und Buddhismuskunde 90.1–2. Vienna: Arbeitskreis für Tibetische und Buddhistische Studien, Universität Wien.

The Jewel Cloud. Ratnamegha (Toh 231). Translated by the Dharmachakra Translation Committee. 2019. 84000: Translating the Words of the Buddha. Current version (2022): https://read.84000.co/translation/toh231.html.

Jones, C. V. 2021. *The Buddhist Self: On* Tathāgatagarbha *and* Ātman. Honolulu: University of Hawai'i Press.

Kano, Kazuo. 2016. *Buddha-Nature and Emptiness: rNgog Blo-ldan shes-rab and A Transmission of the* Ratnagotravibhāga *from India to Tibet*. Vienna: Arbeitskreis für Tibetische und Buddhistische Studien, Universität Wien.

Kapstein, Matthew. 1992. *The 'Dzam-thang Edition of the Collected Works of Kun-mkhyen Dol-po-pa Shes-rab rgyal-mtshan: Introduction and Catalogue*. Delhi: Shedrup Books.

Kemp, Casey A. 2020. "The Definitive Meaning of *Mahāmudrā* according to the Kālacakra Tradition of Yu mo Mi bskyod rdo rje's *Phyag chen gsal sgron*." In *Mahāmudrā in India and Tibet*, edited by Roger R. Jackson and Klaus-Dieter Mathes, 185–203. Leiden: Brill.

Khedrup Norsang Gyatso. 2004. *Ornament of Stainless Light: An Exposition of the Kālacakra Tantra*. Translated by Gavin Kilty. The Library of Tibetan Classics 14. Boston: Wisdom Publications.

The King of Samādhis Sūtra. Samādhirājasūtra (Toh 127). Translated by Peter Alan Roberts. 2018. 84000: Translating the Words of the Buddha. Current version (2022): https://read.84000.co/translation/toh127.html.

Kittay, David R. 2011. "Interpreting the *Vajra Rosary: Truth and Method* Meets Wisdom and Method." PhD dissertation, Columbia University.

Kochumuttom, Thomas. 1982. *A Buddhist Doctrine of Experience*. Delhi: Motilal Banarsidass.

Komarovski, Yaroslav. 2006. "Reburying the Treasure—Maintaining the Continuity: Two Texts by Śākya Mchog Ldan on the Buddha-Essence." *Journal of Indian Philosophy* 34.6: 521–70.

———. 2011. *Visions of Unity: The Golden Paṇḍita Shakya Chokden's New Interpretation of Yogācāra and Madhyamaka*. Albany: State University of New York Press.

———. 2020. *Radiant Emptiness: Three Seminal Works by the Golden Paṇḍita Shakya Chokden*. New York: Oxford University Press.

Kongtrul, Jamgön. 2005. *The Treasury of Knowledge: Book Six, Part Four: Systems of Buddhist Tantra*. Translated by Elio Guarisco and Ingrid McLeod, Kalu Rinpoché Translation Group. Ithaca, NY: Snow Lion Publications.

———. 2007a. *The Treasury of Knowledge: Book Six, Part Three: Frameworks of Buddhist Philosophy*. Translated by Elizabeth Callahan, Kalu Rinpoché Translation Group. Ithaca, NY: Snow Lion Publications.

———. 2007b. *The Treasury of Knowledge: Book Eight, Part Four: Esoteric Instructions*. Translated by Sarah Harding, Kalu Rinpoché Translation Group. Ithaca, NY: Snow Lion Publications.

———. 2012. *The Treasury of Knowledge: Book Six, Parts One and Two: Indo-Tibetan Classical Learning & Buddhist Phenomenology*. Translated by Gyurme Dorje, Kalu Rinpoché Translation Group. Boston: Snow Lion Publications.

van der Kuijp, Leonard W. J. 2016. "Reconsidering the Dates of Dol po pa

Shes rab rgyal mtshan's (1292–1361) *Ri chos nges don rgya mtsho* and the *Bka' bsdu bzhi pa'i don*." Bod rig pa'i dus deb [Journal of Tibetology] 14: 115–59.

Lindtner, Christian. 1986. *Master of Wisdom: Writings of the Buddhist Master Nāgārjuna*. Berkeley: Dharma Publishing.

Lugi, Ligeia. 2010. "Meaning without Words: The Contrast between *Artha* and *Ruta* in Mahāyāna *Sūtras*." *Buddhist Studies Review* 27.2: 139–76.

Mathes, Klaus-Dieter. 2004. "Tāranātha's 'Twenty-One Differences with regard to the Profound Meaning': Comparing the Views of the Two *Gźan Stoṅ* Masters Dol po pa and Śākya mchog ldan." *Journal of the International Association of Buddhist Studies* 27.2: 285–328.

———. 2008. *A Direct Path to the Buddha Within: Gö Lotsāwa's Mahāmudrā Interpretation of the* Ratnagotravibhāga. Studies in Indian and Tibetan Buddhism. Boston: Wisdom Publications.

———. 2019. "A Brief Analysis of Jonang Choklé Namgyal's *Pointing-Out Instruction on the Foundation, Path, and Fruit*. In *Reason and Lives in Buddhist Traditions: Studies in Honor of Matthew Kapstein*, edited by Dan Arnold, Cécile Ducher, and Pierre-Julien Harter, 241–54. Studies in Indian and Tibetan Buddhism. Boston: Wisdom Publications.

Newman, John. 1987. "The Outer Wheel of Time: Vajrayāna Buddhist Cosmology in the *Kālacakra Tantra*." PhD dissertation, University of Wisconsin.

———. 1988. "Buddhist Sanskrit in the *Kālacakra Tantra*." *Journal of the International Association of Buddhist Studies* 11.1: 123–40.

———. 1992. "Buddhist Siddhānta in the *Kālacakra Tantra*." *Wiener Zeitschrift für die Kunde Südasiens* 36: 227–34.

Orofino, Giacomella. 1994a. *Sekkodeśa. A Critical Edition of the Tibetan Translations. With an Appendix by Raniero Gnoli, "On the Sanskrit Text."* Serie Orientale Roma 72. Rome: Istituto Italiano per l'Africa e l'Oriente.

———. 1994b. "Divination with Mirrors. Observations on a Simile Found in the Kālacakra Literature." In *Tibetan Studies: Proceedings of the 6th Seminar of the International Association for Tibetan Studies*, edited by Per Kvaerne, vol. 2, 612–28. Oslo: The Institute for Comparative Research in Human Culture.

———. 2007. "From Archaeological Discovery to Text Analysis: The Khor chags Monastery Findings and the *Mañjuśrīnāmasaṃgīti* Fragment." In *Discoveries in Western Tibet and the Western Himalayas: Essays on His-*

tory, Literature, Archaeology and Art, edited by Amy Heller and Giacomella Orofino, 86–127. Leiden: Brill.

———. 2009. "The Mental Afflictions and the Nature of the Supreme Immutable Wisdom in the *Sekkodeśa* and Its Commentary by Nāropa." In Arnold, *As Long as Space Endures*, 28–47.

Padmakara Translation Group. 2006 [1997]. Shāntideva, *The Way of the Bodhisattva.* Boston: Shambhala Publications.

———. 2002. *Introduction to the Middle Way: Chandrakīrti's "Madhyamakāvatāra" with Commentary by Jamgön Mipham.* Boston: Shambhala Publications.

———. 2005a. *The Adornment of the Middle Way: Shantarakshita's* Madhyamakalankara *with Commentary by Jamgön Kongtrul.* Boston: Shambhala Publications.

———. 2005b. *Nagarjuna's* Letter to a Friend, *with Commentary by Khyabje Kangyur Rinpoche.* Ithaca, NY: Snow Lion Publications.

———. 2018. *A Feast of the Nectar of the Supreme Vehicle: An Explanation of the* Ornament of the Sūtras. *Maitreya's* Mahāyānasūtrālaṃkāra *with a Commentary by Jamgön Mipham.* Boulder, CO: Shambhala Publications.

The Perfection of Wisdom in Eighteen Thousand Lines. Aṣṭādaśasāhasrikāprajñāpāramitā (Toh 10). Translated by Gareth Sparham. 2022. 84000: Translating the Words of the Buddha. Current version (2023): https://read.84000.co/translation/toh10.html.

Petech, Luciano. 1990. *Central Tibet and the Mongols.* Rome: Istituto Italiano per il Medio ed Estremo Oriente.

The Question of Mañjuśrī. Mañjuśrīparipṛcchā (Toh 172). Translated by the Kīrtimukha Translation Group. 2021. 84000: Translating the Words of the Buddha. Current version (2023): https://read.84000.co/translation/toh172.html.

Rangjung Dorje, the Third Karmapa. 2014. *The Profound Inner Principles: With Jamgön Kongtrul Lodrö Tayé's Commentary* Illuminating the "Profound Principles." Translated, annotated, and introduced by Elizabeth M. Callahan. Boston: Snow Lion Publications.

The Ratnaketu Dhāraṇī. Ratnaketudhāraṇī (Toh 138). Translated by the Dharmachakra Translation Committee. 2020. 84000: Translating the Words of the Buddha. Current version (2023): https://read.84000.co/translation/toh138.html.

Reigle, David. 2015. "Dolpopa's Annotations on the *Vimalaprabhā*, Chapters 3–5, Now Published." Academia.edu. https://www.academia.edu/33825163/Dolpopas_Annotations_on_the_Vimalaprabha_pdf.

———. 2017. "The Three Natures in the *Pañcaśatikā Prajñāpāramitā*." Academia.edu. https://www.academia.edu/44024892/The_Three_Natures_in_the_Pancasatika_Prajnaparamita.

———. 2017. "*Kālacakra-mūla-tantra* Section Rediscovered." Academia.edu. https://www.academia.edu/33825152/K%C4%81lacakra-m%C5%ABla-tantra_Section_Rediscovered.pdf.

———. 2018. "Studies in the Jonang Revised Translation of the *Kālacakra-tantra*: 1.1–1.3." Academia.edu. https://www.academia.edu/44024859/Studies_in_the_Jonang_Revised_Translation_of_the_K%C4%81lacakra_tantra_1_1_1_3.

———. 2018 [with added notes 2020]. "The *Uttara-tantra*: Sublime Continuum or Later/Higher Teaching." Academia.edu. https://www.academia.edu/44055193/The_Uttara_tantra_Sublime_Continuum_or_Later_Higher_Teaching.

Roerich, George N., trans. 1976 [1949]. *The Blue Annals*. Delhi: Motilal Banarsidass.

Rongtön Sheja Künrig. 2017. *Adorning Maitreya's Intent: Arriving at the View of Nonduality. A Commentary on the* Madhyāntavibhāga, Distinguishing the Middle from the Extremes. Translated by Christian Bernert. Boulder, CO: Snow Lion Publications.

———. 2018. *Perfect* or *Perfected? Rongtön on Buddha Nature. A Commentary on the Fourth Chapter of the* Ratnagotravibhāga. Translated and introduced by Christian Bernert. Kathmandu: Vajra Books.

The Root Manual of the Rite of Mañjuśrī. Mañjuśrīmūlakalpa (Toh 543). Translated by the Dharmachakra Translation Committee. 2020. 84000: Translating the Words of the Buddha. Current version (2022): https://read.84000.co/translation/toh543.html.

Śāntideva. 1997. *A Guide to the Bodhisattva Way of Life*. Translated from the Sanskrit and Tibetan by Vesna A. Wallace and B. Alan Wallace. Ithaca, NY: Snow Lion Publications.

Schmidt, Erik Pema Kunzang, et al. 2003. *Rangjung Yeshe Tibetan-English Dictionary*. Kathmandu: Rangjung Yeshe Publications.

The Seal of Engagement in Awakening the Power of Faith. Śrāddhābalādhānāvatāramudrā (Toh 201). Translated by the Dharmachakra Translation

Committee. 2021. 84000: Translating the Words of the Buddha. Current version (2022): https://read.84000.co/translation/toh201.html.

Seyfort Ruegg, David. 1966. *The Life of Bu ston rin po che*. Rome: Istituto Italiano per il Medio ed Estremo Oriente.

———. 1981. *The Literature of the Madhyamaka School of Philosophy in India*. Wiesbaden: Otto Harrassowitz.

———. 1989. *Buddha Nature, Mind and the Problem of Gradualism in a Comparative Perspective*. London: School of Oriental and African Studies.

———. 2010. *The Buddhist Philosophy of the Middle: Essays on Indian and Tibetan Madhyamaka*. Boston: Wisdom Publications.

Sferra, Francesco. 1999. *The* Ṣaṭsāhasrikākhyā Hevajratantrapiṇḍārthaṭīkā *by Vajragarbha*. Critical Edition and Translation. Doctorate Thesis. Rome: Università degli Studi di Roma "La Sapienza."

———. 2000. *The* Ṣaḍaṅgayoga *by Anupamarakṣita: With Raviśrījñāna's* Guṇabharaṇīnāmaṣaḍaṅgayogaṭippaṇī. Text and Annotated Translation. Serie Orientale Roma 85. Rome: Istituto Italiano per l'Africa e l'Oriente.

———. 2005. "Constructing the Wheel of Time: Strategies for Establishing a Tradition." In *Boundaries, Dynamics and Construction of Traditions in South Asia*, edited by Federico Squarcini, 253–85. Firenze: Firenze University Press.

———. 2006. *The* Sekkodeśaṭīkā *by Nāropa (*Paramārthasaṃgraha*)*. Critical Edition of the Sanskrit Text by Francesco Sferra. Critical Edition of the Tibetan Translation by Stefania Merzagora. Serie Orientale Roma 99. Rome: Istituto Italiano per l'Africa e l'Oriente.

———. 2009. "*The Elucidation of True Reality*: The Kālacakra Commentary by Vajragarbha on the *Tattvapaṭala* of the *Hevajra Tantra*." In Arnold, *As Long as Space Endures*, 93–126.

Sheehy, Michael R., and Klaus-Dieter Mathes, eds., 2019. *The Other Emptiness: Rethinking the Zhentong Buddhist Discourse in Tibet*. Albany: State University of New York Press.

Shendge, Malati J. 2004. *Ṣaṭsāhasrikā-hevajra-ṭīkā:* A Critical Edition. Delhi: Pratibha Prakashan.

Smith, E. Gene. 2001. *Among Tibetan Texts: History and Literature of the Himalayan Plateau*. Boston: Wisdom Publications.

Snellgrove, David L. 1959. *The Hevajra Tantra: A Critical Study*. 2 vols. London: Oxford University Press.

Stanley, Richard. 1988. "A Study of the Madhyāntavibhāga-bhāṣya-ṭikā." PhD Thesis, Australian National University, Canberra, Australia.

Stearns, Cyrus. 1996. "The Life and Tibetan Legacy of the Indian *Mahāpaṇḍita* Vibhūticandra." *Journal of the International Association of Buddhist Studies* 19.1: 127–71.

———. 2007. *King of the Empty Plain: The Tibetan Iron-Bridge Builder Tangtong Gyalpo*. Ithaca, NY: Snow Lion Publications.

———. 2008a. "Chokle Namgyel." Treasury of Lives, https://treasuryoflives.org/biographies/view/Chokle-Namgyel/2812.

———. 2008b. "Jonang Lotsāwa Lodrö Pel." Treasury of Lives, https://treasuryoflives.org/biographies/view/Jonang-Lotsawa-Lodro-Pel/2823.

———. 2008c. "Kunpang Chodrak Pelzang." Treasury of Lives, https://treasuryoflives.org/biographies/view/Kunpang-Chodrak-Pelsang-/9482.

———. 2008d. "Sabzang Mati Paṇchen Lodro Gyeltsen." Treasury of Lives, https://treasuryoflives.org/biographies/view/Sasang-Mati-Panchen-Lodro-Gyeltsen/2801.

———. 2010. *The Buddha from Dölpo: A Study of the Life and Thought of the Tibetan Master Dölpopa Sherab Gyaltsen*. Ithaca, NY: Snow Lion Publications.

The Stem Array. Gaṇḍavyūha (Toh 44–45). Translated by Peter Alan Roberts. 2021. 84000: Translating the Words of the Buddha. Current version (2023): https://read.84000.co/translation/toh44-45.html.

Summary of Empowerment. Sekoddeśa (Toh 361). Translated by the Vienna Buddhist Translation Studies Group. 2020. 84000: Translating the Words of the Buddha. Restricted trantric text, current version (2023): https://read.84000.co/translation/toh361.html.

The Sūtra on Wisdom at the Hour of Death. Atyayajñānasūtra (Toh 122). Translated by the Vienna Buddhist Translation Studies Group. 2016. 84000: Translating the Words of the Buddha. Current version (2022): https://read.84000.co/translation/toh122.html.

The Teaching of Akṣayamati. Akṣayamatinirdeśa (Toh 175). Translated by Jens Braarvig and David Welsh. 2020. 84000: Translating the Words of the Buddha. Current version (2022): https://read.84000.co/translation/toh175.html.

The Teaching on the Great Compassion of the Tathāgata. Tathāgatamahākaruṇānirdeśa (Toh 147). Translated by Anne Burchardi. 2020. 84000: Translating the Words of the Buddha. Current version (2023): https://read.84000.co/translation/toh147.html.

The Teaching on the Indivisible Nature of the Realm of Phenomena. Dharmadhātuprakṛtyasaṃbhedanirdeśa (Toh 52). Translated by the Dharmachakra Translation Committee. 2018. 84000: Translating the Words of the Buddha. Current version (2022): https://read.84000.co/translation/toh52.html.

Teaching the Relative and Ultimate Truths. Saṃvṛtiparamārthasatyanirdeśa (Toh 179). Translated by the Dharmachakra Translation Committee. 2014. 84000: Translating the Words of the Buddha. Current version (2022): https://read.84000.co/translation/toh179.html.

The Teaching of Vimalakīrti. Vimalakīrtinirdeśa (Toh 176). Translated by Robert A. F. Thurman. 2017. 84000: Translating the Words of the Buddha. Current version (2022): https://read.84000.co/translation/toh176.html.

The Transcendent Perfection of Wisdom in Ten Thousand Lines. Daśasāhasrikāprajñāpāramitā (Toh 11). Translated by the Padmakara Translation Group. 2018. 84000: Translating the Words of the Buddha. Current version (2023): https://read.84000.co/translation/toh11.html.

Tucci, Giuseppe. 1973. *Transhimalaya.* Geneva: Nagel Publishers.

Ui, Hakuju, Munetada Suzuki, Yenshō Kanakura, and Tōkan Tada, eds. 1934. *A Complete Catalogue of the Tibetan Buddhist Canons (Bkaḥ-ḥgyur and Bstan-ḥgyur).* Sendai: Tōhoku Imperial University.

Unraveling the Intent. Saṃdhinirmocana (Toh 106). Translated by the Buddhavacana Translation Group (Vienna). 2020. 84000: Translating the Words of the Buddha. Current version (2022): https://read.84000.co/translation/toh106.html.

Vajra Conqueror. Vajravidāraṇa (Toh 949). Translated by the Dharmachakra Translation Group. 2021. 84000: Translating the Words of the Buddha. Current version (2022): https://read.84000.co/translation/toh949.html.

Wallace, Vesna A. 2001. *The Inner Kālacakratantra: A Buddhist Tantric View of the Individual.* New York: Oxford University Press.

———, trans. 2004. *The Kālacakratantra: The Chapter on the Individual together with the* Vimalaprabhā. Translated from the Sanskrit, Tibetan, and Mongolian. New York: American Institute of Buddhist Studies, Columbia Center for Buddhist Studies, and Tibet House US.

———, 2009a. "The Body as a Text and the Text as the Body: A View from the *Kālacakratantra's* Perspective." In Arnold, *As Long as Space Endures,* 179–91.

———. 2009b. "Why Is the Bodiless (*aṅanga*) Gnostic Body (*jñāna-kāya*) Considered a Body?" In *Journal of Indian Philosophy* 37: 45–60.

———, trans. 2010. *The Kālacakra Tantra: The Chapter on Sādhanā together with the* Vimalaprabhā *Commentary*. Translated from the Sanskrit, Tibetan, and Mongolian. New York: American Institute of Buddhist Studies, Columbia Center for Buddhist Studies, and Tibet House US.

———. 2012. "The Six-Phased Yoga of the *Abbreviated Wheel of Time Tantra* (*Laghukālacakratantra*) according to Vajrapāṇi." In *Yoga in Practice*, edited by David Gordon White, 204–22. Princeton, NJ: Princeton University Press.

———. 2013. "Practical Applications of the Perfection of Wisdom Sūtra and Madhyamaka in the Kālacakra Tantric Tradition." In *A Companion to Buddhist Philosophy*, edited by Steven M. Emmanuel, 164–79. Chichester: John Wiley & Sons.

Wangchuk, Tsering. 2011 (2012). "Dol po pa Shes rab rgyal mtshan on Mahāyāna Doxography: Rethinking the Distinction between Cittamātra and Madhyamaka in Fourteenth-Century Tibet." In *Journal of the International Association of Buddhist Studies* 34.1–2: 321–48.

Wedemeyer, Christian K. 2007. *Āryadeva's Lamp That Integrates the Practices (Caryāmelāpakapradīpa): The Gradual Path of Vajrayāna Buddhism according to the Esoteric Community Noble Tradition*. New York: American Institute of Buddhist Studies, Columbia University.

Zimmermann, Michael. 2002. *A Buddha Within: The Tathāgatagarbhasūtra. The Earliest Exposition of the Buddha-Nature Teachings in India*. Tokyo: The International Research Institute for Advanced Buddhology, Soka University.

Index

About the Translator

CYRUS STEARNS has been a student of Tibetan Buddhism since 1973. His main teachers have been Dezhung Tulku Rinpoché, Chogyé Trichen Rinpoché, and Dilgo Khyentsé Rinpoché. He received a PhD in Buddhist Studies from the University of Washington and is the author and translator of a number of books, including *The Buddha from Dölpo*, *King of the Empty Plain*, and *Hermit of Go Cliffs*. He is an independent scholar and translator living in the woods on Whidbey Island, north of Seattle, Washington.

Institute of Tibetan Classics

The Institute of Tibetan Classics is a nonprofit, charitable educational organization based in Montreal, Canada. It is dedicated to two primary objectives: (1) to preserve and promote the study and deep appreciation of Tibet's rich intellectual, spiritual, and artistic heritage, especially among the Tibetan-speaking communities worldwide; and (2) to make the classical Tibetan knowledge and literature a truly global heritage, its spiritual and intellectual resources open to all.

To learn more about the Institute of Tibetan Classics and its various projects, please visit www.tibetanclassics.org or write to this address:

Institute of Tibetan Classics
304 Aberdare Road
Montreal (Quebec) H3P 3K3
Canada

The Library of Tibetan Classics

"This new series edited by Thupten Jinpa and published by Wisdom Publications is a landmark in the study of Tibetan culture in general and Tibetan Buddhism in particular. Each volume contains a lucid introduction and outstanding translations that, while aimed at the general public, will benefit those in the field of Tibetan Studies immensely as well."

—Leonard van der Kuijp, Harvard University

"This is an invaluable set of translations by highly competent scholar-practitioners. The series spans the breadth of the history of Tibetan religion, providing entry to a vast culture of spiritual cultivation."

—Jeffrey Hopkins, University of Virginia

"Erudite in all respects, this series is at the same time accessible and engagingly translated. As such, it belongs in all college and university libraries as well as in good public libraries. *The Library of Tibetan Classics* is on its way to becoming a truly extraordinary spiritual and literary accomplishment."

—Janice D. Willis, Wesleyan University

Following is a list of the thirty-two proposed volumes in *The Library of Tibetan Classics*. Some volumes are translations of single texts, while others are compilations of multiple texts, and each volume will be roughly the same length. Except for those volumes already published, the renderings of titles below are tentative and liable to change. The Institute of Tibetan Classics has contracted numerous established translators in its efforts, and work is progressing on all the volumes concurrently.

1. *Mind Training: The Great Collection*, compiled by Shönu Gyalchok and Könchok Gyaltsen (fifteenth century). NOW AVAILABLE
2. *The Book of Kadam: The Core Texts*, attributed to Atiśa and Dromtönpa (eleventh century). NOW AVAILABLE
3. *The Great Chariot: A Treatise on the Great Perfection*, Longchen Rapjampa (1308–63)
4. *Taking the Result As the Path: Core Teachings of the Sakya Lamdré Tradition*, Jamyang Khyentsé Wangchuk (1524–68) et al. NOW AVAILABLE
5. *Mahāmudrā and Related Instructions: Core Teachings of the Kagyü Schools*. NOW AVAILABLE
6. *Stages of the Path and the Oral Transmission: Selected Teachings of the Geluk School*. NOW AVAILABLE
7. *Mountain Dharma: An Ocean of Definitive Meaning*, Dölpopa Sherab Gyaltsen (1292–1361). NOW AVAILABLE
8. *Four Tibetan Lineages: Core Teachings of Pacification, Severance, Shangpa Kagyü, and Bodong*, Jamgön Kongtrül (1813–99). NOW AVAILABLE
9. *The Tradition of Everlasting Bön: Five Key Texts on Scripture, Tantra, and the Great Perfection*. NOW AVAILABLE
10. *Stages of the Buddha's Teachings: Three Key Texts*. NOW AVAILABLE
11. *The Bodhisattva Ideal: Selected Key Texts*
12. *The Ethics of the Three Codes*
13. *Sādhanas: Vajrayana Buddhist Meditation Manuals*
14. *Ornament of Stainless Light: An Exposition of the Kālacakra Tantra*, Khedrup Norsang Gyatso (1423–1513). NOW AVAILABLE
15. *A Lamp to Illuminate the Five Stages: Teachings on the Guhyasamāja Tantra*, Tsongkhapa (1357–1419). NOW AVAILABLE
16. *The Perfection of Wisdom Tradition: Three Essential Works*
17. *Treatises on Buddha Nature*
18. *Differentiations of the Profound View: Interpretations of Emptiness in Tibet*
19. *Illuminating the Intent: An Exposition of Candrakīrti's Entering the Middle Way*, Tsongkhapa (1357–1419). NOW AVAILABLE
20. *Tibetan Buddhist Epistemology I: The Sakya School*
21. *Buddhist Epistemology in the Geluk School: Three Key Texts*
22. *Tibetan Buddhist Psychology and Phenomenology: Selected Texts*

23. *Ornament of Abhidharma: A Commentary on the Abhidharmakośa*, Chim Jampaiyang (thirteenth century). NOW AVAILABLE
24. *Beautiful Adornment of Mount Meru: A Presentation of Classical Indian Philosophies*, Changkya Rölpai Dorjé (1717–86). NOW AVAILABLE
25. *The Crystal Mirror of Philosophical Systems: A Tibetan Study of Asian Religious Thought*, Thuken Losang Chökyi Nyima (1737–1802). NOW AVAILABLE
26. *Gateway for Being Learned and Realized: Selected Texts*
27. *The Tibetan Book of Everyday Wisdom: A Thousand Years of Sage Advice.* NOW AVAILABLE
28. *Mirror of Beryl: A Historical Introduction to Tibetan Medicine*, Desi Sangyé Gyatso (1653–1705). NOW AVAILABLE
29. *Selected Texts on Tibetan Astronomy and Astrology*
30. *Art and Literature: An Anthology*
31. *Tales from the Tibetan Operas.* NOW AVAILABLE
32. *A History of Buddhism in India and Tibet*, Khepa Deu (thirteenth century). NOW AVAILABLE

To receive a brochure describing all the volumes or to stay informed about *The Library of Tibetan Classics*, please write to:

support@wisdompubs.org

or send a request by post to:

Wisdom Publications
Attn: Library of Tibetan Classics
132 Perry Street
New York, NY 10014 USA

The complete catalog containing descriptions of each volume can also be found online at wisdomexperience.org.

Become a Benefactor of the Library of Tibetan Classics

The Library of Tibetan Classics' scope, importance, and commitment to the finest quality make it a tremendous financial undertaking. We invite you to become a benefactor, joining us in creating this profoundly important human resource. Contributors of two thousand dollars or more will receive a copy of each future volume as it becomes available, and will have their names listed in all subsequent volumes. Larger donations will go even further in supporting *The Library of Tibetan Classics*, preserving the creativity, wisdom, and scholarship of centuries past, so that it may help illuminate the world for future generations.

To contribute, please either visit our website at wisdomexperience.org, call us at (617) 776-7416, or send a check made out to Wisdom Publications or credit card information to the address below.

Library of Tibetan Classics Fund
Wisdom Publications
132 Perry Street
New York, NY 10014
USA

Please note that contributions of lesser amounts are also welcome and are invaluable to the development of the series. Wisdom is a 501(c)(3) nonprofit corporation, and all contributions are tax-deductible to the extent allowed by law.

If you have any questions, please do not hesitate to call us or email us at support@wisdompubs.org.

To keep up to date on the status of *The Library of Tibetan Classics*, visit the series page on our website, and subscribe to our newsletter while you are there.

About Wisdom Publications

Wisdom Publications is the leading publisher of classic and contemporary Buddhist books and practical works on mindfulness. To learn more about us or to explore our other books, please visit our website at wisdom.org or contact us at the address below.

Wisdom Publications
132 Perry Street
New York, NY 10014 USA

We are a 501(c)(3) organization, and donations in support of our mission are tax deductible.

Wisdom Publications is affiliated with the Foundation for the Preservation of the Mahayana Tradition (FPMT).